# FATHER TED

## the complete scripts

### Graham Linehan & Arthur Mathews

HAT TRICK

BOXTREE

First published 1999 by Boxtree

This edition published 2000 by Boxtree
an imprint of Macmillan Publishers Ltd
25 Eccleston Place London SW1W 9NF
Basingstoke and Oxford

www.macmillan.com

Associated companies throughout the world

ISBN 0 7522 7235 7

Copyright for the scripts as follows:

'Father Ted' Series 1 © Channel 4 1995
'Father Ted' Series 2 © Channel 4 1996
'Father Ted' Christmas Special © Channel 4 1996
'Father Ted' Series 3 © Channel 4 1998

Additional material copyright © Graham Linehan,
Arthur Mathews and Hat Trick International Ltd. 1999.

This collection copyright © Hat Trick International Ltd. 1999.

9 8 7 6 5 4 3

A CIP catalogue record for this book is available from
the British Library.

Picture credits

Hat Trick Productions Ltd: pages vii, 12, 29, 43, 62, 67, 90, 99,
118, 127, 144, 152, 171, 178, 196, 211, 229, 243, 261, 279,
290, 305, 322, 338, 352, 365, 368.

Designed by Dan Newman/Perfect Bound Ltd
Printed by Mackays of Chatham plc.

**The new Father Ted video (catalogue number VC6780)
is also available to buy from all good video outlets.**

# dedications

*I'd like to dedicate this book to my parents – Graham*

*To Paul Wonderful – Arthur*

# acknowledgements

We'd like to thank Geoffrey Perkins for making the first series ten times better than it would have been had we had our own way all the time . . . Mary Bell of Hat Trick for looking after us and looking after the show and realising that doing so amounted to the same thing . . . Denise O'Donoghue and Jimmy Mulville at Hat Trick for trusting us enough to never give us notes . . . Seamus Cassidy for having the guts to commission it after our first sitcom ended up filling the valued 3 a.m. slot on Channel 4 . . . Lissa Evans for being a great studio producer . . . Declan Lowney for not killing us while he was directing the first and second series . . . Andy de Emmony for not killing us while he was doing the third series . . . the ever-dependable crews in Ireland and England which were comprised of some of the best people in the world . . . the various people who worked in the production office, for their patience and hard work . . . the various visiting cast members for consistently 'getting it' . . . Ken Sweeney for his friendship and his sterling work as a sort of SuperExtra . . . John Fisher for his unusual hair . . . Neil Hannon for writing the music, especially the tune for 'My Lovely Horse' . . . the journalists who gave the show a chance . . . the journalists who were so obviously and amusingly enraged by its success . . . *Fawlty Towers*, *The Simpsons* and *Seinfeld* for their influence . . . Paul Wonderful for inspiring at least two characters and being generally hilarious . . . Patrick and Cheryl McCormack for the use of the Parochial House, and for not minding when we turned the front garden into The Somme . . . the fans of the show in Ireland, England and wherever else the thing ended up . . . Dermot Morgan, Ardal O'Hanlon, Frank Kelly and Pauline McLynn for being everything we hoped for and more . . . The Catholic Church . . . and finally, the Big Guy himself, without whom all this would have been a show about three firemen or something, and may not have worked quite so well.

**Graham Linehan** and **Arthur Mathews** met while working as film critic and art director respectively at *Hot Press* magazine in Dublin and started writing together shortly afterwards. As well as their work on *Father Ted*, the writers' credits include: *The All New Alexei Sayle Show, Paris, The Day Today, Brass Eye, The Saturday Night Armistice, Smith and Jones* and *Coogan's Run*.

*Father Ted* has won numerous comedy awards including two BAFTAs, one in 1995 and the other in 1999.

# contents

# introduction

We're great fans of script books, but too many of them seem to be transcribed from the screen by a third party rather than written by the original authors. With this in mind, we've decided to publish the next-to-last drafts of each episode of *Father Ted*, and so provide you with the extra characters and scenes and jokes that didn't make it into the final version for one or another reason. Now, what we've got here doesn't differ too wildly from what ended up on your TV screens, but there's the odd nice surprise. The process of making *Father Ted* was fun – we always had a great crew, and the cast exceeded our wildest expectations – but the process of writing it was even better. We rarely sweated over the scripts contained here – it was more like dropping by the Parochial House, turning on a tape recorder and seeing what happened next. If this book goes some way to illuminating that process, then it'll have done its job. On the other hand, if it just makes you laugh, it'll have done its job too. Enjoy yourselves. We certainly did.

*Graham Linehan and Arthur Mathews, September 1999*

---

**Publisher's note:** The footnotes contained in these scripts reveal significant changes that took place between this penultimate draft of the script and the final version that was broadcast. As well as anecdotal details, they highlight scenes that were deleted or inserted and large amounts of dialogue that was deleted (small amounts of dialogue are footnoted only when their insertion or omission had a marked influence on the development of the plot).

# good luck, father ted

**GRAHAM:** There was an element of debate about which episode of *Father Ted* should be the first in the series. The choice was between this and *The Passion of Saint Tibulus*. In fact, neither was the first to be written; our initial proposal to Hat Trick was in the form of three scenes of what is now Episode Six. In the end we decided that this one should be first because all the central characters have moments where they step up and make their idiosyncracies known; Dougal, Mrs Doyle and Jack are basically just being themselves while the plot revolves around Ted. It's a good 'welcome to the band'. And, because we'd written the last episode first, we had a fair idea of who our characters were already.

We didn't realise we were doing it at the time, but aside from Ted, each central character seems to be a parody of popular perceptions of the Irish. We were certainly sick of the clichés about Ireland – even the nice ones – so it felt good to bend and stretch and exaggerate those stereotypes until they became caricatures. Mrs Doyle is a caricature of our alleged friendliness, Jack is a caricature of our supposed capacity for drink and Dougal is a caricature of our perceived hilarious and delightful light-headedness, God bless us.

In this particular episode I think we might have made a tactical error. Although I like the *Deliverance* joke with the banjo, I'm not sure that it should have been in the first episode. Given the way the rest of the series went, it seems uncharacteristically savage, an inappropriate calling card.

Both Arthur and I make an appearance now and again in the series, and my back makes an appearance in this episode. (I promise I'm only mentioning this because I like the joke.) There's a 'ride' hidden behind Jack and Dougal on the roundabout called 'Goad the Fierce Man' – you can see the fierce man on the ladder. That's me in the red jacket goading him.

**ARTHUR:** Actually, this isn't my favourite episode. In retrospect I would have preferred to open the series with *The Passion of Saint Tibulus* (now Episode Three), but it is still a good introduction. Ted's wish to appear on television is very much to the fore. He cares deeply about all the really superficial things that priests aren't supposed to care about – especially money – and he's utterly useless at hiding the fact. I also like the bit about Dougal comparing fortune telling to 'heaven and hell and everlasting life and that type of stuff'.

John and Mary O'Leary hate each other, they're stuck in this awful marriage, but they would just die if a priest saw them arguing. And they don't just stop fighting when they see a priest; they make this sudden switch to become this extraordinarily loving couple.

## PART ONE

SCENE 1 INT./DAY 1
SET: PAROCHIAL HOUSE

*We see Father Ted Crilly, a middle-aged, pleasant, well-meaning priest, looking at a large notebook. He is wearing a grey cardigan. We can see his clerical collar underneath it.*

TED: Right, so that's Tuesday dealt with . . . now let's have a look at Wednesday.

*Father Jack Hackett, an elderly, blotchy, ugly, ill-tempered priest, looks back at Ted with undisguised disgust from his ancient armchair. Father Jack looks about seventy years old. A cigarette with one long line of ash protruding from it dangles from his hand. An empty bottle of whiskey lies on his lap. His clerical clothes are stained horribly.*

TED: Ah . . . the half seven Mass, I can take that . . .

*Jack glares at him.*

TED: And maybe . . . could you do the half eight at all — ?

*He looks at Jack hopefully. Jack stares back.*

TED: Right, I can take that as well. Now . . . the half past six evening on Sunday . . . ?

*Jack says nothing. He takes a drag on his cigarette and blows the smoke out while still staring at Ted.*

TED: The evening mass, now . . . too early for you . . .? (*No response from Jack.*) No problem . . . I can do that . . . just make a note . . .

*He writes something in his notebook. A young, gormless priest, Father Dougal McGuire, enters the room. There are noticeable globules of shaving foam all over his face and in his hair.*

DOUGAL: Morning, Ted.

TED: Morning, Dougal.

*Ted looks up and notices the foam. He considers the sight.*

TED (*pointing to just below his own ear*): There's . . . a little bit of shaving cream there . . .

DOUGAL (*looking closely at Ted*): No, there's not, Ted.

TED: No, on you, Dougal.

DOUGAL: Where exactly, Ted?

TED: Just . . . there below your ear . . .

DOUGAL (*wiping softly beneath his ear*): Here?

TED: Yes, and there's . . . there's a bit more . . .

*Ted points to just below his own lip. Dougal wipes the foam from his lip.*

DOUGAL: Gone?

TED: No, there's still just a tiny . . . Dougal, it's all over the place.

DOUGAL (*goes to mirror*): How on earth did all that get there? I didn't even shave this morning.

*Ted just looks at him. Dougal wipes himself clean of the rest of the foam. Ted examines his notebook.*

DOUGAL: So what are we doing today, Ted? Confessions and Mass and things like that, I suppose.

TED: Yes, Dougal. Things like that.

*Dougal nods, smiling. He looks around. Pause.*

DOUGAL: It's great being a priest, isn't it, Ted?

*Ted doesn't say anything. He takes a sweet from a bowl beside the telephone. Dougal looks at Jack. Jack looks at Dougal with even more contempt than he displayed to Ted.*

DOUGAL (*whispers*): Is Father Jack getting drained today?

TED: Tuesday.

DOUGAL (*looks out of the window*): It's lovely out.

*Shot of the view outside the window. Storm-force winds batter the trees. Pause.*

DOUGAL: Oh, wait'll I tell you! . . . Funland's coming to Craggy Island!

TED: This fairground thing? I wouldn't have much interest in that now, to be honest.

DOUGAL: They've got a spider baby.

TED: A what?

DOUGAL: A spider baby. It's like a freakshow thing. It's got the body of a spider, but it's actually a baby!

*We see that Father Jack is drifting off to sleep.*

TED: And how is it a baby? Does it have a nappy on or something?

**DOUGAL:** No.

**TED:** Does it have the head of a baby?

**DOUGAL:** Emmmm . . . no.

**TED:** Dougal, if it looks like a spider, and it doesn't gurgle at you or anything, how do you know it's actually a baby?

*Pause.*

**DOUGAL:** They keep it in a pram.

**TED:** Are you absolutely sure about this? You're not confusing it with a dream you had, or something?

**DOUGAL:** Yes, I saw it on the News. Honestly. I . . . oh, wait now . . . Eh, yes, actually, now that you say it, it was a dream, yes.

*Ted sighs and lifts up a diagram. It has a drawing of an outline of a head. The space around the head is filled with a single word – 'reality'. Inside the head is the word 'dream'.*

**TED** (*pointing at diagram*): Dougal. Have you been studying this like I told you to?

**DOUGAL:** I have, I have, Ted. Sorry . . . but we should go anyway, Ted. It'll be great! Last year I had a go at the horse riding and it was fantastic!

**TED:** I didn't know you could ride horses.

**DOUGAL:** Ah, it wasn't a real horse, Ted. It was an old lad with a saddle on him. God, he must have been eighty. He wasn't able to go very fast. I was lashin' him with the whip, but I couldn't get much of a response out of him.

**TED:** And how long were you up on him?

**DOUGAL:** I'd say it was about . . . an hour.

**TED:** So you were up on an eighty-year-old man, riding him around and whipping him for sixty minutes? (*Rubs his eyes.*) You realise that image is going to stay with me for the rest of my life now . . .

**DOUGAL:** Ah, it's great. We should go!

**TED:** No, I don't think I could take the excitement, to be honest.

*Dougal nods, but still looks disappointed.*

**DOUGAL:** See if there's anything on the telly, so.

*Dougal switches on the television. As soon as he does so, it wakes Jack, who sits up with a start, grabs the whiskey bottle, smashes in the television screen and goes back to sleep. Ted gives Jack's prone figure a disapproving glance.*

**DOUGAL:** Or, maybe I'll just go and study the old diagram.

*He picks up the diagram and leaves the room. The telephone rings. Ted picks it up absent-mindedly.*

**TED:** Hello, Father Ted Crilly speaking . . .

SCENE 2 INT./DAY 1
SET: OFFICE/PAROCHIAL HOUSE
*The man on the other end of the telephone is a television producer. His name is Terry MacNamee.*

**TERRY:** Hello, Father. Sorry to disturb you. My name is Terry MacNamee. I'm producing the programme *Faith Of Our Fathers* for Telly Eireann at the moment. We're doing a special about priests who work in isolated communities, and I was wondering if you'd be interested in talking to us . . .

**TED:** Oh! Well, that's . . . that's very exciting . . . *Faith Of Our Fathers* is my favourite programme.

**TERRY:** Well, you're the first person we thought of . . . (*He springs around on his chair and we see a chart with many, many priests' names on it, all of them crossed off. The only remaining one is 'Father Ted Crilly'.*) If you are interested, we could come over. We can also give you a small fee for your trouble.

SCENE 3 INT./DAY 1
SET: PAROCHIAL HOUSE/OFFICE
*Dougal walks into the room behind Ted.*

**DOUGAL:** Who's that, Ted?

*Ted jumps with fright.*

**TED:** Eh . . . it's no one, Dougal.

**DOUGAL:** No one?

**TERRY:** Hello? Father Crilly?

**DOUGAL:** It must be someone, Ted.

**TED:** Eh, just a second . . .

*He puts his hand over the mouthpiece. He takes a sweet from a bag and throws it over to the other side* of the room and Dougal runs for it. Ted continues his conversation with Terry.

**TED:** Sorry about that.

**TERRY** (*looking at charts*): Father, quick question. How do you get to Craggy Island, exactly? It doesn't seem to be on any maps.

**TED:** No, it wouldn't be on any maps, now, Terry, we're not exactly New York! The best way to find it is to head out from Galway and go slightly north until you see the English boats with the nuclear symbols on the side. They go very close to the island when they're dumping the old 'glow-in-the-dark'.

**TERRY:** Oh, one thing. Are there other priests living there with you? (*Looks at a sheet of paper.*) Our researcher doesn't mention anyone else.

**TED:** Oh, well, ah . . .

*He looks at Dougal, who is having trouble unwrapping the sweet. Jack snores loudly, and Ted looks over at him. A line of spittle is falling from his mouth. It rises and falls as Jack snores.*

**TED:** There's no one else here.

**TERRY:** Right, then. We'll see you Saturday. I'll ring when I get there.

**TED:** See you so! Bye . . .

*Ted looks at Dougal. Dougal has finally managed to unwrap the sweet. He chews it slowly, a look of ecstasy on his face. Ted smiles at him. Jack belches.*

SCENE 4 EXT./NIGHT 1
SET: ANT COLONY
*Stock footage from a nature programme. We see close-ups of ants, chewing leaves, fighting and crawling all over each other. The sight is framed as if seen through binoculars.*

SCENE 5 INT./NIGHT 1
SET: PAROCHIAL HOUSE
*We see Dougal looking through a pair of binoculars. He lowers them from his face then brings them back up again.*

SCENE 6 EXT./NIGHT 1
SET: ANT COLONY
*More footage of ants.*

SCENE 7 INT./NIGHT 1
SET: PAROCHIAL HOUSE
*Dougal wraps the strap around the binoculars.*

**DOUGAL:** The ants are back, Ted.

*Ted is on the floor, removing parts from the smashed television. He lays them out to one side.*

**TED:** Never put on the television when Father Jack's asleep, Dougal. You know how he is.

**DOUGAL:** But he's always asleep.

*We see Jack asleep in his chair in exactly the same position as he was in previous scenes.*

**TED:** Well, anyone who's worked as long as he has for the Church deserves a rest. It's actually quite an honour for us to look after him in his old age.

*Father Jack opens his mouth and draws in breath in a noisy, violent way.*

**TED** (*laughs softly*): Dreaming of past glories, no doubt.

*We close-up on Jack's blotched face. The screen goes white.*

SCENE 8 INT./DAY 2
SET: SCHOOL HALL
*We see a nun addressing a hall full of schoolgirls.*

**NUN:** Girls? Girls, pay attention. We've got a special treat today. Father Hackett has very kindly volunteered to take you all for volleyball practice.

*Cut to a slightly younger Jack, who is smoking a cigarette nearby. He looks at the girls in a fixed, disconcerting way. He leans over to the nun and whispers something in her ear.*

**NUN:** . . . Oh, right, Father . . . and he's just reminded me that it's very warm today, so there'll be no need for your tracksuit tops.

*Jack smiles, worryingly.*

SCENE 9 INT./NIGHT 2
SET: PAROCHIAL HOUSE
*We see Jack frowning, still asleep. Ted enters the room, twiddling a screwdriver. He walks over to the television and bends down to look at it. He unscrews the front section and hands it to Dougal. Dougal takes the frame and holds it in front of his face.*

**DOUGAL** (*addresses camera*): Hello, Father Dougal McGuire here, and welcome to this week's *Top of the Pops*. In at number 45 is Father Ted Crilly with 'I've Got The Power'. And still at number 17 for the sixteenth week in a row is Father Jack Hackett with 'I'm A Sleepy Priest' . . .

*Suddenly Jack wakes up with a start. He sees Dougal in the television.*

**JACK:** How did that gobshite get on television?

*The housekeeper, Mrs Doyle, enters. She carries cups and saucers and a pot of tea on a tray.*

**MRS DOYLE:** Hello to you all! Oh, is the television broken again, Father?

**TED:** It is. We had a bit of trouble with —

**MRS DOYLE:** Never you mind! There's nothing wrong with it that won't be fixed with a bit of 'you know what' in the head department.

*Ted smiles kindly at Mrs Doyle.*

**MRS DOYLE:** Who's for tea, then?

**DOUGAL:** Me please, Mrs Doyle.

**JACK:** Tea! Feck!

**TED:** I'm fine, Mrs Doyle.

*Pause. Mrs Doyle looks at Ted.*

**MRS DOYLE:** You won't have a cup?

**TED** (*sighs*): No, honestly, Mrs Doyle, I won't have a cup, I'm fine.

**MRS DOYLE:** You sure now? It's hot.

**TED:** No, I'm not in the mood thanks, Mrs Doyle.

**MRS DOYLE:** All right . . . ah, go on! Will you not have a drop?

**TED:** No, Mrs Doyle, thanks anyway.

**MRS DOYLE:** A small cup?

**TED:** I'm fine.

**MRS DOYLE:** I'll tell you what, Father, I'll pour a cup for you anyway.

**TED** (*places hand over cup*): No, seriously, Mrs Doyle —

*Mrs Doyle pours anyway. It spills over Ted's hand.*

**TED:** Aaaarrrrgghhh!

**MRS DOYLE** (*oblivious*): . . . And you have it if you want.

*Ted rubs his hand and looks at her fiercely.*

**MRS DOYLE** (*turning to Jack*): Now, Father, what do you say to a cup?

**JACK:** Feck off, cup!

*She starts to pour a cup. Jack grunts and mumbles under his breath in Mrs Doyle's face.*

**MRS DOYLE** (*to Ted*): He loves his cup of tea . . .

**JACK:** Feck off!

**MRS DOYLE** (*finishes pouring*): There we go!

*She leaves the cup beside Jack and starts to walk towards the door. He throws the cup after her. It smashes on the wall beside her head but she doesn't notice. She turns suddenly.*

**MRS DOYLE:** Oh, Father Crilly, I almost forgot. There was a 'phone call earlier from a Terry MacNamee.

**TED** (*suddenly alert*): Right!

**DOUGAL:** Who's that, Ted?

**MRS DOYLE:** He's something to do with . . . was it the television?

**TED:** Yes! He's the man who's coming to fix the television.

**MRS DOYLE:** Anyway, he'll be here tomorrow at twelve.

**TED:** Grand . . .

*Mrs Doyle smiles again and leaves. Dougal walks up to the television, stepping around the parts on the floor. He presses the 'on' button a few times.*

**DOUGAL:** Ah, yeah, it's good you called someone, Ted. It's still not working.

*Reaction shot of Ted considering Dougal.*

SCENE 10 INT./NIGHT 2
SET: TED AND DOUGAL'S BEDROOM
*Dougal is in the bedroom, looking into the cupboard mirror. He is playing air guitar with a tennis racket. We notice that Ted's bed, the one nearest the door, has a 'Pope John Paul II, Ireland 1979' duvet cover. Dougal has a Jack Charlton duvet cover. He wears an Ireland jersey and boxer shorts.*

**DOUGAL** (*singing*): . . . 'You're simply the best!' . . . Dow, dow, dow, dow . . .

*Ted walks through the door. He wears normal striped pyjamas. He looks at Dougal.*

**DOUGAL:** . . . Dow, dow, dow, dow . . .

**TED:** Ahem . . .

**DOUGAL** (*jumps*): Oh! Ted! You frightened me there!

**TED** (*amused*): You doing the old pop-star thing there, Dougal?

**DOUGAL:** I am! It was great being on television today, Ted. I think I've caught the old telly bug.*

**TED:** Well, get into bed now and go asleep. You don't want to get overtired.

**DOUGAL** (*climbing into bed*): D'yever want to get into television yourself, Ted?

**TED** (*slightly uncomfortable*): Ah, no. I wouldn't have any interest in that type of thing, really.

**DOUGAL:** Right . . . I can't imagine you'd be much good, actually.

**TED:** What? Why not?

**DOUGAL:** Ah, I don't know . . . You're a bit

---

* It's easy to miss, but in the actual episode, Dougal actually places his air 'guitar' back in its stand when he's finished playing.

serious. And your eyes are a bit crossed. They're a bit wonky. The cameras can pick that up, you know.

**TED** (*shocked*): I am not cross-eyed!

**DOUGAL:** Ah, you are a bit now, Ted. Half the time I don't know if you're talking to me or Father Jack.

**TED** (*angry*): Dougal, will you just . . . get some sleep.

**DOUGAL:** Fair enough, Ted! Just have to say the old prayers.

*Dougal kneels down.*

**DOUGAL:** Our Father, who art in . . .

*Pause.*

**TED:** Heaven.

**DOUGAL:** Right. Hallowed be thy . . .?

**TED:** Name. Listen, Dougal, you know you can praise God with sleep?

**DOUGAL:** Can you, Ted?

**TED:** You can. It's a way of thanking him for a tiring day.

**DOUGAL:** There's a lot of ways you can praise God, isn't there? Like when you told me to praise him by just, you know, going out of the room.

**TED:** That's a good one, yes.

*Ted turns off the light. The two lie in bed, barely illuminated by the moon outside.*

*Pause.*

**DOUGAL:** Ted? . . . Ted?

**TED** (*sighs*): Yes, what?

**DOUGAL:** Did you ever wonder if there were any other planets besides Earth?

**TED:** Goodnight, Dougal.

SCENE 11 INT./DAY 3
SET: PAROCHIAL HOUSE
*We see Jack in his armchair, asleep. There is a sound of muffled conversation from the corner of the room. Jack's eye darts open and he fixes his gaze on something. We pan across to where he is looking. We see the cord of a telephone leading behind the curtain. Ted is there, on the telephone. He spots Jack*

looking at him and wraps the curtain around him.

**TED:** Right! There we go! Sorry, Terry, go ahead . . . You made it, then?

SCENE 12 EXT./DAY 3
SET: TELEPHONE POLE ON THE ISLAND
*Terry is telephoning from the island's sole telephone box – it's actually just a telephone on a pole by the side of the road. He seems totally unprepared for the ferocity of the weather on Craggy Island, and his brightly coloured tie dances madly around his face and neck. A camera team freeze nearby.*

**TERRY** (*shouting over wind as he looks around*): I think so! There don't seem to be any indications that this is Craggy Island. There's no signs or anything!

SCENE 13 INT./DAY 3
SET: PAROCHIAL HOUSE
*We see Ted behind the curtain.*

**TED:** Is there a man looking at you with a T-shirt saying 'I Shot JR'?

SCENE 14 EXT./DAY 3
SET: TELEPHONE POLE ON THE ISLAND/PAROCHIAL HOUSE
*Terry frowns at this question and looks around. He sees a large, strange-looking man staring at him with a fixed, gormless expression. He does indeed wear a faded T-shirt with 'I Shot JR' written on it. It's too small for him and his belly pokes out from under it.*

**TERRY** (*taken aback*): Actually . . . there is.

**TED:** Oh, you're here, so!

**TERRY:** What? This line is very bad, Father. You're a bit muffled.

SCENE 15 INT./DAY 3
SET: PAROCHIAL HOUSE/TELEPHONE POLE ON THE ISLAND
*Ted looks around at his self-made cave.*

**TED:** Oh, yes, I'm . . . ah . . . I have a portable phone and you caught me by surprise when you called, you know? I'm . . . on the toilet.

*Ted grimaces in embarrassment at what he has just said. In the background, out of the window, we see Dougal passing. He sees Ted and looks puzzled.*

TERRY: Oh, right . . . ah . . . so, where can we meet up? Anywhere we can go and get some nice shots? Any local landmarks?

TED: No.

TERRY: What?

TED: No, there's no landmarks here now, Terry.

TERRY: None at all?

*Dougal approaches the window. He looks at Ted, sees something offscreen and then seems to have an idea. He suppresses a laugh and disappears to the right.*

TED: No. The island itself is a kind of landmark. For ships and that. The general rule is that if you're heading away from it, you're going in the right direction.

TERRY: Right, so, ah . . .

TED: There's the field.

TERRY (*putting on a brave face*): Oh, a field! Yes. That sounds . . .

TED: Well, it's not a field, really, but it doesn't have as many rocks in it as most places.

TERRY: Look, that's fine, Father. We'll meet at the field. How do I get there?

TED: Oh, just ask Tom there. He'll help you out.

TERRY: OK, then. Thanks, Father.

*Terry puts down the telephone and looks over at Tom, the T-shirt man. A bird has landed on a post right beside him. Tom notices the bird, produces a shotgun and blows it to smithereens. Reaction shot of Terry, his face frozen. Tom looks back and smiles broadly. He has four teeth in total.*

TOM (*points to where the bird was, and shouts*): Bird!

*Terry exchanges a worried look with the camera team.*

SCENE 16 INT./DAY 3
SET: PAROCHIAL HOUSE
*Ted is still at the window. We see a grotto-sized statue of the Virgin Mary being raised into shot behind him. He turns around and sees it.*

TED: Aaaaaaaaaaaaaaaaaaaaaarrghh!

*He falls back, bringing the whole curtain rail down with him. When the curtain falls, it reveals a cowed Dougal, holding the statue.*

SCENE 17 INT./DAY 3
SET: PAROCHIAL HOUSE
*Ted sits holding a cup of tea. He is trembling, staring ahead of him as if in shock.*

DOUGAL: God, Ted, I'm so sorry. It was just a joke.

TED: T—t—try to avoid doing that again, Dougal. I thought it was really . . . Herself. That's the last thing I need.

TED: Anyway . . . it's time for Jack's walk. (*To Jack.*) Time for your walk, Father! Off around the cliffs!

DOUGAL: Can I bring him to Funland, Ted?

TED: No, he wouldn't like that, now. Bring him round the cliffs. And Dougal, if you're stopping near the edge, put the brakes on. He was just lucky the last time.

DOUGAL: You not coming, Ted?

TED: No, I think I'll stay here and pray for a while.

DOUGAL (*slyly*): O'ho! What're you after, Ted?

TED: I'm not after anything, Dougal! It's not unknown for members of the clergy to pray from time to time, you know.

*Mrs Doyle enters the room pushing a wheelchair.*

MRS DOYLE: Here we are, Father Crilly.

JACK (*sees the chair*): Gerraway!

MRS DOYLE: There's nothing Father Hackett likes better than to get out and about in the fresh air!

*Jack is warding them off with a big walking stick.*

JACK: Grrrrgaaaahhhhggghhh!

*Dougal, Ted and Mrs Doyle try to grab him so they can lift him into the wheelchair. Jack suddenly goes limp, like a protester, but they eventually manage to drag him over. When they land him in the wheelchair, he slides down to the floor in one move. They drag him up again. Ted puts a blanket on his legs and starts to tuck it in.*

**TED:** This'll keep you lovely and warm . . .

*Jack slaps Ted in the face. Mrs Doyle wheels him to the door. Jack then leaps out of the wheelchair, runs back to his armchair, and wedges himself in again. Ted, Dougal and Mrs Doyle, breathing heavily, turn around to look at him.*

SCENE 18 INT./DAY 3
SET: PAROCHIAL HOUSE
*We see Jack being wheeled out of the house by Dougal. He has been tied to the chair at various places. He has one hand just about free and is holding a walking stick. With the hook of the stick, he drags a small table behind him. Ted removes it from the table as it comes through the door. Dougal and Mrs Doyle seem not to notice Jack's reluctance, and act cheerful.*

**TED:** Bye, then! (*To Mrs Doyle as they leave.*) Every single day the same thing . . .

**MRS DOYLE** (*putting on hat and coat*): Ah, once he's out there he has a great time. He loves the old cliffs.

**TED:** Mmm . . .

**MRS DOYLE:** Well, I'll be off then, Father! What are you up to yourself?

**TED:** Oh, I think I'll stay here and have a bit of an old pray.

**MRS DOYLE:** All right, then! Enjoy the rest of the weekend!

*Mrs Doyle leaves. Ted smiles in an excited, sneaky way and closes the door quickly.*

SCENE 18A INT./DAY 3
SET: PAROCHIAL HOUSE HALLWAY
**TED** (*rubs his hands*): Right!

*He puts on a coat and goes the other way.*

SCENE 19 INT./DAY 3
SET: PAROCHIAL HOUSE
*From a distance, we see Ted leaving by the back door and running at full speed across the landscape.*

SCENE 20 EXT./DAY 3
SET: FRONT GATE
*We see Dougal looking around the gate at the house. He turns Jack's chair and wheels it in another direction.*

**END OF PART ONE**

\* \* \*

**PART TWO**

SCENE 21 EXT./DAY 3
SET: ENTRANCE TO FAIRGROUND
*Ted has arrived at a gate set in a stone wall. A sign on the gate reads 'The Field' in professional lettering, while written underneath in thick, black marker-pen ink are the words 'Today, Funland'. Ted sees that Tom, still in his JR T-shirt, is sitting on the wall. We hear Wurlitzer music coming from inside.*

**TED:** God, I didn't know this bloody thing was on here . . .

**TOM:** Hello, Father.

**TED:** Hello, Tom . . . ah, the Telly Eireann lads, did you get them here all right?

**TOM:** I did, yes, Father. They said they were going to film a bit of the island. They'll be back soon.

**TED:** Oh, no, they're not going near the cliffs, are they?

**TOM** (*shakes his head*): They headed off the other way.

**TED:** Thank God for that. (*Looking around.*) Right . . . so I'll wait in the field, so . . .

**TOM:** Father, I've killed a man.

TED (*looking around, not really listening*): Have you, Tom? I'll, ah . . . I'll talk to you about that later. (*Brightly.*) I'm doing an interview for the television!

*Ted walks through the gate.*

SCENE 22 EXT./DAY 3
SET: FAIRGROUND
*Funland is the most pathetic fairground in the world. The names of the rides are written on flimsy cardboard signs: there is 'The Ladder', which is a ladder leaning against a wall. We see a young boy halfway up it while a surly youth wearing a large moneybag watches him. The surly youth has a very weak moustache.*

SURLY YOUTH: Keep your hands on the sides.

*We also see a sign for 'The Whirly-Go-Round – an experience unlike any other'. Cut to reveal four people going around very slowly on a flat, circular platform. Another moneybag-wearing youth occasionally walks across it for no clear reason. Then we see a sign with 'Car Ride' written on it. A group of people wait beside the sign. A beaten-up Ford Escort arrives, two children get out of the car and are replaced by a young man and his girlfriend. The car takes off again. Cut to a ride called 'The Gate of Hell', which is just a surly youth swinging a young boy back and forth on a gate. We also see a crane in the background. Then we see a stall that sells sweets. It is manned by Mr and Mrs O'Leary, a middle-aged couple.*

MR O'LEARY: You stupid, ignorant, bitch!

MRS O'LEARY: Don't you call me a bitch, you bastard! You can't even get it up!

MR O'LEARY: You big, fat, smelly cow!

MRS O'LEARY: Titface! You've got a face like a pair of tits!

MR O'LEARY: Well, at least that's one pair between us.

*Mrs O'Leary produces a knife and tries to stab Mr O'Leary. Mr O'Leary grabs the knife and gives Mrs O'Leary a karate chop on the neck. Ted walks into shot. The two stop fighting before he sees them. He turns around and notices them at last.*

MR O'LEARY (*very cheerily*): Hello, Father!

TED: Oh, hello, John . . . Hello, Mary. Are you not in the shop today?

MRS O'LEARY (*puts a fond arm around Mr O'Leary*): Well, with Funland here, we decided to open a stall for a few days.

MRS O'LEARY: Will you have a packet of Toffos, Father?

TED: No thanks, Mary. I have to meet someone now. Actually . . . to be honest, I'm being interviewed for a television programme.

MR O'LEARY: Really? Oh, that's fantastic.

MRS O'LEARY: You know, Father, I think you'd be brilliant on television.

TED (*very flattered*): Well, thank you very much . . .

MR O'LEARY: You know, Father, I'd say you'd be more than a match for Gay Byrne or Terry Wogan, or any of them.

TED: Oh, it'll be a few weeks before I get to their level, I'd say . . .

MRS O'LEARY: John was just saying to me the other day, 'Wouldn't Father Crilly be brilliant on television?'

MR O'LEARY: I was. In fact, I think you could do anything you turned your mind to, Father. Television, acting in films, writing bestsellers . . .

TED: Oh, go on! I think you only see my good side . . .

MRS O'LEARY: You only have a good side, Father.

*They all laugh good-naturedly. Ted looks at his watch.*

TED: Anyway, I'd better go. I must try and track down this film unit. They'll probably want to do a few close-ups and mastershots and noddys and all that with me. I'll see you soon.

*He moves out of shot. Mr and Mrs O'Leary wave after him.*

MR O'LEARY: Good luck, Father Ted! (*Pause. He turns to Mrs O'Leary.*) Get those feckin' Crunchies out of the car!

*Cut back to Ted, who looks at his watch anxiously. He looks up and his face freezes in horror. Cut to Dougal and Jack, who are having a ride on the Whirly-Go-Round. Jack is still in his wheelchair on* the platform as it slowly turns. Dougal looks over and sees Ted. Ted turns and pretends to examine the wall behind him.

**DOUGAL:** Ted! Ted! Over here, Ted.

*Ted is forced to turn around and acknowledge him. He makes his way to the ride.*

**DOUGAL:** Ted, what are you doing here? I thought you weren't interested in this kind of thing . . .

**TED:** You're supposed to be taking Father Jack for his walk!

**DOUGAL:** . . . Well, ah . . . the cliffs were closed for the day.

**TED:** How could the cliffs be closed, Dougal?

**DOUGAL:** OK, no, it wasn't that. Ahem . . . They were gone.

**TED:** They were gone? The cliffs were gone? Dougal, how could the cliffs just disappear?

**DOUGAL** (*pause*): Erosion.

**TED** (*sighs*): Now, come off of that and off to the cliffs with you.

**DOUGAL:** There's just a few more turns to go, I think.

*Ted stands beside the platform as it turns. Dougal and Jack pass by every couple of seconds. Each time they do, Dougal waves at Ted like a five-year-old waving at his parents. Ted waves half-heartedly back the first time, but after that he just glowers at them.*

SCENE 23 EXT./DAY 3
SET: SOMEWHERE ON THE ISLAND
*We see the camera team relaxing, having a smoke, etc., near a thatched cottage. The cameraman is facing a small bald boy who has a banjo. The cameraman starts playing a guitar, and the bald boy joins in on the banjo. They play 'Duelling Banjos' from 'Deliverance'.*

SCENE 24 EXT./DAY 3
SET: FAIRGROUND
*Dougal and Ted are wheeling Jack through the fairground.*

**TED:** Now, you're to go straight home, do you hear?

*Dougal sulks.*

**TED:** I don't want to hear any more nonsense.

**DOUGAL:** Everyone else is here . . .

**TED:** Dougal, you're a priest! You have to show some decorum.

**DOUGAL** (*whispers*): Wish I wasn't a priest.

**TED:** Dougal! If Father Jack heard you say that!

**DOUGAL:** Sure, he told me once he doesn't believe in God!

**TED:** Dougal!

*Ted walks Dougal out of shot. Jack is left alone. He scowls and makes strange noises. Some young girls pass by. He looks at them and then slowly follows them out of shot, pushing the wheels of his chair with all his might.*

SCENE 25 EXT./DAY 3
SET: OUTSIDE TENT
*Ted and Dougal walk into shot. A sign beside the tent reads 'Tarot Reading's – Fortune's Told'.**

**DOUGAL:** Ted, can I have a go on the 'Crane of Death'?

**TED:** The what?

**DOUGAL:** The 'Crane of Death'. It's called that because there was a fella killed on it last year.

**TED:** . . . Dougal, I'm sick and tired of —

**DOUGAL:** Ted! Ted, look! A fortune teller! Just give us one go here!

**TED:** You shouldn't waste your money on that stuff, Dougal.

**DOUGAL:** There might be something in it, Ted.

**TED:** It's a lot of rubbish. How could anyone believe any of that nonsense?

**DOUGAL:** Come on, Ted. Sure it's no more peculiar than that stuff that they taught us in the seminary. Heaven and Hell and everlasting life and that type of stuff. You're not meant to

---

*Evidence of our obsession with misplaced apostrophes which, of course, meant absolutely nothing on screen.

take it seriously.

**TED:** Dougal! You *are* meant to take it seriously!

**DOUGAL:** Are you? What? Heaven, Hell and everlasting life and all that?

**TED:** Of course.

**DOUGAL:** Tsch!

**TED:** Look, if I let you go in, will you go home straight after that?

**DOUGAL:** Oh, yeah! I promise.

**TED:** Right.

*They enter the tent.*

SCENE 26 INT./DAY 3
SET: TENT
*Ted and a very excited Dougal enter the tent. An old woman sits at the table facing them.*

**WOMAN:** Hello.

*Dougal's smile dies. He looks at the woman, then turns and whispers to Ted.*

**DOUGAL:** Ted, let's go.

**TED:** What's wrong, Dougal?

**DOUGAL:** I'm scared.

**TED:** Oh, for pity's — look, I'll do it and then you can watch.

*Dougal just nods. Ted turns to the woman.*

**TED:** Hello, there!

**WOMAN:** Sit.

**TED:** All righty . . .

**WOMAN:** First, you must cross my palm with silver.

**TED:** Silver? I don't carry huge bags of it around. I'm afr—

**WOMAN:** Give me a pound.

**TED:** Oh! Right!

*The woman takes the money and fans out some cards.*

**WOMAN:** You must choose, and I will interpret. One card at a time, please.

*Ted turns over a card, giving Dougal a jokey*

'spooked' *look as he does so. The first card is the Grim Reaper. Ted turns, sees the card and jumps slightly.*

**TED:** Can I pick another card? I wasn't concentrating.

**WOMAN** (*laughs*): No, no . . . this is a common misunderstanding. The Grim Reaper does not mean death in a literal sense. Rather, it may be the death of an old way of life and the beginning of a new one.

**TED:** Ahhh! I know what that is!

*He remembers Dougal is behind him.*

**TED:** . . . Probably about getting that new light for the bike . . .

**WOMAN:** Another card, please.

*Ted turns over another card. Again, it's the Grim Reaper.*

**TED:** Ah . . . is that good?

**WOMAN:** Well . . . that, ah . . . maybe it will become clear on the next card . . .

*Ted turns over another card. Again, it's the Grim Reaper.*

**WOMAN:** This is really weird. There's only supposed to be one in each pack . . .

*Ted and Dougal exchange worried looks.*

SCENE 27 EXT./DAY 3
SET: ENTRANCE TO FIELD
*Tom is still sitting on the wall. He is reading a newspaper – 'The Craggy Island Examiner'. The headline reads 'Crazed murderer still at large'. The camera team arrive beside him.*

**TERRY:** Hello again, Tom . . . Father Crilly around yet?

**TOM:** He is, yes. He's in there.

*Terry notices a large scar on Tom's hand.*

**TERRY:** Fffewww . . . nasty scar there, Tom. Where'd you get that?

**TOM:** Oh, I was . . . in an argument.

**TERRY:** Oh . . . I hope you won.

**TOM:** I certainly did. (*Pause.*) But that's nothin'. . . . I've had worse than that!

*Tom quickly turns around, bends over and pulls down his trousers. We see the shocked faces of the camera team.*

**TOM:** Would you believe me own dog did that to me?

*One of the camera team puts his hand over his mouth and rushes off.*

**TOM:** Doesn't it look like a face?

SCENE 28 EXT./DAY 3
SET: FAIRGROUND
*Dougal and Ted are looking around anxiously.*

**TED:** Where did he get to? You'll have to get him back home for his drink. It's nearly five . . . Listen, you go that way and I'll go this way. (*Cut to Jack on a metal seat, asleep. Cut to Ted looking around. He sees him and walks over. Back to Jack on the seat. Ted goes up and sits on the seat beside him. He starts shaking him softly.*) Father? Father? We'd better be off.

SCENE 29 EXT./DAY 3
SET: FAIRGROUND
*Cut to Dougal wandering around looking for Ted and Jack. We hear an offscreen voice.*

**VOICE:** Father! Father!

*Cut to reveal the camera team beckoning to Dougal. Dougal goes over to them.*

**TERRY:** There you are, Father. We got here at last.

*Dougal looks confused.*

SCENE 30 EXT./DAY 3
SET: CRANE CHAIR
*Ted is still talking to Jack.*

**TED:** Father, Father? . . . (*Fondly.*) Tsk . . . dead to the world . . . You don't know what's goin' on, do you . . .?

*Jack wakes up.*

**JACK:** Gin! Vodka!

**TED:** That's right, Father, time for your drink . . .

**JACK:** Thunderbird! Yellow packs!

*Jack looks around in confusion, realising where he is.*

**TED:** Come on, we'd better –

*Ted moves to get out of the chair and almost falls into empty space. We see that the crane has lifted them high above the ground.*

**TED:** Arrggghh!!! What the hell are we doing up here?!!!

*Pause.*

**JACK:** Drink!

SCENE 31 EXT./DAY 3
SET: FAIRGROUND
*Dougal is with the television people.*

**DOUGAL:** Are you from the television?

**TERRY:** Eh . . . yes . . .

**DOUGAL:** Great!

**TERRY:** We'll just ask you a few questions . . .

**DOUGAL:** Questions? I'm going to be on television?

**TERRY:** Eh . . . well, yes . . . We'll start off with the history of the island, move on to how life has changed in the last few years for the islanders . . . economically and culturally . . .

*Terry's voice fades out as we close in on Dougal's face. He is open-mouthed and slightly vacant.*

SCENE 32 INT./DAY 3
SET: DOUGAL'S MIND
*Animation. We see the diagram with the silhouette of the head and 'dream' and 'reality' written on it. Question marks appear beside 'reality', then beside 'dream'. Then the words swap places. Then a few animated rabbits come into the scene and start hopping about.*

SCENE 33 EXT./DAY 3
SET: FAIRGROUND
*Dougal is now smiling gormlessly, a million miles away. We hear Terry's voice.*

**TERRY:** . . . Aaaaand, action! Father, how would you say that people's religious beliefs here on Craggy Island have been affected by the advent of television and greater access to the media in general?

SCENE 34 EXT./DAY 3
SET: THE CRANE

*Ted looks panic-stricken.*

**TED:** I've got to get off!! My interview!! Oh, Jesus, my interview!

**JACK:** Drink!

**TED** (*sees something in the distance*): Oh, God! They're talking to Dougal! Nooooo!!!!!

**JACK:** Drink! Drink! Drink! Drink! Drink!

*Jack starts rocking the chair back and forth.*

**TED:** I've got to think of something . . . Come on, Ted, think!

*Jack finally rocks the chair so much that Ted is tipped out of it. Ted falls without a noise.*

SCENE 35 INT./NIGHT 3
SET: PAROCHIAL HOUSE
*We see the floor beside Jack's chair. Bottles of rum and whiskey and wine and cans of beer litter the floor. Jack's callused hand drops lifelessly into view, a can of Castrol GTX rolling from it. Cut to a full view of him. His lap is covered with bottles and he is asleep. The camera pans around and we see a very excited Dougal staring at the television.*

**DOUGAL** (*to someone on his right*): There I am! It's me! I'm on the telly! Look!

SCENE 36 EXT./DAY 3
SET: FAIRGROUND
*Cut to the television. We see Dougal in an interview pose, the crane in the background.*

**DOUGAL** (*on television*): . . . I suppose God is a bit like the Loch Ness monster. Not a lot of people have seen him, but there's the odd photograph . . . He doesn't look like a load of tyres though . . .

*In the background we see an ambulance pulling up, blazing its lights and sounding its siren.*

**DOUGAL:** . . . But, you know . . . does he exist? (*Shrugs.*) Who knows?

*We see the ambulance pulling off.*

**DOUGAL:** See over there? Just under that tree? I was hit by lightning there.

SCENE 37 INT./NIGHT 3
SET: PAROCHIAL HOUSE
*Back in the Parochial House, we see Ted, sitting beside Dougal, covered from head to toe in a full-length cast. We can just see his eyes. He bangs his arm up and down in frustration, groaning loudly. Dougal turns to him.*

**DOUGAL:** I know! It's great, isn't it?

SCENE 38 EXT./DAY 3
SET: FAIRGROUND
*Cut back to the television Dougal.*

**DOUGAL** (*on television*): . . . The spider baby . . . ah, yes. It's got the body of a spider, but the mind of a baby . . .

*As Dougal talks on, the words 'Father Ted Crilly' appear beneath him.*

SCENE 39 INT./NIGHT 3
SET: PAROCHIAL HOUSE
*Cut to Ted, who is sobbing uncontrollably.*

**DOUGAL:** I know! I can't believe it either! I'm on television!

*Jack wakes up. He sees the television and gets a shock.*

**JACK:** That gobshite again! He's never off the air!

*He throws a bottle at the television.*

**THE END**

# entertaining father stone

**ARTHUR:** Our original idea about the titles was that they would all be in the vein of *Good Luck, Father Ted* and *Think Fast, Father Ted*, like the titles of the old 'Mister Moto' films, but we couldn't think of any more than two. In retrospect I'm glad, because it meant we could have more fun with them. This, for instance, is a fairly obvious reference to one of my favourite films, Joe Orton's *Entertaining Mr Sloane*.

The story was inspired by a 'friend' of friends of mine who used to visit them every summer. He was awful. Apart from the fact that he used to cheat at golf, he had this peculiar ability to dominate – and simultaneously ruin the atmosphere in – a room without really doing anything. One of those people who are just there. He wasn't quite as deathly silent as Father Stone, but he was on the way, apparently.

I love the silences – the quietness and calm of this episode. If I had to pick a favourite, this would probably be it. *Father Ted* can be quite frantic, perhaps too frantic on occasion, and this makes for a quiet interlude. We were really enjoying the fact that they were sitting around in silence having a truly terrible time, but after about fifteen pages we realised the episode had to go somewhere, it needed a twist – so we had Father Stone being struck by lightning. That, in turn, provides another indication of their attitude to religion. The only time we ever see Ted pray is when he's in terrible trouble and he calls on God in the last resort. But he always gets it wrong: he even offers God money to help them get rid of Father Stone.

I like the way it ends with Father Stone staying for ever. That's the beauty of sitcoms as opposed to drama: you can end one episode with something terrible happening and then not even refer to it in the next. But we did think of getting Stone back and having a running joke that he'd have a room in the house and stay there indefinitely.

**GRAHAM:** Initially, John and Mary were also going to provide a running joke through every episode, but I'm glad we dropped that idea. I don't think they would have worked in every episode as they're always exactly the same, fighting and then swooning over each other the moment they see a priest. It probably works better to only see them occasionally.

We also rather abandoned another joke after this episode: the weather. It was always in the back of our minds that the weather on Craggy Island would be constantly awful, pouring with rain literally all the time. Logistically, it would have been difficult to sustain, but that wasn't the real reason for losing it. Rather, we just seemed to forget about it . . . But I'm glad we did. It's not a good thing to paint yourself into a corner at the start of a sitcom series.

**PART ONE**
SCENE 1 INT./DAY 1
SET: PAROCHIAL HOUSE

**DOUGAL:** Ted, if you had three wishes, what would they be?

**TED:** Three wishes? . . . God, I don't know really. I suppose . . . world peace, that'd be the first one . . . then maybe an end to hunger . . . and . . . ah . . . (*We see a quick flash of Ted dancing with some girls in a nightclub.*) . . . more money for hospitals and that type of thing.

**DOUGAL:** Fair enough, Ted.

**TED:** And yourself, Dougal . . . What would your three wishes be?

**DOUGAL:** Oh, Lord. I dunno. I'm happy enough, really.

**TED:** You wouldn't want anything at all, Dougal?

**DOUGAL:** No, I don't think so. I can't think of anything, anyway.

**TED:** So you wouldn't even like . . . say, a big car to drive around in?

**DOUGAL** (*incredibly excited*): Eh? Oh, God, I don't know . . . I think that'd be fine. The car'd be fine.

**TED:** You wouldn't like to be . . . a big rock star or something? Like Elvis?

**DOUGAL:** Oh, God, yeah! That'd be great! I'd love to be a rock star! Like Elvis or something!

*Pause.*

**TED:** So, your third wish. If you had one . . .

**DOUGAL:** Oh, that'd be fine. If I had a big car to drive and I was Elvis . . . that'd be grand.

**TED** (*trying something out*): You wouldn't like . . . this cup?

*He lifts up a cup from the table.*

**DOUGAL:** Oh, God, yeah! I'd love that cup! If I had that cup and I was in a big car and I was Elvis! That'd be fantastic!

**TED:** You've never had much of an imagination, have you, Dougal?

**DOUGAL:** Oh, no, Ted, you're right there.

SCENE 2 INT./DAY 1
SET: PAROCHIAL HOUSE
*The room is completely silent apart from the sonorous ticking of the clock. We see Ted sitting in an armchair, smiling politely at someone and drinking tea. Jack is asleep in his armchair. We see whom Ted is smiling at. It is Father Paul Stone, a serious-looking priest. There is a long, long pause. Ted keeps up a rigid, unconvincing smile.*

**TED:** Would you like more tea, Paul?

**STONE:** I'm fine.

**TED:** Right . . . (*Pause.*) Will I turn on the television?

**STONE:** No, I'm fine.

*Pause.*

**TED:** Right, so . . .

*Another long pause.*

**TED:** Have you seen Father Shortall recently?

**STONE:** No.

**TED:** I was just thinking . . . what would he be? Would he be eighty now?

**STONE:** I suppose so.

*Pause. We hear the front door opening outside. Dougal sticks his head in through the door.*

**TED** (*immediately*): Dougal, you want to have a word with me? Fair enough. Won't be a moment, Paul.

*Ted bounds to the door and yanks a confused Dougal out.*

SCENE 3 INT./DAY 1
SET: PAROCHIAL HOUSE HALLWAY
*Ted closes the door and takes deep breaths. With shaking hands, he lights up a fag.*

**DOUGAL:** What's up with you, Ted? Who's that?

**TED:** God, I had to get out of there.

**DOUGAL:** Who is it, Ted?

**TED:** Now, Dougal . . . don't overreact.

**DOUGAL:** Fair enough, Ted.

**TED:** All right . . . (*Deep breath.*) It's Father Stone.

*Dougal falls out of shot.*

**TED:** Dougal! Get up!

**DOUGAL:** Oh, Ted, no, not him!

*Ted lifts Dougal back into shot. Dougal looks as if he's just been stabbed.*

**TED:** It's him all right.

**DOUGAL:** God almighty.

**TED:** I know —

**DOUGAL:** Why didn't you tell him not to come? You said you would! You promised after last time!

**TED:** I tried! But he did what he always does! I said, don't come, Father. It's not a good time for us, and he said, no, I will come, and then I said, no, Father, don't come, there's no room, and that still didn't put him off. God, I can't stand it! Those awful protracted silences!

**DOUGAL:** You could have lied to him!

**TED:** I told him all sorts of lies! I said there was a massive radiation leak and we were all dying of cholera and we were spending all our time throwing bodies into a mass

grave . . . But you know the way he is! He just shrugs it off.*

**DOUGAL:** Oh, God, Ted.

**TED** (*motioning him back to the living room*): Come on, Dougal. You've got to keep me company.

**DOUGAL:** No!!!

**TED:** Dougal!

*He wrestles with Dougal for a moment or two. Dougal keeps trying to slide on to the ground through Ted's arms, but finally Ted manages to half-lift, half-drag him into the living room.*

SCENE 4 INT./DAY 1
SET: PAROCHIAL HOUSE
*Still struggling, Ted and Dougal burst into the room. As soon as they do so, they stand up straight and smile widely at Stone.*

**TED:** Back again!

*No response.*

**TED:** Sorry, Paul, you remember Dougal?

**STONE:** Yes.

*Pause.*

**TED:** 'Course you do. Sure you must be coming here . . . how many years is it?

**PAUL:** A few, anyway.

*Pause.*

**TED:** Five. Yes . . . five years it is. Every summer . . . (*Pause.*) What time are you going back tomorrow?

**PAUL:** Ah, I might stay.

*Pause.*

**TED:** What?

**PAUL:** I might stay.

**TED** (*urgently*): How long?

**PAUL:** Don't know. A few weeks.

**TED:** A few weeks?

---

*For the final version we deleted the previous three sentences and inserted the following line: 'I told him all sorts of lies! Great big massive lies with fecking bells hanging off them!'

**PAUL:** Yeah.

*Dougal falls out of shot again. He gets to his feet slowly.*

**DOUGAL:** Sorry about that, Ted. Fell over.

**TED:** You don't have to get back to your parish, then?

**STONE:** No. Not for a while, anyway.

**TED:** Right . . . except . . . there's only one problem in that . . . Dougal and I were thinking of doing something that . . . Dougal, what were we thinking of doing?

**DOUGAL:** Oh, the thing there.

**TED:** Yes, the thing we were going to do together . . .

**DOUGAL:** Yes.

*Pause.*

**TED:** What was it again? That thing we were thinking of . . .

**DOUGAL:** Big thing it was, Ted. Eh . . .

**TED:** Eh . . . eh . . . eh . . . holiday . . . we're going on holiday!

**STONE:** That's fine. I'll mind the place.

**TED** (*to Dougal*)**:** Wait, it wasn't that we were going on holiday at all. We were going to do something else that means that no one can stay in the house.

*Pause.*

**TED** (*biting his lip*)**:** Oooohhh . . . what was it again?

*Pause. Dougal looks desperate. Ted snaps his fingers, desperately trying to come up with something.*

**TED:** What were we going to do . . .? We were going to . . .

*Pause. Ted is gesticulating wildly in order to bring forth an idea.*

**DOUGAL:** . . . Have the paintings rehung . . .

**TED:** Brilliant! Brilliant . . . memory there, Dougal! Have you noticed? They're all crooked. Look at that one, there. (*Ted goes up to a painting and starts 'adjusting' it.*) God,

what type of angle do you call that?

**DOUGAL:** Ahh, it's a mad angle.

**TED:** So we can't stay here. Too dangerous. Can't be around when people are shifting paintings all over the place.

**STONE:** Where will you go?

**TED:** Eh, we'll be staying in a hotel, probably.

**STONE:** That's all right. I'll go with you.

*Ted looks horrified. He looks at Dougal.*

**TED:** Sorry, Paul, I just have to sort out something with Dougal.

*He rises and motions Dougal to follow him. They go outside the door.*

SCENE 5 INT./DAY 1
SET: PAROCHIAL HOUSE HALLWAY

**TED:** What are we going to do? Think, Dougal, think!

*Dougal looks very blank.*

**TED:** OK, I'll do the thinking. God, what'll we do?

**DOUGAL:** Ted . . . Jack.

**TED:** Oh, God, if he sees him! He'll . . . Christ almighty! I'll have to break it to him gently. You get Paul out of the house and I'll —

**DOUGAL:** You're not leaving me alone with him, Ted!

**TED:** Dougal!

**DOUGAL:** Sorry, Ted, but I have to say no. I just can't. There's no way.

**TED:** Right, so are you going to tell Jack?

**DOUGAL:** I'll get my coat.

*They go back inside.*

SCENE 6 INT./DAY 1
SET: PAROCHIAL HOUSE

**TED:** Paul, Dougal's going for a walk. Would you like to join him?

**STONE:** No, thanks.

**TED:** Will you not go? It's lovely.

**STONE:** No, thanks. I'm fine.

**TED:** Paul, he has to show you something. It's very important.

**STONE:** Is it?

**TED:** Oh, yes. Very important. This could be the most important thing you'll ever see.

**STONE:** Yeah?

**TED:** Oh, yes.

**STONE:** Right.

**TED:** So you'll go?

**STONE:** No, I'm fine. I'll see it again.

**TED:** OK, Paul, to be honest, Dougal doesn't want to show you anything. It's just . . . there's a fire in the house, and you'll have to leave.

**STONE:** A fire?

**TED:** Yes. I didn't want you to get into a panic because it's only a small fire. But it could spread. And if you died in it, I'd never forgive myself. You go out with Dougal, and I'll fight the blaze.

**STONE:** All right.

**TED:** You're going!?

**STONE:** Yeah, if there's a fire.

**TED:** Great!

*Stone gets up. Dougal appears at the door in his coat. Dougal looks terror-stricken.*

**TED:** Don't worry about me, now! Bit of water'll do the trick!

*They leave. Ted looks at Jack with trepidation. He goes to the shelves and takes something off the top.*

SCENE 7 EXT./DAY 1
SET: PAROCHIAL HOUSE
*We see Dougal gently ushering Stone outside.*

**DOUGAL:** Have you seen Father Shortall lately?

**STONE:** No.

**DOUGAL:** I suppose he must be about eighty now.

**STONE:** I suppose so.

SCENE 8 INT./DAY 1
SET: PAROCHIAL HOUSE
*We see that Ted is wearing a crash helmet and protective shoulderpads. He approaches Jack.*

**TED:** Father? Father, you awake?

*Jack awakens in a slow, blinking, peaceful way. He looks at Ted glassily, still half-asleep.*

**TED:** Father. (*Deep breath.*) We have a visitor.

SCENE 9 EXT./DAY 1
SET: PAROCHIAL HOUSE
*Dougal and Stone are standing outside the house.*

**DOUGAL:** So . . . how's everything then?

**STONE:** All right.

*Just as Dougal is about to speak, a figure smashes through the window of the front room. It is Ted, who has obviously been thrown through it with some force. He stands up and brushes himself off. Inside the house, we just about hear Jack.*

**JACK** (*distantly*): Not that bastard! You keep him away from me!

*Ted calmly walks back to the front door of the house, giving Dougal and Stone a little wave.*

**TED:** Bit of a backdraft! . . . Nearly out!

*He walks through the door and into the house. Stone looks at Dougal.*

SCENE 10 INT./DAY 1
SET: PAROCHIAL HOUSE
*Ted and Dougal are sitting down, captive to the unearthly silence. Stone looks at them, his occasional blinking the only sign of life.*

**DOUGAL:** Jack gone to bed, then, Ted?

**TED:** Yes, he was a little tired.

SCENE 11 INT./DAY 1
SET: JACK'S BEDROOM
*We see Jack tied down to his bed, struggling mightily.*

SCENE 12 INT./DAY 1
SET: PAROCHIAL HOUSE
*Again, we see the three men sitting in silence. A very, very long pause.*

**TED:** Well, I suppose my bath'll be ready by now.

*He stands up. Dougal grabs hold of his arm and then his leg, both of which Ted wrestles free from.*

SCENE 13 INT./DAY 1
SET: BATHROOM
*Ted walks into the bathroom in his dressing gown. He closes the door, takes the dressing gown off and gets into the bath.*

**TED:** Ahhhhhhhh . . .

*Ted closes his eyes. He smiles and relaxes. He opens them to see Stone looking down at him.*

**TED** (*Pause. He doesn't quite know what to say*): Can I help you, Paul?

**STONE:** I'm fine.

*Pause. Ted moves his hand to cover his middle. There is another long pause.*

**TED:** Ah . . .

*Pause.*

**TED:** Sorry, Paul . . . I . . . ah . . . I'm having a bath.

**STONE:** I just wanted to go to the toilet.

**TED:** Ah . . . all right, go ahead, Paul.

*Paul walks to the toilet beside the bath, pulls down his trousers and sits down.*

**TED** (*to himself*): Oh, for Jaysus' sake . . .

*Ted covers his eyes.*

SCENE 14 INT./EVENING 1
SET: PAROCHIAL HOUSE
*Stone, Dougal and Ted are sitting in their usual chairs. The unearthly silence is reaching breaking point. Ted gets up.*

**TED:** Right! Time for bed!

**STONE** (*looks at his watch*): It's only half seven.

**TED:** Yeah, but . . . I have to be up at eleven tomorrow. Dougal, you'd better get some rest, too.

*Dougal stands up and runs out of the room at top speed.*

**TED:** Goodnight, then!

SCENE 15 INT./EVENING 1
SET: TED AND DOUGAL'S BEDROOM
*Ted and Dougal are in their beds, staring at the ceiling.*

**DOUGAL:** I can't take much more of this, Ted.

**TED:** I know, I know . . .

**DOUGAL:** Six years. You'd think that by now he'd have got the message. Do you remember that year when we knew he was coming and we pretended to be on a retreat?

**TED:** That was amazing. Anyone else'd go, oh, fair enough, and just not come. God . . . five days hiding in the attic. No food, no water . . . rats everywhere . . . God, if only we'd thought of it this year . . .

**DOUGAL:** How'd you meet him in the first place?

**TED:** He was introduced to me by Father Jim Dougan. We were at a conference and Dougan came up, said, this is Father Stone, and then ran out of the building. Just ran out! I should have known something was up . . . So we started talking . . . Well, I started talking. You know how he is. Just to break the silence, I invited him to stay . . . just for something to say, you know? The next day, *the next day,* he arrived on the island. I wouldn't mind if he just said something. But he just sits there! I mean, what does he get out of it!

**DOUGAL:** I hope he's gone before your birthday party . . .

**TED:** Oh, God, he'll be gone long before then. What is it? Three weeks away?

SCENE 16 INT./NIGHT 2
SET: PAROCHIAL HOUSE (3 WEEKS LATER)
*We see Stone sitting in what is by now his usual chair, wearing a party hat. We see that there are more guests sitting around, all wearing party hats,*

all completely silent. Ted looks very embarrassed. Jack is getting drunk somewhere else in the room. The mood is that of a funeral. One guest, Father Billy Kerrigan, looks at his watch and stands up.

**BILLY:** God, look at the time. Better get going, Ted.

**TED:** Oh . . . fair enough . . .

*Another priest, Father Liam Fay, leans forward.*

**LIAM:** Actually, I'd better be off as well. Can I get a lift from you, Billy?

**BILLY:** No problem. Anyone else need a lift?

*Everyone puts their hand up. They all stand up and follow Billy out of the room. Dougal is one of them.*

**TED:** Dougal . . .

*Dougal turns and sits down again, looking miserable. Stone sits there, not saying anything. The three stare at each other. Jack falls off the table, drunk.*

**END OF PART ONE**

\* \* \*

**PART TWO**

SCENE 17 INT./NIGHT 2
SET: TED AND DOUGAL'S BEDROOM
*It is very dark, but Ted is lit up by light. He is praying.*

**TED:** Please, God . . . please get rid of him. I don't care how you do it. Just, please . . . please get rid of him. Do you want money? Anything you want. Name any charity. Just . . . please! Please get rid of him! . . .

*He starts sobbing.*

SCENE 18 EXT./DAY 3
SET: CRAZY GOLF COURSE
*We see a sign saying 'Craggy Island Crazy Golf – £1.00, Members – 50p'. The sign is being lashed by wind and rain. There seems to be only one hole on the course. It is just a row of cement blocks with a windmill at the end of it. We hear thunder in the distance. Ted and Dougal are playing the hole. It is raining buckets. They look miserable.*

**DOUGAL:** Maybe we should go home, Ted.

**TED:** Think about it, Dougal. Think about who's sitting in the living room.

*Pause.*

**DOUGAL:** I think it's clearing up a bit, anyway.

*He lines up the putt. As he does so, the windmill is blown away by a gust of wind. Dougal is now aiming at an empty space.*

**DOUGAL:** The windmill thing's blown away, there, Ted.

**TED:** Never mind. Just have your go.

*Dougal lines up his shot. Just as he's about to putt, we hear a voice from nearby.*

**STONE:** Golf, yeah . . .?

**TED** (*to himself*)**:** God help us . . . (*To Stone.*) Ah, yes. Crazy golf, Paul . . . Not exactly the U.S. Masters!

**STONE:** No.

*Pause.*

**TED:** Will you have a go, Paul?

**STONE:** No.

**TED:** Ah, you will. It's great fun! Isn't it, Dougal?

**DOUGAL:** Oh, yeah. Fantastic, Ted.

**TED:** You'll have a go, Paul?

**STONE:** No.

**TED:** Go on! Sure it's even easier now the windmill has blown away!

*Ted takes the club from Dougal and more or less forces the club into Stone's hands.*

**TED:** There you go, Paul. Give it a real go! Sure what's the worst thing that can happen?

*Stone raises the club slightly and is hit by a massive bolt of lightning.*

**STONE** (*high-pitched*)**:** Waiieeee!!!!

*Ted and Dougal are gobsmacked. They look at each other.*

**DOUGAL:** Uh-oh.

SCENE 19 INT./DAY 3
SET: HOSPITAL CORRIDOR
*Ted and Dougal are sitting in a corridor, looking worried.*

**TED:** Oh, God, Dougal, it's all my fault!

**DOUGAL:** Don't be silly, Ted. What'd you do, pray for him to be hit by lightning?

**TED:** No, no, of course not . . . Well, I asked him to intervene in some way, but this is a bit much. (*Looks up and addresses God.*) What were you thinking of?

**DOUGAL:** Who would have thought that being hit by lightning would land you in hospital . . .?

**TED:** What? What are you talking about? Of course it can land you in hospital!

**DOUGAL:** Well . . . it's not usually serious, is it, Ted? I was hit by lightning a few times and I never had to go to hospital.

**TED:** Yes, but . . . you're different from most people, Dougal. All that happened to you was balloons kept sticking to you. Most people do have to drop into a hospital after being hit by lightning. Just to be polite, you know? (*Pause.*) God, I hate hospitals.

**DOUGAL:** Did you ever notice that it's usually sick people who end up in hospital?

**TED:** Thank you, John Pilger.

**DOUGAL:** Oh, yeah, they all come here. (*Pause.*) Of course you're a goner the minute you walk through the door. I'd prefer to take my chances in the real world. No matter how sick I was, I'd never go under the hammer.

**TED:** Under the knife, Dougal. Under the hammer is auctioneering.

**DOUGAL:** Oh, right . . . (*Pause.*) Did you ever see that film, Ted, where your man has his head transplanted on to a fly, and the fly's head was transplanted on to the man?

**TED:** Oh, yes . . . what was it called . . .?

**DOUGAL:** *Out of Africa*, I think. Anyway, your man has the head of the fly and he's chasing his wife all over the place and she's hiding the jam and everything, so he won't get stuck in it . . .

**TED:** I'll have to stop you there, Dougal.

**DOUGAL:** Yes, Ted?

**TED:** No reason. I just have to stop you.

*Suddenly, Jack is wheeled by on a trolley. A doctor follows behind.*

**TED:** There he is. The weekly emergency. What is it today, Doctor?

**JACK:** Frig!

**DOCTOR:** We don't know. I think it's a combination of Babycham and Harpic.

*The doctor moves off.*

**TED:** Only things left after the party, I suppose . . .

**DOUGAL:** They've been in there a long time, haven't they, Ted?

**TED:** They have . . . God . . . What's going on?

**DOUGAL:** Do you think he'll die, Ted? He's been in there for a while.

**TED:** They're probably just doing tests.

**DOUGAL:** What type of tests? General knowledge?

**TED:** No . . .

**DOUGAL:** They won't be able to get much out of him in that condition.

**TED:** No, no, medical tests.

**DOUGAL:** Sure what would he know about that, Ted? He's a priest!

*Jack suddenly runs by, holding his IV drip. Some doctors and nurses run after him.*

**TED:** God, would you look at that! He can move when he wants to.

*They see the shopkeepers, John and Mary O'Leary, approaching from the end of the corridor. Mr O'Leary has a bloodstained bandage around his head. Mrs O'Leary has her arm in a sling.*

**MRS O'LEARY:** You stupid bastard. You've really, really done it this time.

**MR O'LEARY:** You started it, you bitch.

**MRS O'LEARY:** God, I should have finished the job. The next time I — (*She notices Ted.*). Ah, Father . . .

**TED:** Hello, John. Hello, Mary.

**MR O'LEARY:** Ah . . . well . . . What are you doing here?

**TED:** A friend of ours had an accident.

**MRS O'LEARY:** Oh, dear.

*Pause. Ted looks at Mr O'Leary's bloodstained bandage.*

**TED:** And what happened to you? That looks a bit nasty.

**MR O'LEARY:** Ah, it's nothing, Father. Just a headache. Don't know why I bothered coming, really.

**TED:** Is that blood there?

**MR O'LEARY:** No. God, no. I don't think so. I just got a slight nick with a knife while Mary was putting the bandage on. It's not a stab wound.

**MRS O'LEARY:** Sure, he's fine.

**TED:** You look like you've been in the wars yourself, Mary.

**MRS O'LEARY:** Ah . . . it's just a sprain, Father. It's nothing. I was lifting a bag of coal. It's not broken . . . (*Pause.*) Or if it is — sure what the hell!

**TED:** Ah, ha!

*Pause.*

MR O'LEARY: Anyway, I hope your friend gets better.

MRS O'LEARY: We'll be off. Goodbye, Fathers.

*They move off, smiling, out of earshot of Ted and Dougal.*

MRS O'LEARY: The next time, I'll make friggin' sure . . .

MR O'LEARY: Shut up, you batty old witch.

*Cut back to Ted and Dougal.*

DOUGAL: They're a lovely couple, though, aren't they? John and Mary?

TED: Ah, they are, all right . . .

*As they talk, we see Mrs O'Leary kick Mr O'Leary in the groin. Mr O'Leary falls on the ground and starts holding his groin and moaning. Mrs O'Leary continues kicking him on the floor.*

SCENE 20 INT./DAY 3
SET: HOSPITAL CORRIDOR
*Ted and Dougal sit in the corridor. Ted looks tired and drawn, but Dougal seems as fresh as always.*

TED: How much longer are they going to be . . .?

DOUGAL (*looks at his watch*): God, Ted, we hardly even know him, when you think about it. Does he have much of a family?

TED: The parents are still alive . . . and I think he has a brother, a doctor in America.

DOUGAL: A doctor. Wow.

TED: You wouldn't think it, would you? But that used to be common enough. The favourite son would become a doctor or something, and the idiot brother would be sent off to the priesthood.

*Pause.*

DOUGAL: Your brother's a doctor, isn't he?

TED: He is, yes.

*A doctor comes out of the room. Ted and Dougal stand up.*

TED: So, how's the patient?

DOCTOR: He's hanging in there. It's mostly shock, but . . .

TED: Great! Well, that's not serious!

DOCTOR: Well, it's quite serious. A bolt of lightning can do a lot of damage.

TED: Can it?

DOCTOR: Yes. His reactions are very poor at the moment.

TED (*slightly desperate*): Oh, he's always been like that. Very poor reactions. That's normal for him.

DOCTOR: Well, actually, he's not reacting at all to any stimulus.

TED: Again, no need to worry. That's always the way with him.

DOCTOR: Look, Father, I'm the doctor. And I know that it's not normal to fail to react to a stimulus.

TED: I'm sure it is. Watch this.

*Ted throws a pen at Dougal. It bounces off Dougal's head. Dougal doesn't react.*

TED: Y'see? It's a thing with priests. We have our minds on more spiritual things.

There's no need to worry.

**DOCTOR:** Well, no, I think I will worry about it . . .

**TED** (*defeated at last*): Oh, God, OK, OK . . . Look, can we see him? I'd like to say a prayer.

**DOCTOR:** Yes, all right, Father. This way . . .

SCENE 21 INT./DAY 3
SET: HOSPITAL WAITING ROOM
*We see Stone, standing in the same position, holding the golf club, his face frozen in a cross-eyed grimace. His hair stands on end. Beside him are IV drips, a heart monitor, etc.*

**DOCTOR:** As you can see, we still haven't been able to remove the golf club.

**TED:** Why isn't he in bed?

**DOCTOR:** It's hard to get him in a comfortable position when he's in that stance. (*Looks at his watch.*) But you're right, he's been on his feet long enough.

**DOUGAL:** He looks like a trophy.

**TED** (*laughs slightly*): You know, he does a bit!

*There is a knock on the door. A woman sticks her head around it. She is Mrs Stone, Stone's mother.*

**MRS STONE:** Sorry, I heard — Oh, no! Paul!

*She runs over and hugs Stone, who teeters slightly. Stone's father, Mr Stone, enters, followed by Granny Stone, a tiny, fierce-faced woman.*

**DOCTOR:** Come on, Mrs Stone, we have to put him into bed. Father, could you?

*Ted and the doctor put him into bed. Dougal stands in front of the heart monitor, transfixed by the bleeping noise and the white dot. Mrs Stone hugs her husband, still weeping. She turns back just as Ted is finished.*

**MRS STONE:** Oh! You must be Father Crilly.

**TED:** I am, yes.

**MRS STONE:** Oh, God bless you, Father. God bless you.

*Mr Stone coughs lightly.*

**MRS STONE:** Father, this is my husband, Dermot.

*Mr Stone grabs Ted's hand with both of his and pumps it up and down many, many times.*

**MR STONE:** Oh, God, Father, it's terrible, it's terrible, God, Father, forgive me Father, forgive me for using the Lord's name, Father, but, Jesus Christ, isn't it terrible, Father!

**TED:** It is, yes —

**MR STONE** (*still shaking Ted's hand*): It is, it is, it is, it is, it is, it's terrible, Father, it is, I couldn't have said it better myself, terrible is the word, terrible is . . . I tell you, terrible is too small a word, Father, God bless you, but it is, it's too small a word, Father. (*Turns to Stone's prone figure.*) Look at what you've done to your mother! You little bastard! You're useless! Get up out of that bed now!

**TED:** Now, Mr Stone . . .

**MR STONE:** I'm sorry, Father. Him causing you this trouble. God forgive me for saying this, but wouldn't it have been better if he'd been killed? And herself all upset. Jesus, what you must think of him. And us, for bringing him into the world . . .

**TED:** Now, Mr Stone . . .

**MR STONE:** I'm going out for a drink. Will you join me?

**TED:** Eh, no, I think I should stay here for the moment . . .

**MR STONE:** Fair enough. See you later, then.

*He stops shaking Ted's hand and walks out.*

**MRS STONE:** . . . And this is Mammy . . .

*Ted turns to smile at the old woman but is met by a gaze of terrible, vicious suspicion from her. His smile dies immediately.*

**TED** (*nervously*): Hello!

*The old woman, still looking very scary indeed, beckons Ted with her finger. Ted walks over to her.*

**TED:** Yes?

*He bends down to hear her.*

**GRANNY STONE** (*whispers*): I know what you're up to.

*Ted bolts upright, looking terrified. He is immediately grabbed by Mrs Stone.*

**MRS STONE:** Oh, God, Father, you know . . . Paul thought the world of you.

**TED:** Ah, well . . .

**MRS STONE:** He did. He never stopped talking about you. It was Father Ted said this and Father Ted said that. He worshipped you, Father.

**TED** (*massively uncomfortable*): Really?

**MRS STONE:** He'd come back from Craggy Island and he'd be counting the days till he could come back. Literally. He had a chart and he'd mark the days as they went by. And just at the very bottom of the chart, Father, there'd be a photograph of yourself.

**TED:** Oh, God . . .

**MRS STONE** (*reaches into her bag*): He used to paint as well, Father. He did this one for you, but he was too shy to bring it himself.

*She takes out the painting. It is a small, framed portrait, quite well done, of a smiling Ted and Stone, their arms around each other's shoulders in a lads' embrace.*

**TED** (*aghast at this*): But, he never gave me any indication . . .

**MRS STONE:** And of course, he had this, Father.*

*She shows him a medallion containing a lock of hair.**

**MRS STONE:** He said that he snipped that off when you were asleep, Father. He would have asked, but he was afraid that you'd say no to him. And that would have broken his heart. He wanted a memento of you to carry around with him wherever he was . . .*

*Suddenly, we hear a loud bleeping noise.*

**MRS STONE:** Oh, God!!!!

*Ted runs over to Stone.*

**TED:** Oh, God, what is it?!

**MRS STONE:** It's his heart! Do something, Father!

*Ted pauses for a moment, looking desperate, then begins to pummel Stone fiercely on the chest. Stone jolts wildly with each punch. Cut to Dougal looking at his watch. He adjusts it and the wild bleeping sound stops. Ted and Mrs Stone look at Dougal. Dougal smiles at them gormlessly.*

**TED** (*grits his teeth*): Dougal . . .

*Ted looks at the old woman. She is still giving Ted the evil eye. The doctor enters.*

**DOCTOR:** Mrs Stone, could you come with

* We deleted these lines from the final version.

me? I need you to fill out some forms.

**MRS STONE:** Will he be all right, Doctor?

**DOCTOR:** We're doing all we can. But he is quite ill. Just hope for the best.

*Ted looks devastated.*

**MRS STONE:** All right, Doctor. Come on, Mammy.

*The old woman turns and gives Ted the evil eye again. The two women leave the room.*

**TED:** She knows!

**DOUGAL:** What, Ted?

**TED:** The old woman! She knows! She knows it's all my fault!

**DOUGAL:** Sure how would she know that, Ted?

**TED:** Oh, they know, Dougal. They have ways. Old women are closer to God than we'll ever be. Why do you think they're always going to Mass? They get to that age and they have a direct line. They don't need the operator any more. Oh, she knows all right . . . But who could blame her for being angry with me? It's all my fault! I mean . . . Why did I do it?!

*He falls to his knees beside the bed.*

**TED:** Oh, Lord, please bring him back! I never wanted you to take him away. There was no need for the lightning! You know I

didn't mean that! That was just silly! Oh, God, please bring him back. Bring him back and I swear, I swear we'll look after him! He can stay as long as he wants —

**DOUGAL:** Ah, now, Ted —

**TED:** Shut up, Dougal! I swear, bring him back and I'll take care of him for the rest of my days! Please! Please do this one thing!!!!

*Ted looks at Stone. No response. He looks up again.*

**TED:** Ah, come on! Please! Please! I swear I'll . . . I'll . . .

*He looks down. Stone is staring at him without expression. He is back to his former self.*

**TED:** Paul! Paul, I don't believe it! You're back! Oh, Lord, thank you! It's a miracle! It's a miracle! DOCTOR! DOCTOR! Paul, are you all right? Can we get you anything?

*Pause.*

**STONE:** I'm fine, thanks.

SCENE 22 INT./DAY 3
SET: PAROCHIAL HOUSE
*We see Ted, Dougal, Jack and Stone, all staring at each other. Pause. After a moment, the credits start to roll in silence. The silence is broken occasionally by slight coughs.*

**THE END**

# the passion of saint tibulus

**GRAHAM:** This episode was very easy to write – we just followed the course of certain events in real life. Whenever a provocative film stirs up controversy, it's a pleasure to watch all the moral guardians who try and protect us from it becoming unpaid, unwitting publicists for the film company. *Je Vous Salue, Marie* – Godard's updating of the Virgin Mary story – caused one hell of a storm in Ireland. A friend of mine went to see it in Trinity College and he was punched by a nun when he came out. She punched him in the face just for watching a film. These people still don't seem to understand the basic concept that the more fuss you make about a film, the more people will want to see it. Would anyone really have been desperate to see *Je Vous Salue, Marie* if it hadn't been banned?

We knew when we were plotting the episode that having Ted and Dougal stage a protest would provide lots of opportunities for jokes. That's how we generally plot an episode – we look for those kind of opportunities and string them together as believably as we can. I'm very happy with their ineffectual protesting in the cinema: 'That'll be enough out of you, now!' – all that stuff. I think Dermot and Ardal even threw in 'Ye dirty pups, ye!' during filming.

This was a contender for the first episode, because in it we explain why Ted, Dougal and Jack have been banished to Craggy Island. I think it actually works better being in Episode Three – it would have been too obvious to fill the audience in on the backstory (a word I use with much embarrassment, by the way) in the first episode.

Mrs Doyle is also beginning to show her true colours here, evolving into a psychotically hospitable character with her demented insistence on offering tea to the bishop. At first we really didn't realise the potential of her character, or of Pauline McLynn's phenomenal ability which I think, develops into tremendous physical comedy later in the series. We did try and give her one stand-out moment in each episode (sometimes, shamefully, failing – as in *Entertaining Father Stone*).

**ARTHUR:** Geoffrey Perkins, our producer, was an enormous influence at the beginning, making sure we didn't stray too far from the point. He also did the wonderful voice-over for Father Hernandez at the beginning of the episode. I really haven't a clue how we decided on having him speak Spanish, which, bizarrely, they understand, and having a translation for the viewers. But I think it works well because Geoffrey's enunciation is so droll.

Bishops being up to no good in the bedroom was still a relatively novel plotline at this point. It was certainly influenced by the news of Bishop Casey's affair, which was greeted with horror by older people in Ireland and unbridled joy by everyone else. It also coincided with the exposure of an affair between a priest called Father Michael Cleary and his housekeeper, but our take on all that was very light with Brennan prancing around with his mistress in full bishop's garb. I'm still not sure why, but we had to lose a shot of Brennan's child making bishop's hat-shaped sandcastles on the beach. This was a pity, because I think that image summed the situation up in one very simple gag.

## PART ONE
SCENE 1 EXT./NIGHT 1
SET: PAROCHIAL HOUSE

*Through the rain-streaked window of the Parochial House, we see Father Dougal McGuire, a young innocent-looking priest, staring out at the night. Occasionally his face is illuminated by flashes of lightning. From the noise, we can assume that the rain is pummelling the earth.*

SCENE 2 INT./NIGHT 1
SET: PAROCHIAL HOUSE

*We see Father Ted Crilly sitting at a table with a handsome, black-haired priest. This is Father José Hernandez, a Cuban. Whenever he speaks, his dialogue is dubbed (no one comments on this). His 'voice' is very deep and smooth; he sounds like a real lady-killer. The two priests are seated around a Cluedo board. They are drinking cups of tea. A large brown candle burns in the centre of the table. Father Jack Hackett, an elderly man whom we can't see clearly as yet, watches television in another part of the room. Cut to Dougal, who is still watching the torrential rain. We see more lightning and hear more thunder.*

**DOUGAL:** Looks like rain, Ted.

*Ted raises his eyes heavenward when he hears this.*

**TED:** Dougal, come on. It's your go.

*Dougal walks over and assumes his place at the table. He rolls some dice. Ted smiles at Hernandez.*

**TED** (*brightly*)**:** I must say, Father Hernandez, it's been wonderful having you over. But I expect you're getting a bit homesick for Cuba by now.

**JOSE** (*dubbed*)**:** Si. Mi pais es muy hermoso.
[Yes. My country is very beautiful.]

**JOSE** (*dubbed*)**:** Pero, Ted, usted es un hombre muy afortunado. En Craggy Island tiene usted dos buenos amigos, el Padre Dougal . . .
[But, Ted, you have a great life here on Craggy Island. You have two good friends, Father Dougal . . .]

*Shot of Dougal choking on something. He gags for a while and then takes one of the Cluedo pieces out of his mouth and looks at it quizzically.*

**JOSE** (*dubbed*)**:** . . . Y claro, el Padre Jack.
[. . . And, of course, Father Jack.]

*We see Father Jack's face for the first time. We hear the sound of flies buzzing. His mouth hangs open, and a thin line of drool hangs from his mouth. His teeth are blackened and broken. His nose is large, red and bruised. One of his eyes rolls up into the socket. A tooth sticks out of the corner of his mouth, pushing his lip up into a permanent sneer. One of his ears looks as if it has been badly burnt. When he breathes, he sounds like a sleeping animal.\**

*Mrs Doyle enters with more tea.*

**TED:** Yes . . . yes, it's . . . it's great here. Although, I must say, sometimes I miss the noise and the lights and the . . . you know, the whole buzz of the big city.

**JOSE** (*dubbed*)**:** Usted estaba en Wexford, verdad?
[You were in Wexford, weren't you?]

**TED:** I was, yes. But, you know, Craggy Island has its charms. The west part of the island was beautiful. Until it drifted off, of course.

**JOSE** (*dubbed*)**:** Se desprendio?
[Drifted off?]

**TED:** Yes. There was a bit of a storm and it came loose. Now, of course, we don't have a west side. It's just north, south and east. But while it was there it was lovely.

**JOSE** (*dubbed*)**:** Sabe usted Ted . . . su ama de llaves es una mujer muy hermosa.
[You know, Ted, your housekeeper is a very beautiful woman.]

*He smiles at Mrs Doyle. She doesn't know how to deal with this, and makes a hasty exit.*

---

\*Obviously, we reined ourselves in on some of this.

JOSE: En ocasiones esto del celibato es muy duro para un hombre . . . je, je, je . . .
[Sometimes, this celibacy is hard for a man . . . heh, heh . . .]

TED: Oh, well . . . you have to take the rough with the smooth, I suppose. Bishop Brennan springs to mind.

JOSE (dubbed): Ah si . . .?
[Oh, yes . . .?]

TED: Yes, Bishop Len Brennan. He's our . . . kind of boss, I suppose. He's the one who thought Dougal and Father Jack would be better off working here . . . on an island with, you know . . . a very small population. Anyway, the rumour is that his housekeeper caught him once, ah, 'in delicto flagrante'. They say, ah . . . they say the union was 'blessed' if you know what I mean.

JOSE (dubbed): No! . . . Nino o nina?
[No! . . . boy or girl?]

TED: A boy, I think. Lives in America now, or so goes the rumour anyway!

DOUGAL: Was it . . . Colonel Mustard . . . in the kitchen . . . with the candlestick?

TED: What?

DOUGAL: Colonel Mustard, in the kitchen, with the candlestick?

TED: But you have Colonel Mustard! You showed him to me earlier! How could it be Colonel Mustard if you have Colonel Mustard?!!

Slight pause.

DOUGAL: Ohhh, right . . .

TED: Father Hernandez, your go . . .

JOSE (dubbed): Si . . . Creo que fue el Reverendo Green . . . con el cuchillo . . . en la estancia.
[Yes . . . I think it was Reverend Green, with the knife, in the drawing room.]

TED: Those Protestants! Up to no good as usual!

Everyone laughs softly.

TED: What's Father Jack looking at?

Shot of Father Jack staring intently at the television.

TED: What's that you're watching, Father?

JACK (barks): What?!

TED: What film are you watching?

JACK: What?!

TED: Isn't that Keifer Sutherland?

JACK: What?!

TED: Is that Flatliners you're watching?

JACK: What?!

JOSE (dubbed): El Padre Jack esta un poco mal de los oidos?
[Is Father Jack a little hard of hearing?]

JACK: What?!

TED: Well, he gets a kind of waxy build-up in his ears. Then we have to syringe them. It's not very nice.

JACK: What?!

JOSE (cringing slightly): Mmmhmm . . .

JACK: What?!

DOUGAL: It's great, though, in a way, 'cause we're never short of candles, you know?

Dougal indicates the very large candle in the middle

*of the table. Hernandez looks at it with something approaching horror.*

**JACK:** What?!

**TED:** Yes, most of that was in his head last week. And up there . . .

*He points to a row of candles on the mantelpiece.*

**TED:** We've nearly enough for a papal funeral! He's a one-man candle factory! Aren't you, Father?

**JACK:** What?!

**TED** *(whispering to Hernandez)*: To be honest, though, he can hear well enough when he wants to. Watch this. *(Louder.)* Father Jack, would you like a glass of brandy?

**JACK:** Yes!

**TED:** You see? He's a terrible man!

**JACK** *(shouts)*: Brandy!

**TED** *(good-humouredly)*: All right! All right!

*Ted gets the brandy and a large bowl-shaped glass and brings it over to Jack. He starts pouring.*

**TED:** Say when . . .

**JACK:** What?!

**TED** *(still pouring)*: Say when . . .

**JACK:** What?!

**TED:** Tell me when you want me to stop pouring.

**JACK:** What?!

**TED:** Say when!

**JACK:** What?!

*Jack's glass is full to the brim.*

**TED:** Oh, right, that's it, is it? You sure you don't want more?!

**JACK:** Yes!

*He grabs the bottle from Ted. Ted gives him a look and starts to move back to the table. The telephone rings, however, and he stops to pick up the receiver.*

**TED:** Hello, Craggy Island Parochial House. Father Ted Crilly speaking. *(His face grows slightly fearful.)* Oh! Bishop Brennan! . . . How are you? Yes . . . No . . . All right . . . Yes, of course . . . Good, yes . . . All right, then . . .

Bye, so! *(He puts the telephone down.)* That was the boss. He's coming over. He says he wants to talk to us about something. *(More to himself.)* It must be important . . . he's had to come back early from his holidays.

*Dougal is examining the Cluedo wallet where the killer, location and weapon card are hidden.*

**DOUGAL:** Ted. Shouldn't there be some cards in here, or something?

*He holds it up. It's empty.*

SCENE 3 EXT./MORNING 2
SET: PAROCHIAL HOUSE HALLWAY
*Hernandez is saying goodbye to Ted and Dougal. He shakes hands with them both.*

**JOSE** *(dubbed)*: Nuevamente, no tengo palabras para expresar mi gratitud.

[Again, I have no words to say how thankful I am.]

**DOUGAL** *(whispers)*: That's a bit ungrateful, Ted.

**TED** *(ignoring Dougal)*: Don't you worry about it, Father!

**JOSE** *(dubbed)*: Sin embargo, lo que si tengo son algunos regalos que les manda la gente de mi pueblo.
[However, I do have some gifts from people of my village.]

*He hands a package to Dougal.*

**JOSE** *(dubbed)*: Por favor, no se vayan ustedes a reir de sencillez de este regalito. Es solo un ejemplo de artesania cubana.
[Please do not laugh at this simple gift. It is just an example of Cuban handicraft.]

*Dougal unwraps the package like a ten-year-old boy.*

**DOUGAL:** It's a video recorder!

**JOSE** *(dubbed)*: Si, lo lamento. Es un modelo muy basico. Solo tiene el sistema de pregrabado con tres semanas de anticipacion.
[Yes, I am sorry. It is a very basic model. It has only a three week pre-record facility.]

**DOUGAL:** No, don't worry about it! It's great!

*He runs inside.*

**TED:** Thanks very much, Father Hernandez. That's wonderful.

**JOSE** (*dubbed*)**:** Y, en cuanto a usted Ted, tengo algo muy especial.
[And for you, Ted, I have something very special.]

*He gives Ted a package. Ted opens it.*

**TED:** You really didn't have to . . .

*He sees that it is a hand-carved wooden sculpture of a male figure with a very large appendage sticking up into the air.*

**TED** (*shocked*)**:** . . . You really didn't have to . . .

**JOSE** (*dubbed*)**:** Es un simbolo cubano de fertilidad. Espero que le traiga tanta suerte a used, como la que me ha traido a mi . . . si? . . . eh? Eh, mi buen amigo . . .?
[It is a Cuban fertility symbol. I hope it brings you as much luck as it brought me, yes? Eh? Eh, my friend?]

**TED:** Ha, ha, yes . . .

**JOSE:** Bueno, adios, Ted.
[Well, goodbye, Ted.]

*He puts on a pair of designer sunglasses and walks out of shot.*

SCENE 4 EXT./DAY 2
SET: PAROCHIAL HOUSE
*Ted waves goodbye. Cut to Hernandez in a Ferrari. He waves and takes off at incredible speed.*

SCENE 5 INT./DAY 2
SET: PAROCHIAL HOUSE
*Dougal is down on all fours, messing around with the VCR. Ted is cleaning up the room.*

**TED:** C'mon now, Dougal. The Bishop'll be here any minute.

**DOUGAL:** Oh, right.

**TED:** Now, do you remember what I told you?

**DOUGAL:** Eh . . .

**TED:** It's very simple. On no account mention what we were talking about last night.

**DOUGAL:** Right. (*Pause.*) What were we

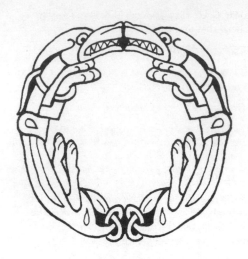

talking about last night?

**TED:** You know . . . the rumours about the Bishop's little mistake.

**DOUGAL:** Right. (*Pause.*) What mistake was that, Ted?

**TED:** His son. His son in America.

**DOUGAL:** Oh, yes. (*Pause.*) He has a son in America?

**TED:** Yes! Well, so they say . . .

**DOUGAL:** Right, OK. (*Pause.*) That's news to me, Ted.

**TED:** We were talking about it last night, Dougal! To Father Hernandez.

**DOUGAL:** Who? Oh, right! The Cuban lad.

**TED:** But you remember now . . . not a word about the son . . .

**DOUGAL:** Oh, right!

**TED:** . . . Just . . . forget about all that, all right? Forget about it. Don't say a word. Have you got that?

**DOUGAL:** I have, Ted.

**TED:** I don't want you saying anything stupid.

**DOUGAL:** The lights are on, but there's nobody home, Ted.

**TED:** Are you sure?

**DOUGAL:** I am indeed, Ted. Don't worry about that at all.

**TED:** Grand. All right. I think that's everything.

*He notices that Jack's hair is a little awry. He approaches him gingerly, producing a comb as he does so.*

**TED:** Father . . . Father, do you think I could . . . ?

*He holds the comb out towards Jack's hair, ready to put it back into place. As the comb approaches, Jack leans away from it, a very threatening look on his face. Ted keeps approaching. Jack starts growling softly but menacingly.\**

**TED:** It's just for the Bishop. We should have you looking your best . . .

*Jack looks like a cobra about to strike. Ted moves the comb forward again, then seems to think better of the whole thing.\**

**TED:** Maybe it's fine. We'll leave it as it is. Let it settle.

*We stay on Jack as Ted moves out of shot. Jack relaxes, and there is a pause. Then, from behind the seat, Ted's head slowly comes into sight. He raises the comb and moves it towards Jack's head. Jack shifts in his seat, oblivious to all this. Ted retreats, then goes to the arm of the chair. From here, he tries to blow Jack's hair into position. It works. Jack spins around, but Ted has gone. Mrs Doyle comes into the room.\**

**MRS DOYLE:** Father Crilly, Bishop Brennan is here.

**TED:** Hell's bells! Right . . . Show him in. *(To Dougal.)* Dougal, please remember, whatever you do, not a word about the son. Honestly, this is the most important thing I'll ever ask you to do. Don't say a word.

**DOUGAL:** There's no danger of that whatsoever, Ted.

**TED:** OK.

*Mrs Doyle brings in the Bishop. He is about fifty, plump and very stern-faced.† He has a large leather carrier-bag.*

**TED:** Ah, hello, Bishop Brennan! Are you well?

*The Bishop barely acknowledges their presence. Jack, in turn, is oblivious to the Bishop's arrival. Dougal smiles happily.*

**TED:** Your Eminence, sit down there beside Father Dougal. Mrs Doyle, could you make some tea for us?

**MRS DOYLE:** Certainly, Father.

*The Bishop sits beside Dougal. Ted sits down in a chair opposite them both. On the little table beside Ted is the Cuban fertility statue. The Bishop stares at it. Ted doesn't know at first what he's staring at. He then turns and notices the statue. He tries to cover the appendage with his hand, but then he realises that he's touching it. He eventually knocks it on to the ground to get it out of sight. There is another pause. Dougal watches the Bishop closely. We hear a clock ticking. Dougal clears his throat ominously. There is a very, very long pause.*

**DOUGAL:** How's the son?

*The Bishop bristles visibly.*

**BISHOP:** What?

**TED** *(panicking)*: The Son of God. How is the Son of God? Everything well in the world of religion?

**BISHOP:** What? The world of religion? What are you talking about, Crilly?

**TED:** You know . . . ah . . . Mrs Doyle! Is that tea ready?! Ha, ha!

*Mrs Doyle enters, carrying a tray.*

**MRS DOYLE:** Here I am! Here I am! . . . Ah, isn't this grand?

*She hands a cup to the Bishop. He puts his hand out to stop her.*

**BISHOP:** I'm fine, thank you, Mrs Doyle.

**MRS DOYLE:** Will you not have a cup of tea, Bishop Brennan?

**BISHOP:** No, no, I'm not staying long. I just want to get right to the point and get the hell out of here.

---

\*These stage directions were deleted from the final version because it was too difficult to play.

† Played in the end by the very non-plump Jim Norton.

**MRS DOYLE:** Are you sure you won't have a cup?

**BISHOP:** Certain, thank you. *(To Ted.)* Now, I –

**MRS DOYLE:** Go on, have a cup.

**BISHOP:** I won't thanks. *(To Ted.)* Now —

**MRS DOYLE:** Everyone else is having a cup. Will you not have one yourself?

**BISHOP:** No. I don't have time. Crilly, I —

**MRS DOYLE:** You'll feel left out. You'll be Bishop Piggy In The Middle.

**BISHOP:** I'm fine, I'm fine.

**MRS DOYLE:** You sure you won't have a cup? Just a drop?

**BISHOP:** No! . . .

**MRS DOYLE** *(sings softly)*: Bishop Piggy In The Middle . . .

*Ted leans over.*

**TED** *(whispers)*: Actually, Your Eminence, just say yes. It's quicker, believe me.

**BISHOP:** All right, then.

**MRS DOYLE** *(pleased)*: Grand!

*She gives him the tea and leaves. The Bishop addresses the three priests.*

**BISHOP:** Well, I hope you're not doing too

much damage here. Jack, are you behaving yourself?

*Jack is smoking a fag. He blows out some smoke contemptuously.*

**JACK** *(under his breath)*: . . . Feck off!

**BISHOP:** What did you say?!

**TED:** Ha, ha! Anyway, Your Eminence, what brings you to the island? Are you thinking of letting us head back to our old parishes?

**BISHOP:** Fat chance! You're here until I tell you otherwise. Do you think I'd let Jack back into a normal parish after what he did in Athlone? Dressing up as a nun to get into a girls' school!* How do you think I felt when I had to explain that to Cardinal Daly?

**TED:** Well, yes, but . . . surely I'm all right . . .

**BISHOP:** No, no. You're here until every penny of that money is accounted for.

**TED:** I told you, that money was just resting in my account until . . .

**BISHOP:** Enough!

**TED:** I don't know where it went!

**BISHOP:** Crilly, I won't tell you again! And as for this . . . cabbage . . . *(Dougal looks very uncomfortable. Ted goes very quiet.)* . . . The mere idea of letting him back into the real world after The Blackrock Incident.

**TED** *(quietly)*: Yes, that was . . . unfortunate.

**BISHOP:** The amount of lives irreparably damaged . . .† The tourist industry shattered in a single blow . . . My God, do you know how many strings I had to pull to stop the Vatican getting involved?

*Jack chuckles to himself. Dougal is ashen-faced.*

**BISHOP:** I don't even want to talk about it. I just want to get this film thing over with.

**TED:** Film? What film?

---

*We deleted this sentence from the final version.

†The following lines were inserted in final version:

**DOUGAL:** They were only nuns.

**BISHOP:** Nuns are people too.

**BISHOP:** This . . . whatever it's called . . . film. *The Passion of Saint Tibulus.* His Holiness banned it, but because of some loophole the bloody thing's being shown here on this godforsaken hellhole.

**DOUGAL:** Oh, yes, that's right. Is it any good, do you know?

**BISHOP:** I don't care if it's any good or not! All I know is that we have to be seen to be making a stand against it. That's where you and Larry and Moe come in.

**TED:** What do you mean?

**BISHOP:** I know that normally you wouldn't be able to organise a nun-shoot in a nunnery, but it's up to you to make the Church's position clear. Make some kind of protest. Even you should be able to manage that.

**DOUGAL** (*touched*): Thanks very much.

**BISHOP:** This is very important. Don't make a balls of it. I'll be in touch.

*He gets up and starts to head out of the room. Ted tries to attract his attention.*

**TED:** . . . Ah . . . ah, Your Eminence? This isn't really my area.

**BISHOP:** Nothing's your area, Crilly! You don't have an area! Unless it's a kind of play area with sandcastles and buckets and spades. Just do what you're told, all right?

*He leaves the room, slamming the door. There is a quiet pause.*

**DOUGAL:** Bye, then!

SCENE 6 EXT./DAY 2
SET: CINEMA
*Establish cinema.*

SCENE 7 INT./DAY 2
SET: CINEMA
*The Ormonde is a once-natty but now slightly dilapidated old cinema. Ted and Dougal are finding some seats near the back. The only other cinemagoers are an old woman in peasant garb at the front and an old man with a dog. Ted and Dougal take their places.*

**TED:** Look at this . . . This is silly . . . there's only one person in the cinema, for God's sake . . .

**DOUGAL:** Why wouldn't Jack come along, Ted?

**TED:** I asked him, he said he'd be along sooner or later . . . God . . . I don't see the point of this at all . . .

*A middle-aged, well-dressed man, Michael Cocheese, comes out in front of the screen. He has fair, wavy hair and wears a bow-tie.*

**COCHEESE** *(well spoken)*: Well, Ladies and Gentlemen, hello. I'm Michael Cocheese, owner of The Ormonde and film critic for *The Craggy Island Examiner*. I'm pleased to say we've got a bit of a treat lined up today for all you fans of French cinema.

*The old woman sits up straighter when she hears this.*

**OLD WOMAN:** Is this subtitled?

**COCHEESE:** Pardon?

**OLD WOMAN:** Is this subtitled or is it dubbed?

**COCHEESE:** Ah, it's subtitled.

*The old woman, without a word, stands up and makes her way out of the cinema. Cut to Ted and Dougal, watching her go.*

**DOUGAL:** Ted, should we start protesting now, or what?

**TED:** Yes, I suppose so.

**DOUGAL:** Or maybe we should wait 'til we see a bit of the film?

**TED:** No, we'll just get it over with . . .

**DOUGAL:** Maybe it's not so bad. It could be another *Commitments*.

**TED:** It doesn't matter whether it's good or bad, Dougal. It's just the morality that we don't agree with. Right, let's go . . .

*They start booing in a terribly unconvincing way.*

**DOUGAL:** Boo! . . . Boo! . . . Give it up, lads!

**TED:** Come on now, you!

*We see Cocheese looking at Ted and Dougal, confused.*

**TED:** That'll be enough out of you, now!

**DOUGAL:** Boo! . . .

**TED:** Terrible film . . .

**COCHEESE:** What? Who's that?!

*We see the dog turn around and look at Ted and Dougal.*

**DOUGAL:** Booo! . . .

**TED:** You dirty, filthy beggars!

*Cocheese stands up and makes towards Ted and Dougal.*

**COCHEESE:** Now, look, you! . . . Oh, Father Ted, Father Dougal. It's yourselves.

**TED:** Hello, Michael, how are you?

**COCHEESE:** Oh, I'm grand. How's Father Jack? I haven't seen him since we had *Caligula\** on . . .

**TED:** Oh, he's grand. He was a bit tired so he didn't come along today.

**COCHEESE:** Right. But what are you up to, though? You're making a fair racket.

**TED:** Oh, it's a long story . . . We have the Bishop over, you know, Len Brennan . . .

**COCHEESE:** Ohhh, that gobshite.

**TED:** . . . And he's going mad because of the film.

**DOUGAL:** He told us to come down and kick up a fuss.

**COCHEESE:** Right. It's just, you're making a bit of a racket. Could you try to keep it down? You have to think about other people.

*He indicates the empty cinema.*

**TED:** No problem.

**DOUGAL:** You can count on us, Michael!

*Cocheese smiles and starts to walk off.*

**TED:** Michael! Michael!

*Cocheese turns back. Ted grabs his elbow gently.*

**TED:** Are we still OK for the old . . . *(He smiles*

---

\*In the final version this became a 'Sharon Stone season' because we thought there was a risk people would have forgotten *Caligula*.

*and points at his collar.)* . . . half price?

**COCHEESE:** No problem at all. Enjoy the film.

**TED** *(jokingly)***:** Boo!

**COCHEESE:** Now, you!

*Ted and Dougal laugh good-naturedly.*

### END OF PART ONE

* * *

### PART TWO

SCENE 8 INT./NIGHT 2
SET: TED AND DOUGAL'S BEDROOM
*Ted and Dougal lie in their beds, looking at the ceiling, very confused looks on their faces. Dougal has a teddy bear with a clerical collar round its neck.*

**TED:** What was all that about?

**DOUGAL:** You're asking the wrong person now, Ted. I couldn't make head nor tail of it.

**TED:** I know for a fact that Saint Tibulus wore more clothes than that. Sure wasn't he from Norway or somewhere? He'd have frozen to death.

**DOUGAL:** Do you remember the bit when Saint Tibulus was trying to take that banana off the other lad?

**TED:** That wasn't a banana, Dougal. Anyway, look, I'm going to sleep. Good night, Dougal.

*Ted turns off the light. Pause. After a moment, Dougal starts mumbling in his sleep.*

**DOUGAL** *(offscreen)***:** I'll have a B, please, Bob . . . Beethoven . . . C, please, Bob . . . Carnivorous . . . F, please, Bob . . .

**TED** *(moans)***:** . . . Not *Blockbusters* again . . .

**DOUGAL:** Fettuccine . . .

*Ted puts the pillow over his head.*

SCENE 9 INT./MORNING 3
SET: TED AND DOUGAL'S BEDROOM
*The light shines through the window. Ted wakes up, blinking. He yawns and looks at the little novelty Pope-clock beside the bed.*

**TED:** Oohhh, let's see . . . six a.m. . . . Oh, great, another eight hours' sleep . . .

**DOUGAL:** You awake, Ted?

**TED:** Mmmmhh . . .

**DOUGAL:** This is fantastic, isn't it, Ted? Another great lie-in for the lads.

**TED:** It is . . .

**DOUGAL:** Do you know what'd be terrible, Ted? Wouldn't it be terrible if Bishop Brennan came in and told us to go down to the cinema and start protesting again?

*Suddenly, the door bursts open and the Bishop storms in like a force of nature. Ted and Dougal sit bolt-upright in their beds.*

SCENE 10 EXT./MORNING 3
SET: CINEMA
*Ted and Dougal stand outside The Ormonde carrying placards. They're cold and still half-asleep. The placards read 'Down With This Type Of Thing' and 'Careful, Now'.*

**TED:** This is ridiculous. The flippin' place doesn't open for another seven hours.

**DOUGAL:** Ted . . . Ted, what about what the Bishop said? Didn't he want us to chain ourselves to the railings?

**TED:** How are we going to do that?

**DOUGAL:** O'Leary's might have something.

**TED:** Yeah, you go off and get something. I'll stay here and guard this closed cinema against anyone who might want to see a film that's not on for another seven hours.

*Dougal moves off.*

SCENE 11 INT./DAY 3
SET: PAROCHIAL HOUSE
*The Bishop walks into the room. He sees Jack, sitting in his usual chair. The Bishop looks warily at him. Jack is eating something.*

**BISHOP:** Jack, what are you up to? Why aren't you at the film?

**JACK:** . . . Feck off!

**BISHOP:** What?! What did you say?

*Jack gives him a sarcastically innocent look.*

**BISHOP** (pause): Listen . . . did you see my bag, my travel bag?

*Jack gives the Bishop a 'puzzled' look. He is still chewing.*

**BISHOP:** Well, if you see it, give it to me. My bloody passport and everything's in there . . . all right?

*Jack nods in a compliant sort of way, but when the Bishop leaves, he smiles evilly and reaches down beside his chair. He brings the Bishop's bag into view and opens the zip. He starts rummaging through the bag, grunting slightly like a foraging animal. He takes out a videotape and puts it to one side. We see 'Holiday '94' written on the side. He then takes out a passport, opens it and laughs nastily at the photo of the Bishop. We see it, too – it shows Brennan looking numbly at the camera, wearing his Bishop's hat. He rummages about a bit more and we then see, from his point of view, a plastic bag inside a pouch that has 'Duty Free' written on it. A blast of dramatic music plays as we see Jack's eyes widen. Cut back to the videotape with 'Holiday 94' written on it resting beside him.*

SCENE 12 INT./DAY 3
SET: HARDWARE SHOP
*We see Mr and Mrs O'Leary in the middle of a heated argument.*

**MR O'LEARY:** Ahhh, ya fat old bitch!

**MRS O'LEARY:** Don't you talk to me like that, you big pile of shite! You ignorant prick!

**MR O'LEARY:** You watch that filthy mouth of yours!

**MRS O'LEARY:** I'll watch nothing! I'll stick this up your arse!

*She holds up a huge knife. Suddenly, Dougal enters the shop.*

**DOUGAL:** Hello, you two!

**MR O'LEARY** (suddenly cheery): Father, how's tricks?

**MRS O'LEARY:** We haven't seen you in a while, Father. We were just going to have some tea, if you'd like a drop?

**DOUGAL:** Oh, no, I'm fine there, Mrs O'Leary.

**MR O'LEARY:** What can I 'do you for', Father?

**DOUGAL:** I was looking for a pair of handcuffs, actually.

*Pause.*

**MR O'LEARY:** A pair of handcuffs? What do you need them for?

**DOUGAL:** Oh, nothin' much. They're for me and Ted.

*Pause.*

**MRS O'LEARY:** You and Father Ted?

**DOUGAL:** Yes. We're just tryin' something out.

*Pause.*

**MR O'LEARY:** Well, actually, funnily enough, I think we have a pair. Sergeant Thornton left them here when he retired.

**DOUGAL:** Retired from what?

**MR O'LEARY:** From the police.

**DOUGAL:** The police? Was Sergeant Thornton a policeman?

**MR O'LEARY:** Em, he was, yes. Why did you think he used to wear the uniform?

**DOUGAL:** I thought he was just having a laugh.

*Mr O'Leary has no idea what to say to this.*

**MR O'LEARY:** Anyway, Father, here's the handcuffs.

*He gives them to Dougal. Dougal hands over the money.*

**DOUGAL:** Bye now!

*Exit Dougal.*

**MR O'LEARY:** Bye, Father! (Pause.) What are you doing standing there, you stupid bitch?!

**MRS O'LEARY:** Don't you call me stupid, you toerag! I'll friggin' kill you!

*She lunges at Mr O'Leary. We leave them there, locked in combat.*

SCENE 13 EXT./DAY 3
SET: CINEMA
*Ted and Dougal are handcuffed to the cinema railings. Their placards are beside them. A constant stream of people is filing casually past them into the*

cinema. *Ted is protesting in an apathetic sort of way.*
*A middle-aged farmer, Jim Halpin, passes by.*

**JIM:** Hello, Father Crilly, Father McGuire.

**TED:** Hello, Jim.

**JIM:** I saw your picture in the paper.

**TED:** What?

**JIM:** Here. Have a look.

*He gives the paper to Ted. Dougal reads it over Ted's*
*shoulder. They are both highly excited. We can see a*
*headline in the paper, which reads 'Priests protest*
*against blasphemous film'.*

**JIM:** So, it's a blasphemous film is it, Father?

**TED:** Oh, it is.

**JIM:** What type of thing is it?

**DOUGAL:** It's mad stuff.

**TED:** It's very immoral. You wouldn't like it,
Jim.

**JIM:** Is it a type of nudey thing, Father?

**TED:** Oh, you wouldn't believe the amount of
nudity in it.

**JIM:** Is it nudey men or women mostly? Or a
bit of both?

**TED:** Oh, every type of thing.

**JIM:** And you see the lot, do you, Father? It's
not just the top half you see?

**TED:** There's nothing left to the imagination,
Jim.

**JIM:** Right. Well, I'll be off, then.

**TED:** Bye, Jim!

*He walks straight into the cinema. Ted is amazed*
*and disgusted. Two very meek old ladies, Mrs*
*Sheridan and Mrs Glynn, pass by.*

**MRS SHERIDAN:** Ah, hello, Fathers.

**TED:** Hello, Mrs Sheridan, Mrs Glynn.

**MRS GLYNN** (*reads poster*)**:** *The Passion of Saint*
*Tibulus.* What's that? Is it a musical or a
western or what?

**MRS SHERIDAN:** We always go on
Tuesdays. Gets us out of the house.

**MRS GLYNN:** We saw a great one a few

weeks ago. *The Crying Game.*

**MRS SHERIDAN:** Oh, that was brilliant.

**MRS GLYNN:** There's a great bit in it where
there's this girl, and then you find out it's not
a girl at all, but a man.

**MRS SHERIDAN:** Yes. He takes his lad out.

**TED:** What?!

**MRS GLYNN:** He takes his lad out. You only
see it for a second, but you get the message!

**MRS SHERIDAN:** I didn't know what it was
for a second! It's been so long since I've seen
one!

**MRS GLYNN:** I thought it looked like your
Billy's!

**MRS SHERIDAN:** No, Billy's is rounder at
the top. Anyway, Father, bye!

*They both go inside.*

**DOUGAL:** Should we be stopping them going
inside, or what, Ted?

**TED:** It just shows, doesn't it? No one takes a
blind bit of notice of what the Church says any
more.

*Another old man, Pat Harty, passes by.*

**TED:** Ah, hello, Pat.

**PAT:** Father Crilly, hello.

**TED:** Pat, how's your wife? I hear she hasn't
been well.

**PAT:** She's dead, Father.

**TED:** Oh no! That's terrible! When did she . . .

**PAT:** Ah, a few hours ago.

**TED:** Really?

**PAT:** Yes. Anyway, that's just the way.

*Pause.*

**PAT:** What's the film like, Father?

**TED:** What?

**PAT:** Is it any good? I was reading about it in
the paper.

**TED:** Now, Pat. I don't think you should be
thinking about going to the film if your wife's
just died.

**PAT:** Yeah, Yeah. It's just, ah . . . I was always a bit of a fan of Saint Tibulus.

**TED:** Well, now . . .

**PAT:** Sure, I might wander in. I'll contact you about the funeral details, Father . . .

*He heads off into the cinema.*

**TED:** . . . This isn't going too well . . .

*Cocheese comes out of the cinema.*

**COCHEESE:** Well, Fathers, I must say, this is extraordinary. This is the most successful film we've had since *Jurassic Park*. It's breaking all sorts of records due to all this publicity over your protest.

**TED:** Well, we certainly didn't plan it like that . . .

*Cocheese looks up the road.*

**COCHEESE:** Oh, look who it is!

**TED:** Oh, thank God, a bit of support.

*It's Jack. He walks towards the three men, not acknowledging their presence.*

**TED:** Fair play to you for turning up!

*Jack walks straight past them and enters the cinema.*

**TED:** Brilliant.

**COCHEESE** (*running after Jack*): Come on, Father, I'll get y'a seat right at the front . . .

*Pause.*

**TED:** Right. I've had enough. Dougal, we're leaving. Give us the keys.

*Dougal looks very puzzled.*

**DOUGAL:** Keys?

SCENE 14 INT./DAY 3
SET: PAROCHIAL HOUSE
*Ted and Dougal sit beside each other, still chained to a big lump of railing complete with section of wall. They look exceptionally cowed. Jack sleeps noisily in his chair. Cut to the Bishop sitting at the table, poring over a map of the world that he has spread out in front of him.*

**TED:** Ah . . . what's this now, Your Eminence?

*When the Bishop talks, he is very, very, very calm.*

**BISHOP:** Why am I looking at a map of the world? Well, how can I explain it . . .?

*He sits down on the edge of the table.*

**BISHOP:** Firstly, a resumé of the last few days. I don't know if you remember . . . I came in here and I had this idea about you mounting a dignified protest about this film. Do you remember that?

**TED** (*uncomfortably*): Yes.

**BISHOP:** Good. Just to make the Church's opposition to the film clear. But, and this is the part that I think is interesting . . . you've actually managed to make it the most successful film that has ever been shown here! Isn't that great?

**TED:** Ah –

*The Bishop gives Ted a look that shuts him up immediately.*

**BISHOP:** People are coming from all over the country to see the film. They're even coming from Gdansk! And, this is wonderful . . . look at this . . .

*He takes a poster from a tube and unfolds it. It's the promotional poster for 'The Passion of Saint Tibulus'. It features a photograph of Dougal and Ted tied to the railings, and a shot of Jack giving a thumbs-up in the cinema. The slogan on the poster reads 'The film they tried to ban!'.*

**BISHOP:** Look. There's you, there's Forrest Gump. And there's Father Jack actually watching the film. What a turn-up for the books! Ha, ha! Right. Now, I think the best thing would be for you three to continue your careers as priests-cum-film promoters outside of my jurisdiction. Don't you think? Ted, I thought you might like to go to America. (*Looking at map.*) What part, do you think?

**TED:** Oh, ah . . . (*Hopefully.*) Las Vegas?

**BISHOP:** Oh, sorry, Ted, I meant South America! I tell you what, there's a little island off the coast of Surinam, and, ha, ha, there's a couple of tribes there . . . you'll like this . . . they've been beating the shit out of each other since 1907. We've never found the right man to bring them together in a spirit of Christian harmony. But I think you're the man.

**TED:** Well, thanks very much, but –

**BISHOP:** No need to thank me. One question. Do you know how to make arrows?

**TED:** Ah, no –

**BISHOP:** Never mind, never mind. It'll come in time. Anyway, Dougal . . . on to you. Isn't it funny how some of these places in the Philippines can keep on going without any sort of proper sewerage system?

**DOUGAL:** Oh, you're right there, Your Honour.

**BISHOP:** The amount of diseases that leads to. I read somewhere that they still have diseases over there that we got rid of in the eighteenth century. And of course the clergy aren't immune from all this. Their place is with their flock. Swimmin' about in the river with the rest of them.

*He turns on the sleeping Jack.*

**BISHOP:** Jack. Where can we stick you?

*He notices Jack is asleep.*

**BISHOP:** Jack! Wake up!

**TED:** I wouldn't do that, Bishop.

**BISHOP:** You shut up! Jack! Wake up!

*He leans over and shakes Jack. We see a huge close-up of Jack's eye opening. We see only the white of his eye. Then, his pupil swings down from behind his eyelid and fixes on the Bishop. Cut back to the Bishop leaning over Jack.*

**JACK** (*a roar from the very depths of hell*)**:** Feck off!

*He punches the Bishop. The Bishop falls over. He stands up, adjusting his clothes. He has a bloody nose.*

**BISHOP:** Oh, that's it, Jack. I've got you now. I've got all of you! You think this place is bad . . . Wait'll you see your new parishes. Wait'll you see!

*He leaves the room and slams the door. Dougal and Ted look despondent. Jack is still just waking up.*

**TED:** Well . . . that's it, then. I suppose . . . I suppose all we can do now is pack . . .

**DOUGAL:** I don't want to go to the Philippines, Ted . . . I can't even spell the Philippines . . . I know it begins with an 'F'.

**TED:** I know, I know . . . if only there were some way we could persuade the Bishop to change his mind. If only we had something we could bargain with . . . or . . . oh, I don't know . . .

*Meanwhile, Jack has switched on the VCR.*

**TED:** Did you get a film out, Father? I tell you, the last thing I want to see now is a film . . .

*Nonetheless, Ted looks at the screen.*

SCENE 15 EXT./DAY X
SET: BEACH
*This is the video that Jack, Dougal and Ted are watching. We don't see anything interesting at first, but then we see the Bishop come into shot. He is laughing, running along the beach, wearing a pair of swimming trunks. We then see that he is chasing a young woman in a bikini, who is laughing and playfully putting the Bishop's hat on her head as she runs. He catches her and wrestles playfully with her as she tries to hold the hat out of reach. Cut to the Bishop lying on a deckchair looking proudly at something offscreen. The camera turns to reveal the Bishop's son making large arched sandcastles with the Bishop's hat.*

SCENE 16 EXT./DAY X
SET: BEACH
*Cut to the Bishop on a swing, this time in full regalia, the woman pushing him. The Bishop holds the boy in his lap. The film ends.*

SCENE 17 INT./DAY 3
SET: PAROCHIAL HOUSE
*Cut back to Dougal, Ted and Jack.*

**TED:** Well . . . that was great!

**DOUGAL:** You're right there, Ted.

*Pause.*

**TED:** Will we 'phone him now or will we watch it again?

*Pause.*

**TED:** Ah, we'll watch it again.

*They press 'play' on the video and settle back in their seats.*

**THE END**

# competition time

**ARTHUR:** The 'All-Priests' Stars in Their Eyes Lookalike' competition was inspired by the All Priests' Roadshow in Ireland, otherwise known as the Holy Show. Basically, it's a bunch of very good-natured priests who tour the country, singing and telling jokes and doing their various turns. Not by any means the strangest manifestation of faith in Ireland; I recently saw a film containing footage from an Irish newsreel of 1964. One item it contained was the Annual Blessing of the Jets at Dublin Airport. Priests were blessing jets on the runway. . .Even better was the Annual Blessing of the Scooters, when about 200 mods had their minds put to rest in the space of an afternoon. The competition host himself, Henry Sellers, is very much the Irish light entertainer abroad – the Henry Kelly/Terry Wogan/Eamonn Andrews type.

**GRAHAM:** The idea of having a trio of doppelgänger priests on a nearby island hit us like a bolt out of the blue. An idea like that is worth a hundred gags, because it dictates what you should be writing about. You set up the rivalry, involve them in a confrontation with high stakes and have lots of gloating at the end. That system also took care of the plots of *Song For Europe* and *Escape From Victory*. Oh, and just to set the record straight once and for all – Dick Byrne is not a sexual reference. If we had had any idea people would think that, we'd have changed his name immediately.

One thing that is puzzling about this episode is how Jack managed to get himself dressed up as Elvis at the beginning. I mean, it's a complete mystery how he did it. In fact, it's the sort of thing you don't really want to go into, so perhaps I shouldn't have brought it up. Just pretend I didn't say anything.

**PART ONE**
SCENE 1 INT./MORNING 1
SET: PAROCHIAL HOUSE
*We see the door of the room. Ted is behind it, but we don't see him, or Dougal and Jack, to whom he is talking.*

**TED:** All right, you ready?

**DOUGAL:** Ready when you are, Ted!

**TED:** You'll like this, Dougal. OK! One, two, three! Here I come!

*He jumps into the room, facing the wall, his arms outstretched. His black leather jacket has 'Elvis' written on the back. He is dressed as Elvis circa 1968 – his 'guitar man' phase – black leather, greased black wig, pointed boots and a guitar. He spins around and the smile on his face immediately disappears when he sees Dougal and Jack. Cut to reveal that they are dressed in exactly the same way. Ted can't believe this. Pause.*

**DOUGAL:** Who're you supposed to be, Ted?

**TED:** What do you think you're doing? You two can't go as Elvis!

**DOUGAL:** You . . . Wait a second, you're Elvis as well!

**TED:** Of course I'm Elvis! I've got 'Elvis' written on my back! I don't believe this —

**DOUGAL:** Bit of a coincidence, all right. Great minds think alike, I suppose.

**TED:** I've been saying for the last two weeks I was going as Elvis!

**DOUGAL:** Ahh! That's probably where I got the idea . . .

*Ted walks over to Dougal. The leather creaks noisily whenever he moves.*

**TED:** This is great, this really is. The first 'All-Priests' Stars In Their Eyes Lookalike' competition I thought I'd have a chance of winning. I don't believe it. Look! I even cleared a space for the trophy beside the one we got for coming third in the ludo championships.

*We see a 'trophy' on the mantelpiece. It comprises four coloured discs – they look like ludo pieces – stuck to each other in a vertical line on a plastic base.*

**DOUGAL:** You might still win, Ted, you never know.

**TED:** But what if you're on before me? I'll look like an eejit! Everyone'll think I copied the idea off you!

**DOUGAL:** Well, Ted, to be fair . . . it is a bit weird you happened to think of it as well.

**TED:** I thought of it first! It was my idea!

**DOUGAL:** I believe you, Ted. (*To himself.*) Thousands wouldn't.

**TED:** Forget it! Just forget it! You do whatever you want! I'll just have to be Mother Teresa again.

*He sits down in a sulk. Jack, who has been watching him all this time, takes another drag on his cigarette and exhales. Pause.*

**JACK:** Who're you supposed to be?

**TED** (*trying to suppress his anger. Pause.*)**:** Elvis. I'm Elvis.

**JACK:** I'm Elvis!

**TED:** I know you are, Father! We're all Elvis! That's the problem!

*Mrs Doyle enters the room.*

**MRS DOYLE:** Tea, Fathers?

**JACK:** Feck off!!!

**MRS DOYLE:** There's nothing nicer than a cup of tea in the afternoon . . . (*She notices*

Ted's appearance.) . . . Oh, you look a bit different, Father. Have you had a haircut, or something?

**TED:** No, I'm Elvis Presley.

**MRS DOYLE:** Are you, Father? Well that's a turn-up for the books.

**DOUGAL:** It's for the 'All-Priests Lookalike' show tomorrow.

**MRS DOYLE:** Ah, now I see. Well, I must say I'm looking forward to that. Is Father Kiernan coming?

**TED** (*quietly*): He won't be, no.

**MRS DOYLE:** He's a great laugh. Always full of the joys of spring. I remember him last year, telling all his stories. He had me in stitches. It's true what they say about chubby men, isn't it? They are jollier than the rest of us. They have a way of looking at things —

**TED:** He shot himself.

**MRS DOYLE:** Did he? Oh, that's terrible. I suppose that's often the way with fat men. They laugh to hide the tears. But sure that's life. Happy one moment, then, I suppose, you just go . . . and shoot yourself, and . . . there you go. Anyway! Tea!

*She starts pouring. She looks at Ted. Pause.*

**MRS DOYLE** (*cagily*): Will you have a cup, Father?

**TED:** No, thanks. I'm fine.

**MRS DOYLE:** Go on!

**TED:** No, thanks . . . Well, actually . . . all right. Just a drop.

*Pause.*

**MRS DOYLE:** What?

**TED** (*holding his hand out for the cup*): I'll have just a little bit.

**MRS DOYLE** (*pulling cup away slightly*): Ah, now, you don't really want any, Father.

**TED:** No, I do!

**MRS DOYLE:** No, I'm forcing it on you, Father.

**TED:** No, you're not . . .

**MRS DOYLE:** No, I am. (*She slaps herself on the wrist.*) You're just a big dictator, Joan!* Can't take no for an answer!

**TED:** But I'm not saying no, Mrs Doyle.

**MRS DOYLE:** Ah, you're saying no with your eyes, Father.

**TED:** . . . I'll just have a little cup, Mrs Doyle.

*Mrs Doyle wags her finger at him and smiles.*

**TED** (*cannot believe this*): Please, Mrs Doyle . . .

**MRS DOYLE** (*to Dougal*): Cup of tea, Father?

*The telephone starts ringing. Ted, shaking his head in wonder, goes to answer it.*

**TED** (*picks up the telephone*): Hello?

SCENE 2 INT./DAY 1
SET: RIVAL PAROCHIAL
HOUSE/PAROCHIAL HOUSE
*We see a middle-aged priest, Father Dick Byrne, on the telephone. In the background we see a housekeeper handing out tea to two other priests, a young simple-minded type, Father Cyril McDuff, and an old crotchety type, Father Jim Johnson. Cutting back and forth between Ted and Dick, we see that the action is identical on either side of the line.*

**DICK:** Ted! How are you?! Dick Byrne here!

**TED** (*not too happy*): Ah . . . hello, Dick. How are things on Rugged Island?

**DICK:** Not so bad, Ted! You all set for tomorrow?

**TED:** The show? Em . . .

**DICK:** Looking forward to not getting your hands on the trophy again?

**TED** (*slightly angry*): Actually, I think the trophy's going to Craggy Island this year.

**DICK:** That'll be the day, Ted. What have you got planned?

---

*Oh, my God! Her first name! This is a very good example of the kind of information one carelessly flings about in the early days of writing a sitcom, without realising that it has the potential to be a lovely dark secret for years and years.

TED: Ah, now, I shouldn't say . . . it'd be giving you an advant—

DICK: Mother Teresa?

*Furious pause.*

TED: No!

DICK: I tell you what, keep it as a surprise. Actually, I'm only joking really. I do think you might be in with a chance this year, Ted.

TED (*calms somewhat*): Oh, well . . . Do you really, Dick?

DICK: No.

*Ted is so enraged that he misses the cradle when he puts the telephone down, and has to slam it a few times to get it into place. On the other end of the line, we see Dick sniggering to himself.*

CYRIL (*very Dougal-like*): Who's that, Dick?


SCENE 3 INT./DAY 1
SET: PAROCHIAL HOUSE
*Ted is furious. He storms over to Dougal.*

TED: I'm asking you one more time, Dougal! Don't go as Elvis!

DOUGAL: What?

TED: We have a chance, for once, of having the Lookalike championship trophy in this house. If we all go as Elvis, none of us will win!

DOUGAL: Can't I go as Elvis?

TED: Look, Dougal, I've been looking forward to this for ages. I know all the moves and everything! And remember who's judging this year!

DOUGAL: Who, Ted?

TED: Henry Sellers!

DOUGAL: No! He's coming here! Wow!

TED: I told you this, Dougal! Father Dunne is bringing him over.

DOUGAL: I've never met a celebrity before.

TED: You met the Pope.

DOUGAL: Did I?

TED: Don't you remember? When we went to Rome.

DOUGAL (*thinks*): That was the Pope? The fella living in the art gallery?

TED: The Vatican, Dougal! It was The Vatican!

DOUGAL: All the same, Ted, I wouldn't say he's a 'celebrity' in the true sense of the word, you know?

TED: Dougal, the Pope is God's representative on earth.

DOUGAL: Huh! . . . You'd think he'd be taller.

TED: What, like a giant? A giant Pope, Dougal? Is that what you'd have preferred? Maybe next time they'll make Hulk Hogan Pope. Would that help you at all?

DOUGAL: Still, though, Henry Sellers, coming here . . . . Ha . . . . (*Pause.*) Aaaaaaaaaaaaarrrrgghhhhhhhhhhh!!!!!!!

*He starts running around in circles*

DOUGAL: Aaaaaaaaaaaagggghhhhhh!!!! Henry Sellers? *The* Henry Sellers?

TED (*puts his hands on Dougal's shoulders*): Dougal, calm down. We have to concentrate on the Elvis problem. Look, why don't we toss for it? Whoever wins can be Elvis.

DOUGAL (*calming*): . . . Yes . . . All right.

*Ted takes out a coin and prepares to toss it.*

TED: Right. Heads or tails?

*Dougal pauses for a long time.*

TED: Heads or tails, Dougal?

DOUGAL: Heads . . . (*Ted tosses the coin.*) . . . No, tails!

*The coin falls to the ground.*

DOUGAL: Heads! Tails! (*He bends down to the coin.*) Heads!

TED: Dougal! You have to give me a choice between the two!

DOUGAL: Sorry, sorry. Got a bit excited there, Ted.

TED: All right, we'll go again. Heads or tails?

DOUGAL: Heads.

TED: You sure now?

DOUGAL: Absolutely pos— tails.

TED: Right.

*Ted flips the coin.*

DOUGAL: No, heads! Tails! Heads!

TED: Dougal!

DOUGAL: Heads!

TED: Dougal, calm down.

DOUGAL: Tails! Heads! Tails! Heads!

*Dougal is staring strangely. His head quivers in a weird way.*

TED: Dougal! Dougal! Are you all right?

DOUGAL (*calming*): I'm fine. Sorry, Ted. I'm not the best at making decisions . . . Or am I?

TED: Look, Dougal. You toss the coin, all right? I'll take . . . heads. Heads it is! Toss the coin, there.

DOUGAL: All right.

*Dougal flips the coin straight at the ludo trophy. The top two pieces break and fall off. Ted looks as if he's about to explode.*

TED: Right! Forget it! Forget it! Forget it!

*Ted storms off. Dougal looks at the coin on the ground, then checks that Ted has left the room. He does an Elvis-style karate chop.*

DOUGAL: Yesss . . .


SCENE 4 INT./NIGHT 1
SET: PAROCHIAL HOUSE
*Ted is reading 'The Sunday Independent'. He makes a point of not looking at Dougal. Dougal is watching television. Jack sleeps. They are all dressed normally again. Ted is determinedly not looking at Dougal. Dougal looks at Ted with a worried expression.*

DOUGAL: Ted, Henry's on. Ted?

*Ted ignores him. We see the television.*


SCENE 5 INT./DAY X
SET: QUIZ SHOW
*Henry Sellers, the host of 'Morning Quiz', is interviewing a contestant, a very old woman who seems to be having trouble seeing him. She looks slightly to his left.*

HENRY: So, back to you for a five-point question, Monica. The capital of England . . . is it New York, London or Munich?

*Pause.*

HENRY: I'll give you a clue. You live there.

*Pause. Quick shot of Henry displaying a slight expression of weariness. We hear a 'ding-dong' sound.*

HENRY: Jane, do you know?

*Cut to the other contestant. She seems embarrassed.*

JANE: I leaned on the button by mistake.

HENRY: All right, back to Monica . . .

*Pause. Monica stares ahead.*


SCENE 6 INT./NIGHT 1
SET: PAROCHIAL HOUSE
*Cut back to Dougal watching the show.*

DOUGAL: He's great, isn't he, Ted? Henry? And he'll be here any second! Are you excited, Ted? Henry Sellers! Look at him askin' the questions there.

*Ted turns his head away. Dougal looks upset. Cut back to the programme.*

HENRY: 'A stitch in time saves . . .' How many?

*The 'ding-dong' noise sounds again. Henry turns to Jane.*

JANE (*holding her hand up*): Sorry!

*Cut back to Dougal and Ted.*

DOUGAL: Any idea why he left the BBC, Ted? (*No response.*) Probably just got fed up asking questions. I suppose we can ask him ourselves when he comes. I'll ask him. (*No response. We hear applause and end-of-show music from the television.*) Oh, it's over, Ted. Do you want to have a look at another one? (*Dougal holds another video. No response.*) I suppose it's not as much fun when you know the answers . . . (*Pause.*) Ted, look, why don't you be Elvis. Since you thought of it first I suppose it's only fair. I'll go as Mother Teresa.

*Ted at last looks at Dougal. His expression softens.*

TED: Ah, Dougal . . . no, no, I'm sorry. I'm being selfish. I'm sorry. You go as Elvis.

**DOUGAL:** No, Ted, it's not fair on you. You had your heart set on it.

**TED:** No, seriously, Dougal. You go.

**DOUGAL:** Really? Great! Thanks, Ted!

*Ted looks a little put out at this, but he doesn't know what to say. Dougal puts in another video.*

**TED:** . . . Unless you'd prefer to go as Mother Teresa . . .

**DOUGAL:** Ah, not really, Ted, no. Anyway, there's only one Mother Teresa, Ted, and that's you.

**TED** (*not meaning it*)**:** Thanks, Dougal. Oh, well . . . at least we've got the honour of taking care of Mr Sellers. And remember, it's very important that we be extremely nice to him. That'll increase the chances of us winning a hundred per cent. We'll fill him up with food and drink until it's coming out of his ears . . . (*Turns to Jack.*) You'll be nice to Mr Sellers, won't you, Father?

*Jack is looking at Ted strangely. He seems confused and a little wary.*

**JACK:** Wha . . .?

**TED:** Father, are you all right. You look —

*Ted sees something on the floor.*

**TED** (*picks up a bottle*)**:** Ah, no, Father! Not Toilet Duck! You know what that does to you!

*Jack looks up at Ted with increased puzzlement and horror.*

**TED:** You'll be seeing the pink elephants again! (*Holds up three fingers.*) How many fingers am I holding, up Father?

SCENE 6A INT./EVENING 1
SET: PAROCHIAL HOUSE
*We see Ted from Jack's point of view. Ted's hand appears incredibly large, about the size of the fake hands you see at football matches.*

**JACK** (*still frightened*)**:** Three?

**TED:** Well, you're not too bad. Maybe you're immune to it now.

*The doorbell rings.*

**DOUGAL:** That'll be him! That's Henry! Oh, God!

**TED:** Dougal, calm down! He's just a normal person like you or me. Well, like me, anyway.

*Mrs Doyle sticks her head in.*

**MRS DOYLE** (*very excited*)**:** He's here!

*She steps back to allow Henry into the room. He is well dressed in a light blue suit. He walks up to Ted with his hand out.*

**HENRY:** Hello, there! Henry Sellers!

**TED:** Hello, Mr Sellers. Father Ted Crilly. It's an honour to have you here!

**HENRY:** Well, it's lovely to be here. (*To Dougal.*) Hello Father . . .?

*Dougal has gone rigid. He stares at Henry, unable to move a muscle.*

**TED:** Sorry, Mr Sellers. This is Father Dougal McGuire.

*Dougal continues to stare.*

**TED:** Father Dougal . . . Say something to Mr Sellers!

*Slight pause. Ted gives Dougal a little kick.*

**DOUGAL:** Ow! How old are you?

**TED:** Dougal! Don't be asking Mr Sellers how old he is!

**HENRY:** Ha, ha, ha! That's quite all right. I'm thirty-seven, Father.

*Ted muses on this for a moment and then brings him over to Jack.*

**TED:** And over here is Father Jack Hackett . . .

*Henry approaches Jack. We see this from Jack's point of view. Henry is bathed in a strange light, and he is dressed up as a garden gnome. Cut to Jack's terrified expression.*

**JACK:** Aaaaaggghhhhhhhhh!!!!!!

*Jack stumbles from his chair, trying his best not to go near Henry, and practically kills himself trying to get out of the room.*

**TED:** Bye, Father! . . . (*To Henry.*) He's just gone out for his walk.

*As Ted talks, we see a terrified Jack running past the window at top speed. Henry looks puzzled.*

**TED** (*to Henry*)**:** Can we get you anything at all, Mr Sellers?

**HENRY:** Call me Henry. Eh, if you'd have something to eat . . . Maybe a sandwich?

**TED:** Mrs Doyle, could you bring in some sandwiches . . .?

**MRS DOYLE:** Right, Father. How many, Father?

**TED:** Oh, ah, two hundred.

**HENRY:** Oh, honestly, I'm —

**TED:** Oh, you're absolutely right, Henry. Three hundred. Sure I might have one myself!

*She leaves. Ted sits down. Dougal is looking in a very fixated way at Henry's 'hair'. Henry is looking straight ahead, but still seems very aware of Dougal's eyes.*

**DOUGAL:** Is there something wrong with your head?

**TED:** DOUGAL!!!

**DOUGAL:** What? It's just his hair looks a bit . . .

**TED:** Dougal, shut up!!!

**DOUGAL:** Why? I didn't say anything. I just said that his hair looks a bit mad . . .

**TED** (*quickly changing the subject*)**:** Is Father Dunne with you?

**HENRY:** He is. He's just bringing in the b— oh, here he is . . .

*Father Barty Dunne, a jolly, good-natured priest, arrives, carrying some luggage. He holds out his hand to Ted.*

**BARTY:** Ted!

*Ted rises again.*

**TED:** Barty, How are you? Sit down, there . . .

**BARTY:** Good to be on Craggy Island, again. God, I haven't seen you in ages. I remember the last time . . . ha, ha, we had that, ha, ha, funny incident, ha, ha, I suppose . . . ha, ha . . . you've forgotten all about it . . . HA! HA! It was the type of thing . . . ha, ha, ha, HA! HA!

**HENRY:** What's this . . .?

**TED:** Ah, the last time Father Dunne was here, Father Hackett lost his slippers . . .

**BARTY:** It was a bit of a . . . ha, ha, ha . . . He had us all lookin' for them . . . ha, ha, ha . . . Bit of a . . . ha, ha, ha, ha, ha . . . It was a bit like the type of thing . . . ha, ha . . . ha, ha, ha, ha . . .

**TED:** We found them after a while.

*Henry nods, smiles kindly. He looks around, to see Dougal still rigid. Barty distracts him again.*

**BARTY:** I suppose . . . ha, ha, ha . . . I suppose it's a bit like . . . ha, ha, ha, ha . . . I suppose it's a bit like . . . ha, ha, ha, ha . . . ha, ha, ha, ha . . . It's a bit . . . ha, ha, ha . . .

**TED:** How long was the car journ—

**HENRY** (*immediately*): Four hours.

*Ted nods understandingly.*

### END OF PART ONE

\* \* \*

### PART TWO

SCENE 7 INT./EVENING 1
SET: PAROCHIAL HOUSE
*There is a mountainously huge pile of sandwiches on a tray on the table. Henry, Ted and Barty sit around the room. They each have a small plate, with half-eaten sandwiches on each one. Dougal is still dumbstruck.\* Ted and Barty each have a glass of whiskey. Henry is drinking tea. Barty drones on, and the rest look very, very bored.*

**BARTY:** . . . I suppose . . . in all honesty . . . ha, ha, ha, ha, ha, ha . . . with the thing there! . . . Oh! Ha, ha, ha, ha, ha! . . .

**DOUGAL** (*unable to speak*): Mmbrorlrorrr!!!

*Henry smiles uncertainly at Dougal.*

**TED:** So, Henry, what's it like being a TV star?

**HENRY:** Well . . .

**BARTY:** You must be, you must be, you must be . . . ha, ha, ha, ha, ha, ha, ha . . . I suppose you must be . . . ha, ha, ha, ha, ha . . . with the television . . . ha, ha, ha . . . with the way things are goin' . . .ha, ha, ha, ha, ha, ha . . . ah, Lord . . .

**TED:** I have to say again, Henry, we're just so delighted to have you here. Can I get you anything else?

**HENRY:** No, no, I'm fine.

**TED:** More sandwiches?

\*We have a feeling Dougal is dumbstruck because we didn't know what to do with him.

**HENRY:** Hmmm? (*He turns and sees the sandwich mountain.*) Oh . . . you've . . . brought more in. No, really, I'm fine.

**DOUGAL:** Everything OK with your hair?

**TED:** Dougal, will you please stop talking about Henry's hair!!! I'm sorry Henry, it's just that your hair looks so natural, Dougal can't stop talking about it. It really is a beautiful head of hair . . . Anyway, what I was saying was . . . Anything you want at all, we can get it for you. There's no problem. And I mean that. Anything that you want. Anything that you want – that it would be at all possible for us to get you – just ask us. And I mean anything. (*Pause.*) There's no problem there at all. Anything.

**HENRY:** Well, I tell you what, I've been having a bit of difficulty getting the British papers over here. Would it be possible —

**TED:** Can't help you there, Henry. (*Pause.*) But anything else. Anything you want. Just ask. Except, obviously, the British papers.

**HENRY:** Well, I must say, your Craggy Island hospitality is very impressive. There must be something about priests and islands. Something in the air that makes them extremely generous and kind.

**TED** (*modestly*): Ah, well . . .

**HENRY:** Tell me, Father, do you know a Father Dick Byrne at all?

**TED** (*concerned*): What?

**HENRY:** Father Dick Byrne. He lives over there on Rugged Island. He's there with a . . . Father Johnson and a Father McDuff?

**TED:** What about them?

**HENRY:** Oh, they're always inviting me to come and stay with them. And they've sent me all types of presents and gifts. They're big fans of the show. I believe they're taking part in the Lookalike competition tomorrow . . .

**TED:** Hmmm . . . Well, to be honest, Henry . . . to be quite honest . . . and I don't know how to put this kindly, but . . . I think they're just buttering you up, there.

**HENRY:** What, for the competition, you mean? I'm sure they wouldn't do that.

**TED:** Well, you know . . . you should watch yourself with that lot.

**HENRY:** Their island's quite near this one, isn't it?

**TED:** Why? You're not thinking of visiting them, are you?

**HENRY:** Well, it is nearby, isn't it?

**TED:** Well, to be honest, Henry, you'd be making a mistake to visit them.

**HENRY:** Why is that Father?

*Pause.*

**TED:** They're lepers.

**HENRY:** They're what?

**TED:** They're lepers. The three of them. Rugged Island is a leper colony.

**HENRY:** You're not serious. A leper colony?

**TED:** Well, no. It's not leprosy. But there is something wrong with them. Did you never think how strange it was, three priests living on an island together?

**HENRY:** I suppose . . .

**TED:** No, there's something not quite right there . . . You'd be better off staying well away from them.

**BARTY** (*getting up*): Ted, where's the old . . . eh . . . ha, ha, ha, the old . . . eh . . . ha, ha, ha . . .

**TED:** The old? Oh, yes . . . you go upstairs and it's first on the left . . .

*Barty leaves. Pause. Dougal is still looking at Henry's hair.*

**DOUGAL:** It's a wig!!!

*Ted stands up, grabs Dougal by the shirt collar and the seat of his pants and frogmarches him outside before he can say anything else. Henry looks on, very puzzled. Mrs Doyle enters with a tray. On it is a bottle of sherry and four glasses.*

**MRS DOYLE:** Time for a little nightcap, everyone! Oh, and you're running out of sandwiches. I'll bring in some more . . .

*Mrs Doyle starts pouring sherry into each of the glasses.*

**HENRY:** I won't have one, thanks.

**MRS DOYLE:** Oh, now don't be silly! You will!

**HENRY:** No, really, I shouldn't.

*Ted returns.*

**TED:** Ah, go on. It'll help you sleep.

**HENRY:** . . . No, it's not a good idea. You go ahead.

**TED:** You've been saying no all day. A little drop won't do you any harm.

**MRS DOYLE:** The tiniest drop. Just a weeny, tiny bit.

*She hands him the glass. He takes it reluctantly.*

**TED:** The day a bit of sherry does anyone any harm is the day Ireland doesn't win the Eurovision!

*They laugh at the idea.*

**MRS DOYLE:** Ah, go on.

**HENRY:** No, I —

**MRS DOYLE:** Ahhhh, go on. Go on. Go on, go on, go on, go on, go on, go on, go on —

**HENRY:** No, seriously . . .

**MRS DOYLE:** Go on. Go on. Go on, go on, go on, go on, go on, go on, go on, go on, go on, go on, go on, go on, go on, go on, go on, go on, go on, GO ON!!!!

**HENRY** (*jumps with the shock*): Well . . . Just a drop, then.

*Henry smiles nervously. He puts the glass slowly to his lips. Fade to black.*

SCENE 8 INT./NIGHT 1
SET: PAROCHIAL HOUSE
*Fade back up to reveal that there are books strewn all over the floor, broken, overturned furniture and other indications that a disaster has occurred. Cut to Henry, who seems to have undergone a complete personality change. He is standing at the fireplace swigging sherry from the bottle, roaring and shouting his head off. Ted, Dougal and Barty are hiding behind the sofa.*

**HENRY:** What a shower of BASTARDS!

**BARTY** (*to Ted, very concerned*): Oh, Lord, Ted, why'd you give him a drink?

**TED:** I didn't know this would happen!

**BARTY:** That's why he was sacked from that programme! He's a terrible alcoholic! He's been on the wagon for a year . . . My God, Ted!

**TED:** How was I supposed to know?!

**HENRY:** Sack me? Sack me?! I made the BBC! I made it!

*He falls to the ground and starts sobbing uncontrollably. Ted makes a tentative move towards Henry.*

**TED:** Henry? Maybe if you have a bit of a rest you'll feel better . . .

**HENRY:** Get away from me, priest!

**TED:** The thing is, I think it's time we should all head up to bed . . .

*Henry walks over to the television and, with a single kick, smashes in the screen.*

**TED:** Good man, Henry! There's never anything on, anyway. Sure I'll give it a kick myself.

*He gives it a pathetic little kick.*

**HENRY:** You want a fight?

**TED** (*looks nervously at his watch*): Well, y'know, I'd love a bit of an ould scrap, but . . .

**HENRY:** Bloody priests!

**TED:** O'ho!

**HENRY:** Bunch of sanctimonious bastards. Made my life a bloody misery . . .

**TED:** Well, sorry about that, Henry . . . Are you sure you wouldn't like to —

**HENRY:** Arrrrrrrghhhh!

*Henry turns over the table.*

**TED:** Well, I suppose we could stay up a little longer if you want . . .

**HENRY:** I've had enough of you bastards! I'm off! Don't try to stop me!

**TED:** Well, Henry, it's a *bit* late . . . Ha, ha . . .

*Henry takes a run-up to the window and leaps through it. We hear his scream dwindling as he disappears into the night. Ted and Barty run to the window and watch him go.*

**DOUGAL:** It's true what they say, though, isn't it? You should never meet your heroes. You'll always be disappointed.

SCENE 9 EXT./DAWN 2
SET: NEAR WOODS

**DOUGAL:** God, Ted, imagine if we're not able to get him back. He'd be like Big Foot, except he'd be a BBC television presenter.

*Ted and Dougal have joined Sergeant Deegan, a gruff, serious policeman. They hide behind some rocks.*

**DEEGAN:** D'ye see him? There . . . by the trees . . .

*He hands Ted a pair of binoculars. Ted looks through them and we see the woods from his point of view. At first we don't see anything. Then a figure in the distance, wearing a bright shirt and tie, runs from one entanglement of trees to another. It is a brief, dark, fleeting movement.*

**TED:** Got him! There he is!

*He passes the binoculars to Dougal. Dougal has a look.*

**TED:** Sorry about all this, Sergeant.

**DEEGAN:** Oh, no problem, Father. I've been through this before . . . rock stars, actors, television personalities. They give up the drink and drugs and come over to places like this. The solitude can get to them. What happened to this fella?

**TED:** Well, he was fine one minute, and then he had a sip of sherry . . .

*The sergeant laughs at Ted's naïveté.*

**DEEGAN:** Relapse. That's when they're at their most dangerous. Right, y'ready? I want you two to bang these sticks together and shout a bit. That'll scare him out of the woods so I can get a clear shot.

*He lifts a rifle into shot.*

**TED:** You're going to shoot him?!

**DEEGAN:** A tranquilliser dart, Father. It'll just put him to sleep for a bit.

**TED:** Still . . . it seems a bit extreme.

**DEEGAN:** It's the best way, Father, believe me.

**TED:** Well, you know best.

**DEEGAN:** God . . . this reminds me of Vietnam.

**TED:** Were you in Vietnam, Sergeant?

**DEEGAN:** No, no . . . I mean, you know, in the films . . . All right . . . (*He takes quick, sharp breaths in quick succession.*) . . . Let's go!

*The three come out of cover and walk towards the woods. Ted and Dougal bang sticks against tins.*

**TED:** Come on, Henry! Out you come!

**DOUGAL:** Go on out of it, there!

*They make some more noise. Suddenly, Henry, a distant shadowy figure, runs out of the woods to the side.*

**TED:** There's nothing of interest to you in there now, Henry. (*Ted sees Henry.*) There!

**DEEGAN:** Got him.

*Deegan raises the gun and fires. There is a 'phut' noise and Henry falls to the ground. Suddenly, another figure breaks from the woods and runs in the opposite direction.*

**TED:** It's Jack!

**DEEGAN:** I've got a clear shot, Father! Do you want me to get him?

**TED** (*smiling kindly*): No . . . let him go. He'll

make his own way back.

*They watch as Jack runs off into the distance.*

**DEEGAN** (*shakes his head*): Look at him go. Beautiful.

SCENE 10 INT./DAY 2
SET: PAROCHIAL HOUSE
*We see Henry asleep on the sofa. Ted and Dougal stand over him. Ted has a cup of tea in his hand. Henry makes a few grunting noises and then wakes up.*

**HENRY:** Uhhhh . . . Oh, God, my head . . .

**TED:** Here you are Henry. A nice cup of tea.

**HENRY:** Where am I? Oh, my God. What? What happened last night? I remember having a sip of sherry . . .

**TED:** Nothing to worry about, Henry.

**HENRY:** I hope I didn't do anything to embarrass you, Father.

**DOUGAL:** Ha, ha, ha, ha, ha, ha, ha, ha!!!!

**TED:** Dougal! No, no, you were fine, Henry.

*The telephone rings.*

**TED:** Oh, no . . . that'll be Dick Byrne. I do feel kind of sorry for him, though. Marooned out there with those eejits and they've absolutely nothing in common.

SCENE 11 INT./DAY 2
SET: RIVAL PAROCHIAL
HOUSE/PAROCHIAL HOUSE
*We see Father Dick Byrne talking to Cyril and Jim as he waits on the telephone for Ted to pick up.*

**DICK:** . . . absolutely nothing in common. Ah, Ted! Hello!

**TED:** Hello, Dick . . .

**DICK:** Ted! We were just talking about you.

**TED:** Really?

**DICK:** Yeah, we were saying how great you were.

**TED:** Really?

**DICK:** No!!!!!

**TED:** Hilarious, Dick.

**DICK:** I was just calling to make sure you're going to turn up tonight . . .

**TED:** Why wouldn't I turn up?

**DICK:** Well, you know, it might be a little embarrassing to come last again.

**TED:** I won't be coming last, Dick. It'll be you who'll be coming last! In fact, I was wondering if you'd like to put a little bet on the show tonight. Raise the stakes a bit . . .

**DICK:** Put your money where your mouth is, Ted. What are we talking about here? A pound? Two pounds?

**TED** (*moves telephone to other ear*): Five pounds?

**DICK** (*pause. Moves telephone to other ear*): Five pounds?

**TED:** You're not scared are you, Dick?

**DICK:** Of course I'm not scared. Five pounds it is! See you tonight!

*He puts down the telephone.*

**CYRIL:** Who's that, Dick?

**JIM:** Drink!

*Dick looks at the telephone, concerned.*

SCENE 12 INT./DAY 2
SET: PAROCHIAL HOUSE
*Ted puts his head in his hands. Henry is leaving the room.*

**HENRY:** I'd better get cleaned up for tonight, brush my teeth . . . I've got this weird taste of raw meat in my mouth for some reason . . .

**TED:** Right you are, Henry! (*Henry leaves.*) Oh, what did I do that for? We haven't a hope in hell.

**DOUGAL:** Why can't we all go as Elvis, Ted?

**TED:** 'Cause we'll all look the same! Anyway . . . (*He looks at his watch.*) Jack should be back any minute for his afternoon drink.

*We hear a crash outside the room.*

**JACK** (*from outside*): Drink!

**TED:** There he is.

*Jack comes into the room. He looks wrecked. Puffy, bloated and exhausted.*

**DOUGAL:** God, Ted! He looks very rough! We'll have to get him sobered up if he's going to do the contest.

*Dougal walks towards Jack. Ted stops him.*

**TED:** Dougal. Wait . . . I've got an idea.

*Cut to Jack looking at them both, breathing heavily.*

SCENE 13 EXT./EVENING 2
SET: PAROCHIAL HALL
*Establish hall.*

SCENE 14 INT./EVENING 2
SET: PAROCHIAL HALL
*A priest dressed as Ziggy Stardust is performing on stage. He has nearly finished his act. Henry is sitting at a small desk to the side of the stage, making notes.*

**PRIEST** (*sings*): Ziggy played . . . geeetaarrrrrrrr . . .

*Applause. He bows and walks off. Henry and Father Barty Dunne walk onstage.*

**BARTY:** Fantastic! Father Harry Fitzpatrick, there. He looks a bit . . . ha, ha, he won't mind me saying this . . . ha, ha . . . ha, ha, HA, HA, HA!!!! Ah, no . . . Anyway, Henry . . . marks for Father Fitzpatrick?

**HENRY:** Very good. (*He holds up a card with a number on it.*) I'll give him seven out of ten.

*Everyone applauds, except Father Fitzpatrick, who is watching in the wings.*

**FATHER FITZPATRICK:** Bastard.

**BARTY:** O'ho! Not bad at all. 'Ziggy played guitar' . . . ha, ha . . . anyway, that means the lads from Rugged Island are still in the lead with nine out of ten! A big hand for Diana Ross and two of the Supremes!

*We see Dick, Cyril and Jim all with blacked faces and wigs. They look absurd. They turn to each other and shake hands.*

**BARTY:** Now, now, don't start celebrating yet! We've still got one more act to go! Ladies and Gentlemen, please welcome to the stage . . . aha, ha, ha, ha, ha . . . the lads . . . ha, ha,

ha, ha . . . I suppose, it's a bit like . . . ha, ha, ha, ha . . . Anyway, from these very shores, Father Ted Crilly, with Father McGuire and Father Hackett . . .

*Applause. The light goes down. The stage is in complete blackness.*

**TED'S VOICE:** Elvis Presley was a simple truckdriver from America. But one day in the 1950s, he invented rock 'n' roll!

*The lights come up to reveal Dougal revealed as a young Elvis circa 1955, complete with pink jacket, guitar and blue suede shoes. He mimes to 'Hound Dog' for a short while. The music stops, the stage goes black and we hear Ted's voice again.*

**TED'S VOICE:** Elvis became famous. Then

they forced him into the army. Then, he came out. Then, ten years later he came back with a comeback special.

*The lights come on and Ted is revealed in his leather Elvis costume. He mimes 'Guitar Man'. The music stops, and the stage goes black once more.*

**TED'S VOICE:** Elvis was back! From then until the end of his life he played in Las Vegas and became once again the 'King Of Rock 'n' Roll'!

*The lights come on to the strains of 'My Way'. Jack is revealed in Las Vegas costume, sitting in an armchair, looking like a fat, bloated Elvis circa his death. He has a burger in his hand and is smoking. He looks around as if he doesn't know where he is.*

**TED'S VOICE:** Ladies and Gentlemen, that was 'The Three Ages of Elvis' . . . Thank you!!

*The audience applauds.*

**BARTY:** Fantastic. Ha, ha . . . Lord God almighty! Three Elvises! Anyway, over to you Henry for the marks . . .

*Cut to Henry. The atmosphere is tense. A smile slowly crosses his lips. He holds a card up slowly. We see that it is the maximum 'Ten'. There is wild applause. Cut to Dick, who looks disgusted. He gets up to leave and motions to Cyril and Jim to join him.*

SCENE 15 INT./NIGHT 2
SET: PAROCHIAL HOUSE
*Ted is being congratulated by Barty and Henry.*

**BARTY:** Brilliant, Ted. It was fantastic. It was a bit like . . . ha, ha, ha . . .

**TED:** Thanks very much, Barty.

*Dick and Cyril arrive. Dick hands over a fiver to Ted.*

**DICK** (*very angry*): Five pounds, Ted!

**TED** (*taking the money*): Ah, Dick. Hard luck.

**CYRIL:** Did we not win, Dick?

**TED:** No, I'm afraid you didn't, Cyril. This year the trophy goes to Craggy Island! But you have every chance of winning next year.

**DICK:** Do you really think so Ted?

**TED:** No!!!

**DICK:** Come on Cyril. Let's go.

*Father Jim wanders into shot holding an empty glass.*

**JIM:** I'm out of feckin' whiskey.

**DICK:** There's plenty at home, Father.

*The three priests leave briskly.*

**DOUGAL:** That Cyril McDuff's an awful eejit, isn't he, Ted?

*Mrs Doyle arrives with a tray of glasses.*

**HENRY:** Well, I suppose since I didn't make a fool of myself the last time, I might have a drop of champagne. Cheers!

**TED:** Henry, no!

*Too late. Henry downs the champagne.*

**HENRY:** Don't worry yourself, Father. I'm fine. If I can't celebrate tonight, then when can I? The bastards! What the hell is going on?! The bastards! How dare they fire me! I'm Henry Sellers! I'm Henry Sellers!

*He runs to the window and jumps out. Dougal walks up to Ted.*

**TED:** Well, there he goes again.

**DOUGAL:** You're right there, Ted.

**TED:** Ah, we'll get him in the morning. Well done again, Dougal. How do you like the trophy?

*They turn to look at it. We see them from the trophy's position.*

**DOUGAL'S VOICE:** Ah, it's great. And it's all because of you, Ted!

**TED'S VOICE:** Put it there, Dougal!

*Cut to the two of them standing on either side of the trophy. They shake hands. From this vantage point, we see that the trophy is absolutely tiny, about the size of a thimble. They turn to look at it again.*

**THE END**

# and god created woman

**ARTHUR:** This was a favourite among fans of more mainstream comedy, while people who were really keen on *Father Ted* were more ambivalent. It's not surprising really, as this is far less surreal than many other episodes. It's also something of a cliché, but we felt we had to do it. You can't really write twenty-odd episodes of *Father Ted* without using the Priest-Meets-Glamorous-Woman plotline.

Mrs Doyle's bad language speech gave us another aspect to Mrs Doyle's character – a kind of suppressed sexual obsession masquerading as disgust. We were beginning to discover things about Mrs Doyle ourselves here. Like the fact that she deeply distrusts any woman who isn't a nun and doesn't have a mole and a moustache. That made it easier to locate her attitude towards different women later on in the series. We should point out that 'Ride me sideways!' was Pauline's line – she threw it in during rehearsal. When Dermot closed the door on her, he was laughing so much that we had to cut away sharpish.

**GRAHAM:** I disagree very much with Arthur about this episode. I think it's a good mixture of surrealism (the blue card for Jack, the meeting with Tom, the incredibly quick Mass) and really nice observational comedy (Ted's attempts to appear literary and his inability to say goodbye to Polly at the start). The plot could have had a turn or two more, I suppose, and the part with the housewarming party didn't quite work as well as we thought it would, but I think it's the best ambassador for the first series.

The scene with the nuns interviewing Ted was inspired by Saturday morning television interviews with pop-stars, when children would ask the same questions every week about the stars' most embarrassing moments and what their inspirations were. The 'Zoe Ball' role is taken by Rosemary Henderson (Sister Assumpta), who is just one of the many fabulous comic actors in Ireland. We liked her so much we reinvented her character for *Cigarettes and Alcohol and Rollerblading*.

The joke about Ted not being able to say goodbye to Polly Clarke is based on our attempts to leave aftershow parties at places like the BBC. What happens is, you tend to meet someone you vaguely know (or maybe, like Polly, someone vaguely famous), have a nice, thorough chat with them and then say goodbye. Then about three minutes later you find yourself having to dredge up extra conversational nuggets when you meet them outside waiting for a taxi. That's why, I think, famous people always pretend they haven't seen you the second time. Or else it's my personality.

**PART ONE**
SCENE 1 INT./DAY 1
SET: BOOKSHOP
*We see a poster inside the bookshop – a photograph of a glamorous, Edna O'Brien-type novelist underneath the words 'Polly Clarke', signing copies of her new book. A few well-dressed people stand around the bookshop, drinking glasses of wine. Some people are putting on their coats and leaving. We see Ted talking to Polly Clarke.*

**TED:** . . . Now, I love a bit of Oscar Wilde, I suppose. He always does it for me.

**POLLY:** Ah, Wilde . . . 'The only thing worse than being talked about, is not being talked about.'

**TED:** Exactly! You know, I don't think Wilde could have put it better himself.

**POLLY:** Well, it was him who said that, actually.

*Pause.*

**TED:** Yes, but . . . he wouldn't have said it in that kind of ladylike way . . .

**POLLY:** Oh, you're a charmer, Father . . .

**TED:** Miss Clarke, I don't suppose you'd sign a copy of the latest for me?

**POLLY:** I'd be delighted.

**TED** (*as she writes*): Father Ted C— Just Ted Crilly, actually. Don't bother with the Father.

**POLLY** (*writing*): I envy you, really, Father. You must have great peace of mind being a priest. That's what I'd love . . . a feeling of serenity.

**TED:** Oh, I have serenity coming out of my ears. Too much serenity, really. A bit of excitement would suit me down to the ground. It must be great being a writer, though, jetting around the world, being interviewed, going on television . . .

**POLLY:** Don't forget writing, Father.

**TED:** Hmm? Oh, right . . . Well, thanks again for the autograph. I have to go – we've got some nuns coming to visit us on the island so we're all very busy . . .

**POLLY:** OK, Father . . . (*Someone hands her another book to sign.*) . . . Bye, bye!

**TED:** Goodbye now. Good luck with the book.

*Ted moves off.*

SCENE 2 INT./DAY 1
SET: LIFT
*Outside a lift. Ted is looking at the page where Polly has signed the book. It reads 'To Father Curley, Best Wishes, Polly Clarke'. The lift doors open and Ted steps in.*

**TED** (*quietly to himself*): Ah, feck . . .

*Polly walks into the lift just as Ted says this.*

**TED:** Ah, there you are again!

**POLLY:** Ah, Father Curley . . .

**TED** (*jokingly*): Going down? Ha, ha . . .

**POLLY** (*smiles*): Thanks . . .

*The lift doors close. Slightly embarrassing moment. Ted opens the book and looks at the erroneous inscription.*

**TED:** Eh . . .

*Polly smiles at him. Ted looks at her but then chickens out.*

**TED:** Thanks again for the autograph.

**POLLY:** You're welcome.

*Pause. The lift doors open. They step out.*

**TED:** Well . . .

**POLLY:** Ha . . .

**TED:** Good luck with the book again!

**POLLY:** Thanks very much, Father . . .

**TED:** Bye, then!

**POLLY:** Bye, Father!

*They move off in opposite directions.*

SCENE 3 EXT./DAY 1
SET: CAR PARK
*Ted arrives beside his car. He puts his keys into the door. Polly arrives beside Ted. She takes out keys and puts them into the door of the car beside Ted's. She notices him. More embarrassment ensues.*

**POLLY:** Well hello . . . again!

**TED:** Ah, hello!

**POLLY:** We're going to have to stop meeting like this!

**TED:** Ah, ha!

**POLLY:** Well . . . goodbye again!

**TED:** Bye! Good luck with the book!

*They get into their respective cars. Ted waves from inside.*

**TED:** Bye, bye.

*They rev up their engines and move off, waving at each other.*

SCENE 4 EXT./DAY 1
SET: TRAFFIC LIGHTS
*We see Ted waiting at the traffic lights. There is one more car directly in front of him, another car beside that in the other lane. A car pulls up alongside his. Ted turns to see Polly Clarke in the neighbouring car. She turns at exactly the same time. They smile and nod at each other, but the scene is obviously fraught with embarrassment. Pause. Ted waves slightly.*

**TED** (*mouths the words*)**:** See you soon, then!

*We see Polly smiling and nodding from the neighbouring car. Cut back to Ted, who turns to the lights again. He is very aware of Polly's presence beside him. Cut to the traffic lights, which are still red.*

**TED** (*talking through clenched teeth*)**:** Change . . . please change . . . for God's sake . . .

*He turns again to Polly and smiles. He holds up the book.*

**TED** (*mouths the words*)**:** Good luck with the book!

*He turns again.*

**TED:** Please change. Please. Please change. God, please make the lights change. Hail Mary, full of grace, the Lord is with thee . . .

*The lights change. Ted immediately slams his foot down on to the accelerator and the car lurches into the one in front. Ted is mortified.*

**TED:** Oh, God almighty!!!

*The man in front gets out of the car. He looks very angry. Polly doesn't notice the commotion and drives off.*

**TED:** Oh, Christ!

*The man gestures angrily at Ted. Ted rolls down the window to talk to him.*

**TED:** Sorry about that.

*The man comes into shot and blocks our view of Ted. He is a very broad-shouldered, beefy type. We see the man's arm coming back, then we hear a punch, and Ted's cry of pain and surprise.\**

SCENE 5 INT./DAY 1
SET: PAROCHIAL HOUSE HALLWAY
*Ted walks through the front door. He has a bloody nose. He walks towards the living room and steps inside.*

SCENE 6 INT./DAY 1
SET: PAROCHIAL HOUSE
*We see Polly sitting on the sofa. She is reading an issue of 'Cosmopolitan' magazine. Ted walks into the room. She looks up and sees him. He sees who it is and walks straight out again.*

SCENE 7 INT./DAY 1
SET: HALLWAY
*Ted looks up at the ceiling, addressing God.*

**TED:** All right, what's going on?

*He turns and walks into the room again.*

SCENE 8 INT./DAY 1
SET: PAROCHIAL HOUSE
*Ted walks into the living room. Polly looks very puzzled, but not displeased.*

**TED:** Miss Clarke . . . ?

**POLLY:** Father, what are you doing here?

**TED** (*still dazed*)**:** Oh . . . I'm the parish priest here.

**POLLY:** That's extraordinary. Looks like someone's trying to keep us together!

*Ted looks befuddled.*

**POLLY:** I've rented a cottage on the island, you see. But it's not ready yet. The builders suggested I stay here for the night. Is that OK?

---

\*Our director, Declan Lowney, decided to speed all this action up, and consequently make it one of the funniest moments in the episode.

TED: . . . Yes, yes . . . This is amazing . . . God . . . we were both going the same way. But of course, you're very welcome to stay.

*Mrs Doyle enters.*

**MRS DOYLE:** Oh, hello, Father. You've met your visitor, then . . .

TED: Mrs Doyle, Miss Clarke will be staying the night. Could you show her where the spare room is?

**MRS DOYLE** (*coldly*): What?

TED: Could you show her to the spare room?

**MRS DOYLE:** Yes . . . it's just . . . I was going to make some tea . . .

TED: Well, you can do that later, Mrs Doyle. (*To Polly.*) I think tea is a bit common for Miss Clarke's tastes!

*Ted and Polly laugh. Mrs Doyle does not appreciate this remark.*

**MRS DOYLE** (*to Polly*): All right. Come on.

TED: Have a shower and . . . I mean, have a shower if you want . . . I don't want you to have a shower, but . . . it might . . . you might want to get out of your clothes . . . Well, obviously, that's no concern of mine . . . but, ah . . . Mrs Doyle?

*Mrs Doyle ushers her out. Ted sits down and looks at the issue of 'Cosmopolitan' left behind by Polly. He picks it up and flips through it. His eyebrows raise and we cut to see that he is looking at the 'Or are you just pleased to see me?' Wonderbra advertisement. He is looking at this as Dougal's head appears over the sofa directly behind him.*

DOUGAL: Ted . . .

TED (*throws the magazine into the air*): Aaaaaaaaggghhhh!!!!!

*Ted leaps into a standing position.*

DOUGAL: Who was that, Ted?

TED (*clutching his heart*): For God's sake, Dougal!! What do you think you're doing?!

DOUGAL: I was hiding, Ted.

TED: Hiding from who?

DOUGAL: Hiding from yer one. I heard her coming in so I hid behind the sofa.

**TED:** Dougal, I'm still slightly confused . . . Why did you do that?

**DOUGAL:** Oh, I wouldn't know what to say to her. I thought I'd better wait until you got home.

**TED:** She's only a woman, Dougal.

**DOUGAL** (*very uncomfortable*): Oh, I don't . . . I don't know many women, Ted.

**TED:** What about your mother?

**DOUGAL** (*incredulous pause*): My mother? She's not really a woman, Ted. She's not like the women you see on the telly. Like The Gladiators. She wouldn't be one of them.

**TED:** Well . . . I . . . I'm sure that's their loss. But what about Mrs Doyle? She's a woman.

**DOUGAL:** Ah, Ted, come on . . .

**TED:** No, Dougal she is. She's just as much a woman as one of The Gladiators or the lady who runs Pakistan. You're just saying that because she's not conventionally attractive. You can't think like that anymore, Dougal . . .

**DOUGAL:** Mmm . . .

**TED:** . . . This is the twenty-first century, remember.*

**DOUGAL:** Anyway, who's that one you were talking to?

**TED:** She's a novelist. I've just been to her book signing. Apparently she's taken a cottage on the island . . .

*We hear a scream from upstairs. Dougal and Ted look at each other, then run out of the room.*

SCENE 9 INT./DAY 1
SET: SPARE BEDROOM
*Polly stands in the room looking a little shaken. Mrs Doyle seems unsure what to do. Ted and Dougal enter and look at the bed. We see Jack lying on his back on the bed dressed only in socks, vest and underpants. He looks like a beached whale. There is a half-empty bottle of whiskey in his hand. He snores loudly. This is a fairly unsettling sight.*

*Like computers that haven't been checked for the Millennium Bug, this joke will stop working the moment the calendar flips to 1/1/00.

**POLLY:** I'm sorry, Father. I just got a bit of a shock.

**TED:** Come on now, Father . . . (*He turns to Polly.*) This is Father Hackett. He gets a bit confused sometimes. (*To Jack.*) Come on, Father!

*Jack rolls away from him.*

**TED:** No, Father. Not your room! Not your room! No! Come on, now . . .

*Jack moans and then lashes out at Ted, striking him across the face. Ted falls out of shot then immediately stands up again. Jack goes mad, thrashing about wildly.*

**JACK:** Arse! Arse! Feck!!! Arse!! Feck!! Arrrgghhhh!!!

**TED** (*to Dougal*): Father!

*Dougal doesn't respond to this.*

**TED:** Dougal! Give us one of the cards! Quickly!

*Polly turns to look at Dougal, who immediately averts his gaze. He moves past her, keeping his head fixed in this position. He stands by Ted, taking some cards out of his pocket and fanning them. We see they are all different colours.*

**DOUGAL:** What colour, Ted?

**TED:** Blue, Dougal! Quickly!

*Dougal gives Ted a blue card and immediately shows it to Jack. Jack continues screaming until he sees the card, when he suddenly calms and stops.*

**TED:** There we go. (*To Polly.*) The old blue has a great calming effect.

*They lift him out of bed and lead him past Polly.*

**JACK:** Hehhh . . .

**TED:** That's right. That's Miss Clarke. Dougal . . .

**JACK** (*as he is led out of sight*): Woman!

**TED:** It is a woman, Father. You're right on the button.

*Mrs Doyle and Polly are left behind.*

**MRS DOYLE** (*smiles coldly*): Well . . . Have a lovely stay.

*She leaves the room. Polly, as quietly as possible, closes the door and locks it.*

SCENE 10 INT./NIGHT 1*
SET: TED AND DOUGAL'S BEDROOM
*We see Ted reading 'Bejewelled with Kisses'. He looks up over his glasses at Dougal. Dougal is reading Polly's copy of 'Cosmopolitan', his eyes wide.*

**DOUGAL** (*under his breath*): . . . Jaysus . . .

**TED:** It might not be a good idea reading that Dougal. You'll get confused.

**DOUGAL** (*pauses and, turns page*): God, Ted, Kim Basinger is forty.

*He shows Ted a full-page photograph of a glamorous Miss Basinger.*

**DOUGAL:** I hope I look this good when I'm forty. My God.

*Ted starts to say something, then thinks better of it and returns to his book. He talks to Dougal absently while looking at it.*

**TED:** So . . . what do you think of Miss Clarke?

**DOUGAL:** Oh, she's very nice. I think we hit it off.

**TED:** Dougal, you were hiding from her. I don't think that fits the definition of 'hitting it off'. She is very nice, though . . . It'll be great to have someone here on the island I can talk to . . . about books and films and poetry and so on . . .

**DOUGAL** (*a little hurt*): You can talk to me, Ted.

*Ted looks at Dougal.*

**DOUGAL:** Seriously, Ted. Let's talk about something.

**TED:** . . . OK. What do you want to talk about?

*Long pause. Dougal looks at Ted vacantly.*

**DOUGAL:** What?

**TED:** All right, I'll pick something . . . ehhhh . . . What's your biggest fear in life?

**DOUGAL:** I wouldn't like to be hit on the head with a football.

**TED:** You . . .

_____
*We deleted this scene from the final version.

**DOUGAL:** I don't think about it all the time. Only when I'm passing by football pitches.

*Pause. Ted doesn't know what to say.*

**DOUGAL:** God! I'm glad I talked to you about that . . . I feel much better now.

**TED:** I . . . yes . . . I can understand . . . Anyway, I think I'll go to sleep. You'd better sign off yourself, Dougal. Big day with the nuns tomorrow. Put the magazine away, now.

**DOUGAL:** Right so.

*Ted turns off the light. Pause.*

**DOUGAL:** Ted?

**TED:** Yes, Dougal?

**DOUGAL:** What's female circumcision, Ted? . . . Ted?

*Pause. After a moment, we hear Ted pretending to snore.*

SCENE 11 INT./MORNING 2
SET: PAROCHIAL HOUSE
*Ted looks immaculate. His hair is as smooth as plastic. His face is as smooth as a baby's bottom and he wears a blacker-than-black jacket. He checks himself in the mirror, then looks at his lapel badge. He rubs it, looks uncertain, then picks up a spray from the mantelpiece and sprays it. He shines it with his sleeve. He starts walking around the room, trying out various poses/ways of walking, etc. He mouths little phrases to himself, as if rehearsing a conversation. He laughs urbanely, practises a 'thoughtful look', etc. He keeps adjusting his jacket. He walks to a chair and leans on it in what he imagines to be a casual yet stylish way. He tries various poses here. Then he remembers something and goes to the bookcase. He starts taking down books and leaving them on the table. They are 'War and Peace', 'Crime and Punishment', 'The Odyssey' and 'The Commitments' by Roddy Doyle. He reconsiders the Doyle book and puts it back on the shelf. He leans on the chair again, tries a few poses and finally settles on one. The door opens and he opens his mouth in a smile. Dougal enters. Ted's smile disappears and he resumes his normal stance.*

**TED:** Ah. Hello, Dougal.

**DOUGAL** (*looks at the books*): Ah, good idea, Ted. You throwing out the ones you couldn't get through?

**TED:** No, no, Dougal, I'm just . . . putting them in alphabetical order.

**DOUGAL:** Fair enough.

**TED:** You taking Jack for his walk, then?

**DOUGAL:** Suppose so, Ted. Do you want to come at all?

**TED:** No . . . no, I'd better . . . prepare for the nuns.

*Mrs Doyle enters, pushing Jack in his wheelchair.*

**MRS DOYLE:** Here we are, Father. It's a lovely day out.

**JACK:** My arse.

**MRS DOYLE** *(to Dougal)***:** Do you want him on automatic or manual, Father?

**DOUGAL:** Em . . . automatic, I think. Nice day . . . might as well take it easy.

**TED:** That's right, Dougal. You take your time.

**MRS DOYLE:** Fair enough.

*Mrs Doyle produces a steel bar-like contraption and attaches it to Jack's wheelchair. It bends in the middle, and at its end, hanging from a piece of string, is a small bottle of whiskey. It hangs just in front of Jack, carrot-and-stick-like. Jack immediately starts pushing the wheels of the chair forward. Dougal casually walks after it. Mrs Doyle waves goodbye. She turns to Ted when they're gone, looking slightly disgusted.*

**MRS DOYLE:** Well, Father, I never thought we'd have anyone like her staying here.

**TED:** Hmm? Oh, Miss Clarke? I know. It's very exciting, isn't it? A famous novelist!

**MRS DOYLE:** You haven't read any of her books, have you, Father?

**TED:** Well, actually, I'm a bit of a fan, Mrs Doyle. That's where I was the other day. At her book signing.

**MRS DOYLE:** Well, I'm surprised at that, Father. I didn't think you'd like that sort of thing. I read a bit of one of them once. God, I couldn't finish it. The language . . . unbelievable.

**TED:** It's a bit gritty, Mrs Doyle. But sure that's the modern world.

**MRS DOYLE:** It was a bit much for me, Father . . . 'Feck this and feck that' . . .

**TED:** Yes, Mrs Doyle.

**MRS DOYLE:** 'You big bastard' . . . Oh, dreadful language . . . 'You big hairy arse' . . . 'You big fecker' . . . Fierce stuff altogether. And of course, the F word, Father. The bad F word. Worse than feck. You know the one I mean.

**TED:** I do, Mrs Doyle.

**MRS DOYLE** *(pause)***:** 'F you!', 'F your effing wife!' Awful stuff. I don't know why they have to use that type of language. *(Pause.)* 'I'll stick this effing pitchfork up your hole!' That was another one.

**TED:** OK, Mrs Doyle. I see what you mean.

**MRS DOYLE:** 'Bastard' this and 'bastard' that. You can't move for the 'bastards' in her books. It's wall-to-wall bastards!

**TED:** Is it? Anyway —

**MRS DOYLE:** 'You big bastard'. 'You fecker.' 'You bollocks.' 'Get your bollocks out of my face.' . . . God, it's terrible, Father.

**TED** *(starts to usher her out)***:** Yes . . . you go and get ready for the nuns, Mrs Doyle . . .

*Ted finally manages to slam the door shut. He leans against it, breathing heavily. Then he goes back to the books on the table and starts to pose around them again. He looks down and adjusts his fly. He pulls it down and then can't pull it up again. He turns and hops slightly as he tries to pull it up. Behind him the door opens and Polly comes in. She sees the books on the table and smiles. She picks one up and starts looking at it. Ted is still hopping up and down. He finally turns, pulling up the zip.*

**TED:** Ahhhh . . . there you go . . . Aaaaghhhhh! *(Ted tries to assume his 'stylish' pose again. He has a little trouble with this.)* Hello there Miss Clarke! . . . Did you have a nice sleep?

**POLLY:** Oh, I slept like a log. It's so peaceful here . . . God, I need a bit of peace after the year I've had.

**TED:** I see . . .

**POLLY:** I've had quite a rough time of it recently. My husband left me for another woman. I suppose it was my fault. The sex was getting a little boring and I never did anything to spice it up.

**TED** (*massively uncomfortable*): Tcha! Isn't it always the way . . .

**POLLY:** Near the end I tried a few things. I'd dress up in some really revealing lingerie, and when he came through the door I'd just leap on top of him and have sex there in the hall.

*Pause.*

**TED:** So, you had a good sleep, then.

**POLLY:** Yes, I . . . Oh, God, sorry, Father! I probably shocked you!

**TED:** Oh . . . go . . . go away with . . . no, I've heard far more shocking things in confession down through the years.

*He walks away from Polly in a very strange, uncomfortable way.*

**POLLY** (*sighs*): Do you ever think of the future, Father?

**TED:** Oh, I used to think about it. The future. And then the future became the present, so I was obviously thinking about it a lot then. And now it's in the past, so I don't really think about it that often.

**POLLY:** The future is in the past?

**TED:** Well, it wasn't then, of course. It was the future . . . But when you're a priest, to be honest, the whole time is like a continual present, you know?

*Polly smiles at him. She then looks down at the books on the table.*

**POLLY:** Do you like Dostoevsky?

*Ted smiles blankly. Polly smiles and holds up 'Crime and Punishment'.*

**TED:** Oh! Oh, him? Oh, yes, that's one of my favourites, all right. I must have read that book . . . ten times.

**POLLY:** I see you're reading it again. There's a bookmark here on page seven.

*Ted smiles and nods.*

**POLLY:** Did you feel his sense of commitment wane towards the end?

**TED:** Well, yes.

**POLLY:** When did you feel that began to happen?

**TED:** Towards the end. (*Pause.*) Around the time he stopped writing about crime and went on to the punishment bit. It began to drag a bit there for me.

**POLLY:** I always felt that if Joyce, Keats and Lawrence were sitting in a room together and Dostoevsky came in, there'd be a bit of a fight for the last piece of pudding!

*She laughs. Ted joins in, throwing his head back. He turns slightly and we see him pull a 'what the hell did that mean?' expression.*

**POLLY:** It's great having someone to talk to about these things . . . My husband, there was a man who really was afraid of Virginia Woolf.

*Ted nods.*

**TED:** Was she following him or something?

**POLLY:** Ha, ha, ha, ha!!!

**TED** (*uncertain*): Ha, ha, ha, ha . . .

**POLLY:** Would you . . . I don't suppose you'd like to come up to the cottage later? For a drink? And maybe more book talk!

**TED:** Oh, that would be delightfug.

**POLLY** (*laughs*): Sorry?

**TED:** I'd be delightegetted.

**POLLY:** Right. See you later then, Father. About seven.

TED: Seven. Seven o'clock. Right.

*She leaves. Ted smiles to himself, then looks up at the ceiling.*

TED: It's just a drink!

### END OF PART ONE

* * *

### PART TWO

SCENE 12 INT./DAY 2
SET: PAROCHIAL HOUSE
*We see a close-up of Ted, smiling in a fixed way. He sips from a cup of tea. Cut to a wide shot of the room. We see five nuns sitting on chairs together, smiling and looking at the ground. Pause.*

TED: So! You had no trouble getting here.

ASSUMPTA: No, no. I drove Sister Julia in the Renault and Sister Margaret took the Mini.

TED: It's great having the old car, all the same . . . Any more tea at all?

*The nuns talk as one, and do so as quietly as possible. We can't make out any words but the gist of it seems to be that they don't want any more tea.*

TED: Sister Margaret, will you not have something?

*Margaret goes bright red. All the other nuns turn exactly the same shade at exactly the same time.\* Sister Margaret begins to speak as softly as possible.*

MARGARET: . . . No, thank you, Father.

TED: Sorry?

ASSUMPTA: She's fine, Father. Ah, what time does the Mass tonight start, Father?

TED: Oh, at seven o'clock.

ASSUMPTA: That's grand. We don't want to be up too late.

TED: Well, seven isn't too . . . (*His eyes widen.*) Aaaargh!!

*The nuns jump slightly with fright.*

ASSUMPTA: Father! Are you all right?

---

*\*We were going to smother them in make-up to get this effect but in the end, we decided to leave it to the performances of the actresses.*

TED: Yes . . . yes. Oh, dear, there's just . . . seven o' clock . . . I may have to leave early.

ASSUMPTA: During the Mass? Oh, you couldn't leave during the Mass, could you, Father?

TED: No, it's just . . .

*A very old nun whispers something in Sister Assumpta's ear.*

ASSUMPTA: Sister Julia says that you say a lovely Mass. She says that you said one of the nicest Masses she ever heard.

*Another nun whispers something to Assumpta.*

ASSUMPTA: Sister Teresa says she thought last year's Mass here was fabulous. She says she'd give it ten out of ten. And she's very hard to please. She's seen you do . . . what? Is it about fifty Masses since then?

*Teresa nods. She looks very embarrassed.*

ASSUMPTA: Show Father Crilly the photographs, Teresa. You'll like these, Father . . .

*Teresa takes some photographs out of her bag. She hands them meekly to Assumpta, who shows them to Ted.*

ASSUMPTA: There's you at last year's Mass here . . . and that's you doing the Mass the year before . . . And . . . what's that? . . . your sister-in-law's funeral . . . my personal favourite . . .

*We see that all the photographs are incredibly dull shots of Ted saying Mass. They are all more or less identical, except for one, which has Ted sporting a ridiculous-looking, bushy beard.*

ASSUMPTA: That's when you had the beard . . . Sister Julia was saying the other day that you're the best priest that she's ever seen saying Mass. And she's been to Mass about half a million times.

TED (*flipping quickly through the photographs*): Really?

ASSUMPTA: Actually, Father, you couldn't sign a few for us?

TED: The photographs?

ASSUMPTA: Yes.

**TED:** Ah . . . all right . . .

*He produces a pen and starts signing them. We see that some of the nuns are putting their hands up.*

**ASSUMPTA:** Could you put on my one, 'To Sister Assumpta'?

**TED:** Sure . . .

**ASSUMPTA:** Father, Sister Margaret wants to ask a question . . .

**TED:** Yes?

**MARGARET:** Where do you get your ideas for your sermons?

**ASSUMPTA:** Where do you get your ideas for your sermons?

**TED:** Oh, just . . . overheard conversations, the News, whatever. Listen, I have to be honest here . . . I mightn't be able to—

*Two nuns have their hands up.*

**ASSUMPTA:** Sister Julia, do you have a question?

**JULIA:** What's your most embarrassing moment saying Mass?

**ASSUMPTA:** What's your most embarrassing moment saying Mass?

**TED:** Well, I suppose it was the time I forgot my sister-in-law's name . . . That got me a bit hot under the collar.

*Everyone laughs kindly.*

**TED:** Anyway, listen . . . the thing is, I might not be able to say this evening's.

*Very pregnant pause.*

**ASSUMPTA:** What, Father?

**TED:** I have something quite important to do.

**ASSUMPTA:** Not more important than saying Mass, surely?

**TED:** It's just that someone I know very well is . . . dying.

**ASSUMPTA:** Oh dear. Is it serious?

**TED:** Yes. In this particular case, the person who's dying is quite seriously ill. It's a good friend of ours . . .

*The door opens and Dougal wheels Father Jack in.*

**JACK:** Nuns! Reverse! Reverse! Reverse! Reverse!

*Dougal immediately wheels Jack back out through the doorway. After a moment, he returns.*

**ASSUMPTA:** Hello, Father McGuire! Father Crilly's just been telling us about your friend dying.

**DOUGAL:** Who's that, Ted?

**TED:** Oh, old Jim.

**DOUGAL:** Is he dying? Poor old Jim. He won't like that.

**TED:** Oh, he's terribly down.

*Pause.*

**DOUGAL:** Wait a second . . . Jim Halpin?

**TED:** Yes.

**DOUGAL:** I was just talkin' to him and he didn't say anything about it.

**TED:** Oh, well, that's Jim. Brave is not the word.

**DOUGAL:** He's just outside. Hold on, I'll get him.

**TED:** What?! What's he doing outside? He . . . he should be home in bed.

**DOUGAL:** I met him earlier. He wanted a lend of some sugar. Jim! C'mere for a mo', will you?

**TED:** Dougal, at this moment, the man needs peace. Don't—

*Jim enters the room.*

**TED:** Hello, Jim.

**JIM:** Hello, Father. Hello, Sisters.

**DOUGAL:** Jim, you never told me you were ill.

**JIM:** What? I had a cold a few weeks back.

**DOUGAL:** A cold? Ted said you were dying.

**JIM:** Dying? Oh, no. I don't think so, anyway.

*Everyone looks at Ted.*

**TED:** Ah . . . well, I was talking to Doctor Sinnot the other day, and he said that you . . . that you might be dying. He wasn't a hundred per cent sure himself, now. So don't go worrying yourself unnecessarily.

**JIM:** God almighty! I'd better give him a call.

*He moves towards the telephone.*

**TED:** I wouldn't go calling him, Jim.

**JIM:** Why not?

**TED:** He can't use the phone. He's . . . gone deaf.

**DOUGAL:** Doctor Sinnot's gone deaf, Ted? That's terrible!

**TED:** It is, all right.

*Dougal sees something through the window.*

**DOUGAL:** O'ho, wait a second, Ted! There he is now!

*Dougal opens the window.*

**DOUGAL:** Doctor Sinnot! Doctor Sinnot! (*Turns to Ted.*) He heard that all right, Ted. Doctor! C'mere for a second!

**TED:** Actually, wait . . . I've just remembered. Jim's actually not dying, and Doctor Sinnot's not deaf. I was thinking of two completely different people.

**ASSUMPTA:** Oh . . . so you will be able to do the Mass tonight, Father.

**TED:** I will, yes. Thanks to Father Dougal for clearing up that little misunderstanding.

*He puts a friendly arm around Dougal's shoulders. Pause.*

**DOUGAL:** Ted . . . Ted, you're hurting me . . .

SCENE 13 INT./DAY 2
SET: SACRISTY
*Dougal is helping Ted get into his vestments.*

**TED:** All right, listen, Dougal, I'm going to have to go straight after this, so you'll have to take care of the nuns.

**DOUGAL:** Fair enough, Ted . . . What'll I do with them?

**TED:** Whatever you want . . . Just try not to kill them or anything.

**DOUGAL:** Ha, ha! No chance of that, Ted!

**TED:** Remember Sister Janita?

**DOUGAL:** Oh, right . . . That was a bit too close for comfort, all right.

**TED:** Well, just be careful this time. (*Looks at his watch.*) . . . Oh, God . . . Right, are they all in there?

*Dougal looks through the door into the church.*

**DOUGAL:** They are. Like peas in a pub.

**TED:** Pod. Right. See you later.

*Dougal leaves the sacristy. Ted takes a deep breath, then walks out into the church. The door swings open wide, and then closes slowly. We see the door closing, and as we do, we hear Ted's muffled voice coming from without. Then we hear the nuns say something simultaneously. Then Ted says something. The door is just about to click shut when Ted opens it and comes charging into the sacristy, tearing off his vestments. He looks pleased and focussed.*

**TED:** Right . . .


SCENE 14 EXT./DAY 2
SET: CHURCH
*Ted exits the church at top speed, taking out his car keys as he does so. He runs towards his car, but as he approaches it, we see his expression change to one of horror. We see that the two cars belonging to the nuns are blocking his car at both ends, effectively stopping it from moving anywhere. He can't believe it, especially since there is tons of room all along the road. He gets in the car and starts the engine. We see him cursing like crazy. He turns around as if to reverse. We see the back bumper edging into the front bumper of the other car. He then edges forward into the other car. He turns the wheel around many, many times, edging the car backwards. Then he turns the wheel*

*just a little bit more. We hear a 'crack'. Ted stops. He turns off the engine, holds the wheel and spins it as easily as one would a bicycle wheel. We see Ted, but can't hear him, and he is clearly saying 'fuck' again and again. He gets out of the car, still repeating the word. As he opens the door, we can finally hear him.*

**TED:** Flip! Flip! Flip! Flip! Flip! Flip!

*Ted starts running down the road. After a while, he hears a vehicle in the distance behind him. He stops running and holds his thumb out. We see a Renault van in the distance. He adjusts his collar so that it's clear he's a priest. The van keeps approaching. Ted takes a deep breath.*

**TED:** Please, please, please, please, please . . .

*The van keeps coming down the long, straight road. This takes a minute or so. We see Ted in the foreground, the van in the distance, getting larger by the second – rather like Omar Sharif's appearance in 'Lawrence of Arabia'. After a while, the van runs straight into Ted and knocks him on to the hood. We see Ted with his face pressed against the windscreen. Inside the van we see Tom, looking shocked. He puts on the brakes, and Ted slides off the hood and on to the road. He lies there as we hear the car door opening. Tom runs around to the front of the car.*

**TOM:** Sorry, Father! Didn't see you there!

**TED** (*from the ground*)**:** No problem, Tom. Can you give me a lift?

SCENE 15 INT./DAY 2
SET: CAR
*We see the two driving along at a 'brisk' pace. Ted is holding on to the dashboard. There is no suspension in the car and Ted is being thrown about wildly. A dog is beside Ted, barking his head off. Ted is constantly trying to bring a seatbelt down around him, but it extends only about half a foot before stopping.*

**TED** (*very, very nervous*)**:** Ho, ho!!!

**TOM** (*to dog*)**:** Headcase! Shut up! Shut up, Headcase! Shut up! Will ya shut the feck up! Shut up! Shut up!

**TED:** Thanks again for the lift, Tom.

**TOM:** No problem, Father. I just have to stop at the post office for a moment.

**TED** (*looks at his watch*)**:** Well it's just, I am in a

bit of —

**TOM** (*stopping the car*)**:** Won't be a second, Father. Could you hand me that parcel?

*Ted gives him a long parcel.*

**TED:** It's just — I'm supposed to be meeting someone — God, that's heavy . . .

**TOM:** Back in a mo', Father. Shut up, Headcase!!

*Tom unbuckles his buckle, which isn't attached to a seatbelt, and puts it on the dashboard.*

SCENE 15A EXT./DAY 2
SET: POST OFFICE
*He leaves the car and walks into the post office. The dog continues barking. We hear three gunshots and some muffled shouting. Tom comes out of the post office carrying a bag and the long parcel.*

SCENE 15B INT./DAY 2
SET: CAR
*He gets into the car, putting the seatbelt back in place.*

**TOM:** Sorry about that, Father. Right! (*To the dog.*) You! Shut up!

**TED:** You're not up to your old tricks again, are you, Tom?

**TOM:** No, no, Father. It's my money, I just didn't want to fill out the forms.

*The car rips off at top speed.*

SCENE 16 EXT./NIGHT 2
SET: COTTAGE
*Blackness. We hear Tom's van pulling up and a loud crash!!*

SCENE 17 EXT./NIGHT 2
SET: COTTAGE
*Ted appears at the doorway, looking fairly dishevelled. He tries to tidy himself as best he can. The door opens. Polly stands there, smiling. She looks devastating in a slinky, black, low-cut dress.*

**POLLY:** Father Curley! You came!

*Ted starts to reply, takes in Polly's appearance, and then can't say anything.*

**POLLY:** C'mon and have a drink. What would

you like. Sherry? I think I've got everything you might want in here.

*Ted can't say anything. He follows her into the living room, a huge smile on his face. When he gets in, however, his smile dies. In the room we see Dougal, Jack, the nuns and a few assorted guests milling about, drinking, etc.*

**DOUGAL:** Ted, Ted! Over here!

*Ted moves over to Dougal and the nuns.*

**DOUGAL:** This is great, isn't it?

**TED:** What are you doing here?

**DOUGAL:** What? Well . . . you know, we were invited . . .

**TED:** Invited? . . .

**DOUGAL:** Same as you, Ted. Can't have a housewarming on your own, can you, Ted?

**TED** (*massively disappointed*): No . . . no, I suppose you can't . . .

*Assumpta approaches Ted.*

**ASSUMPTA** (*coldly*): Very short Mass tonight, Father. We were all a bit disappointed, weren't we, Sisters?

*She looks at the other nuns. They all look very unfriendly, especially Teresa, who stares at Ted with a look of disgust.*

**ASSUMPTA:** We mightn't be back next year. They say Father Clippit does a good long Mass. Three hours, he does, on a good night, since his stroke. That's value for money.

**TED:** Well, Sister, you see . . .

**ASSUMPTA** (*looks conspicuously at her watch*): Oh, sorry, Father. I'm in a hurry.

*She walks off. Ted looks up to see Polly engaged in deep conversation with the old nun. Dougal is struggling with a huge bag of family-sized crisps.*

**DOUGAL:** God, how do you get these open?

*He crushes the sides of the bag and it explodes, showering a downcast Ted with crisps. Fade out.*

SCENE 17A INT./NIGHT 2
SET: COTTAGE
*We fade back in as everyone is leaving the party. Polly stands beside Ted. The nuns file out past them.*

**TED:** I'll see you back in . . .

**ASSUMPTA:** Hrrmmphhh . . .

*Jack walks past. He looks very strange, as if a rubber raft has inflated inside his jacket. Ted stops him.*

**TED:** Now, Father . . .

*Ted reaches inside Jack's jacket and starts to remove bottles of whiskey, six-packs, and some more bottles of various different types of alcohol. Ted puts the booty on a nearby table. Jack moves off grumpily and Ted starts to follow him out, when he is stopped by Polly.*

**POLLY:** Father, before you go, could I have a quick word?

**TED** (*brightens*): Oh . . . right . . . (*To Dougal.*) Dougal, you go on ahead, I'll see you in a while . . .

**DOUGAL:** Right so, Ted.

*Dougal leaves. Ted closes the door after him. He turns to see Polly sitting down on the sofa. She pats the space beside her and Ted sits down there.*

**TED:** So . . .

**POLLY:** Would you like a drink, Father Curley?

**TED:** Oh, yes . . .

*Polly goes to the drinks cabinet and pours them both drinks. She walks back to Ted and hands him his.*

**POLLY:** It was nice talking to you today, Father.

**TED:** Well, if you can't talk to a priest, who can you talk to? We're taught how to listen. Not that we had 'listening classes' or anything! It's not as if we didn't know how to listen, already. Because that's just being there and someone talking to you . . . which is, you know, quite easy . . . unless you're deaf . . . not a lot of work involved there . . . no swotting for exams with the old listening . . .

**POLLY:** Father, remember I was telling you that I had reached a crossroads in my life.

**TED:** Yes, yes, I do.

**POLLY:** Well, what do you think I should do? I need advice.

**TED** (*puts on his 'caring priest voice'*): . . . Is it a busy crossroads at all?

POLLY: You, know, Father, that's interesting. I think one road leads back to where I was. And that's a busy road. A glamorous road. Overflowing with traffic and people and bright lights. And the other road is a quiet country road with serenity and peace and fulfilment.

TED: I see.

POLLY: Which one would you choose, Father?

TED: Ah, that's an easy one.

POLLY: Yes, Father. The choice is obvious . . .

TED: Bright lights! Glamour! Film premières! . . .

POLLY: Well, I was thinking . . .

TED (smiling): Parties! Cocaine busts! Las Vegas! . . .

POLLY: No . . . Father? Father?

TED (smiling in a faraway manner): Hmm? Sorry?

POLLY: Father, what I wanted to say was . . . I know I've made the right choice!

TED: I know you have, Polly! And I'm with you all the way!

POLLY: I'm going to become a nun!

Pause.

TED: Oh . . . feck!

POLLY: What, Father?

TED: Feck! Feck! Fecking great news! Just . . . fecking . . . marvellous!

POLLY (continuing enthusiastically): I was talking to Sister Julia earlier. She's ninety-seven years old. Did you ever wonder what it would be like to be a ninety-seven-year old nun, Father?*

TED (can't think what to say): No.*

POLLY: She's ninety-seven. She's deaf. She's half-blind, she's never been with a man in her life, and she's one of the most joyful people I've ever met.*

TED: Oh . . . yes. Although it's not obvious at first, I suppose. She's not exactly Mr Motivator.*

POLLY: Father, thank you.*

TED: Eh . . . *

POLLY: For helping to show me that the religious life is the one for me.*

Pause.*

TED: Are you absolutely sure you're making the right decision? Don't you want to give that other road just a few more miles?*

POLLY: I'm heading off tomorrow, Father. I'm not going to leave it a day longer.*

TED (very disappointed): Oh . . . *

POLLY: I'll be sorry to leave Craggy Island. It's silly I know. I've only been here a day! But I'll always remember you. When I look into my Bible in twenty years' time, I'll probably still be thinking about . . . Father Ted Curley.

TED: Crilly.

POLLY: What?

TED: Father Ted Crilly. (He offers her his hand.) How are you? Now, I'd better be off.

He stands up and walks out of shot. Polly looks after him, confused.

SCENE 18 INT./NIGHT 2
SET: PAROCHIAL HOUSE
Ted comes into the room, looking at his copy of Polly's book. He lets it drop on to the table. Jack is laughing wildly at the sight of Dougal, who has his head stuck down the back of the sofa.

TED: Oh . . . Dougal, not again.

DOUGAL (muffled): Sorry, Ted. I was looking for change.

Ted sighs.

TED: Ah, well . . . back to the everyday grind . . .

He starts trying to pull Dougal out of the chair. Roll credits.

**THE END**

---

*We deleted these lines from the final version.

# GRant unto him Eternal Rest

**GRAHAM:** This was the first episode to be conceived, and it contains the three scenes with which we presented *Father Ted* to Hat Trick. If I remember correctly, they were the scene where Ted enters the bedroom to find Jack dead, the scene with the monkey priest and the crying priest, and a portion of the mausoleum scene at the end. I always say that the reason Jack had so few words in his vocabulary is because he started off his life by being dead, so even 'Feck! Drink! Arse! Girls!' is quite chatty for him.

Now, I know how difficult this might be to believe, but it wasn't until the show was being edited that someone pointed out the similarity between Ted discovering Jack's body and a similiar scene in *Fawlty Towers*. It's terribly similar, but I swear it wasn't a conscious lift. Furthermore, if we were going to deliberately copy another show, I hope we wouldn't be stupid enough to plagiarise the all-time great British sitcom.

Perhaps because of it being the first one we wrote, Ted and Dougal behave in slightly uncharacteristic ways here. The reflective moment in the mausoleum when Dougal and Ted discuss their beliefs is unusual, especially when Ted recites James Joyce. And towards the end Ted and Dougal are on the verge of going out of character when they leave the room to buy floor polish, the substance that 'killed' Jack in the first place. In the early days of a sitcom, when you're still insecure about whether it's funny or not, it's always tempting to make someone behave out of character for the sake of a gag. It's not too bad, as these things go, but I hope I wouldn't do it now.

**ARTHUR:** This was quite an easy episode to write and was probably helped by the fact that it's a very old-fashioned idea: beneficiaries of a will having to do something unusual in order to inherit the money. Dougal's 'Last Rites' speech features references to Costacurta, Baggio and Roberto – Ardal and myself were big fans of Channel 4's coverage of Italian football. The character of the monkey priest was born entirely out of a desire to see a man walk into a room with another man, holding his hand limply and walking like a gibbon. Like Father Hernandez in *The Passion of Saint Tibulus*, he seems to be able to make himself understood. It's almost as if priests are a sort of species in *Father Ted*; it doesn't matter what they're doing or saying, other priests can always understand them.

**PART ONE**
SCENE 1 INT./MORNING 1
SET: PAROCHIAL HOUSE
*Camera centres on Dougal, then pulls back to reveal him sitting beside a nun, Sister Monica. She is a youngish, respectable, Dana type. There is a slight, embarrassed pause.*

**DOUGAL:** So, then. You're a nun?

*Ted walks into the room.*

**TED:** Right, Sister Monica, I've left your bags in the hall. I thought before we leave you to the boat, we might go and see the Holy Stone.

**MONICA:** The what?

**TED:** The Holy Stone of Clonrichert.

**DOUGAL:** Oh, great!

**TED:** Yes, it's good to go now 'cause there'll be no tourists. Although that's a pity in a way, 'cause when the tourists are here there's a van that sells ice-cream and fizzy drinks and all that. And sometimes the local shop gets in these magnificent souvenir combs.

**DOUGAL:** Yes, they're fantastic combs. (*He produces a comb.*) I got this one last year. You can see there they've written 'I Saw The Holy Stone of Clonrichert'.

*The nun smiles politely and nods.*

**TED:** The Stone's great, though. We've seen it, I think, about three hundred times.

**MONICA:** Well, why not. It'd round off the weekend.

**TED:** If you thought the ludo night was exciting, then this'll drive you over the edge! It's all been leading up to the Holy Stone . . .

**MONICA:** What's so holy about it anyway, Father?

**TED:** Ah, it's just a general kind of holiness. Father Dougal stood beside it for about ten minutes once and he got a marvellous sense of serenity.

**DOUGAL:** Yes, I got a great buzz off it.

**MONICA:** Why is it called the Holy Stone of Clonrichert? I thought Clonrichert was in Fermanagh . . .

**TED:** It is. The Stone used to be up there all

right, but apparently it wasn't doing great business. So! A treat in store for you!

**MONICA:** Yes . . . I . . . wonderful. I'll just freshen up.

*She leaves the room. Dougal waits until she's gone, then turns to Ted.*

**DOUGAL:** She'll be putting on make-up, I suppose. Impress the lads.

**TED** (*discreetly*): Ah, no. She's probably gone to the toilet or something.

**DOUGAL:** Aren't nuns great, though, Ted? It's good because you don't feel as nervous with them as you do with real women.

**TED:** Oh, you're right there.

**DOUGAL:** Even though I only got the courage to talk to her a minute ago it's nice to have a nun around. Gives the place a bit of glamour, you know?

**TED:** Yes . . . a woman's touch . . .

*Dougal looks puzzled at this.*

**TED:** Anyway, listen, I'll just go and rouse Jack, tell him we're off.

*Ted leaves the room. Dougal takes out his comb, reads the inscription again and starts running it through his hair. Monica comes back in. Dougal smiles at her. There's a pause, as Dougal searches for something to say.*

**DOUGAL** (*conversationally*): Ted says you were touching him.

*Reaction shot of Monica.*

SCENE 2 INT./MORNING 1
SET: JACK'S BEDROOM
*Jack's bedroom is a mess. Dust and cobwebs everywhere, stains on the bedspread. Paintings on the wall covered in so much dust that you can't make them out. Clothes strewn here and there, etc. Father Jack Hackett sits in his chair, staring lifelessly at the wall. He may very well be dead. There is a knock on the door. Ted opens the door and marches in purposefully.*

**TED:** Father Jack! Are you all right there? Ready for another day?

*He walks into the room and absent-mindedly starts picking things up.*

**TED:** You really should let Mrs Doyle clean up in here . . . Well, you're looking a lot better today, anyway. A good night's rest always does you the world of good, doesn't it?

*He sits in a chair beside Jack and leans towards him.*

**TED:** We're off with Sister Monica now, so when you get dressed, could you ask Mrs Doyle to have dinner ready for about five? We'll be back before then, anyway. Ah, but just in case the milkman calls, the money is under the statue of Our Lord being embarrassed by the Romans. All right, then?

*He then walks into an adjoining room. The other door opens and Dougal comes in. He notices Jack.*

**DOUGAL** (*quietly*): Morning, Father.

*There is no response. As Ted talks, Dougal walks over to Jack and examines him closely. He waves a hand in front of his face, then steps back.*

**TED** (*offscreen*): Would you like a cup of tea before I go? I know you won't mind us leaving you alone because Dougal got the new Al Pacino video for you, *Carlito's Way*.* It's probably not as violent as the ones you usually like, but, well . . . give it a go.

*Ted comes out of the room carrying a teapot.*

**TED:** Dougal. What are you doing?

---

*Carlito's Way was changed to Reservoir Dogs in the final version. In fact, Carlito's Way is nowhere near a violent enough film for this joke to work. We think we picked it because we'd seen it the night before we wrote it!

**DOUGAL:** This looks very bad, Ted.

**TED:** What?

**DOUGAL:** He's very drunk.

**TED:** Still? He must've been at it all night . . . (*Looking around.*) Where does he hide it?

**DOUGAL:** I haven't seen him this bad since that wedding in Clones. Do you remember, Ted? Didn't he disappear off with Sister Concepta?

**TED:** Oh, God, yes . . . The Blue Nun.

**DOUGAL** (*notices something*): I think it's worse than that, Ted . . .

*Dougal raises a bottle of floor-polish. He turns it over and shakes it. It's empty.*

**TED:** Oh, Godddd . . .

*He holds the teapot out to Dougal.*

**TED:** Hold this. (*To Jack.*) Now, Father, this is very bad. Do you not remember the last time? With the Windolene?

*Dougal is holding the teapot not by the handle, but around the sides.*

**TED** (*rousing him*): Father Jack. Father Jack, are you there?

**DOUGAL:** Ted . . .

**TED:** Imagine the damage floor-polish would do to you. Dear God . . .

**DOUGAL:** Ted . . .

**TED:** What is it?

**DOUGAL:** I'm in tremendous pain, Ted.

**TED:** Put it down, then! God, Dougal. Right, we'd better get him. Dougal, get him under the arms . . . Father Jack, come on now, we can't let Sister Monica see you like this.

*They lift him out of the chair, and start to walk him around the room slowly.*

**TED:** Come on, Father, big steps . . .

*Suddenly, Monica comes into the room.*

**MONICA:** What's the matter?

**TED:** Ah, Sister Monica, there you are. Ah, it just takes Father Jack's motor a little time to get going in the mornings.

**MONICA:** He doesn't look well.

**TED:** No, he's grand. We're just taking him on a little trip to the toilet. Will we go on a little trip to the toilet, Father?

**MONICA:** Put him down there in that chair and we'll have a look at him.

**TED:** Well, he doesn't like to be fussed over.

**MONICA:** I really think you should let me look at him.

*Ted and Dougal settle Jack back in the chair. Monica picks up his wrist to feel his pulse.*

**MONICA** (*alarmed*): Oh, Holy Mother of God . . . he's dead!

**DOUGAL:** What's the problem there, Sister?

**MONICA:** Father Jack, he's dead! There's no pulse, and he's stone cold.

**TED:** Ah, come on, Father Jack, you're not dead are you?

**MONICA:** He's very definitely dead.

**TED** (*sternly*): Come on now, Father! The joke's over!

**MONICA:** Father, he's gone. I think you should go and get help. Father Dougal here can give him the sacraments.

**TED** (*walking out*): Well, I'll call Dr. Sinnot, but I really think we're making a load of fuss over nothing.

*Reaction shot of Dougal looking very worried. When he's gone, Monica blesses herself and bows her head. Dougal looks at her, then looks at the body, then at her again. She raises her head slightly, looks at Dougal. Dougal smiles at her, waves.*

**MONICA** (*whispers*): The last rites, Father . . .

**DOUGAL:** Oh! Of course. Right. Shouldn't we wait for Ted . . . ?

**MONICA:** There's no need, really. Is there any anointing oil?

**DOUGAL:** No, I think himself drank it last week.

*Reaction shot as Monica takes this in.*

**DOUGAL:** You sure you wouldn't like to do the honours . . . ?

**MONICA:** What?

**DOUGAL:** No, of course you wouldn't. I suppose . . . I suppose I'm wearing the trousers as far as this goes . . .

*He addresses Father Jack.*

**DOUGAL:** 'We are gathered here today, to join two . . . people . . .' No, wait a second . . . that's not it . . .

*Slight pause. Monica is pretending not to notice. Dougal looks very panicky. Finally, he goes for it.*

**DOUGAL:** Well, Father. Best of luck. (*He looks expectantly at Monica.*) Oh. There's more. Of course . . . well, ah . . . sorry I didn't get a chance to see you off . . . I don't know whether I should be looking at you here or, or up there. I'll look up there . . .

*Reaction shot of Monica. Dougal is now addressing the roof.*

**DOUGAL:** Anyway, you're up there anyway. With Our Lord, and Stalin and Bob Marley and the rest of them. And of course my own parents. Actually I'd like to take this opportunity to say hello to them. Hello Mammy and Daddy. Hope they're looking after you up there.

**MONICA:** The Latin, Father . . .

**DOUGAL:** Oh, right! Of course . . . ah, totus tuus, minimus, cannus, costacurta, baggio, roberto et dino . . .

*Ted comes back.*

**MONICA:** Did you ring the doctor, Father?

**TED:** Yes. Well, it looks bad, all right. I gave Doctor Sinnot the symptoms over the phone, and he says he's probably dead, all right. The pulse not being there is bad enough, but the heart stopping is the real danger sign.

**DOUGAL:** That happened to my uncle and he was fine afterwards.

**TED:** His heart stopped? For how long?

**DOUGAL:** A week.

**TED:** A week? Really? And he was fine afterwards?

**DOUGAL** (*thinks a second*): Actually, no. Now I think of it, he died.

*Pregnant pause.* *

**MONICA** (*to Ted*): Ah, Father Dougal's just giving him the last rites.*

**TED** (*horrified*): Oh Jesus! Actually, maybe I should take over!*

*Ted and Monica pray over the body. Dougal watches them, slightly impatient. He looks at his watch.* *

**DOUGAL:** . . . Ted . . . the Holy Stone closes at three, Ted.*

**TED** (*fierce whisper*): Dougal!*

*Pause.* *

**DOUGAL** (*under breath*): . . . Jawohl, mein Führer . . .*

SCENE 3 INT./DAY 1
SET: PAROCHIAL HOUSE
*The room is very quiet. About six priests stand around, slowly eating sandwiches and drinking tea. Monica is also present. The mood is solemn, but friendly. The priests are (1) a black 'Shaft' type priest who resembles an extra from a blaxploitation movie of the 1970s, with large handlebar moustache and huge Afro haircut; (2) a nervous priest who moves like a small bird; (3) an elderly priest who has no distinguishing characteristics; (4) another elderly priest; and, finally, Ted and Dougal. Mrs Doyle walks from cleric to cleric, a tray of tiny sandwiches in her hands. Her mood is sunny, as usual. In another part of the room lies Jack in his coffin. Meanwhile, Monica is talking to the Shaft priest.*

**MONICA:** . . . is absolutely great to see. I mean the level of commitment amongst the African Church in bringing the faith to the people is just wonderful. It's marvellous, isn't it?

**SHAFT PRIEST** (*heavy accent*): Sure, I wouldn't know. I'm from Galway.

*He walks away. Cut to Mrs Doyle offering the elderly priest – Father Paul Cleary – a tiny sandwich from her tray.*

**MRS DOYLE:** Will you have a sandwich, Father?

* We deleted these lines from the final version.

**CLEARY:** No, thanks, Mrs Doyle, I'm fine.

**MRS DOYLE:** Have a try. They're tomato and jam.

**CLEARY:** No, no. Thanks, anyway.

**MRS DOYLE:** Ah, go on, have one. They're only small.

**CLEARY:** No, thanks, I'm grand.

**MRS DOYLE:** Are you sure you won't have one?

**CLEARY:** No, thanks, Mrs Doyle. I ate before I came.

**MRS DOYLE:** Would you like one for later? I can put one in a bag.

**CLEARY:** Ah, no, thanks —

**MRS DOYLE** (*produces a tiny plastic bag*): Here's a little bag you can take one home in. You can eat it later, or you can eat it now, if you want. Whatever suits you.

**CLEARY:** Well . . .

**MRS DOYLE:** Ah, you'll have it now!

**CLEARY:** Ah, sure, I might as well!

*Cut to Ted beckoning to Mrs Doyle.*

**TED:** Mrs Doyle!

*Cut back to Cleary reaching for a sandwich, but Mrs Doyle has already set off in Ted's direction.*

**TED:** I think Father Mackey wants a sandwich!

*Cut to the second elderly priest hiding in a corner of the room. He is desperately trying to signal to Ted that he doesn't want Mrs Doyle to come over. Too late. She starts off towards him. We see the priest trying to hide behind his hand.*

**MRS DOYLE** (*approaching him*): Father Mackey, will you have a sandwich? . . .

*The door flies open and two men enter. The first, Father Jim Sutton, a man around the same age as Ted, has obviously been crying. The second, Father Fintan Fay, who has a limp grasp of Father Jim's hand, walks in a crouching position, like a monkey. The monkey priest is very old.*

**JIM** (*close to tears*): I'm terribly sorry I'm late . . . Ted . . . the car . . . the car broke down . . .

**TED** (*quietly*): That's all right. (*Taking the monkey priest's hand.*) Father Fay, how are you?

**MONKEY PRIEST:** Egghh, eghhh, ngaaa, egghhh.

**TED:** He did. It was very quick.

**MONKEY PRIEST:** Ngaaaa?

**TED:** Ah, yes, I suppose so . . .

**JIM:** Oh, Christ, Ted!

*He falls into Ted's arms.*

**JIM:** Why him, Ted? Why is it always the good ones?

*He looks up to heaven and punches his fist into the air.*

**JIM:** You Bastard!

**TED** (*very concerned*): Now, Father Sutton . . .

*Sutton falls to his knees and starts to weep uncontrollably.*

**JIM:** He could have been Pope, Ted. The feckin' Jesuits, they have it all tied up . . .*

**TED:** Yes . . .

*Ted leads Jim to the casket.*

**JIM:** Imagine, Ted. A Polish Pope! It should have been Jack! But it's not what you know, is it? It's who you know.

**TED:** It's sad all right. Ah, but look at him. He looks so serene.

*Shot of Jack in the casket looking as scary and ugly as ever. Sutton is still distraught.*

**JIM:** Oh, God . . .

*He starts banging his fists on the side of the coffin, becoming increasingly hysterical each time.*

**JIM:** No! No! No! No! He's dead, Ted! We'll never see him again!

**TED:** Well, we'll see him in the next world . . .

**JIM** (*very sceptically*): Oh yeah, sure.

*Meanwhile, the monkey priest has climbed halfway up the bookcase.*

**JIM:** Oh, God, no! Get him down, get him

---

* This is complete nonsense – another example of our painstaking research procedure.

down!

**TED:** There's nothing of interest to you up there, Father!

*Scenes of chaos then ensue as the priests attempt to get the monkey priest down. He starts throwing books at them. They duck for cover. Fade out as the noise continues.*

SCENE 4 INT./EARLY EVENING 1
SET: PAROCHIAL HOUSE
*Dougal has just finished putting the last book back in its place. The room now looks back to normal. Dougal turns and notices Jack's empty chair. He looks at it nervously. Gradually, he edges towards the chair. He looks around, and then sits down gingerly in it. He smiles and surveys the room, pleased with himself. He then starts doing an exaggerated, childish, squint-eyed impression of Father Jack holding a glass and smoking.*

**DOUGAL:** Ehhhh . . . give me lots of drink . . . ehhhh . . .

*Ted and Monica enter the room while Dougal is thus engaged. Ted walks over to stand directly in front of Dougal. Dougal doesn't notice because his eyes are closed.*

**DOUGAL:** Uhhhhh . . . Feck off, Ted! . . . You big fool . . . ehhh . . .

**TED:** What are you doing, Dougal?

**DOUGAL** (*jumping a mile*): Whaaa!

**TED:** I don't think you should be getting up to that kind of nonsense. Now, come on, up you get.

*Dougal stands up, looking sheepish.*

**TED:** We should leave the chair idle for a while. (*He looks at the chair.*) Would y'ever look at that. The seat's completely bald. (*Rubbing it.*) Smooth as a baby's behind.

**DOUGAL** (*big smile*): You'd know all about that, Ted!

**TED** (*shocked*): What?

**DOUGAL:** When you're baptising them. The babies.

**TED:** Oh! I'm just going to give Sister Monica a lift to the boat.

**MONICA:** Thank you, Father.

**TED:** O'ho, no, it's the least we could do. You were always terribly good to Father Jack. It's the least we could do.

*Mrs Doyle knocks lightly on the door before sticking her head in.*

**MRS DOYLE:** Father Crilly? There's a woman here to see you.

**TED:** A woman, Mrs Doyle? You mean a nun.

**MRS DOYLE:** No, no, it's a woman. A young woman. Very well turned out.

**DOUGAL:** I'll be off then!

*Before Dougal can escape, the woman in question strides confidently into the room. She looks like someone out of 'LA Law'. Her name is Laura Sweeney.*

**SWEENEY:** Hello, Father Crilly?

**TED:** Yes?

**SWEENEY:** I'm from Corless, Corless and Sweeney.

**TED:** Oh, we're fine for coal, thanks.

**SWEENEY:** Oh, no, it's nothing to do with coal. My name is Laura Sweeney. (*She shakes hands with Ted.*) This must be Father McGuire!

*Dougal stares at the floor, his face bright red.*

**DOUGAL:** . . . Hhhhrhhhmm . . . uh . . . mmh . . .

**SWEENEY:** Anyway, I think you'd both better sit down. I've got a bit of a shock for you.

**TED:** Before you say anything, I just want to assure you that that was a routine relocation of funds . . .

**SWEENEY:** No, no . . .

**TED:** . . . The money was simply resting in my account for a while before I moved it on to—

**SWEENEY:** No, you don't understand. This is about Father Hackett. Please, sit down and I'll explain everything to you.

*Dougal and Ted sit down. Miss Sweeney produces an official-looking document.*

**SWEENEY:** It may come as a surprise for you to learn that Father Hackett left a will.

**TED:** Really? What does it say?

**SWEENEY:** Well . . . if I may . . .

*As she reads from it, we stay on Ted and Dougal.*

**SWEENEY:** 'I, Father Jack Hackett, being of sound mind and body, leave my entire fortune to Father Ted Crilly and Father Dougal McGuire to be distributed equally amongst them . . .'

**TED:** What?!

*He stands up and reads over her shoulder. Dougal looks at Ted expectantly. Monica appears in the doorway, two heavy suitcases in her hands.*

**MONICA:** Eh, I'll be off now, then . . .

*No response.*

**MONICA:** I'll make my way to the boat myself, then? . . .

**TED** (*without looking at her*): . . . Yeah, yeah . . .

**MONICA:** Bye, Fathers . . .

*They don't hear her. Monica leaves, her suitcase weighing her down.*

**TED:** Dougal! Look at this! He's left us some money!

**DOUGAL:** That's very nice of him. How much?

**TED** (*reads*): Half . . . half a million.

*Ted faints and falls out of shot. Dougal grabs the paper before he does so.*

**DOUGAL:** Half a million pounds!? Each?!! (*Disappointed.*) Oh . . . no, between us. It's only a quarter of a million each, Ted. Ted?

*Dougal sees that Ted has fainted.*

SCENE 5 INT./EARLY EVENING 1
SET: PAROCHIAL HOUSE
*Ted is lying on a sofa. Miss Sweeney and Dougal sit on the other chairs in the room. Ted is pressing a damp cloth to his head. Miss Sweeney is putting papers into her case. Mrs Doyle is nearby, pretending to dust some shelves so as to be able to listen.*

**SWEENEY:** . . . So that's that. It looks like you're going to be very rich men . . .

**TED:** Grand.

**SWEENEY:** There's just that sole requirement, which I'm surprised Father Hackett didn't discuss with you himself . . .

**TED:** Oh? . . .

**SWEENEY:** When is the funeral again?

**DOUGAL:** Again? Well, we haven't had the first one yet. I didn't think there'd be two funerals.

**SWEENEY:** No. Sorry, maybe I didn't make myself clear . . .

**TED:** It's tomorrow morning.

**SWEENEY:** Right, well, you know about Father Hackett's terrible fear of being buried alive.

**DOUGAL:** There's no chance of that now, is there? He's dead.

**TED:** Oh, God, yes, he was terribly frightened of that. That's why he wouldn't do Confession – he didn't like enclosed spaces. Of course, he also just didn't want to do it . . .

**DOUGAL:** A load of people telling you their sins . . . Who'd be bothered with that?

*Ted looks at Dougal.*

**SWEENEY:** Well, Father Hackett's fear was so great that he stipulated that you two must spend the night before the burial with him. Just in case he wakes up.

**TED:** Well, that's hardly likely, is it?

**SWEENEY** (*chuckles*): Of course, but nonetheless, it's in the will. In order to claim the inheritance, you and Father McGuire have

to spend the night with Father Hackett.

**TED:** OK, OK. Right. Well, I suppose it's the least we can do. Anyway, we can discuss it with the solicitor.

*A pregnant pause ensues.*

**SWEENEY** (*testily*): I am the solicitor.

*Another pregnant pause. Ted smiles at Dougal, then back at the solicitor.*

**TED** (*incredulous*): No, you're not . . .

**SWEENEY:** I'm sorry, but I am the senior partner in Corless, Corless and Sweeney.

**TED:** Now, come on, now . . . just because we're from the island, you think you can have a bit of fun with us.

**SWEENEY:** I assure you—

**TED:** All right, all right, very funny. The big thickos from the island. But we're not as thick as we look. Eh? Are we, eh?

**DOUGAL** (*laughing*): No way, José!

**SWEENEY:** Wait a second – why do you think I've been talking to you for the last hour and a half?

**TED:** Look, you're a lovely girl, but I really think we should talk to the solicitor.

**DOUGAL:** If you're a solicitor, then I'm Boy George.

*There is another frozen moment.*

SCENE 6 INT./EVENING 1*
SET: PAROCHIAL HOUSE
*Dougal is filling a flask with hot water. He is singing Culture Club's 'Karma Chameleon' to himself. Ted enters the room with a rucksack and a pile of candles. He has a bandage over his eye.*

**TED:** You ready yet, Dougal?

**DOUGAL:** Not yet, Ted. Be with you in a moment. How's your head?

**TED:** Oh, not too bad. She was aiming for my eye, I think. It's true what they say, though, about these career women being aggressive.

---

*We relocated this scene to the crypt, glued the next scene to it and lost the tea-in-the-face gag in the final version.

**DOUGAL:** Yes, she was very aggressive, wasn't she, Ted?

**TED:** And the language out of her! You wouldn't hear that from a docker.

**DOUGAL:** Ah, you would, Ted. They use very bad language.

**TED:** Effing this, and effing that.

**DOUGAL:** It was worse than that, Ted. She was saying fu—

**TED:** Now, Dougal! But anyway, who would have thought Jack had half a million pounds?

**DOUGAL:** And he never said a word about it.

**TED:** . . . There it was, lying in a bank account all these years . . .

**DOUGAL:** But . . . explain to me again, where'd he get it in the first place?

**TED:** As far as I can understand it, he was just an astute saver. He tried to avoid giving money to charity, he wouldn't wear trousers in the summer, so that obviously saved a couple of bob on wear and tear, all sorts of little savings all over the place. It all adds up, you know.

*Ted leaves the room. Dougal puts a teabag into the thermos, closes the lid and shakes it roughly. He*

*then opens the lid and searches for the teabag with a fork. He rattles the fork around.*

**DOUGAL:** C'mere, y'bollicks . . .*

*He slowly lifts the thermos up, looking into it as he does so. He continues to lift it, until suddenly a cascade of tea explodes into his face.*

**DOUGAL:** Arrrrgggh!!!

### END OF PART ONE

\* \* \*

### PART TWO

SCENE 7 INT./NIGHT 1
SET: CRYPT
*Dougal's face is as red as a lobster. He and Ted sit on either side of an imposing coffin. Dougal looks at Ted, hoping for him to begin a conversation. Ted is deep in his own thoughts. Dougal thinks for a second. He then reaches in his pocket and takes out his comb. He reads the inscription again. Then he combs his hair. He puts the comb away. He looks to Ted again. No sign of life. He thinks for a second, then takes the comb out again.*

**TED** (*absently*): I suppose, though, we only really knew him in his twilight years.

*We can see Dougal in the background, trying to see whom Ted's talking to.*

**TED:** But I think we saw the best of him. A really lovely man, a true Knight of the Church . . . gentle, lovely sense of humour, patient, good natured . . .

**DOUGAL:** Sorry, Ted, who's this now?

*Pause.*

**TED :** Who would you say I'd be talking about at this particular moment, Dougal?

**DOUGAL:** I'm not sure. I didn't catch the start.

**TED:** Father Jack, of course!

**DOUGAL:** Oh, right. Yes.

**TED:** A great priest.

---

*Note that this line is completely out of character.

SCENE 7A INT./DAY X
SET: PAROCHIAL HOUSE
*Shot of a bolt-upright Jack, lying stiffly on his chair, unable to bend his body so that it fits its contours. He smokes a cigarette and in his other hand holds a glass of whiskey. Cut back to Ted and Dougal.*

SCENE 7B INT./NIGHT 1
SET: CRYPT

**DOUGAL:** First priest to denounce The Beatles.

**TED:** That's right.

**DOUGAL:** He could see what they were up to.

**TED:** And he loved children, of course.

**DOUGAL:** He did, yes.

*Pause.*

**TED:** They were terrified of him, though.

**DOUGAL:** Well, he had that stick. He'd be waving that stick. Maybe they thought he'd hit them.

**TED:** I heard that when he was teaching in Saint Colm's he was a great believer in discipline.

FLASHBACK
SCENE 8 INT./DAY X
SET: SCHOOL
*Shot of a young Jack, cigarette hanging from his mouth, viciously kicking a student who lies in a foetal position on the ground.*

SCENE 9 INT./NIGHT 1
SET: CRYPT

**DOUGAL:** Would you say he was a good teacher?

**TED:** A friend of mine had him, Father Jimmy Rannable. He studied under him for a couple of years. He told me once, he said, no one, no one had such a huge effect on him as Jack did.

**DOUGAL:** Father Jimmy Rannable . . . Oh, yeah! Whatever happened to him?

**TED:** Do you remember the Drumshank Massacre?

**DOUGAL:** Yes . . . ?

**TED:** That was him.

**DOUGAL:** Oh . . .

*Pause.*

**TED:** Another thing about Father Jack . . . He loved a bit of competition. Great sense of fair play . . .

FLASHBACK
SCENE 10 INT./DAY X
SET: PAROCHIAL HOUSE
*Shot of Jack playing chess with Ted. Jack scowls at Ted and the board in a very intimidating manner. Ted gingerly picks up a piece, thinks, and places it on another square. He then leans back and gives Jack a 'what-do-you-think-of-that?' kind of look. Jack looks at the board for a moment or two, then kicks it into the air. Then he leans over and punches Ted in the face.*

SCENE 11 INT./NIGHT 1
SET: CRYPT

**TED:** . . . And a great traditionalist. Didn't really agree with a lot of the modern thinking within the Church.

SCENE 12 INT./DAY X
SET: CLASSROOM
*Shot of Jack standing beside a blackboard. There is a sheet hanging over it. Jack is obviously shouting at the top of his voice. He whisks away the sheet to reveal the word 'Hell!'. Then he throws a match into a little pot that goes up in flames. He puts his fingers to the sides of his head and does an impression of the devil. We see a classroom of very young children, crying.*

SCENE 13 INT./NIGHT 1
SET: CRYPT
*Ted in reflective mood. Pause.*

**TED:** Funny . . . one moment you're there, the next . . . Someone once said, Dougal, that life is just a thin sliver of light between two immensities of darkness . . . Makes you think . . .

**DOUGAL:** It does, Ted . . .

*Long pause.*

**DOUGAL:** . . . About what?

**TED** (*angrily*)**:** About death, Dougal, about death.

**DOUGAL:** That's a bit morbid, isn't it? What started you off thinking about death?

*Ted buries his face in his hands. He recovers after an instant and becomes reflective again.*

**TED** (*sighs*)**:** Ah, well . . . it's nice to have this time with him, though. Maybe sometimes we weren't as thoughtful as we could have been. At least now we're able to spend some time with him. Treat him with the respect he deserves . . .

**DOUGAL:** You're right there, Ted . . . (*Pause.*) Do you fancy an oul game of charades?

**TED:** Why not, I suppose?!

**DOUGAL:** All right, you go first.

**TED:** Right. (*He stands up.*) Right, I've got one. I'll start with an easy one.

*He begins to mime 'a film'.*

**DOUGAL:** Fishing. Gone fishing. Something to do with boxing? One-handed boxing?

**TED:** No, no, Dougal, it's a film.

**DOUGAL:** You're not supposed to tell me, Ted.

**TED:** OK, OK . . . (*He begins to mime again.*)

**DOUGAL:** Film. One film.

**TED:** No, one word.

**DOUGAL:** Ah, come on now, Ted. You're making it a bit easy for me . . . I'm not an eejit . . . Right, one-word film . . . can't be too many of them . . . *Salem's Lot*?

*Ted shakes his head. He points to his teeth.*

**DOUGAL:** Teeth. Mouth. Tongue. Is there a film called *Tongue*? *Tom Tongue*.

*Ted starts pretending to swim, baring his teeth as he does so.*

**DOUGAL:** Tongue fish. Swim tongue. *Swim, Tongue Fish!* Fish. *Attack of the Giant Killing Fish*? Tongue. Tonguefish. *The Deep. Piranha. Jaws 2*?

*Ted nods and points desperately at Dougal.*

**DOUGAL:** Ah, I'm close, then. *Ghostbusters 2*? *Superman 2. Batman Returns. Lethal Weapon 2* . . . ah . . .

**TED:** It's *Jaws!* You had it!

**DOUGAL:** No, I had *Jaws 2*. Different film. Very different film. Different shark.

*Ted glowers at Dougal. Fade to black.*

SCENE 14 INT./NIGHT 1
SET: CRYPT
*When we fade up again, Dougal and Ted are lying in their sleeping-bags. Ted's eyes are closed. Dougal stares up at the ceiling, looking around in a nervous manner.*

**DOUGAL:** Ted? . . . Ted? . . . Are you still awake?

**TED:** Yes, yes . . .

**DOUGAL:** Can I ask you a question?

**TED** (*sighs*)**:** Oh, not again . . . Look, Dougal, when a man and a lady are very much in love . . .

**DOUGAL:** No, no, I wasn't going to ask that, Ted. I was going to ask . . . do you believe in an afterlife?

**TED:** Do I what?

**DOUGAL:** Do you believe in an afterlife?

**TED:** Well, Dougal, what would you say? Considering that for the last twenty years I've been walking round administering the sacraments and being a general type of spiritual light in people's lives . . .

**DOUGAL:** You're sort of uncertain?

**TED:** No, in fact, I'm actually the opposite of uncertain. Generally speaking, priests tend to have a fairly strong belief in the afterlife.

**DOUGAL:** I wish I had your faith, Ted.

**TED:** Dougal, how did you get into the Church? Was it, like, collect twelve crisp packets and become a priest?

**DOUGAL:** It's just that at times like this, you start thinking about things. Like maybe settling down. Finding the right girl . . .*

**TED:** Hold on. Now, hold on. This is obviously . . .*

**DOUGAL:** Sometimes you wonder if there's really a God . . .*

**TED:** Just hold it there, Father McGuire. Look, think about it a second. How do cars work? How does a record-player work?*

**DOUGAL:** Well . . . I wouldn't know, exactly . . .*

**TED:** Well, there you go – all these things are done by God.*

**DOUGAL:** But, if you're wrong, Ted . . . if there's no afterlife.*

**TED:** Look, of course there's an afterlife. Sure, if there was no afterlife our time here on earth would be completely meaningless. We'd be just going through the motions with no hopes, and no reason for living. We'd just be like isolated planets in a lonely Godless universe . . .*

**DOUGAL** (*cheerily*)**:** I suppose you're right, Ted. I feel a lot better now. Thanks very much. Goodnight!*

*Dougal snuggles into his sleeping-bag and closes his eyes. Ted does the same, but after a moment opens his eyes again and stares at the ceiling, terrified.**

*We deleted these lines from the final version.

SCENE 15 INT./NIGHT 1
SET: CRYPT
*A blue light is starting to creep through the one window in the crypt. Dougal and Ted are still in their sleeping-bags.*

**DOUGAL:** . . . Ted?

**TED:** Dougal, please let me go to sleep. The birds'll be up in a second and they'll be screeching their heads off.

**DOUGAL:** Oh . . . all right . . .

**TED** (*sighs*)**:** What is it, then?

**DOUGAL:** I was just wondering. What are you going to do with your share of the money?

*Ted turns around and looks at the ceiling, suddenly interested.*

**TED:** I . . . well . . . Luckily there's a lot of great charity organisations that are always grateful for money . . . Concern, Food for Africa, St Vincent de Paul . . .

*Fade out as he speaks. We hear funky music and see Ted's soft-focus fantasy.*

**SCENE 16 INT./NIGHT 1**
**SET: NIGHTCLUB**
*Ted is wearing sunglasses and dancing in a club*
*with some beautiful women. They laugh and hug*
*him. Ted laughs and jokingly raises an*
*admonishing finger. Cut to Ted at a craps table. He*
*throws some dice and obviously gets a seven. He*
*jumps with joy while the women at the table go*
*crazy, hugging and kissing him.*

**SCENE 17 INT./NIGHT 1**
**SET: CRYPT**

**TED:** . . . Maybe a few pounds for Comic
Relief . . . What's the use of money if you can't
use it for good, eh, Dougal?

**SCENE 18 INT./NIGHT 1**
**SET: CRYPT**
*Cut back to Dougal in the crypt, licking his lips.*

**TED:** So, some good'll come from Jack's
death.

**DOUGAL:** It's hard to believe he's gone.

**TED:** You're right there . . .

**SCENE 19 EXT./DAWN 2**
**SET: THE ISLAND**
*Assorted shots of the island. Everything looks bleak*
*but somehow beautiful, rather like the closing*
*moments of John Huston's 'The Dead'. Over all*
*this, we hear Ted's voiceover.*

**TED** (*offscreen*): It's beginning to snow again.
The flakes, silver and dark, are falling
obliquely against the lamplight. It's probably
snowing all over the island – on the central
plain, on the treeless hills, falling softly on the
graveyards, on the crosses and headstones,
upon all the living . . . and the dead.

**JACK** (*offscreen*): Will you shut the feck up!

SCENE 20 INT./DAWN 2
SET: CRYPT
*Ted jumps up in the air with shock. He spins around and sees Jack standing next to him, his burial shroud around his shoulders. Jack is holding his head as if it's about to explode.*

**TED:** Argggghghhhhhhhhhhhhhh!!!!!!!!!

*Ted faints. His scream has woken Dougal, however. Dougal stands up and rushes over to Ted's prone body.*

**DOUGAL:** Ted! Ted! What's wrong? Father Jack, what happened to him? Ted! Did you see what happened, Father Jack? What—

*Dougal realises whom he's talking to and immediately passes out.*

SCENE 21 INT./DAY 2
SET: PAROCHIAL HOUSE
*Unpleasant close-up of Father Jack's big, fat face. He is snoring, his eyes are squeezed shut – he even sleeps in a menacing way – and he is back in his old chair. Cut to Ted, watching him with a kind of awe.*

**TED:** So . . . there is he, risen from the dead. Just like . . . ah . . . that fella . . . E.T. (*Pause.*) Your face is looking a lot better, Dougal.

*Cut to Dougal. White flakes are peeling from his face. It is also horribly puffed-up and tender-looking.\**

**DOUGAL:** Oh, really?

**TED** (*not terribly convincingly*): Mmm . . .

**DOUGAL:** Thanks, Ted.

*Jack lets rip with another loud snore.*

**DOUGAL:** There's one thing I'm a bit confused about, though.

**TED:** Yes?

**DOUGAL:** Is Jack dead, then? Or what?

**TED:** Apparently not. I think the floor-polish brought about all the symptoms of death . . . such as . . . no heartbeat, rigor mortis, decomposition. But he was lucky. The effects just seemed to wear off.

**DOUGAL:** Well . . . it's good to have him back, isn't it, Ted?

\*The hot tea, remember?

**TED** (*unconvincing nod*): Mm . . .

**DOUGAL:** Who needs half a million pounds, anyway?

**TED:** Yes, our life is the spiritual life.

**DOUGAL:** . . . Pity, though, to think of all that money just lying about.

**TED:** It is, actually . . . and I can't see himself putting it to much use.

**DOUGAL:** It could be doing good work, couldn't it? Couldn't it, Ted?

**TED:** It could.

*Pause.*

**TED:** But . . . to be honest, Dougal . . . I don't like talking about it, but . . . it's just a matter of time, really . . . he's not a young man and . . . you know . . . and I suppose it won't be so bad when he's gone. The money will be some kind of comfort to us, I suppose.

**DOUGAL:** Well, that's something.

**TED:** That's right. Now . . . (*He stands.*) will you come down to the shops with me? I think we need some more floor-polish.

*They walk to the door.*

**DOUGAL:** Yes. Maybe we should get a few different brands? Just to try them out?

**TED:** Yes, and we can leave them around the house. So they don't get lost.

*They leave the room. We hear Dougal's voice fading as he gets further away.*

**DOUGAL:** Or just put them in Jack's room, ask him to keep an eye on them . . .

*They leave the room. Close-up of Jack. He wakes up suddenly.*

**JACK:** Drink!

*He realises that no one's around and looks surly. He looks directly at the camera and scowls. Pause.*

**JACK:** Feck OFF!!!!!!!

**THE END**

# hell

**GRAHAM:** This episode was inspired partly by the dreadful holidays my parents would take me on when I was young. I don't know what was going through their heads but we went to some really terrible places, campsites with stinky outdoor showers and a whole new range of kids to be bullied by. There's a tradition in British comedy of going on holiday to really crappy places which goes way back to the early *Carry On* films right up to *Withnail and I* and beyond. Arthur showed me the *Likely Lads* movie which, like this episode, featured a terrible caravan holiday. As we always felt that *Ted* was a sitcom in the British tradition although it was set in Ireland, it seemed appropriate to try and follow that tradition.

There was a very simple structure in this episode; it revolved around the three 'moments'– the encounters with the romantic couple which were complicated further by the arrival of Graham Norton's character, Father Noel Furlong (Arthur's inspired casting, that). We also used one of our favourite devices – that of the unbelievably obvious expositional opening, which is used when Tom learns the basics of door-opening/sewage-unloading. One reviewer commented, 'It's embarrassingly obvious what's going to happen' – and missed the point brilliantly.

The scene where Dougal can't get to grips with the difference between a small cow and a faraway cow isn't in this draft because we thought of it on location. I think it's probably the all-time most-quoted joke of all three series. It replaced the rather fine noughts and crosses gag that was great on paper, but just didn't work when filmed.

**ARTHUR:** I'd never met Graham Norton but I'd heard him on the radio and thought he might add something to the character. We didn't see him as being camp at first; we just liked the idea of a priest who is simply incredibly excited to be around young people, so excited that he interprets their really quite sensible lifestyles as unbelievably dangerous and exciting. He's based on someone our good friend Paul Wonderful had met. Paul's a great performer and a very, very funny man and it was really his impression of this mad priest that led to Father Noel being created. To set the record straight once and for all, Noel is not having sex with the teenagers in his charge. A lot of people thought this, including Graham Norton, but take it from us, Noel's completely asexual.

Part of this episode *was* hell for the actors. The whole sewage plot at the beginning started as an in-joke on Dermot and then backfired on him and Ardal and all of us. We'd used a rain machine in the first series (in *Entertaining Father Stone*) and Dermot was standing under it, feeling miserable, when he said jokingly, 'What are you going to do to me next? Cover me in shit, I suppose.' So we spent the next few months wondering how we could cover Ted in shit . . . When the time came, the special effect liquid shit we ended up using was freezing cold. We didn't know this and we were trying to get a funny performance out of Dermot and Ardal and they were in agony, *blinded* by the cold. We felt terrible for them; they really were in shock afterwards.

## PART ONE

SCENE 1 EXT./DAY 1
SET: ROADWAY

*Pre-credit sequence. A man is speaking to Tom, who is still wearing his 'I Shot JR' T-shirt, as they stand at the door to a large articulated truck. The container behind the cab is silver and cylindrical and has 'Craggy Island Sewage Works' written on it. Tom watches the man with his usual expression of incredible concentration.*

**MAN:** Now, Tom, this is the first time you've been trusted with such a large consignment of raw sewage. Are you sure you'll be all right?

**TOM:** I will, yeah. Don't worry about me at all.

**MAN** (*pointing into truck*): And remember, Tom, this is the button that opens the doors, and this is the button that makes the sewage shoot out.

**TOM:** Right. That one opens the doors, and that one makes the stuff come out.

**MAN:** No, no, no . . . the other way around.

**TOM:** Right y'are!

*Cut to Tom gripping the wheel of the truck and starting to drive off. Opening titles roll. We see a close-up of a 'The Holy Stone of Clonrichert' day-by-day calendar. It reads July 18. A hand comes into shot and rips it away so that it reads July 19. Cut to Ted looking at the calendar, a puzzled expression on his face.*

SCENE 2 INT./DAY 1
SET: PAROCHIAL HOUSE

**TED:** July nineteenth . . . why does that date strike me as important?

*Dougal is sitting at the table playing magnetic fishing. He lifts a fish up out of the makeshift 'pool'.*

**DOUGAL:** Yes! (*To Ted.*) Ah, July nineteenth . . . I wouldn't know, Ted, y'big bollocks.

**TED:** I'm sorry?

**DOUGAL:** I said, I wouldn't know, Ted, you big bollocks.

**TED** (*beat*): Have you been reading those

Roddy Doyle books again, Dougal?

**DOUGAL:** I have, yeah, Ted. I read all of them this morning, you big gobshite.

**TED:** Well, that's all very well, Dougal, but you have to remember they're just stories. Normal people like us don't use that type of language. Remember, this is the real world.

**DOUGAL** (*reeling in one of the fish*): Oh, you're right there, Ted.

**TED:** Anyway, July nineteenth . . . any idea why that should be important?

**DOUGAL:** Would it be the day the Ice Age ended?

**TED:** No, I don't think they could be that precise about the Ice Age, Dougal.

**DOUGAL:** I'll look it up in the diary.

*Dougal places his little fishing rod in a special holder so that it's still hanging out over the 'pool'. He checks the 'lines' on one or two other rods he has already placed there. He goes to the bookcase and grabs the diary.*

**DOUGAL:** The nineteenth of July . . . 'On This Day' . . . 'Galway liberated from Indians' . . . 'Church condemns cars for first time' . . . Aha! Ted. 'Ice Age ends'.

**TED:** No, it's nothing to do with that type of thing, Dougal. It's something to do with us. Is it something we always do on July the nineteenth?

**DOUGAL:** Do we go to the shops?

**TED:** Well, we might. But that wouldn't be specific to July the nineteenth, Dougal. We'd tend to go to the shops a bit more often than that.

**DOUGAL:** What could it be, Ted? Maybe it's something to do with Jack?

**TED:** Maybe . . . it . . . Oh, God! It's not his bath is it???!!!

**DOUGAL:** Oh, God, Ted, no! It couldn't be!

**TED:** No, wait, wait, calm down . . . sure he only just had his bath. Remember? Just before Christmas?

**DOUGAL:** Oh, thank God for that . . . God almighty!

*They stand there for a moment, breathing heavily, hands on their hearts. Mrs Doyle comes in.*

**MRS DOYLE:** Time for tea, Fathers.

**TED:** Mrs Doyle, does anything strike you as important about July nineteenth?

**MRS DOYLE:** It doesn't matter what day it is, Father. There's always time for a nice cup of tea. Sure didn't Our Lord himself on the cross pause for a nice cup of tea before he gave himself up for the world?

**TED:** No, he didn't, Mrs Doyle.

**MRS DOYLE:** Well, whatever equivalent they had for tea in those days. Cake, or whatever. And speaking of cake . . . I have cake!

*She holds up a container full of cake.*

**TED:** I'm fine for cake, Mrs Doyle.

**MRS DOYLE:** Are you sure, Father? There's cocaine in it . . .

**TED:** There's what?

**MRS DOYLE:** Oh, no, not cocaine. What am I on about . . . I meant, what do you call them . . . raisins.*

---

* For the final version we inserted three pages of dialogue here about Mrs Doyle forcing cake on Ted and then keeping it back from him. Why we added it in, we don't know. It had the effect of making the first scene run on far, far too long.

**TED:** No, this date thing is bothering me now. July nineteenth . . . July nineteenth . . . July nineteenth . . .

*The door opens and Jack enters. He is wearing a one-piece Victorian-style black bathing suit – possibly with dog collar? He stands at the doorway with a bucket and spade in his hand and a knotted hankerchief on his head. Ted, Dougal and Mrs Doyle stare at him for a moment.*

**TED:** Aha! Holiday!

SCENE 3 EXT./DAY 1
SET: PAROCHIAL HOUSE
*Dougal is throwing things into a small trailer attached to the back of the car, totally randomly – a toothbrush, a hurling stick, a sleeping-bag, a kettle, some snorkelling gear, skis, etc.*

**TED:** C'mon Dougal. Better get moving. (*Dougal runs to the car and gets in the front seat. Jack is in the backseat.*) Right! Let's go!

*He moves his hand to the ignition.*

**DOUGAL:** Ted, where'll we go on holiday?

**TED** (*stops short*): Oh . . . God . . . I dunno . . .

**DOUGAL:** Pierson's?

**TED:** Pierson's? No, that's only up the road. Anyway, Mr. Pierson doesn't really like people staying with him on their holidays. It's not actually a guesthouse.

**DOUGAL:** Isn't it?

**TED:** No, no. Do you not remember the big argument we had with him last year? When we tried to stay the second week . . . Wait! Do you know where we'll go?! Father O'Rourke has that caravan. He said we could use it any time we wanted!

**DOUGAL:** Oh, God, Ted, not again. It's very small, that caravan.

**TED:** No, he got a new one! Apparently it's twice as big! Let's go!

*He starts the ignition and begins to drive away. Jaunty 'holiday' music plays.*

SCENE 4 EXT./DAY 1
SET: CARAVAN PARK
*The car pulls up outside a huge, shiny, new-looking mobile home. Dougal sticks his head out of the window, impossibly excited.*

**TED:** He said it's the one at the end.

**DOUGAL:** Ted! Ted! There it is! It's huge!

**TED:** Dougal, calm down. (*To Jack.*) We're here, Father!

**JACK:** Feck off!

*They get out of the car. Ted stretches and looks around, then stares at the back of the car.*

**TED:** Dougal . . .

**DOUGAL:** Yes, Ted?

**TED:** Where's the trailer? With all the stuff in it?

*Cut to reveal that the trailer is, indeed, nowhere to be seen.*

SCENE 5 EXT./DAY 1
SET: PAROCHIAL HOUSE
*We see the trailer exactly where it was originally.\**

SCENE 6 INT./DAY 1
SET: MOBILE HOME
*Ted, Dougal and Jack walk in. Jack immediately goes to sit in a corner.*

**JACK:** Drink!

**TED:** Yes, Father, I promise you. In a minute.

**DOUGAL:** It's great, isn't it, Ted?

**TED:** It's very nice, all right.

*Jack lights up a cigarette. Ted stretches. Dougal sits forward in his seat excitedly. They are all grouped down one side of the mobile home.*

---

\* We inserted a new scene here which opened with Ted saying to Dougal, 'Next thing you'll be telling me you forgot to lock the front door', and was followed by a scene of the Parochial House being burgled.

SCENE 7 INT./DAY 1
SET: SHOWER UNIT
*A small mini-shower-type thing. A man, Mr. Gleason, steps out, leaving a woman, Mrs Gleason, behind the frosted glass.*

**WOMAN:** Wait a second, you have to do my back.

**MAN:** No, I'm wrinkling up like a raisin in there. See you in a sec.

*The man walks out of the room, naked. He starts to dry his hair.*

SCENE 8 INT./DAY 1
SET: MOBILE HOME
*The man comes into the main part of the home, still naked. Ted and Dougal stop talking and look at him. Jack stops smoking his cigarette for a moment. The man walks, still towelling his head, with his bottom to the camera – he still hasn't noticed the three, and sits beside Ted. Ted just looks at him, confused. The man stops drying his hair and takes the towel away. He turns to Ted, Dougal and Jack and looks at them. They look back at him. There is a 'moment'.*

SCENE 9 EXT./DAY 1
SET: CARAVAN PARK
*Ted is talking to a policeman, who is writing something in a notebook.*

**TED:** . . . Father Ted Crilly, Craggy Island Parochial House, Craggy Island . . .

*We see the man and woman in their dressing gowns watching the priests with scowls on their faces. Cut to Dougal looking down at the ground nearby. Cut back to Ted at the police car, which is starting to drive away.*

**TED:** Honestly, Officer, I can't apologise enough . . . (*The car drives off. Ted looks at Dougal.*) Oh, Ghodddd . . . that was so embarrassing . . .

**DOUGAL:** Ted, if that one's not our one, which is?

*A caravan in the background pulls away to reveal a tiny, tiny caravan, slightly unbalanced to one side. Dougal and Ted look around, framing the caravan between them. We cut before they turn around to notice it.*

SCENE 10 INT./DAY 1
SET: CARAVAN

*Ted and Dougal are squeezing into a very small space. The caravan is absolutely tiny. Jack jumps in front of them and sticks himself into a corner. Ted and Dougal look around before sitting across from Jack. They are all very close to one another. Jack stares right into Ted's eyes in a disconcerting manner.\**

**DOUGAL:** Sure this is great! It is bigger than last year's one. What do you want to do first, Ted?

**TED:** Well, we'll take it easy first. Don't want to go mad on the first day. I think we should just, you know, get settled in to the old caravan. (*They look around the caravan for a moment.*) Right. That's enough of that. Where'll we go?

**DOUGAL:** There's a booklet here, Ted.

**TED:** Right, let's see . . .

*He picks up a tiny booklet that is incredibly small and bears the words 'Things to do in Kilkelly'. He looks at it briefly.*

**TED** (*reading*): 'Places of interest' . . . 'Saint Kevin's Stump' . . . That sounds good . . . 'The Magic Road' . . .

*He turns over another page, but sees that there are no more pages in the booklet. He tosses it away.*

**TED:** Two places of interest. Still, that's one more than Craggy Island has.

**DOUGAL:** What's The Magic Road?

**TED:** It's one of these bizarre natural wonders where everything's gone haywire and nothing works the way it's supposed to. It's sort of like you, Dougal, except it's a road. There's a few of them around the country.

**DOUGAL:** I still don't understand. It's a kind of mad road?

**TED:** Yes. It's what's called a 'strange phenomenon'. If you stopped a car on it and took off the handbrake, it'd go uphill. And water would flow up it.

**DOUGAL:** That's almost as mad as that thing you told me about the loaves and the fishes.

**TED:** No, Dougal, that's not mad. That's when Our Lord got just one or two bits of food and turned it into a big pile of food and everyone had it for dinner.

**DOUGAL:** God, he was fantastic, wasn't he?

**TED:** Ah, yeah, he was *brilliant* . . . OK, let's try and find the magic road.\*

*Ted opens the door of the caravan. Outside it's pouring with rain. Ted closes the door.*

**TED:** All right, come on . . . will we play some Scrabble?

**DOUGAL:** Yeah! Brilliant!

**TED:** Did you bring the Travel Scrabble, Dougal?

**DOUGAL:** I brought the normal Scrabble and the Travel Scrabble. The Travel Scrabble for when we were travelling and the normal Scrabble for when we arrived.

**TED** (*impressed*): Good man, Dougal . . .

**DOUGAL:** Oh, no, wait a second. Now I think of it, I didn't bring either of them.

**TED:** Right.

**DOUGAL:** God, I'm an awful eejit. I wish we had something else. They should have more 'travel' versions of games, shouldn't they, Ted? I mean I've got this great idea for golf in a car — †

**TED:** I don't want to hear the rest of this, Dougal.†

**DOUGAL:** No, I know it sounds mad, but if you got very small clubs —†

**TED:** No, I don't want to hear this . . .†

**DOUGAL:** No, all you need is a fairly big ball . . .†

**TED:** No, Dougal. No. All right? No, stop.

---

\* After this, we inserted a scene of them putting Jack to bed by putting a cardboard box over his head.

† We deleted these lines from the final version.

---

\* We decided to abandon this idea of Jack staring at Ted for the final version.

I'm going to set you on fire if you don't stop talking about playing golf in the car.[†]

*Pause.*[†]

**DOUGAL:** Oh, all right.[†]

**TED:** So . . . what are we going to do for the next two weeks? This isn't exactly Disneyland.

**DOUGAL:** God, no, it's not even *close*. Will I put on the kettle?

**TED** (*sighs*)**:** Yeah, go on.

*Dougal fills the kettle and turns it on. The three of them watch the kettle.*

**DOUGAL:** That must be one of those ones that clicks off automatically.

**TED:** Yes. (*Pause. After a few moments, the water begins to steam slightly.*) Bit of steam there. (*Pause. He turns to Dougal.*) Incidentally, did you bring any teabags?

**DOUGAL:** No.

**TED** (*sighs*)**:** Right . . .

*Ted takes out a cigarette and watches the kettle.*

SCENE 11 INT./DAY 1
SET: CARAVAN
*The kettle is boiling. It clicks off.*

**DOUGAL:** Kettle's boiled, Ted. Will I put a bit more water in and turn it on again?

*Ted is lying with his head back. He looks very bored.*

**TED:** No, I liked it best the first time . . . and it's sort of gone downhill from there.

*Ted puts his head back again. Fade out.*

SCENE 12 INT./DAY 1
SET: CARAVAN
*Fade back. Ted has his hands over his eyes.*

**TED:** . . . Ninety-nine, one hundred! Coming, ready or not! (*Cut to main part of the caravan. Dougal has put some cushions around him and has pulled the curtain over his head. Ted walks up to him. He seems very unexcited as he taps Dougal's shoulder.*) Found you.

**DOUGAL:** Gahhhhh!!!! All right, Ted. Your go!

*Dougal runs out of shot.*

**DOUGAL** (*offscreen*)**:** One, two, three, four, five . . . (*Ted looks at where Dougal was, sighs, then arranges the cushions around him and puts his head behind the curtain.*) . . . six, seven, eight . . .

*Fade down.*

SCENE 12A INT./DAY 1*
SET: CARAVAN
*Fade up. Ted is smoking, looking bored. Suddenly inspiration strikes.*

**TED:** I know! Father Larry Duff!

**DOUGAL:** Ah, Larry!

**TED:** He often comes around this area when he gets a break. I'll give him a call on his mobile. I got him one for Christmas and he's always complaining that no one rings him on it.

**TED:** He must have it turned off.

*Fade down.*

SCENE 12B EXT./DAY 1
SET: ROAD
*Cut to a priest driving a car. He hears a high-pitched bleeping noise and looks around in confusion. Then he turns back to the road and screams. Cut to stock footage of a car veering out of control and going over the edge of a huge cliff. Cut back to Ted still on the mobile phone.*

SCENE 12C INT./DAY 1
SET: CARAVAN
*Ted switches off the mobile.*

---

\* In the final version we inserted the faraway cow scene as follows:

*Close-up of a bunch of toy plastic cows... the kind you'd get with a toy farm set. Pull back to reveal Ted and Dougal. Dougal frowns, puzzled.*

**TED:** . . . OK, one last time. These are small and the ones out there are *far away. Small . . . far away...*

*Dougal smiles and shakes his head, uncomprehending.*

**TED:** Ah, forget it!

*Ted throws them down in disgust.*

*Fade down.*

*Fade up.*

*Cut to wildebeest galloping across a plain – as though seen through Dougal's binoculars. Reveal Dougal looking through the window with binoculars. He turns to Ted.*

**DOUGAL**: Ted, you know the way your eyes sometimes play tricks on you?

SCENE 12D INT./DAY 1†
SET: CARAVAN
*Fade up. Ted is sitting beside Dougal. He has a black marker in his hand. He looks fairly vexed. Dougal looks puzzled.*

**DOUGAL:** Wait . . . so . . . I put the thing here . . .

**TED:** No! No, no, no, you can't put the thing there! You have to draw one in where there isn't already one of mine . . .

*Cut to reveal that they are looking at a game of noughts and crosses. Experimental crosses and noughts are placed randomly all over the paper. A hand comes into shot and points at a nought.*

**DOUGAL:** So I put an X here . . .

**TED:** No! . . .

*Fade down.*

SCENE 13 INT./DAY 1†
SET: CARAVAN
*Ted and Dougal are lying around in different parts of the caravan, bored, bored, bored.*

**TED:** God . . . how long have we been here now?

**DOUGAL:** Ah, about twenty minutes. (*Pause.*) Will we have a bit of an old pray?

**TED:** No, I'm not really in the mood, Dougal.

**DOUGAL:** Ah, I suppose you're right. Sure

---

† We deleted this scene from final version.

we're on holiday! We can forget about God and religion and all that nonsense.

**TED:** Yes, Dougal.

*Fade out.*

**END OF PART ONE**

\* \* \*

**PART TWO**

SCENE 14 EXT./DAY 1
SET: FIELD
*Fade up to reveal Dougal and Ted standing around in a featureless field, apart from a large rock in the centre of it. Ted and Dougal are looking at a stump.*

**DOUGAL:** Why is it called Saint Kevin's stump?

**TED** (*looks at brochure*): Doesn't say . . .

*Pause. Ted and Dougal look bored.*

**DOUGAL:** So, is this what all holidays are like, Ted?

**TED:** Actually . . . yeah. (*Pause.*) Anyway, we'd better get back to Jack.

**DOUGAL:** Ah, he's fine. He said he'd stay put by the cliffs.

**TED:** I'm always worried leaving him near the cliffs, Dougal.

**DOUGAL:** Ah, Ted, he's nowhere near the edge. Sure what could happen to him?

SCENE 15 EXT./DAY 1
SET: MAGIC ROAD
*We see Jack on his wheelchair at the bottom of a path that extends behind him up a hill. He is asleep. He wakes up suddenly.*

**JACK:** DRINK!

*He starts beating his fists up and down. We see one of the wheels on the wheelchair starting to turn backwards slowly. Jack's chair then starts* rolling backwards up the hill, away from the camera. We see a sign that reads 'The Magic Road' beside the path.

**JACK:** DRINK! DRINK! DRINK!

He continues to roll up the path.


SCENE 16 EXT./DAY 1
SET: FIELD
Ted and Dougal are still standing around.

**DOUGAL:** Can we walk up to the rock and back, Ted?

**TED** (sighs): Well . . .

**DOUGAL:** Come on, Ted, we're on holiday. Live a little.

**TED:** All right. But we'd better get back to Jack soon.

They start walking towards the rock.


SCENE 17 EXT./DAY 1
SET: MAGIC ROAD
From the same point of view that we saw earlier, we see that Jack is now heading towards the cliff at tremendous speed.

**JACK:** DRINK! DRINK! DRINK! (He finally reaches the cliff edge and disappears backwards over it. Dwindling.) DRINK! DRINK! DRINK!

We hear a distant splash.

SCENE 18 EXT./DAY 1
SET: FIELD
Ted and Dougal have just reached the rock.

**TED:** Well, here we are.

**DOUGAL:** Will we walk over to that fence now?

**TED:** No, we might just blow up with excitement if we do that now. Anyway, we should save something for next week.

Ted turns and tries to lift himself up on to the rock. He sticks his head over it, then Dougal does the same. We see, from their point of view, the couple from the mobile home kissing passionately, some picnic gear beside them. Mr. Gleason has his hand up Mrs Gleason's jumper. He pauses, sensing something, then looks up. Ted and Dougal look at him. There is a 'moment'.

SCENE 19 EXT./DAY 1
SET: CARAVAN PARK
Ted is talking to a policeman again. Dougal stands beside him.

**TED:** . . . Father Ted Crilly . . . Craggy Island Parochial House . . . sure you know all that . . .

**DOUGAL:** Ted, maybe we should tell him about Jack.

**TED:** No, Dougal.

**POLICEMAN:** What's that about?

**DOUGAL:** It's just we were with another priest, and he's gone missing.

**POLICEMAN:** Well, do you want to report it or not?

**TED:** Ah, no. He'll turn up.

**DOUGAL:** Should we not report it, Ted? Just in case?

**TED:** Ah . . . (The policeman looks at him.) It won't cost anything, will it?

**POLICEMAN:** No.

**TED:** OK, so the man you're looking for, even though there's no need to look for him because he'll turn up any second, is Father

Jack Hackett . . . Ah God, how would you describe him . . .

**DOUGAL:** Mid-fifties . . .

**TED:** . . . To mid-eighties . . . tremendous smell of vegetables off him, for some reason . . .

**DOUGAL:** . . . Angry man, very angry man . . .

**TED:** . . . Hates children . . . likes the odd drink . . . and, ah, if you find him, don't come up on him from behind. He won't like that at all.*

**POLICEMAN:** We'll look out for him. Right . . . anything else I can do for you while I'm here? Want to confess to any robberies or unsolved murders or anything?

**TED:** No, I don't think so, anyway . . . Dougal?

**DOUGAL** (*thinks for a second*)**:** . . . No . . .

**TED** (*jokily*)**:** No, we're fine for the old unsolved mur—

*The policeman gives them a cold look. Ted shuts up. They wait for a moment, looking abashed, as the policeman moves away.*

**DOUGAL:** What do you think's happened to Jack, Ted?

**TED:** I don't know, Dougal. God . . . some holiday this is turning out to be. C'mon. At least there'll be a bit more room in the caravan.

*They move off.*

SCENE 20 INT./DAY 1
SET: CARAVAN
*We see four Aran-jumper-wearing individuals,*

---

* It's always nice to come across an opportunity like this. The convention of giving a description to a policeman provides you with what we call, when we're drunk, a 'joke basket'– a chance to deliver a bunch of gags in an interesting manner and learn some fun new stuff about Jack in the process. We were just as interested as anyone else to discover that he had 'a tremendous smell of vegetables off him'.

*quite young, two men and two girls. With them is Father Noel Furlong, a jolly priest who is about forty. Noel has a thing of being incredibly excited when he's around young people. Ted and Dougal enter. They're surprised, but not very happy. The kids and the priest are singing a rousing rendition of 'Ebony and Ivory'.*

**NOEL:** Ted!

**TED** (*looking very crestfallen*)**:** Noel . . .

**NOEL** (*friendly*)**:** What in goodness name are you doing here?

**TED:** Well, this is our caravan, actually, Noel.

**NOEL:** Well, Father O'Rourke said we could use it.

**TED:** Well, that's what he said to us as well.

**NOEL:** I think he must say it to everybody. Sure that's the type of man he is. Generous to a fault, the fault being that he's too generous. Anyway, plenty of room for everyone. Sit down and we'll have a bit of an old song. What'll we sing? Will you sing one, Ted?

**TED:** No, I won't, thanks.

**NOEL:** Ah, you will!

**TED:** I'd rather not.

**NOEL:** Will you dance, then? Come on. Tony, stick on the *Riverdance* album.

**TED:** Honestly, Noel, I'm a little tired. I won't —

**NOEL:** What? Ah, maybe you're right. Actually, we're all a bit exhausted from the old singing. We had a great old session last night. And then of course, we had to go to the *local*. I mean it must have been about *nine*, but there's a few people around here who'd put *Oliver Reed* to shame. What? (*He looks at one of the singers.*) Gerry Fields knows who I'm talking about! Ah? What? Eh? (*The singer ignores him.*) Ho-ho! Anyway, we arrived back at, God, it must have been half ten, and some of us crawled in – *Janine Reilly* knows who I'm talking about there. Don't you?! Don't you?! (*The girl looks at him without interest.*) . . . And then of course some of the wild bunch started up! What!? Who's that I could be talking about? *Eh? Heh? Tony Lynch?* He knows! Ahhhhhhhh, ha, ha, look at him there! All sweetness and light! Well he wasn't like that last night when he crawled into bed at *ten past eleven*!!!! *(He puts out his hand to Dougal.)* Hello. Father Noel Furlong. You're a fine young fella! What age would you say I am!? What age!? Go on, guess! *(Ted puts his eyes to heaven.)* Ted, don't tell him, you know! He knows! Look at him there dyin' to tell him! Go on! What age would you say?

**DOUGAL** *(thinks)*: Forty?

**NOEL** *(face freezes, turns to red.)*: Ted, haven't seen you for ages, how are you?

*Ted opens his mouth to answer.*

**NOEL** *(sings)*: 'You saw the whole of the moon!' *(The Ceol Na Gael crowd immediately start singing along.)* 'I was grounded!' Come on, Tony Lynch, sing up! 'You saw the crescent . . .'

*We see Ted, looking very, very tired indeed. Fade out. We come back as they are finishing.*

**NOEL** *(very stridently)*: 'Dirty old tooooooowwwwwwwnnnnnnn! Dirty old . . . towwwwwwn!' Oh, God, Ted, they have me worn out. They're a mad crowd. What time is it? *(He looks at his watch.)* Half ten! Oh, God. And I'll tell you, Nuala Ryan, I'm not going down to the pub with you! *(We see Nuala, asleep with her mouth open.)* No! I won't! Don't you give me that look! No, we should all go to bed. *(Tony goes out through the door.)* Where's Tony Fields off to? Probably to get some heroin!

**TONY**: No, I'm just going to the toilet, Father.

**NOEL**: Oh, right . . . Anyone need to go to the toilet? Nuala . . . are you OK?

**NUALA** *(waking up)*: I'm fine, Father.

**NOEL** *(trying to be discreet)*: Janine, do you need to go?

**JANINE**: No, I'm fine, thanks.

**NOEL**: Anyone else? Ted, Dougal, are you OK?

**TED**: We're grand, thanks Noel.

**NOEL**: Are you sure now? Ted? You don't need a little tinkle?

**TED**: I'm fine, Noel. I'll go again.

**NOEL**: There's no need to be embarrassed if you want to go. We all have to go sometime. There's no need to be ashamed of a thing like that.

**TED**: No, I'm not ashamed at all, Noel. I just don't want to go.

**NOEL**: There's no shame in it. You know that.

**TED**: Yes. Honestly, Noel, I'm fine.

**NOEL**: You're all like camels! Anyway, we'll get the sleeping-bags.

**TED**: Will it not be a bit cramped, Noel?

**NOEL**: Not at all! The more the merrier!

*Shot of an unconvinced Ted.*

SCENE 21 INT./NIGHT 1
SET: CARAVAN
*We see the Ceol Na Gael crowd, Ted and Dougal and Father Furlong all in sleeping-bags in the caravan. It is incredibly cramped. Ted is trying to sleep. There is a foot jammed up against his face. Dougal is also completely squashed. In the background we hear Father Furlong talking away to the Ceol Na Gael crowd, who are all fast asleep. He, however, is as full of energy as ever.*

**NOEL**: . . . Saint Colm's had a great old football team in the mid Fifties. There was the three-in-a-row team, and they won the Father Fitzgibbon Cup three years in a row. Father Fitzgibbon . . . thing about him was that he looked like a cup. Big ears. Like handles. TED, D'YE REMEMBER HIM? TED! TED! ARE Y'ASLEEP!? DO YE REMEMB—

**TED**: YES, I REMEMBER HIM, NOEL!

**NOEL**: Ooooooohhhh hoooooo! Who's a bit of a Moaning Michael tonight? God almighty, it's very late. I think what we should all do now is TELL A FEW GHOST STORIES.

**DOUGAL**: Ted?

**TED**: Yes.

**DOUGAL**: I'm going mad.

TED: Yes, yes, let's get out of here. Let's go home.

*Ted and Dougal extract themselves from their sleeping-bags and start to leave.*

NOEL: Who's that now? Is that Gerry Fields heading off to the disco?

TED: Ah, no, Noel. It's only us. We might head out for some fresh air.

NOEL: Right so, Ted. Don't forget to bring us back some!

TED: Hah, right so! (*Under his breath.*) You big feckin' eejit . . .

SCENE 22 EXT./EARLY MORNING 2
SET: CARAVAN PARK
*Ted and Dougal leave the caravan, Ted grabbing a carrier-bag on his way out. Outside Ted lights up a fag.*

DOUGAL: What about Jack?

TED: Chances are he's gone back to Craggy Island. He's got an incredible homing instinct. Hmmmmm . . . I wouldn't be surprised if we opened the front door to find him there with a big smile on his face and his arms outstretched to welcome us back.

DOUGAL: What?

TED: Well, maybe not with the smile on his face or the outstretched arms. Or the welcome back. But he's probably there. Oh God.

*He sees Mr. Gleason walking towards them with a towel around his waist. He hasn't seen them yet.*

TED: Oh, God, it's your man! Dougal, quick, I don't want him to see us!

*They duck into the small pre-fab toilet and listen at the door.*

DOUGAL: Everything all right there, Ted?

TED: Give it another minute.

*Cut to a full-on view of the pair. We see behind them the top half of Mrs Gleason, who is sitting on the toilet. Pause. They slowly turn around. Mrs Gleason looks at them. There is a 'moment'.*

*Ted and Dougal run out of the toilet and make towards their car. Mrs Gleason comes out after them.*

MRS GLEASON: Gerry! Gerry!

*We see Mr. Gleason, still wearing the towel. He turns and sees Ted and Dougal running away. He runs after them. Ted and Dougal get to the car. Ted tries to open the door.*

TED: Open! Please open!

DOUGAL: You're all right, Ted. He's a fair bit away yet. (*We see Mr. Gleason running towards them.*) Might be worth speeding up there a bit, Ted.

*Ted finally opens the door. They jump in and start the engine. Gleason jumps on to the bonnet.*

TED: Sorry about that!

MR GLEASON: Bloody perverts!

SCENE 23 INT./DAY 2
SET: CAR
*Ted and Dougal have obviously been driving for some time. They both look embarrassed. Hold on this for a moment. Then cut to reveal that Mr. Gleason is still sprawled over the bonnet, completely naked. He glowers at them through the windscreen. Dougal smiles back at him and gives him a little wave.*

DOUGAL: Ted, maybe we should stop and let him off. He's probably very cold now that

his towel's blown off.

**TED:** I've been thinking about that for ages. It's just . . . I'm sure he'll start giving out to us.

**DOUGAL:** We could pretend we didn't see him.

**TED:** I don't think he'd believe us. I mean, we can hardly see the road with him spread all over the windscreen.

**DOUGAL:** Ah, Ted. We'd better let him off.

**TED:** Oh . . . all right, I suppose so.

*Ted stops the car. Mr. Gleason gets to his feet. He seems a bit groggy.*

**MR GLEASON:** Get out of the car.

**TED:** Ah, hello again!

**MR GLEASON:** Get out of the car!

*He tries the door but Ted has locked it. Mr. Gleason looks at them for a second and then spots something by the side of the road – a dirty old Coke bottle. He smashes the bottle. Dougal and Ted jump with fright. He then walks towards the car, ducks out of sight and we hear a hissing sound.*

**TED:** Ah, now . . . (*Mr. Gleason goes to another tyre and punctures that as well.*) Now, come on there! There's absolutely no need for that

type of nonsense!

*Mr. Gleason sticks the bottle into a third tyre.*

**DOUGAL:** He's puncturing the tyres, Ted.

**TED** (*to Mr. Gleason*): Well, I can tell you, you're not impressing anyone!

*Mr. Gleason punctures the fourth tyre. He stands up and walks back in the direction they came from, still naked. Ted and Dougal sit there. The hissing continues as the car slowly sinks lower.*

SCENE 24 EXT./DAY 2
SET: COUNTRY ROAD
*Ted and Dougal walk along. They both look exhausted and cold.*

**DOUGAL:** God, Ted, I'm so tired. Maybe we should go back.

**TED:** No, no, no, no, no . . . I'm not going anywhere near Noel Furlong again. God knows what they're getting up to by now.

SCENE 25 EXT./DAY 2
SET: CARAVAN PARK
*We see the caravan rocking from side to side and up and down. We dimly hear music coming from within.*

SCENE 26 EXT./DAY 2
SET: CARAVAN
*All of Noel's gang are Irish dancing to the tune of 'Riverdance'. The music is very loud and they are all bunched so closely together that the scene is one of absolute madness.*

SCENE 27 EXT./DAY 2
SET: CARAVAN PARK
*The caravan topples over on its side with a loud bang. The music stops.*

**NOEL** (*reprimanding in a jokey way*): Oooooooohhhhh!!! Now who did that?

SCENE 28 EXT./DAY 2
SET: COUNTRY ROAD
*Cut back to Ted and Dougal. Dougal hears something and turns round.*

**DOUGAL:** Ted, Ted! It's a truck, Ted! It can give us a lift!

**TED** (*close to tears*): . . . Ohhhh!, thank Goddd . . .

*They stick out their thumbs. We see that it's the articulated lorry that we saw at the start of the show. The truck pulls up. Tom sticks his head out of the window.*

**TOM:** Hello, Fathers!

**TED:** Tommy! Thank God! Tom, we need a lift!

**TOM:** Fair enough, Fathers! Hold on there and I'll open the doors!

*Ted turns to hug Dougal. Tom turns to look down at the buttons and frowns. He rubs his chin thoughtfully. Ted hears a noise from the bowels of the lorry. He looks up and sees a funnel jutting out of the truck and pointing directly at him and Dougal. The rumbling gets louder. Ted looks at Dougal, sighs, and looks back up at the funnel. Suddenly, we see gallons of sewage shooting out on to Dougal and Ted. This continues for a moment or two.*

**TOM:** Sorry about that, Fathers.

*He opens the passenger door. Dougal and Ted slowly, miserably, tramp round and climb in. The truck drives off, the three men staring ahead over the dashboard.*

*As the truck moves out of shot, we see a sign that it had been obscuring. It reads 'Pleasure World. Europe's most exciting adventure playground. 200 yards. Free entry to priests.'\* An arrow points in the opposite direction. Roll closing credits.*

POST-CREDIT SEQUENCE
SCENE 29 EXT./DAY 3
SET: LUXURY YACHT
*Establish yacht.*

SCENE 30 INT./DAY 3
SET: LUXURY YACHT
*We see Jack asleep, seaweed in his hair. He suddenly wakes up.*

**JACK:** Wha?! Arrrgh!

*He stops shouting when he focuses on the sight before him. Three young women, all wearing swimming costumes, look at him with concern.*

**WOMAN 1:** Father, you're awake! Thank God! It took us ages to pull you on board. Are you all right? (*The third woman stands beside a drinks cabinet. She opens it to reveal many, many bottles of different types of drink.*) Will you have something to drink?

*Jack, coming out of his daze, looks at the camera.*

**THE END**

---

\* We really liked this final, cruel twist but it wasn't used because there was something confusing about it. It might have had to do with the arrow pointing in the opposite direction. Had they passed Pleasure World and ignored it, or what? Finally, we couldn't decide on whether it worked or not, so we erred on the side of caution.

# think fast, father ted

**ARTHUR:** This was bumped into the second series from the first series. The dancing priest was inspired by a real priest in Northern Ireland who felt that dancing was the way forward. I remember a Unionist being very angry and feeling that he was being goaded by this priest – who was dancing just outside the man's front garden. We loved the whole idea and just elaborated on it, ending up with a priest who wakes up, starts dancing and doesn't stop until he goes to bed – and then drops dead.

**GRAHAM :** As you may or may not have already noticed, one way we had of creating characters was simply to put a word like 'monkey', 'dancing', 'laughing' or 'boring' in front of the word 'priest'. One of the great things about priests is that they all dress the same. So you can take a concept, impose it on a priest and it becomes funny almost automatically. Try it at home! The boring priest, Father Purcell, is about as basic an example of this as you could hope for.

The studio audience liked that, but they weren't so keen on the concertina car that Ted wrecks by giving it 'a little tap'. I thought it would get a real howl, but it didn't. In retrospect it's possibly because the joke lacks immediacy – there's a slight delay before you realise exactly how many times he must have had to give the car a little tap to achieve that result.

## PART ONE

SCENE 1 INT./DAY 1*
SET: PAROCHIAL HOUSE
*Credits. Music as normal. Everything as normal, in fact, except that the show is called 'Father Ben'. Before the helicopter crashes we cut to . . .*

*Dougal watching television. He seems excited.*

**DOUGAL:** Ted! Ted! Quick! *Father Ben*'s on!

*Ted comes into the room. He's also excited.*

**TED:** Oh, great! I love this!

SCENE 2 INT./DAY 1*
SET: FATHER BEN'S HOUSE
*The set on the show looks very like the Parochial House, but with perhaps one or two subtle differences in taste. A priest, Father Ben, is reading a newspaper. Another priest, Father Brendan, comes in. He is wearing a pair of shorts on his head.*

**BRENDAN:** God, Ben, I'm such an eejit that I've put the shorts on my head!

**BEN:** God almighty! You really are a big fool, Brendan!

SCENE 3 INT./DAY 1*
SET: PAROCHIAL HOUSE
*Ted and Dougal are laughing mightily.*

**TED:** God almighty! This really is top-notch stuff.

**DOUGAL** (*laughing his head off*): Brendan's such an eejit!

**TED:** God, I know someone *just* like Father Ben. Big thicko.

*Cut to real credits.*

SCENE 4 INT./DAY 1
SET: PAROCHIAL HOUSE
*As we hear the closing music to 'Father Ben' we see Father Jack, asleep in his chair. His mouth is open and he is making his usual strange sleeping sounds. After a moment, a drip of water lands on his forehead, then another, then another. Cut to Ted and Dougal, who are chuckling away. Ted stands up and switches off the television.*

---

*We moved scenes 1–3 to the beginning of Episode Six, *The Plague*, in the final version.

**TED:** Right, Dougal, come on. We can't sit around watching TV all day. It's a big waste. Chewing-gum for your eyes.

**DOUGAL:** No, thanks, Ted.

**TED** (*beat*): What do you want to do? (*He checks his watch.*) I tell you what . . . Will we break out the old crisps? We could spend half an hour eating crisps and have a break for ludo about ten.

**DOUGAL:** Then what?

**TED:** More crisps.

*Cut back to Jack still asleep. A thin stream of water is now pouring on to his head. The water drips from his dangling hand into a glass beside his chair. Ted puts a big box full of packets of crisps on the table, punches a hole in the side and fishes out a pack, throws it to Dougal, then gets one for himself.*

**DOUGAL** (*holding up a crisp*): This is what I do, Ted. I get a cheese-and-onion one *and* a salt-and-vinegar one, and I eat it in the same go!

*He pops it into his mouth to demonstrate.*

**TED:** No need to do that anymore, Dougal. Father Dunning gave me these. Cheese-and-onion *and* salt-and-vinegar flavour. In the same crisp!

*He displays a bag, which has 'Cheese, salt, vinegar and onion flavour' written on it.*

**TED:** Now *this* . . . is the life.

*Suddenly, a torrent of water cascades on to Jack. Somehow, he manages to sleep through this. Cut to*

*Ted and Dougal.*

**TED:** That leak is getting worse. Dougal, get . . . Dougal!

**DOUGAL** (*looking at a crisp*): What's that, Ted?

**TED:** Get that bucket. We'd better move himself and put the bucket under the leak.

**DOUGAL:** Fair enough!

*Dougal brings the bucket over to Jack. He puts it down, then helps Ted lift the chair. Jack is still asleep. They have some difficulty lifting the chair while avoiding the water.*

**TED** (*looking up at the roof*): God, that'll probably cost a fortune to fix. Where are we going to get the money? Think, Dougal . . . how will we raise some money . . . ?

**DOUGAL:** Hmnnnn . . .

**TED:** Ah, I think I know. Yes! Aha!

**DOUGAL:** Aha!

**TED:** Are you thinking what I'm thinking, Dougal?

**DOUGAL:** I think so, Ted!

**TED:** Yes!

**DOUGAL:** But . . . well, I don't know, Ted . . .

**TED:** What?

**DOUGAL:** I mean, Ted . . . it's a big step. And where are we going to get the guns . . . ?

**TED:** What are you talking about?

**DOUGAL:** Well . . . Oh, wait now . . . actually . . . I might have been thinking about something different.

**TED:** You thought we were going to rob a bank, didn't you, Dougal?

**DOUGAL:** I did, yeah.

**TED:** This isn't a Bruce Willis film, Dougal. I was thinking more along the lines of a raffle. What'll we have as a prize, though?

**DOUGAL:** Oh, you've got me there, Ted.

**TED** (*thinks*): We should be able to get something . . . it's not as if we're asking for raffle prizes every day of the week. Under the rules of the diocese, I think we're allowed something every couple of years . . .

*Jack has been moved out of shot. Dougal puts the bucket down. The leak stops.*

**DOUGAL:** That's funny, Ted.

*Cut to Jack, who has fallen asleep again in the background. Water starts cascading on to his head.*

**TED:** God, we'll have to move him out of the room. Is the thing there? The thing for waking him up?

**DOUGAL:** Here it is.

*Dougal hands Ted a steel, bar-like thingy. It is telescopic, and Ted extends it to its full length. He and Dougal go to the other side of the room and start poking Jack in the shoulder with it. There is no response for a moment. Then Jack wakes up with a roar and grabs the device.*

**TED** (*from the other side of the room*): Father! Father! It's only us!

**JACK:** Get to feck!

**TED:** We're going to have to move you, Father!

**JACK:** Drink!

**TED:** Father! No! Don't drink that! It's —

*Jack drinks, then spews it out immediately.*

**JACK:** FECKIN' *WATER!*

SCENE 5 INT./DAY 1
SET: PAROCHIAL HOUSE
*We see Ted on the telephone. Dougal is beside him, craning his head in order to listen.*

**TED:** . . . And I was looking up the records, and the island hasn't been given anything to raffle since those two bags of coal in 1964 . . . I think we're entitled . . . under the rules of the diocese . . .

*He suddenly gives Dougal the thumbs-up. Dougal doesn't react.*

**TED:** . . . Oh, that'd be great . . . oh, that's wonderful! Yes, perfect! Thanks very much, Your Grace . . . yes . . . thanks again. All right, bye, Bishop Brennan! Bye!

*Ted puts down the telephone. He claps his hands together happily.*

**DOUGAL:** No luck then?

TED: Lots of luck, Dougal! They're giving us a car!

DOUGAL: A car! That's a brilliant prize! A car!

TED: Oh, it's not that unusual. Father Finnegan got a car last month. You know him, don't you, Dougal? The dancing priest? Dances for peace.

DOUGAL: Is he still going?

TED: He is indeed. He danced six thousand miles last year. New York to Los Angeles. He was mugged about once every fifteen miles.

DOUGAL: That's terrible! He's all right now, though . . . ?

TED: Oh, he's fine now, God bless him. (*He rubs his hands together.*) Great! We'll have the roof sorted out in no time! Hear that, Father? We'll have the roof back to normal before you know it!

*Cut to a grumpy Jack in a showercap, giving them the finger.*

SCENE 6 EXT./DAY 1
SET: PAROCHIAL HOUSE
*We see Mrs Doyle standing outside the house, looking around expectantly. We hear an engine sound and then see Ted and Dougal appear in the driveway in a car. It is shiny and new, with 'For Reg' on the number plates. The car stops and Ted and Dougal get out looking very pleased.*

MRS DOYLE: Cup of tea, Fathers?

TED: Eh, no thanks, Mrs Doyle. (*He nods at the car.*) What do you think of her?

MRS DOYLE (*distracted*): Yeah, great. Are you sure you won't have a cup?

TED (*ignoring the question*): It's not ours, Mrs Doyle, unfortunately.

DOUGAL: No. It's a prize in our big raffle.

MRS DOYLE: Oh, right. Will I pour it for you, then?

TED: Go on inside, Mrs Doyle. Let me take the tray.

MRS DOYLE: Oh . . . all right then, Father. I'll put the kettle on in case you want some more when you get in.

*Mrs Doyle goes inside. Before Ted and Dougal can follow her, Dougal spots something.*

DOUGAL: Ah, God, look at that, Ted, there's a dent in the car.

TED: What!?

*He looks for somewhere to put down the tray and cups. He can't find anywhere so he throws them into a bush.*

TED: Where's the dent, Dougal?

DOUGAL (*pointing at the front of the car*): Just there, Ted.

TED: God, how did that happen?

DOUGAL: It must have been when we hit that fella on the bike.

TED: Don't mention that to anyone, Dougal. He was all right, anyway. I saw him getting up . . . (*He examines the dent.*) Well . . . well, it's not too bad . . . Sure I can just straighten that out with a little tap. There should be a hammer there in that box.

DOUGAL: Good thinkin', Ted.

*Dougal goes to a box beside the door and searches through it. He takes out a hammer. Ted takes it and taps at the dent. He pauses, then taps a little harder.*

TED: Ooops! Didn't mean to do that. I'll just tap it the other way.

*He continues tapping. Fade out. Fade back in again. It is early in the evening. We see Dougal, sucking his cheeks in and exhaling thoughtfully*

DOUGAL: It's no use, Ted. You'll never get it absolutely right.

*Cut to Ted, still tapping away at the car. The car is now a total wreck. It looks as if it has been hit in the side by a train. Ted stands up.*

TED (*very frustrated*): I thought I had it back there a while ago, you know? It was looking all right there for a while but like an eejit I had to keep bangin' away . . .

DOUGAL: You're a perfectionist, Ted, you know? It's not your fault. It's not too bad, though.

TED: Let me have another look at it.

*Ted steps back to have a look. He muses for a second, but there's no way around the fact that it looks like*

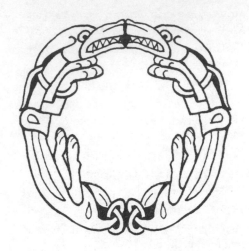

*James Dean's car after his fatal accident. Ted is unnaturally calm. Pause.*

**TED:** No . . . no, we can't give that away as a prize.

**DOUGAL:** Look, let's sleep on it, Ted. See how you feel in the morning.

**TED:** Maybe you're right. (*Pause.*) OK, then.

*They enter the house.*

SCENE 7 EXT./NIGHT 1
SET: PAROCHIAL HOUSE
*It is very late at night. All the lights are off. It's very peaceful and quiet. Suddenly, we hear Ted's scream and a single light goes on. We hear Ted's voice.*

**TED:** OH, JESUS! WE'RE DEAD! OH, GOD ALMIGHTY!

SCENE 8 INT./NIGHT 1
SET: TED AND DOUGAL'S BEDROOM
*Ted is sitting up in bed, terrified. Dougal looks at him, worried.*

**DOUGAL:** Ted, calm down, there! Come on!

**TED:** Calm down! Calm down? We've just destroyed a car that's worth seven grand! It looks like it's been bombed!

**DOUGAL:** Come on, Ted. It'll look better in the morning.

**TED:** Dougal, try and understand! WE'RE DEAD! The bishop'll kill us! We're dead! We're

dead! We're dead! We're DEAD!

*Ted is totally hysterical. Dougal rushes over to him, unsure as to what to do. Finally, he slaps him in the face. Ted recovers after a moment.*

**TED:** Thanks, Dougal . . . I probably needed that but . . . don't ever do it again.

**DOUGAL:** It was just you were getting a little hysterical there, Ted.

**TED:** Fair enough, but . . . don't ever do it again. Now, what are we going to do . . . ?

**DOUGAL:** We could run away.

**TED:** No . . . no, they'd just find us again. They always do.

**DOUGAL:** Oh . . . oh, you're right there, Ted . . . (*Pause.*) What about that other fella that has the car? The dancing priest . . .

**TED:** Finnegan! Yes! It'd be the same kind of car and everything!

**DOUGAL:** How could we get him to give it to us, Ted?

*Pause.*

**TED:** Maybe . . . maybe we could just get a lend of it . . .

**DOUGAL:** But when someone wins it in the raffle, Ted, they won't want to give it back.

**TED:** Well . . . now, this is going to sound very immoral, Dougal, but stay with me. What if . . . what if we rigged the draw so that we won it? Then we could bring it back?

**DOUGAL:** Oh . . . oh, that'd be terribly wrong, Ted. I don't think we should do that.

**TED:** It wouldn't even be cheating, really. It'd be just . . . structuring the raffle in such a way that the return comes to the benefactors rather than the beneficiaries.

**DOUGAL:** Hmmm . . .

**TED:** Dougal, seriously, listen . . . think of it this way . . . If Bishop Brennan finds out we wrecked the car, he *will* kill us, you know? And murder's a terrible, terrible sin, Dougal. So, by committing this *little* sin, we'll actually be *saving a Bishop's soul!*

*Long pause. Dougal thinks.*

**DOUGAL:** Fair enough, then, Ted.

SCENE 9 INT./DAY 2
SET: PAROCHIAL HOUSE
*Ted and Dougal are finishing putting on their coats.*

**TED:** Come on, Father.

*Jack comes round the corner in his coat as Ted opens the door and they start to exit.*

SCENE 10 EXT./DAY 2
SET: PAROCHIAL HOUSE
*Ted, Dougal and Jack appear at the front door and run to the wrecked car, which is parked a short distance from the house. As they do so, they are attacked by thousands of squawking birds. Ted runs at the front, followed by Dougal who holds Jack by the arm. A huge crow pecks Jack on the cheek. Jack roars. When they get into the car, they behave as if they have experienced nothing more unusual than heavy rain.*

**TED:** Right! Off we go!

SCENE 11 EXT./DAY 2
SET: FINNEGAN'S HOUSE
*We see the wrecked car, still barely able to move, squeaking to a halt outside the house. It pulls up behind a new-looking car, also with 'For Reg' plates. Ted gets out.*

SCENE 12 INT./DAY 2
SET: CAR OUTSIDE FINNEGAN'S HOUSE
*We see Jack and Dougal in the back seat. Jack is sneezing loudly. Dougal is cowering away from him. There are thousands of crumpled tissues all over the back seat.*

**TED:** God, look at it. It's the same colour and all. Dougal, you mind Jack here. I'll be as quick as I can.

**DOUGAL:** But, Ted —

*Ted slams the door. Dougal is alone with Jack. Appalling sounds come from Jack's direction. Dougal looks nervous.*

SCENE 13 INT./DAY 2
SET: FINNEGAN'S LIVING ROOM
*We see Father Liam Finnegan dancing a twist in the manner so beloved of parents at school discos. Sixties-*

*type beat music plays. There is a light knock at the door of the room. It opens and Ted sticks his head around.*

**TED:** Liam . . .

**LIAM:** Ted! Come on in! (*Ted enters.*) Will you join me?

**TED:** What, me? Dance? O'ho, no . . . I'm not much of a dancer, now.

**LIAM:** Come on, Ted. Prayer isn't the only way to praise God, you know. And it keeps you fit as well!

**TED:** Oh . . . all right, then . . .

*Ted starts dancing in tiny, quick movements. He and Liam face each other, jiving away.*

**LIAM:** You said something on the phone about taking a loan of the car.

**TED:** I did, yes. You'd be doin' me a great favour, Liam —

**LIAM:** Ah, don't be silly. Just look after it. Don't give it away in a raffle or something!

*He laughs. Ted looks a little frightened, then he laughs, too. He laughs too loudly and a little too long.*

**TED:** Someone said you were on television recently. In some documentary. You were dancing in Belfast or something?

**LIAM** (*coldly*): That wasn't me. That's some other fella. Some young fella. Ripped off the idea. Don't like talking about him.

*Uncomfortable pause.*

**LIAM:** How is Dougal and old Father Jack?

**TED:** Fine. They're out in the car.

SCENE 14 EXT./DAY 2
SET: CAR
*We see the car jolting wildly as Jack sneezes.*

SCENE 15 INT./DAY 2
SET: FINNEGAN'S LIVING ROOM
*Ted is jiving towards the door.*

**TED:** All right, Liam! I'd better be heading off!

**LIAM:** Fair enough! Bye, Ted!

*Ted dances out through the door. Liam dances a little*

*more, then suddenly clutches his heart and falls to the ground.*

SCENE 16 EXT./DAY 2
SET: FINNEGAN'S HOUSE
*Ted runs out of the house, shaking the car keys in triumph. He runs towards the car, looking joyful. He looks in at Dougal and knocks at the window.*

**TED:** Way-haaaaayyyyyy!!!!

**DOUGAL** (*winds down the window*): No luck, then?

*Ted looks at him, deflated.*

### END OF PART ONE

* * *

### PART TWO

SCENE 17 INT./NIGHT 2
SET: CAR
*Ted and Dougal are in the car. Dougal is drawing his name in the condensation on the window.*

**TED:** Dougal, you'll leave a mark on the window.

*Dougal stops.*

**DOUGAL:** Are we there yet?

**TED:** Dougal, it's a long drive. We won't be there for a while. (*Pause.*) I must say, Father Finnegan's looking well for a man of his age. Dancin' away there . . . you should have seen him. Ah, sure everything's fine now. Father Ted Crilly saves the day once again! How are you doing back there, Father?

*He turns to check and Jack sneezes in his face.*

**TED:** Aaaaaghhhh!!!

*Ted is momentarily blinded. The car swerves to the other side of the road for an instant.*

**TED** (*wiping his eyes*): My God! My God, what have you been drinking, Father?! God, it's like acid!

*Ted finally gathers himself together.*

**TED:** We really have to take care of this car. We can't afford any accidents . . . this is the only one we have now . . . dear God. Father, try this. This'll clear you up.

*He hands Jack a nasal inhaler. Jack breaks the top off and drinks the contents.*

**DOUGAL:** Aren't cars great, though, Ted?

**TED** (*not really listening*): . . . Yes . . . they are, all right . . .

*Pause.*

**TED:** Look . . . maybe you should have a rest, Dougal. It's a long drive. You have a little sleep.

**DOUGAL:** Right so, Ted.

*Dougal puts his head back into the seat and closes his eyes. Jack is asleep beside him. The car speeds into the night.*

SCENE 18 INT./DAY 3
SET: CAR
*We see Dougal still asleep. The camera moves to show Jack asleep beside him. Then Ted is revealed, also asleep. The car travels on. We see the countryside dwindling behind. Ted shifts to get more comfortable.*

SCENE 19 EXT./DAY 3
SET: ROAD
*The car roars by.*

SCENE 20 INT./DAY 3
SET: CAR
*Another shot of the three of them sleeping happily. Ted slowly stirs himself. Then one eye opens. He stretches and smacks his lips. Ted looks at the wheel of the car, then at Dougal and Jack. He turns again and looks out through the windscreen.*

**TED:** God, almost drifted off there . . . oh, great, we're nearly home!

*Jack and Dougal wake up.*

SCENE 21 INT./DAY 3
SET: PAROCHIAL HOUSE
*Ted is looking at a notebook. He taps a pen against his teeth. Dougal sits beside him. Jack is asleep nearby, water still pouring on to his head.*

**TED:** Right, the raffle. Let's go through it again. It's crucial we do it absolutely right . . .

**DOUGAL:** Fair enough, Ted . . .

**TED** (*produces a hat*): OK . . . I'll fill the hat with a load of tickets with the same number on them. Say, eleven.

**DOUGAL:** Eleven . . . two ones. That's easy to remember, Ted . . .

**TED:** . . . Then when I'm doing the draw, we'll make sure that you have that number.

**DOUGAL:** Right. So we won't have to cheat at all?

**TED:** Well, that's actually how we're cheating . . .

**DOUGAL:** Oh, right. OK, so. Let me get this right . . . You'll be wearing the hat?

**TED:** No, no. I won't be wearing any hats. The *tickets* will be in the hat.

**DOUGAL:** Gotcha. But you'll put on the hat to give me the signal?

**TED:** I won't be giving you any signals, Dougal! I'll just pull out your ticket from the hat, you say 'That's my number', and then come up and collect the prize!

**DOUGAL:** There's a prize, Ted!? What is it!?

**TED:** THE CAR!!! (*Ted takes a breath.*) Dougal. Look. All you have to do is, when I call the number, you say 'Yes, that's my ticket', and come up on stage. Just remember that. Right?

**DOUGAL:** Right!

*He gives Ted the thumbs-up. Ted returns to his notebook. Mrs Doyle enters, carrying a tray.*

**MRS DOYLE:** Here's the sandwiches for tonight, Father. Ooops, wait. I forgot to do my test.

**TED:** What test is that, Mrs Doyle?

**MRS DOYLE:** I always take one sandwich at random and try it. If it doesn't meet my standards, the lot of them go in the bin.

*She pulls out a sandwich and bites into it. Beat. Her face slowly screws up into a grimace. One eye flickers. She starts making gagging sounds. She starts to swallow it as if it's a piece of wood with nails sticking out of it. She thumps chest and makes unpleasant noises. Her head suddenly jerks back. Pause.*

**MRS DOYLE** (*recovering immediately*)**:** They're fine.

*She leaves the room. Dougal approaches Ted.*

**TED:** So! Are we all sorted?

**DOUGAL:** Rarin' to go, Ted! Oh, who's doing the disco?

**TED:** Father Billy O'Dwyer.

**DOUGAL:** 'The Spinmaster'! Great!

**TED:** Actually, I'm looking forward to this. Bet you I sell a load of tickets.

**DOUGAL:** Bet I sell more than you, Ted.

**TED:** Hmm . . .

*Dougal pauses beside the open door.*

**DOUGAL:** Do you know what it's a bit like, Ted? (*Acting cool.*) It's a bit like *The Sting* and I'm Robert Redford and you're Paul Newman.

*He smiles and walks the wrong side of the open door, so that he's obscured by it. He emerges after a moment, looks sheepishly at Ted and walks out on the right side of the door.*

SCENE 22 INT./NIGHT 3
SET: PAROCHIAL HALL
*We see a priest, Father Billy O'Dwyer, setting up some DJ equipment. Ted approaches him.*

**TED:** Ground control to the 'The Spinmaster'!

**BILLY:** O'ho! Ted, how are ya?!

*Ted climbs up on stage to have a word with him.*

**TED:** Fine, fine . . . God, it's like NASA. How do you keep track of it all?

**BILLY** (*proudly*)**:** Oh, it's quite simple, really. Y'see here we have the two turn-tables, which I control from the mixing-desk here. Treble, bass . . . This switch helps you flip between the two records if you want to get a bit of a jam going. This is a new thing I got – Japanese thing that makes the sound a bit more tonal.

**TED:** Oh, I tell you, I can't wait. What records have you got for us?

*Pause.*

**BILLY:** Records.

**TED:** Bit of The Bee Gees, I suppose. Get them all jumping.

*He sees that Billy has his head in his hands.*

**BILLY:** Oh, God . . .

**TED:** Billy! What's up with you?

**BILLY:** I've forgotten the records, Ted.

**TED:** What?! Do you not have any at all!!?

**BILLY:** I knew there was something . . .

**TED:** Billy, what am I going to do? The whole island's coming to this thing!

**BILLY:** Hold on a sec, now . . . wait a sec . . . I might have one. I think I have one in the car.

*He leaves the stage. Dougal and Mrs Doyle arrive. Mrs Doyle has a tray with teacups, etc . . .*

**MRS DOYLE:** Tea, Father?

**TED:** Ah, Mrs Doyle! Would you like to be the first to buy a raffle ticket?

**MRS DOYLE:** Oh, I'd love to, Father! I haven't taken part in a raffle in donkey's years!

**TED** (*flips through the book of tickets*)**:** How many will you have?

**MRS DOYLE:** Just the one, Father.

**TED** (*disappointed*)**:** Just one? You should buy a couple, Mrs Doyle. You'll have better chance of winning.

**DOUGAL:** Well to be honest . . . (*He winks knowingly.*) . . . You won't have much chance of winning this one . . . no matter how many tickets you get!

**TED:** Dougal! Mrs Doyle has every chance of winning!

**DOUGAL** (*slyly*)**:** Does she? I don't think so, Ted.

**TED:** Shut up, Dougal! Go on, Mrs Doyle. It's

for charity. Buy a few.

**MRS DOYLE:** No, I don't think I will. I'll just have the one.

**TED** (*sighs*)**:** 50p.

**MRS DOYLE:** 50p! (*Reluctantly.*) Well . . . OK, then, Father.

*She hands Ted the money.*

**TED:** Grand.

**MRS DOYLE:** I only need the one ticket, anyway. My lucky number, never lets me down.

**TED** (*flips through book*)**:** O'ho! I see! Which one is that?

**MRS DOYLE:** Eleven.

*Dougal gasps.*

**TED:** What?

**MRS DOYLE:** Eleven. It's always been lucky for me.

**TED:** Eh, we're out of elevens, Mrs Doyle.

**MRS DOYLE:** But I thought I was your first customer . . .

**TED:** Yes, but . . . I think this one came without elevens . . . Tell, you what, Mrs Doyle. I'll give you a number ten and a number one, and that'll add up to eleven. And you can have them both for 50p.

**MRS DOYLE:** No, I don't think so, Father. I'd better have the money back.

**TED:** Mrs Doyle, it's for charity. It's for the roof.

**MRS DOYLE:** Sorry, Father.

*She holds her hand out, patiently. Ted sighs and gives her the money. She leaves. Ted looks at Dougal.*

**TED:** Incredible woman . . . Now, where's Jack got to?

**DOUGAL:** He's with Father Purcell.

**TED:** Oh, God. I'd better rescue him. He'll be going mad!

**DOUGAL:** Oh, they're fine, Ted. They're having a chat.

**TED:** That'll be a one-sided chat if ever there

was one, Dougal. Purcell's the most boring priest in the world. He was working in Nigeria in some village a few years ago and he woke up one morning to find that everyone in the village had gone off. Oh, they'd had enough of him. Went off in a big boat that sank after about a mile and they were eaten by alligators, God love them. Anyway . . . just in case the same thing happens to Father Jack . . .

*Ted moves off.*

SCENE 23 INT./NIGHT 3
SET: CHANGING ROOM
*Father Jack is being talked to by Father Austin Purcell, an extraordinarily dull man. Jack looks at Austin with absolute hatred, looking around for an escape route. Austin doesn't seem to notice. Ted sticks his head around the door, raffle tickets in hand.*

AUSTIN: . . . So we run the gas off the electricity and the electricity off the gas and we save two hundred pounds a year. But a few weeks later, God, I'll never forget it . . . we got a new boiler.

*Ted coughs lightly. Jack looks at Ted hopefully.*

TED: Are you all right there, Fathers?

JACK: Help me.

AUSTIN: Hello, Ted! I was just telling Father Jack about the thing there last year. How did you fare with yours?

TED: Ah . . . I don't really know what —

AUSTIN: 'Cause if it's giving you any trouble at all they'll take it back. Oh, it's no trouble to them. Sure that's what they're paid for! They have *no* morals and they have *no* respect for human life. What they have, and no one can deny this, is the finest collection of boilers in the world. And I include Canada in that.

TED (*hasn't a clue what he's talking about*): Fine! Actually, Austin, if you don't mind, I need Father Jack for a moment.

JACK: Thank Christ!

*Jack runs to the door and exits quickly.*

TED: While I'm here, I don't suppose you'd like a few raffle tickets?

AUSTIN: Ah, God, I remember the first time I saw the boiler. Beautiful.

TED: A ticket, Father?

AUSTIN: . . . but you never know with these things – unless, of course, you get them wholesale and try to move them into the space that was occupied by, say, a wardrobe, or a big ceramic hob . . .

TED: Would you like a ticket, Austin?

AUSTIN (*pausing to look at the tickets*): Did you get them printed specially, Ted? 'Cause you know you can buy them in a shop. Any number you want . . . one . . . seven . . . twenty . . . three . . . nine . . . one hundred and twelve . . . anything you want up to . . . four hundred and nine, I think it is. If you want any more they can send off for them. They send them back in an envelope. Normal type of thing, rectangular, four corners . . .

*Ted gives up. He smiles and backs out of the room, closing the door slowly behind him. Austin doesn't seem to notice and talks on regardless.*

AUSTIN: . . . That's the way I like them, anyway, the old envelopes. No round envelopes for me! No way, José! Sid Vicious! That was a great name, wasn't it? He got into trouble with the drugs . . . .

SCENE 24 INT./NIGHT 3*
SET: PAROCHIAL HALL HALLWAY
*Ted looks around.*

TED: Father? Father? Oh, where's he gone . . . ?

SCENE 25 INT./NIGHT 3
SET: BACKSTAGE PAROCHIAL HALL
*We see Jack wandering around, completely lost. He turns a corner and we see that the hallway is lined with crates of beer.*

JACK: Oh, yessss!

SCENE 26 INT./NIGHT 3
SET: PAROCHIAL HALL
*Ted is standing alone, no one is buying tickets from him. He sees Dougal, selling tickets hand over fist.*

DOUGAL: There you go! Anyone else? All righty . . .

*We deleted this scene from the final version.

*Ted looks at Dougal, annoyed. Cut to the stage. Ted comes up to the microphone.*

**TED:** Sorry about the wait, folks. Bit of trouble with the old disco. Ah, luckily, though, I've got a few old pals to come up and do a few songs. Please welcome Father Tiernan, Father Cafferty, Father Rafter and Father Leonard!

*Head-and-shoulder shots of four priests. We hear Kraftwerk music starting up and the camera pulls back to reveal that they are standing behind impressive synthesisers. They move only very, very slightly as they play, looking at the audience with no expression on their faces.*

SCENE 27 INT./NIGHT 3
SET: SIDE OF STAGE
*With the sound of German synthesiser pop in the background, Ted sees Father Billy and runs up to him.*

**TED:** Billy! Where've you been?

**BILLY:** Sorry, Ted. I got the record!

**TED:** All right, all right. Listen, how about a ticket . . . 50p each, or four for a pound . . .

**BILLY:** Gambling, Ted. Ruined my father, and my grandfather. Both of them, Ted. Died without a penny to their name. That's not going to happen to me, Ted.

**TED:** Oh, come on, Billy. Have a few.

**BILLY:** No, Ted. It's like a disease. You don't want to get into that kind of thing.

**TED** (*a tad frustrated*): God, it's just for charity. It's not real gambling.

**BILLY:** Oh, go on, then.

**TED:** Great. How many tickets will you have?

**BILLY:** Give us two thousand.

*Pause.*

**TED:** Two thousand?

**BILLY:** Go on, there. I'll do you a cheque.

**TED:** That's a good lot of tickets, Billy.

**BILLY:** Ah, it's fine. Sure I'll have a much better chance of winning the car! There you go . . .

*He rips out the cheque and hands it to Ted. Pause.*

**TED:** No . . . no, I can't take this. It's too much.

**BILLY:** I can handle it, Ted. I've got a few friends who loan me cash from time to time.

**TED:** No, no, you keep this. You shouldn't be throwing this kind of money around.

*He moves as if to rip up the cheque. Dougal comes up to him.*

**DOUGAL:** Ted, I need another ticketbook. This one's run out.

**TED:** Already!! How could you have sold out already?!

**DOUGAL:** Don't ask me! I can hardly keep a straight face back there!

*He grabs a ticketbook from Ted and moves off. Ted turns to Billy. Pause.*

**TED:** What was it again, Billy, two thousand?

SCENE 28 INT./NIGHT 3
SET: BACKSTAGE PAROCHIAL HALL
*Jack has just finished a can of beer. Cut to reveal that the hallway is covered with empty beercans. Jack tries to shake the can and looks inside it, then throws it on the ground.*

**JACK:** Need more drink!

*He stumbles towards a door and swings it open. We see the prize car just outside the door.*

**JACK:** Ah, ha, haaaaaa!

SCENE 29 INT./NIGHT 3
SET: PAROCHIAL HALL
*The disco is going full blast. Father Billy is playing 'Ghost Town' by The Specials at top volume. The hall is now quite full. The song ends, and Billy picks up the needle and returns it to the start of the record again. Cut to Ted and Dougal by the side of the stage.*

**TED:** Right, here we go. You know what to do?

**DOUGAL** (*taps his head*): It's all in there, Ted.

**TED:** OK, let's go . . .

*He moves on to the stage and motions for Billy to turn the music off. Billy does so. Ted moves towards the microphone.*

**TED:** Thank you, Father Billy! And now . . . let's get on to the important stuff! The raffle!

The last raffle I was at was very interesting because the people who ran the raffle actually won the prize! So it's not unusual for that to happen every now and again. Right? OK . . .

*Cut to Dougal in the audience. Cut back to Ted. He produces a hat, then pulls out a number.*

**TED:** And the winning number is . . . number eleven!

*Dougal looks at his ticket, disappointed.*

**TED** (*worried*): Number eleven!

*Dougal looks around to see if anyone else has the ticket.*

**TED:** Number eleven! If anyone has that number could they please come up on stage!

*Pause.*

**TED:** What's that, Father McGuire? You say you have the winning ticket?

**DOUGAL:** What?

**TED:** Well done! A big round of applause for our very own Father Dougal McGuire!

*Dougal joins Ted on stage. Ted whispers to him.*

**TED:** God almighty, Dougal! What were you doing?!!

**DOUGAL:** Sorry, Ted. I was looking at the ticket upside down.

**TED:** It was number *eleven*, Dougal! It looks the same both ways!

**DOUGAL:** Ah, now, it doesn't really, Ted. They've got the little standy-out things at the top.

*Ted ignores him and turns to the crowd.*

**TED:** Well, congratulations, Father Dougal! What a magical thing to happen, you living here and . . . winning the car . . (*He decides he'd better shut up.*) Anyway, wasn't that a fantastic evening? We've raised enough money to repair our roof and we had a great time as well. So thank you all for coming. And now, if I could ask you all to stand for our national anthem!

*He gestures to Billy. Billy looks down at the turntable for a moment, then puts on 'Ghost Town' again. Everyone in the hall stands respectfully. Ted turns to Billy. Billy shrugs apologetically.*

SCENE 30 INT./NIGHT 3
SET: PAROCHIAL HOUSE
*We see Billy on the telephone.*

**BILLY:** For God's sake! I'll have the money next week! Please! Please!!!!! One more chance, that's all I ask!!!!

*Mrs Doyle comes up and offers tea. Father Billy puts his hand over the telephone.*

**BILLY:** Thanks very much, Mrs Doyle. (*He returns to the telephone.*) Have some pity, for God's sake!!!!

*Other guests chat away as Mrs Doyle mingles among them with her sandwiches. Cut to Dougal listening to Austin. Dougal looks across the room to see if he can see Ted anywhere. He can't manage to extract himself from Austin.*

**AUSTIN:** Ah, they have you every way. I was in the AA there. The insurance is very expensive . . .

**DOUGAL:** Oh, right . . .

**AUSTIN:** . . . I ended up having to crash the car in the end, just to get the money back. But then they had witnesses, of course, who said that I steered it into the wall on purpose, so there was talk of me going to jail for a while . . .

*Cut back to Ted. Mrs Doyle approaches him. She looks shocked. She taps him on the shoulder.*

**TED:** Mrs Doyle, what can I do for you?

**MRS DOYLE:** Terrible news, Father.

**TED** (*concerned*): What is it, Mrs Doyle?

*He pulls up a chair and gets her to sit in it.*

**MRS DOYLE:** It's Father Finnegan. He's had a heart attack.

**TED:** No!

**MRS DOYLE:** The doctor warned him to cut it down to twelve hours a day, but *he just couldn't stop dancing!!!*

**TED:** Oh, that's . . . that's terrible!

*Dougal approaches.*

**DOUGAL:** What's up, Ted?

**TED:** Father Finnegan had a heart attack.

**DOUGAL:** He hasn't! Are there any more chipsticks?

*Ted and Mrs Doyle look disapprovingly at Dougal. Jack enters the room. No one notices him.*

**DOUGAL:** Does that mean we can keep the car?

**TED:** Dougal! That's a terrible thing to say! The man has just – wait a second! You're right! We can keep the car!

*Ted notices Jack. He has a crate of beer under one arm and an air-freshener tree-thing hanging from his face. He looks very drunk. Ted and Dougal look horrified. They walk over to Jack, who puts his hands over his crate of lager in a protective movement.*

**JACK:** Feck off!

**TED:** Father . . . where did you get the air-freshener from?

**JACK:** Car . . .

**TED:** Oh, God.

**JACK:** Drived the car!

**TED:** Not the new car!

*Pause.*

**JACK:** Yeah!

**TED:** Tell me from the beginning, Father. Where'd you drive the car?

**JACK:** To shops! Drink!

**TED:** How fast were you driving? Were you driving fast?

**JACK:** Slow!

**TED:** You were driving slowly? Thank God.

**JACK:** Corner. Stopped the car. Got out. Fag! Turned around. TRUCK!

**TED:** A truck!

**JACK:** Two!

*He brings his hands apart and smashes them together.*

**TED** (*devastated*): All right . . . all right, where is it? Maybe we can salvage something from it.

SCENE 31 EXT./NIGHT 3
SET: PAROCHIAL HOUSE
*We see the car from the front. It looks pristine,*

*although there is a slight dent over the front bumper. Dougal walks behind the car. Ted bends down and examines the dent.*

**DOUGAL:** Ah, Ted. It's not that bad.

**TED:** Yes . . . God, I thought it'd be much worse than that . . .

*He stands up and sees something. We get a side view of the car, which reveals that the back has been completely squashed into the front.*

**TED:** Oh, bollocks. Dougal, how is this 'not that bad'?*

**DOUGAL:** Well, remember, Ted, when you tapped the other car and it ended up looking a bit like this one?*

**TED:** Yes . . . *

**DOUGAL:** Well, could you kind of do the opposite of that, and maybe, tap this one *back* so that it looks like a new one.*

**TED:** I *could* probably do that, Dougal. But probably by the time I've finished, we won't need cars 'cause we'll all be flying around in spaceships. Oh, well, at least we've still got the raffle money to fix the roof.*

SCENE 31A INT./NIGHT 3
SET: PAROCHIAL HOUSE
*Billy is still on the telephone.*

**BILLY:** Please! Just give me twenty-four hours! Please!

*He hangs up, looking desperate. He sees a big bucket with 'Raffle Money' written on the side. He contemplates this.*

SCENE 32 INT./NIGHT 3
SET: PAROCHIAL HOUSE
*On television, we see a weather report.*

**WEATHERMAN:** . . . So because of that low pressure, we'll probably be seeing a lot more rain, at least until July, or possibly until August . . .

*Ted, Dougal and Jack sit around the room, watching the television. Each has an individual stream of water falling on to his head. They all wear showercaps. They look absolutely miserable.*

*We deleted these lines from the final version.

**TED:** God almighty . . . how could someone be so *dishonest* as to steal raffle money from a priest.

**DOUGAL:** Well, it was a rigged raffle, though, Ted.

*Ted tries to respond but can't think of any way to refute this. He looks enormously frustrated.*

**TED:** Oh, well, I suppose it's not too bad. As long as a tree doesn't fall through the roof or something!

*Outside we hear a thundercrack. The lights go off. There is a long, slow, creaking sound. They all watch the window, from where the noise is coming. The creaking sound gets louder, then stops.*

**TED:** Ha. I thought there —

*We hear a crash and the lights go out.*

*Roll closing credits.*

POST-CREDIT SEQUENCE

SCENE 33 INT./NIGHT 3
SET: PAROCHIAL HOUSE
*Father Austin Purcell is talking to camera.*

**AUSTIN:** . . . Here's a piece of advice my Father gave to me, and this not only refers to lagging, but any form of insulation. He said, 'Don't ever . . .' No . . . it was 'Always . . . always make sure . . .' No, sorry, it was 'Never . . .' Ah. I've forgotten. Never mind. What's your favourite humming noise? Is it . . . hmmmmmmmm . . . or is it *hmmmmmmmmmmmmmmm* . . . I think hmmmmmmmmm . . . is my favourite, but sometimes, if I'm in a bit of a funny mood, I prefer *hmmmmmmmmmmmmmmmm*. That would be the sound of a fridge. But the first one would be the sound of a man humming . . . you never hear women humming. I've often wondered what a more feminine hum would sound like . . . mmm . . . mmmm. I knew a woman once, but she died soon afterwards . . . What was Hitler on about? That's no way to run Europe. Great roads, but if you've got no car, you might as well have some kind of ski-lift. They go way up in the air . . .

**THE END**

# tentacles of doom

**ARTHUR:** One of the things we liked best about the characters in *Ted* was that they didn't think too much about religion; they were frightened it would drive them mad and because they didn't have any theological knowledge, they were absolutely terrified of anyone mentioning the subject. So the arrival of three bishops was bound to throw them into a panic. I think I'm right in saying that upgrading the status of a relic – in this case the Holy Stone of Clonrichert, which gave Dougal 'a great buzz' in Series One – is something that doesn't happen. Upgrading happens with saints, when they go through stages before beatification, but I don't think it's the same with relics. I don't even think the Church is keen on relics any more.

Anyway, we needed three bishops to conduct the upgrading – one for each of our boys to destroy. Once we'd decided on that, the structure of this episode was fairly easy. Jack being taught to say, 'That would be an ecumenical matter' was the inspired suggestion of (by now ex) producer Geoffrey Perkins. We were just going to have him saying 'Yes' and 'No', but that phrase really lifted it. There was a third line, 'Temptation comes in many guises', but it didn't add anything so we dumped it in the end.

**GRAHAM:** I like Jack's spiffy look. Normally he was absolutely hideous – you don't really see on TV just how revolting he was. Frank Kelly was actually a very lonely man on filming days; he would have to eat lunch on his own because his make-up was so horrific that nobody could bear to sit opposite him. He was like the sun; you couldn't look directly at him for any amount of time. He had a river of wax coming out of his ear; dried chapped stuff around his mouth and a milky-white contact lens…Just in case you never noticed, take a look at the space behind Jack's chair. We asked the design people if they could make it look as if the area had been 'infected' by Jack sitting there for so long. The wall is going black, and there's all manner of matter stuck there.

There's a subplot in this draft involving Ted being asked to prepare a paper by one of the bishops. It made the show about five minutes overlong and really didn't go anywhere. When we took it out, it barely caused a ripple in the rest of the show. Really, if you can take out a plot strand without having to rewrite anything, then it probably shouldn't have been there in the first place.

**PART ONE**

SCENE 1 INT./DAY 1
SET: PAROCHIAL HOUSE BATHROOM
*Ted is standing by the toilet, fixing something in the cistern. Dougal is standing beside him.*

**TED:** That might do it. (*He presses the handle, but it doesn't flush.*) Ah, for pity's . . .

*He goes round to the front of the bowl. He pushes the handle again, but still nothing happens. He puts his head into the bowl. He looks around inside for a moment. At this point, Dougal pushes the handle. The toilet flushes. Ted's head remains out of sight, in the toilet, until the flushing sound ceases. Pause. He finally takes his head out, soaking wet, and looks at Dougal.*

**DOUGAL:** That's working now, Ted.

*Ted turns slowly, takes a deep breath and tries again. This time it doesn't work.*

**DOUGAL:** It's broken again . . .

**TED** (*still angry*): Maybe it only works when my head's in it.

**DOUGAL:** Ted, maybe we should call a plumber.

**TED:** No, no, there's no need to get them involved. It's just a tiny, simple thing. Anyway . . . I'd be a little embarrassed to tell them how I . . . broke it in the first place . . . you know . . . that I was trying to give it a more powerful flush.

**DOUGAL:** Well, Ted, I have to say, it was fine for me. It was a good powerful flush, I thought.

**TED:** Yes, but you know . . . I'm thinking

more about Jack. When he's involved you want to get that stuff away as (*He thrusts his arm forward.*) . . . as *fast* and as . . . as *hard* as possible. Best thing would be for us to flush here, and then have it pop out somewhere in Sierra Leone.

**DOUGAL:** You're right there, Ted.

**TED:** Oh, wait now . . . wait now . . . aha, aha, aha, aha, aha, aha . . .

*He reaches into the cistern and fumbles about. He finally emerges with a bottle of Jack Daniels.*

**TED:** I thought Jack might have stashed something in here.

*He reaches down and pulls out another, and another.*

**TED:** Right! Try it now.

*Dougal flushes. It makes an incredibly loud flushing sound, so loud that Dougal and Ted would not be able to talk over it if they tried. They give each other a high five.*

SCENE 2 EXT./DAY 1
SET: PAROCHIAL HOUSE GATE
*We see a drain just outside the gate. A jet of water shoots out of it and goes about twenty feet into the air.*

SCENE 3 INT./DAY 1
SET: PAROCHIAL HOUSE
*Jack is reading a book. We see that it is called simply 'Girls'. There are a few pictures on the cover of girls circa 1960. They look like models who would adorn the cover of knitting magazines.*

JACK (*to himself*): Girls . . .

*Dougal comes in. Ted follows, a towel tied around his head like a turban. He is looking at a letter.*

TED: Oh, God . . . Bloody hell . . . tsk . . .

DOUGAL: Good news, Ted?

TED: No, very, very bad news. It's The Holy Stone of Clonrichert. They're making it a Class Two relic.

DOUGAL: Oh, great!

TED: There's nothing great about it, Dougal. It means they'll be sending a few bishops over to do a ceremony. And you know what they're like. We'll have to be on our best behaviour. It must be even holier than we thought. It might have something to do with that fella from England last year. He touched it and he grew a beard.

DOUGAL: Wow, that's weird. That'd be nearly enough to upgrade it to a Class One.

TED: A Class One is rare enough, Dougal. That's bringing people back to life, and time travel and cloning dinosaurs. Very rare . . .

DOUGAL: But . . . there must be millions of relics all over the world. How do they know which ones to do?

TED: Oh, there's all these things they have to think about . . . The history of the relic, how the publicity will affect the Church. All sorts of considerations would go into making a decision like that.

SCENE 4 INT./DAY 2
SET: A ROOM SOMEWHERE
*Cut to reveal a plush library-like room. Two priests are in the room. One is smoking a cigarette and reading a magazine. The other is at a computer. He hits a button and looks up.*

PRIEST 1: How about . . . The Holy Stone of Clonrichert?

PRIEST 2 (*doesn't look up from the magazine*): Whatever.

SCENE 5 INT./DAY 2
SET: PAROCHIAL HOUSE
*Ted looks glum.*

DOUGAL: Ah, come on, Ted, cheer up. It may never happen.

TED: Well . . . it is happening. They're definitely coming.

DOUGAL: Oh, right. Ah, well, who cares anyway. They come in, they strip the wallpaper down, fumigate the place and they're gone. What's so bad about that?

TED: Dougal . . . they're *bishops*.

DOUGAL: . . . Ohhh, right . . . yes, yes.

TED: Dougal, what is this confusion you have with bishops? Are you *absolutely* sure you know what bishops actually do? *Nothing* to do with fumigating houses or anything like that. Have you got that?

DOUGAL: Got it! Come on, Ted, let's play a game and get your mind off it. (*He holds up two boxes.*) Chess or Buckaroo?

TED: Eh . . .

DOUGAL: Actually, I wouldn't mind a game of the old chess today.

TED: Really?

DOUGAL: No, only joking, Ted! Buckaroo of course. But only if you're ready for another thrashing!

TED: You've never actually beaten me, Dougal.

DOUGAL: Oh, right . . .

*We see Jack on all fours, sticking his head into the*

*fire to get a light.*

**TED:** Ah, Buckaroo! The Sport of Kings! I suppose it won't be so bad, really. The bishops will have a look around, see that we're just a normal, everyday parish and go away. Nothing to worry about at all.

*Ted notices Jack, who turns from the fireplace with the now-lit cigarette in his mouth. Also, his hair is smoking and his face is reddened and blackened. He sits down and calmly continues smoking his fag. Ted absently puts a final object on to the toy donkey. It 'buckaroos', sending little plastic bits everywhere.*

SCENE 6 INT./NIGHT 2
SET: TED AND DOUGAL'S BEDROOM
*Dougal is in bed. He wears a T-shirt with 'It's a priest thing. You wouldn't understand' on it. Ted is in bed, reading an official-looking letter.*

**TED:** So, the ceremony's on Thursday, and they'll be arriving tomorrow. (*He puts the letter away.*) Now, Dougal, this is crucial. Listen to me, all right?

**DOUGAL:** Right, Ted.

**TED:** These bishops are very important. I'll try and stay around you all the time, just in case. So I can stop you saying anything that you shouldn't say to them.

**DOUGAL:** Like what?

**TED:** Well, something like what you said to Bishop Linsey when he asked where I was when Kennedy was shot.

**DOUGAL:** Oh, yeah . . .

**TED:** I mean, you overreacted slightly there . . . That's just a question people *ask*. He wasn't accusing me of *anything*. And, of course, there's Jack.

**DOUGAL:** Couldn't we hide him somewhere for a couple of days?

**TED:** No. They'd hear him shoutin' 'girls'.

**DOUGAL:** Maybe we could train Jack to say something apart from 'drink' or 'feck' or 'girls'. Like, remember the dog on *That's Life* a few years back?

**TED:** Dougal, Father Jack may be bad, but he isn't a *dog* . . .

*We hear a scratching from somewhere outside.*

**TED:** There he is now. I think he wants to go outside.

*Ted gets up and goes to the door. Then he pauses.*

**TED:** Wait though . . . maybe we *could* . . . teach him to say one or two things, nothing too specific, some all-purpose sentences like . . . 'That would be an ecumenical matter.' Yes, . . . I can't think of any religious question that couldn't be answered by saying that. It's what I always say when people ask *me* questions. That's the great thing about Catholicism. It's very vague and no one really knows what it's about. I think this might work, Dougal. Yes, it will work! I know it will!

**DOUGAL:** It won't work, will it, Ted?

**TED:** It won't, no, but we've got to *try!**

SCENE 7 INT./DAY 3
SET: PAROCHIAL HOUSE
*Jack sits in his chair, looking his usual self. Ted goes over to the table, picks up a large card and returns, speaking to Jack as he does so.*

**TED:** Right, Father . . . we're going to have a little elocution lesson.

**JACK:** Drink!

**TED:** Now, come on, Father. You can't be saying 'drink' all the time when the bishops are here.

**JACK:** Feck!

**TED:** No, you can't say that either, Father.

**JACK:** Girls!

**TED:** Look, Father, go back to 'drink' for the moment.

**JACK:** Drink!

**TED:** Right. I want you to have a look at this.

*Ted holds up the large card. It has the following written on it in felt-tip ink:*

1. That would be an ecumenical matter.

*In the final version we inserted a scene where a blind-folded knife-thrower who is throwing knives at Larry Duff is distracted by Larry's mobile phone ringing.

*2. Yes.*

*He shows it to Jack and points at the first word of number 1.*

**TED:** Right, Father, have a go at the first one here. 'That . . .'

**JACK:** Drink!

**TED:** No, no . . . 'That' . . .

**JACK:** Drink!

**TED:** No, try and concentrate, Father. 'That . . .'

**JACK:** Drink!

**TED:** That . . .

**JACK:** Drink!

**TED:** That . . .

**JACK:** Drink!

**TED:** That . . .

**JACK:** Drink!

**TED:** That . . .

**JACK:** Drink!

**TED:** That . . .

**JACK:** Drink!

**TED:** That . . .

**JACK:** Drink!

**TED:** Father, now, come on, I know you can do it. There'll be a little drink in it for you if you can do it.

**JACK:** Drink?

**TED:** Yes, I promise, Father. So . . . try again. 'That . . .'

*Jack moves his mouth as if to say 'That'. He puts his tongue to his top teeth and tries to get the sound out.*

**JACK:** Th . . . th . . . thhhhhhhh . . . thhhhhhhhdrink!

**TED:** Come on, Father! You almost got it there!

**JACK:** Thhhhhhhhh . . . thhhhhhhhhhh . . . thhhhhhhhhh . . . THAT!

**TED:** Great!

**JACK:** THAT!

**TED:** Brilliant, Father, well done! OK, let's keep going here . . . 'That would . . .'

**JACK:** That . . . drink!

*Ted's look of happiness dissipates. He knocks over the easel.*

SCENE 8 INT./DAY 3
SET: BATHROOM
*Ted sticks his head around the door.*

**TED:** Mrs Doyle, you've left the cooker on.

*Cut to reveal Mrs Doyle giving Dougal a very soapy bath.*

**MRS DOYLE:** Oh, right, Father, I'll be there in a second.

*Ted leaves.*

SCENE 9 INT./DAY 3
SET: PAROCHIAL HOUSE
*We see a Clonrichert calendar on the wall. A date on it is circled in red, with 'Bishops!!!' scrawled beside it. Ted comes into the room. He walks over to the table and munches on a biscuit. Mrs Doyle comes into the room.*

**MRS DOYLE:** Right, Father, everything's

ready. There's a big vat of tea steaming away, and I've got the Ferrero Rochers arranged in a big triangular pile. Oh, God, Father, I'm so excited! Taking on three bishops all at once! Oh, I can't wait!

*Ted moves to another part of the room, but Mrs Doyle continues to talk to the space he last occupied.*

**MRS DOYLE:** I think this is going to be the finest moment of my career, Father. It's almost as if my whole life was leading up —

**TED:** Mrs Doyle . . .

*Mrs Doyle looks around in confusion.*

**TED:** Mrs Doyle, I'm over here.

*Mrs Doyle turns, but is still not looking in the right direction.*

**MRS DOYLE:** Oh, so you are, Father.

*Ted comes up close to her.*

**TED:** Mrs Doyle —

**MRS DOYLE:** Aiiiee!!

**TED:** Mrs Doyle, have you your contacts in?

**MRS DOYLE:** Tsk, no. A dog ran off with them. I thought I'd get away with it but I suppose I'll have to wear the glasses. Ah, I don't like wearing them, Father. I always think they make me look like a frustrated old bag!

*Mrs Doyle fumbles in her handbag for her glasses.*

**TED:** Ha, ha, ha . . . aahhh . . . I can't imagine that, Mrs Doyle. I'd say they look fine on y. . . (*She puts them on and turns to Ted. They magnify her eyes hugely. She blinks and it looks like two trapdoors opening and shutting.*) Aaaaaaggghhhh!!!!!!

**MRS DOYLE:** God almighty! Are they that bad, Father?

**TED** (*recovering*): No . . . no, I was just thinking about a scary film I saw. They're fine, they really are.

*Ted looks at her queasily.*

**TED:** Great . . .

**MRS DOYLE:** Ah, that's much better. I'll just go and check on the tea.

*She moves out of shot. Ted flicks some dust off his shoulder. We hear Mrs Doyle's voice from out of shot.*

**MRS DOYLE:** Father? I have absolutely no idea where the door is.

*Cut to reveal that she has taken only one step away from Ted, and is facing the wrong way as she speaks.*

SCENE 10. INT./DAY 3
SET: PAROCHIAL HOUSE
*We see a clock on the wall that says three o'clock. Cut to the view of a windswept, barren road seen through a pair of binoculars. Cut to Dougal with binoculars looking through the window. He puts the binoculars down.*

**DOUGAL:** No sign of them yet, Ted.

*Cut to Ted.*

**TED** (*confused*): Dougal . . . Dougal, they're here.

*Cut to a wide shot of the room. We see three bishops. Two sit down but one, Bishop Facks, paces the room in a slightly threatening way. Ted is also in the room.*

**DOUGAL:** Oh, right, yeah. Sorry about that.

*The bishops are Bishop O'Neill, a serious, slightly boring bishop; Bishop Facks, an aggressive priest who emphasises every point by poking people in the chest and fidgeting with pens, etc; and Bishop Jordan, a nervous bishop with a severe heart condition.*

**TED:** Sorry, Bishop O'Neill. You were saying . . .

**O'NEILL:** Yes. Very simple ceremony. We'll just need a little incense.

**TED:** Incense . . . oh . . . I don't think . . . I think we're out of it. Dougal, have we any incense, do you know?

**DOUGAL** (*slightly confused*): There was a spider in the bath last night.

**TED:** No, *incense, incense!*

**DOUGAL:** Oh, right. No, I don't think so. (*Laughing slightly.*) Ha, ha, remember, Ted, remember what happened last week when we ran out of incense and got the Windowlene and . . .

*Ted coughs very loudly indeed until Dougal shuts up. Pause.*

O'NEILL: Well . . . I'm sure we can find some.

TED: Have you done much upgrading around the country recently?

FACKS: We recently elevated a mushroom field in Cavan to a Class Three.

TED: Great.

O'NEILL: Our work takes us all over the country.

JORDAN: We're trying to organise a large meeting at the end of the year where all ranks of the clergy can discuss their views with representatives of the lay community . . .

*We see Dougal and Ted, their attention drifting.*

JORDAN: What do you think, Father Crilly?

*Ted is looking around, not paying attention. He notices everyone looking at him.*

TED: Sorry, what?

FACKS: Do you think a close relationship between the lay community on this particular matter is desirable? Or should a certain distance be maintained?

TED: Eh, yeah . . . good question. Well, you know, involve the lay community, but keep them at a distance.

FACKS: How much of a distance?

*Pause.*

TED: . . . Couple of miles?

*Mrs Doyle enters the room, her head up, looking around in confusion. She carries a tray.*

MRS DOYLE: Here we are, now, tea for everyone!

*She walks straight through the room and out through the other door. Pause.**

O'NEILL: I'm interested in your views on this matter, Father Crilly . . . Do you think you could draw up a paper?**

TED: What?*

JORDAN: Maybe a ten-page summary of your ideas?**

*Through the window we see Mrs Doyle. in the front garden with her tray, looking around in confusion.**

TED: Well, I eh . . .*

FACKS: Is there a problem?**

TED: Well, it's just that, you know, no one told me that I'd have to do any work.**

JORDAN: Ha, ha. But that would be splendid, if you could do that for us.**

TED (*very unhappy*): All right.**

JORDAN: Sorry?**

TED: I said, *yes.**

*Facks touches the 'buckaroo' and it jumps up suddenly.*

JORDAN (*jumps slightly*): Oooh!

TED (*confused*): Are you all right, Your Grace?

JORDAN: Yes, I . . . I had a minor heart attack last year so I have to take it easy. I got a bit of a fright there.

TED: Oh . . . right . . .

JORDAN: It's not a problem. Just . . . give us a bit of a warning if you're going to do anything sudden —

*Dougal suddenly jumps in front of Jordan with his hands up.*

DOUGAL: Aaaaaaaarrrggghhh!!!!

JORDAN: Aaahhh!!!

TED: Dougal! What are you doing?!

DOUGAL: Sorry, Ted. I just remembered *Aliens* is on after the News.

TED: For God's sake, Dougal! I'm terribly sorry, Bishop Jordan.

*O'Neill tends to Jordan, who is trying to get his breath back. Ted leads Dougal away.*

TED: Did you not hear what he was saying about his heart?

DOUGAL: It's just . . . it's the director's cut. (*To everyone.*) C'mon, everyone. Let's all have a big lads' night in!

---

*We deleted these lines from the final version.

**TED:** Dougal, just – just sit down. (*To Jordan.*) A *heart attack*. That's a rare enough thing, I'd say.

**O'NEILL:** There were certainly a lot of prayers said for Bishop Jordan around the country.

*O'Neill prattles on. As he does so, Dougal leans over to Ted.*

**DOUGAL:** I don't know why we can't look at *Aliens*.

**TED** (*fierce whisper*)**:** Dougal! Bishop O'Neill is speaking . . .

**DOUGAL:** But they'd love it, Ted!

**TED:** Dougal, we're not watching *Aliens*!!!

**END OF PART ONE**

\* \* \*

**PART TWO**

SCENE 11 INT./DAY 3
SET: PAROCHIAL HOUSE

**FACKS** (*contemptuously regarding a magazine*)**:** I think our priority must be to fight back against the anti-clerical bias in the media. (*He pokes Ted.*) Do you know what I mean, Father? Do you see what I'm getting at?

**TED:** Yes, yes . . .

*Mrs Doyle enters with her tray full of Ferrero Rochers.*

TED: Ferrero Rocher?

O'NEILL: Aha! I think you are spoiling us, Father Ted!

*Ted gives Mrs Doyle a signal but she doesn't see it.*

TED (*sighs*): Mrs Doyle . . .

MRS DOYLE: Oh, right . . .

*Mrs Doyle walks further into the room unsteadily. She holds the sweets just out of reach of Bishop Jordan. He reaches over with a grunt and takes one. She navigates her way around the rest of the room in much the same way, always holding the sweets out too far for anyone to reach.*

TED: Sorry about that. You were saying . . .?

FACKS (*stabbing his shoulder with his index finger*): Ah, yes . . . I was saying we should fight back against the media. We have to make our voice heard!

JORDAN: Where is Father Hackett?

FACKS: Would that be Father Jack Hackett?

TED: Eh, yes . . .

FACKS: A friend of mine, Father Cave, was taught by him in Saint Colm's and still has very vivid memories of him.

SCENE 12. INT./DAY X*
SET: AN OFFICE
*A priest is looking at himself in the mirror. We see there are loads of explosives tied to his chest. He closes his jacket over them, picks up a gun and walks out. We see loads of photographs of Jack all over the wall. After a moment, we hear an explosion.*

SCENE 13. INT./DAY 3
SET: PAROCHIAL HOUSE
*Ted stands up.*

TED: Mrs Doyle, could you get Father Hackett for us, please?

MRS DOYLE: Certainly, Father.

JORDAN: I must say, Mrs Doyle, they keep you on your feet. My housekeeper isn't the best, I'm afraid. Sometimes I think that it's me

*We deleted this scene from the final version.

that should be making the tea for her!

*Mrs Doyle laughs heartily. Everyone else laughs along. However, Mrs Doyle has now become hysterical.*

MRS DOYLE: Ha . . . ha . . . ha . . . making the tea for her . . . ha, ha, ha, ha . . .

TED: Mrs Doyle . . .

MRS DOYLE: Ha . . . ha . . . ha . . . HA, HA, HA, HA . . .

TED: Ah, Mrs Doyle . . .

MRS DOYLE: HA, HA, HA . . . Making the tea for her . . .HA, HA, HA, HA, HA!!!

*Ted nods at Dougal. They grab the still-laughing Mrs Doyle and carry her out of the room. Ted comes back in.*

TED: Sorry about that! Ah, here's Father Hackett now . . .

*After a second a completely transformed Jack enters; he is dressed relatively neatly – although his clothes seem 'off' somehow, perhaps a size too small? His hair is Brylcreemed so that it's very slick, and he smiles in a strange, forced way.*

TED: He was very much looking forward to your visit, weren't you, Father?

JACK (*with a strange look at Ted*): Yes!

TED: Ah, ha. Well, this is Bishop O'Neill . . . (*The bishop makes a move forward.*) Don't get up, Bishop . . .

JACK: *Yes!*

TED: This is Bishop Jordan . . .

JACK: *Yes!*

TED: . . . and this is Bishop Facks . . .

JACK: *Yes!*

JORDAN: They're looking after you, then, Father?

*Jack looks at Ted, who gives an imperceptible nod.*

JACK: That would be an ecumenical m —

*Ted interrupts him with a halting, coughing noise.*

*Pause.*

JACK: *Yes!*

O'NEILL: I was just saying, Father, how I'm

looking forward to discussing the social effects of some of the Church's thinking as regarding issues of personal morality.

*Jack steals a quick look at Ted.*

**TED** (*under his breath*): Ecumenical . . .

**JACK** (*immediately*): That would be an ecumenical matter.

**O'NEILL:** Yes, I . . . I suppose it would. Good point, Father.

**JACK:** *Yes!*

**FACKS:** That's what we need, a more positive attitude like Father Hackett's.

**TED:** What?

**O'NEILL:** I agree. I can see Father Hackett making a valuable contribution over the next few days.

**TED:** Oh, God . . .

*Ted gives a fake smile. Dougal seems happy. Jack looks uncertain, but still with his fixed smile.*

**JACK:** *Yes!*

SCENE 14. INT./NIGHT 3*
SET: TED AND DOUGAL'S BEDROOM
*Ted is sitting with a laptop computer. He is examining a bruise on his arm.*

**TED:** God almighty! Bishop Facks is a big poking fan, isn't he?

**DOUGAL** (*examining a bruise of his own*): Oh, you're right there, Ted.

**TED:** What the hell am I going to write about, Dougal? What do I know about the relationship between the clergy and the lay community? And tomorrow . . . Oh, God . . . I don't know how long Jack can keep it up. I had to feed him another *gigantic* bottle of whiskey as a reward . . . Anyway . . . 'The lay people and the clergy' . . . Oh, God, this is turning into a nightmare.

**DOUGAL:** 'Lay people' . . . who are they again?

**TED:** People who aren't the clergy.

**TED:** Oh, right, yeah. Like Tom Hanks.

**TED:** He'd be one, yeah.

**DOUGAL:** Hitler . . . Ruby Wax, Denzel Washington . . .

**TED:** Yes . . .

**DOUGAL:** Bjork . . .

**TED:** . . . Yeah, the thing is, Dougal, he doesn't want me to *name* everyone who's not actually a member of the clergy.

**DOUGAL:** No?

**TED:** No. That'd take a hundred million years. No, I have to think of something of interest to say about them. God, this is so hard. And on top of all this we've got the Mrs Doyle problem.

**DOUGAL:** God, yeah. Where do you think she got to?

*Ted shrugs.*

SCENE 15. EXT./NIGHT 3*
SET: A FIELD
*We see a cow and hear Mrs Doyle offscreen.*

**MRS DOYLE:** Ah, go on, Father, have a cup. Will you not have a little cup? Just a drop?

*We see Mrs Doyle standing beside the cow, the tea tray in her hands.*

SCENE 16. INT./NIGHT 3*
SET: TED AND DOUGAL'S BEDROOM
*Ted is still frowning at the computer. Suddenly, inspiration strikes.*

**TED:** Yes. Yes. *Yes!* That's it! I'll start by describing how economic necessity has forced people to pay more attention to the day-to-day pressures of life at the expense of their spiritual health. If I cross reference that with the experiences of the clergy in the mid Fifties, I think gradually a coherent picture of where the Catholic religion is heading will emerge! Yes! It's so simple! And I tell you, Dougal, I'm not moving from this spot until I've finished it, even if it takes me all night.

*He starts typing wildly. Dougal looks impressed.*

*We deleted this scene from the final version.

SCENE 17. INT./DAY 4*
SET: PAROCHIAL HOUSE
*Ted is talking to Bishop Jordan.*

**JORDAN:** Yess . . . well, thanks very much for doing that report.

**TED:** Well, I enjoyed doing it.

**JORDAN:** There's just one thing, Father. You seem to have just done a big list of people who aren't priests.

**TED:** That's right, yes.

**JORDAN:** I was really hoping more for an examination of the relationship between lay people and the clergy.

**TED:** Were you? Oh, no! I thought you just wanted the list. Still, never mind. If you're ever compiling a list of people who aren't priests, it could come in very handy.

*Jordan nods unenthusiastically and moves off. Dougal comes up to Ted.*

**DOUGAL:** That other idea not work out, Ted?

**TED:** Nope.

_____

*We deleted this scene from the final version.

SCENE 18. EXT./DAY 4
SET: FIELD
*We hear O'Neill's voice.*

**O'NEILL:** Heavenly Father, hear our prayer . . .

*As we hear these words, we see a sign that reads 'The Holy Stone of Clonrichert – Admission £20.00. Students and O.A.P.'s £19.00'.*

*Cut to O'Neill blessing the rock. The other bishops stand beside him. Ted, Dougal and Jack are also present. Everyone wears ceremonial vestments, although Ted's, Dougal's and Jack's are very basic.*

**O'NEILL:** . . . We pray that this rock be upgraded to a Class Two relic . . . (*Pull back to reveal the rock for the first time. It is tiny, about the size of a fist, but is at waist level on a plinth.*) . . . and by the grace of God bring healing to all who pass within a radius of two and a half to three feet of it, at Your discretion. And may all who are healed in such a way give glory to you, Our Lord, through your earthly form of the Class Two relic.

**EVERYONE:** Amen

**DOUGAL:** Eamon.

*Silently O'Neill bows his head and steps back. He blesses himself.*

**O'NEILL:** Right!

*The priests relax and mingle.*

**TED:** Great stuff. Right, will we head off?

**FACKS:** I'll stay here and have a little chat with Father Hackett.

*Jack's eyes widen, the rest of his face still frozen.*

**TED:** Oh. That's probably not a good idea. Father Hackett is very tired.

**FACKS:** Oh, nonsense. You'll stay and have a chat, won't you, Father?

**JACK:** *Yes!*

**TED:** No, Father. You're very tired, aren't you?

**JACK:** That would be an ecumenical matter!

*Facks looks puzzled. Jordan butts in and takes Ted by the arm.*

**JORDAN:** Come on, Father . . .

*A nervous Ted is led away by Jordan. Facks and Jack are alone.*

**FACKS:** Well, here it is. Fantastic, isn't it?

**JACK:** *Yes!*

**FACKS:** I suppose a lot of people would think it old-fashioned, this business of blessing relics . . . but we have to fight back against that kind of cynicism, Father. These days, you can't open a newspaper without seeing some trendy anti-clerical article written by some bearded Leftie.

**JACK:** *Yes!*

**FACKS:** What, Father?

**JACK** (*thinks*)**:** That would be an ecumenical matter.

**FACKS:** Of, course, Father. But we should act now, before it's too late.

*He looks away from Jack, out to sea.*

**FACKS:** All this materialism. People nowadays seem obsessed with earthly, unspiritual pleasures.

*Jack notices that the bishop's back is turned away. He reaches into his sleeve and extracts a clear, plastic tube. He sucks at the tube and some whiskey shoots up into his mouth. His eyes cross as he drinks it. He quickly moves it back up his sleeve. The Bishop turns around.*

**JACK:** Temptation . . . ecumenical matter . . . yes!!!

**FACKS:** How right you are, Father. How right you are . . .

*As he says this, he taps Jack once on the shoulder with his index finger. Jack starts a little bit. He doesn't like that at all.*

SCENE 19. EXT./DAY 4
SET: COUNTRY ROAD
*Dougal and O'Neill are in front, Ted and Jordan about ten feet behind.*

**O'NEILL:** So, Father, *do you* ever have any doubts about the religious life? Is your faith ever tested?

**DOUGAL:** Tested?

**O'NEILL:** Yes. Anything you've been worried about, any doubts you've been having about any aspects of faith, anything like that?

**DOUGAL:** Well, yes. You know the way God made us all, right? And he's looking at us from heaven and everything . . .

**O'NEILL:** Mmm, mmm . . .

**DOUGAL:** . . . And then his Son came down and saved everyone and all that . . .

**O'NEILL:** Yes.

**DOUGAL:** . . . And when we die we're all going to go to heaven?

**O'NEILL:** Yes, what about it?

**DOUGAL:** That's the bit I have trouble believing in.

*Over to Ted and Jordan. They approach the driveway of the house. Ted looks nervously ahead of him at Dougal and O'Neill.*

**JORDAN:** When you come face to face with death, it makes you think about things. I saw that film recently – *Apollo 13* – and it reminded me of my own brush with death. Do you know what I mean?

**TED:** You mean . . . you were in space when you had your heart attack? I didn't . . .

**JORDAN:** No. How could I be in space?

**TED:** I don't know . . . sorry. No, I suppose not.

**JORDAN:** No, I meant I know what it's like to be close to death.

**TED:** I'm sure you do. I've never been close to death myself, thank God, but a lot of my relatives are dead. Are you coming in?

**JORDAN:** I'll be in in a second. It is very bracing around here, isn't it?

**TED:** Bracing. Yes, actually I need to use the old W.C., so I'll go on . . .

**JORDAN:** Yes, you do that. I'll take the air. I feel very close to nature these days.

**TED:** Oh, yes, well you're in the right place if you want to be close to nature. It's all over the shop around here. Right, I'll see you soon . . .

*Ted goes to the house. Jordan takes a deep breath and exhales.*

SCENE 20. EXT./DAY 4
SET: DOOR OF THE HOUSE
*Dougal unlocks the door.*

**DOUGAL:** . . . So then, if God has existed forever, what did he do with all that time before he made the earth and everything? You know?

**O'NEILL:** Well, we all have doubts.

**DOUGAL:** And what about when you weren't allowed to eat meat on Fridays? How come that's all right now, but it wasn't then? Did people who ate meat on Friday then go to Hell or what? It's mad.

*Cut to a very thoughtful bishop. Ted comes up.*

**TED:** He's not bothering you, is he?

**O'NEILL:** No . . . no, it's . . . fascinating.

**TED:** Well, just call me if you need help. Now, I just need to . . . 'see a man about a dog'.

*He flashes a look at Dougal and then goes up the stairs.*

SCENE 21 EXT./DAY 4*
SET: COUNTRY ROAD
*Facks is talking to Jack. He is leaning over him and poking him repeatedly in the shoulder. Jack looks from him to the poking finger, his expression a mixture of slight pain, irritation and anger.*

**FACKS:** But do you see what I mean, Father? Do you see what I mean? Do you see what I'm getting at?

*Jack's face is now red with anger. He clenches his teeth and raises his hand. Suddenly, Facks stops poking him. He turns around.*

SCENE 22 INT./DAY 4*
SET: BATHROOM
*We see Ted standing up, buttoning his trousers.*

SCENE 23 EXT./DAY 4
SET: DRIVEWAY
*We see Jordan walking outside. He stands over the grate that we saw the water shooting from earlier, covering it with his cassock. He looks around.*

*We deleted this scene from the final version.

**JORDAN** (*deep breath*): Ahhhhh . . .

SCENE 24 INT./DAY 4
SET: BATHROOM
*Ted finishes washing his hands. He goes to the door, remembers something, then goes back and flushes the toilet.*

SCENE 25 EXT./DAY 4
SET: DRIVEWAY
*There is a strange gurgling from below. Jordan's cassock starts to billow slightly. Suddenly, we hear a great rush of water shooting up. The cassock billows up around him as he tries to keep it down. The water roars in every direction. Close-up on his face.*

**JORDAN:** Aaaaaaaarrrrrgggggghhhhh!!!!!!

*He clasps his chest and keels over. The water gradually eases down and out of sight.*

SCENE 26 INT./DAY 4
SET: PAROCHIAL HOUSE
*We see a Marilyn Monroe poster on the wall. It is the still from 'The Seven Year Itch' that shows her skirt billowing up. Cut to Dougal and O'Neill entering. They bump into Ted as he is about to go outside to join Jordan.*

**TED:** Ah, there you are. I hope you had a nice chat.

**DOUGAL:** It was great.

**O'NEILL:** I think I reached some very interesting conclusions.

**TED:** Good. What exactly?

**O'NEILL:** Well, it's nonsense, isn't it?

**TED:** Sorry? What is?

**O'NEILL:** Religion.

**TED:** Eh . . .

**O'NEILL:** I've been struggling with my conscience for some time. But Father McGuire clarified the whole thing for me, really. God, Heaven and Hell . . . it's all a load of rubbish. Only a child could believe it, really. It's scarcely more credible than Santa Claus or the tooth fairy.

**TED:** Dougal! What have you been up to?

*An innocent-looking Dougal shrugs. Suddenly,*

*there is a scream from outside. Mrs Doyle runs in and addresses the air beside the three men.*

**MRS DOYLE:** Quick! It's Bishop Jordan! I think he's dead!

*She runs outside, followed by the three men, feeling her way as she goes.*

SCENE 27 EXT./DAY 4
SET: DRIVEWAY
*Mrs Doyle turns the corner and points to the ground.*

**MRS DOYLE** (*pointing*): There! Oh, dear Lord, what's happened to him?

*The three look to where she is pointing. Cut and we see what they are looking at. It is a dustbin on its side.*

**TED:** Mrs Doyle . . .that's a dustbin.

**MRS DOYLE:** What? Oh, I mean . . . there!

*She turns and points. We see the bishop on the ground behind them. Ted and Dougal turn and look at each other.*

**O'NEILL:** God almighty! This is terrible! Where's Bishop Facks?

SCENE 28 EXT./DAY 4
SET: FIELD
*Jack is calming down slightly.*

**FACKS:** We have to straighten out the media. That's the important thing, Father. And we have to do it . . .

*He turns around and raises his finger in the air. Close-up on the finger. Close-up of a primed, ready-for-action Jack. Facks brings his finger down and pokes Jack severely in the shoulder with it.*

**FACKS:** Now!

*Jack's eyes widen in pure rage.*

**JACK** (*Standing, arms raised to either side.*): Aaaaaaarrrrrrrrrrrgggggghhhhhhhh!!!

*Facks cowers on the ground. Jack grabs The Holy Stone in rage.*

SCENE 29 EXT./DAY 4
SET: FRONT DOOR OF PAROCHIAL HOUSE
*Ted and Dougal stand at the doorway. Out comes*

*O'Neill, in civvies. He also has a backpack slung over his shoulder. He grabs Dougal's hand and shakes it warmly.*

**O'NEILL:** Dougal. Thank you.

**DOUGAL** (*blank*): Ah, you're welcome, Bishop.

**O'NEILL:** No, no, Eddie.

**TED:** Are you sure you won't reconsider your decision —

**O'NEILL:** No. It's too late anyway. I'm off to India for two months with a few friends. Ah, there they are . . .

*He runs off. Cut to see a brightly coloured van. The side door opens and three hippie-type girls wave him in. O'Neill steps inside, waves, and then slides the door closed. Next out is Facks. As he walks haltingly past them, we see that he is severely bow-legged.*

**TED:** See you again, then! (*Embarrassed.*) Will it . . . will it still be a Class Two when they remove it?

*Facks just looks at him. He walks off towards an ambulance.*

**DOUGAL:** Bye!

*A coffin is next. Ted and Dougal go quiet. It is wheeled out by two men.*

**TED** (*touches coffin*): Eh . . . God bless you . . .

*The ambulance, the hearse and the van all drive away. Ted and Dougal close the door.*

SCENE 30. INT./DAY 4
SET: PAROCHIAL HOUSE
*Ted and Dougal walk into the room. They don't say anything. Ted looks at Dougal. Pause.*

**TED:** Went pretty well, I thought.

**THE END**

# the old grey whistle theft

**ARTHUR:** The original idea behind this episode was to give Dougal a friend. The second idea was to have law and order breaking down, and the two elements came together – not easily, but because they had to. It was tough to write and we felt that that might come across. Funnily enough, however, it turned out to be one of the best-loved episodes in this series.

It was nice to give Dougal a friend if only to get him out of the usual partnership with Ted, where he exists usually to misunderstand things, ask silly questions, come to mistaken conclusions and so on. This gave him an extra dimension, a bit of life outside Ted. We were glad to do this because it was sometimes easy to take Ardal for granted. He spent the first series feeling slightly insecure, I think, because people weren't giving him any acting notes. The truth was, we didn't need to. Whenever he widened his eyes and opened his mouth slightly, he simply became Dougal; everything he said sounded like Dougal and everything sounded funny. His line readings were invariably perfect, partly because of this quality but also because he shared our sense of humour. The character of Dougal was very delicate as he had the potential to be very annoying. As far as that goes, casting Ardal was the best decision we ever made.

**GRAHAM:** This was a big ol' son of a bitch to write. It went through about seven drafts and to us, never seemed to get any better. Somehow, despite our worries, a combination of elements – Joe Rooney as Damo, the illogical but funny ending, the image of Mrs Doyle standing in the darkness – made people forgive the plot, which was even more inconsequential than usual. (Although how this episode could be more inconsequential than anything that had gone before or after is probably only evident to Arthur and I.)

Mr Benson came in part from the penchant Irish parents have for using the phrase, 'The Man'. Whenever children are being loud or generally misbehaving in a restaurant or any other public place, you'll hear Irish parents scaring their children by pointing to the waiter/park keeper/whoever and saying, 'Here comes The Man! You've made The Man angry!' Mr Benson is the ultimate manifestation of 'The Man'.

**PART ONE**

SCENE 1 INT./DAY 1

SET: PAROCHIAL HOUSE

*Ted and Dougal are standing beside a picnic basket, which is on the table. Ted is putting various snacks into the basket. Jack is asleep in another corner of the room.*

**TED:** . . . So he was already having an affair with the sister, and this was when his wife was seriously ill in hospital . . .

**DOUGAL:** Wow.

**TED:** Incredible, isn't it? But then, of course, who does he get pregnant but the babysitter, so he doesn't know whether to stay with the wife, or the sister, or run off with the babysitter.

**DOUGAL** (*beat*): When's his next confession?

**TED:** Tuesday. I'll keep you posted. (*Pause. Dougal goes to the basket. Ted looks at a list.*) Right! Let's see! Jam . . .

**DOUGAL:** Check . . .

**TED:** Pepperoni . . .

**DOUGAL:** Check . . .

**TED:** Mustard . . .

**DOUGAL:** Check . . .

**TED:** Bread . . .

**DOUGAL:** Check . . .

**TED:** Great. We're all packed then.

**DOUGAL:** No, no . . . (*He reaches into the*

basket and takes out a piece of paper.*) They're all on this list.

**TED:** Right, so we both made lists . . . No problem. I'm sure I put them all in anyway. (*He smiles.*) I must say, I'm really looking forward to this.

**DOUGAL:** Ah, me too, Ted. It's good to take a day off every now and again. It shouldn't be just work, work, work, should it?

**TED:** Yes. It's not as if everyone's going to join some mad religious cult just because we go on a picnic for a few hours.

**DOUGAL:** God, Ted, I heard about those cults. Everyone dressing in black and saying that Our Lord's going to come back and judge us all.

**TED:** No . . . Dougal, that would be us, now. You're talking about Catholicism, there.

*Mrs Doyle enters. She carries two heavy canvas shopping bags.*

**MRS DOYLE:** Right. Here's the sandwiches, Father. The rest are in the hall.

**TED:** Great.

**MRS DOYLE:** I hope you like them, Father.

**TED:** Oh, I'm sure I will. I love an old sandwich from time to time. Doesn't matter what flavour it is as long as it's not egg. (*Mrs Doyle's smile freezes almost imperceptibly. She looks at Ted but her eyes glaze over slightly.*) . . . 'Cause you know how much I hate egg. Oh, God, even the smell of it brings me out in a terrible rash. I tell you I wouldn't eat an egg sandwich if you paid me – they're just horrible stinking things. As I've told you earlier, anything but egg, Mrs Doyle, and how I wanted anything at all except egg. They're egg, aren't they, Mrs Doyle?

**MRS DOYLE:** Yes.

**TED:** Great.

**DOUGAL:** I'll eat them, Mrs Doyle. I love egg. Sometimes I think I like egg so much that one day I'll turn into a big, giant egg.

**TED:** Oh, well, never mind. I'll just have a few Pepperoni. Right! Dougal! You ready?

**DOUGAL:** Ready as I'll ever be, Ted! I don't

think I've ever looked forward to something as much as I've looked forward to this picnic.

**TED:** OK, so!

**DOUGAL:** Oh, wait, I just remembered. I can't go.

**TED:** What? Why not? . . .

*The doorbell rings. Dougal goes 'Oh!' and starts putting his coat on. Ted leaves the room.*

SCENE 2 EXT./DAY 1
SET: PAROCHIAL HOUSE
*Ted answers the door. Standing outside is a young priest of Dougal's age. He has a slightly sulky demeanour.*

**PRIEST:** How'ya. Is Dougal in?

*Dougal, carrying a football, rushes up behind Ted and runs past him. The young priest and Dougal immediately run off, Dougal bouncing the football along the ground. They chatter excitedly to each other as they disappear. Ted looks after them, puzzled. He is about to go back inside when he hears a voice.*

**VOICE:** Hello, Father!

*Ted turns to see the local policeman, Sergeant Hodgins, standing on the other side of the wall.*

**TED:** Ah, hello, Sergeant.

**HODGINS:** Hello, Father. Just doing the rounds.

**TED:** On the trail of some crazed murderer, no doubt!

**HODGINS:** What was that?

**TED:** Sorry?

**HODGINS:** Something about a crazed murderer? Where? When did this happen?

**TED:** No, I was only joking.

*Pause.*

**HODGINS:** Oh, right. Well, if you ever hear anything about a crazed murderer on the loose, report it. That'd give me somethin' to do, you know.

**TED:** Yes.

**HODGINS:** Very quiet here, you know. Not much crime.

**TED:** It is very quiet, all right.

**HODGINS:** So, you know, if you hear anything . . . doesn't have to be a murder or a kidnapping, you know. Anything. A disappearance! That'd be great! Lord Lucan! Anyway . . . anything at all . . . a car wrongly parked, anything. Give me a call. By the way, that licence up to date on your car?

**TED:** Eh, it is yes.

**HODGINS** (*very disappointed*)**:** Yeah, thought it might be.

**TED:** Bye, Sergeant.

*Ted closes the door. Hodgins sighs and looks round, totally bored.*

SCENE 3 INT./DAY 1
SET: PAROCHIAL HOUSE
*Ted walks back into the living room. Mrs Doyle comes in.*

**MRS DOYLE:** Who was that young priest, Father?

**TED:** Hmmmm? Oh . . . I don't know . . .

**MRS DOYLE:** So Father McGuire's not going on the picnic.

**TED:** No. Never mind. I'm meeting Larry Duff and a few of the lads from Saint Colm's. I'd better give him a call, make sure they know where they're going.

SCENE 4 EXT./DAY 1
SET: ROADSIDE/ROADBLOCK
*We see some soldiers and policemen with machine guns beside a car at a roadblock. They point the guns at four priests who have their hands in the air. One of them is Larry Duff. He slowly moves his hands down to a telephone, checking it's OK with a soldier who has a gun trained on him.*

**LARRY:** Hello? Ah, hello, Ted!

**TED:** Larry. How are you?

**LARRY:** Ah, grand. Got a bit of a problem, though. We mightn't be able to make the picnic.

**TED:** Ah, God, Larry, why?

**LARRY:** You know Father Williams who was driving us over?

**TED:** Billy? What about him?

**LARRY:** Well, they found a big box of machine guns in his house.

**TED:** Really? God, I didn't think he'd be interested in that type of thing.

**LARRY:** Ah, yeah, you think you know someone. Anyway, there you go. Bye, Ted!

*He puts the telephone down. In the background a priest runs out of shot. One of the soldiers sees this and lets loose with machine-gun fire. Larry looks at the scene with a blank expression.*

SCENE 5 INT./DAY 1
SET: PAROCHIAL HOUSE
*Back to Ted.*

**TED:** Well. Just me, I suppose.

*He spots something and looks back at Jack. Then very gingerly he bends down and brings two bottles of wine into shot. He very quietly puts the two bottles into the basket. Jack stirs, and Ted freezes. Then he lets go of the bottles and picks up a third. He very gingerly places it in the basket. We hear an almost inaudible clink as one of the bottles touches another.*

**JACK** (*wakes suddenly*): Drink!!!

**TED:** Ah, it's not drink, Father. It's fizzy water.

*Jack gives him a very suspicious look.*

**JACK** (*thinks*): Jacobs Creek Chardonnay, 1991.

**TED:** No, I promise you, F— (*He looks at the bottle.*) My God – you can tell that just from the sound?

**JACK:** Drink!!! Drink!!! Drink!!!

**TED:** Well, I thought I might go on a little picnic, Father . . . on my own.

*Jack stares at him. We stay on his face as Ted speaks.*

**TED:** Outside. You wouldn't like it, Father. Honestly, you'd be happier here. You'd . . . there's . . . I . . . ah . . .

SCENE 6 EXT./DAY 1
SET: PICNIC AREA
*We see a sign that reads 'Picnic Area'. The picnic area is a wind-blasted, rocky, awful-looking place. Ted and Jack are directly under the sign, which is bending dangerously and creaking loudly in the wind. Jack is sitting in his wheelchair, watching Ted with interest. Ted is holding up a large picnic rug. The wind is howling, wrapping the rug around Ted's body. Jack just looks at him. The sign suddenly spins and hits Ted on the back of the head. Ted falls over, still wrapped in the blanket.*

**TED:** The flipping thing . . . Could you do something, Father?

*Jack stands up, walks over to Ted, bends down and picks up a packet of cigarettes lying beside Ted. He then walks back to his seat, lighting a fag, sits down and calmly observes Ted's tribulations. Ted finally struggles over the blanket and holds it down. He gets some rocks and, with enormous effort, places them on each corner of the rug. Then he lies there, breathing deeply.*

**TED** (*out of breath*): Right! There we go.

*He kneels down and takes out the bottles of wine. He puts them beside him, some distance away from Jack. He turns to the picnic basket and takes out some bread. When he turns back, we see that the three bottles of wine are overturned and empty. Ted looks at Jack, who is twiddling his thumbs innocently.*

SCENE 7 EXT./DAY 1
SET: FIELD
*Dougal, and his friend Father Damo Lennon, are sitting on an old stone wall. A large house is some distance in the background. Father Damo Lennon is smoking. Dougal has his hands in his pockets and is kicking the wall in a lackadaisical manner.*

**DAMO** (*offering Dougal a fag*): Do you want one?

**DOUGAL:** Ah, no, thanks, Father Lennon. (*Pause.*) What time is your tea ready?

**DAMO:** Frosty usually has it about six.

**DOUGAL:** Who?

**DAMO:** Frosty. Father Frosty.

**DOUGAL:** Oh, wow . . . Frosty! Brilliant!

**DAMO:** What do you call your fella?

**DOUGAL:** Who, Ted? Ah, no . . . Just Ted, but . . . it's the way I say it, you know.

**DAMO:** He's an awful eejit, isn't he?

**DOUGAL** (*uncertain*): Yeah . . . ha, ha . . .

**DAMO:** Who do you like better, Oasis or Blur?

**DOUGAL:** Eh, Blur.

**DAMO:** Wha?

**DOUGAL:** Oasis! I mean . . . Oasis.

*We see a door open in the house behind the wall. A middle-aged priest steps outside. It is Father Frost.*

**FROST:** Your tea's ready.

**DAMO** (*very rudely*): I'll be in in a minute!

*Dougal looks very impressed.*

SCENE 8 EXT. DAY 1
SET: PICNIC AREA
*Jack is now comatose. He snores loudly. Ted has finally managed to set everything up. He has a variety of flasks, a water purifier, bread, plates, etc.*

**TED** (*rubbing his hands*): Great! Here we go!

*He takes out a book, 'The life of Mel Gibson', and settles back to read it. We hear an offscreen voice.*

**VOICE:** What the fup are you doing here?

*We see that a very nasty-looking middle-aged man is standing over Ted. His equally horrible wife stands beside him. They are Mr. and Mrs Joyce.*

**MR JOYCE:** This is my fuppin' spot. Get the fup off.

**MRS JOYCE:** Hit him, Frank.

**TED:** But there's lots of room. Could you not just go over there?

**MR JOYCE:** No fuppin' way!

**MRS JOYCE:** F.U.P.O.F.F.

**MR JOYCE:** Yeah fup off! We come here every fuppin' Sunday.

**TED:** But today's Saturday.

**MR JOYCE:** That doesn't fuppin' matter. The fact that we come here on Sunday means that this is our fuppin' spot. So fup off.

**MRS JOYCE:** Hit him Frank. I'll hit him.

**MR JOYCE** (*to Ted*): She fuppin' would, too. And so would I, you fuppin' backstard.

**TED:** Why are you talking like that?

*The man points to the picnic-spot sign. It has a list of rules and among them is 'No swearing'.*

**MR JOYCE:** So fup off. You grasshole.

**TED:** I don't know why . . .

**MR JOYCE:** That's fuppin' it. I'm callin' the fuppin' man. (*He starts shouting.*) Hey! Hey! Hey! Hey! Hey! Hey!

*We see a tiny hut about fifty or sixty yards away. A door suddenly opens and we see a man sitting in a chair. He leaps out of the chair and starts blowing his whistle furiously. He bolts the front door behind him and runs to a nearby bush. He goes behind the bush and raises a megaphone to his mouth.*

**MR JOYCE:** Hey! Hey! Hey! Hey!

**BENSON:** I'm here, Mr. Joyce.

**MR JOYCE:** Listen, this backstard priest is in our spot.

**BENSON:** What's the problem there?

**TED** (*shouting*): But we were just . . .

*As he speaks, he raises his plastic fork to indicate something. Mr. Joyce jumps backwards.*

**MR JOYCE:** Watch it!

**TED:** What? I wasn't going to—

**BENSON:** Put the fork down! Put the fork down!

*The sound cuts out. Pause. Ted looks at the fork and drops it. It blows away, making a dwindling plink sound as it goes. Benson starts advancing slowly towards Ted.*

**BENSON:** Now put your hands very slowly down to your sides – slowly! Keep them where I can see them.

*Benson is close enough to speak to them normally.*

**BENSON:** I'm putting the megaphone down, now, all right? Nice and easy . . .

*He places the megaphone very deliberately on to the ground. He approaches Ted, palms held up.*

**BENSON:** We don't want anyone getting excited. We're all friends here. Let's not do anything silly. All right? (*The atmosphere is very tense.*) I'm going to reach into my pocket now. All right? Everything's fine . . . (*He reaches into his pocket and takes out a packet of cigarettes. He offers one to Ted.*) Cigarette?

**TED:** Ah, no, thanks.

**BENSON** (*lighting up*): I guess you're right. These things'll kill me someday. OK, Father . . . here's the story . . . I like to keep a quiet picnic area here. I want everyone who comes here to have fun – enjoy a few sandwiches, a bottle of lemonade, have a few laughs, and then go home.

**TED:** I think that's what I'll do now. I'll go home.

**BENSON:** You do that. Slowly.

**TED:** Right. Bye, then.

*Ted turns around, secretly terrified. He starts to throw everything into the basket. Meanwhile Benson turns to the couple.*

**BENSON** (*to the Joyces*): All right, come on, get on with the picnic. Nothing to see here. Nothing to see here . . .

SCENE 9 INT./DAY 1
SET: PAROCHIAL HOUSE
*Ted is unpacking the picnic basket, looking very annoyed. Dougal enters. He keeps his head to one*

*side so that we only see him in profile. Ted doesn't notice this at first.*

**TED:** Ah, there you are. You wouldn't believe the day I had. You wouldn't – my *God*. That Mr Joyce is the *rudest* man . . . (*Dougal nods, still only showing Ted his profile. He sits down.*) And that Benson fella. Unbelievable . . . blowing that bloody whistle all the time. Someone should take it and . . . Where did you go off to, anyway?

**DOUGAL:** I just went off with Father Damo Lennon. He's over with Father Frost.

**TED:** Oh, yes. Father Frost said they might come over for a bit of a holiday.

**DOUGAL:** Father Damo's great.

**TED:** Maybe I'll . . . Why are you walking like that?

**DOUGAL:** Like what, Ted?

**TED:** Like what?

**DOUGAL:** Oh, right. Sorry, Ted.

*Dougal turns quite sheepishly. We see that he is wearing a tiny earring.*

**TED** (*turning*): Right, I . . . Dougal, what's that?

**DOUGAL:** What? Oh, this . . . Nothing.

**TED:** Dougal, it's an earring.

**DOUGAL:** Oh, right, yeah. It is, all right.

**TED:** Dougal, what's got into you? You can't go round wearing an earring.

**DOUGAL:** Ah, Ted. All the young priests have them. Father Damo has one.

**TED:** What? Did he give you the idea?

**DOUGAL:** Yeah. He's great.

**TED:** Well, what next? I suppose he'll be giving you crack cocaine or something.

**DOUGAL:** Crack cocaine . . . ah come on, Ted.

*Dougal looks disgusted, then his eyes light up.*

**TED:** Well you'll have to take it out.

**DOUGAL:** Ah, Ted.

**TED:** Come on now, Dougal. You're helping with Mass later. I'm not having you looking like that. What'll your parents think when they get here?

**DOUGAL:** Ah Ted, you don't know what's going on with young people.

**TED:** I was young once, you know. God, when I think of the things we used to get up to in the seminary. Me and a bunch of the other lads there, once we mitched off to see a Dana concert.

**DOUGAL:** Dana? God, Ted, no one listens to Dana anymore. You'd want to be mad to listen to her!

**TED:** Father Bigley listens to Dana, and he's not mad.

**DOUGAL:** Why is he in that home then?

**TED:** He's in that home because . . . because of those fires. But that's nothing to do with Dana. Anyway, come on, take the earring out.

**DOUGAL:** Oh, all right. God, Ted, I should be able to do what I want. I am almost twenty-six. You still treat me like I was twenty-four.

**TED:** Well, Dougal, if you go round wearing earrings, then what do you expect? I'll start treating you like a twenty-six year old when you start acting like a twenty-six year old. Anyway, time for your bath.

**DOUGAL:** Is it? Oh, right. (*He gets up to leave.*) Just remember, Ted. Today's youth are the young people of tomorrow.

*He leaves. Ted looks a bit puzzled.*

SCENE 10 EXT./ NIGHT 1
SET: PICNIC AREA
*We see the following from a mystery protagonist's*

point of view. We are outside Benson's hut. It is very quiet. As 'we' approach, we hear Benson snoring. The door opens. We enter. The camera points down and closes in on the snoring Benson. We see Benson's whistle, attached to a row of keys, hanging on a nail behind him. Close in on the whistle. A hand comes into shot and tries to take it off the nail. It rattles noisily as it does so. We constantly turn to see if Benson has woken. But he has not, even though the noise is terrible. Finally, the hand takes it off the nail. The camera turns around and points out of the hut. We hear a panting sound as we run away at great speed from the hut. The camera shakes and judders as we run. This run lasts slightly longer than it perhaps should. Soon we pass by a man and his dog.*

**MAN:** Hello, Father!

**VOICE** (*completely out of breath*): Ung!

*'Our' hand comes into shot and waves at him. The camera shakes as we run on a little further.*

### END OF PART ONE

\* \* \*

### PART TWO

SCENE 11 EXT./DAY 2
SET: JOHN AND MARY'S SHOP
*Ted is about to cross the road when he hears a noise from above. He looks up and squints into the sky. Cut to see a helicopter hovering about fifty feet in the air. Hodgins is sitting at the open side door.*

**HODGINS:** Hello, Father!

**TED:** Ah, hello . . .

**HODGINS:** How are things?

**TED:** Fine . . . fine . . .

**HODGINS:** Good. (*There is a lull in the conversation.*) Well, I'll be off. See you later, Father! (*To the pilot.*) Go, go, go, go!!!!

*The helicopter flies away. Ted stands there, confused.*

SCENE 12 INT./DAY 2
SET: JOHN AND MARY'S SHOP
*We see that Mary has John's head in a bucket of water.*

**MARY:** You bastard!

*She pulls John's head out of the bucket.*

**JOHN:** Slag! Mmmmfbrrr. . .

*Mary shoves his head back into the water again. Ted enters. Mary keeps John's head in the water.*

**MARY:** Hello, Father!

**TED:** Hello, Mary . . . Ah . . .

*Mary looks to where Ted is looking.*

**MARY:** Oh.

*She releases John. John stands up, gasping for air as he does so.*

**JOHN:** . . . Haaaaaaaaaallloooo, Father.

**TED:** Hello, John.

**JOHN:** Mary was just washing my hair. She has lovely soft hands.

**TED:** I was just looking for some firelighters.

**JOHN:** Oh yes. What type? Inflammable or non-inflammable?

**TED:** Eh, inflammable.

**MARY:** I'll get them. They're out the back.

*Mary leaves.*

**TED:** I didn't know Sergeant Hodgins had a helicopter.

**JOHN:** Oh, yes. He's had to get one in because of this whistle thing.

**TED:** Whistle thing . . . ?

**JOHN:** Yes. Look . . .

*He hands Ted a copy of 'The Craggy Island Examiner' and Ted looks at it. The headline reads*

'*Mr Benson's whistle stolen. Full story pages 2, 3, 4, 7, 8, 11, 13, 14, 15, 20*'.

**MARY** (*from back*): Isn't it terrible, Father?!

**JOHN:** The whole island's talking about it. Who would have thought law and order would break down here on Craggy Island?

**MARY** (*still out back*): God help us all, Father!

**TED:** Well, if it was just a whistle that was stolen . . .

**JOHN** (*not listening*): I've had to buy a shotgun and everything. (*He lifts the shotgun over the counter. As he speaks, he casually holds the shotgun so that it's pointing at Ted. Ted does a little nervous dance, trying to stay out of the line of fire.*) I wouldn't hesitate to use that, now. If that man comes in and tries to steal any of the whistles I have here, I'd blow his feckin' head off his shoulders. Ha, ha! (*Ted joins in the laughter uncertainly. Mary comes back in with the firelighters.*) Look Father. I've even got it cocked so I get a jump on him.

**TED:** Is it not dangerous to have it cocked like that, John?

**JOHN:** Not at all, Father. As long as you don't suddenly drop it or something.

*He slams the gun, pointing at Ted, down on the counter. Ted jumps slightly.*

**MARY:** There you are, Father. If they don't work, bring them back and we'll give you a refund.

**TED:** OK, so. Thanks very much.

*He leaves. We see Mary grabbing the barrel of the gun and trying to wrest it away from John.*

SCENE 13 EXT./DAY 2
SET: JOHN AND MARY'S SHOP
*Ted closes the door behind him. An old woman, Mrs Glynn, approaches Ted.*

**MRS GLYNN:** Father, did you hear about the whistle being stolen?

**TED:** Yes, I . . .

**MRS GLYNN:** I never thought I'd see such a thing. What next? Someone'll be murdered, I suppose. And then the porn kings and drug barons will move in. And then where'll we be? Drive-by shootings and the like. It'll be like *Boyz N the Hood*. And then they'll have all the hoors selling their wares on the street, and the pimps'll be using crack to keep the hoors under control.

*We hear a muffled gunshot from inside the shop.*

**MRS GLYNN:** I'm going home now, and I'm going to lock myself in the basement until they catch him. Goodbye, Father!

**TED:** Eh . . . goodbye . . .

SCENE 14 INT./DAY 2
SET: PAROCHIAL HOUSE
*Dougal and Father Damo are sitting in front of the television, playing a computer game – 'Streetfighter 2'. Jack is asleep. Ted comes in. He carries the newspaper.*

**TED:** Unbelievable . . . they really are making too big a deal about all this. Look! A pull-out supplement about whistles!

*We see the supplement. It has a picture of a whistle on the cover and beneath it the word 'Whistles'.*

**TED:** And there's even a crossword clue here that says 'Two across – Mr Benson had one stolen last night – seven letters'. I don't know —

*Ted finally notices that no one is paying attention to him.*

**TED:** Ah, Dougal. Aren't you going to introduce me to your friend?

**DOUGAL:** This is Father Damo.

**DAMO** (*without looking*): Howya?

**TED:** Hello, Father. Playing the old computer game there? (*Damo and Dougal stifle a laugh. Ted's a bit confused at this. The telephone rings. Ted picks it up.*) Hello, Father Ted Crilly speaking . . . Yes, ah, Father Frost. Yes, yes, I'll tell him. (*He puts his hand over the mouthpiece and addresses Damo.*) Eh, Father Damo, Father Frost says you're to go home. Your tea's ready.

**DAMO:** Tell him I'm not goin'. I'm havin' dinner here.

**TED:** Are you? Oh . . . (*To the telephone.*) Eh, hello, Father, eh . . . he says he's having dinner here. (*Pause.*) Father Damo, Father

Frost says you're to go home immediately.

**DAMO:** *Aw shite!* Didja tell him I'm having dinner here?

**TED:** Eh, yes . . .

**DAMO:** Well, tell him to feck off then.

*Pause. Ted blinks for a moment, trying to think of how to relay this information to Frost.*

**TED:** Father Damo's happy enough here for the moment. Right. OK. (*To Damo.*) Eh, Father Frost says if you don't come home for tea, he'll come down here and get you.

**DAMO:** Tell him that's fine. I don't care what he does. He's not my boss.

**TED:** Right. (*To the telephone.*) Eh . . .

**DAMO:** (*standing up*): Oh, all right, all right. I'm goin'. Tell him I'm goin'. Seeya Dougal.

*He goes out through the door and gives Dougal a secretive signal to follow him. Dougal does so.*

**DAMO:** Dougal, mind this for me.

**DOUGAL:** Oh, yeah, right.

*Damo gives Dougal a packet of cigarettes.*

**DAMO:** Give them back to me later. Frosty hates smokin'.

**DOUGAL:** OK, Damo. See ya!

*Dougal puts the fags in the pocket of his jacket. To make more room, he takes something out. It is a set of rosary beads. He looks embarrassed.*

**DAMO** (*sarcastically*): Prayin', yeah?

**DOUGAL:** What? Oh, no. They're eh, . . . they're Ted's.

**DAMO:** I'll see ya.

*He leaves.*

**TED** (*from inside*): Dougal!

**DOUGAL:** Oh, *God*. What does he want now?

*Dougal 'tsks' theatrically and does an exaggerated 'cool' walk into the room.*

SCENE 15 INT./NIGHT 2
SET: TED AND DOUGAL'S BEDROOM
*We see Dougal, asleep. He starts mumbling.*

**DOUGAL:** Consonant, vowel, consonant, vowel, consonant, vowel, consonant, vowel.

*Cut to Ted, a pillow over his head. He takes it off and lies on it, facing away from Dougal. It's no use. He turns on the light, and starts to get dressed. He takes his jacket off the back of a chair and puts it over his arm as he walks out of the room.*

**DOUGAL:** Consonant . . . put your clothes back on, Carol, I can't concentrate.

SCENE 16 INT./NIGHT 2
SET: PAROCHIAL HOUSE HALLWAY
*Ted, in silhouette, opens the door to the room. He fumbles with the switch and finally manages to turn the light on. When he does so, we see Mrs Doyle standing right beside him, holding out a tea tray.*

**MRS DOYLE:** Tea, Father?

**TED:** Good God almighty!!!

**MRS DOYLE:** Oh, sorry, Father, did I give you a fright?

**TED:** What are you doing up?

**MRS DOYLE:** Oh, I always stay up, Father. Just in case any of you need a cup of tea.

**TED:** Mrs Doyle, there's really no need. You should get some sleep. How long have you been doing this?

**MRS DOYLE:** Oh, about three years now.

**TED:** But we never get up at night.

**MRS DOYLE:** Well, you're up now, aren't

you, Father? Unless I'm hallucinating from lack of sleep. That's happened before, all right.

**TED:** Well, I was just going to go for a walk. So . . .

**MRS DOYLE:** OK, so, I'll stay here.

**TED:** There's really no need.

**MRS DOYLE:** Ah, go away with you. Have a nice walk, Father.

*Ted thinks of saying something, then decides against it. He leaves the room, closing the door softly behind him. Mrs Doyle stands there, looking straight ahead, the tea tray in her hands. After a moment she looks at the light switch and turns it off. We see her standing there, in exactly the same position, in the darkness.*

SCENE 17 INT./NIGHT 2
SET: PAROCHIAL HOUSE HALLWAY
*Ted is at the hall door. He opens the door and puts on the jacket. It's far too small for him.*

**TED:** Ah, God . . . (*He's about to take it off when he feels something in the pocket. It's Damo's packet of cigarettes.*) Oh, Dougal . . .

*He opens it and examines the contents. He frowns, reaches in and pulls out Benson's whistle. Ted looks at it for a moment.*

SCENE 18 INT./DAY 3
SET: PAROCHIAL HOUSE
*Ted and Dougal are eating cornflakes at breakfast.*

**TED:** Dougal . . . is there anything on your mind? (*Dougal looks at Ted, a blank look on his face.*) Let me rephrase that . . . You don't want to talk about anything? Something bothering you in some way?

**DOUGAL:** Like what, Ted?

**TED:** Well, let me put it this way. Have you done anything you might be a bit embarrassed about? (*Dougal looks vacant.*) Have you done anything bad, recently? Anything wrong?

**DOUGAL:** Wrong?

**TED:** Wrong, yes. Do you remember, Dougal: right and wrong? You know, the differences between the two. Page one of *How to be a Catholic.*

**DOUGAL:** Eh . . .

**TED:** Just think – 'Things that are wrong' . . . Anything happening there? What is 'wrong'?

**DOUGAL:** Eh . . .

**TED:** Honestly, Dougal, this is very basic stuff. What is wrong? Or is everything perfectly acceptable?

**DOUGAL:** Just give me a second, Ted. Eh . . .

**TED:** Arson. There's one. Murder. Infidelity. Swearing . . .

**DOUGAL:** Swearing, yeah . . .

**TED:** Anything else?

**DOUGAL:** Eh . . . (*He bites his lip.*) . . . Ummmmmmm . . . (*One eye twitches. Ted is holding his breath, silently urging Dougal on. Dougal opens his mouth and says with complete uncertainty.*) . . . lying?

**TED:** Yes! Well *done*, Dougal!

**DOUGAL:** Thanks, Ted. I —

*Dougal looks a bit unsteady.*

**TED:** Are you all right?

**DOUGAL:** I'm fine, Ted. I just need to sit down.

*Ted takes Dougal by the arm and leads him to a chair.*

**TED:** Sorry about that, Dougal. Probably pushed you a bit far there . . .

**DOUGAL:** No worries, Ted.

**TED:** But . . . another thing that's wrong is stealing. What I'm trying to say is . . . it's wrong to steal. It's just something you don't do.

**DOUGAL:** Right. Except you.

**TED:** Yes. What?

**DOUGAL:** You're allowed to steal.

**TED:** What are you talking about?

**DOUGAL:** The money from that Lourdes thing . . .

TED: Different thing, Dougal. First of all, the money was just resting in my account before I moved it on.

DOUGAL: It was resting for a long time, Ted.

TED: It was, yes, but —

DOUGAL: Good long rest.

TED: Dougal – let's forget about me. All right? This is about you. Is there anything you want to tell me? (*He takes out the whistle and gives it to Dougal.*) About this, for example.

*Mrs Doyle enters. Ted instinctively grabs the whistle back from Dougal and puts it in his pocket.*

MRS DOYLE: Father, Sergeant Hodgins and Mr Benson are here.

TED: Dougal, I heard a noise there. Could you go and get the . . . shears.

DOUGAL: Right y'are, Ted.

*Dougal runs out of the room. Benson, in a wheelchair, is pushed into the room by Hodgins.*

HODGINS: Hello, Father. Sorry to have to disturb you, but, ah . . . I felt we should meet, talk about this . . .

BENSON: You've heard about the whistle business, Father?

TED: God, yes. It's all a big load of fuss over . . . (*Benson and Hodgins glare at him.*) . . . what is obviously a very serious matter.

HODGINS: Yeah, a bit of excitement at last. This is the first bit of excitement since we thought the Boston Strangler might be a local man. Wow! We were *way* off there!

TED: What happened to you? The thief didn't break your legs or something?

BENSON: No, Father. When I woke up, and saw that my whistle had been stolen, I went into a state of shock and lost the use of my legs. Well, one of them. This one's fine. But the other one . . .completely lost all feeling. Look.

*He takes Hodgins's baton and whacks himself on the leg with it, then immediately doubles up in pain.*

BENSON: Oaaaaaaagghhhh, Sweet Jesus!

HODGINS: Yes. The shock also affected his memory, Father. It's actually the other leg which doesn't have any feeling.

BENSON: Anyway, Father, come on. Have you heard anything?

TED: About what?

BENSON: About my whistle. Did you hear anything during Confession?

TED: No, no, now, come on. The Confessional is sacrosanct.

BENSON: So you have heard something, Father?

TED: No, I haven't heard anything.

BENSON: I've had that whistle for fifty years. It saved my grandfather's life.

TED: Did it really?

BENSON: Yes. He was being executed by the British. They had him up against a wall and they shot him. And the bullets all hit the whistle in his coat pocket and bounced off him.

TED: Really? The bullets bounced off him?

BENSON: Yes.

TED: God almighty! So he survived?

BENSON: No, no. They just reloaded and shot him again.

HODGINS: Listen, Father, I didn't want to say anything, but . . . Jim saw someone.

TED: Yes?

BENSON: He didn't get a good look, but did notice something . . . the collar. Jim says it was a priest. Who stole the whistle.

*Dougal comes into the room with the shears.*

DOUGAL: Oh, right. That'd be Ted.

TED: What!

DOUGAL: Do you remember, Ted? You were talking about stealing something, and then you showed me the whistle. You put it in your top pocket there.

(*Pause.*)

TED: Dougal, come on, now. Dougal sometimes gets confused . . . things get sort of mixed up in his mind and he . . .

DOUGAL: . . . Was the whistle sort of bent, with an inscription underneath that read 'To Billy from Padraig'?

BENSON: That's exactly right.

DOUGAL: Oh, right. That's the one Ted had.

TED: No, Dougal.

DOUGAL: It is, Ted. Try your top pocket. Go on, Ted, seriously. I bet you it's there. I'm sure it is. Give it a go.

*Ted, defeated, reaches into his pocket and fumbles around.*

DOUGAL: It's more to the right, there.

TED: *Yes, Dougal.* Thank you.

*After a moment, he takes out the whistle. Hodgins and Benson stare at him.*

TED: Hah! Yes! Right! Well there's an obvious explanation.

BENSON: Is there, Father?

TED: Oh, yes.

DOUGAL: What is it, Ted?

TED (*incredibly calm*): Well, I just have to go away for a couple of minutes. Then I shall return with a full and frank explanation.

BENSON: It better be a good one.

TED: It will be completely satisfactory. Just excuse me for a few moments.

*Ted leaves the room.*

SCENE 19 INT./DAY 3
SET: TED AND DOUGAL'S BEDROOM
*Ted enters very slowly. He sits down on his bed and puts his head in his hands. He concentrates very hard.*

SCENE 20 INT./DAY 3
SET: PAROCHIAL HOUSE
*Benson and Hodgins seem a little uncomfortable. Dougal is not sure what to say.*

DOUGAL (*to Hodgins*): So I hear your babysitter got pregnant . . .

*Hodgins looks confused. He is about to say something when Mrs Doyle enters suddenly.*

MRS DOYLE: More visitors, Father.

*In come two priests, one of whom is Father Damo. He is being marched in by an older priest, Father Frost.*

DAMO: Gerroff!!!

FROST: Right. Ah, I believe there's a Mr Benson who's had a whistle stolen?

BENSON: That's right. That'd be me.

FROST: Well, I have the culprit here.

BENSON: What?

DAMO: Yeah, yeah, I stole it. So what, it's only a whistle.

BENSON: But . . . why?

HODGINS: Yes. Why? Are you unhappy, Father Lennon?

*Damo shrugs and says something under his breath.*

FROST: I saw him with it on Tuesday morning. Then I heard Mr Benson's whistle had gone missing. I asked him about it and he said that he hadn't seen it, but he thought Father McGuire was the culprit. Sorry about that, Father McGuire.

DOUGAL: Well it was my fault for stealing it.

FROST: But you didn't steal it, Father.

DOUGAL: Oh, right.

FROST: He hid it in a packet of cigarettes, apparently.

DOUGAL: Oh, right. That must be how we

got a hold of it. 'Cause Father Damo gave me the cigarettes to mind.

*The door bursts open. Ted comes in.*

**TED:** Right! Right, I have a full explanation.

**BENSON:** Ah, Father, we were just . . .

**TED:** Hello, Father Damo, Father Frost. I was just about to tell everyone why I stole the whistle.

**FROST:** No, Father . . .

**TED:** No, no, I have to get it off my chest. It's been bothering me ever since I took it.

**DOUGAL:** Ted . . .

**TED:** Sh . . . Dougal. Fifteen years ago . . . I met a young boy, an orphan. His parents had been killed in some sort of bizarre accident involving trees . . . a tree fell on them, that's it. They were both crushed. This young boy has nothing, nothing to his name, except a dream.

**DOUGAL:** Ted. . .

**TED:** Shut up, Dougal. His dream was to own his own stable. With prizewinning horses in every . . . bit of the stable. But then, tragedy struck. A strange disease took hold of him, one that affected his speech so that he could only communicate by raising his eyebrows. Once for yes, twice for no. 'If only I had a whistle,' he thought. 'So that I could train my horses to win the Grand National and the Derby . . .This young, brave man wrote to me two weeks ago asking . . .

**DOUGAL:** Ted, Father Damo took the whistle . . .

**TED** (*immediately*): Did he? Oh, right. Well, that's that cleared up. See you all soon!

**HODGINS:** What's that about the horses?

**TED:** What? The horses . . . ah, nothing. I was going mad. Listen, you'd better go. I have to do another one of those Masses.

**BENSON:** Wait!

*They all look at him. He is holding the whistle and gazing at it in wonder. He slowly puts his hands on the arms of the wheelchair. Slowly, he pushes himself up on to his feet, his eyes wide as if experiencing a miracle.*

**BENSON:** Ah! I . . . I can walk! I can walk! I can waaalllkkk!!!!

*He walks unsteadily out of the room with his hands in the air.*

**TED** (*to Dougal*): Dougal, don't put too much faith in people who are 'cool'. Most of the time they're just on the fast track to a life of crime. Father Lennon will probably end up like that corrupt cardinal in *The Godfather III*.

**DOUGAL:** Oh, you're right there, Ted.

**TED:** So, have you learnt something from your experience?

*Pause.*

**DOUGAL:** No.

**THE END**

# SONG FOR EUROPE

**GRAHAM:** While *Father Ted* was written very much with both an Irish and British audience in mind, we still had to be careful that we didn't alienate any of our British viewers by using plotlines that would only mean something to the Irish. Therefore, we had to use only those aspects of Irish life that were noteworthy enough to cross the Irish sea. For instance, the way Ireland kept winning the Eurovision Song Contest, and the oft-reported urban myth that stated we were going to pick a bad song in order to deliberately lose the contest and thereby avoid the expense of hosting it again.

We had two structures to fall back on here. The first was the rivalry with Dick Byrne, which had its own pattern, and the second was provided by the process of writing a song (writing the music and lyrics, going into a studio, doing a video and, finally, performing it live). It featured one of our all-time favourite characters, Jeep Hebrides.

Funnily enough, the scene when Ted and Dougal are wondering what the song should be about is a mirror image of Arthur and me doing the same thing when we were writing the episode. I said, 'What'll the song be about?' and Arthur replied, 'How about a lovely horse?' Five minutes later, when I was able to stand up again, we gave Dougal the line.

There's a little nod to *Seinfeld* in this episode: 'Not that there's anything wrong with that type of thing' is an 'Irishified' lift of a catchphrase from a brilliant episode called *The Outing*. (If you don't like *Seinfeld,* by the way, you get no muffins round at my house. I think it might be the best sitcom ever written.)

**ARTHUR:** The mumbling presenter was handed to us on a plate by Steve Coogan who used to do a fantastic impression of one of his relatives, who apparently mumbled like that. Our initial idea was that Steve might play the part himself, but we also wanted Jon Kenny in the show. He and his partner Pat Shortt (who plays the mad Tom) are the funniest comic actors in Ireland.

## PART ONE

SCENE 1 INT./DAY 1
SET: PAROCHIAL HOUSE

*Ted is humming softly to himself while reading a newspaper. Mrs Doyle has stopped her polishing and listens to him dreamily. Dougal sticks his head around the door.*

**DOUGAL:** Ted, did you see my record collection?

**TED:** Your record collection?

**DOUGAL:** Yeah.

*Ted picks up an old single that is beside him. He shows it to Dougal.*

**TED:** Here it is. And Dougal, you have to have more than one record for it to be a 'collection'. What you have is a 'record'.

**DOUGAL:** Oh, right, yeah.

*He goes to the record player and starts fiddling around with it. Ted starts humming again Mrs Doyle stops what she's doing and looks up at Ted. She cocks her head and listens in a dreamy way.*

**MRS DOYLE:** You know, you've a beautiful voice, Father.

**TED:** What? Ah, no I don't, really.

**MRS DOYLE:** No, you do. It's gorgeous.

**TED:** Well, thanks very much.

**MRS DOYLE:** Did you ever think of turning professional?

**TED:** Well, no, I'm a priest.

**MRS DOYLE:** You know, Father. I don't think I've heard anything more beautiful in my life. Sing something else there . . . Go on.

**TED:** Well, I don't normally do requests!

**MRS DOYLE:** Ah, sing something for me, Father.

**TED** (*enormously flattered*): No . . .

**MRS DOYLE:** Do, Father, go on, please.

**TED:** Well, ha ha . . . (*He hums 'Wherever I Lay My Hat', drifting in and out of the lyrics.*) 'By the look in your eye, I can tell you're gonna cry . . . dum, dum, dum . . . I'm the type of guy . . . Wherever I lay my hat, that's my home.'

*He finishes, then pauses.*

**MRS DOYLE:** I didn't like that so much Father. I was a bit disappointed with that one, to be honest.

**TED** (*crestfallen*): Well, yes, thank you, Mrs Doyle.

**MRS DOYLE:** God, I'm surprised at that . . . that wasn't very good at all.

**TED:** Yes . . .

**MRS DOYLE:** I used to love that song, but that version was *catastrophic* . . .

**TED:** Well, Mrs Doyle, I tell you what, I won't book Carnegie Hall just yet.

**MRS DOYLE:** I don't think they'd let you play Carnegie Hall with a voice like that.

*She scurries out through the door. Dougal perks up.*

**DOUGAL:** Carnegie Hall. Oh, Ted, here's one . . . How do you get to Carnegie Hall?

**TED:** Practise!

*Pause.*

**DOUGAL:** What?

**TED:** That's the old joke, isn't it? How do you get to Carnegie Hall? Practise.

**DOUGAL:** Huh?

**TED:** Oh, I see. Eh, you'd have to go to New York, Dougal.

**DOUGAL:** Oh, right. Do you mind if I put on my record?

**TED:** No, go ahead.

**DOUGAL:** I've got Eurosong fever, Ted.

**TED:** Oh yes?

**DOUGAL:** Oh, God, yeah. I love the Eurosong competition, Ted. I can't wait. I've got it all planned out. I'm going to keep the night free, get a big bag of popcorn and watch the whole thing.

**TED:** 'Keep the night free'. Right, so you'll have to reschedule . . . what exactly? Your annual address to the United Nations?

**DOUGAL:** What, Ted? (*Ted ignores him.*) God, Ted, I'm so excited. What time is it now?

**TED:** Half one.

**DOUGAL:** Half one. And the competition is on in . . . (*He looks at his watch.*) . . . May.

**TED:** That's eight months away, Dougal.

**DOUGAL:** I know! Isn't it incredible? It only seems like a couple of months back that the last one was on. God, Ted. Imagine winning the Eurosong! Wow! When you think of all the stars who've won it.

**TED:** Like who?

*Dougal looks blank.*

**DOUGAL:** Ted, you know they're looking for entries for this year's competition?

**TED:** Are they?

**DOUGAL:** Yeah.

**TED:** Yes, well . . .

**DOUGAL:** Why don't we . . .

**TED:** Dougal, don't say . . .

**DOUGAL:** I mean . . .

**TED:** Dougal . . .

**DOUGAL:** Come on . . .

**TED:** No.

**DOUGAL:** Imagine if we won, Ted. We'd be famous. Like Nelson Mandela and his mad wife.

**TED:** Dougal, we don't have the time to be entering Eurosong '96. Anyway, we'd have to write a song. That needs a certain type of person with a very special talent . . . Cole Porter, George and Irene Gershwin*, Chris de Burgh. Any old eeejit can't just take up the art of songwriting just like that. (*The telephone rings. Ted picks it up.*) Hello. Father Ted Crilly speaking.

*We see who is on the end of the line. It is Father Dick Byrne.*

**DICK:** Hello. Dick Byrne here.

**TED** (*darkens*)**:** Ah, hello Dick.

**DICK:** Well, Ted, are you enterin' this year?

**TED:** What?

**DICK:** Eurosong '96. The young fella here has

---

*Ted obviously believes it was a husband and wife team.

me driven mad with it.

*Cut to Father Cyril McDuff looking fondly at an album entitled 'The Best of the Eurosong Contest'.*

**DICK:** Anyway, we thought we'd give it a go. Why don't you have a try as well, I'm sure you'd win . . .

**TED:** Well, thanks very much, but . . .

**DICK:** . . . If all the other contestants were killed! Ha, ha!

**TED:** Well, I'm sure we'd do just as well as you would, Dick.

**DICK:** No, you wouldn't.

**TED:** Yes, we would.

**DICK:** No, you wouldn't.

**TED:** Yes, we would.

**DICK:** No, you wouldn't.

**TED:** Yes, we would.

**DICK:** No, you wouldn't.

**TED:** Yes, we would.

**DICK:** No, you wouldn't.

**TED:** Yes, we would.

**DICK:** No, you wouldn't.

**TED** (*very annoyed*)**:** Yes, we would, yes we would, yes we would.

**DICK:** No, you wouldn't times a thousand!

**TED:** Y—

**DICK:** Jinx! No comebacks!

*An enraged Ted realises he's beaten and slams down the telephone.*

**TED:** Dougal, get the guitar . . .

**DOUGAL:** But I thought you didn't . . .

**TED** (*roars*)**:** I said get the guitar!!!!!!

*Dougal hops slightly with the shock.*

SCENE 2 INT./NIGHT 1
SET: TED AND DOUGAL'S BEDROOM
*Ted and Dougal are in the bedroom. Dougal sits by a keyboard. Ted has a guitar. They sit on the edge of their beds.*

TED: Right, what'll we write it about?

DOUGAL: How about a lovely horse?

TED: OK. We'll call it . . . 'My Lovely Horse'. (*He writes this down on a piece of paper.*) . . . My Lovely Horse . . . by . . . Father Ted Crilly.

DOUGAL: And Father Dougal McGuire . . .

TED (*a bit more reluctantly*): . . . And Father Dougal McGuire . . . right. Will we write the lyrics first? Or will we do the music?

DOUGAL: Eh . . . lyrics. Then we'll fit the tune around it.

TED: Right. Here we go!

*Both of them just sit there, looking off into the middle distance. Pause.*

DOUGAL: Maybe we should do the music first.

TED: Right! Here we go!

*He strums one chord on his guitar. Pause.*

DOUGAL: I liked that.

TED: Was that all right?

DOUGAL: Yeah, it was a bit sad.

TED: Good, good. I'll write it down. That was an 'A' I think. (*He writes it.*) OK, so . . .

*Pause.*

DOUGAL: I think . . . I think I have a line.

TED: Right! Lyrics! Go ahead, there, Dougal.

DOUGAL: What's it called again?

TED: 'My Lovely Horse'.

DOUGAL: All right, how about this . . . 'My lovely horse, I want to hold you so tight, I want to rub my fingers through your tail, and love you all night . . .'

TED: Dougal . . .

DOUGAL: 'I want to be with you all the time and kiss you on the head —'

TED: Dougal, Dougal, stop there. We want to keep out of the whole area of, you know, actually being in love with the horse.

DOUGAL: Oh, right.

TED: It's more that we're friends with the horse. We want to jump around with it a little and, you know, just have a good laugh with it.

DOUGAL: Right. Chase rabbits.

TED: Yes, except I don't think horses actually chase rabbits. What does a horse do? That's a good start. Think about what horses actually do.

*Pause.*

DOUGAL: What about something like 'Take this lump of sugar, baby, you know you want it.' That'd be like something the rap fellas'd write.

TED: Forget about them, Dougal. Forget all about Icy Tea and Michael Jackson and those fellas. They won't help us. Anyway, come on . . . we're not moving from here until we finish the song. You ready?

DOUGAL: Ready, Ted! Let's do it!

TED: Now, Dougal, don't take it too seriously. It's only a bit of fun, all right?

*We see a Pope-clock twisting to show the passage of time.*

SCENE 2A INT./NIGHT 1
SET: TED AND DOUGAL'S BEDROOM
*Fade up on Ted and Dougal. Ted is standing up with a cigarette in his mouth. Dougal is on the bed with the keyboard. There are cans and bits of paper on the floor, the room is filled with cigarette smoke and the atmosphere is much like the Rolling Stones' studio after fifteen hours of non-stop rehearsal.*

*Dashes indicate censorious bleeps.*

TED: Just play the f—king note!

DOUGAL: The first one?

TED: No, not the f—king first one! The f—king first one's already f—king down. Play the f—king note you were f—king playing earlier! I've been f—king playing the f—king first one. We've got the f—king first one!

DOUGAL: So . . .

TED: Just play the f—king note you were just f—king playing there! The f—king thing you were just f—king doing! Play the f—king note!!!

*The Pope-clock spins again.*

SCENE 2B INT./NIGHT 1
SET: TED AND DOUGAL'S BEDROOM
*Cut to reveal Ted and Dougal splayed out on their beds asleep. Dougal's keyboard is still on and is doing a slow samba rhythm. Ted is slumped over his guitar. Fade out.*

SCENE 3 INT./DAY 2
SET: PAROCHIAL HOUSE
*Ted is sitting on a stool with his guitar. Dougal stands beside him, behind the keyboard. An expectant Mrs Doyle and a grumpy Father Jack are on the sofa, watching them. Dougal presses one button and a drumbeat starts. He then stands back, not touching the keyboard for the rest of the song. Ted starts playing his guitar – the same note for each line.*

**TED:** 'My lovely horse,
Running through the fields
Where are you going
With your fetlocks blowing in the wind.'

*Shot of Jack and Mrs Doyle taking this in.*

**DOUGAL AND TED:** (*chorus*)
'I want to shower you with sugar-lumps
And ride you over fences

Polish your hooves every day
And bring you to the horse dentist.
My lovely horse
You're a pony no more,
Running around with a man on your
back, like a train in the night.'

*Ted does the one note again, and then moves his hand up the fretboard to do the final note. It goes wrong.*

**TED:** Oh, wait, wait . . .

*He tries again. It sounds off.*

**TED:** Wait, I can do this.

*He tries again. This time it sounds reasonably OK. The song ends. Ted puts the guitar upright and leans on it. Pause.*

**TED:** It needs a bit of work here and there, but what do you think in general?

*Ted and Dougal look expectantly at Jack and Mrs Doyle. Mrs Doyle cannot conceal her look of distaste. Jack looks at her, looks at them, reaches around the side of the sofa, picks up a shotgun and shoots the guitar.*

**TED** (*looks at shattered guitar*): Right . . .

SCENE 4 INT./DAY 2
SET: PAROCHIAL HOUSE
*Ted and Dougal are sitting on the sofa, looking glum.*

**TED:** Father Jack's right. It's a terrible song. It really is. God almighty, what were we thinking?

**DOUGAL:** Ah, it's not that bad, Ted.

**TED:** Well, the lyrics are fine. There's no problem there. But there's no tune. It's just one note over and over again. Oh, God . . . and I went and booked time in that studio. I hope we can cancel.

**DOUGAL:** Ted. Can I put on my favourite Eurosong? Maybe that'll cheer us up.

**TED:** Yes. That might help. What is it?

*Dougal goes to the stereo and puts on his record.*

**DOUGAL:** Nin Huugen and the Huugen Notes. It came fifth in the 'Song for Norway' competition in 1976.

**TED:** Where on earth did you get that?

**DOUGAL:** Ah, you know me, Ted. I've always had an interest in rare, hard-to-find records.

**TED:** Dougal, can I remind you again, you've only got one record. That's not really an 'interest'. Maybe if you developed an interest in records that weren't hard to find, you might actually be able to find some records.

*Dougal has put the record on, and it's quite tuneful.*

**TED:** That's not too bad, actually.

**DOUGAL:** Oh, actually, that's the B side. I'll turn it over.

**TED:** No, leave it, leave it . . .

**DOUGAL:** It's nice enough, isn't it?

**TED:** Yes. If only we'd come up with something like that.

*Pause. A strange sly look comes over Ted's face.*

**TED:** I suppose not many people would have heard that song.

**DOUGAL:** Suppose not. First time I've heard it, anyway.

**TED:** A lot of people wouldn't really have much of an interest in the B side of songs that came fifth in 'A Song for Norway'. What are the band doing now?

**DOUGAL:** Oh, God, Ted, it's a terrible story. They all died in a 'plane crash along with all the people who were involved in the song – the producer, the studio engineer, their manager . . .

**TED:** . . . The people who owned the publishing rights?

**DOUGAL:** Oh, yes.

**TED:** Tsk, that's terrible. (*Pause.*) Eh, Dougal . . .?

**DOUGAL:** Yeah?

**TED:** Wouldn't it be nice to commemorate all those talented people by keeping their music alive?

**DOUGAL:** What?

**TED:** Say, if we borrowed that tune for 'My Lovely Horse'. It'd help us out and commemorate their memory at the same time.

**DOUGAL:** So we wouldn't just be stealing the tune?

**TED:** Dougal, there's no way, just because we take their tune and put our lyrics over it, that we're stealing the tune.

**DOUGAL:** No?

**TED:** No. You'd have to be mad to jump to that conclusion. What we're doing is celebrating their memory. Secretly. Don't tell anyone, incidentally.

**DOUGAL:** Right. And I suppose, if the song wins and we make money out of it, we could give it to their relatives.

*Pause.*

**TED:** . . . Yyyyyyyyeah . . . we'll play it by ear.

SCENE 5 EXT./DAY 2*
SET: RECORDING STUDIO
*We see Jeep Hebrides, engineer at Craggy Island Recording Studios. He is an old hippy with long hair – there seems to be something stuck in it – who seems to be a little dazed and confused, but he's a friendly type. He is staring intently at a dancing flower – one of those toys that moves whenever it 'hears' sound.*

*We deleted this scene from the final version.

**JEEP:** What do you want with me? (*The flower dances and stops.*) Stop messin' with my head.

*The door opens and Ted sticks his head around the door.*

**TED:** Jeep, how are you?

*Jeep looks at the flower.*

**JEEP** (*to flower*): Oh, wow. I'm fine, man. (*He notices Ted.*) Huh!

**TED:** Father Ted Crilly. We booked the studio?

**JEEP:** Oh, yeah, it's just . . . I'm supposed to have some priests coming in.

**TED:** That's us, Jeep.

**JEEP:** Yeah? OK, come in, man . . .

*They all enter the other half of the studio.*

**JACK** (*as soon as he enters*): Drink!

*Jack starts opening drawers, rummaging behind things etc in his search for drink. He continues to do this throughout the remainder of the scene. There are drums, speakers etc. littering the studio. Dougal looks at Jeep and notices, as we do, that there is a whole burger in his hair. Along the wall, we see photographs of Chris de Burgh, The Cranberries, U2, Enya, Bob Geldof and Van Morrison etc.*

**DOUGAL** (*whispers*): Ted . . . Ted, he's got a burger in his hair.

**TED:** I know. Shh . . . (*To Jeep.*) Haven't seen you at mass recently, Jeep!

**JEEP:** Haven't been to mass in years, man. The whole Catholic thing is a joke.

**TED:** Ah, ha!

*Dougal points out the photographs along the wall.*

**DOUGAL:** Wow! Are these all the people who've recorded here?

**JEEP:** No. (*Beat.*) I go in there, man.

**TED** (*looking at photographs*): Oh, look! They're signed!

**JEEP:** No, man. I did that. Sometimes I have to see my name written down or I freak out.

*He goes through a door and into the booth. There is a thick pane of glass between him and the priests.*

**TED:** Where'll we set up, Jeep?

*Jeep looks back at Ted. He can't hear what they're saying, he looks puzzled.*

**TED** (*louder*): Where do you want us to set up?

*Jeep looks confused, he comes back out of the booth.*

**JEEP:** What? Sorry, man. I couldn't hear you through the glass. It's soundproof.

**TED:** Should you not have headphones or something?

**JEEP:** Headphones? Oh, yeah!

*He picks up a pair of earphones and puts them on.*

**TED:** Should you not go in there, Jeep?

*Jeep doesn't respond.*

**TED:** Jeep, take the headphones off.

**JEEP:** What?

*Ted signals for him to take the headphones off. Jeep does so.*

**JEEP:** Ha, ha . . . sorry, man. I couldn't hear you with the headphones.

**TED:** I was just saying, maybe you should go in there.

**JEEP:** Oh, yeah.

*He goes into the other part of the studio again.*

**TED:** Got it now, Jeep?

*Jeep looks at them blankly. He mouths, 'What?'*

**TED** (*to Dougal*): Jeep hasn't missed a Glastonbury since it started.

SCENE 5A INT./DAY 2*
SET: RECORDING STUDIO
*Jeep has headphones on and a huge joint hanging from his mouth. Hie eyes are closed. He smiles, opens his eyes, takes off the headphones and applauds.*

**JEEP:** That was great, guys. You won't get it more perfect than that. I think we can call it a day.

*Ted and Dougal look at him strangely. Dougal is fiddling with his keyboard. Ted has his guitar on and has one hand on a machine head.*

**TED:** Eh, we're still setting up, Jeep. We haven't actually recorded anything yet. Maybe you should go back into the booth.

*We deleted this scene from the final version.

**JEEP:** Oh, yeah, OK, But, still, guys, well done. Seriously.

*He leaves the room. We see him examining the ashtray, picking it up and looking puzzled.*

SCENE 5B INT./DAY 2*
SET: RECORDING STUDIO
*Back to Ted and Dougal.*

**TED:** Right, Dougal, you ready?

**DOUGAL:** I think so. Which button do I press again?

**TED:** The one with 'Song' written on it. OK, let's go.

*Ted strums the guitar, nods to Dougal who presses a key with 'Song' written on it. The instrumental Norwegian track starts playing. Ted starts singing and stops playing the guitar.*

**TED:** 'My lovely horse,
Running through the fields'

SCENE 5C INT./DAY 2*
SET: ANOTHER ROOM/RECORDING STUDIO
*We hear the song, muffled, nearby. We see Jack in another room, sitting on a plush red leather sofa. He uses a knife to rip the lining. He then pulls out some stuffing, searching frantically.*

**JACK:** DRINK!

SCENE 5D INT./DAY 2*
SET: RECORDING STUDIO
*Ted and Dougal are coming to the end of the song.*

**TED AND DOUGAL** (*chorus*)**:** 'Running around with a man on your back,
Like a train in the night'

*Ted does the one note again, and then moves his hand up the fretboard to do the final note. It goes wrong.*

**TED:** Oh, wait, wait . . . (*He tries again. It sounds off.*) . . . Wait. I can do this . . . (*He tries one more time. It sounds OK.*) . . . How was that?

*Jack comes into shot with a trumpet. He points it right at Ted's head and blasts it incredibly loudly. Ted falls out of shot with the shock.*

**JACK:** DRINK!

SCENE 5E INT./DAY 2*
SET: RECORDING STUDIO
*From left to right, Ted, Dougal and Jack are standing at the door. Jack looks very impatient. We see this from over Jeep's shoulder as he says goodbye.*

**JEEP** (*to each*)**:** Bye, man. Bye, man. Bye, man.

*He closes the door. They walk to Ted's car, get in and drive away. After a moment, another car, exactly the same make as Ted's, pulls up. Father Dick Byrne, Father Cyril McDuff and Father Jim Johnson get out and go up to the door. They knock, and after a second Jeep opens it. We see, over his shoulder, the three of them standing in the same positions as Ted, Dougal and Jack.*

**JEEP:** Wuaaaaghhhh!

SCENE 6 INT./NIGHT 2
SET: TED AND DOUGAL'S BEDROOM
*Ted and Dougal are in bed, staring happily at the ceiling.*

**TED:** Well, I don't want to jump to any conclusions and get us all excited, but I think we're definitely going to win.

**DOUGAL:** Really? Great!

**TED:** There'll be a lot to think about . . . promotional gifts for journalists, the American tour dates . . . I think a big flyposter campaign . . . and of course, the obligatory video . . .

**DOUGAL:** A video! Wow! Are priests allowed to be rock stars, though, Ted?

**TED:** Oh, yes. I remember one lad at the seminary . . . Father Benny Cake. He recorded a song and it went to number one in England.

**DOUGAL:** Really?

**TED:** Yes. He didn't want people to know he was a priest, so he called himself . . . God, what did he call himself? . . . Anyway, I think the song was called 'Vienna'.

**DOUGAL:** Why didn't he want people to know he was a priest?

**TED:** Ah, people thought if you were a priest, you were a bit of a 'square'. You were 'uncool'.

**DOUGAL:** And then we came along!

*We deleted this scene from the final version.

**TED:** Right! Anyway, Dougal, you go to sleep. Sweet dreams.

*He turns off the light. Close in on Dougal's face.*

SCENE 7 EXT./NIGHT/DAY X
SET: VARIOUS
*The following are the scenes from Dougal's ultimate rock video. This is a 'lifestyle' video with a dash of performance at the top. Each scene is shot in a very grey, dull kind of way, complete with the occasional zoom.*

*1. Ted and Dougal enter the shot from either side and start singing. They wear glittery jackets with very big lapels. The camera moves up and into a spotlight above the stage. Fade to . . .*

*2. Ted and Dougal playing table tennis in a grotty-looking youth-club-type place. Ted plays a really, really bad shot and the ball flies out of shot. They laugh happily.*

*3. Ted and Dougal on a horse, both wearing helmets.*

*4. Ted and Dougal in what looks like a yacht. The camera zooms back, in time to the music, to reveal that the yacht is absolutely tiny.*

*5. A horse looking around. Dougal looking around.*

*6. Ted and Dougal in a miserable-looking indoor swimming pool. A woman is in the pool, another woman is sitting at the edge. Ted's and Dougal's hair is completely dry. The four throw a ball to each other.*

*7. Ted and Dougal on a tandem.*

*8. Ted and Dougal looking at each other and singing as the camera circles them in a park.*

*9. Dougal and Ted standing beside the horse and laughing for no apparent reason.*

*10. Dougal (or Ted) hugging the horse.*

*11. The horse, Ted and Dougal all sitting down at a picnic.*

*12. For the instrumental part, we see a badly cut-out photograph of the horse's head – quite scary, in fact, with psychedelic colours radiating from it.*

SCENE 8 INT./NIGHT 2
SET: TED AND DOUGAL'S BEDROOM
*Cut back to Ted. Asleep. He frowns unhappily, then wakes up with a start. Dougal also bolts up at the same time. They look at each other.*

**TED:** We'll have to lose that guitar solo.

**END OF PART ONE**

* * *

**PART TWO**

SCENE 9 EXT./NIGHT 3
SET: LARGE HALL
*We see a banner outside the hall that reads 'A Song for Ireland '96'.*

SCENE 10 INT./NIGHT 3
SET: DRESSING ROOM
*Dougal and Ted are tuning up. They are very excited.*

**TED:** Well, Dougal, are you nervous?*

**DOUGAL:** Oh, I never get nervous, Ted.*

**TED:** You've never been nervous? Never in your life?*

**DOUGAL** (*thinks*): I don't think so.*

**TED:** What about when you were doing your tests. At the seminary. You must have been nervous then . . .*

**DOUGAL** (*laughs silently*): God, no, Ted. They were just a laugh.*

**TED:** But your whole future depended on those tests.*

**DOUGAL** (*worried*): Did they? God almighty . . . *

*There is a knock on the door. Two middle-aged men enter. One is the M.C., Fred Rickwood. The other is the show's producer, Charles Hedges. He looks at a clipboard while holding his other hand out to shake Ted's.*

**CHARLES:** Hello, Father . . . Crilly. I'm Charles Hedges. I'll be producing the show. This is . . .

**TED:** Oh, you don't have to tell me. Mr Rickwood, it's great to meet you. I thought you did a brilliant job presenting last year's show.

*Fred mumbles in a speedy, incomprehensible manner. Ted cocks his head as he hears this, looking puzzled.*

---

* We cut this from the final version and replaced it with Mrs Doyle putting make-up on Dougal.

*Pause.*

**TED:** What?

*Fred speaks again.*

**TED:** Ha, ha. Yes.

*Fred raises his voice, but speaks just as quickly. Ted smiles and nods.*

**TED:** Mmmmmm . . .

*Fred comes out with another stream of gibberish before walking to the door and giving them the thumbs-up before leaving.*

**TED:** Ah, I have to say he sounded a lot better on last year's show.

**CHARLES:** Oh, once he gets on stage he's fine.

**TED:** Have you known each other long?

**CHARLES:** Well, he's been my partner for ten years.

**TED:** Oh, right. Do you run the production company together?

**CHARLES:** No, no, I mean, he's my lover.

*Pause. They look at each other for a moment.*

**TED:** He's . . . he's quite a catch. Ah, this is my partner, Father Dougal McGuire. Not my sexual partner! I mean, you know, my partner that I do the song with.

**CHARLES:** Yes. I guessed that.

**TED:** Right. Of course you did. Not that there's anything wrong with that type of thing!

**CHARLES:** I thought the Church thought that 'that type of thing' was inherently wrong.

**TED:** Ah, yes. It does. (*Pause.*) The whole gay thing. I suppose it's a bit of a puzzle to us all. (*Pause.*) I suppose it must be great fun, though . . . not the, eh, you know . . . but the nightclub scene and all that. The whole rough and tumble of . . . homosexual activity and . . . having boyfriends when you're a man. Like, with girlfriends, you couldn't bring them out to a match . . . but I'm sure with a man, he'd be dying to go. (*Pause.*) Anyway, don't worry about what the Church thinks. Sure they used to think the earth was flat. It's like . . . you know . . . sometimes the Pope says things he doesn't really mean. You know. We all get things wrong. Even the Pope!

**CHARLES:** What about Papal infallibility?

**TED:** Yes. I suppose so, but, ah . . . is that for everything, do you know? The infallibility?

**CHARLES:** I don't know!

**TED:** Right! Right! Of course, ah . . . anyway . . . (*Long, long pause.*) Nothing to do with me. (*Pause. Ted is mortified. He looks around.*) Look at Dougal! Bored out of his mind! (*Cut to a bamboozled Dougal.*) We could go on all night talking about gay issues, but, God . . . poor old Dougal! No interest in the subject whatsoever!

**CHARLES:** Anyway, I'm looking forward to your entry, Father.

*Pause.*

**TED:** Oh, right! The song! Yes, eh, me too.

**DOUGAL:** Do you think we'll win?

**TED:** It's not up to him, Dougal. It's the public who decide.

**CHARLES:** Not this year.

**TED:** No?

**CHARLES:** No. We've decided that this year I'll pick the winner. The old phone-in system wasn't really working out.

**TED:** Was it not? The song the public chose has won five years in a row.

**CHARLES:** Yes, but . . . ah . . . well, it's just . . . very complicated . . . and . . . eh . . . you're looking forward to the show then?

*Pause.*

**TED:** Oh, yes! It's a big thrill for us. A bit of a novelty, too, I suppose, seeing as we're priests.

**CHARLES:** Well, not really. There's another act tonight that's very like you. Father Dick Byrne and Father Cyril McDuff.

**TED:** God . . . I didn't think they'd make it this far . . .

**DOUGAL:** Flip! They'll win, Ted! We might as well give up now.

**TED:** That's a very defeatist attitude, Dougal.

**DOUGAL:** Actually it is. Sorry about that, Ted.

*Dick bursts through the door. Dougal moves beside Ted. Cyril comes in as well, looking lost as usual.*

**DICK:** But he's right, Ted!

**TED:** Dick!

**DICK:** You ready to be beaten, then?

**TED:** Hah! It's probably a terrible song altogether.

**DICK:** No, it's not! It'll be better than your one, Ted, you big fool.

**TED:** Take that back!

**CHARLES:** I'll, eh . . . get going.

**TED** (*turning into a priest again*): Oh, right. See you later, Charles. Thanks for everything so far. It really is a tremendous honour to be here.

**DICK** (*ditto*): Yes, I'm sure we'll all have a great time. (*There is a respectful silence for a moment as Charles leaves.*) I won't take it back! I bet we get a million points! And I bet you get minus seven thousand!

**TED:** Oh, yes? How much? How much do you bet?

**DICK:** Four pounds.

**TED:** You're on.

**DICK:** This is just on us winning, now. Obviously, that million points thing was an exaggeration.

**TED:** Oh, right, yeah.

*A paper ball hits Dougal on the back of the head. Dougal looks around and sees Cyril looking innocent. Dougal looks around to see if anyone else is in the room. He is very confused.*

**DICK:** All right, come on, Cyril! We're off to win the contest! Seriously, though, Ted, even if you don't win, I'm sure the song's very good.

**TED:** Do you really, Dick?

**DICK:** Nooooooooooo!

*He and Cyril duck out through the door. Ted turns to the camera and pulls a hugely enraged face.*

**TED:** Oooooh! I really hate Father Dick Byrne!

SCENE 11 INT./NIGHT 3
SET: SIDE OF STAGE
*Ted and Dougal are beside our host, Fred Rickwood. He is in a slightly crouched position. His tie is loose, and his suit badly crumpled.*

**TED:** Good luck tonight, Fred.

*Fred mumbles something incoherently.*

SCENE 12 INT./NIGHT 3
SET: STUDIO CONTROL
*We see engineers, technicians, banks of television monitors, etc. Charles is sitting in his luxurious producer's chair.*

**CHARLES:** Let's go!

*We see very impressive television graphics, accompanied by a voiceover.*

**VOICEOVER:** And now, live from the Theatre Royal, 'A Song for Ireland 1996', and here is your host, Fred Rickwood!!!!

SCENE 13 INT./NIGHT 3
SET: SIDE OF STAGE
*Fred sucks on his cigarette one more time, steps on it and shuffles out of shot.*

SCENE 14 INT./NIGHT 3
SET: STAGE
*We see the television pictures of Fred striding on to the stage. He walks with an impressive stroll and his suit and tie are now immaculate. He waves to the audience, does a quick boxing shuffle and runs confidently to his microphone.*

**FRED:** Helloooo and welcome to the thirty-fifth 'A Song for Ireland', the contest in which we select Ireland's entry for Eurosong '96. It's not often that priests appear on the show, but tonight we've got two acts comprised of clerical duos. We've also got some exciting new acts from all over the country, and a few names that will be very familiar to all of you out there in TV land. A word about the emergency exits – you'll find them on your left, and just behind the stalls. In the event of a fire, please make your way calmly to one of these.

SCENE 15 INT./NIGHT 3*
SET: CONTROL ROOM
*We see Charles at the mixing desk.*

**CHARLES:** What a pro.

*We deleted this scene from the final version.

SCENE 16 INT./NIGHT 3*
SET: THE AUDIENCE
*We see Jack and Father Jim sitting beside each other in identical wheelchairs. The two identical Mrs Doyles adjust the blankets on the priests' laps. This irritates them and they wave their identical sticks in an identical manner at the two identical Mrs Doyles. The shot should be completely symmetrical.*

SCENE 17 INT./NIGHT 3
SET: SIDE OF STAGE
*Ted and Dougal are full of nervous tension. They can see Dick and Cyril at the opposite side of the stage waiting to go on. Dick is posing and looking very aloof. Between them and Dick, in the centre of the stage, Fred continues his introduction.*

**TED:** Look at Dick Byrne there, showing off. He won't be too happy when we win and he comes last.

*Ted catches Dick's eye. Dick gives him the two fingers. Ted returns it. They continue like this for a while.*

SCENE 18 INT./NIGHT 3
SET: STAGE
*Fred glances to the side just in time to see Ted's two-fingered gesture. Ted sees him and immediately turns his hand around to give him a friendly salute. Fred is doing his spiel.*

**FRED:** . . . So . . . please welcome on stage the Euro-hopefuls from Rugged Island, Father Dick Byrne and Father Cyril McDuff.

SCENE 19 INT./NIGHT 3
SET: SIDE OF STAGE
*Ted and Dougal, unimpressed.*

SCENE 20 INT./NIGHT 3
SET: STAGE
*Music starts. Dick and Cyril are revealed under single spotlights – Cyril slightly in the background on keyboard, Dick in the foreground, standing in a very dramatic way, his arms held apart, his head bowed low. The music swells slightly, and Dick raises his head and starts singing.*

**DICK:** 'When I was young, I had a dream
And though the dream was very small
It wouldn't leave me.'

*We deleted this scene from the final version.

SCENE 21 INT./NIGHT 3
SET: SIDE OF STAGE
*We see Ted and Dougal looking very superior.*

**TED:** Dougal, Dougal . . .

*He gets Dougal's attention and does a very childish impression of Dick Byrne.*

SCENE 22 INT./NIGHT 3
SET: STAGE
*Back to Dick. A single tear runs down his cheek.*

**DICK:** 'To be a beggar or a king
To play the poet or the fool
And now you see me . . .'
(*Chorus*) 'And now the miracle is mine!!!!'

*At this line, the rest of the stage is lit up and we see an entire backing band: a line of priests around a microphone singing along, violinists, etc. It all looks very impressive.*

SCENE 23 INT./NIGHT 3
SET: SIDE OF STAGE
*Ted is still doing his silly impression. He and Dougal see the impressive stage set-up and freeze, their mouths agape.*

SCENE 24 INT./NIGHT 3
SET: STAGE
*Back to Dick. He continues the chorus. As he does so, his actions are very dramatic and passionate.*

**DICK:** 'The battle fought, the war begun!!!!!
And now I've nothing left but time!!!!! But still I reach out . . . to the sun!!!!!'

*The song drops down again.*

SCENE 25 INT./NIGHT 3
SET: SIDE OF STAGE
*Ted has had enough.*

**TED:** Hmrprh . . . I need a fag.

*He walks off, leaving Dougal there.*

SCENE 26 INT./NIGHT 3
SET: OUTSIDE A LIFT
*Ted is standing outside the lift. The doors open and a technician comes out. He is whistling something. Ted looks at him, puzzled, then gets into the lift.*

SCENE 27 INT./NIGHT 3
SET: A LIFT
*Ted walks into the lift. He presses a button and the doors close. We hear lift muzak. Ted cocks his head, listening to it. He freezes, then goes into a panic. He starts hitting all the buttons frantically.*

**TED:** . . . Oh, Ghoddddd . . .

SCENE 28 INT./NIGHT 3
SET: SIDE OF STAGE
*Ted runs into shot and grabs Dougal.*

**TED:** Dougal!!!! We can't do the song!

**DOUGAL:** What? Why not, Ted?

**TED:** I just heard it in the lift! They're piping it in in there! I heard someone *whistling* it!

**DOUGAL:** Well, that's good, isn't it? Shows what a great song it is.

**TED:** No, no no! They'll know we ripped it off!!! It must be more famous than we thought! We'll be found out! Oh God!

**DOUGAL:** Wh— what'll we do, Ted?

**TED:** Why did this have to happen to us? What did we ever do to deserve this? (*He thinks.*) Wait! Wait! I have an idea!

**DOUGAL:** What, Ted?

**TED:** Let's pray! We'll pray and ask God to help us.

**DOUGAL:** But Dick's probably thought of that! He probably prayed that we wouldn't win!

**TED:** God, yes! A pre-emptive pray! Maybe we can cancel out his pray with our one!

**DOUGAL:** Song's nearly over, Ted.

**TED:** Oh, no! We'll have to . . . Dougal . . . I think we'll have to resort to plan B.

*Shot of a puzzled, then horrified Dougal.*

SCENE 29 INT./NIGHT 3
SET: STAGE
*Dick is now on his knees, coming to the end of the song. He repeats the chorus, bows his head and the lights go out with the sudden end of the song. The lights come on and Dick stands up to rapturous applause. He gestures to the rest of the band and*

*bows etc., etc., as he and Cyril move off. Dick shoots a smug look at Ted.*

**FRED:** Well, how about that! Wonderful . . . (*He applauds.*) . . . OK, now to our next act, Father Ted Crilly and Father Dougal McGuire!

*Ted and Dougal walk on to applause. They look very dispirited. Dougal goes up and stands beside Ted. They then proceed to do the original version of 'My Lovely Horse'. Ted plays the same note over and over. As they do the song we see various people listening . . .*

*1. The two Jacks listening from the side of the stage, disgusted. Mrs Doyle has her head in her hands.\**

*2. Fred, at the side of the stage, rumpled up once more, smoking a fag. He says something impenetrable and uncomplimentary.\**

*3. Dick and Cyril rolling about on the floor, laughing their heads off.\**

*4. Tom still in his 'I Shot JR' T-shirt, watching a television that's plugged into a lightbulb in his horrible, bare house.\**

**TOM:** Brilliant! Mammy? Oh, she's dead.\*

*5. The people in the producer's box, including Charles. They look at the screen with their mouths open, completely frozen.\**

*Back to Ted and Dougal. They can hear Dick and Cyril laughing in the distance and look very uncomfortable. They come to the end of the song. Ted goes for that one different note on his guitar. It goes wrong.\**

**TED:** Wait, wait . . . (*He tries again.*) I can do this. Wait . . . (*Last time. He does it. No applause.*) Ah . . . thank you.

*They walk off to complete silence.*

SCENE 30 INT./NIGHT 3
SET: DRESSING ROOM
*We hear lots of laughter. Close-up on a champagne bottleneck. The cork pops off to a tremendous cheer. We gradually pull back to see that Ted is pouring the champagne into glasses belonging to Jack, Mrs Doyle, Dougal and Charles. Jack takes the bottle when Ted has stopped pouring.*

---

\*We deleted these lines from the final version and replaced them with the lyrics to 'My Lovely Horse'.

**TED:** Well, we did it Dougal! Don't ask me how, but we did it!

**CHARLES:** Well, the reason you won, Father, is quite simple. Yours was the best song.

**TED:** Well, I suppose so. Although I didn't really think the audience was going for it.

**CHARLES:** Audiences?! What do they know?!!!!

*Fred mumbles something impenetrable and congratulatory.\* Slight pause.*

**TED:** Yes! (*He raises his glass. Everyone cheers.*) Ah, there's Dick Byrne! (*Dick and Cyril wander into shot.*) Well, Dick. Yet again, Rugged Island capitulates to sheer, raw talent.

**DICK** (*immediately to Charles*): What's going on? Our song was miles better than theirs!

**CHARLES:** Ah, well, we, ah, we thought . . .

**DICK** (*to Charles*): I mean, for God's sake! It was just one note over and over again!

**CHARLES:** Yes, we, ah . . . we admired its . . . (*Fred mumbles something incomprehensible.*) Yes, exactly. Fred put it better than I ever could.

**TED** (*unconvincingly*): Hah! So there!

**CHARLES:** I mean, your song was good, but . . . a bit overblown. That can alienate people, you know . . .

**DICK:** But they were going mad for it . . .

**CHARLES:** Yes . . . but . . . ahem . . . oh . . . well, you know . . .

**DICK:** I mean, what's going on?! It's almost as if you wanted Ireland to lose the next Eurosong contest!

*Charles and Fred exchange glances.*

**CHARLES** (*long pause*): Ha. Ha. Nonsense. Why would we do that?

**DICK:** I don't know. Maybe because it was costing you so much to stage . . .

**TED** (*shakes his head sadly*): Dick, Dick, Dick, Dick . . . Now come on. Does that really sound plausible? I really think you should go and count your sour grapes before . . . they hatch.

---

\*One of the things he mumbles is 'Shave a bullock'.

*Dick goes to leave.*

**CYRIL** (*to Dougal*): Better luck next time.

**DICK:** We lost, Cyril.

**CYRIL:** Really?

**DICK:** Come on . . .

*Dick and Cyril leave.*

**CHARLES:** Well done, again, Father. And I'm sure you'll do very well in the Eurosong contest.

*He moves off.*

**TED:** I think so! Next stop, Europe!

*Charles goes over to Fred, who is standing beside the window. From the window beyond we can hear angry shouting.*

**CHARLES:** We'd better sneak them out the back. That's a nasty crowd.

SCENE 31 INT./NIGHT 4
SET: BACKSTAGE AT EUROSONG
*The following is shot as if we're watching it on television. We see Ted and Dougal sitting together on a yellow sofa. They have their spangle suits on and look quite excited. Jack is behind them, sprawled over a chair, completely out of it. Mrs Doyle is sitting behind looking very enthusiastic. Dougal and Ted smile and look at a monitor situated somewhere above and behind the camera – this is the classic Eurovision 'waiting for the points' pose.*

**VOICE:** And now could we please have the points for Ireland?

*We then hear, in a series of different accents and languages, each country give Ireland no points – 'Nil points, nada punten, keinen pune, no points, zero points'. Gradually the smiles die from their faces. The credits roll as Ted and Dougal examine their sleeves, look around, puff out their cheeks, scratch their heads, avoid each other's eyes, etc., etc. Mrs Doyle also looks very embarrassed.*

**THE END**

# the plague

**ARTHUR:** This was our *Fawlty Towers* episode. It's similar in that it relies on a great deal of physical comedy, with people running around and throwing themselves down stairs, and most of the action is set in real time. Not that we were ever in the *Fawlty Towers* league; we got better, but we were never *that* good, and our plots were never that airtight. The surreal nature of *Father Ted* meant that our plots didn't have to make perfect sense. The plots may be more satisfying when they do make sense, but as long as they didn't test the audience's patience too much and kept delivering the jokes, we were usually forgiven. This plot is incredibly simple and it depends on a *complete* cheat: that the rabbits can get around the house without anyone noticing, and can breed in those kind of numbers from just one rabbit . . . overnight. Jim Norton (Bishop Brennan) had a terrible time with those rabbits. They did their business all over the place in the scene where he and Jack are in bed, and all the showers at the TV studios had broken down – Jim was not best pleased . . .

**GRAHAM:** We had some incredibly stupid complaints about Jack calling the rabbits 'hairy Japanese bastards'. They bleeped it out in Canada because they thought it was racist, and in Britain someone phoned in and said it was an insult to his Japanese wife. I really don't understand that. First of all, Jack thinks they're rats – which shows how ludicrous the whole thing is – and the fact that he calls them 'hairy Japanese bastards' makes about as much sense as Dougal calling his rabbit Sampras because of the tennis/rabbit connection. It's just a senseless joke, a surrealistic silly jape – but you can never underestimate the desire some people have to be offended.

I dimly remember an old *Star Trek* episode called *The Trouble With Tribbles* which had a similar plot to this. Luckily, we didn't see it in the run-up to writing this show or we might have thought it too similar.

**PART ONE**

SCENE 1 EXT./NIGHT 1*
SET: THE ISLAND
*A particularly spooky part of the island. A man, woman and their daughter – posh, southside Dublin types – all in expensive hiking gear, are walking along a misty clifftop.*

**WOMAN:** Come on. Nearly there. (*Pause.*) It's a bit creepy, isn't it?

**MAN:** Oh, come on, Jane. There's nothing out there that can—

*A branch snaps behind them. They turn around and see, in the mist, the outline of a man. Close-up as the man's face comes out of the mist. It is Father Jack. We see, from Jack's point of view, a look of pure horror dawning on their faces.*

**THE FAMILY:** Aaaaaaaarrrrggggghhhhhh!!!!!!!

SCENE 2 INT./DAY 2
SET: PAROCHIAL HOUSE
*Dougal is looking at a cage on the table. Inside it we see a rabbit. Dougal looks at it lovingly, and then picks up a book with a big picture of a rabbit on it. The book is called 'My New Rabbit'. Jack is asleep in the background. Ted enters.*

**TED:** Ah, there he is, anyway.

**DOUGAL:** He's great, isn't he?

*Ted approaches the rabbit.*

**TED:** He is all right. Does he have a name?

**DOUGAL:** I don't think so. Mrs Guthrie didn't mention one, anyway.[†] God, I dunno . . . how about 'Ted'? That's a good name for a rabbit.

**TED:** What? No, that's not a good idea, Dougal. Don't forget I'm called Ted as well.

*Dougal thinks and then points at Ted in a 'you're right' gesture.*

**DOUGAL:** Well, I could call you 'Father Ted'.

**TED:** No . . . seriously, Dougal . . . try and come

up with something a bit more original.

*Mrs Doyle comes in with a tea tray.*

**MRS DOYLE:** Hello, Fathers.

**TED AND DOUGAL:** Hello, Mrs Doyle!

*Mrs Doyle collects some cups and goes out again. Dougal looks after her for a few moments, a thoughtful look on his face.*

**DOUGAL:** How about 'Mrs Doyle'?

**TED:** No, Mrs Doyle isn't a good name for a rabbit. You need something like 'Popsy' or 'Bruce'.

**DOUGAL:** Oh, right. (*Pause.*) Wait! I've got one!

**TED:** Yes?

**DOUGAL:** You know the way he's got big floppy ears flopping all about the place.

**TED:** Yes?

**DOUGAL:** Well, why don't we call him 'Father Jack Hackett'?

**TED** (*has had enough*): Perfect! Father Jack it is!

*Jack wakes up.*

**JACK:** What?

**TED:** Nothing, Father. Dougal's named his new rabbit after you.

**JACK:** What?

**DOUGAL:** Are you all right, Father Jack?

**JACK** (*confused*): What?

**TED:** He wasn't talking to you, Father. He was talking to the rabbit.

**JACK:** What?

**DOUGAL:** I think Father Jack wants a drink.

---

*Scenes 1-3 from *Think Fast, Father Ted* that featured the television show *Father Ben* were transferred to here in the final version.
† Mrs Guthrie the pet-shop owner was dropped from the final version and was referred to as 'the woman in the pet shop' instead.

JACK (*immediately happy*): Drink!

TED: Will we get him some water?

JACK: Water? Feck!

TED: No, Dougal, honestly. This will get very confusing.

DOUGAL: Ah, Ted. I've got used to calling him Father Jack. Could we not call Father Jack something else?

TED: Great idea! What'll we call him? Flipper? Flipper the priest. Flipper the priest it is!

JACK: What?

TED: No, Dougal, c'mon now, it won't work. Call him after someone you like.

DOUGAL: Someone I like?

*Dougal muses. The telephone rings. Ted picks it up.*

TED: Hello, Father Ted Crilly speaking.

SCENE 3 INT./DAY 2
SET: BISHOP'S HOUSE
*We see Bishop Len Brennan in a large bath on a cordless telephone. His 'bishop stuff' is hanging neatly beside the bath. On the wall there is a massive painting of Len, kitted out to the nines, looking more like a Napoleonic figure than a religious one.*

BRENNAN: Crilly, it's me.

TED: Oh, feck!

BRENNAN: What?

*Ted freezes in horror.*

TED: Ooo ees thees? Zere is no Creely heere.

BRENNAN: Crilly!

*Ted slams down the telephone.*

TED (*to Dougal*): God almighty! I just said 'feck' to Bishop Brennan!

DOUGAL: O'ho! He won't like that.

TED: It might be all right, though. I disguised my voice so he'd think he dialled the wrong number.

*The telephone rings. Ted picks it up.*

BRENNAN: Crilly!

TED: Ah, Bishop Brennan. I think you must have got the wrong number when you called there.

*Ted looks at Dougal and crosses his fingers hopefully. Dougal does the same in a supportive way.*

BRENNAN: What?! What are you on about now? When I was talking to you there, you swore at me, then put on a foreign accent and then hung up.

TED: Did I? I don't think so. You must have got the wrong number.

BRENNAN: No, I didn't. It was definitely you. God forbid there's more than one Ted Crilly in the world.

TED: O'ho, no! When God made me, he kept the mould and . . . didn't make anyone else with it . . .

BRENNAN: Shut up, Crilly! I'll make it quick. What would the words 'Jack', 'sleepwalking' and 'bollock naked' suggest to you?

TED: Oh, no . . .

BRENNAN: This is the third time in the last six months! You may have heard of Brian Noonan, a very important Junior Minister and a personal friend of mine. And I can tell you, the last thing he and his family needs is a vision of an elderly priest wearing only a pair of socks and a hat! I'll be over on Thursday to examine what kind of security you have – and Crilly?

TED: Yes?

BRENNAN: If you ever try to bullshit me like that again, I'll rip off your arms.

*He clicks the telephone off and puts it to one side. As he does so, we get a very brief glimpse of a woman emerging from the water at the other end of the bath.*

SCENE 4 INT./DAY 2
SET: PAROCHIAL HOUSE
*Ted puts the telephone down.*

TED: He's coming over.

**DOUGAL:** Oh, no. Why is he always bothering us? You'd think he'd have his hands full running that betting shop.*

**TED:** No, Dougal. Bishop Brennan is a bishop. There's a clue in his name – Bishop Brennan?*

**DOUGAL:** Oh, right. What was he calling about, anyway?

**TED:** Father Jack's been sleepwalking in the nude again.

**JACK:** What?

**TED:** Bishop Brennan is coming over to have a word with you, Father. About your nude sleepwalking.

**JACK:** Nudie Father Jack!

**TED:** That's right, Father. Can you think of any reason why you might be doing that?

*Jack looks clueless.*

**TED:** You're not having any doubts about your vocation, are you, Father?

**JACK** (*disgusted*): What?

**DOUGAL:** Maybe it's the Diet Whiskey, Ted . . .

*Ted picks up a bottle with 'Diet Whiskey' written on the side.*

**TED:** I don't think so. Anyway, he hasn't touched this. You don't like this, do you Father?

*Jack grabs the bottle and throws it to the other side of the room, where it smashes.*

**TED:** We really should talk about it, and remember you can always share your problems with us. Father Dougal and myself will always lend you a friendly ear. Isn't that right, Dougal?

**DOUGAL** (*beat*): Sorry, Ted?

**TED:** Don't forget, Father, we're your friends, and we're always here for you, no matter what you've done. Would you like to talk about it now?

**DOUGAL:** Well, Ted . . . *Byker Grove* . . .

**TED:** Oh, God, yes, after *Byker Grove*.

*Ted and Dougal excitedly take their seats and hit the*

---

*We deleted this from the final version.

remote control. Jack watches them grumpily as the 'Byker Grove' music starts up.

SCENE 5 INT./DAY 2
SET: PAROCHIAL HOUSE
*Dougal is playing with the rabbit on the floor. He throws a little stick.*

**DOUGAL:** Go on, boy. Go on! Get it, boy!

*Ted walks in.*

**TED:** C'mon, now, Dougal, get him in his cage. We don't want Bishop Brennan seeing him.

**DOUGAL:** Ah, Ted, he might like him.

**TED:** No, he won't, Dougal. Bishop Brennan doesn't like rabbits at all, now.

**DOUGAL:** Why not?

**TED:** It's a strange story. About ten years ago, he was in New York and he was trapped in a lift with about twenty rabbits for the whole night. They started nibbling his cape and everything.

**DOUGAL:** How did they get in?

**TED:** I suppose they must have burrowed in. You know rabbits. (*Ted sees the rabbit at his feet and picks it up.*) God almighty. They can move fast enough.

**DOUGAL:** Why do you say that, Ted?

**TED:** Well, he just shot across the room to me there. (*Ted notices that Dougal still has his rabbit as well.*) Wait now. That's your rabbit.

**DOUGAL:** Yeah.

**TED:** So where did this one come from?

**DOUGAL:** Eh, Ted . . .

*Cut to Jack, asleep. There is another rabbit on his head.*

**TED:** I don't like the look of this at all. Don't let your rabbit get mixed up with the other lads.

**DOUGAL:** All right. Come on, Sampras . . .

**TED:** Wh— what did you call him?

**DOUGAL:** Sampras. Like Pete Sampras.

**TED:** Why?

**DOUGAL:** Well, you know . . . rabbits, tennis . . . you know . . . that whole connection there.

*Pause.*

**TED:** Ah, right! (*Ted turns and pulls a 'what the hell was that all about?' face.*) Come on, we'd better round them up. We'll just release these spare ones into the wild. (*He picks up the two rabbits and puts them in a box. He looks at Sampras.*) Ah, look at him there. All alone with no other rabbits for company. He must feel like Brian Keenan when they took John McCarthy off to another cell. Anyway, he'll get used to it . . .

*The camera closes in on the rabbit. Fade out.*

SCENE 6 INT./DAY 2
SET: PAROCHIAL HOUSE
*Fade back in on the rabbit. Time has passed. We pull back slowly from the close-up of the rabbit to reveal that the room is hugely populated by rabbits. They crawl all over the chairs and tables, and chew the carpets, etc. Jack is looking at them warily. Ted comes in, yawning, some letters in his hand.*

**TED:** Morning, Father. (*He goes to the table and starts reading the letters.*) Bills, bills, bills . . .

*Dougal enters.*

**DOUGAL:** Morning, Ted!

**TED:** Morning, Dougal.

**DOUGAL:** What'll we do today, Ted?

**TED** (*walks to his armchair and sits*): Well, Bishop Brennan'll be here soon, so we'll have to get that rabbit of yours somewhere he won't see him. God, he'd go mad if he knew there was a rabbit around the place.

**DOUGAL** (*sits on sofa*): Fair enough, Ted!

**TED:** I hope he's in a good mood. Len can be a bit scary when . . . when, when . . . (*He looks around at all the rabbits.*) Aaaaggghhh!!!!

**DOUGAL:** Ted! What's wrong?

**TED:** Rabbits!

**DOUGAL:** Rabbits? Where – oh, wow!

**TED:** Where the hell did these ones come from?!

**DOUGAL:** It's like a big rabbit rock festival. Well, I suppose we'll just have to get used to it.

**TED:** Get used to it? Dougal, we have to get rid of these before Bishop Brennan arrives.

**DOUGAL:** Oh, right, yeah.*

**TED:** I'll call Mrs Guthrie. *

**DOUGAL:** She's gone on holiday, Ted.*

**TED:** Damn. What'll we do?*

**DOUGAL** (*frowns*): Well . . . if we . . . there's something we can do, if . . . wait a second, let me . . . I know . . . I know, I've got it, Ted!

**TED:** What?

**DOUGAL:** Well, the way I see it . . . if there's . . . ah . . . wait a second, what's the problem again?

**TED:** THE RABBITS!

**DOUGAL:** Oh, yeah, yeah! Sorry, Ted. Ah, why don't we try and give them to Father Duff? He's always going on about how he'd love a few rabbits running about the place.

**TED:** You're right! I used to think it was just a mad thing to say, but now— (*He picks up the telephone.*) Come on . . . come on . . . Larry?

SCENE 7 INT./DAY 2
SET: FATHER DUFF'S HOUSE
*We see Father Larry Duff on the telephone.*

**LARRY:** Ted! How's it hanging?

**TED:** Eh, it's hanging fine, Larry. Listen, we've

*As Mrs Guthrie was cut, in the final version Dougal said that he couldn't take the rabbit back because he bought it from a travelling pet shop that wouldn't return until spring.

got a bit of a problem here . . . Do you remember how you're always saying you'd love to have a few rabbits around the place?

**LARRY:** I do, Ted. That's one of my all-time fantasies. I'd love to have a few dozen rabbits all over the place.

**TED:** Well, today's your lucky day! We've got loads of the things!

**LARRY:** Sorry, Ted, won't be able to take them.

**TED:** Really? Oh, God, why not?

*Cut from close-up to reveal that Larry is surrounded by Rottweilers.*

**LARRY:** I sort of gave up on the rabbits idea – it just seemed too far-fetched – so I got twelve Rottweilers instead.

**TED:** Oh, right.

**LARRY:** I'd love to take the rabbits, but I'd be afraid the Rottweilers might maul them.

**TED:** Yes, yes, I understand. Bye, Larry.

*Larry puts the telephone down. Cut to close-up again. We hear a dog growling.*

**LARRY:** Bad dog . . . Don't you look at me like that . . . you're a very bad d—

*The dog lunges and Larry disappears out of shot with a scream.*

SCENE 8 INT./DAY 2
SET: PAROCHIAL HOUSE
*Ted steps away from the telephone.*

**TED:** He can't take the rabbits. He's got twelve Rottweilers.

**JACK** (*to Ted*): Hey! Hey! You!

**TED:** Yes, Father?

**JACK** (*pointing at the rabbits*): Wh— . . . rats . . . d— . . . wh— . . .

**TED:** Oh, yes, Father, we can see them, too. You're not hallucinating.

*Jack takes this in, then looks at the rabbits.*

**JACK** (*to rabbits*): Hairy Japanese bastards . . .

*Ted and Dougal exchange a look. Jack gets up and leaves. Cut back to Dougal and Ted.*

**TED:** Do you know what this is like, Dougal? It's like a plague or something. A big rabbit plague. I wonder if God is punishing us for something. Maybe it's because I said feck to Bishop Brennan.

**DOUGAL:** God, if he sends down a plague of rabbits just because you said feck to Bishop Brennan, imagine what he'll do when he finds out about all the money you robbed from that charity!

**TED:** Dougal, that money was just resting in my account. I was keeping it there until I moved it on—

**DOUGAL:** Ted . . .

**TED:** . . . It was basically a non-profit-making subsidiary account . . .

**DOUGAL:** The rabbits have gone, Ted.

*Cut to a wide view of the room. All the rabbits have gone.*

**TED:** Where'd they go?

**DOUGAL:** They followed Father Jack out of the room.

**TED:** That's amazing. So it wasn't that the last rabbit was in heat at all. I've always thought Father Jack gave off a kind of furry smell. The rabbits must think he's some sort of rabbit God.

**DOUGAL:** Great! So if we just keep Father Jack out of the way . . .

**TED:** But Bishop Brennan's coming to see Jack. No, we'll have to get them out of here.

**DOUGAL:** Hey – Paddy Jordan!

**TED:** Paddy Jordan! Yes! He'd definitely take them for us! Definitely!

SCENE 9 EXT./DAY 2
SET: GREYHOUND TRACK
*We see Paddy Jordan, a middle-aged fat man in a white coat and hat. Paddy, Ted and Dougal are at a small distance from the track and at a higher level, so we can see it clearly. There is a small, expectant crowd there, too. It is just grass, and a hundred metres long, like an athletics track. There are about seven lanes, with a box-like cage construction at the top of each one. We hear a buzzer. A badly constructed full-size cloth greyhound emerges on a rail running along the track. Then the trapdoor on each of the cages shoots up. The cloth greyhound hurtles along the side of the track as two or three rabbits emerge slowly from the cages. The other rabbits remain inside. We see the rabbits sniffing around. Cut back to the greyhound, which hits a bar at the end of the track and spins into the air before crashing to the ground. Ted, Dougal and Paddy stare as the rabbits slowly go about their business. Hold on this for just a moment too long.*

**PADDY:** God, no, Father. They're even worse than the hares.

**TED:** Yes . . . they're not exactly 'going for it', are they? I tell you what – I'll go and give Tom a call. He might be able to help us.

*Ted goes out of shot. Dougal and Paddy look at the rabbits.*

**PADDY:** To be honest, Father, I think I'm going to have to close down the track.

**DOUGAL:** Why?

**PADDY:** It's just a really, really bad idea.*

SCENE 10 INT./DAY 2
SET: TOM'S HOUSE†
*Tom opens the door – as usual, he wears his 'I Shot JR' T-shirt – and says into camera . . .*

**TOM:** Hello, Father!!

---

*This didn't work because it was a joke on top of a joke. The idea was that Paddy has already been racing hares, and that the rabbits were much worse. Luckily, we changed this on location and the version that ended up on-screen (with Dougal's line about having some money on 'that little beauty') was much better.
† A new scene was inserted before this with Ted and Dougal waiting for Tom to answer the door.

*Ted and Dougal enter the room. It is a bombsite. A big pile of rubble is in the centre of the room; there are plastic bags piled up in one corner, a faded poster of Farrah Fawcett Majors on the wall, a shredded mattress in one corner and the word 'Redrum' painted in red on the wall. The room is divided by a partition with a Perspex window, through which we can see shelves full of tools, and a doorway into this other smaller room.*

**TOM:** Would you like something to eat, Father? I could do you a salad.

**TED:** Ah, no thanks, Tom. Some other time. Well, I have to say, you've done wonders with the place.

**TOM:** Right, Father, you said you had some rabbits for me?

**TED:** Yes, they're in the car.

**TOM:** Right! With you in a mo'.

*Tom goes into the room with the shelves. Ted and Dougal talk in the foreground. Tom is in the background looking through the shelves.*

**DOUGAL:** Ted, what's Tom going to do again?

**TED:** I don't know, really. He just said he'd take care of them.

*Ted and Dougal don't notice, but in the background we can see Tom pick up a hammer and start swinging it around, testing it.*

**TED:** I'd say he'll just collect them all together and put them somewhere safe.

*Tom puts down the hammer, frowning, and picks up a baseball bat. He starts testing it, swinging it around wildly, knocking things off the shelves and stumbling around. Despite the noise, Ted and Dougal still don't notice.*

**DOUGAL:** Ah, right. So he's just going to look after them.

**TED:** Yes. Basically, I think he'll just put them in a big pen where they can run around and have a bit of a play . . .

*Tom puts down the baseball bat and picks up a huge chainsaw. He starts yanking the chain. It splutters once or twice.*

**TED:** Ah, yeah, Tom's the man for a job like this. He'll try and keep the rabbits as comfortable as possible while they—

*Ted's words are drowned out by the sound of the chainsaw. Tom raises it in the air as Ted keeps talking, Dougal nodding at what he's saying, voicing his agreement from time to time. We can't hear any of this, of course. After a moment or two, the chainsaw conks out and Tom looks disappointed.*

**TED:** . . . so there's absolutely nothing to worry about.

*Tom looks up and sees something out of shot. He disappears towards the door.*

**TED:** He's taking his time, though. I wonder wh—. . . Ah, there he is . . .

*Ted's voice trails off as he sees Tom walking slowly out of the room with a long Samurai sword poised for action.*

**TOM:** All right, Father! Let's go for it!

**TED:** Ah, that's a very impressive sword, Tom. Eh, I just wonder . . . Where exactly are you going to put the rabbits?

**TOM:** In the vice, Father.

**TED:** In the vice?

**TOM:** Yeah . . . I'll show you . . . I've been practisin' with this toy one.

*He takes out a toy rabbit from under his arm.*

First you stun it . . .

*He whacks its head off the side of the workbench.*

Then you stick it in the vice . . .

*He sticks the rabbit's head in the vice and tightens it with the handle.*

You grab the legs there, Father . . .

*Ted very reluctantly grabs the legs and pulls the rabbit out from the vice. We see Tom lifting the sword.*

**TED:** Tom, you know the phrase 'to take care of something' . . .

**TOM:** Yes, Father . . .

**TED:** I realise now you meant that in a sort of Al Pacino way, whereas I was thinking more along the lines of Carla Lane.

**TOM:** Don't worry, Father. They won't know what's going on.

**TED:** No, Tom, I really don't think—

**TOM:** Come on, Father! Let's go! You can have a go if you want!

**TED:** No, honestly, Tom. It's a bit cruel.

**TOM:** I could run them down in me van!

**TED:** Dougal, I think we'd better be off . . .

**DOUGAL:** What's the problem, Ted?

**TOM:** Do you have nothing at all I can kill, Father?

**TED:** No, sorry about that, Tom.

**TOM:** Ah, feck! Feck it altogether!

*Tom is breathing very heavily. He clenches the Samurai sword tightly and stares in a fixed way at Ted and Dougal. Pause.*

**TED** (*somewhat nervous*): Well! We'll be off! Bye, Tom!

*They open the door very slowly and, without making any sudden moves, back out, smiling and nodding at Tom. He watches them go, red-faced. Outside the door, Ted immediately speeds up.*

**TED:** Run, Dougal. Run quite fast, quite fast.

*They jog out of shot.*

### END OF PART ONE

\* \* \*

### PART TWO

SCENE 11 INT./DAY 3
SET: JACK'S BEDROOM
*Ted leads Bishop Brennan into the room. We don't see any of the room's contents yet.*

**TED:** . . . Well, I'm sure it won't happen again.

**BRENNAN:** It better not. Priests walking

around in the nude is the last thing we need.

**TED:** Yes, you're right. But as you can see, we've added a few modifications to Jack's bed.

*We see Jack's bed. It looks more like a deranged cot, with bars around the sides that extend into downward and inward curving spikes. Barbed wire is around the top.*

**BRENNAN:** Yes . . . (*He points at the barbed wire.*) That's new, isn't it?

**TED** (*nods*): Combined with the spikes, it'll make escape almost impossible. We've also got these new pyjamas . . . (*He holds up a one-piece pyjama suit.*) Very easy to put on, hard to get off, so that's the nudity sorted.

*Brennan holds up a length of thick rope from inside the cot.*

**TED:** Ah, yes, the rope. I'd like to see him chewing through that! . . .

*Brennan makes a 'mmm' face and leaves the room. Ted looks at the rope. He speaks quietly, to himself.*

**TED:** . . . again . . .

SCENE 12 INT./DAY 3
SET: PAROCHIAL HOUSE HALLWAY
*Ted and Brennan have come downstairs.*

**TED:** . . . plus, in the unlikely event of him getting out, this tracking device should give us a speedy recapture. That cost fifty pounds. Maybe we could get that back from the diocese . . .? (*He looks at Brennan hopefully. Brennan gives him a nasty look.*) Ha, ha . . . only joking . . .

*They enter the living room. Dougal is there.*

**DOUGAL** (*very cheery*): Ah, hello, Len!

**BRENNAN:** Don't call me Len. I'm a bishop.

**TED:** He's right, Dougal. Your Grace is more appropriate.

**DOUGAL:** Oh, Your Grace, right.

**BRENNAN:** Anyway, yet again, I am dragged away from my warm fireside to come and deal with the cast of *Police Academy*. Now, Jack, you behave yourself. (*To Jack.*) Are you listening to me, Jack?

**JACK:** No.

*Jack pours himself a large drink from a bottle of whiskey.*

**TED:** Oh, would you like a drink, Len? Your Grace! Your Grace!

**BRENNAN:** Yes . . . very well.

**TED:** I'll just . . .

*Ted goes over to Jack. He attempts to take the bottle from him, but Jack grunts angrily and refuses to let go. There is a slightly embarrassing struggle. Brennan looks on.*

**DOUGAL** (*to Brennan*): It must be fantastic being a bishop. Do you have any tips?*

**BRENNAN:** Tips?*

**DOUGAL:** Y'know. For the racing.*

*Ted struggles a bit more, then quickly gives up and turns around.*

**TED:** How about a cup of tea, Your Grace?

*Mrs Doyle enters. She carries a saucer of water and some lettuce.*

**MRS DOYLE:** Time for dinny-poos! Here's . . .

**TED** (*jumps*): Ah, yes! Thank you, Mrs Doyle.

*Ted takes both and sits down in his chair. He starts drinking the water casually and munching the lettuce. Mrs Doyle and Brennan look at him strangely. Ted behaves as if nothing is wrong.*

**MRS DOYLE** (*notices Brennan*): Ah, there you are, Bishop Brennan. I thought I should tell you – your car is parked outside.

**BRENNAN:** Yes, I know it is. I parked it there.

**MRS DOYLE:** The tyres look a bit flat. I'll give them a little blow up for you with the pump . . .

**BRENNAN:** No . . .

**MRS DOYLE:** What type of air would you normally put in them? We have ordinary and . . . well, that's all we have, actually. I don't think there's any other kind, really. Oh, and if you're looking for the wipers, I have them in the kitchen.

**BRENNAN:** What?

**MRS DOYLE:** They looked as if they needed a

---

*These lines were deleted from the final version.

wash. The only thing is, I'm afraid I broke the side window while I was snapping them off.

**BRENNAN:** Leave my car alone! Don't touch it again!

**MRS DOYLE:** Just one question, Your Grace . . . Eh, is your car diesel, or petrol?

**BRENNAN:** Just leave it, Mrs Doyle!

**MRS DOYLE:** No, this is just curiosity, Your Grace. Diesel or—

**BRENNAN:** Diesel! It's diesel!

**MRS DOYLE:** Right. So it's not petrol.

**BRENNAN:** No.

**MRS DOYLE:** Right, so it'd do a terrible

amount of damage if I put petrol in.

**BRENNAN:** Yes, it would. It would completely ruin the car's engine.

**MRS DOYLE:** Well, ha, ha! I certainly won't be doing that! Ha, ha!

*She turns and we see her horrified expression as she scurries out of the room.*

**TED:** I expect you must clock up a fair few miles during the year. Goin' round the old diocese . . .

**BRENNAN** (*interrupting*)**:** Crilly, where is my room?

**TED** (*finishing off the lettuce*)**:** Oh, it's the spare room, Your Grace. First on the right.

*He gets up to leave. On the way, he passes the rabbit cage. There is a half-eaten leaf of lettuce.*

**BRENNAN:** This lettuce . . .

**TED** (*sees the lettuce*)**:** Oh, no, I honestly couldn't. I just had some. You have it . . .

**BRENNAN:** No, I mean . . . what's it doing here? You don't keep rabbits, do you?

**TED:** No, no . . .

**BRENNAN:** It's just . . . I don't like them at all. I had an experience with some once. And it . . . it wasn't very nice . . . they got into a lift with me. They started nibbling my cloak . . . and everything.

**TED:** Well, you have absolutely no need to worry, Your Grace. That's just where we . . . grow the lettuce.

**BRENNAN:** You grow lettuce? Indoors? In a cage?

**TED:** That's right. It's safer and, ah, no one can steal it. As well as that, it, you know . . . brightens up the room.

*Brennan looks at them for a second. He then walks towards the door. He looks down. There is a little mound of rabbit droppings just in front of it.*

**BRENNAN:** What . . . is . . . this?

**TED:** That? Oh that's the eh . . . caviar.

**BRENNAN:** Caviar?

**TED:** Yes. Well, it's not every day we have a bishop staying with us, Your Grace. So we thought we'd get a bit of caviar out for you.

**BRENNAN:** So what's it doing lying in little piles on the floor?

**TED:** Oh, eh, eh . . . Japan.

**BRENNAN:** What?

**TED:** It's the Japanese tradition to eat off the floor. Great fun. And you don't need as many chairs.

**BRENNAN:** Right. So what you've done is you've spread some caviar down there so I can get down on my hands and knees and eat off the floor.

**TED** (*beat*)**:** Yes.

**BRENNAN:** What do you think I am, Crilly? A pony? I'm going to bed. (*To Jack.*) And you, keep in your room!

**JACK:** Feck off!

*Brennan marches out of the room.*

**TED:** Dougal, where'd you put them?

**DOUGAL:** The rabbits? Ah, ha, ha . . . somewhere really safe, Ted.

**TED:** Where?

**DOUGAL:** Guess. It's almost like the type of place you'd never even think of.

**TED:** God, where'd that be? That small room behind the kitchen?

*Dougal shakes his head.*

**TED:** The coal cellar?

*Dougal shakes his head.*

**TED:** Jack's room? Great idea!!!

**DOUGAL:** Nope, it's not Jack's room.

**TED:** God, I don't know . . .

**DOUGAL:** Think about it, Ted. Where'd be the last place you'd think I'd put them?

**TED:** The last place? God . . .

**DOUGAL:** Somewhere you wouldn't expect at all . . .

**TED:** Well, let's see . . . (*Ted thinks. Then his expression changes to one of horror. Hesitant, nervous.*) Well, now, I'd say the last place I'd think you'd put them would actually be Bishop Brennan's room.

**DOUGAL:** Bingo! Think about it, Ted. If you were trying to find some rabbits, where's the last place you'd look? I put them in the last place he'd ever expect them – in his own room! He'd never imagine there'd be a load of rabbits in there!

*He steps back and moves his hands apart.*

**DOUGAL:** Eh? Eh?

*Ted raises his hand and grimaces. Dougal misunderstands this as a congratulatory gesture and waves him away humbly. Ted puts his hands up to his own head in horror, and again Dougal misunderstands, laughs and winks. This 'dance' goes on for a moment or two. Then Ted moves his hands up to Dougal's neck, thinks better of it and dashes out of the room.*

SCENE 13 INT./NIGHT 3
SET: PAROCHIAL HOUSE LANDING
*Brennan is just about to open the door. Ted appears over the top of the stairs.*

**TED:** Your Grace! Your Grace!

*Brennan stops and looks at Ted.*

**BRENNAN:** Crilly. What is it?

**TED** (*slightly out of breath*): . . . Just wanted to say, the whole bishop thing, fair play to you.

*Brennan doesn't say anything.*

**TED:** I mean, you probably get a lot of this, but I just wanted to say, you know . . . Well done. Who would have thought that someone from Limerick would get this far? Ha . . . you know . . . all the ones you studied with in the seminary, the other priests . . . they must be feeling pretty sick at the moment! They'd be looking at the TV goin' 'How did that awful eejit get to be a Bishop?!' Ha, ha. But you know, that's no mystery to me. You have this sort of . . . bishopy air about you. Everything about you says 'I am a bishop.' You know, I think even if you were naked, like, you know, totally . . . naked . . . I think someone who didn't know you would still be able to go . . . 'That man's a bishop.' Even if you were naked. (*Pause.*) Can I just shake hands with you? (*He does so.*) Well done.

**BRENNAN** (*puts a hand on Ted's shoulder*): Crilly . . . I hate you. So all that means absolutely nothing to me.

*He goes to enter the room. Ted quickly turns and intentionally falls down the stairs. He throws himself down them in one huge jump, going out of shot.*

**TED:** Aggghhh! Oh, God, I've fallen down the stairs!

*Brennan closes the door and goes over to look down the stairs.*

**BRENNAN:** Crilly! What happened!

**TED** (*out of shot*): God, would you believe, I just fell down the stairs there.

**BRENNAN:** Well . . . are you injured?

**TED:** I'm not sure. There's a twinge all right. My arm! I can't move!

**BRENNAN:** Do you want someone to call an ambulance, Crilly?

**TED:** Ah, no. I'll just lie here for a while. Rest is probably the best thing for me now. Ah, yes . . . bit of a rest . . . Oh, did you see that documentary on Hiroshima last night? Who would have thought an atomic bomb could do so much damage?

**BRENNAN:** Crilly, I am going to bed.

*Brennan turns towards the door again. Suddenly, Ted arrives back in shot. Brennan sighs and turns to face him.*

**TED:** I'm all right! Bishop Brennan, I'm fine now. Thanks. Phew!

**DOUGAL** (*shouting, from downstairs*): Did Len find the rabbits, Ted?

*Pause. Brennan and Ted look at each other. Ted's face is frozen in horror.*

**BRENNAN** (*very angry*): What did he say?!

**TED:** Oh, God, look, I'd better tell you—

**BRENNAN:** Did he call me Len again!?! (*He shouts down.*) YOU ADDRESS ME BY MY PROPER TITLE, YOU LITTLE BOLLOCKS!

**DOUGAL** (*from downstairs*): Sorry . . . ah . . . Bishop Len Brennan . . .

**BRENNAN** (*calming somewhat*): What was he on about, anyway?

**TED:** Oh, God knows! (*He shouts down.*) Dougal, you big eejit! What are you on about now?! Ha, ha!

**DOUGAL:** I was just asking—

**TED:** Oh, shut up, Dougal, you big, mad fool!

*Ted turns to see that Brennan is halfway into the room. He runs back.*

**TED:** Bishop Brennan. Could I go in first?

**BRENNAN:** Why?

**TED:** I really need to go to the toilet. Eh, all the rest of the toilets in the house are broken. It's just number ones—

**BRENNAN:** I DON'T WANT TO KNOW!

*Brennan moves out of the way and Ted goes in.*

SCENE 14 INT./NIGHT 3
SET: BISHOP BRENNAN'S ROOM
*Ted comes in and looks around, confused.*

SCENE 15 INT./NIGHT 3
SET: PAROCHIAL HOUSE LANDING/BISHOP BRENNAN'S ROOM
*Brennan looks at his watch and sighs. Finally, Ted comes out.*

**TED:** Oh, God . . . I really needed that, I can tell you.

*Brennan shoves Ted out of the way and goes into his room.*

SCENE 16 INT./NIGHT 3
SET: BISHOP BRENNAN'S ROOM
*Brennan comes in. He looks around, confused. Pause.*

**BRENNAN:** But . . . there's no toilet in here.

*He looks ever so slightly nervous.*

SCENE 17 INT./NIGHT 3
SET: OUTSIDE BISHOP BRENNAN'S ROOM
*Ted leans against the door, looking drained. Dougal appears up the stairs.*

**TED** (*whispers*): Dougal, where are they? They're not in there.

**DOUGAL** (*whispers*): Are they not?

**TED:** No. It's a completely rabbit-free area. Are you sure you're not getting confused?

**DOUGAL:** No, I definitely put them in there, Ted.

**TED:** Then where are they? Where the hell are they? If Len runs into them, we're finished. And we'll be in a parish where it's a two-thousand-mile walk to the nearest newsagent.

**DOUGAL:** Wait! What about Jack's room? Maybe they smelled him, and they just had to see him one last time.

**TED:** That's possibly a slightly over-romantic way of putting it but . . . it's a good guess. Come on!

SCENE 18 INT./NIGHT 3
SET: JACK'S BEDROOM
*They enter the room. It is dark, but we hear the scuffling sounds of rabbits crawling all over the place.*

**TED:** God, Dougal, you're right! There's loads of them. How did they get in?

**DOUGAL:** They must have burrowed in. You know rabbits, Ted.

**TED:** We'll have to do it in shifts. Get them out of the house and as far away as possible. Try not to wake Father Jack, Dougal. He can be unusually violent when you wake him suddenly.

**DOUGAL:** Ted, why can't we just leave them in there?

**TED:** Because, Dougal, my nerves are shot. I won't be able to relax until the only rabbit left is the one sitting in your head working the controls.

*Dougal goes into the small room adjoining Jack's.*

**DOUGAL** (*offscreen*): There's more in here, Ted. Oh, look at this one. Doesn't he look like that fella, Harvey Keitel?

**TED:** Harvey Keitel? God, Dougal . . . (*He follows him out of shot.*) How could a rabbit look like Harv— . . . God almighty! . . .

*Pause.*

**DOUGAL:** Y'see?

**TED:** . . . He's the *image* of him. Amazing . . . Anyway, we haven't the time to think about things like that . . . Get that one there. Get that one before he . . .

*We see, in silhouette, Jack standing up. He climbs out of his cot. We hear a lot of ripping and tearing.*

SCENE 19 INT./NIGHT 3
SET: FRONT DOOR
*We see Jack's hand coming into shot and trying the front door blindly for a moment or two in the dark. No luck. The hand retreats.*

SCENE 20 INT./NIGHT 3
SET: JACK'S BEDROOM
*Ted and Dougal come out of the adjoining room, holding rabbits. They stop in their tracks.*

**TED:** Where've they gone?????!!!!

**DOUGAL:** Ted, where's Jack?

*We see the cot. Jack's pyjamas are shredded and hanging from the barbed wire. Ted and Dougal put down the rabbits and run out.*

SCENE 21 INT./NIGHT 3
SET: PAROCHIAL HOUSE HALLWAY
*Ted comes to a sudden halt.*

**TED:** Oh . . . my . . . God . . .

*We see that the door to Brennan's room is ajar.*

**TED:** We have to get them out! Oh, God, Dougal!

SCENE 22 INT./NIGHT 3
SET: BISHOP BRENNAN'S ROOM
*The room is completely dark. Dougal's and Ted's silhouettes appear at the door. Then they close it gently.*

**TED** (*whispers*): Dougal, get as many as you can! Come on!

**DOUGAL:** I am, Ted . . . c'mon, lads!

**BRENNAN:** Huh? . . . Who's . . .

*The light suddenly comes on. Brennan is half-asleep, surveying the scene. We see Ted and Dougal, their arms filled with rabbits, frozen as they stare back at him. Also, there are dozens of rabbits crawling all over the bed and floor. This is held for one, awful moment. Then Brennan looks down and sees, in bed beside him, Jack, who is staring at him in confusion. Neither of them is wearing pyjamas. Again, we hold on this. Finally, after what seems an age . . .*

**TED:** Ah, just a bad dream, Your Grace. It'll be over in a mo'.

*Brennan blinks for a moment, then nods and puts his head back down on the pillow. Ted and Dougal look at each other. Then Brennan wakes up again, sits bolt upright and screams.*

SCENE 22A EXT./NIGHT 3*
SET: PAROCHIAL HOUSE
*Cut to an exit shot of the Parochial House as his scream fills the night.*

POST-CREDIT SEQUENCE*
SCENE 23 INT.
SET: VARIOUS
*Ted sitting down, reading. Loads of rabbits hop around the living room. Ted is oblivious to all this.*

*Jack trapped in his cot. He peers out from behind the bars like an overgrown baby.*

*Dougal throwing a tennis ball to a rabbit. Cut to a close-up of the rabbit. We see that it has a tiny tennis racket stuck to it and wears a headband and tennis gear.*

*Extreme close-up of Brennan. He may be in some kind of hospital. His face is locked in a grimace of absolute terror.*

**THE END**

---

* We deleted this scene from the final version.

# ROCK A HULA TED

**ARTHUR:** There's really no point in pretending otherwise, is there? Niamh Connolly was inspired by Sinead O'Connor. Sinead's actually very friendly towards the show and came to the recording of the Christmas Special. And we must have had a great effect on her – she's become a priest. Archbishop Michael Cox, put a curse on our friend Paul Wonderful after he appeared on *The Late, Late Show* with a song called 'Bless Me, Father'. A week later he was ordaining Sinead O'Connor in a ceremony in a hotel room in Lourdes.

The Lovely Girls Competition is a low-budget version of The Rose of Tralee, a competition held annually in County Kerry, which used to be hosted by Gay Byrne. Girls, mainly of Irish extraction, come from all over the world and do a little turn, talk about world peace and so on. As with everything on Craggy Island, this is a low-budget version.

**GRAHAM:** We wanted to do a spoof of rock stars who saw themselves as preachers, and of the politically correct opinions being bandied about at the time. But it wasn't enough to satirise right-on opinions. We wanted to poke fun at the opposite viewpoint as well, which is how we arrived at the idea of a Lovely Girls Competition.

I love the 'take your bra off' stuff. Arthur and I love the word 'bra'; it's a brilliant word that just stops in mid-air. We just can't get enough of it. I'd love to have had a whole episode in which Ted and Dougal continually had to say the word 'bra': 'Maybe her bra's on too tight,' 'Dougal! Where did you put the bra?'. Oh, well . . .

Father Bigley's a character who didn't quite come off. We wanted to construct a character who would never appear on-screen because, from the way they described him, he'd be such a weird-looking Mister Potato Head that he couldn't possibly exist. We wanted to have him in every episode, adding an appalling physical attribute each time, but in the end, we couldn't find anymore than one or two occasions on which to do so.

**PART ONE**
SCENE 1 INT./DAY 1
SET: TELEVISION STUDIO
*A television chat-show. Very like 'The Late Late Show'. A Gay Byrne type is interviewing a rock star, Niamh Connolly. She has short, black hair and wears a black T-shirt with blue jeans.*

**NIAMH:** . . . and societies in Ancient India were ruled by women.

**INTERVIEWER:** Really?

**NIAMH:** And men weren't allowed around women without a licence, and they were put in a corner and were told off for being sexist.

**INTERVIEWER:** . . . Aaaaaanyway, you're going to do a song from your new album for us . . .

*Cut to Ted and Dougal watching this. We see Mrs Doyle walking behind them. She is carrying a big hod full of bricks. She is bent under the weight of the load. Ted and Dougal don't see her, their attention held by Niamh. On one of the walls of the room, although our attention shouldn't be drawn to it at first, is a red fire-alarm bell.*

**TED:** What an eejit. She's never happy unless she's giving out about something.

**DOUGAL:** You're right there, Ted.

*Cut back to the television.*

**INTERVIEWER:** I believe this new song is about the Catholic Church?

*Cut back to Ted.*

**TED:** Oh, here she goes!

**NIAMH:** That's right. It's about how the Church in Ireland secretly had lots of potatoes during the famine. And they hid the potatoes in pillows and sold them abroad at potato fairs.

**INTERVIEWER:** Really?

**NIAMH:** Yes. And then the Pope closed down a lot of factories that were making potatoes and turned them into prisons for children. And the nuns hid up trees and hit people unless they went to Mass . . .

*Cut back to Ted.*

**TED:** God almighty! She says that as if there's something *sinister* about it all. *What* is the problem with her?

**DOUGAL:** She seems to be taking the whole Catholic thing a bit seriously.

**TED:** Yes, Dougal.

**DOUGAL:** I mean, it's just a bit of a laugh . . .

**TED:** Stop talking, Dougal. I tell you what, though, it's this militant feminism lark that really gets my goat.

**DOUGAL:** Mad!

**TED:** This idea that the Church has some kind of negative attitude to women.

**DOUGAL:** Ted! She's doin' her song.

*Cut back to the television. Niamh is at the microphone, singing.*

**NIAMH:** 'Big men in frocks
telling us what to do
they can't get pregnant
like I do . . .'

**TED:** Mrs Doyle, you're a woman. What do you think of all this stuff? Do you think the Catholic Church is a bit sexist?

*We see only a head-and-shoulders shot of Mrs Doyle as she answers this question. She doesn't look at Ted and Dougal as she answers, and they are unseen in this shot.*

**MRS DOYLE** (*her face red from exertion*)**:** God, no, Father. I always thought that the Church is extremely responsive to my views. I mean, I remember once I was having terrible problems at home, and the Church gave me great

support then. I mean, there's a lot of people who . . . (*Suddenly, we see Ted and Dougal, who have stood up while out of shot, walking past behind her. They pay absolutely no attention to her at all.*) . . . run the Church down. But they're just a load of old moaners. Moan. Moan. Moan. Anyway, thanks for asking, Father, but no . . . (*Ted and Dougal walk back into shot carrying bags of crisps, munching them and chatting to each other. They go back to their seats.*) . . . I really have no complaints at all.

*She looks down at them. Ted and Dougal look up at her, as if they'd forgotten she was talking.*

**TED** (*not interested at all*): Yeah? Great.

*Mrs Doyle staggers off. Cut to Niamh on television. A woman is 'translating' her lyrics into sign language as she sings.*

**NIAMH:** 'You give us all your rules
But that's not the way it was,
When women ruled the land
of Tir Na Nog . . .'

*The signing woman doesn't know the sign for Tir Na Nog, so she just shrugs. The fire-alarm thing*

over Ted's head suddenly rings once.

**TED:** Oh, no!!!!

**JACK:** DRINK!!!!!

*As Jack says this, a bottle hits Ted on the back of the head.*

**TED:** Oooo, God . . . one second late and he goes mad. Here you go, Father. Your afternoon drink.

*Ted gets a full bottle and carries it over to Jack. Jack puts down the magazine he has been looking at and we see him for the first time. His hair is very long and he has grown some type of goatee-and-sideburns affair.*

**TED:** . . . You know you really should get a haircut. You're letting yourself go a bit, Father. You don't want to go too far down that Bob Geldof road.

**DOUGAL:** Oh, God, Ted, that's a bad road.

**TED:** It is indeed, Dougal, and there's no coming back once you're gone down it, as Bob himself would tell you. Ha, ha . . .

*He nudges Jack playfully. In one quick move, Jack brings up his walking stick and whacks Ted in the face with it.*

SCENE 2 INT./DAY 2
SET: PAROCHIAL HOUSE
*A priest, Father Liam Deliverance, is looking up at Ted's bookshelves, in a contemplative stance.*

**LIAM:** What'd ye pay for the shelves, Ted?

*Cut to Ted pouring a cup of tea.*

**TED:** God, Liam, I don't really remember . . .

**LIAM:** These won't last you. (*He points at one of the supports.*) Look at that. You could talk that into coming down.

**TED:** Well, they've lasted fine until now . . .

**LIAM:** Give us a go.

*He reaches up and starts pulling as hard as he can on one of the higher shelves. At one point his feet come off the floor.*

**LIAM:** I can feel it beginning to go, Ted.

**TED:** Don't . . . ah, Liam . . .

*Liam lets go of the top shelf and starts slamming his foot down on to one of the lower ones. Bang! Bang! Bang! Bang! Bang! It breaks and all the books on that shelf tumble on to the floor.*

**LIAM:** Ah, look at that, Ted. It's falling apart.

**TED:** Liam, how about a little cup of tea?

**LIAM:** Fair enough.

*He walks over to Ted, who pours some tea from a teapot.*

**TED:** So, what'd you want to talk about?

**LIAM:** You were planning on going to the Lovely Girls Festival this year, weren't you?

**TED:** Oh, I was, yes. Never miss a Lovely Girl Festival. My absolute favourite time of the year. How's Miss Lovely Girl 1995 doing?

**LIAM:** Oh, God, Ted, we had to strip her of her title.

**TED:** God almighty. Why? Oh, no, she didn't have a drink in public, did she?

**LIAM:** No, no. We found out she'd been in a film called *Stallion Farm*. I heard it's a bit rude. Anyway. I'm chairman of the organising committee this year, and I was wondering if you wanted to judge it.

**TED:** Judge it!!!! God, Liam, I'd love to! Oh! . . . and there's the dinner afterwards isn't there?

**LIAM:** Oh, yes. You have the honour of taking the winner out for a meal.

**TED:** And I think . . . who pays for it? It's not me is it? Did I hear that somewhere . . .?

**LIAM:** That's right. We had that idea a few years ago. *You* have the honour of taking her out to dinner and *she* has the honour of paying for it.

**TED:** Oh, lovely.

**LIAM:** How much did that stereo set you back?

*He bends over the stereo.*

**TED:** Oh, about a hundred pounds.

**LIAM:** I could have got you one for half price.

**TED:** Careful Liam . . . So, what were you saying?

**LIAM:** Ah, yes. When you take the lovely girl out to dinner, could you persuade her to wear one of me Mammy's dresses? She could use the publicity.

**TED:** Oh, right! How's the business going?

**LIAM:** Great! She sold one last week.

**TED:** Good. How many is that sold this year?

**LIAM:** That'd be one.

*We hear a snap. Liam turns around and holds up the arm of the record player.*

LIAM: Y'see? Now, that's no good at all. I can get you a great one from Father Clonkett. I could get you a few of them if you want.

TED (slightly annoyed): Don't worry about it, Liam.

LIAM: Basically, we thought it'd be a bit of a laugh getting a priest to judge it this year. Also, it eliminates any sexual aspect to the thing.

Ted doesn't know how to take this.

LIAM (jokily): Or am I wrong? I hope you won't be tempted by all those lovely girls!

TED: Oh, no chance of that, Liam! Ha! Ha!

LIAM: 'Cause we've had problems with that sort of thing before, you know!

TED: O'ho! Ha! Ha!

LIAM (suddenly dead serious): No, Ted, we really have had problems with that before.

TED (serious): Oh, right! No, you've nothing to worry about there, Liam.

LIAM: Anyway, I'll be off. (He goes to the door.)

TED: Bye, Liam.

LIAM: How much did this door cost you, Ted?

TED: Ah, I don't know, Liam. It came with the house.

Liam swings it open and closed a few times. Very roughly. He smiles back at Ted, then leaves, closing the door. Ted sighs and goes to sit down. Suddenly Liam's foot comes through the door. Liam looks through the hole he's made.

LIAM: Cowboys, Ted. They're a bunch of cowboys.

At last he leaves. Ted picks up a newspaper and browses through it. Dougal enters. He has a copy of a glossy magazine called 'Rock Cupboard'*. Ted puts down his paper. He notices a picture of Niamh on the front of Dougal's magazine. She is wearing boxing gloves and is staring angrily out from the cover. The headline reads 'I am still very angry – the Niamh Connolly interview'. One word is written on both gloves so that together they read 'Clit Power'.

---

*Rock Cupboard is an affectionate nod to Ireland's Hot Press magazine, for which Arthur worked as Arts Editor.

TED: Oh, God, look at her there. She's all over the place. (Dougal sits down.)

TED (squints at the headline): 'Clit Power'? What does that mean?

DOUGAL: Dunno.

TED: I used to know a Father Clint Power. Maybe she's having a go at him. What's the interview like? The same old nonsense, I suppose.

DOUGAL: Ah, I didn't read much of it. She's goin' around Ireland at the moment. She wants to buy a house on an island and live in it. She has her eye on some Godforsaken place off the west coast.

TED: Really? Did it mention what island she had her eye on, Dougal?

DOUGAL: It did, yeah, but I don't remember the name of it.

TED (swallows, stands up): Could you have a look there?

DOUGAL: 'Course I can, Ted.

Dougal flicks through the magazine.

DOUGAL: Ah, it's . . . ah . . . let me see . . . it's . . . Ahhhh . . .

SCENE 3 INT./DAY 2
SET: PAROCHIAL HOUSE
We see Niamh being interviewed on television by a wall in a street.

NIAMH: . . . Craggy Island. Yes. Craggy Island. Craggy Island is the place for me. (Shot of Ted and Dougal looking miserable.) I've always wanted somewhere peaceful to record my music and Craggy Island might just be the place. I see it as being a safe haven for those wishing to escape the hypocrisy of the mainland.

Cut to Ted and Dougal watching television, worried looks on their faces.

TED: Oh, God . . .

NIAMH: I want to create a world free of sexual and religious intolerance . . .

Ted and Dougal look at each other, worried.

TED: For f—

**NIAMH:** . . . Free of sexist patriarchal systems and hypocrisy.

**TED:** Oh, no, no, no! That's terrible news!

*He marches over and turns off the television.*

**TED:** Right. Basically, I think we'll just have to stand our ground. If she's on the island, I'm bound to bump into her somewhere. I'll just tell her that the people of Craggy Island will not stand for a world free of sexual and religious intolerance!

**DOUGAL:** No way, José.

*Mrs Doyle comes in. She looks dirty and tired.*

**MRS DOYLE** (*slightly out of breath*)**:** Father . . . I, ah . . the roof should be all right now. I hoovered upstairs and I did the attic – top to bottom – and – ooooh, what else? . . . Oh yes, I washed your car. Also, I built a little greenhouse near the garage. Would that be all for today?

*Cut to Ted and Dougal. They obviously haven't heard a word of this. Ted turns and notices Mrs Doyle.*

**TED:** Ah! Mrs Doyle! Any chance of a cup of tea for your two favourite priests?

*Mrs Doyle takes this in, then nods, exhausted, and backs out of the room. Once there, she collapses.*

SCENE 4 INT./MORNING 3
SET: TED AND DOUGAL'S BEDROOM
*We see Dougal asleep in bed. Pull back to see Ted fully dressed beside him, busying himself. Dougal stirs.*

**DOUGAL:** Uuuuhhhhh . . . Ted, . . . What time is it? (*He searches for his watch.*) God, Ted, it's only eleven. What are you doing up?

**TED:** I want to get away early to the Lovely Girls Competition.

**DOUGAL:** God, Ted. I wouldn't mind goin' but I don't think I'd know what to say to a lovely girl.

**TED:** God, there's no end of things you can talk about . . . What their father does for a living, if they have a boyfriend, dressmaking . . . anything to do with clothes or perfume, basically. Clothes is easiest to talk about because men wear

clothes but we don't wear perfume.

**DOUGAL:** Except Father Bigley.

**TED:** Except Father Bigley. Anyway, if y'ever meet a woman, I'm sure you'd be able to deal with it. Just be yourself, Dougal. Be yourself, make them feel at ease, and the golden rule, always let them have their way! It's easier in the long run. (*Dougal nods.*) Anyway, better be off. Don't want to keep those lovely girls waiting!

*Ted leaves. Dougal picks up another notebook and starts writing . . .*

**DOUGAL:** 'Be . . . yourself . . .'

SCENE 5 EXT./DAY 3
SET: MARQUEE
*Establishing shot of marquee. We see a banner reading 'Lovely Girls Festival '96'.*

SCENE 5A INT./DAY 3
SET: MARQUEE
*In the foreground we see four men standing in a circle. They have pints of beer in their hands and white shirts over beerbellies. Lots of 'lovely girls' walk around smiling at everyone. The men look at them appreciatively and grunt at each other.*

**TERRY:** Eh? Eh? She's comin' for you, Billy.

**BILLY:** Ha! Is she, yeah? O'ho, God . . .

**DANNY:** She's got her eye on Paddy . . .

**PADDY:** Ohhhh, ho . . . there we go now . . .

*Ted comes into shot.*

**DANNY:** Hello, Father.

**TED:** Hello, lads, how's it goin' there?

**PADDY:** O'ho, we're gettin' the eye from the girls, Father.

**ALL:** Oh, oh . . .

**TED:** Has Cupid been firing his arrows in the direction of the Casey brothers?

**ALL:** Oh, ho hooooooo!!!

**TED:** I hope you won't be getting into any mischief.

**TERRY:** Oh, you know us, Father.

**TED:** I do! And that's the trouble!

**ALL:** O'hoooooo!!!!!

*Ted looks at his watch.*

**TED:** Lads, lads, sorry, but I'd better run. The competition's starting any second.

*Ted starts to move off, but he sees Jack nearby.*

**TED:** Oh, no . . .

*They all raise their beers as he dashes out of shot. One of the women comes up to the group.*

**WOMAN:** Hello.

*The men look down at the ground and don't say anything, mortified with embarrassment. After a moment, she shrugs and walks away; as she does so, they watch her go and say, almost simultaneously . . .*

**DANNY:** O'ho . . .

**TERRY:** Oh, ho, ho, ho . . .

**BILLY:** Ooooohhhhh!!!!! . . .

**PADDY:** Oh, hooooo . . .

SCENE 5B EXT./DAY 3
SET: ANOTHER PART OF MARQUEE
*We see Jack holding a tin with 'Live Aid' written on it. He looks very innocent. Someone puts money in it. Jack shakes the tin and runs to the bar. Ted approaches him.*

**TED:** Now, Father, that's not on. Impersonating Sir Bob. And what would all those other Live Aid people think? Peter Gabriel and Queen and the other bands who were on earlier in the day. And Phil Collins flying all the way to Boston. (*Ted takes the box*

*from him. Jack punches him in the stomach, takes the box back and walks out of shot. Ted is completely winded, but manages to glance at his watch.*) Oh, God! (*He staggers off.*)

SCENE 6 INT./DAY 3
SET: BESIDE THE STAGE
*Father Liam Deliverance is looking at his watch beside the makeshift stage. Ted comes into shot.*

**LIAM:** Ted, for crying out loud. The girls won't stay lovely for ever, you know.

**TED** (*out of breath*)**:** Sorry, Liam, Father Jack just punched me in the stomach . . . God . . .

**LIAM:** Come on, get up there!

*Ted makes his way with difficulty to the stage, completely out of breath. We see four lovely girls in frocks with large sashes walking around on the stage and smiling. Ted can't speak. He doubles over, trying to get his breath back. He breathes very heavily. Liam puts the microphone in his hand. Ted climbs up on stage.*

**TED** (*into microphone*)**:** Hello . . . (*He takes a breath.*) . . . Lovely girls . . . Look at them there . . . walking around . . .

*Ted stops talking and tries to get his breath back again. However, he does this into the microphone, and we pull back for a shot of the lovely girls walking around, with Ted's amplified heavy breathing on top of it. The girls look slightly worried by this.*

SCENE 7 INT./DAY 3
SET: PAROCHIAL HOUSE HALLWAY
*We hear the doorbell. Dougal comes into the hall. He is right beside the door but he looks up the stairs.*

**DOUGAL:** Mrs Doyle? Someone at the door, Mrs Doyle! (*The doorbell rings again.*) Mrs Doyle!

SCENE 8 EXT./DAY 3
SET: PAROCHIAL HOUSE
*We see the door open very slowly. Dougal peeks out.*

SCENE 9 INT./DAY 3
SET: MARQUEE
*Ted is talking to Imelda, one of the contestants.*

**TED:** Well, Imelda, you're a lovely girl.

Although you had a bit of bad luck recently. I hear your dog was knocked down by a car and he was killed, is that right?

**IMELDA:** No, that was . . . that was my father.

*Ted nods at this, and looks through his notes for something else.*

**TED:** And it says here you're twenty-two . . .

**IMELDA:** No, nineteen . . .

**TED:** Oh, right. And you were born in Mayo. That's a lovely part of the world . . .

**IMELDA:** . . . Eh . . . eh, Dundalk . . .

**TED:** I see. Ah well, it says here that you're a black belt in karate. So what would you do if I came at you like this . . . ?

*He rolls up the notes and holds them over his head, as if to stab her with them. Imelda is terrified and screams.*

**TED:** Imelda, Imelda! Sorry! Are you all right? I tell you what, could you have a look through my notes and stop on any piece of information that's actually true . . .

**IMELDA:** I will indeed, Father.

*She looks at the notes. Pause. She turns the page and looks some more. Ted sighs.*

SCENE 10 INT./DAY 3
SET: PAROCHIAL HOUSE
*Dougal and Niamh are sitting down. Dougal looks terrified.*

**NIAMH:** You haven't told me your name, Father.

**DOUGAL:** Mmmm . . . Be yourself . . . Father Dougal McGuire!

**NIAMH:** Oh, right. This is a beautiful house. I love the crude religious imagery.

**DOUGAL:** Uh . . . ah . . . uh . . . eh. Are you all right there? Is your bra all right?

**NIAMH:** What?

**DOUGAL:** Your bra? Is it comfortable? Do you have a bra?

*Niamh gives him a look.*

**DOUGAL:** It's not too tight? 'Cause you can loosen it if you want. Take it off, sure.

**NIAMH:** I . . .

**DOUGAL:** Or would you like some tea? I tell you what. I'll go and make some tea, and you take your bra off.

*Dougal leaves the room. Niamh watches him go, flabbergasted.*

SCENE 11 INT./DAY 3
SET: MARQUEE
*Danny, Terry, Billy and Paddy are still standing in the same place.*

**ALL:** O'ho . . .

**BILLY:** O'hooooo . . . Wh— Isn't that Bob Geldof there?

*We see Jack sneaking into the marquee.*

**TERRY:** No, it— Wait a second! It is, you know! He's lookin' a bit rough.

**PADDY:** Ah, he'd have lost all his money in that Live Aid thing.

**BILLY:** I'm not sure if it is Bob Geldof. Hang on there a second. (*He walks out of shot.*)

**BILLY** (*offscreen*): Excuse me, are you . . . ?

**JACK** (*offscreen*): Feck off!

*Billy comes back into shot.*

**BILLY:** Ah, it's him all right.

SCENE 12 INT./DAY 3
SET: MARQUEE
*Ted is at the microphone.*

**TED:** And now . . . walking!

*Cut to a wide shot of the girls in a line, walking between traffic cones.*

**TED:** O'ho! Look at them there. Walking around. Look out there, Mary! Doesn't Mary have a lovely bottom!

*Liam stands up from behind the table and beckons to Ted.*

**LIAM:** Careful there, Ted. That might offend the girls.

**TED:** Right, Liam.

*Ted turns back to face the crowd.*

**TED:** Well, of course, they *all* have lovely bottoms!

*Ted looks at Liam who nods and gives him the thumbs-up.*

SCENE 13 INT./DAY 3
SET: PAROCHIAL HOUSE
*Dougal leans over the kitchen door.*

**DOUGAL:** Actually, Mrs Doyle is the one who makes the tea, and she's out . . .

SCENE 13A EXT./DAY 3
SET: PAROCHIAL HOUSE
*We see a mound of earth beside a hole. A pick-axe appears briefly over the top of it and is then swung down again.*

**MRS DOYLE:** Nyyaaaaaah!!!

SCENE 13B INT./DAY 3
SET: PAROCHIAL HOUSE
*Back to Niamh and Dougal.*

**NIAMH:** Wh— Why don't you just make the tea?

**DOUGAL** (*confused*): But . . . Mrs Doyle makes the tea.

*Pause. Niamh shakes her head.*

**NIAMH:** Anyway, I'd better just tell you the reason I'm here. I'm looking for a house around this area, and I really, really like this one . . .

*Pause. Dougal thinks very deeply about this, then looks at his notes.*

SCENE 14 INT./DAY 3
SET: MARQUEE
*Ted is examining a sandwich with a small measuring device. A lovely girl looks at him hopefully.*

**TED:** I'm sorry, Jean, but your sandwich exceeds the required six centimetres in width. So that means it's between Imelda and Mary in . . . the Lovely Laugh Tiebreak. (*Applause.*) Right. In order to hear your lovely laugh, I'll have to tell you a joke! So, here we go! I'll have to do my Robin Williams impression now! OK, here we go. Here's the joke now. (*Ted's voice deepens as he reads from his notes*).

Secretary: 'Sir, the invisible man is waiting in reception.'

Got that?

Boss: 'Tell him I can't see him now!'

*Ted holds the microphone up to Imelda and Mary to capture their laughter. They both do a 'tinkling' laugh for Ted.*

**TED:** I think I have to say that Imelda's laugh was nicer. Sorry, Mary, but that leaves Imelda as the winner! (*Imelda goes mad. The other girls* look disappointed. *Ted puts a tacky crown on Imelda's head and gives her a rolled-up scroll.*) There's your Certificate of Loveliness, and of course you'll be going to dinner tomorrow at Craggy Island's top seafood restaurant, The Thai Cottage. And, Imelda, who'll you be inviting to dinner?

**IMELDA:** I'll be bringing my mother.

*Pause.*

**TED:** Just have another go at that, Imelda . . .

**IMELDA:** Oh! Sorry! Yes, I'll be inviting you, Father.

**TED:** Yes, you will. You know you're paying? It's not me. It's not me who pays.

**IMELDA:** Oh, right.

### END OF PART ONE

▲ ▲ ▲

### PART TWO

SCENE 15 INT./EVENING 3
SET: PAROCHIAL HOUSE
*Ted arrives, taking off his coat and scarf. Dougal comes down the stairs.*

**DOUGAL:** Ah, there you are, Ted. How did the Lovely Girls Competition go?

**TED:** Brilliantly well, Dougal. And, as is the tradition, I get a free dinner tomorrow night!

**DOUGAL:** Great! Is Jack with you?

**TED:** Oh, God . . . Jack . . .

SCENE 15A INT./EVENING 3
SET: MARQUEE
*We see Jack surrounded by lots of lovely girls. They seem very enamoured with him.*

**LOVELY GIRL:** Wow! You really knocked Michael Hutchence* unconscious?

**JACK:** I *battered* him!

*He demonstrates.*

---

*Oops.

SCENE 15B INT./EVENING 3
SET: PAROCHIAL HOUSE
*Ted and Dougal come into the living room.*

**TED:** So! Anything happen while I was away?

**DOUGAL:** No, I can't think of anything. Oh, yer one. Niamh Connolly called.

**TED** (*panicking slightly*)**:** What, Niamh Connolly? Oh, God. What did you say to her?

**DOUGAL:** Don't worry, Ted. It was fine. I just followed your advice about talking to girls and it was grand. She's upstairs now.

**TED:** She's still here!

**DOUGAL:** Yeah. I think she's in the toilet, actually. (*Niamh comes into the living room.*) Hello, again. I was just telling Ted you were in the toilet.

**NIAMH:** Hello.

**TED** (*slightly sniffy*)**:** Hello, there. Father Ted Crilly. You must be Miss Connolly. Though I suppose that's sexist now! Calling a young lady 'Miss'! Well, I'm sorry but it's too late for me to change my ways now. You can't teach an old dog new tricks!

**NIAMH:** Yes. Well. It's getting a bit late.

**TED:** Oh, right, well, I won't keep you! Bye so!

**NIAMH:** Bye! (*Pause. They all look at each other.*) Goodbye, Father.

**TED:** Yes, goodbye.

*Pause.*

**DOUGAL:** Oh, that's the other thing, Ted. I sold Niamh the house.

**TED:** What?

*Niamh exits to the kitchen.*

**DOUGAL:** Well, actually, I gave it to her.

**TED:** You . . . wh— . . . No, wait a minute. You . . .

**DOUGAL:** Niamh's going to turn it into a studio! She says we can have all the recording time we want!

**TED:** Wait now, wait now. You *gave* her the house. How could . . . ?

**DOUGAL:** Oh, wait a second! Ted, where are we going to live?!

*Ted bites his lip and makes a strangling gesture. Niamh re-enters the living room.*

**TED:** Miss Connolly. Look, there's been a terrible mistake—

**NIAMH** (*not really listening*): Look, I have to record a duet with Peter Gabriel over the 'phone. Hope you don't mind if Alan and big Mike show you out.

**TED:** Well, Miss Connolly, I'm sorry, but we're not going anywhere.

*Two large men in black tour jackets and baseball caps come into the room. They both advance ever so slightly.*

**TED:** All right, I'm not sticking around to be insulted by you! Come on, Dougal, we're leaving. You can *have* the house. I wouldn't stay here if you gave me a million pounds!

SCENE 15C EXT./EVENING 3
SET: OUTSIDE THE DOOR
*We see the door being slammed behind them.*

**TED:** Wait a minute. What did I say there? I meant to say 'Please give us back the house.' What did I say? Why are we outside?

**DOUGAL:** Ted, where are we going to stay?

SCENE 16 EXT./NIGHT 3
SET: PAROCHIAL HOUSE/TENT
*We see a tiny tent beside the house. A faint light glows inside.*

SCENE 17 INT./NIGHT 3
SET: TENT
**TED:** God almighty, I go away for a few hours, and you've managed to make us homeless. Take me through it again. What exactly happened?

**DOUGAL:** I was just sticking to your rules, Ted. Number one, be yourself . . .

**TED:** No, no, no, no! 'Be yourself' is just something people *say*! Never be yourself with women! Never, never, never! What then?

**DOUGAL:** Well, I tried to make her more comfortable, like you said . . .

**TED:** Yes . . .

**DOUGAL:** So I asked her to take off her bra.

*Long pause.*

**TED:** We'll come back to that one. But how did you manage to give away our house? I mean, Dougal . . .

**DOUGAL:** What about the golden rule, Ted? Always give them what they want.

**TED:** No, that's the silver rule, Dougal. The golden rule is, if anyone ever says anything to you again, think about what you're saying, and then don't say it, and then run away somewhere. Right. All right. This is a long shot, but it's our only chance. I'm going to leave this pen and paper here, and hopefully in the morning God will have written down what we should do.

**DOUGAL:** That is a long shot.

**TED:** It's our only hope. (*He looks up to heaven*). C'mon God!

*He puts the pen and paper down. Fade down.*

SCENE 18 EXT./MORNING 4
SET: PAROCHIAL HOUSE
*We see Ted and Dougal's tent. It is morning and we hear the birds singing.*

SCENE 19 INT./DAY 4
SET: TENT
*Ted wakes up and picks up the paper.*

**TED:** Aaaaaggggghhhhhhh!!!!!!

*Dougal wakes up with a start.*

**DOUGAL:** TED! TED, WHAT IS IT? DID GOD WRITE BACK?!!!!

**TED** (*crumples up the paper*): No, he didn't! Bollocks anyway! (*He looks up.*) All right, I'm going to have to take care of this myself. I'll persuade her that we're really hip priests who agree with her about absolutely everything. We'll show her that we're more of a forward-thinking parish than she thinks.*

**DOUGAL:** What do you mean by a 'forward-thinking parish' exactly?*

**TED:** I mean one that isn't too constrained by some of the more old-fashioned views of the Church.*

**DOUGAL:** But we'd still believe in God and all that?*

**TED:** Oh, I think so. The belief-in-God thing, that's very important to the Church. That'll be one of the last things to go. But on the whole, for now, I think we just have to stick with the New Testament. The Old Testament stuff won't go down well. That stuff about if your wife goes to the toilet, she has to be thrown down a big pit. To be honest, Dougal, I've always had a few doubts about that one myself. And all that stuff about pulling out your right eye if it offends you.*

**DOUGAL:** That's a strange one, isn't it, Ted? I mean, if you're seeing something with your right eye, surely you'd be seeing it with your left one as well.*

**TED:** Yeah. Your right eye would have to be nearly on the other side of your head.*

**DOUGAL:** Like Father Bigley.*

**TED:** Like Father Bigley. But still, I think if we stick to all the post-ripping-out-your-eyes stuff it'd be safer. Just think: this is the modern world – this is the modern Church. Right!*

*They come out of the tent.**

SCENE 20 INT./DAY 4
SET: PAROCHIAL HOUSE
*Niamh, Ted and Dougal are in the living room.*

**TED:** Basically . . . the thing is, the house. It really wasn't Dougal's to give away. So if you

could give it back to us, it'd be great. I think you'd be interested in the kind of work we're doing here. We're a very progressive parish.

**NIAMH:** I hope it's not some kind of hideaway for paedophile priests. That whole thing disgusted me.

**TED:** Well, we're not all like that, Niamh. Say, if there's two hundred million priests in the world, and five per cent of them are paedophiles, that's still only ten million.

*Niamh doesn't know what to say.*

**TED:** No, Niamh, what we wanted to do here was create a world free of intolerance and hypocrisy.

**NIAMH:** Really, Father?

**TED:** Oh, yes. Niamh, if there's one thing I hate . . . (*Dramatic pause.*) it's hypocrisy.

*Ted's attention is drawn to the window behind Niamh, where we see Father Liam Deliverance. He gives Ted the thumbs-up then holds up a newspaper, 'The Craggy Island Examiner'. The headline reads 'Father Ted gives thumbs-up to Lovely Girls' bottoms'.*

**NIAMH:** I mean, the sexism that is rampant within the church . . . it's . . . appalling.

**TED** (*worried*): Yes, yes . . .

---

*We deleted these lines from the final version.

**NIAMH:** It really distresses me. It really gets my goat.

*Liam opens the newspaper to another page. We see a picture of Ted pulling a comical Kenneth Williams-type face as he's kissed on the cheeks by two lovely girls. Liam moves away from the window. Ted looks more worried.*

**TED:** Anyway, we're very different on Craggy Island . . We don't like any of . . . that kind . . . of thing . . .

*Liam arrives, holding the newspaper and carrying two evening dresses.*

**LIAM:** Ah, Ted . . . (*He notices Niamh.*)

**LIAM:** Who's this lovely girl? Now, Ted you're only allowed to pick one!

**NIAMH:** Don't call me a lovely girl. I've sold twenty million records.

**LIAM:** What? Anyway, Ted. What do you think? (*He holds up the dresses.*) This one or this one? I like this one . . .

**TED:** That's a nice one, Liam.

**LIAM:** But I like the colour of this one. Oh, I just don't know . . .

**TED:** Liam, they're both great. I'm sure whichever one you'll pick, it'll look lovely.

**LIAM** (*touched*): Thanks, Ted.

*He runs off, excited, Ted turns to Niamh.*

**TED:** You see? All sorts of alternative lifestyles catered for. This is a refuge for priests like Liam. Where else could he give a sermon while he's dressed as Joan Crawford? Please don't take our house, Niamh! Please don't stop our good work here!

**NIAMH:** I had no idea. To be honest with you, Father, I've always had a bit of a blinkered view of priests.

*Ted is standing beside the red bell.*

**TED:** Well, you've probably got that old-fashioned perception of the drunken, old, lecherous priest. I promise you, Niamh, that stereotype is long gone.

*Ted glances at his watch and immediately puts his hands up to the bell just as it goes off. He holds it so that it just makes a very faint 'clinkety-clinkety'*

noise. *It does so a few times and then stops. Pause. Ted looks up. We hear a bump. Then we hear footsteps from above. Ted and Niamh follow the footsteps as we hear their owner running around upstairs. Pause. We hear the footsteps coming down the stairs. Ted is still following where the noises are coming from with his eyes. Pause. Jack suddenly bursts through the door.*

**JACK:** Drink! (*He sees Niamh.*) Woman!!!

**TED:** Hello there, Billy!!

*Ted turns Jack around and leads him out into the hall.*

**TED:** Won't be able to chat with you today, Billy. See you later.

**JACK:** Wha— . . .?

*Ted pushes the front door open and pushes Jack out. He then walks back into the room.*

**TED:** Father Billy would be more of an old-style priest. He sometimes comes over for a good old debate.

*We see Jack looking through the window, puzzled.*

**NIAMH:** But . . . he came from upstairs . . .

**TED:** Yes. He usually gets in through the upstairs window.

**NIAMH:** Why?

**TED:** Well, he sometimes likes hiding around the house, so he can spring a topic on me. Like . . . he might hide in the bathroom and I'd be going to the toilet and he'd jump out and say 'Women priests!' And I'd have to think really fast and say 'I'm in favour of them!'

*Pause as Niamh takes this in.*

**TED:** Anyway, the main thing I wanted to say is . . . we're all huge, huge fans here. I think we have every record you've ever made.

SCENE 21 EXT./DAY 4
SET: PAROCHIAL HOUSE
A. *Ted bounds out of the door and runs at top speed out of shot.*

B. *Parochial house driveway. Ted running towards the gate.*

C. *Road. Ted running down the road.*

D. *John and Mary's shop. Ted running into shop. Pause. He runs out again, a number of records in his arms.*

E. *Road. Ted running up the road.*

F. *Parochial house driveway. Ted running through the gate and up the driveway.*

G. *Parochial house. Ted runs into the house.*

SCENE 22 INT./DAY 4
SET: PAROCHIAL HOUSE
*Ted runs in.*

**TED:** Here . . . you . . . here . . . records here . . .

*Ted is gasping for breath.*

**NIAMH:** What would you like me to put on them?

**TED** (*still dying*)**:** Don't care.

*Niamh nods and sighs. Mrs Doyle comes in.*

**MRS DOYLE:** Father, I've finished digging that drainage ditch.

**TED** (*still out of breath*)**:** No . . . Mrs Doyle . . .

**MRS DOYLE:** But I have to say, I keep passing out, so I might go and have a little rest. I know you wanted me to clean the roof slates tonight but . . .

**TED** (*still gasping*)**:** Mrs Doyle . . . No . . . don't.

**MRS DOYLE:** So I thought I might as well do them tomorrow when there's less chance of me falling off and being killed.

*Niamh looks at Ted, outraged. Ted smiles in a sickly way.*

SCENE 23 INT./NIGHT 4
SET: RESTAURANT
*We see Mrs Doyle, Imelda and Niamh.*

**IMELDA:** But . . . will Father Ted be coming later?

**NIAMH:** *No.* He has to stay home so Mrs

Doyle can come out. That's the only reason I let him have the house back. One night off every week for Mrs Doyle.

**MRS DOYLE:** Maybe I should just check on them . . .

**NIAMH:** Sit . . . down. (*She raises a glass*). Now come on, let's enjoy ourselves, sisters! No men around and we can do whatever we want! . . . (*Mrs Doyle starts eating.*) . . . Is that meat?

*Mrs Doyle freezes. Imelda looks worried.*

**IMELDA:** Do I still have to pay for this?

SCENE 24 INT./NIGHT 4
SET: KITCHEN
*Ted and Dougal are in the kitchen. The kettle is boiling. Steam is billowing out. Pots rattle on the stove as their contents bubble dangerously. Ted and Dougal run around the kitchen in complete confusion and panic. Dougal has a pair of oven mittens on.*

**TED** (*looking at the kettle*)**:** There's no button! Where's the button!?

*Dougal takes his hands, still in the mittens, out of the oven. They are on fire.*

**DOUGAL:** Ted! Ted! I'm on fire!!!!!

*Ted picks up the kettle and throws the water on Dougal's hands. The fire goes out and Dougal screams. The noise from all the different kitchen utensils is awful. Ted and Dougal huddle together in the centre of the room, clutching each other in fright.*

**TED:** I just want my tea!!!!!!!

**THE END**

# CIGARETTES AND ALCOHOL AND ROLLERBLADING

**ARTHUR:** Obviously Lent suggested the structure for this one. Finding a vice for each of them to give up was easy as far as Jack (alcohol) and Ted (cigarettes) were concerned, but Dougal was the wild card. We had no idea that rollerblading was one of his skills – it must have rubbed off on him from our visit to friends in New York, the rollerblading capital of the world. To make this episode work, we had to get Mrs Doyle out of the house, and she obliged by going on a Lenten pilgrimage to Croagh Patrick. It's a real hill, and people really do climb it in their bare feet.

As regards martyrs, we had a gift with a Dubliner called Matt Talbot, who became our Matty Hislop. Talbot was a terrible alcoholic who later renounced the booze and, as a penance for his wayward early life, went on to drape himself in chains and give himself a really terrible time. He loved tea, for example, so he'd brew himself a lovely hot pot and then wait until it was stone cold before drinking it. That was in the 1920s. Nowadays he'd be considered mad and given psychiatric help, but in Dublin there's a bridge and a street named after him.

**GRAHAM:** We thought it was funny that they should all fail immediately with their Lenten vows, but it meant that we didn't have anywhere for the plot to go. That's why we brought in Sister Assumpta (Rosemary Henderson) and her penances. When plotting an episode, we usually write a list of ten plot points before we write any dialogue, but this time . . . I have a feeling we started writing the script before we'd worked everything out, found ourselves in a corner and had to write our way out of it. . . but that sometimes works too.

## PART ONE

SCENE 1 EXT./DAY 1
SET: PAROCHIAL HOUSE
*Filmed from a distance, we see a silhouette of a figure bent low as he carries a large cross over the grounds of the Parochial House. Dramatic biblical music plays. Ted – for it is he – moves it into an upright position. The horizontal part of the cross suddenly slides down and conks Ted on the head. He drops out of shot. Slight pause. We hear a thunderbolt. It starts to rain very heavily.*

SCENE 2 INT./DAY 1
SET: PAROCHIAL HOUSE
*Mrs Doyle is cleaning up. Ted comes in rubbing his head; he is soaking wet.*

**MRS DOYLE:** I see you put the old cross up, Father. What's that about?

**TED:** Oh, I thought people might have been sort of getting confused about where the Parochial House is. So I thought, I'll put a big cross up in the middle of the garden. I just hope people know it means that I'm a priest and not just some madman.

SCENE 2A EXT./DAY 1
SET: PAROCHIAL HOUSE
*A couple walk by the house. They see the cross.*

**MAN:** Look at that. Some madman's put up a cross.

SCENE 2B INT./DAY 1
SET: PAROCHIAL HOUSE
*Mrs Doyle gives the window a final wipe. When she's finished with it, it looks utterly filthy.*

**MRS DOYLE:** Lovely. Well, that's everything, Father. I'm heading off tomorrow.[†]

**TED:** Really? Where are you . . . oh, Croagh Fiachra![†]

**MRS DOYLE:** Oh, yes, Father, Croagh Fiachra. Every Lent I head off. It was wonderful last year. People from all over, giving up the simple pleasures to give thanks to the Lord. A lot of priests there, too.

---

\* In the final version Mrs Doyle then fell off the windowsill.
† We deleted this from the final version.

Climbing up that mountain in their bare feet. Standing for hours in the cold and going without food for days and days. Have you ever been yourself, Father?[†]

**TED** (*begins to shake his head, then catches himself*): . . . Many, many times.[†]

*Dougal walks in. He is dressed in rollerblading gear. He clanks along with some difficulty in the huge wheeled boots.*

**DOUGAL:** Ted, I'm off rollerblading.

**TED:** Right so, Dougal.

*Dougal trundles out through the door. The telephone rings. Ted goes to answer it.*

**TED:** Hello. Craggy Island Parochial House. Father Ted Crilly speaking.

*Cut to the other end of the line. It is Father Dick Byrne. He is in an uncharacteristically serious mood.*

**DICK:** Hello, Ted. Dick Byrne here.

**TED:** . . . Dick . . .

**DICK:** I just wanted to call and wish you all the best for Lent this year.

**TED:** What? Oh, Lent, yeah. What are you giving up? Being the biggest eejit in the priesthood?!!!

**DICK:** No, seriously, Ted. If we can just put aside the joking for a moment, Lent is a solemn time of the year. I know we've had our disagreements in the past, but at the end of the day, we're both brothers in Christ.

**TED** (*mood changing*): Oh . . .

**DICK:** So, anyway, over here, we're making a special effort this year. I'm giving up cigarettes, Father Johnson is giving up alcohol, and Father McDuff is giving up skateboarding. And I have to say, the atmosphere of serenity and devotion to Our Lord in the Parochial House is very special this year.

**TED** (*a bit more serious*): Right.

**DICK:** So, would you like to do something similar? Why don't you give up the old cigarettes, and get the other two there to make an effort as well. Would you do that, Ted? Will you join us and go the extra mile this year?

**TED:** Well, Dick, I suppose you're right. Our chosen path is one of devotion to Our Lord. I suppose we should make a special effort, too.

**DICK:** Well, Ted, it'll be worth it. I'll see you soon. God bless you Ted.

**TED:** Goodbye, Dick. God bless *you*, Dick.

*We cut back to Dick. He raises a cigarette to his lips, draws on it and chuckles. He then laughs more hysterically. It echoes in a sinister way.*

SCENE 3 INT./DAY 1
SET: PAROCHIAL HOUSE
*Dougal and Jack sit on the sofa, looking at Ted. Dougal looks glum. Jack is just trying to focus.*

**TED:** . . . So that's it. I'm giving up the fags, Father Jack, I think, can lay off the old drink for a while, and no more rollerblading for you 'til Easter, Dougal.

**DOUGAL:** . . . Easter's miles away . . .

**TED:** It is, but it wouldn't be a sacrifice if it was too easy, would it? Don't forget why we're doing this.

**DOUGAL:** I know, I know . . . because of the sacrifice Our Lord made for us on . . .

**TED:** Yes, yes, but more importantly . . . I'm not havin' Dick Byrne beat me in a giving-things-up competition. And that's what this is, a giving-things-up competition. We've got to show him what we can do, especially after that Scrabble fiasco.

**DOUGAL:** You've never told us what happened there, Ted.

**TED** (*angry and embarrassed*): Oh . . . he . . . I don't know how he did it, he must have been cheating, he *must* have . . . but . . . he managed to get all his words to say, 'Useless Priest. Can't say Mass.' So, is that all right? No more drinking, rollerblading or smoking until Easter. Understood?

**DOUGAL:** But . . . I like rollerblading.

**TED:** Dougal, come on! What would Our Lord think of you if he knew you didn't want to give up rollerblading?

**DOUGAL:** Bet *he* didn't have to give up rollerblading.

**TED:** Dougal, which is worse? Being nailed to a cross or having to give up rollerblading?

**DOUGAL:** I'm not saying being nailed to a cross is easy. All I'm saying is at least he had the choice.

*Mrs Doyle enters with a bottle of whiskey on a tray.*

**MRS DOYLE** (*playfully*): Who wants their afternoon drink?

*Jack wakes up suddenly. He looks delirious with delight.*

**JACK:** DRINKKKKKK! O YES!!!!!!!!

**TED:** No Mrs Doyle. I'll have that.

*Jack looks confused.*

**JACK:** No?

**TED:** No, Father. It's Lent, remember. You said you'd give it up for a couple of days.

**JACK:** WHAT?!

**TED:** Do you not remember? You said you'd offer it up for Our Lord.

**JACK:** ARNOLD? WHO'S ARNOLD?

**TED:** No, no, 'Our Lord'. Well, I suppose I made your vow for you. Because I know that deep down you'd like to make a little sacrifice.

**JACK:** SACRIFICE? ARSE!

**TED:** Come on, Father. It's Lent, remember?

**JACK:** I DON'T CARE!

**TED:** Father, it's a very special time for us all . . .

**JACK** (*stumbles to the drinks cabinet*): DRINK!

**TED:** You won't find any there, Father! I've put them in a very safe place.

**JACK:** WHERE?

SCENE 4 EXT./DAY 1
SET: CLIFF FACE
*We see a remote-looking cliff face with a cave near some dangerous, choppy-looking waters and rocks below. It should look absolutely impossible to reach.*

SCENE 5 INT./DAY 1
SET: CAVE
*Inside the cave we see an absolutely mountainous pile of full whiskey bottles. Seagulls squawk outside.*

SCENE 6 INT./DAY 1
SET: PAROCHIAL HOUSE
*Jack has gone into a sulk.*

**TED:** Now, Father, don't be like that, OK, here we go. No more cigarettes for me until Easter.

*He holds up some fags, gets a pair of scissors and snips them at the filter. He throws them in the bin. Pause.*

**TED:** Great. There's no problem with that at all. (*Longer pause.*) God, do you know what? I don't miss them at all. This is easy.

*Pause.*

**TED:** Ah, yes. I'm not even thinking about smoking. Not even *thinking* about it. (*Pause.*) Ha.

*Fade to black. A caption comes up: 'Five minutes later'. We see Ted, sitting in his chair staring ahead in a fixed way, his hands gripping fiercely on to the armrests. He looks like someone experiencing massive G-force. Cut to Jack, who is in a similar state, and then to Dougal who is shaking slightly.*

**DOUGAL:** It's beginning to kick in, Ted!

**TED:** I know! Me too! God, this is terrible! I don't like this at all.

**DOUGAL:** Maybe we can stick with it, Ted. I mean, we've come through worse together, and don't forget Dick Byrne . . .

*Cut to Ted as he listens to Dougal. His eyes seem to glaze over. Cut to his point of view. We see that Dougal has been replaced by a giant cigarette with arms and legs. The arms are gesticulating, but all Ted can hear is . . .*

**DOUGAL/CIGARETTE:** Blah, blah, blah, blah . . .

*Cut back to Ted, who is now smiling gormlessly. Cut back to Dougal, who is again his normal self.*

**DOUGAL:** Don't you think so, Ted?

**TED** (*rousing himself*): I certainly do, Dougal. Absolutely. Anyway, how are you doing, Father Jack? You all right there? Do you want me to . . .

*Cut to Jack. He is looking at Ted strangely. Cut to reveal that Ted looks like a giant pint of Guinness from his point of view. As the glass of Guinness gesticulates, white foamy bits splosh from the top.*

**TED/GUINNESS:** Blah, blah, blah, blah . . .

*Cut to Jack looking at Ted with an expression of delight. Cut back to the now-normal Ted, who is faltering slightly as he looks at Jack.*

**TED:** Father? Father?

**DOUGAL:** Is he all right?

**TED:** Oh yes, I think he's just . . . circling the airport. (*The front doorbell rings.*) Better get that. You all right, Dougal?

**DOUGAL:** What? Oh, yeah . . .

*Cut to Dougal looking at Ted. Then we see, from his point of view, that Ted has turned into a giant rollerblade skate; it slowly moves out of the room and turns towards the door. Dougal blinks dazedly.*

SCENE 7 EXT./DAY 1
SET: PAROCHIAL HOUSE DOOR
*We see John and Mary outside. Mary has a package.*

**JOHN:** Now don't make a show of yourself in front of him: 'Yes, Father Crilly, No, Father Crilly. Oh, you're so great, Father Crilly.' Oh, it makes me sick.

**MARY:** I don't know what you're talking about. You're feckin' worse: 'Oh, Father, you're brilliant. Oh, Father, you should be Pope.' It doesn't impress him – it just sounds stupid. God, you are an awesome *divot*.

*Ted opens the door.*

**JOHN AND MARY:** Ah, Father . . .

**TED:** Hello, John, hello Mary.

**JOHN:** Father . . . you look wonderful. Is that a new outfit?

*Ted, confused, looks down at his bog-standard shirt and collar.*

**TED:** Eh . . .

**MARY:** My God, Father, you said a beautiful Mass on Tuesday. And the sermon! I think you'd be a brilliant writer. You should win awards for everything you've ever done ever in your life.

**TED:** I didn't do a Mass on Tuesday.

**MARY:** Did you not? Oh . . . (*Very embarrassed.*) Anyway, we just thought you might like some Easter eggs from the shop.

**TED:** Oh, that's terribly nice of you. Thank you very much indeed.

**JOHN:** I think it comes to about eight pounds.

*Ted's smile disappears.*

**TED:** Oh . . . right.

*He hands over the money.*

**MARY:** Yes, we thought we should get them to you. We're going on holiday, and we're not quite sure when we're getting back.

**JOHN:** Yes. We're going to Rome.

**MARY:** We're really looking forward to it. We might see your friend there.

**TED:** Who's that? Sophia Loren?!!!

*They all laugh their heads off.*

**MARY:** Ah, ha . . . No, Father. The Pope.

**TED:** He's no friend of mine!!!!

*Ted laughs. John and Mary don't. There is an uncomfortable silence.*

**TED** (*abashed*): Actually, that might have sounded a little disrespectful. sorry.

**JOHN:** No problem, Father.

*John puts a cigarette in his mouth. Close-up of Ted's eyes widening. Cut back to John. He draws on the cigarette in slow motion, this is accompanied by an exaggerated furnace-like inhaling noise. Then he exhales. The exhalation goes on for far too long, smoke billowing out everywhere. Ted watches as the smoke curls and forms the words 'lovely fags'. Cut back to Ted in real time. He screams and slams the door on the couple. They look at each other.*

SCENE 8 INT./NIGHT 1
SET: TED AND DOUGAL'S BEDROOM
*We see Ted tossing and turning in his bed. He finally switches the bedside lamp on and sits up. He looks at Dougal, who is sound asleep, mouth agape. Ted gets up and walks to the door.*

SCENE 9 INT./NIGHT 1
SET: JACK'S BEDROOM
*Ted peeks in. He sees Jack in bed snoring in a fairly horrific way. Ted closes the door.*

SCENE 10 INT./NIGHT 1
SET: PAROCHIAL HOUSE
*Ted sits down at the table. He picks up a bin and rummages in it. He takes out a filter and the other half of a cigarette. He places them together. Cut to a shot from the back. He fiddles around with something. After a moment, he leans down on something and we hear the sound of a stapler, stapling.*

SCENE 11 EXT./NIGHT 1
SET: PAROCHIAL HOUSE
*We see Ted's silhouette running from the house. He runs towards a tiny shed nearby. Halfway there, he stops and looks around. Suddenly, the horizontal part of the cross slides into shot and conks him on the head, before sliding the rest of the way down. After a moment of groaning, he gets up and moves off.*

SCENE 12 INT./NIGHT 1
SET: SHED
*Ted comes into the shed. It is very dark.*

**TED:** Ahhhh . . . here we go now.

*He lights a match, which illuminates the interior of the shed. Ted freezes, the match not quite touching the stapled-together cigarette. Cut to what he's looking at: Jack, a bottle of carpet-cleaner almost to his lips, and Dougal, dressed in full rollerblading gear and frozen in the act of lacing up one of his boots. There is a 'moment'.*

SCENE 13 INT./DAY 2
SET: PAROCHIAL HOUSE
*Ted is on the telephone, waiting to be taken off hold. Dougal watches him, slightly abashed. Jack is gripping on to the armrests with an expression of horror.*

**TED** (*to Dougal*)**:** Well, I have to say, I'm very disappointed in us all. One day! You'd think we could go *one* day without giving in to temptation. God almighty, when I think of all the sacrifices Matty Hislop made.

**DOUGAL:** Who?

**TED:** Matty Hislop. He was a notorious drunkard who found God and then decided to punish himself for his sins. Oh, he did all kinds of things . . . like . . . he had a terrible allergic reaction to cats, so instead of avoiding them, he'd carry a kitten around in his pocket and sniff it from time to time. His head would just inflate like a balloon!

**DOUGAL:** God almighty!

**TED:** Also, they say he used to glue his hair to the ceiling in his kitchen and hang there for days and days. And he used to save money in a little cardboard box, and after he'd saved enough for a holiday, he'd throw the money into the Liffey and eat the box. I mean, Dougal, surely you can knock the old rollerblading on the head for a couple of weeks.

**DOUGAL:** I know, Ted, it's just . . . I used to be happy with the old bike, you know? I used to get a great buzz just goin' down to the shops. But after a while it just wasn't enough. I kept goin' for bigger and bigger thrills. But I can handle it, Ted. I could quit any time I want.

**TED:** But you tried to quit yesterday and you couldn't.

**DOUGAL** (*beat, then breaks down*)**:** You're right, Ted! I admit it! I have a problem!

**TED:** Come on now, Dougal, there's no need for that. Not now that I'm getting outside help, anyway. (*He turns back to the telephone.*) Come on, come on, why do the nuns always have the most awful music when you're on hold . . . ? If I hear 'Ave Maria' one more time . . . Excuse me? Excuse me?

SCENE 14 INT./DAY 2
SET: CONVENT
*We see a nun holding the telephone normally as she sings 'Ave Maria' into it. On the wall behind her there is a religious painting of a man with his hand in a toaster. This is Matty Hislop. He looks in great pain, but is being rewarded by a light from Heaven shining on his face.*

**NUN:** Ave Mariaaaaaa . . .

**TED:** Excuse me?

**NUN:** Yes?

**TED:** How much longer am I going to be on hold?

**NUN:** She'll be with you in a second, Father. (*Continues singing.*) Ave Mariaaaaa . . .

*A hand comes into shot and takes the telephone. It belongs to a nun who is sitting in front of a computer. We see many other nuns beside her, like a row of telephone operators, stretching into the distance.*

**NUN 2:** Hello?

**TED:** Ah, hello there! Listen, my name is Father Ted Crilly. We were wondering if you

could send someone out? We're just having a very small problem keeping our Lenten vows. We need someone to keep us on the right path. We almost had a bit of a lapse last night, but . . .

*Nun 2 starts rattling information into the computer.*

**NUN 2:** . . . You just need someone to help you with your vows.

**TED:** Yes.

**NUN 2:** What is it you wish to give up, exactly?

**TED:** Cigarettes, and alcohol and . . . eh rollerblading.

**NUN 2:** Rollerblading. I don't really have a rate for rollerblading. I have skiing. How would you feel about giving up skiing?

**TED:** Eh . . .

**NUN 2:** Well, I'll put that down as a general Sports/Outdoor activity.

*The nun types this into the computer.*

**NUN 2:** All right, we have a special going this month . . . the Lenten package . . . That would be . . . (*She tots this up.*) one hundred and fifty . . . plus VAT . . . plus booking fee . . . two hundred pounds.

**TED:** Two hundred pounds! I'm not trying to buy cocaine!

**NUN 2:** All right, I suppose . . . (*Looking at the computer.*) We have a basic package for . . . fifty pounds.

**TED:** Oh, that'd be much better.

**NUN 2:** How do you wish to pay? We accept all major credit cards.

*Another telephone rings.*

**NUN 2:** Oh, can you hold on a moment, Father?

*She hands the telephone back to the 'hold' nun.*

**NUN:** Ave Maria . . .

SCENE 15 INT./DAY 2
SET: PAROCHIAL HOUSE
*Jack jolts in his chair. He makes a slight, cut-off, strangled noise. Ted looks at him.*

**TED** (*into the telephone*): Oh, listen, I'll have to call you back.

*Dougal joins Ted as they walk over to examine Jack.*

**DOUGAL:** What's up with him, Ted?

**TED:** Hmmmm . . . it looks like the last of the alcohol has left his system. I think he might actually be sober. (*To Jack.*) Is that it, Father? Seeing things as they really are, at last?

**JACK:** Oh . . . my . . . God.

**TED:** Yes, that's it all right. I suppose sobriety for Father Jack must be sort of like taking some mad hallucinogenic.

*Jack looks up at them as if noticing them for the first time.*

**JACK:** Where's the other two?

**TED:** The other two? Ah, I see . . . the old vision must be back to normal. No, Father, there's only two of us.

**JACK:** . . . Two? Oh, thank God.

**TED:** That's right. Two of us and one Mrs Doyle.

**JACK:** And what is it you do again?

**TED:** We're priests, Father.

**JACK:** What?! Priests? I'm not still on that feckin' island, am I?

**TED:** Well, yes . . . How do you feel, Father? It's good to sober up every now and again, isn't it? Or at least, every twelve years.

*Jack goes to the telephone and examines it.*

**JACK:** PHONE!

**TED:** Yes, that's right, Father.

*Jack looks very pleased.*

**JACK** (*pointing*): CURTAINS!

**TED:** Yes, well done.

**JACK:** FLOOR!

**TED:** All coming back to you is it, Father?

**JACK** (*points at Ted*): GOBSHITE!

*Ted's smile disappears.*

**JACK:** YES! I REMEMBER! I REMEMBER!

**END OF PART ONE**

\* \* \*

**PART TWO**

SCENE 15A INT./DAY 3
SET: PAROCHIAL HOUSE
*Mrs Doyle enters. She is dressed to go out and carries a small holdall. In the background we see Jack wandering around looking at things as if seeing them for the first time.*

**MRS DOYLE:** I'll be off now, Fathers.

**TED:** Oh, right. Off to Croagh Fiachra.

**DOUGAL:** Where's that, Ted?

**TED:** It's a big mountain. You have to climb up it with no socks on, and then when you're up there, they chase you back down with big planks. Great fun.

**MRS DOYLE:** Oh, I don't want it to be any fun, Father. I want a good miserable time, keep me on the straight and narrow. I met a couple there last year, and it did them the world of good. They were a bit obsessed with the old S-E-X. Couldn't stop thinking about it. Then they went to Croagh Fiachra and that got it out of their system fast enough, I can tell you. God, I'm glad I never think of that type of thing, Father. That whole sexual world. God, when you think of it . . . it's a dirty, filthy thing, isn't it, Father? How does anyone ever do it? Can you imagine, Father, looking up at your husband with him standing over you with his chap in his hand wanting you to degrade yourself. God almighty . . . try and imagine that, Father.

*Ted looks perturbed.*

**MRS DOYLE:** Imagine that, Father. A naked man looking down on you with only one thing on his mind. Just think about that for a second, Father.

**TED:** N— . . . Well, no, I don't . . .

**MRS DOYLE:** Are you thinking about it, Father? It's disgusting, isn't it? Just picture it, there, Father. Get a good mental picture of it. Do you see what I mean? Can you see him there, ready to do the business?

*We hear the doorbell ringing.*

**TED:** DOORBELL! . . . I mean, doorbell, Mrs Doyle.

*Mrs Doyle leaves.*

**JACK:** Hey! Hey, you! YOU!!! (*He holds up a spoon.*) What the hell is this?

**TED:** Ah, that's a spoon, Father.

*Jack nods, still confused, and puts it down.*

**TED:** C'mon Dougal, this'll be her now. (*A nun enters.*) Hello, there. We . . . Sister Assumpta?

**ASSUMPTA:** Hello, Father.

**TED:** I didn't know you were doing this? How are you?

**ASSUMPTA:** Oh, I'm fine, Father.

**TED:** Dougal! Dougal, you remember Sister Assumpta . . .

**DOUGAL:** Ah, no . . .

**TED:** She was here last year, and then we stayed with her in the convent. In Kildare. Do you remember?

*Dougal thinks, then shakes his head.*

**TED:** Ah, you do. You were hit by the car when you went down to the shops. You must remember all that. And then you won a hundred pounds with the lottery card. You must remember.

*Dougal bites his lip as he tries to remember.*

**ASSUMPTA:** And weren't you accidentally arrested for shoplifting? I remember we went down to the police station to get you. And then the police station went on fire and you had to be rescued by helicopter.

**TED:** Do you remember?

*Something seems to register in Dougal's face, but then it goes.*

**TED:** You can't remember any of it? The helicopter? When you fell out of the helicopter over the zoo? The tigers? Do you not remember? (*Dougal slowly shakes his head.*) You were wearing your blue jumper.

**DOUGAL:** Ahhhh!!! Sister Assumpta, yes, hello there.

**TED:** And you remember Father Jack.

*Assumpta steps back slightly.*

**ASSUMPTA:** Oh yes.

**JACK** (*pointing*): NAN!

**TED:** No, no, it's 'nun', Father.

**JACK:** NUN!

**TED:** Father Hackett has just had a bit of a head-on collision with the real world. Anyway, I have to say I had no idea you were with the Matty Hislop crowd.

**ASSUMPTA:** Oh, yes. Ever since I read his pamphlets, abstinence has been both my keeper and my reward.

**TED:** Yeah? Great. Anyway, all we want is the basic fifty quid job. The bare essentials. Keep us all off the booze and fags. And rollerblading.

**DOUGAL** (*very grandly*): I'm afraid rollerblading is my own particular vice . . .

**ASSUMPTA:** Well, we'll do our best. I'm looking forward to it.

**TED:** You know . . . I sort of am myself. Do us a bit of good to exercise the old willpower. You looking forward to it, Father Jack?

**JACK:** I'm off for a wank!

*Jack leaves the room. Pause.*

**ASSUMPTA:** What did he s—

**TED:** Walk. He's off for a walk. He loves a good, long walk. I think, maybe, it'll just be me and old Dougal tomorrow. Father Jack's very old.

**JACK** (*from upstairs*): Nobody come upstairs while I'm having a wank! (*Really long pause. Everyone looks very thoughtful.*) All right?

**TED:** YES, ALL RIGHT!

SCENE 16 INT./MORNING 4
SET: TED AND DOUGAL'S BEDROOM
*We see the alarm clock reads 5.00. Cut to reveal Assumpta standing beside the bed with a klaxon. She is dressed even more austerely than on the previous night. She presses a button and Ted and Dougal, frightened out of their minds, leap out of bed into a standing position in one quick movement.*

**TED:** GOD ALMIGHTY!!!

**ASSUMPTA** (*stridently*): Good morning, Fathers. Breakfast in five minutes!

*She leaves the room. Dougal and Ted stand panting, looking at each other in confusion. They look at the door, then at each other again.*

**TED:** What . . . what was that thing? Is there a fire? Is there a fire in the house?

**DOUGAL:** I suppose it's just time to get up.

**TED** (*picking up the clock*): It's five a.m. Dougal! Look at this! Five a.m.!

*Dougal comes over to look at the clock. They both stare at it for a moment too long.*

**DOUGAL:** I've never see a clock at five a.m. before.

**TED:** Neither have I. God, there must be some mistake. She probably set her clock wrong. The flight from Dublin probably gave her very minor jetlag and she thinks it's twelve thirty midday.

**DOUGAL:** What'll we do?

**TED:** Well, she's obviously made a mistake. Let's just go back to bed.

**DOUGAL:** Fair enough. What are you doing?

*We see Ted is writing something on a piece of paper.*

**TED:** I'll just write her a note saying we usually don't get up 'til later.

**DOUGAL:** Good thinkin', Ted.

*He opens the door and sticks the note on the other side. We see it. It says, 'You got the wrong time, Assumpta!!! See you at twelve p.m.' Ted comes back into the room. He walks to the bed and gets in. They both snuggle up under the blankets. Suddenly the klaxon sounds again, and we cut to reveal that Assumpta has somehow got into the room and is standing beside the bed again. Ted and Dougal leap out of bed in shock.*

SCENE 17 INT./MORNING 4
SET: PAROCHIAL HOUSE
*Dougal and Ted look shattered. They sit down at the table, looking at their table mats.*

**TED:** I suppose a bit of breakfast and we'll be fine.

**DOUGAL:** Oh, God, I hope so, Ted.

*We see Assumpta appearing in the background with two bowls.*

**TED:** Sister Assumpta? You know, we really are only down for the fags, booze and rollerblading . . . deal. The getting-up-early thing, I mean, it's great but . . . (*He looks down at the bowl and stops talking. We see the contents of the bowl. It's water. Pause.*) . . . This is water.

**ASSUMPTA:** That's right, Father.

**TED:** All right, all right. Having a bit of a laugh with the big thickos from the island. Where's our real breakfast?

**DOUGAL:** I'd love a Pop Tart, Ted.

**TED:** That's right. Father Dougal loves his Pop Tarts first thing in the morning.

**ASSUMPTA:** I don't think Pop Tarts have any place in Our Lord's plan for the world.

**TED:** I think Pop Tarts have as much a place as anything else. Maybe Our Lord doesn't personally take an interest in them, but I'm sure he delegates it to someone almost as important.

**DOUGAL:** But he'd know about them?

**TED:** Oh yes, he'd know about everything. He wouldn't OK Pop Tarts unless they were part of his plan for the world.

**DOUGAL:** What about Coco Pops?

*As Ted answers this, we cut to a shot that shows Assumpta with Ted and Dougal on either side of her in the foreground, listening to this nonsense, barely able to believe it.*

**TED:** Again, the same thing. He mightn't have come up with the idea, but he'd be the one who'd give it the green light. No one would be able to sneak an idea like that past him. He'd know all about it.

**DOUGAL:** Oh, right. But if you look at something like, say, Sugar Puffs or Lucky Charms, it's hard to see how . . .

**ASSUMPTA** (*has had enough*)**:** FATHERS! COULD YOU PLEASE . . . could you please stop having this conversation. Finish your breakfast and come outside for your daily punishment.

**TED:** Oh, fair enough, I suppose. We'll just finish the . . . daily what? I'm sorry? Daily? . . . What did you just say there?

**ASSUMPTA:** Your daily punishment. Matty Hislop's ten-step programme to rid yourself of your pride. The single greatest obstacle to inner fulfilment.

**TED** (*unsure*)**:** Well, that sounds great . . .

SCENE 18 INT./DAY 4
SET: PAROCHIAL HOUSE
*We see Assumpta looking down at something, the Parochial House in the background*

**ASSUMPTA:** How are you two doing?

**TED** (*out of shot*)**:** F— f— fine, thanks.

**ASSUMPTA:** Fine? I hope it's good and cold.

*Cut to Ted and Dougal in two baths filled with water. They are naked and freezing.*

**TED:** No, no! When . . . w–when I say fine, I mean freezing cold. I mean fine in the sense of feeling really, really awful.

**ASSUMPTA** (*holds up a bucket*)**:** Are you sure you don't need more ice?

**TED:** NO! No, actually, to be honest with you, I might enjoy that too much. Very refreshing, the old ice.

**ASSUMPTA:** I'll go and get more, just in case . . . Soon we'll be able to begin the ten steps.

**TED:** What? Wait a second – this isn't the first one? There's still ten to go?!

**ASSUMPTA** (*laughs*)**:** Oh, Father, of course. This is just to cleanse you . . . it's a form of preparation.

**TED:** For what? Are we going into space? (*She moves off.*) I can't feel my legs!

*An outraged Ted turns to Dougal. Dougal smiles at him, with not a care in the world. Ted takes this in. Cut to Jim passing by. He notices Ted and Dougal.*

**JIM:** Ah, hello, Fathers.

**TED:** Hello, Jim.

**DOUGAL:** How's it goin' there, Jim?

**JIM:** Ah, fine. In the old bath, I see. (*Ted nods at this. Long pause.*) See you so.

*Jim moves off. He sees something before he moves fully off. Cut to what he is looking at. It is the cross that Ted put up. Now, the horizontal part has slid almost to the very bottom of it, so that it looks like an inverted cross. Jim looks at it, worried, looks back at Ted, then gradually starts to run away. Pause.*

**TED:** I'm beginning to think this might have been a big, big mistake. Well, ten steps left. Hopefully, it'll just involve having a bit of a pray.

*Dougal looks at him.*

SCENE 19 EXT./DAY 4
SET: OUTSIDE HOUSE
*We see Assumpta driving a tractor. Cut to an overhead shot of the same in which we see Ted and Dougal being dragged behind the tractor. Then we see the tractor going as fast as it can, pulling the lads into the distance.*

SCENE 20 EXT./DAY 4
SET: OUTSIDE HOUSE
*Assumpta is giving Ted a Chinese burn. Ted screams in pain.*

*We see Assumpta standing beside a wheelbarrow full of stones. She has one stone ready to throw. Cut to Ted and Dougal tensed. She wrongsteps them, and they duck and jerk to one side. Then she throws the stone and it hits Ted's shoulder. She looks very put out by this. She picks up another one. Ted and Dougal tense up again.*

*Assumpta giving Dougal a Chinese burn. He seems completely unperturbed. He looks at her, confused.*

*Assumpta sitting beside a table. There are some bowls of food on it. Ted and Dougal approach, looking like animals coming out of a forest, very nervous. They come close to the food on the table. Assumpta then takes out a gun and shoots at them. They run like crazy out of shot.*

SCENE 21 INT./DAY 4
SET: TED AND DOUGAL'S BEDROOM
*Dougal hops into the bedroom, completely contented. Ted follows, looking utterly exhausted and miserable.*

**TED:** Ohhhhh . . . God, I'm looking forward to this . . .

*He stiffens himself and makes a dramatic drop*

backwards on to the bed. We hear a sickening 'clack' sound. Ted, now in incredible pain, opens his mouth in silent agony. Dougal pulls back the blanket on his own bed. We see that instead of the usual mattress, there is a large flat 'brick mattress'.

**DOUGAL:** Ted, guess what she's replaced my mattress with.

*Ted, his face frozen in the same expression of utter pain, manages a barely audible gurgling noise.*

**TED:** Ohhhhh . . . That's it. That's it, she's obviously insane. Dougal, I've had enough. I don't care who she calls . . . If we have to go through this kind of misery one more day, God knows what'll happen. We might die! We're getting out of here.

**DOUGAL** (*dressing*): Where'll we go?

**TED:** No problem. We know loads of people.

**DOUGAL:** What about Mehwengwe? His parents are away for the week. He's got the whole place free *and* he's got satellite.

**TED:** Dougal, he lives in Addis Ababa.

*Pause.*

**DOUGAL:** What about Dick Byrne, Ted?

**TED:** Oh no, I'm not calling him . . . I know, Larry Duff. I'm sure he'll put us up for a while.

*Ted reaches to the telephone beside him and dials.*

SCENE 22 INT./NIGHT 4
SET: DARKENED ROOM
*Close-up of a hand passing a ring around a circuitous line of copper wire. Pull back to reveal that the hand belongs to Larry, and he is just reaching the end of an incredibly long, twisty puzzle. A sign above it reads 'First Prize – £10,000'. Just before he reaches a sign that says 'End' his mobile phone rings and he starts slightly. The thing in his hand shudders and we hear a buzzer sound. Larry jumps with fright. We hear an audience going 'Awwwwwwwww'. Larry looks furious.*

SCENE 23 INT./NIGHT 4
SET: TED AND DOUGAL'S BEDROOM
*Ted puts the telephone down.*

**TED:** Oh, wait a second, no. He told me not to call him tonight because he had this big

important thing on. Well, I suppose it'll have to be Dick Byrne. He'll hide us until she's gone. We'll leave a note saying that we've had to go to a funeral or something . . .

**DOUGAL:** What about an autopsy?! Could we say we had to go to an autopsy? That'd be more exciting.

**TED** (*writing note*): No, Dougal, a funeral would be more believable.

**DOUGAL:** Oh, right.

**TED:** OK, now, listen, we're going to have to do this as quietly as we can. Don't suddenly panic and make any noise. If we take it easy, we won't wake her.

*They go through the open door.*

**DOUGAL:** What was that?

**TED:** Run!!!!!

*We stay on the open door as we hear them crash down the stairs like two out-of-control pianos. Their descent ends in a painful-sounding crunch. (N.B. The following sounds dwindle with distance but are still very loud.)*

**TED:** AGH!

*We hear the front door opening and closing with a slam, then footsteps crunching away. A car starts with a very loud and hesitant splutter. It then roars away. Then it roars back. The doorbell rings. It rings again. Then the door opens.*

**TED** (*from downstairs*): Dougal!

**DOUGAL:** Sorry, Ted! I went the wrong way.

**TED:** Come on!

*The door closes. Footsteps. Car splutter. Dwindling roar. Silence. Pause.*

**ASSUMPTA** (*offscreen*): Who's up?

SCENE 24 INT./NIGHT 4
SET: TED AND DOUGAL'S BEDROOM
*Assumpta comes into the room holding her klaxon. She presses it.*

**ASSUMPTA:** Come on, Fathers, we have to get an early start or we'll miss the rain . . .

*She notices that they have gone. She picks up a note on Ted's bed.*

**ASSUMPTA:** Right!

*She storms out of the room.*

SCENE 25 INT./NIGHT 4
SET: CAR
*We see Ted and Dougal pulling up outside the Rugged Island Parochial House.*

**TED:** Right. They're probably asleep. I'll just knock very gently on the door.

**DOUGAL:** Oh, right. So you won't wake them up.

**TED:** Eh . . . no. I'll have to wake them up so they can let us in.

**DOUGAL:** Well then . . . shouldn't you just knock loudly?

**TED:** Oh, right. Yes, good point, Dougal.

*They get out of the car.*

SCENE 26 INT./NIGHT 4
SET: PAROCHIAL HOUSE
*Assumpta comes into the living room and walks to the telephone. She picks it up and starts to dial, then looks up and sees the Easter eggs on top of the wardrobe. She pauses, then puts the telephone down, looking worried.*

SCENE 27 EXT./NIGHT 4
SET: RUGGED ISLAND PAROCHIAL HOUSE
*A corner of the house. We hear muffled laughing*

*and mucking about coming from somewhere.*

**TED** (*coming around the corner*): . . . I knocked as hard as I could, Dougal. C'mon, we'll try round the back. (*They turn the corner and hear the muffled noises.*) What's that?

*They see a window with light coming out of it. They creep up and look through. Inside they see Dick, Cyril, and Jim. Dick is smoking away happily. Jim is drinking from a bottle of whiskey and Cyril is in full skateboarding gear. Cyril does a little trick with the skateboard and Dick and Jim applaud happily. Ted and Dougal turn slowly to look at each other.*

SCENE 28 INT./DAY 5
SET: PAROCHIAL HOUSE HALLWAY
*Ted and Dougal come into the hallway. They look tired and defeated.*

**TED:** I should have known. I should have seen it. You can't trust Dick Byrne. As priests go, he's a really bad priest.

**DOUGAL:** Ted, we've still got thirty-eight days of Lent to go.

**TED:** I know, I know . . . Still, maybe we should just stand up and take it like men.

*They walk into the living room.*

SCENE 29 INT./DAY 5
SET: PAROCHIAL HOUSE
*Ted and Dougal come in then stop in their tracks. Cut to reveal Assumpta, Easter-egg wrappers shredded around her feet, chocolate smeared over her mouth, looking very guilty indeed. There is a 'moment'.*

**ASSUMPTA:** This isn't what it looks like.

*Ted looks at Dougal. He walks to the table and sits down. He touches his fingertips together and puts them to his mouth.*

**TED:** Well . . . this certainly puts a new spin on things, doesn't it?

**ASSUMPTA:** You won't tell anyone? Will you? I couldn't help it! They're just so *chocolatey* . . . And I can't go back to the other nuns before Easter. Please don't tell them that I gave into temptation.

**DOUGAL:** She's been eating chocolate!

**ASSUMPTA:** Oh, God, please, Father. If there's anything I can do to make it up. You must be so disappointed in me!

**TED:** Well . . . ahem . . . *here's* a mad idea.

SCENE 30 INT./DAY 5
SET: RUGGED ISLAND PAROCHIAL HOUSE
*A hallway. Music plays in the background. The doorbell rings and Dick Byrne comes into shot. He half-walks/half-dances to the door. He opens it. Assumpta is standing outside. Dick Byrne pulls on his fag, exhales . . .*

**DICK:** Ah, Sister. How can I help you?

SCENE 31 INT./DAY 5
SET: PAROCHIAL HOUSE HALLWAY
*Mrs Doyle enters. She is in a cheery mood. She calls inside to the living room.*

**MRS DOYLE:** I'm back, Fathers.

*We see that there is smoke oozing from under the door of the living room.*

**MRS DOYLE:** Oh, my God!

SCENE 32 INT./DAY 5
SET: PAROCHIAL HOUSE
*Mrs Doyle sticks her head round the door. She looks puzzled. We see that the living room is so filled with smoke that it's positively foggy. We see Ted with a line of about six cigarettes in his mouth. We see a row of bottles, all upside down and linked to intravenous tubes. They lead into Jack, who is looking delighted. Cut to window. We see a helmeted Dougal speeding by every now and again.*

SCENE 33 EXT./DAY 5
SET: RUGGED ISLAND PAROCHIAL HOUSE
*We see the Rugged Island priests all in their underpants, freezing. Assumpta walks among them as they sing Matins. Occasionally she whips them with a big branch. We segment the screen so we can see the different activities in both places. Credits.*

**THE END**

# new jack city

**ARTHUR:** Our idea here was to introduce someone even more unpleasant than Jack, but I think some people found Father Fintan Stack just *too* unpleasant. I don't mind him, and I like the way he does all these horrible pointless things like drilling holes in the walls. This is Graham's least favourite episode. It's not top of my list either, and I think the instance of Larry Duff (in the final, televised version) is the weakest. Yet the episode has its moments. I love the scene when they're driving back with Jack who actually throws himself out of the car because he simply can't wait to get his hands on a drink.

**GRAHAM:** I like the scene where Ted invites two other priests round to watch the Sports Day video, and they just end up gossiping about their fellow priests – this is when the several Father Windy Shepherd-Hendersons are mentioned. You can find them, and every other priest named in the series, on a website called the Craggy Island Examiner. It has nothing to do with us, but, interestingly, contains masses of information that we'd forgotten. I'd forgotten, for example, that there were at least four Windy Shepherd-Hendersons. But you really can't forget Fintan Stack, or the wonderful way Brendan Grace played the character. It was especially interesting how he interpreted his lines. We had written them as angry lines, but he played the part in a light, delicate, almost effeminate way, which makes the character far more threatening.

Apart from Brendan, I'm really not keen on this episode, but I think it's worth it for the title alone. I *love* that title. And I like Ted listening to the racing on the radio in the beginning, having placed his bet on a horse called Divorce Referendum. I wish we'd also had him put an accumulator on one called Abortion Referendum . . .

## PART ONE

SCENE 1 INT./DAY 1
SET: PAROCHIAL HOUSE

*Ted is sitting at the table listening to the radio, which is on the table. He seems very excited and has a rolled-up newspaper in his hand. We hear racing commentary coming from the set.*

**COMMENTATOR:** . . . and it's Divorce Referendum in the lead followed by Glory Be to God . . . Glory Be to God nipping at Divorce Referendum's heels . . . Glory Be to God creeps ahead of Divorce Referendum!

**TED:** C'mon, Divorce Referendum! C'mon, Divorce Referendum!

**COMMENTATOR:** Divorce Referendum struggling to stay the pace as Glory Be to God increases its lead . . .

**TED:** Oh, no! C'mon, for pity's sake! C'mon!

**COMMENTATOR:** Divorce Referendum edges in front! Divorce Referendum is way in front!

**TED:** YES!! YES!! COME ON, DIVORCE REFERENDUM!

**COMMENTATOR:** The finishing line is in sight! Divorce Referendum is speeding towards victory!

**TED:** HA, HA!!!!!

**COMMENTATOR:** Oh no!

*Ted freezes.*

**COMMENTATOR:** Disaster for Divorce Referendum as he turns in the opposite direction and simply runs off the course! Glory Be to God takes advantage of the opening and steams home!

*Ted's mouth is open. He stares at the radio in bewilderment.*

**TED:** OHHHHH . . . FLIP!! YOU FLIPPING, FLIPPING . . . FLIPPPER! IT'S THE KNACKER'S YARD FOR YOU, PAL! OHHHHHHH, FFFFFFFLIP!!!!!

*He hears the front door opening and quickly changes the channel, assuming a thoughtful expression at the table.*

**VOICE:** . . . So what role do you see the Church assuming in coming months?

*The door opens and Dougal pushes in an empty wheelchair.*

**DOUGAL:** What you listening to there, Ted?

**TED:** Oh, it's a thing about, ah . . . the Church and . . . you know . . . God and . . . so on.

**DOUGAL:** Ah, right.

*Ted turns off the radio. Dougal sits down and starts idly flicking through a copy of a magazine. Ted looks up. We see a shot of the empty wheelchair.*

**TED:** Where's . . . eh . . . where's Father Jack, Dougal?

**DOUGAL:** Where's Father Jack?

**TED:** Yes. Father Jack. Where is he?

**DOUGAL:** He's in his . . . (*He looks at the empty chair.*) Ah . . .

**TED:** Yes . . . Where is he?

**DOUGAL:** He's, ah . . .

**TED:** He's supposed to be in the wheelchair, Dougal.

**DOUGAL:** Yes . . .

*Dougal thinks for a second, looks at Ted, then looks at the wheelchair.*

**TED:** You've lost him again, haven't you, Dougal?

**DOUGAL:** I have, Ted, yeah.

**TED:** So you took him out for his walk and you lost him. Again.

**DOUGAL:** That must have been what happened, all right.

**TED:** Well, what have you got to say for yourself?

**DOUGAL:** Well, like I said the last time, it won't happen again.

**TED** (*sighs*)**:** Well, Dougal, I'll hold you to that. Try not to let it happen again.

*Pause.*

**DOUGAL:** What? . . .

*Ted looks at him for a moment.*

**TED:** Well?

**DOUGAL:** Yes, Ted?

**TED:** Are you not going to look for him?

**DOUGAL:** Ah, he'll come back on his own, Ted. Sure what's the worst can happen to him?

**TED:** Well, he could have an accident and be killed.

**DOUGAL:** Oh, right, yeah.

*Dougal stands up and wraps his scarf around him*

*again. But then he sees something.*

**DOUGAL:** Wait a second, Ted . . . Is that not Jack there?

*We see Jack lying on the ground near his chair, breathing noisily. He is dressed to go out, in hat, scarf, etc.*

**TED:** What? (*He stands up and goes over to where Jack is lying.*) Ah, Dougal, you didn't even get him out the door, did you?

**DOUGAL:** I thought the old wheelchair felt a bit lighter today, yeah.

**TED:** C'mon, let's get him up.

*They lift him into his chair. Ted takes his hat off. He takes a handkerchief and wipes the inside of the brim. We see that there is a vast amount of brown grease on the hankie when Ted takes it away. He takes off Jack's scarf, then goes to put the hat and scarf away.*

**TED:** Take off his gloves, there, Dougal.

**DOUGAL:** Right, so, Ted. (*He bends over Jack. Pause.*) Ted?

**TED:** Hm? . . .

**DOUGAL:** Ted . . . they're not gloves.

*He holds up Jack's hands. They are exceptionally hairy. Ted walks over and examines them.*

**TED:** God. They're very hairy hands altogether.

**DOUGAL:** Hairy is the word, Ted. Actually, Ted, I think the word is 'very hairy'.

**TED:** This is just typical. Father Dillon and Father Shanahan are coming up on Saturday. What are they going to think when they see the wolfman here?

**DOUGAL:** What do you think's wrong with him, Ted?

**TED:** I don't know.

**DOUGAL:** Do you remember the time his head went septic?

**TED:** Yes. I didn't think a whole head could go septic. Y'know, a *whole head*. But that's Jack for you. Anyway, I'd better look in the book . . . They really are exceptionally hairy.

*Ted goes and takes a large, ancient-looking book*

*from the library. In the background we see Dougal take out a comb. He gingerly combs Jack's hairy hands. Ted puts the book on the table and opens it.*

**TED:** Right . . .

*Ted has opened the book at a page that shows a row of six photographs. The first is of a normal human hand, the sixth one is of an ape's hand. The ones in between show the various stages of progression.*

**TED:** Hold up his hand there, Dougal.

*Dougal does so. Ted looks at the book.*

**TED:** Hmmm . . . He got up to stage four after drinking that brake fluid . . . but this looks like a stage six.

*He slams the book shut. Mrs Doyle enters, carrying a tray.*

**MRS DOYLE:** Hello to the lot of yous.

**TED:** Hello, Mrs Doyle.

**MRS DOYLE** (*looking at Jack*)**:** Ah, would you look at him there with his hairy hands.

**TED:** . . . Yes . . . I think we'll have to call Doctor Sinnot.

**MRS DOYLE:** He'll know what to do. I had to go to him a couple of weeks ago.

**TED:** Really? I didn't know you were ill, Mrs Doyle. What was wrong with you?

**MRS DOYLE:** Oh, I'm afraid it was a bit of a woman's problem. I was having a bit of trouble with—

**TED:** Right! I'd better phone him now, actually, before it gets too late.

*He goes over to the table, leaving Mrs Doyle before she can say any more. There are two telephones on the table, one black and one red. Ted picks up the red one and presses a single button on the front of it.*

SCENE 2 INT./DAY 1
SET: OFFICE
*We see a red telephone, exactly the same as Ted's, and hear it ringing. An ominous light starts flashing on it. In the background we see Doctor Sinnot examining a patient. He looks over at the telephone, a nervous expression on his face.*

SCENE 3 INT./DAY 1
SET: PAROCHIAL HOUSE HALLWAY
*We see Doctor Sinnot closing the front door behind him. He looks very tense, but businesslike. He carries a medical bag and a suitcase. Ted and Dougal are there to greet him.*

**SINNOT:** Right, so it's the hairy hands?

**TED:** Yes.

**SINNOT:** Both of them?

**TED:** Yes.

**SINNOT:** And you say it looks like a stage six?

**TED:** It looks like it, yeah.

**SINNOT:** Hmmm . . . All right, I'll change upstairs.

*Sinnot heads upstairs.*

**DOUGAL:** Why's Jack so scared of doctors Ted?

**TED:** I think they just remind him of illness. He doesn't like thinking about his own mortality. That's why he always hated visiting the sick.

**DOUGAL:** Oh, God, yeah, he hates the sick, all right. And the poor, he hates them as well.

**TED:** Yes. The poor really get on his nerves.

**DOUGAL:** And the needy.

**TED:** Them as well. What was it he always used to say about the needy? He had a term he used for them . . .

**DOUGAL:** A shower of bastards.

**TED:** That's it. Anyway, listen, when we bring the doctor in, you're to act completely normal. Just pretend like he's a normal visitor. We can't let Jack suspect that anything's up.

*Dougal nods. We hear a noise from the stairs. Ted looks up.*

**TED:** Ah, doctor. Ready to go in? C'mon, Dougal. Remember, act perfectly normal.

*The doctor comes into shot. He is dressed in protective gear that makes him look like Dustin Hoffman in 'Outbreak'. He follows Ted and Dougal inside.*

SCENE 4 INT./DAY 1
SET: PAROCHIAL HOUSE
*The doctor stands at the doorway, talking to Ted. We see there is a large crack in the visor of the helmet.*

**TED:** So, it's off to Saint Clabbert's again, Doctor?

**SINNOT:** Yes. Well, the way I see it, it's more for your safety than for his. That hair thing can be very contagious.

**TED:** So . . . how long do you think you'll have him?

**SINNOT:** Hard to say. It could be a while . . . Actually, Father, you should be prepared . . . It might be better for him if . . . if he doesn't come back.

**TED** (*brightens*): Great! I mean, oh, no . . .

**SINNOT:** He is very old, and the nuns at Saint Clabbert's are trained to look after priests in their twilight years.

**TED** (*obviously delighted*): Yes, of course . . . Oh, well, just have to grin and bear it, I suppose. I'll break it to him gently. Thanks, Doctor.

*He waves and closes the door.*

SCENE 5 INT./DAY 1
SET: PAROCHIAL HOUSE
*Jack is in his chair. Ted comes in and approaches.*

**TED:** Father, do you remember that great time you had in Saint Clabbert's?

**JACK** (*suddenly shocked*): Huh?

**TED:** Do you remember the fun you had with all the nuns fussing over you?

*Jack's face goes into a fixed, frozen look of absolute terror.*

**TED:** Well, Doctor Sinnot thinks another little spell in there would do you the world of good . . .

*Another shot of Jack wearing exactly the same expression.*

**TED:** I know you might have to give up the odd glass of sherry for a while, but that'll be good for you.

*Pause. Another shot of a frozen Jack.*

**TED:** What do you say, Father? You ready to have just a great big laugh with all the nuns?

*Another shot of Jack. Ted waits for an answer. He cocks his head slightly.*

**TED:** Sorry, Father?

*Jack is now beyond help. He stares ahead in that frozen way.*

**TED:** Well . . . well, I'll just go and get you all packed.

*Ted leaves the room, pausing one more time to look at the frozen Jack. When Ted leaves, Jack shakes himself out of his horrified trance and runs out, bumping into a confused Dougal at the doorway. Then he exits through the front door at top speed. Cut back to Dougal. Ted comes in.*

**TED:** Right, if we— Dougal, where's Father Jack?

**DOUGAL:** I just saw him running out the door there.

**TED:** Oh, God. Where's he gone?

SCENE 6 EXT./DAY 1
SET: NEAR PAROCHIAL HOUSE
*We see Jack driving away from the house in a one-man tractor-mower that is far too small for him. A flurry of grass shoots out of the side of it as he drives. He bounces in his seat, urging it to go faster, and looks behind him to see if Ted and Dougal are following. It makes a pathetic 'chucka-chucka' noise as it goes.*

SCENE 7 INT./NIGHT 1
SET: TED AND DOUGAL'S BEDROOM
*Ted and Dougal are in bed. It's very quiet.*

**DOUGAL:** So, Jack's up there in Saint Clabbert's anyway.

**TED:** Indeed he is. And you know, despite the *Born to be Wild* act with the old Flymo there, I think secretly he's de-*lighted*.

**DOUGAL:** God, it's weird the way you get used to something, isn't it, Ted? It seems like only yesterday he was here, shouting at us and drinking his head off.

**TED:** Dougal, it *was* yesterday.

**DOUGAL:** Yeah, but, you know, that's why I said it seemed like yesterday.

**TED:** Oh, right, because it *was* yesterday.

*Pause.*

**DOUGAL:** What time are Father Dillon and Father Shanahan coming on Wednesday?

**TED:** Around six.

**DOUGAL:** Six o'clock?

**TED** (*sighs*): Yes.

**DOUGAL:** Right.

**TED:** It's just as well Jack won't be here, you know. He can get very irritable around strangers. That was the thing about Jack . . . always very bad around strangers.

**DOUGAL:** And people he knew.

**TED:** Yes. Very bad around strangers and people he knew. Oh, don't forget, the lads'll be bringing the video of the sports day, so don't be late.

**DOUGAL:** Oh, great! That was a brilliant day.

*He turns off the light.*

**TED:** Night, Dougal.

**DOUGAL:** Night, Ted.

*Ted settles down. Pause.*

**TED:** Oh . . . damn it . . .

*He puts the light back on. He takes a notebook from his bedside table and starts flicking through the pages, grabbing a pen as he does so. Meanwhile, Dougal has got out of bed. He stretches and yawns and grabs a towel from the end of the bed. He undoes a few buttons on his pyjama top. He also turns on the radio and starts to whistle. Ted watches this quietly.*

**TED:** Dougal, no. It's not morning yet. I just put the light back on.

*Pause.*

**DOUGAL:** Oh, right.

SCENE 8 INT./DAY 2
SET: PAROCHIAL HOUSE
*Ted, wearing a dressing gown, walks into the room and stretches. He walks over to the table, where a bowl of breakfast cereal is waiting for him. He sits down and starts to eat. Just as he is about to put the first spoonful in his mouth, he looks up and freezes. Cut to an oldish priest, Father Fintan Stack, sitting where Jack usually sits. He is smoking a fag and observing Ted dispassionately.*

**TED:** Ah . . . hello . . . ah, Father . . . Father, ah . . . who are you?

**FINTAN** (*gruffly*): Who are you?

**TED:** Father Ted Crilly. Pleased to meet you.

*He stands up and walks over, holding his hand out. Rather than shaking it, Stack takes an envelope out and hands it to Ted.*

**TED:** Oh . . . what's this?

*He looks at Fintan uncertainly and wanders back to the table, opening the letter.*

**TED:** Oh, it's from the Bishop . . . Oh, right . . . oh . . . so . . . so, you'll be taking Father Jack's place . . .

*Fintan just looks at Ted, smoking his fag. Ted smiles and uncertainly resumes eating.*

**TED:** Well, this is a bit of a surprise. Ah, has Mrs Doyle shown you round the house?

*No response. Thinking Fintan might have said something . . .*

**TED:** . . . Sorry?

*No response.*

TED: Anyway, well . . . ah . . . welcome to Craggy Island. Ah . . . meals are at eleven, one, half two, three, five, seven and nine. And if you ever want a quick snack, just ask Mrs Doyle. Ah, there's . . .

*Fintan stands up and walks over to where Ted is. Without paying attention to anything Ted says, he takes the bowl Ted is eating from and pulls at it. Ted holds on to it for a moment and then lets go. Fintan takes the spoon, then walks back to his seat, calmly eating.*

TED (*after a moment's hesitation*): Ah . . . that's actually mine . . . ah . . . Well, you go ahead there . . .

*Dougal walks in.*

TED: Ah, Dougal, this is Father Fintan Stack. He'll be staying with us now that Father Jack's gone.

DOUGAL: Oh, right, yeah.

*Dougal nods a hello.*

FINTAN: This the brains of the operation?

DOUGAL: Ah, no, that'd be Ted.

FINTAN: I want to listen to some music, all right?

TED: Yes, yes, go ahead there and—

FINTAN (*already up*): I wasn't asking for permission.

*He takes a tape from his pocket and walks over to the stereo. He puts something on and presses 'play'. Incredibly loud Jungle blasts out of the speakers. Fintan goes back to his seat. Dougal and Ted look at each other as the music pumps out.*

SCENE 9 INT./NIGHT 2
SET: TED AND DOUGAL'S BEDROOM
*Ted and Dougal are in bed. We hear the repetitive beats of Jungle in the adjacent room.*

TED: So . . . Dougal . . . What do you think of Father Stack?

DOUGAL: . . . Eh . . .

TED: In his note from the Bishop, it says that they've never been able to find a suitable parish for him . . . He's not a very nice man, is he?

DOUGAL: God, Ted, I've never met anyone like him, anyway. Who would he be like? Hitler or one of those mad fellas.

TED: He's nearly worse than Hitler. You wouldn't find Hitler playing Jungle music at three o'clock in the morning. . . . God, he nearly makes Jack seem normal.

DOUGAL: You know, he nearly does. You'd—

*Dougal is interrupted by a massive roar. Ted holds his hand up and they listen for a moment, heads cocked. Pause.*

TED: All right, carry on.

DOUGAL: I was just saying, you'd almost sort of miss Father Jack.

TED: I mean, he had his funny little ways. But, you know, whenever Jack'd hit us or whatever, he'd never do it out of spite. He'd only do it because, you know . . . he thought it was funny . . . or whatever.

DOUGAL (*laughs*): I suppose . . . thinking about it now, it was sort of funny, wasn't it?

TED: Yes, ha, ha! . . . Do you remember that time he . . . ha, ha! . . . gave you a big kick up the B-O-T-T-Y!?

DOUGAL: Ha, ha. And do you remember . . . do you remember when you were bending over him . . . !?

TED: . . . Yeah, ha, ha! . . . Yeah . . .

DOUGAL: . . . And he held your nose until you had to open your mouth, and then he put a big spider in it. Ha, ha, ha!

TED (*stops laughing*): No, that wasn't funny, Dougal. When he kicked you up the arse, that was funny. But it wasn't funny when he put the spider in my mouth.

DOUGAL: Ah, it was, Ted . . .

TED: No, it wasn't, Dougal.

DOUGAL: Ah, Ted.

TED: Dougal, did you have the spider in your mouth or was it me?

DOUGAL: It was definitely you, Ted. The look on your face!

*Dougal does an impression of Ted's face.*

**TED:** Dougal! Anyway, he's gone now . . . God, it's funny how you get used to someone's little ways . . .

SCENE 9A INT./EXT
SET: VARIOUS
*Flashback. Beautiful, emotional music plays – perhaps 'Seasons in the Sun' – as we see a number of incidents involving Jack. All the scenes are shot in a very 'romantic', idealistic soft focus.*

*Ted and Jack putting up a sign that reads 'Home Sweet Home'. Ted holds the nail and Jack levels a hammer at it. He brings the hammer back and then whacks Ted on the head with it. He then goes to finish the job but Dougal and Mrs Doyle hold him back.*

*Ted in a bathroom. He walks towards the bath and suddenly Jack appears over the edge. He attaches a pair of clothes pegs to Ted's nipples. Ted turns to the camera and screams. The pegs are attached firmly. Jack laughs happily.*

*Ted lining up a moderately difficult putt on a very nice green. He aims, draws back the putter and hits the ball softly. It starts to roll towards the hole. Ted*

*makes a 'come on, come on' gesture. Then Jack drives a car into shot and knocks Ted down. Ted is splayed some feet away from the car. Jack, behind the wheel, laughs his head off.*

*Ted drifts back into reality and loses the faraway look on his face. We hear the noise from downstairs worsening.*

**TED** (*getting out of bed*)**:** Ah, God, I've had enough. It sounds like he's drilling holes in the walls or something. I'm going to have a word.

**DOUGAL:** Careful, now!

SCENE 10 INT./NIGHT 2
SET: PAROCHIAL HOUSE
*Ted walks into the living room. He turns to see Fintan drilling holes in the walls of the room, a fag hanging from his mouth. There are already many big, ugly holes dotting the walls. He turns to Ted and stops drilling.*

**FINTAN:** What?

*Ted can't think of anything to say. He leaves the room. Fintan continues drilling.*

**END OF PART ONE**

* * *

**PART TWO**

SCENE 11 INT./DAY 3
SET: PAROCHIAL HOUSE HALLWAY
*Ted opens the front door and sticks his head in.
There are two other priests behind him.*

**TED:** Right . . . come on . . . I think he's gone
out.

**VOICE 1:** What's up with you there, Ted?

**VOICE 2:** Ted's gone mad!

*The two men laugh. Ted comes in and ushers them
in. They are Father Ken Dillon and Father Rory
Shanahan.*

**TED:** All right, this way, lads.

**RORY:** Lead on, MacTed!

SCENE 12 INT./DAY 3
SET: PAROCHIAL HOUSE
*Ted sticks his head in and we see that Fintan is
nowhere to be seen.*

**TED:** Right. Coast's clear.

*The other two follow Ted.*

**KEN:** Father Jack's not here?

**TED:** No, he has that hair thing again. He's
up in Jurassic Park.

**RORY:** Oh, right. Saint Clabbert's. Father

Walton's up there, I hear.

**TED:** Sit down there . . . (*The other two sit
down.*) Sherry all right . . . ?

**RORY:** Grand job.

**KEN:** Lovely.

*Ted starts to pour some sherry.*

**RORY:** Did you know Father Coogan, at all,
Ted?

**TED:** Oh, God, yes. Tom Coogan. He was in
Africa for a while, wasn't he?

**RORY:** He was. And he was with Father
Shortall in Athlone.

**KEN:** And he was parish priest in Kenmare
then.

**RORY:** And I think at one stage he was in
Lucan.

**KEN:** And wasn't he in Boston for a while?

**RORY:** Yes. A great old pal of mine, Jim
Doolan, was with him in Boston.

**KEN:** And he was back in Wicklow for about
a year.

**TED:** I think Windy Shepherd-Henderson
was parish priest while he was in Wicklow.

**KEN:** Is that Windy Shepherd-Henderson
that was in Tralee with Larry Buckley?

**TED:** No, that was another Windy Shepherd-
Henderson. There were about four of them.

**KEN:** Oh, at least. One of them was with
Father Daley in Chicago.

**RORY:** Father Daley from Clones? Wasn't he
the first man on the scene when Malcolm X
was assassinated?

**TED:** No, that was Father Burke. Father
Daley used to have the lump on the side of
his head in the shape of Connaught.

**KEN:** Ah, yeah, like Father Carolan there. He
lost the use of his ears in an accident.

**RORY:** He's deaf?

**TED:** No, no, he just lost the use of his ears.
He used to be able to wiggle them. Now
they're just completely paralysed.

**KEN:** Remember Father O'Reilly? Isn't he in

Clare now? They had to move him there after he owned up to that O.J. Simpson thing.

**RORY:** Father Costello in Athlone is related to that fella, the Japanese fella. Judge Ito. The little humpty fella with the fake beard. Father Merrigan from Ardee did his wedding, I think.

**TED:** Father Merrigan, isn't he dead now?

**RORY:** No, no, he always just lookcd dead.

**KEN:** Ted, did you say Larry Duff was coming to this thing?

**TED:** Actually I'll give him a call on his mobile. (*He picks up the telephone.*)

SCENE 12A INT./DAY 3*
SET: SMALL THEATRE
*We see a blindfolded knife-thrower taking aim in a hushed theatre. We see Larry revolving on a circular board. The knife-thrower takes aim. We hear Larry's mobile phone ringing. We see the knife-thrower jump slightly as he is startled by the noise. He throws the knife and we hear a thunk. A woman screams in the audience.*

SCENE 12B INT./DAY 3
SET: PAROCHIAL HOUSE
*Cut back to Ted still on the telephone. After a while he puts the receiver down.*

**TED:** He must have it turned off. (*He looks around.*) Where's Dougal got to?

**RORY** (*holding up a tape*): C'mon, Ted, you got the video player there?

**TED:** I do!

*He puts in the video and presses 'play'. The priests settle down to enjoy themselves. They are very excited. All through the following scene, we hear the priests chattering excitedly among themselves.*

*Cut to the video. We see a line of priests, all in their usual uniform, running along in an egg-and-spoon*

---

*In the final version this scene was moved to Episode Three, Tentacles of Doom. This scene was changed to show Larry making a house of cards. He is interrupted by the telephone ringing and when he picks up a stapler instead of the phone, he staples his ear to his head and then falls out of shot, knocking down the house of cards as he does so.

*race. Ted is one of them.*

**ALL:** Oh, look! O'ho! There y'are now!

*We see another line of priests in a sack race. Dougal is one of them. In the background we see two priests throwing a frisbee to each other.*

**TED:** God, where's Dougal at all?

*Cut to a priest running around a real track. He carries a baton. He passes it to another priest, who runs on.*

*We see another priest running, then doing a long jump into a sandpit. He looks up, waiting for some scores, then punches the air triumphantly.*

**TED:** Good old Father Smith. He broke the priest record with that one.

*Fintan walks in from the kitchen, smoking a fag. He walks to his chair and sits looking at them. Ted's smile disappears. Rory and Ken remain 'up'. We see a priest doing a shot putt. He throws.*

**RORY:** Rayyyyyyy!!!

*He notices Fintan's glare and shuts up. The mood darkens considerably. A very long pause.*

**FINTAN:** What are we watching?

*Long pause. The three priests are very uncomfortable.*

**KEN:** We're looking at the sports day.

**FINTAN:** Yeah? . . . Lots of young fellas runnin' around in shorts . . . (*Pointing at Rory.*) That's the kind of thing you like lookin' at, is it? Young fellas runnin' around a field in shorts.

*Rory and Ken look very embarrassed. They are blushing wildly.*

**FINTAN** (*pointing at Ken*): And I bet you like that, too. The only thing is, you're probably imaginin' what they'd look like without shorts. What do you think that'd look like? Young fellas runnin' around in the nude? (*Pause.*) You're sittin' there imaginin' that, aren't you? Thinkin' about it with a big smile on your face. You dirty fecker.

**RORY:** Well, I have to say . . . I think that you are a very rude man.

**FINTAN:** If you ever say that to me again, I'll put your head through the wall.

*There is another long, uncomfortable pause.*

**TED:** Father Stack, if you're trying to embarrass us, you're not succeeding.

**FINTAN:** Yes, I am.

*Dougal walks in from the kitchen. He looks very disorientated. His hair is dishevelled and he doesn't look very well.*

**TED:** Dougal, where were you?

**DOUGAL** (*very drunk*): TED! TED, HOW ARE YA!

*He goes to hug Ted. Ted reels from Dougal's breath.*

**TED:** Dougal, what the . . . ?!

**DOUGAL:** Guess what, Ted!

**TED:** What?

*Pause.*

**DOUGAL:** What?

**TED:** Have you been drinking, Dougal?

**DOUGAL:** Yeah, I have! I've been drinking like a mad eejit, Ted. Oh, wait!

*He looks at Fintan and winks broadly. Very deliberately.*

**DOUGAL:** No, I haven't.

**TED:** Dougal, I am ashamed of you!

**DOUGAL:** Ted, Ted. Ted. Ted. Ted, c'mere, Ted. (*He whispers.*) You're me best friend. God, I love being a priest! We're all going to heaven, Ted! Rayyy!

**FINTAN:** Perhaps I should explain. Your little friend and I were enjoying a bottle of whiskey which I found upstairs.

**TED:** Oh, well, that, that is the last straw!

**DOUGAL** (*holding up a bunch of keys*): I'm driving! I'm driving home! I'm perfectly capable!

*Dougal falls over.*

**FINTAN:** Oh, by the way, I got the keys of your car and I drove it into a big wall. If you don't like it, tough. I had my fun and that's all that matters.

**DOUGAL** (*from the floor*): Ted, Ted, I can see up your trousers, Ted.

**TED:** Well, frankly, I thought giving Dougal alcohol was the last straw. But it must just have been the second-last one, because this must definitely be the last bit . . . of . . . straw left in the . . . thing. There's *no* straw left, basically, is what I'm saying.

**RORY:** Ted, it's a little late . . .

**KEN:** Yes . . . I really think we should go.

**TED:** Oh . . . you don't have to.

**RORY:** I think we should.

**FINTAN:** Bye, girls . . .

*The two men get up to leave. Fintan gets up and 'mock' chases them out through the door. Ted follows them. Ted walks back into the room. He seems very cross, but is trying not to show it.*

**FINTAN:** Pair of wankers.

**TED:** Oh! I . . . Dougal, come on, I think we've had enough of Father Stack's company for this evening.

**DOUGAL:** To the pub, Ted!

*Ted grabs Dougal, and they leave the room. After they go, Fintan takes out a knife and begins to rip one of the cushions.*

SCENE 13 INT./NIGHT 3*
SET: PAROCHIAL HOUSE HALLWAY
*Ted and Dougal come into the hall. Ted puts on his coat, then attempts to do the same for Dougal.*

**DOUGAL:** Ted, Ted, what's going on?

**TED:** We're going to kidnap Jack from Saint Clabbert's.

**DOUGAL:** Kidnapping. Wow! How much will we get for him?

---

*In the final version we inserted a new scene, 12C, here which showed Mrs Doyle coming into the living room where Fintan is swaying to Jungle, smoking a fag and drinking some whiskey. Oblivious to all this, she holds up a sign reading, 'Will you have a cup of tea?' He shakes his head and carries on dancing so she holds up a second sign that says, 'Ah, go on.' He shakes his head. This continues for a while, with Fintan dancing and Mrs Doyle holding up the sign until she finally gives up and leaves.

**TED:** We're not doing this to make any kind of profit, Dougal. He's not the Lindbergh baby. We're just going to get him back so that we can jettison Father Stack. Are you with me?

**DOUGAL:** I'm with you, Ted!

**TED:** Then let's go!

*Ted opens the door and walks out. Dougal closes the door after him and walks back down the hall. After a moment, we hear the doorbell ring. Dougal walks back to the door and opens it.*

**DOUGAL:** Hello?

*A hand comes into shot, grabs Dougal and pulls him out.*

SCENE 13A EXT./NIGHT 3
SET: SAINT CLABBERT'S
*We see a sign that reads 'Saint Clabbert's Old Priests Home'. Ted and Dougal are crouching under a window, whispering.*

**TED:** Right. The best thing to do is find an open window, and creep in. The last time, he was in a room on the ground floor. That's where they keep the more 'difficult' ones.

**DOUGAL:** That's a bit mad, Ted. Why don't we just go to the nuns and say we want him back?

**TED:** Because Doctor Sinnot said he's sick and old, and moving him might be dangerous. But I got a second opinion.

**DOUGAL:** Ah, right. From who?

**TED:** Mrs Doyle.

**DOUGAL:** But, Ted, I'm not sure if this is a good idea, Ted. I mean . . . kidnapping . . .

**TED:** No, we're just bringing him back home to where he belongs. It's a bit like *Lassie Come Home* except with Father Jack as Lassie.

**DOUGAL:** Who are we, then?

**TED:** What? I don't know. The other people in the film. You're Roddy McDowell and I'm . . . Liz Taylor.

**DOUGAL:** Right. Well, that's fine. I just wanted to get all that straight in my mind.

*The light turns off in the home.*

**TED:** Right! Let's go!

SCENE 14 INT./NIGHT 3
SET: MAIN ROOM
*The room is completely dark. A door opens and we see Ted and Dougal silhouetted for a moment.*

**TED** (*whispering*): C'mon, Dougal. Get in, get in.

**DOUGAL** (*loudly*): I'm right behind you, T—

**TED:** Dougal! Shut up! We have to keep it quiet. Right. See if there's a light switch anywhere round there.

*A moment's fumbling. Then the light suddenly comes on, revealing a frozen Ted and Dougal, Dougal's hand on the light switch, and about a dozen elderly priests in armchairs, all of whom wake up suddenly and start shouting at the top of their voices.*

**OLD PRIESTS:** DRINK! FECK! ARSE!

*They wave sticks, growl menacingly and bark out confused commands. Basically, it is Jack × 20. A lot of noise.*

**TED:** Turn off the light! Turn off the light!

*Dougal does so, and the noise immediately dies. Suddenly a woman's voice sounds from outside somewhere.*

**MONICA** (*muffled*): What's all that noise?

**TED:** Dougal, quick, over here!

*Pause. The door opens and the light comes on. Sister Monica stands there. All the priests immediately start shouting. We see that Ted and Dougal are sitting in two free seats, also shouting.*

**OLD PRIESTS:** FECK! ARSE! DRINK! . . .

**MONICA:** Now, calm down, all of you! Some people are trying to get some sleep.

*She turns off the light. All the priests stop shouting.*

**DOUGAL:** Arse! Fe—

*There is a 'thump' sound and Dougal shuts up. The nun pauses at the door, then finally closes it.*

SCENE 15/NIGHT 3
SET: OUTSIDE SAINT CLABBERT'S
*We see three figures stealing across the grounds towards a car. Ted and Dougal push the third figure into the car. Then we cut to Ted getting in on his side, Dougal getting into the passenger seat. They*

*both look around to the back seat and jump with shock. The priest in the back seat is not Father Jack, but Father Walton, another elderly priest almost completely covered in hair. He looks very like Lon Chaney in the early werewolf films, except that the hair covers his eyes.*

**TED:** Dougal! That's not Father Jack! Hello, Father Walton.

*He hears Ted's voice, but seems confused.*

**WALTON:** Feck off . . .

**DOUGAL:** Will he not do, Ted?

**TED** (*ponders this for a few moments*): Emmm . . . no. I don't think so. No. Anyway, look at him. He's gone hair mad. It'd be very dangerous to move him around.

**DOUGAL:** OK, so.

**TED** (*in wonder*): God, a stage twelve. I never thought I'd see one. Right. Come on, let's get Father Jack!

SCENE 16 INT./NIGHT 3
SET: MAIN ROOM
*A flashlight illuminates the face of a Jack-type.*

**BILLY:** ARSE!

*The flashlight switches off, then on. We see another Jack-type.*

**RONAN:** FECK!

*Off, on. Another Jack-type.*

**MICHAEL:** DRINK!

*Then a quick succession of Jack-types, illuminated by the torch, all of them saying either 'Drink', 'Feck', 'Arse' or 'Girls'. Soon they fly by in a blur of bad language. Then we see a slightly younger, clean-cut priest.*

**WILLIAM** (*well spoken*): I really shouldn't be here.

*Finally the light switches on to Father Jack.*

**JACK:** DRINK! FECK! ARSE! GIRLS!

SCENE 17 EXT./DAY 4
SET: PAROCHIAL HOUSE
*The car turns and starts up the driveway towards the house. We hear from within the sound of Father Jack.*

**JACK:** DRINK! DRINK! DRINK!

*Before the car stops, Jack opens the door and throws himself out of the car. He gets up immediately and runs towards the house.*

**JACK:** DRINK! DRINK! DRINK! DRINK!

*He runs towards the house at top speed. Then he gets to the front door and bashes into it. He starts banging at the door.*

**JACK** (*with each blow*): DRINK! DRINK! DRINK! DRINK!

*He runs back slightly to Ted and Dougal, excited out of his mind, pointing towards the house.*

**JACK:** DRINK! DRIIIIINK!

*Ted runs towards the house, pulling out some keys.*

SCENE 18 INT./DAY 4
SET: PAROCHIAL HOUSE HALLWAY
*Ted opens the door and Jack bursts in.*

**JACK:** DRINK!!!!!!!!!!!

*Jack runs into the hall. He looks around in excitement.*

**JACK:** DRINK!! DRIIIIINK!!!!!!!

**TED** (*recovering slightly*): Try upstairs, Father . . .

*Jack runs upstairs.*

SCENE 19 INT./DAY 4
SET: PAROCHIAL HOUSE
*We see Fintan sticking the end of his cigarette into a lacy cushion. There are lots of cigarette holes all over it already. Ted comes into the room. Fintan keeps his back to him.\**

**TED:** Ah, Father Stack, you burning holes in the cushions again?*

**FINTAN:** Yeah. Got a problem with that?

**TED:** None at all. You go ahead and enjoy yourself.

**FINTAN:** What was all that noise?

**TED:** Oh, that was Father Jack. He's the fella you replaced.

**FINTAN:** Yeah? Well, tell him to get lost, then. I'm here now.

**TED:** Oh, I thought you might like the pleasure of telling him that yourself. I thought you also might like to tell him what happened to his bottle of whiskey. Once he realises it's gone, I'm sure he'll—

**JACK** (*from upstairs*): Aaaaaaaaaaarrrrrrr rrrrgggggggggghhhhhhhhhhhh!!!!!!!!!!!!!!!

**TED:** Ah, well, I'll let him fill in the rest.

**FINTAN:** Oh, I'm suppose to be scared, is that it?

*Jack suddenly appears through the door, breathing heavily. Fintan turns around to face them. Jack, Ted and Dougal all stop talking and just stare at him. Cut to reveal that Father Stack is covered in hair. He is very hairy indeed. He looks at them.*

**FINTAN:** What?

*Ted, Dougal and Jack all look at each other.*

SCENE 20 INT./DAY 4
SET: PAROCHIAL HOUSE
*Ted and Dougal sit side by side on the sofa.*

**TED:** Listen to that, Dougal.

**DOUGAL** (*puzzled*): I don't hear anything, Ted.

**TED:** That's what I mean. The sound of silence.

**DOUGAL:** No . . . I still don't hear anything. I was going to say, though, I'm really sorry I didn't disinfect Jack's chair like you told me. It's probably all my fault that lad got the hair thing.

**TED:** Oh, don't worry about it, Dougal. I'm sure he's fine up there in Jurassic Park. Best place for him, really. Keep him out of trouble. (*He looks over to Jack's chair. We don't see Jack.*) Do you remember him, Father? Father Stack? You didn't like him very much did you? Anyway, how are you getting on in there? It's a great little invention isn't it? And you won't have to go to Saint Clabbert's.

*Cut to Jack in a bizarre large plastic bubble. We see his hands have gone hairy again.*

**JACK** (*very muffled*): DRINK!

**TED:** Sorry, Father, can't hear you. Anyway, time for bed. C'mon, Dougal.

*Ted and Dougal leave. We see Jack yelling from inside the bubble, but we can't hear him. Ted turns off the light.*

SCENE 21 EXT./NIGHT 4
SET: SAINT CLABBERT'S
*We see a silhouette of the house. The light of the ground-floor priests' room is on. We hear voices inside.*

**MONICA:** Good night, Fathers.

**PRIESTS:** DRINK! ARSE! FECK! . . .

*The light goes off and they stop. After a moment, incredibly loud Jungle starts up.*

**THE END**

---

*In the final version this scene was changed so that Fintan is jumping on a photo of Ted by Jack's chair when Ted comes into the room. Ted's first line was then changed as follows: 'Ah, Father Stack, you jumping on my picture again?'

# flight into TERROR

**GRAHAM:** This was our disaster-movie episode. Arthur was in Dublin, so we agreed that I leave London for a while and write an episode over there. I had recently developed a fear of flying that I believe came in part from the success of *Father Ted*. The better the show did, the more convinced I was that something terrible was going to happen. So I didn't enjoy the flight to Dublin. When I arrived, I talked about my ridiculous worries with Arthur and we both felt there was a plot to be taken from it.

The show seemed to write itself, as if we were listening to the characters and merely transcribing what they said. It also took just two days to write and nearly everything from the first draft ended up on screen. Structurally, it echoes episodes of *Dad's Army* as the characters are in a static situation which generates practically no action, a great deal of talk and a high joke density. There's really no ingenuity in the structure at all, but having all the priests trapped in the same place was perfect for developing really stupid ideas. I'm particularly proud of the essay competition. And we had to have the monkey priest back again because we loved the idea of a monkey let loose on a plane. I also managed not only to wangle myself a part, but also make sure that the final image of the second series was a long take of my huge face.

**ARTHUR:** Pauline McLynn is one of the paper-throwing nuns sitting behind Ted in the plane. Apart from a pre-recorded scene at the beginning, she wasn't in this episode at all, but she wanted to be a part of it because it was the final episode in Series Two, so here she is, really heavily disguised and throwing bits of paper at Ted.

## PART ONE

SCENE 1 INT./DAY 1
SET: PLANE

*A chartered plane. The seats are full of priests. Ted, Dougal and Jack walk down the aisle, Ted is checking the seat numbers.*

**TED:** Twenty-two, twenty-three . . . Ah! This is us, Dougal.

**DOUGAL:** Great! You sure you don't want the window, Ted?

**TED:** No, to be honest, now, I'd be a bit nervous near the window.

**DOUGAL:** What's up with you, Ted?

**TED:** Never liked flying, Dougal. If God had meant us to fly, he wouldn't have put the airports so far from the towns.

*They sit down with their duty free. Jack sits on an aisle across from them. Father O'Shea is sitting beside him. He looks rather snooty, and is certainly unhappy to have Jack sitting there. Jack sits, breathing noisily through his nose. O'Shea looks disgusted.*

**O'SHEA:** Excuse me. Excuse me, you're sitting on my . . .

*He yanks his coat from under Jack. Jack continues breathing through his nose.*

**O'SHEA:** Could you . . . could you not breathe through your nose like that? You're making a noise.

*Jack breathes more heavily, making a disgusting, rasping noise. He then reaches in his pocket and takes out a cigarette.*

**O'SHEA:** Oh, now, I'm afraid this is a no-smoking—

*Jack immediately delivers an almighty punch to the man's head, which snaps back immediately into a very deep unconscious state.*

*Across the way, Ted is talking to Dougal.*

**TED:** Well, did you enjoy that, Dougal?

**DOUGAL:** I did, yeah. Kilnettle is great, isn't it? It must be the holiest shrine in the world.

**TED:** Top ten, anyway.

**DOUGAL:** Funny, isn't it, Ted? Our Lady appearing like that on a golf course. Where exactly did it happen again?

**TED:** Thirteenth hole. She appeared to a fella on the green there. Only about a yard from the pin. Apparently he was putting for a birdie and the ball hit her foot.

**DOUGAL:** God almighty. Then what happened?

**TED:** He just took a drop ball, put it down to experience.

*A priest passes by. This is Father Joe Briefly.*

**JOE:** Hello, Ted. On the old plane, I see!

**TED:** Ah, I am. Same as yourself!

*They both laugh. Joe continues on his way.*

**DOUGAL:** Who's that, Ted?

**TED:** Father Joe Briefly. An old pal of mine from Saint Colm's. We had a nickname for him there . . . what was it? Very funny . . . ha, ha . . . Oh, yes, we used to call him Himalaya Joe, because he had all this hair between his toes and it reminded us of the Abominable Snowman. Ha, ha! Oh, that was very funny. Ha, ha, ha, ha, ha . . .

**DOUGAL:** Ha, ha! Did you have a nickname, Ted?

**TED** (*immediately stops laughing*)**:** No, I didn't.

*Ted goes strangely quiet and serious.*

**DOUGAL:** Ah, you must have had one, Ted.

**TED:** No.

**DOUGAL** (*standing*)**:** Father Briefly!

**TED:** Dougal!

**DOUGAL:** Father Briefly! Do you remember at all what Ted's nickname was at Saint Colm's?

**JOE:** Well, let's see, what was it now . . . ?

*All the priests are looking at Ted and Briefly.*

**TED:** Don't worry about it, Joe! I'll tell him myself!

*Briefly makes a 'fair enough' gesture and sits down. An angry Ted turns to Dougal.*

**TED:** All right, shut up, Dougal. It was 'Father Fluffy Bottom'. The other priests caught a glance of my 'rear end' in the showers after a game of football once and, well, I had a bit of downy fluff around that whole area. (*Bitterly.*) 'Father Fluffy Bottom'. Oh, yes, hilarious stuff.

**DOUGAL:** Right. So, what did you do in the end, shave it off?

**TED:** Shave it off? Ha, ha . . . not at all . . .

**DOUGAL:** Ah, right. (*He stands up.*) Ah, Father Briefly? It was 'Father Fluffy Bottom'!

**TED:** Dougal!

**JOE:** Ah, yeah, right. 'Cause he had a big load of fluffy hair on his behind. What'd you do in the end, Ted? Shave it off?

*All the priests in the plane laugh. Ted is mortified.*

**TED:** No, I didn't! You can't get razors with a long-enough handle to go down . . . your back.

*Everyone laughs again.*

**TED:** Well, do you remember what we called you, Joe? Himalaya Joe! Because of all the big black hair in your toes. Do you remember? Ha, ha, ha, ha!!!

*No one laughs. Very pregnant silence. We stay on Ted as we hear the following.*

**JOE:** That was actually a medical condition, Ted.

*There is a terrible silence. Ted has obviously brought up a taboo subject. Ted makes a jokey 'aha!' noise to ease the tension, but it doesn't work. He turns around and slinks into his seat.*

SCENE 2 INT./DAY 1
SET: PLANE
*Fade up on Ted and Dougal. Dougal is looking out of the window.*

**DOUGAL:** God, Ted, you're missing this. Everything looks so small. All the cars look like ants.

**TED:** They *are* ants, Dougal. We haven't taken off yet.

**DOUGAL:** Ah, right . . .

*Pause. Suddenly, a rolled-up piece of paper hits Ted on the back of the head.*

**TED:** What— Who did that?

*He turns and we see, from his point of view, a very small nun sitting beside a large nun, some young innocent-looking priests, and a shifty looking young priest wearing a pair of shades who is smiling sneakily. Ted, annoyed, turns back. Dougal is taking some stuff out of a bag.*

**TED:** Someone's messing at the back there. What's that, Dougal?

**DOUGAL:** I got it at the gift shop back at the airport.

*We see that it is a heavy, black sticky-tape dispenser that has 'Greetings from the Shrine at Kilnettle' written on it.*

**TED:** God, Dougal, we've already got a tape dispenser back at the house. What do you want that one for?

**DOUGAL:** Ah. But it's not an ordinary one, Ted. Watch.

*Dougal pulls out a bit of sticky tape and rips it off. A voice comes from the tape dispenser.*

**DISPENSER:** You have used one inch of sticky tape. God bless you.

*Ted regards Dougal for a moment.*

**TED:** Dougal . . . That . . . is . . . brilliant. Already, I can see hundreds of uses for that. Did you get anything else?

**DOUGAL:** Oh, yeah. This.

*He takes out a rubber mobile phone in a Cellophane bag. A piece of card is attached to the top with a drawing of a happy dog on it. Ted takes it and examines it.*

**TED:** What does it do?

**DOUGAL:** Squeeze it there. It's a joke telephone.

*Ted does so. It makes a squeaky noise. Ted squeaks it once or twice more.*

**TED:** Dougal . . . this is a dog toy.

**DOUGAL:** What? No, it's not. It's a joke telephone.

**TED:** Dougal, it's a toy for dogs. This is something people give their dogs on their birthday.

**DOUGAL** (*a teeny bit annoyed*)**:** Ted. Seriously, now. It's a *joke telephone*. Look, you give it someone and tell them it's a phone, and they'll try to make a phonecall on it.

**TED:** Dougal, who'd be fooled by this? Even dogs would know this isn't a phone. It's coloured yellow, for God's sake.

**DOUGAL:** Well, Ted, listen . . . we'll agree to differ, all right?

**TED:** No, we won't, Dougal, because you're very, very *wrong*. Did the picture of the dog on the packet not give you any sort of clue? Why do you think he's looking so happy? He's looking happy because someone got him a yellow rubber telephone that makes a noise.

**DOUGAL:** No, no, he's . . . he's laughing because someone's trying to make a phonecall on the telephone.

**TED:** No, Dougal . . . dogs don't have that kind of a sense of humour. They're not as advanced as us. I wish you'd spend your money sensibly. I mean, look at this, for example . . .

*He takes out a bag and reveals what's inside. It is a little box with a model golfer on top. He is addressing a ball a couple of centimetres from a flag with '13' on it. It is incredibly garish.*

**TED:** Put a coin in there, Dougal.

*Dougal takes a coin from his pocket and puts it into a slot in the box. A little Virgin Mary pops up from a tiny flap in front of the hole.*

**DOUGAL:** That is *fantastic!* What is it? A little money-box.

**TED:** Yes. God, it'd be easy to make something like this look cheap and tacky, but look at it there. Pure class.

**DOUGAL:** You're right there, Ted.

*Ted tries to push the little Virgin Mary back into the flap and the whole thing falls apart in his hands.*

**DOUGAL:** Thing broke there, Ted.

*Ted stares at the thing in disbelief. Another rolled-up piece of paper hits him on the back of the head. He turns, and we see the same line-up as before – the innocent priests, the smiling priest with the shades and the two nuns.*

**TED:** All right, now, come on! A joke's a joke!

*The plane starts rumbling.*

**DOUGAL:** Here we go!

**TED:** Oh, God!

**DOUGAL:** What's up with you, Ted?

**TED:** Ah, it's just the tension of taking off. I'll be OK in a minute.

*He closes his eyes tight and grips the edge of his seat.*

**DOUGAL:** It'd be terrible to be killed in a plane crash, wouldn't it, Ted?

**TED:** Yes.

**DOUGAL:** God, or if you just somehow fell out of a plane. Like if the floor just disappeared from under you and you just fell. I mean, you'd be falling for ages and ages and ages and ages and ages. And you'd be screaming your head off.

*As Dougal is saying all the above, Ted bends down to take something out of his bag. He picks up the dog toy and squeezes it a couple of times so that it makes a squeaking noise. Dougal immediately shuts up and watches it intently, a dog-like expression on his face – in fact, it is an exact copy of the expression last seen on the dog's face on the packet. Fade out.*

SCENE 3 INT./DAY 1
SET: PLANE
*We see Dougal and Ted. Ted is reading the Michael Barrymore biography. Ted can't concentrate,*

though. He shifts about, looking very nervous.

**DOUGAL:** Feeling a bit better, Ted?

**TED:** Not really, Dougal, no. I tell you what, maybe I'll give Larry Duff a call. He developed a fear of flying after all those crashes he was in, so he went to a hypnotherapist to cure it. Told me to give him a call whenever I'm feeling a bit nervous.

*Ted picks up Dougal's dog toy and presses some 'buttons'. It squeaks noisily.*

**DOUGAL** (*pointing*): Ahhhhhhhhhhh!!!!!!!!!! Ha, ha, ha!!!!!!

**TED:** Oh, for God's sake.

*He reaches down and finds the real telephone, then starts dialling. Dougal continues laughing. The plane judders slightly.*

**TED:** Ahhh!!!!! What was that?

**DOUGAL:** Just a bit of turbulence, Ted.

**TED:** Oh, right . . . right . . . God, I wish I wasn't so nervous. Larry told me once you have more chance of being trampled by a herd of stampeding donkeys than you do of being killed in a plane crash.

SCENE 4 EXT./DAY 1
SET: A FIELD
*We see a sign that reads 'Glasrowan Donkey Derby'. We hear the 'bleep bleep' of a mobile phone. We also hear a diminishing rumbling sound. The camera slowly moves down and we see the mobile phone some distance away from a muddied hand. There are hoofprints all over the ground. Pull back to reveal that the hand belongs to Larry, groaning in pain, moving his hand uselessly towards the mobile phone. The rumbling sound gets louder again.*

**LARRY** (*holding his head up to see*): Oh, God, no! Not again!

SCENE 5 INT./DAY 1
SET: PLANE
*Ted turns off the telephone.*

**TED:** Funny. He's not picking up.

*Down the corridor come Father Noel Furlong and Father Fintan Fay. Noel looks his usual spritely*

self and Fintan, as usual, holds on to his hand and walks like a monkey.

**NOEL:** Ted!!!

**TED:** Ah, hello, Noel. Father Fay. How are you?

**FINTAN** (*pointing at Ted's book*): Oooh, ooh, ahh, eek, ooh . . . Ahhh . . .

**TED:** Ah, yes! It's very good, actually.

**FINTAN:** Oooh, ahh, eeh, eek, ook . . .

**TED:** Oh, yes, I'm a big fan, all right. Or should I say 'Awright!'?

**FINTAN:** Oook, eek, aaak, oowk, eek . . .

**TED:** No mention of it so far, no.

**FINTAN:** Ahh . . .

**NOEL:** Oh, God, Ted, he has me driven mad. He wants me to bring him up to see the cockpit.

**FINTAN** (*jumping up and down*): OOOOOH!!!!! OOOOOHHH!!!!

**DOUGAL:** The cockpit! Ted? Ted, can I have a look, too?

**TED:** Well, I'm not sure . . .

**NOEL** (*noticing something*): Oh, God, what's he up to now?! You're a mad priest!

*We see Fintan. He has managed to locate a red uninflated life-jacket and is wearing it. It suddenly inflates and he falls over. He blows the whistle on the life-jacket loudly. Noel takes it off him.*

**NOEL:** Oh, God, look, he's going mad with the excitement. I'd better go. Dougal, you might as well come with us.

**DOUGAL:** Great!

*Ted stands up to let Dougal pass. Dougal moves out of shot with Fay and Noel. Ted shouts after them.*

**TED:** Dougal, don't touch anything! We don't want an action replay of the Sealink incident.

**DOUGAL** (*calling back*): Fair enough, Ted!

SCENE 6 INT./DAY 1
SET: COCKPIT
*Fintan, Noel and Dougal enter the cockpit. Inside*

*there is a pilot.*

**PILOT:** Ah, there you are, Father. You wanted the official tour!

**NOEL:** Oh, God, yes. It's all he's been talking about all day.

**FINTAN:** Ooooogh, aaggh, eeegghhh!!

**NOEL:** Y'see? Will you calm down, you little monkey-man!

**PILOT:** Well, basically, these are the main controls. Over here you have the meters for engines one, two and three . . .

*Dougal turns to his side and sees a big red button. Over it are written the words 'Do Not Press'. Dougal's eyes widen. The camera gets closer and closer to the button as we keep cutting to Dougal's sweating face. The sound of his heartbeat fills the soundtrack. Finally, the camera is on top of the button. Dougal's heartbeat is deafening.*

**PILOT:** Father?

**DOUGAL:** What?! What! I wasn't going to press it!

**PILOT:** Sorry? I was just asking, have you ever been in a cockpit before?

**DOUGAL:** No, but I was on the bridge of a Sealink ferry once. It's funny, but I was there and I—

*Noel coughs ostentatiously, giving Dougal a meaningful look. Dougal seems to understand.*

**DOUGAL:** It was very interesting.

SCENE 7 INT./DAY 1
SET: PLANE
*Ted is trying to get to sleep. Another rolled-up piece of paper hits him on the back of the head.*

**TED:** Right! That's it!

*He stands up and walks to the back of the plane. He walks straight up to the priest with the oval shades, who's laughing his head off.*

**TED:** What's so funny? What's so funny? Hey, come on now, the joke's over!

*He pushes the priest slightly. The priest takes off a pair of earphones and looks up in Ted's general direction.*

**SHIFTY:** Wh— who's there?

**TED:** What do you mean, who's there? Are you blind? I'm the man you've been pelting with rolled-up pieces of paper for the whole journey!

**SHIFTY:** But I haven't.

**TED:** What's so funny, then? What's the big laugh?

**SHIFTY** (*indicates his earphones*): I was listening to comedy on these. It's *Mr Bean*.

**TED** (*takes this in*): Oh, right.

**SHIFTY:** And, yes, I am blind, as a matter of fact.

**TED:** Is it since birth or a more recent thing?

**SHIFTY:** Since birth.

**TED:** Really? Oh, that's . . . very interesting . . . I suppose your other senses make up for it. I hear that sometimes, with blind people, their other senses become more alert. So to speak. I suppose you can smell things from up to ten miles away. And hear things before they happen.

**SHIFTY:** No.

**TED:** No sixth sense of any kind? Although with you I suppose it'd be a fifth sense, 'cause you've only got the four. Unless you've got another one missing I don't know about! How about sense of touch? That OK?

*Ted playfully touches the by-now-quite-nervous man on the shoulder. The man doesn't respond.*

**TED:** Ha! Ha!

*He pats the man on the shoulder again and then*

*slaps his knee gently a few times. Pause.*

**SHIFTY:** Could you please go away now?

**TED:** Yes, I'll . . . I'll do just that.

*He starts to move off, looking mortified with embarrassment. Another piece of paper hits him on the back of the head. He turns around and we see the two nuns, who until now have been incredibly serene, laughing like two haggard old witches.*

**NUN:** Ha, haaaa!!!!

*Ted looks at them in horror.*

SCENE 8 INT./DAY 1
SET: COCKPIT
*Noel, Fintan and Dougal are still with the pilot. Dougal is staring intently at the 'Do Not Press' button.*

**NOEL:** He's a great laugh, isn't he? Will you not calm down, you big ninny?

**FAY:** OOOOOH! EEEEEK!!!!

**NOEL** (*to Fintan*): Come on, now. We'll head back. Say thank you to Mr Pilot!

**FAY:** OOGH! AAAGGH! EEEGH!

*He tries to lead Fintan out of the cabin. As Fintan is led out, he sees his reflection in one of the instrument panels. He goes mad and starts jumping around.*

**NOEL:** Oh, God, he must have seen his reflection!!!!!

**PILOT:** What?

**NOEL:** He's not supposed to see his reflection! He doesn't know he's a priest!

*Fintan goes mad. He storms around the cockpit, pressing buttons and shouting wildly.*

**PILOT:** Come on now, Father. Settle down now!

*Fintan finally grabs on to the pilot's head, putting his hands over the pilot's eyes.*

**PILOT:** Get him off me! I can't see!

*Noel tries to prise Fintan loose. Chaos. The pilot finally manages to shout . . .*

**PILOT:** FATHER MCGUIRE! FATHER, PRESS THE EMERGENCY BUTTON!

*Dougal, who has been staring at the 'Do Not Press' button in a reverie, finally notices the fracas.*

**DOUGAL:** What?

**PILOT:** The emergency button! The emergency button!

*We see a very clearly marked button with 'emergency' written above it. It is beside the button with 'Do Not Press' on it.*

**DOUGAL:** What does it look like?

**PILOT:** The one with 'emergency' written over it!

*Dougal looks at the buttons, puzzled.*

### END OF PART ONE

* * *

### PART TWO

SCENE 9 INT./DAY 1
SET: PLANE
*Ted is sitting down, his teeth gritted as another rolled-up paper ball hits him on the back of the head. Then another. Then another. Then another. Then another.*

**TED:** Right!

*He stands up and marches towards the two nuns, looking very determined indeed. When he reaches them, the big nun stands up. She is huge, unable even to stand up straight in the plane. Ted walks*

straight past them and towards the toilets.

**TED** (*to himself*)**:** Ahh, just go to the old toilet.

SCENE 10 INT./DAY 1
SET: TOILET
*Close-up of the toilet door. A bolt slides, it opens in the usual folding way, and Ted steps in. He stops short, looking confused. Cut to reveal that the 'cubicle' is the size of, say, a small bedroom, with the toilet in the other corner. It is very clean and white. Beside the toilet stands an attendant, very well dressed.*

**TED:** Ah . . . sorry, is this the toilet?

**ATTENDANT:** First-class toilet, Sir. Do you have a first-class ticket?

**TED:** Ah, no . . .

**ATTENDANT:** Then I'm afraid you have to go across the way.

*Ted mouths an 'oh . . .' and starts to leave.*

SCENE 11 INT./DAY 1
SET: PLANE
*Dougal walks out of the cockpit. We see a brief glimpse of the chaos within as the door opens and closes. He walks to the seat, sees that Ted isn't there, and walks to the toilets. He sees two doors side by side. He knocks on one.*

**DOUGAL:** Ah, Ted?

SCENE 12 INT./DAY 1
SET: ANOTHER TOILET
*This toilet is so small that Ted has to assume a sort of question-mark shape in order to fit in it. He looks massively uncomfortable. He is trying to do up his belt.*

**TED** (*generally annoyed*)**:** What?

**DOUGAL:** Can I have a quick word, Ted?

**TED:** Oh, yes . . . yes . . .

*He tries to wash his hands in the sink sticking into his back but only gets some water on his shoes. He gives up and tries to come out. It takes an age of pushing and pulling before he finally tumbles out.*

**TED:** God almighty . . . What's wrong with you, Dougal?

**DOUGAL:** Slight problem, Ted.

**TED:** What?

**DOUGAL:** Well, apparently, someone, ah . . . someone pressed a button in the cockpit that, ah . . . It was something to do with the fuel, I think. I think the person might have emptied one of the fuel tanks by mistake. Anyway, it means that there's not enough fuel to make it to the airport.

**TED:** Right, so that would mean, what? An emergency landing or something?

**DOUGAL:** Yeah. An emergency landing.

**TED:** Right.

**DOUGAL:** But the thing is, we don't have enough fuel to get somewhere where we can make an emergency landing. Also, there's only two parachutes on board . . .

**TED:** Wait a second, before you go on. What did you say this film was called again?

**DOUGAL:** Eh, no, it's not a film.

**TED:** It's not a film?

**DOUGAL:** No.

**TED:** Right. So, this is actually happening.

**DOUGAL:** Yes.

**TED:** This is actually happening now. To us.

**DOUGAL:** Eh . . . it is, yeah.

**TED:** Right. This is just a mad guess out of the blue here, but did you press the button?

**DOUGAL** (*aghast*)**:** Ah, now, Ted, come on!

**TED:** Did you, Dougal?

**DOUGAL:** Yes.

SCENE 13 INT./DAY 1
SET: COCKPIT
*Ted bursts in, followed by Dougal. Fintan has been blindfolded, and stands quite calmly in one corner of the cockpit.*

**NOEL:** Hello, Ted! Have you heard the news?

**TED:** Yes, Noel. (*To the pilot.*) Has anyone pressed this button?

*Ted points at the 'emergency' button.*

**PILOT:** No.

**TED:** Well, shouldn't someone give it a go?

**DOUGAL:** Careful, Ted. There might be a fine for improper use.

**TED:** Dougal, this is *definitely* an emergency!!! I think basically the most important thing is to keep the other priests calm. Not a word of this when we get back inside.

*He presses the button.*

SCENE 14 INT./DAY 1
SET: PLANE
*At the front of the plane, a sign with 'emergency' written on it in red starts flashing on and off. An electronic voice says 'Emergency, Emergency, Emergency' accompanied by a repetitive buzzing noise. The priests look panicky.*

SCENE 15 INT./DAY 1
SET: COCKPIT
*Ted looks at the button.*

**TED:** Nothing happened. What does it do, exactly?

**PILOT** (*shrugging*): Never needed it before. Father, who gets the parachutes?

**TED:** God, yes, it's a tough decision.

**DOUGAL:** Oh, you're right there, Ted. Maybe we should just not tell anyone about them. Throw them off the plane, pretend they never existed.

**TED:** No . . . I don't think we should do that. I've got a better idea . . .

*The camera zooms slowly in on Ted, accompanied by music, as he smiles and nods. It zooms out again.*

**TED:** Right . . . here's my idea . . . Basically, what we should do is this . . .

SCENE 16 INT./DAY 1
SET: PLANE
*We see Ted at the top of the aisle. He has a pen and a piece of paper in his hand. Everyone else has a pen and a piece of paper as well.*

**TED:** . . . So, no more than two hundred words on why you think you should get a parachute.

*Father Joe Briefly puts his hand up.*

**JOE:** So we should just write how great we are?

**TED:** Yes.

*Father O'Shea puts his hand up.*

**O'SHEA:** I got my housekeeper pregnant a couple of years ago and forced her to leave the country. Should I mention that?

**TED:** No, I wouldn't . . .

*Joe puts his hand up again.*

**JOE:** Are you going to take marks away for spelling mistakes?

**TED:** No. Only if we end up in a tie-break situation.

*O'Shea raises his hand again.*

**O'SHEA:** Who'll own the copyright on this?

**TED:** What?

**O'SHEA:** Say if I survived and I wanted to write a newspaper article or a book about this – could I use extracts from this thing I'm going to write or would you own the copyright on it?

TED: As far as I know, you own the copyright. But frankly, I think the chances of us surviving are very, very low.

O'SHEA: Oh, right.

GALLAGHER: Should we not just have a bit of an oul pray? Maybe God will help us in some way.

*This results in a slightly uncomfortable silence as the priests look around in embarrassment.*

TED: Aaaaanyway, we should start writing. Everyone has pens and everything?

O'SHEA: Can I use my laptop computer?

TED: Well, I don't think you're allowed to use them on planes. Aren't they dangerous or something? I think it might interfere with the radar . . .

O'SHEA: Yes, but we're going to crash anyway.

TED: Right, I see what you mean. Yes, go ahead and use it.

*Ted resumes his seat. Everyone starts writing. There is a serious atmosphere, as in a schoolroom during an exam. While everyone is preoccupied with their essays, we see Jack calmly walking down the aisle with two parachutes. He goes out of shot.*

DOUGAL: Ted, you're very calm about all this. Have you gone mad or something?

TED: It's just . . . I've always hated flying, but now we're in an emergency situation, the fear just seems to have transformed itself into affirmative action. You know what I mean?

DOUGAL: I do, Ted.

TED: Do you?

DOUGAL: No.

TED: Well, never mind. Right! (*Ted stops writing and stands up.*) Put your pens down, please.

*The priests do so, except for O'Shea, who is still tapping away on his laptop.*

TED: Father O'Shea? You didn't stop writing so I'm afraid you're disqualified.

O'SHEA: What? Awww . . .

*He slams down the lid of his laptop and goes into a sulk.*

TED: Father Cave, do you want to go first?

*Father Cave stands up.*

CAVE: I haven't written this down because . . . because it comes from the heart. (*He turns to the priest next to him.*) Father Gallagher. I've worked with you and been your friend for a long time, and now . . . I think it's important to say I love you. I love you like I've loved nobody else. (*Pause.*) I don't want the parachute! Give it to him!

*He bursts into tears and sits down. Father Gallagher looks very embarrassed.*

TED: Right . . . well done, Father Cave. Eh, Father Fay?

FINTAN (*looks at his paper*): OOK, EEK, OOOH, OOOH, AHK, AHK!!!!

*Pause. Then everyone mumbles in an impressed way.*

TED (*impressed*): Well, beat that . . . Joe?

JOE: I think I should get the parachute because I am great. In fact, I think I should get both the parachutes in case one of them doesn't work.

*The other priests don't like this. They inhale disapprovingly.*

TED: Not a popular one there, Joe. Father Flynn, what did you write?

FLYNN: I didn't write anything, because I'm not very good at that type of thing, but I did a drawing.

TED: Did you? Well, let's have a look.

*Flynn stands up and shows a quite accomplished drawing of himself, completely naked with a dog on a lead. He has drawn it so that his back is to the viewer, so we can see his bottom in the drawing. He looks at the viewer with one hand over his mouth in an 'I'm being naughty' gesture.*

FLYNN: What do you think?

TED: Well . . .

FLYNN: It's me in the nip! With a dog!

TED: How . . . how does that help you win the parachute?

**FLYNN:** What do you mean, parachute? I wasn't really listening at the start there. Why would I need a parachute?

**TED:** The plane's in trouble. This is a competition to see who gets a parachute.

**FLYNN:** Oh . . .

*He looks at the drawing. He seems embarrassed. He folds the drawing away discreetly and sits down without saying another word.*

**TED:** Okay, Father Jack, you next . . . Father Jack? Where's Father Jack?

**O'SHEA:** The parachutes!!! The parachutes have gone!!!

SCENE 17 INT./DAY 1
SET: DOORWAY
*We see Jack standing by the open doorway. We hear the roar of the wind going by. Jack attaches one parachute to a drinks trolley and pushes it out through the doorway. Then he jumps out.*

**JACK:** DRIIIIIIIiiiiinnnnnkkkkkkk!!!!!!!!!

SCENE 18 INT./DAY 1
SET: PLANE
*Fade up. Everyone looks annoyed. Dougal wakes up from a nap, looking happy, then he frowns and 'tsks' loudly.*

**DOUGAL** (*put out*): Awww . . . I just remembered that we're all going to die.

**TED:** Dougal, I just wanted to say . . . I know sometimes I'm a little short with you, sometimes I'm not as patient as I should be, but I just want you to know . . . in the end, we're the best of friends.

*Pause.*

**DOUGAL:** I don't understand.

**TED:** Well, I'm just saying that even though I might act like you get on my nerves, I suppose I secretly think it's quite funny.

**DOUGAL:** What is?

**TED:** You know . . . the way you mix things up sometimes and don't really get what's going on.

**DOUGAL** (*frowns*): Who are you talking about?

**TED:** You.

**DOUGAL** (*waits for more*): What about me?

**TED:** I'm just saying I like you, Dougal.

**DOUGAL:** Ah, but sometimes I get on your nerves.

**TED:** I know! I said that!

**DOUGAL:** Did you?

**TED:** Yes!

**DOUGAL:** Thanks very much. Who were you saying that to?

**TED:** YOU! I JUST SAID IT THERE!

*Long pause.*

**DOUGAL** (*looks around*): Hey! We're on a plane!

*Ted has to rest his brain for a moment. The pilot rushes in and goes up to Ted.*

**PILOT:** Father, do you know what a Section Tubing Stabilising Dart is?

**TED:** No.

**PILOT:** Do you know what a Shell Diversifier ER 20 is?

**TED:** No.

**PILOT:** Have you ever used a Jet Wrench Three-ply Shortstick?

**TED:** No.

**PILOT:** If you had a choice between two Oxygen Discharge Multi-enforcers – a 751 and a 98 Sten Magnet – which one would you choose?

**TED:** I don't know.

**PILOT:** Do you know who I am?

**TED:** You're the pilot.

**PILOT:** Great. I know what I did there, I started too big. Do you know what a fuel reserve is?

**TED:** Well, I imagine it's some sort of back-up to the main fuel tanks.

**PILOT:** That's exactly what it is. Well . . . we have a fuel reserve, but the line connecting it to the . . . ah, the thing at the front.

**TED:** The engine.

**PILOT:** The engine, yeah . . . that line is broken. The thing is . . . if we could somehow fix that line . . . we might have a chance. Even sticky tape would do, but I've asked around and there's none on the plane.

**TED:** That's where you're wrong! Dougal, give me that thing you bought. (*Dougal gives Ted the yellow telephone.*) This is the answer to all our problems.

**PILOT:** You shouldn't make any calls, Father. It interferes with radar—

**TED** (*throwing the telephone at Dougal*)**:** The sticky-tape dispenser!

*Dougal hands it to him.*

**PILOT:** Brilliant! So all you have to do is get out of the plane, climb out on to the wheel so that you're under the fuselage, and attach the line!

**TED:** And we'll be saved.

**PILOT:** Yes!

**TED:** Great! So all I have to do is climb out of the plane . . . hang on.

**PILOT:** What?

**TED:** I have to get out of the plane, then climb under it?

**PILOT:** Yes. There's really no one else I'd trust, Father. You've already proved you can keep a level head . . .

**TED** (*beat*): Then . . . I'll do it!!!

**DOUGAL:** But Ted—

**TED:** Dougal, I told you, this has brought out a new side of me. I love all this! When everything's going OK, I just keep imagining all the terrible things that can happen, but when one of those things actually happens, it's just a rush! I am fearless. Like that film with Jeff Bridges.

**DOUGAL:** I haven't seen that one.

**TED:** Not a lot of people have, Dougal, so it's probably a bad reference. Anyway, let's go, Captain!

**PILOT:** I'm not a captain.

**TED:** And I'm not a person who goes under planes to fix fuel lines! I think from now on, we're anything we want to be!

*Big close-up of their hands as they shake them in a manly way. Dougal looks at them.*

**DOUGAL** (*puzzled*): Can I still be a priest?

SCENE 19 INT./DAY 1
SET: DOORWAY
*Ted is sitting with his legs dangling down a square hole in the floor. The pilot and Dougal look at him with admiration and concern.*

**PILOT:** You're a very brave man, Father.

**TED:** I'm just doing a job. Dougal . . . hand me the sticky tape!

**PILOT:** I'd better get back to the cockpit. Good luck, Father Ted!

*Dougal hands him the tape. Ted disappears down the hole. There is a pause. We hear tape being pulled out.*

**DISPENSER** (*offscreen*): You have used three inches of tape. God bless you.

*Another strip is pulled out.*

**DISPENSER:** You have used four inches of tape. God bless you.

*Another.*

**DISPENSER:** You have used two and a half inches of tape. God bless you.

*Another.*

**DISPENSER:** You have used three and a half inches of tape. God bless you.

**TED** (*offscreen*): To be honest with you, Dougal, I can see how this might get a little annoying.

**DISPENSER:** You have used two inches of tape. God bless you.

**TED:** Ahh, shut up. Wait, I think . . . Yes! I've done it! Dougal, the line's sealed up! We're saved!

**DOUGAL:** Great!

**TED:** Everything's OK! We're going to live!

**DOUGAL:** Everything's completely back to normal, Ted! It's just a completely average, day-to-day, common-or-garden airplane journey.

*Pause.*

TED: Aaaaaaaaaaaaagggggghhhhhhhhhh!!!!!
WHAT AM I DOING ON THE FECKIN'
WHEEL? Aaaaaaaaagggggghhhhhhh!!!!!!!!!!

*Dougal looks worried.*

SCENE 20 INT./DAY 1
SET: PAROCHIAL HOUSE
*Dougal is on the telephone.*

DOUGAL: Oh, right. Oh, right, thanks a lot.

*He puts the telephone down. Mrs Doyle comes in.*

DOUGAL: Still no sign of Father Jack, Mrs
Doyle.

MRS DOYLE: Oh, I hope he's all right. And
Father Crilly . . . I really hate seeing him like
this.

DOUGAL: Well, he's starting to loosen his
grip. I'd say he'd be down in about a week.

*Cut to reveal Ted, still gripping tightly on to the
shaft above a massive airplane wheel, which takes
up almost half of the room. He is gripping on to it
with all his might. His face is frozen in an
expression of pure horror. His hair is standing on
end.*

MRS DOYLE: Anyway, how would you like
a sandwich? I've cut it into the shape of an
airplane.

*We see that she has indeed.*

DOUGAL: No, thanks, Mrs Doyle. I think
Ted and I have had enough of planes to last

us a lifetime! Ha, ha, ha? Haven't we, Ted?

*Shot of an unresponsive Ted. Dougal shuts up and
eats his sandwich. Roll closing credits.*

POST-CREDIT SEQUENCE:
SCENE 21 EXT./DAY 1
SET: FIELD
*As the credits roll, we see Jack stuck up a tree,
entangled in his parachute. Nearby, just out of
reach, is the drinks trolley dangling from the other
parachute. There are no other trees for miles
around. Jack vainly struggles to reach out to the
drinks trolley.*

SCENE 22 INT./DAY 1
SET: PLANE
*Back on the plane, the pilot's voice comes over the
intercom.*

PILOT: This is your pilot speaking. The
emergency is over. We will be landing in
twenty minutes.

*Everyone cheers. We cut to Cave and Gallagher.
They cheer, but then something hits them. They sit
down, looking very embarrassed. One of them
starts whistling.*

**THE END**

# a christmassy ted

**GRAHAM:** We wanted to put back the writing of Series Three for a while, so we suggested writing a Christmas Special as a stopgap, thinking it'd be easier. We were *waaaaaaaaay* off. This was infinitely harder to write than any other episode. It took forever to sort out and, to be perfectly honest, I think that comes across in the sprawling plot. Christmas Specials are dangerous anyway; by definition they have to revolve around Christmas, therefore losing an element of spontaneity, and they're invariably longer than normal episodes. That, I think, was the major problem here: we stretched the mad elastic of Craggy Island beyond sustainability. I even remember that it ran over time by four minutes and we begged Channel 4 to let us keep the extra time. Now I wish we hadn't.

However, it does have moments that, on reflection, are among the best in *Father Ted*. (I heard that a pregnant woman went into labour because she laughed so much at Mrs Doyle falling off the windowsill . . . at least, I assume she was pregnant.) But they're moments which would have been used better had they been peppered across a whole series, rather than packed willy-nilly into the one show.

**ARTHUR:** I think Graham's too hard on this one. I quite liked it at the time, and so did a lot of other people. Ratings-wise, it was a highly successful episode. Yet in hindsight there *is* a fairly fundamental flaw in the plot: to my mind it reads like two episodes strung together. We never made a proper, convincing connection between Christmas and the Golden Cleric Award that sends Ted into such a spin. The arrival of the mysterious Todd Unctuous, for instance, doesn't seem to belong in the same story as the priests in the lingerie section of the department store. No pun intended, but we *did* stretch the latter scene too far. Yet I liked the former, and especially Todd's *Mission:Impossible*-style attempts to steal Ted's Golden Cleric Award. When in doubt, use a film reference . . . (We should have put the *Mission Impossible* theme music to the scene.)

David Renwick, who writes *One Foot in the Grave*, really knows how to extend a show beyond the half-hour format – his Christmas Specials are tightly plotted and brilliantly sustained. I wonder if it's more possible to do that when the comedy is set within the real world . . . Perhaps Craggy Island is just too mad and too surreal to handle an hour of comedy.

## PART ONE

SCENE 1 INT./DAY X
SET: BALLYKISSANGEL BAR
*We see Ted sitting at a bar, flooded with sunlight. He finishes a drink.*

**TED:** You know, I've been doing a lot of thinking recently and . . . well, I just don't think I'm cut out for the priesthood . . . I think it's time you and I faced facts.

*Cut to reveal Assumpta – Dervla Kirwan – from 'Ballykissangel', sitting behind the bar.*

**ASSUMPTA:** But Father, you're one of the best priests in the country, if not *the* best.

**TED** (*shakes his head*): Assumpta, Assumpta, Assumpta . . . why are we running from this? You know what I'm talking about, don't you?

**ASSUMPTA:** Yes, I . . . I suppose I do.

**OFFSCREEN VOICE:** I'll be off, then. (*Cut to reveal Father Clifford – Stephen Tompkinson – standing at the door with loads of bags.*) I said I'll . . .

**TED:** Yeah, yeah . . . bye.

**ASSUMPTA:** Bye.

*He leaves, looking sad.*

**ASSUMPTA:** C'mere you . . .

*Ted leans forward. They are about to kiss when we cut to . . .*

SCENE 2 INT./NIGHT 1
SET: BEDROOM
*Ted, a smile on his face, is being shaken awake by Dougal.*

**DOUGAL:** Ted, Ted . . .

**TED:** What? What is it?

**DOUGAL:** Would you like a peanut?

*He is holding out an open bag of peanuts.*

**TED:** A peanut? You woke me to offer me a peanut? God, Dougal!!

**DOUGAL:** Oh. Sorry, Ted.

**TED:** Go to bed! (*Dougal moves off.*) Now . . . where were we?

*He falls asleep again with a smile.*

SCENE 3 EXT./DAY X
SET: FIELD HILLTOP
*Ted is running through a dark place, chased by three giant peanuts with legs. He is terrified.*

SCENE 4 INT./NIGHT 2
SET: PAROCHIAL HOUSE
*Dougal is standing beside a large Christmas tree. Ted is lying down underneath it, only his legs visible. Mrs Doyle is putting up Christmas decorations over the window. Jack is asleep in his chair.*

**TED:** OK, here we go. One, two, three!

*The tree lights come on.*

**DOUGAL:** Yay!

**TED:** They on?

**DOUGAL:** They are, Ted. (*The lights go off.*) Oh, wait now.

**TED:** What?

**DOUGAL:** They've gone off again.

**TED:** Tsk . . . how about now?

**DOUGAL:** No – yes! They're on! Oh. No, Ted, they've gone aga— There you go! They're back, Ted! Keep doing whatever you're — Oh, wait, they're gone.

*Ted is now standing beside Dougal, although Dougal hasn't noticed.*

**DOUGAL:** That's it, Ted! Keep it like that for just a — Dohhh!!! Gone again! Back! Gone! Back! Gone! Back! Gone! Back! Gone!

**TED:** Dougal . . . you go and sit down. They're supposed to do that.

**DOUGAL:** Oh, right. Ah, can I open another

window on the Advent calendar first?

**TED:** All right, then. But remember, you're just allowed to open today's window.

**DOUGAL:** Great! (*He goes to the calendar and opens a window. It is a little shepherd.*) Brilliant! . . . A shepherd! Fantastic stuff! Oh, God, can I not open the other two?

**TED:** No, Dougal.

**DOUGAL:** God, I can't wait to find out what's behind tomorrow's one! I bet it's a donkey or something!

**TED:** So you've changed from your initial prediction. What was it? Ruud Gullit sitting on a shed.

**DOUGAL:** Heh . . . yeah . . .

**TED:** Where do you *get* these things? Do you know what, I'd say it's probably just a lovely angel. (*Turning to Jack, very friendly.*) What would you say is behind tomorrow's window, Father Jack?

**JACK:** A pair of feckin' women's knickers!

**TED:** Yes, well . . . who knows?

**JACK:** Knickers!

**TED:** Yes, father.

**JACK:** WOMEN'S KNICKERS!

**TED:** Yes, Father, yes, message understood. God almighty . . . Dougal, leave the calendar until tomorrow.

*Dougal guiltily retreats from the calendar, picks up a 'Shoot' annual and starts reading. Cut to Mrs Doyle. She finishes putting the decorations over the window.*

**MRS DOYLE:** There!

*She turns around to step carefully down off the ledge, loses her balance and falls out of shot.*

**TED:** Ah, dear. Another year gone – it's hard to believe, isn't it? (*He sighs.*) What's it all about, Dougal?

**DOUGAL** (*looks at the annual*): Well, it doesn't really have a story, Ted. It's just football and stuff.

**TED:** No, Dougal, I mean life. I mean, you slave away attending to the needs of your parishioners and what does it get you? A one-

way ticket to palookaville. (*He pauses and sighs.*) You know, I looked in the mirror this morning and I saw a middle-aged, grey-haired man staring back at me.

*Long pause. Long, long pause. Stay on Dougal. Finally . . .*

**DOUGAL:** Who was that, Ted?

**TED:** Me, Dougal.

**DOUGAL:** Oh, yes, of course.

**TED:** It's just, I had a postcard from Father Jez Flahavan yesterday. He's in Montana. He makes fifty thousand dollars a year and another two thousand in tips.

**DOUGAL:** Brilliant. How does he manage that?

**TED:** I don't know . . . lap dancing or something . . . And Father Buzz Dolan in Canada. He has his own show on cable. And I heard he's landed a bit part in the new Bond movie. It all started when he won that Golden Cleric award.

**DOUGAL:** Wow!!!

**TED:** God, it'd be great to be famous. Do you know what I'd love about being famous? People listen to you, they listen to what you have to say. And I've got a lot to say.

**DOUGAL:** What about when you're doing your sermons? People listen to you then, don't they?

**TED:** No, Dougal, I mean people I *respect*. I suppose the main thing I'd like . . .

**DOUGAL** (*talking over Ted's line*): God, I hope there's a good film on Christmas day.

**TED** (*simultaneous with Dougal's line*): . . . Would be to give a big speech . . . You just talked over me there. Even you don't listen to me.

**DOUGAL:** Ah, I do, Ted, that's not fair.

**TED** (*simultaneous*): Well, I don't know, it seemed to me that you just . . .

**DOUGAL** (*simultaneous with Ted*): Anyway, I suppose I should go and feed Sampras . . .

**TED** (*simultaneous*): . . . Completely ignored what I was saying there . . .

**DOUGAL** (*simultaneous*): . . . He's been looking

a bit sick recently, I suppose . . .

**TED** (*simultaneous*): . . . And just started on a completely unrelated topic . . .

**DOUGAL** (*simultaneous*): . . . He's just a bit homesick for the old warren.

*Dougal walks away while Ted is in mid-sentence. Mrs Doyle has righted herself. She pats her hair into place.*

**MRS DOYLE:** So, Father, you looking forward to Christmas?

**TED:** Oh, I am indeed, Mrs Doyle. A nice, quiet Christmas, that's what I want. A nice, quiet Christmas with no unusual incidents or strange people turning up. That would suit me down to the ground. A nice, quiet, everyday, normal Christmas.

*Pause. Everyone just stands around, looking at each other. After a moment, the doorbell rings.*

**TED:** Oh! There's the door.

*Ted leaves the room.*

SCENE 5 INT./NIGHT 2
SET: PAROCHIAL HOUSE HALLWAY
*Ted opens the front door. On the ground, we see a baby in a little cot. There is wistful music. Ted gasps. He looks around and can't see anybody else. He bends down to pick the baby up, but a woman suddenly appears.*

**WOMAN:** I'm sorry. Er, is this Mrs Reilly's house?

*She picks up the baby.*

**TED:** No. That's er, just down the road.

**WOMAN:** Oh. Thanks very much.

*She walks away. Ted closes the door.*

SCENE 6 INT./NIGHT 2
SET: PAROCHIAL HOUSE
*Ted comes back into the living room.*

**DOUGAL:** Who was that, Ted?

**TED:** Oh, someone looking for Reilly's. She had a baby. For a second I thought someone had just left it on the doorstep.

**DOUGAL:** God, Ted, can you imagine what would have happened if she'd left it with us?!

**TED:** Hah, yes, we'd have been trying to look after it and everything, and getting into all sorts of hilarious jams. The whole thing would have been very, very, funny.

**DOUGAL:** Well, it wouldn't have been that funny, Ted.

**TED:** Actually . . . no.

SCENE 7 INT./DAY 3
SET: DEPARTMENT STORE
*Mrs Doyle is standing beside a salesman. The salesman is demonstrating some kind of moulinex-type thing with 'teamaster' written on the side. He is chirpy.*

**SALESMAN:** . . . and the liquids just come out here. You've already punched in your selection for sugar and milk, so all the work is taken out of it, leaving the modern woman plenty of time for running a business or skiing. With a simple turn of the switch, she can access coffee, hot chocolate or Horlicks. Takes all the misery out of making tea. What do you say to *that*?

*Dramatic close-up of Mrs Doyle, her face set in a very tough, Clint Eastwood-type way.*

**MRS DOYLE:** Maybe I *like* the misery.

*The salesman's smile disappears.*

SCENE 8 INT./DAY 3
SET: DEPARTMENT STORE
*Ted and Dougal are walking through the shop. Ted is looking at his shopping list.*

**TED:** I thought I'd buy some perfume for Mrs Doyle.

**DOUGAL:** Good idea, Ted. Perfume is the ideal 'woman' present, isn't it?

**TED:** Yessss. Well, that's why God invented perfume, so you don't have to put any thought into it whatsoever. Oh, where'd you manage to stick Jack in the end?

**DOUGAL:** Oh, they've got this great place, Ted, where you can put people who don't want to go shopping. They can just stay there and have a laugh.

**TED:** Really? I've never heard of that. Were there other people there?

**DOUGAL:** Oh, loads of people, Ted. He'll be fine.

*They move out of shot.*

SCENE 9 INT./DAY 3
SET: DEPARTMENT STORE/CRECHE
*We see Jack sitting against a wall. There are about a dozen children in with him, playing with blocks and messing about. Jack smokes a fag and looks quite happy.*

SCENE 10 INT./DAY 3
SET: DEPARTMENT STORE/LINGERIE
*Dougal and Ted are still walking.*

**TED:** Perfume . . . perfume.

**DOUGAL:** You think you'd be able to smell it. Ted . . . where exactly are we now?

**TED:** Well, we're in the . . . in the . . . (*Ted looks around, suddenly terrified.*) . . . Oh, my God.

*Cut wide, a blast of very dramatic music, and we reveal a sign over their heads that reads 'lingerie'. Frilly feminine fancies surround them. Ted looks around, panicking slightly.*

**TED:** We're in lingerie. Dougal, we're in lingerie.

**DOUGAL:** What's the problem there, Ted?

**TED** (*as he ushers Dougal along*): Well, think about it Dougal. Two priests hanging around near women's secret things. It just doesn't look good.

*They start walking quickly.*

**TED:** Where's the exit? Oh, God, look, we're in bras! (*Dougal looks around, wide-eyed.*) This way . . . oh, no, that's . . . more underpants! Why in God's name do they need so many kinds of underpants! What, do they parade around in them, looking in mirrors all the time?

*Dougal thinks about this, drifting off. They round a corner and see two other priests looking at lingerie.*

**TED:** Billy? Terry?

**BILLY:** Ted? Ted Crilly?

**BOTH:** How's it going? Hello, there . . .

**TED:** Good to see you both. This is Father Dougal McGuire.

**BILLY:** Hello, Father Dougal.

**DOUGAL:** Hello, Father Dougal!? . . . What?

**TED:** No, that's you, Dougal, You're Father Dougal.

**DOUGAL:** Oh, right.

**TED:** We got lost a bit in the store. That's how we ended up here. We got lost. I suppose that's what happened to you as well.

*Billy and Terry exchange a glance.*

**BILLY:** Hmmmm . . . ? Lost? Yeaaaahhhh, that's it.

**TERRY** (*simultaneous with Billy*): We got lost, that's it.

**TED:** I don't suppose you'd know the way out of here?

**BILLY:** Eh . . . this way?

**TED:** No, we just came that way.

**TERRY:** It's Ireland's biggest lingerie section, I understand.

**TED:** Really?

**TERRY:** Yes . . . I read that . . . somewhere . . .

**TED:** Well, I just think it'd be a good idea to get out as quickly as possible. Four priests hanging around the frillies section . . .

**BILLY:** Yes, I . . . I see what you mean.

**TED:** Let's try this way . . .

*To dramatic music, they start walking through the aisles.*

SCENE 11 INT./DAY 3
SET: DEPARTMENT STORE/CRECHE
*Jack is idly playing with building blocks, still surrounded by kids. We can see that he has spelt out the words 'Feck', 'Arse', 'Drink' and 'Girls' with the blocks.*

SCENE 12 INT./DAY 3
SET: DEPARTMENT STORE/LINGERIE
*Back to our heroes. Everywhere they look, though, they just see more lingerie.*

**TED:** Ohhh, wait a second, we've been here . . . I remember those bras the first time round.

**DOUGAL:** God, they all look the same to me.

**TED:** No, no. These ones have double padding and the black lace outline with the little cotton supports and the extra strength straps. If we pass by any bras with a middle arch support and single padding, along with a white lace outline, we'll know we're on the right track.

**BILLY:** Someone's coming!

**TED:** Damn!

*Before they can bolt away, they see another four priests coming around the corner.*

**TED:** Oh my God.

*They walk up to the priests and exchange greetings, shaking hands in a military, manlike way. The new priests are Father Deegan, Father Cleary, Father Reilly and Father Fitzgerald.*

**TED:** What happened to you?

**CLEARY:** We were looking for the toilets and we wandered in here by mistake. How do you get out? It's huge!

**TERRY:** It's Ireland's biggest lingerie section, I understand.

**TED:** All right. This is the situation. Eight priests wandering around a lingerie section. If it was just one or two of us, well, that'd be embarrassing, but with the eight of us . . . I think we're talking national scandal.

**DEEGAN:** What are we going to do? All the aisles look the same.

**TED:** It's no use panicking. We're in this thing, let's try and get out of it. Billy, you go on point. Father Cleary, Father Deegan, I want you at the back. All right, let's go. And keep it quiet.

SCENE 13 INT./DAY 3
SET: DEPARTMENT STORE/LINGERIE
*Our heroes are walking through the aisles in a line, like a platoon of soldiers. They walk slowly, clutching their shopping to their chests. Close-ups on the sweating, nervous faces of all the priests in turn. One of them wipes his face with a white cloth, realises it's a pair of frilly underpants, and throws it away with a yelp. A muzak version of 'The End' by the Doors is coming through the department store speakers. After a moment or two of this, Billy, walking at the front, a cigarette dangling from his mouth, raises his finger in warning. They all hunker down and wait. Ted passes along the line.*

**TED** (*to priests as he passes*): You all right? Shaping up? Hang in there . . .

*He gets to Billy.*

**TED:** What is it?

**BILLY:** I thought I heard something. Maybe I'm just going crazy. I've been in this damn lingerie section so long . . .

**TED:** No, wait . . .

*We hear a rustling sound. All the priests stay low and quiet, keeping their eyes on where the sound is coming from – a neighbouring aisle that runs parallel to their one. Through the lingerie, we see glimpses of some people walking along.*

**TED:** I don't think they've seen us. Take a rest, Father. Father Reilly, you're on point.

*He passes by one priest who is breathing heavily.*

**TED:** Father Deegan, you all right?

**DEEGAN:** There's no way out! There's just no way out! They're gonna get us! They're gonna get us!

*Ted grabs Deegan around the head and puts a hand over his mouth, muffling him. He looks over at the shapes of the two girls, who stop talking for a moment. Everything is very still. Then the girls continue talking and walk away.*

**TED:** Damn it, Father Deegan!

**DEEGAN:** Sorry. I . . . I . . .

**TED:** We've been in tighter corners than this and we've always gotten out. Haven't we? *Haven't* we?

**DEEGAN:** I only left the seminary two weeks ago! If they find out, I'll never get a decent parish! They'll send me off to some bloody kip! What are we going to do!!!

**TED:** Father Deegan. I'll make you a promise. One day, you and I, we're gonna be sitting in your lovely, new parish, drinking iced tea on the lawn, and all this will be a memory. I want you to hold on to that thought. Can you do that for me?

*Deegan swallows his tears and nods.*

**TED:** Good man. All right.

*Ted raises his finger and gestures for everyone to move. At the back of the line, there's a scream, and Father Cleary falls to the ground. Ted rushes back to Father Cleary.*

**TED:** Father Cleary, what happened?

**CLEARY:** I was messing about with one of those bras, and the strap flew back and hit me in the eye. I . . . AAAhhh!! I think I've twisted my ankle as wel . . .

**TED:** All right. Father Deegan, Father Reilly, give Father Cleary a hand here.

**CLEARY:** No, it was my stupid fault for

messing with the bras. Leave me here, I'll only slow you down.

**TED:** Dammit, man, we're a team. We're sticking together.

*Deegan and Reilly grab him and help him to walk. They turn a corner but Ted stops them and ducks back. He peers around the corner and we see an exit with 'Exit 4' written over it. There are a good few people looking through the shelves nearby.\**

**TED:** It's the exit. God, look at all those people.

**BILLY:** They'd definitely see us coming out. Maybe if we actually buy some underpants, it won't look so strange.

**TED:** They're women's underpants!

**BILLY:** Oh, yes, sorry . . .

*A voice comes over the tannoy.*

**VOICE** (*very boring monotone*): Please visit our restaurant on the first floor where we have a beautiful selection of Christmas-style food and beverages.

*Ted sees something. He goes over to a metal box-like thing on the wall. An idea hits him.*

**TED:** C'mere.

*Everyone groups around.*

**TED:** Who's got the most boring voice?

**BILLY:** What?

**TED:** Of the lot of us, who's got the most boring voice?

**FITZGERALD** (*incredibly boring voice*): That'd be me, Ted . . .

*Murmurs of agreement.*

**TED:** Father! Listen to me.

**FITZGERALD:** I have an awful, dreary, monotonous voice, God help me . . .

**TED:** Yeah, yeah, listen . . .

**REILLY** (*exciting, dramatic voice*): Ted, did you say you wanted a dramatic, exciting voice?

**FITZGERALD:** No, he said 'boring'. He wanted a boring voice.

**REILLY:** Then you must excuse me for my

*\*We moved scene 14 to here in the final version. The rest of this scene became scene 14A.*

impetuous interruption!

**TED:** Right, this is what I want you to do . . .

*Ted starts whispering to Father Fitzgerald. Nearby, Dougal turns to Billy.*

**DOUGAL:** What's goin' on?

**TERRY:** I think Ted has a plan.

**DOUGAL:** No, I mean in general.

**TERRY:** We can't find our way out of the lingerie section.

**DOUGAL:** Oh, right.

*Back to Ted and Fitzgerald. The latter approaches the steel box-thingy and presses a button. He speaks into a microphone sticking out of it and his voice is relayed around the store on a tannoy.*

**FITZGERALD** (*incredibly boring voice*): Ladies and gentlemen, could you please bring your purchases to the checkout as the store is about to close. Hurry up! Come on there! Hurry up will you!

*We see people looking nervous and annoyed as the tannoy badgers them. One person walks back in the opposite direction to everyone else.*

**TED:** Not that way, for feck's sake! The other way!

*The person turns and walks back. Ted looks around the corner. The area around 'Exit 4' is now completely cleared, not a soul in sight. The priests cheer and hug each other.*

*Ted runs across to the doors and opens them – a huge wind blows through. One by one he pushes the priests out and into the wind.*

**TED:** Go! Go! Go! Go! Go! Go! Go!

*Cut to outside where the priests cheer and hug each other.*

SCENE 14 INT./DAY 3
SET: DEPARTMENT STORE/CRECHE
*Jack stands up and walks shakily to the door. He waves to the kids and staggers out. Pause. Slowly, one by one but soon developing into a chorus, the kids start talking.*

**KIDS:** . . . feck . . . arse . . . feck . . . feckity, feck, feck, feck . . . arse . . . feckin' arse . . . (*Louder.*) . . . Feck . . . .ARSE . . . FECK . . . FECKING FECKING FECK!

SCENE 15 INT./DAY 4
SET: PAROCHIAL HOUSE
*Dougal is opening another window on the Advent calendar. He looks hugely expectant. It's the Three Wise Men pointing at a star.*

**DOUGAL:** Oh . . .

*He is obviously hugely disappointed.*

**TED** (*reading a newspaper*): What's wrong, Dougal?

**DOUGAL:** It's just . . . three lads pointing at a star. That's a bit disappointing.

**TED:** Why?

**DOUGAL:** Well . . . what's that got to do with Christmas?

*Ted closes the paper. We see the headline: 'Pope denies claims'.*

**TED:** Well, there's nothing in the Catholic scandal supplement about the lingerie episode. I think we got away with it.

*The telephone rings. After a while, Ted answers.*

**TED:** Hello. Craggy Island Parochial House. Father Ted Crilly speaking.

*Cut to a very posh room with a bishop on the other end of the line. We see a caption that reads 'The Vatican' at the bottom of the screen. In the background we see more bishops having a laugh and drinking cans of lager and wine bottles from the neck. They all look rather dishevelled. Party music plays.*

**BISHOP:** Hello, Ted! Tom McCaskell here!

**TED:** Tom, how are ya? And *where* are you? You left in an awful hurry.

**BISHOP:** Ah, I'm in Rome.

**TED:** When will you be back?

**BISHOP:** When things have died down a bit. I might have to head off to South America for a while. You know she's going to write a bloody book about it?!

**TED:** Ah, now that's not fair.

**BISHOP:** Did they ever catch up with you about that Lourdes thing? It looked a bit dodgy there for . . .

**TED:** Ah, ah, let me stop you there, Tom, that money was just resting in my account . . .

**DOUGAL:** Oh, ho!

**TED:** Shut up, Dougal!

**BISHOP:** Anyway, Ted . . . we owe you a big favour for getting the lads out of trouble the other day. We'd like you to have a Golden Cleric!

**TED:** A Golden Cleric? You're not serious?

**BISHOP:** I'm deadly serious.

**TED:** Ahaaa!!! What . . . what can I say? God, I don't feel worthy. When I think of all the other priests who've won it.

**BISHOP:** Well, you . . .

*A bishop sitting behind a massive drum kit starts whacking it.*

**BISHOP:** Alberto! Alberto, please.

*The drummer stops with an 'oops, sorry' face.*

**BISHOP:** You deserve it. You managed to avert a tricky situation and prevent another scandal in the Church. Father Billy and the rest of the lads will drop the award over to you tomorrow.

**TED:** . . . And is there, sorry about this, but is there any kind of cash prize with that?

**BISHOP:** No.

**TED:** Oh.

**BISHOP:** Actually, Ted, I'm a *wee bit* disappointed you asked that. Just a *wee bit* disappointed. Did I teach you nothing?

*Tom puts down the telephone and turns to the chaos. One bishop is starting to drink a pint in one go. Tom joins in with the others in clapping and cheering him on. The drummer joins in on the high-hat. Cut back to the Parochial House.*

**TED:** Dougal, fantastic news! . . .

**DOUGAL:** You're getting married?

**TED:** What? No, of course I'm . . . Was that a joke?

**DOUGAL:** Er . . . yes . . .

**TED:** No, I've just been awarded a Golden Cleric!

**DOUGAL:** Hurray!

**TED:** Oh, God, I'll have to write a speech! Oh, it'll have to be brilliant. It's not every day you win an award.

**JACK:** Award!!!!

TED: No, Father, you can't have one.

JACK: Why not?!! Award! Award! Award! Award! Award!

TED: All right, Father, all right . . .

*He goes to the mantelpiece and takes a teacup from it. He goes to Jack and presents it to him.*

TED: There you go, Father.

JACK: Yes! Photo! Photo!

TED (*sighs*): Dougal, take a photograph.

*Dougal gets a camera and points it at Ted and Jack. Jack shakes hands with Ted, the other hand holding the trophy. They both look at the camera, like politicians, and Dougal presses the button. Flash and freeze on this image of Jack and Ted. When we go back to normal, Ted takes the trophy and puts it back on the mantelpiece.*

DOUGAL: Oh, Ted, can I stay up tomorrow night to watch the scary film?

TED: What? Oh, no, no. The last time you watched a scary film, you had to sleep in my bed. I wouldn't mind, but it wasn't even *that* scary a film.

DOUGAL: Ah, come on, Ted. A Volkswagen with a mind of its own driving all around the place going mad! If that's not scary, I don't know what is!

TED: Dougal, that's a children's film! If you can't deal with that, how on earth would you be able to take a film about a burglar creeping into people's houses and killing everybody?

DOUGAL (*suddenly looks terrified*): Is that what this one's about?

TED: Yes.

*Dougal looks terrified.*

SCENE 16 INT./DAY 4
SET: PAROCHIAL HOUSE
*We see a close-up of Dougal's hands. He holds a bottle of gum. He draws out a star shape on a piece of paper with the nozzle of the gum. He then spills out some gold sparkly stuff on the paper. It sticks to the gum and forms a star shape.*

*Cut to Dougal. The sparkly stuff is all over his face and shirt, along with bits of paper, etc. He is looking at the television as he works, the decorative materials on his lap.*

SCENE 17 INT./DAY 4
SET: PAROCHIAL HOUSE
*We see what Dougal is watching. We see a few shots of priests turning to the camera and smiling in front of cheap and cheerful backdrops.*

VOICE: If you want to meet priests your own age . . . (*We see two priests, standing back to back, their jackets thrown over their shoulders, miming a gossipy conversation.*) . . . or just listen in on the latest gossip . . . (*The screen is divided into three separate shots. We see a priest listening to a Walkman, another pretending to take a photograph, another reading a magazine and pretending to look interested.*) . . . then call priest chatback, and speak to priests . . . you want to know.

SCENE 18 INT./DAY 4
SET: PAROCHIAL HOUSE
*Cut to a wider view of the room. We see that there are now lots and lots of decorations all round, all over the walls. Mrs Doyle is on the window ledge again. She starts to step down from it, thinks better of it, then turns around and holds on to the side of the window. As she starts to lower herself when the side of the window comes off with a cracking noise and she falls backwards on to the floor. Everyone fails to notice this. Ted walks in with a glass case.*

TED: Right. I got the presentation case for the award.

DOUGAL (*slightly bored with more award talk*): Great, Ted. Fantastic.

TED: I'll put my award here, over the creaky floorboard. (*As he puts it above the fireplace, the floorboard creaks loudly.*) If any burglars come in and try to rob my award, we'll hear them. Very few priests are given this award, you know. It'll mean that I'll be one of the top priests in the country when I get my award.

DOUGAL: Oh, right.

TED: Did you hear there what I was saying? I'm one of the top priests in the country. Did you hear that? . . . I said it there a second ago.

DOUGAL: Oh, I did, yeah.

*Dougal has even more paper stuck to his hands and face. He's having trouble shaking it off.*

MRS DOYLE (*righting herself*): Well, it's not before time, Father. I always thought you were one of the best priests in the country!

TED: Well, thanks very much, Mrs Doyle. (*Pause.*) One of the best? . . . (*Very jokily.*) Or maybe *the* best? Go on, Mrs Doyle, honestly, would you say I'm the best priest in the country at the moment?

MRS DOYLE: Wwwwwellll . . .

*Mrs Doyle seems reluctant to answer.*

TED: Well, what would you say? Honestly, if you don't think I'm the best priest in the country just say so!

*Another shot of Mrs Doyle.*

TED: I honestly won't mind!

MRS DOYLE (*still struggling*): I'd say, Father, you might be the . . . second best.

*Ted nods. He doesn't say anything, he just nods.*

MRS DOYLE: I mean . . .

TED: No, it's all right, Mrs Doyle. I'm not the best priest in the country, I'm only the second best. There's someone better than me, apparently.

MRS DOYLE: Well, I am thinking of those priests who work in very poor areas . . .

TED: Oh, yes, of course. *Those* fellas! Father Archbishop Desmond Tutu and the like.

MRS DOYLE: I think Archbishop Tutu is a Prostestant man.

TED: Oh, right, great, so a *Protestant* is better than me. Anyway, there's no need to continue this. I'm not the best, I'm only the *second* best.

Apparently, the Golden Cleric is a *runner-up* prize. Well, I'm *so* sorry. Obviously, I'm just an *idiot.*Obviously, I can't even say Mass properly.

MRS DOYLE: Father, I was just . . .

TED: No, don't take it back. That's what you said. You said I'm not the best priest in the country. That's fine. I just want to know where I stand. Obviously, I'm going to have to jack it in now.

MRS DOYLE: What?

TED: I'm leaving the priesthood.

MRS DOYLE: But, Father!

TED: No, that's it. I'm going to write a letter to Bishop Brennan and ask for early retirement. And maybe when I go, you can ask the other priest, Father Perfect Peter The Perfect Priest, to come here and you can work for him! Since he's obviously (*dripping sarcasm*) *such a great priest.*

*He storms out of the room and slams the door. A piece of decoration falls down. Mrs Doyle looks at the decorations worryingly. Ted re-enters and collects his coat. He leaves and slams the door again. A paper bell falls off the back of the door. Mrs Doyle looks more worried. Ted enters again, embarrassed. He sheepishly collects his keys and painstakingly closes the door quietly. All the decorations fall to the floor with a series of jangles and pops. Mrs Doyle picks up one of the decorations, and gets back on the dangerous window. Dougal now has an entire square of paper affixed to his face.*

SCENE 19 EXT./DAY X
SET: BEACH
*We see Ted in silhouette, walking along the beach, looking out at the waves. A few similar shots, with Ted just walking along, with lots of fades and beautiful, melancholic sunset shots. Sad music plays. Close-up of Ted. He looks very sad. After a while, we hear Mrs Doyle's voice.*

MRS DOYLE (*her voice, echoing, faraway*): . . . the second best priest in the country . . . the second best priest . . . second best . . . second best . . . second best . . .

*Ted picks up a stone and skims it across the water with a loud whacking noise, it hits an old man in a rowboat, who until then was fishing peacefully.*

**TED:** Sorry about that!

**MAN:** Ye feckin' eejit! Wait there, until I get *ye*!

*The man starts rowing towards the shore. Ted runs away.*

**MAN:** O'ho, wait'll I get you now. Ye little pup, ye.

*Ted runs towards the camera.*

SCENE 19A INT./DAY 4
SET: BLUE SCREEN
*Mrs Doyle's disembodied face floats towards the screen.*

**MRS DOYLE:** . . .the second best priest . . . second best priest . . . second best priest . . .

*Then the old man in the boat's head joins her.*

**MAN:** You feckin' eejit. O'ho, wait'll I get you now . . .

*Jack's head floats by, laughing hysterically. Then Assumpta from Ballykissangel's head floats by followed by Father Clifford's.*

**ASSUMPTA:** I'm not going out with you. You're just the *second* best priest in the country.

*Then Clifford's ('Ballykissangel') head floats towards us, laughing in an evil mocking way.*

**CLIFFORD:** Ahh, ha, ha, ha, ha!!!

*Then, Dougal's head comes by, just looking confused. When it gets close to the camera, it doesn't know where to go, so it turns around and goes back again.*

SCENE 20 INT./DAY 4
SET: PAROCHIAL HOUSE
*Mrs Doyle is up on the dangerous windowsill, fixing the decorations. She turns and starts to get down off the window, remembers her usual trouble with it, and stops. She puts one hand on the window to steady herself and leans against it, starts to put her foot out to get down. The window swings open and she falls into the front garden.*

SCENE 21 INT./DAY 4
SET: PAROCHIAL HOUSE
*Ted goes into the living room. The television is on, and Ted looks over. We hear the end of the Priest Chatback advertisement. Ted looks at it, then at the telephone. Then he goes over and dials, half-singing the number to himself to remember it.*

**TED:** Hello? Priest Chatback?

*The screen splits. On one side we see a twin-reeled tape recorder clicking on in a dingy office. Beside it is an ashtray with a lit fag burning.*

**VOICE** (*recorded voice*): Welcome to Priest Chatback. If you are under eighteen or not a priest, please hang up now. Calls cost forty-nine pence per minute and terminate in Sierra Leone. If you wish to speak about the Pope's visit to Mexico, say 'yes' now. (*Bleep.*) If you want to speak about the role of women within the church, say 'yes' now. (*Bleep.*)

*At this last one, Ted raises his eyes to heaven.*

**VOICE:** If you want to speak about being vaguely unhappy but not being able to figure out exactly why, say 'yes' now. (*Bleep.*) If you want to speak about your addiction to sherry, say 'yes' now . . .

**TED:** Oh, wait! Yes! YES! YES! Hello?

*The screen splits into three. It now features two other priests as well as Ted. Both men are on the telephone and in different locations.*

**PRIEST 1:** Hello? Is that someone else?

**PRIEST 2:** Hello? (*Ad lib extra 'Hello's'.*)

**TED:** Hello? (*Ad lib extra 'Hello's'.*)

**PRIEST 1:** Hello?

**PRIEST 2:** Hello, yes?

**TED:** Oh, yes, hello, there. Is this 'Being vaguely unhappy but not being able to figure out exactly why'?

**PRIEST 1:** No, this is 'How to break the news of a death'.

**PRIEST 2:** We were just talking about techniques. I say it's best to just get it over with quickly. 'Your husband's dead, and he's not coming back. Get used to it.'

**PRIEST 1:** Yes, but sometimes a few little hints help. Like, ah '. . . Do you remember how your husband *used* to love a good laugh?'

**PRIEST 2:** Hmmm, you have a point, but . . .

**TED:** Oh, well, you see. My problem is, I should be on top of the world because I'm about to be given an award, but, well . . .

**VOICE:** Duuhhh . . . stupid priests! Duhhhh!

*Suddenly the screen is divided into four. In the new frame we see two teenagers in grungy-looking gear and with Oasis haircuts. Trying to suppress giggles, one talks while the other listens.*

**PRIEST 1:** Hey! Who's that?

**PRIEST 2:** Have some respect!

**TEENAGER:** Duuuuhhhhhhh!!!

**PRIEST 1:** This is a priest-only line! Are you priests?

*Ted sighs and hangs up. Mrs Doyle enters.*

**MRS DOYLE:** Oh, by the way, Father, when you left for your walk, we got a phone call. I think you were supposed to do a funeral today?

*Ted thinks for a moment, then puts on an 'oh my God' face.*

**TED:** The funeral! I completely forgot about it!

**MRS DOYLE:** It's all right. Father McGuire said he'd do it.

**TED:** Oh, great. Well, that's th— DOUGAL'S DOING A FUNERAL?!!! YOU LET DOUGAL DO A FUNERAL???!!

SCENE 22 EXT./DAY 4
SET: GRAVEYARD
*We see Dougal in his 'official' gear. Behind him, a hearse is on fire and halfway into an open grave. An ambulance is nearby, injured people limping into it. People lie around on the ground, being given assistance. A very angry man looks at Dougal.*

**DOUGAL:** Sorry about that.

*The hearse explodes.*

SCENE 23 INT./NIGHT 4
SET: TED AND DOUGAL'S BEDROOM
*Ted is sitting in bed, writing on a laptop computer. A single lamp illuminates his workplace. It looks as if the rest of the room is in darkness. We hear shuffling coming from Dougal's bed.*

**DOUGAL** (*offscreen*): Oh . . . mmmm . . .

*Shuffle, shuffle. Ted sighs, trying to concentrate.*

**DOUGAL:** Hmmm mummprhh . . . Oh, it's no use, Ted! I'm so excited about Christmas. I can't sleep.

**TED:** Dougal, you'll never get to sleep like that. (*Cut to Dougal on an exercise bike.*) You'll have a better chance if you get off the bike.

**DOUGAL:** Oh, right. What are you up to yourself, Ted?

**TED:** I'm writing my speech for tomorrow. God, it's brilliant so far. This will be my Gettysburg Address. I might try and put it on the Internet and everything.

**DOUGAL:** What do you put in speeches? You normally thank everybody, don't you.

**TED:** Not in this case, Dougal. I got this award through my own initiative and hard graft. There's nobody else to thank but me. Actually, that's a good idea . . . I'll thank myself . . .

*He taps at the keyboard. He takes some papers off the computer and tidies them into line. It looks like a fairly weighty tome.*

**DOUGAL:** Wow. Is that the speech?

**TED:** What? No, these are just my notes. Here, for instance, here's a list of people who've really fecked me over down through the years. Father Jimmy Fennel . . . he needs taking down a peg or two . . . Father P.J. Clabbert . . . Wait . . . he's on the wrong list . . . He should be under 'Liars' rather than 'Twats' . . . Oh, at last. At *last* I get a chance to shine out, to stand out from the crowd. To be recognised.

**DOUGAL:** I recognise you. Look. It's Ted.

**TED:** No, Dougal . . .

**DOUGAL:** There you are there, now.

**TED:** Dougal, I mean recognition of my abilities, my achievements.

**DOUGAL:** Oh, right. What achievements are these?

*Pause. Ted thinks. We hear the dripping of a tap from the kitchen. They both stand there for a long, silent moment.*

**TED:** Shut up, Dougal. Oh, I hope Larry Duff's coming, catch my big moment. I'll give him a ring now, actually. I really hope he makes it. Larry's tremendous fun. He *loves* award ceremonies.

*Ted dials.*

SCENE 24 EXT./DAY 4
SET: SKI SLOPE/BLUE SCREEN
*Cut to Larry happily skiing along. We hear his phone*

ringing. Larry is distracted. Cut to stock footage of skier having horrific fall down slope. It should take a very long time. As he falls, he cries out in pain.

**LARRY** (*from afar*): Oh, dear God in Heaven . . . Ooof . . . agh! My leg! . . . Oh, Holy Mother of God . . . agh . . . Oh, Jesus, Mary and Joseph . . . all the Saints in Heaven, help me . . . God almighty . . .

SCENE 25 INT./NIGHT 4
SET: TED AND DOUGAL'S BEDROOM
*Cut back to Ted.*

**TED:** Oh, wait, no, I think he's on holiday. Well, I won't disturb him.

**DOUGAL:** All right, I'm going to try one more time to get to sleep. (*He closes his eyes, then opens them.*) Gaaaaahhhh!!! It's no use!

**TED:** Dougal, here's a good way to get to sleep. Just try and clear your head of all thoughts.

**DOUGAL:** Well, I'll give it a go, but I don't think . . . Zzzzzzzzzzzzz . . .

*Ted looks at him, then back at the computer. He starts writing.*

**TED:** Heh, heh, heh . . .

## END OF PART ONE

\* \* \*

## PART TWO

SCENE 26 INT./DAY 5
SET: PAROCHIAL HOUSE
*We see another window of the Advent calendar being opened. It is a nativity scene.*

**DOUGAL:** Aaaaggghhh!!! BRILLIANT! A LOAD OF PEOPLE IN A STABLE! The one thing I didn't expect!

**TED:** Dougal . . .

**DOUGAL:** Oh, wow! Unbelievable!

**TED:** Dougal, aren't you going to open your presents?

**DOUGAL:** Presents! Oh, wow! I completely forgot about the presents! First the calendar, now presents! It can't get any better than this!

*He runs up to his presents. He is incredibly excited. He*

*rummages through them and he rips one open. We can't see what it is. He yells with delight.*

**DOUGAL:** Aaaargh! BRILLIANT!

*Ted hands Mrs Doyle a present.*

**TED:** Happy Christmas, Mrs Doyle . . .

**MRS DOYLE:** Oh, Father, you shouldn't have. What is it? It's a . . .

*She opens it. It is the tea-making machine we saw earlier. She stares at it without expression.*

**TED:** I was racking my brains, thinking, 'What would Mrs Doyle really love?' So I thought . . . you know, something to take the misery out of making tea.

**MRS DOYLE:** Oh . . . thank you, Father, it's . . . it's just what I wanted.

**TED:** Yes, Mrs Doyle, the days of housekeepers making tea are over. We can't live in the Dark Ages any more. You've made your last cup of tea in this house.

*Mrs Doyle takes this in.*

**MRS DOYLE** (*recovering slightly*)**:** I'll just put it in . . . in the kitchen, so . . .

**TED:** No need, Mrs Doyle. We can leave it in here and just get the tea ourselves.

**MRS DOYLE:** Oh. OK, so. I'll just go into the kitchen, then and . . . stand beside the cooker and . . . look out of the window for a while . . .

*She turns so her back is to the camera, and walks slowly out of the room, as if she's walking in a funeral procession.*

**TED:** If I know people the way I think I do, she really loves that present.

**DOUGAL** (*offscreen*)**:** Ah, Ted, it's brilliant!

**TED:** You like it?

**DOUGAL:** Ah, yeah . . .

*Cut to Dougal. He is dressed in full matador's gear.*

**DOUGAL:** . . . I mean, how did you know?

**TED:** Don't think I hadn't noticed all those little hints you left lying about the place.

SCENE 27 EXT./DAY 5
SET: PAROCHIAL HOUSE
*We see a finger coming into shot and pressing the*

doorbell. *The person who pressed the bell steps back and looks up - we see all this from behind. We see a huge banner across the front of the house that has on it the words, 'Ted, get me loads of matador stuff. Dougal.'*

SCENE 28 EXT./DAY 5
SET: PAROCHIAL HOUSE
*Jack approaches Ted, a fag hanging from his mouth.*

**JACK:** Present. C'mon. C'MON, PRESENT! PRESENT!

*Ted reaches down for Jack's present.*

**JACK** (*snaps fingers*)**:** C'mon, c'mon, c'mon.

*Ted lifts up a bottle of whiskey. Jack grabs it.*

**TED:** Happy Christ . . .

**JACK** (*walking off*)**:** Yeah, yeah, yeah . . . feck off . . .

*Ted is looking out of the window.*

**TED:** Who could this be? The ceremony doesn't start until two.

*The door opens. Mrs Doyle enters.*

**MRS DOYLE:** Father, it's . . .

*A priest barges past her.*

**TODD:** Teeeeeeeeeedddddddd!!!

*Ted obviously doesn't know who he is, but fakes it.*

**TED:** Ahaaa!!! Ahhhh!! Helloooooo there!!!

*Todd hugs Ted. We see by Ted's face that he doesn't know who he is.*

**TODD:** You finally did it! You won the Golden Cleric. I haven't missed the ceremony, have I?

**TED:** What? Oh, right. No, not at all.

**TODD:** You haven't changed a bit, you rascal! Ha, ha!!

*He attempts to engage Ted in some playful pretend boxing.*

**TED:** Ha, ha! No, and you! Look at you! You haven't changed either!

**TODD:** What? Well, what about the hair?

**TED:** Oh, right, the hair . . . it's a different . . . shape . . .

**TODD:** Colour.

**TED:** Colour, yes. Of course, because it used to be . . . reeeed-black.

**TODD:** Blond.

**TED:** Blond! Blond, yes.

*Todd sees Dougal.*

**TODD:** Hello, there!

**DOUGAL** (*brightly*): Hello, there you back!

**TODD** (*to Dougal*): I suppose he's told you all about me!

**DOUGAL:** No. (*Beat.*) Who are you?

**TODD:** Who am I?

*Todd looks at Ted and makes an 'introduce us' gesture. Pause. Ted begins to say something, then reaches for an address book and opens it.*

**TED:** Actually, you might as well stick your name and address in the old book. Especially the name. It's very important that the name is very, very clear.

**TODD:** Ah, I'd love to, Ted, but I can't really write. One time last year I was running with scissors, and I fell. The nerve that controls handwriting was completely severed.

**TED:** There's a nerve that controls handwriting?

**TODD:** Apparently. And things like . . . you know . . . conducting.

*He attempts to demonstrate by miming 'conducting', but grimaces in pain as soon as he starts. Ted nods. Pause.*

**MRS DOYLE:** Father, aren't you going to introduce me to the new Father?

**TED:** Oh, right. This, as . . . this is . . . Actually

. . . (*Long pause.*) I tell you what. See if you can guess.

**MRS DOYLE:** Guess?

**TED:** Yes. Give it a go there.

**MRS DOYLE:** God, Father, it could be anything.

**TED:** Still, though. Give it a try.

**MRS DOYLE:** Father Andy Reilly.

**TODD:** No, ha, ha.

**MRS DOYLE:** Father Desmond Coyne. Father Kevin Cecil. (*Todd shakes his head.*) Father George Byrne. Father David Nicholson. Father Declan Lynch . . .

**TODD** (*enjoying this*): I'll give you a clue . . .

**MRS DOYLE:** NO CLUES! I'll get it in a second . . . Father Ken Sweeney . . . Father Neil Hannon . . . Father Keith Cullen, Father Kieran Donnelly, Father Mick McEvoy, Father Jack White . . .

*Ted looks at Mrs Doyle and sighs. He sits down and covers his face with his hand. Fade down.*

SCENE 29 INT./DAY 5
SET: PAROCHIAL HOUSE
*Fade up. It is much later. Ted and Dougal are sitting down now, looking tired and bored.*

**MRS DOYLE:** . . . Father Henry Big Bigeen. Father Hank Tree. Father Hiroshima Twinky. Father Stig Bubblecard. Father Johnny Hellsapoppin' . . . Father Luke Duke. Father Muhammad Stiff. Father Billy Furry. Father John Hoop. Father Hairycake Lynam. Father Chewy Louie. Father Rebulah Conundrum. Father Peewee Stairmaster. Father Tighthead Lips. Father Rick Cocksinger . . . Father Jemimah Racktool. Father Gerry Twigg. Father Spodo Comodo. Father Canabramalamar. Father Todd Unctious . . .

**TODD:** Yes! Well done!

**TED:** What? Really? Is that it? She's got it!

**TODD:** C'mon Ted! You knew already!

**TED:** Ha, ha, yes, I'm simply amazed that she got it right in . . . (*He checks his watch.*) Wow! Well under an hour! Well done, Mrs Doyle! So . . . Todd. Todd, Todd, Todd. Old Todd. There you are now. Todd. Good old Todd. Are you all right for tea, Todd? Would you like a hot toddy . . . Todd? Anything you want, Todd. Anything at all. Todd. (*He winks.*) Todd.

**TODD:** What time is the ceremony, Ted?

**TED:** Well, Todd, it's due to start around two. But it's not really a 'ceremony'. I'm sure it'll be a very quick, simple affair.

SCENE 30 EXT./DAY 5
SET: PAROCHIAL HOUSE
*Lots of priests and nuns are milling around in a hive of activity. The following scenes are done in a series of quick montages, the style very naturalistic. There is a kind of 'roadie' priest at the microphone.*

**ROADIE PRIEST:** ONE, TWO, ONE, TWO . . . (*To the sound priest.*) Sean, I'm getting feedback from the monitor. Can you? . . . One, two . . . Yeah, that's good.

*A priest unwrapping a load of candles. Another priest watches.*

**WATCHING PRIEST:** They're the wrong candles. These're feckin' christening candles. You want a number 12 candle for this.

*The other priest looks annoyed. Cut to Dougal and Ted, sitting amongst all the chaos.*

**DOUGAL:** Excited, Ted?

**TED:** Ah, yes.

**DOUGAL:** Something to tell the grandchildren about.

*Ted gives Dougal a look. Cut to a priest, drinking casually from a styrofoam cup, looking at some cue cards that are being held up by another priest for him to check out.*

**PRIEST:** Dominus albe turum . . . Change 'Dominus' to 'Cannus'. (*He motions for the priest to flip to the next card. The priest does so.*) I want you faster than this when we're on, Charlie. 'Teus Medras In Tumo Caneto'. God, who wrote this stuff?

*Another priest raising a chalice. A priest behind him guides his elbow.*

**PRIEST BEHIND:** You're going to have to bring it up quicker.

*He shows him how to do it.*

**FRONT PRIEST:** You're goin' to have to cue me. I'll be lookin' at Cyril, so I won't have to

see the audience.

**PRIEST BEHIND:** Uh-huh. That's no problem.

*Back to Ted and Dougal. A priest wearing a pair of earphones approaches Dougal.*

**TED:** Oh, God, I'm so nervous. I've never spoken in front of this many people before.

**DOUGAL:** Just imagine them naked, Ted. That's supposed to calm you down.

**TED:** I'm not imagining all these people naked! My brain might explode. Where's Todd, by the way? I thought he wanted to see this . . .

**EARPHONES:** Hi. Who's Ted and who's Dougal?

**DOUGAL:** Ah, I'm Ted, that's Dougal there.

**TED:** No, Dougal . . . sorry about that. I'm Dougal, he's Ted.

**EARPHONES** (*to Dougal*)**:** We need you by the stage, Father . . .

**TED** (*to Dougal*)**:** Why does he need you by the stage? He must mean me.

SCENE 31A INT./DAY 5
SET: PAROCHIAL HOUSE
*Jack is asleep. Todd kicks open the door. He has a notebook and is writing notes. He looks at the display case for the award, and scribbles something down. A floorboard creaks. He takes out a very flash-looking hip flask from his jacket, unscrews the top and is about take a slug.*

**JACK** (*through a sleepy haze, his eyes still closed*)**:** Drink? Driiiink?

*Todd looks at him, puzzled. He walks over and holds the flask near his head. He moves it towards Jack.*

**JACK:** Drink? Driiink? Driiink?

*As he moves it towards him, Jack's 'Drink?' becomes louder and he becomes more agitated in his sleep. When he draws it away, Jack gets quieter.*

**JACK:** Drink! Driiink . . . driiink . . .

*Todd puts the hip flask back in his coat pocket.*

**JACK** (*sadly*)**:** Drink? Drink? Driiiink!

*He slumps back into sleep again. Todd continues taking notes.*

SCENE 32 EXT./DAY 5
SET: SIDE OF STAGE
*Ted is placed by the side of the stage. The earphones priest waits beside him. We see a wide view of the impressive set-up. On stage is a very handsome priest, Father Dick Mayo. Standing beside him is a co-presenter nun, Sister Helen Locklear.*

**DICK:** Welcome to the fifth annual presentation of the Golden Cleric.

**HELEN:** Every year, the Catholic Church gives an award to a priest for outstanding achievement . . .

**DICK:** The award is presented to individuals who have helped advance the cause of the church through their actions . . .

**HELEN:** This year's winner is someone who has overcome controversy in the past. . .

**TED:** Nonononononononono . . .

**HELEN:** . . . when rumours of financial irregularities . . . threatened his career in the Church.

**TED:** Shush, shush, nonononononono . . .

**DICK:** But after a thorough investigation, no charges were brought . . .

**TED** (*offscreen, distant*): *. . . money was resting in my account. . .*

**HELEN:** Even though authorities were confused by what they saw as 'bizarre irregularities' in his accounts . . .

**TED** (*offscreen*): *Yes, they've had enough of that now . . .*

**DICK:** But he has overcome these personal setbacks to become this year's winner of the Golden Cleric! Father Ted Crilly!

*Ted goes up and accepts the award. He walks to the microphone. Cut to Father Billy standing beside Father Terry.*

**BILLY:** Oh, God, I hope he doesn't start going on about himself and settling old scores in public. He always used to do that in the debating society in Saint Colm's.

**TED:** Well. (*Pause.*) Well, well, well . . . (*He looks at the audience.*) I see a lot of familiar faces here today. Some more welcome than others. It looks as though I've had the last laugh on a lot of people who didn't really think I had it in me to be a brilliant priest. But what I would say to

those people is; look at me now. I am truly, as James Cagney said in that film about gangsters, 'on top of the world, Ma!'

*Cut to Billy who has put his hand over his eyes in a sort of 'Ohhhh, God' gesture. Fade out. Fade back. A little bit later. Billy and Terry look irritated and bored. Cut back to Ted on the platform.*

**TED:** . . . but I eventually escaped from his headlock. And now where are you, Father Eamonn Hunter? Working with some pygmies in the South Seas. And where am I? Accepting a Golden Cleric Award for being a top priest.

*Fade out. Fade back. We notice there's less people in the seats. Ted natters away, oblivious.*

**TED:** 'Yes, of course', he thought. 'It'd be a great idea to pour water on this young novice's mattress'. But of course, thirty years later, the smile has been very much wiped off Father Barry Kiernan's face. I believe he couldn't take the demands of the priesthood, and became a mandrax fiend.

*Fade out. Fade back. There are only a few priests left-the ones from the lingerie section.*

**TED:** . . . and now we move on to 'liars'. Ahem. Father Peter Sorton. Father Desmond Cairns . . .

SCENE 33 INT./EVENING 5
SET: PAROCHIAL HOUSE
*Ted is examining the award. A few remaining priests – Fathers Terry, Billy, Reilly, Fitzgerald, Cleary, Deegan and an older priest – look on. There is a slightly embarrassed atmosphere.*

**BILLY** (*unconvincingly*): Well . . . great speech, Ted.

**TED:** It went well, didn't it?

**OLD PRIEST:** You were wandering around in there for three hours?

**TERRY:** Yes. It's Ireland's biggest lingerie section, I understand.

*Mrs Doyle comes in with a tray.*

**MRS DOYLE:** Tea for everyone?

**TED:** Right . . . Oh, Mrs Doyle, put all that away and relax. We're going to try out the Tea-master.

**BILLY:** How's it work, Ted?

**MRS DOYLE:** But . . . b-b-b– . . . can I just put in the milk?

**TED:** Look, you just put the cup in there, slide in one of these cartridges and the tea just comes out here.

**TERRY:** God, that's fantastic.

**TED:** Yes, well, now that I've got an award, I can't be seen drinking tea that's just been made in a pot. Hah! The idea!

*Everyone groups around the machine, leaving Mrs Doyle on her own. With her upper lip trembling madly, she leaves the room, unnoticed.*

**FITZGERALD** (*boring voice*)**:** It just seems just too good to be true. What's the catch?

**TED:** Sorry, Father? To be honest, your voice is just so boring, I couldn't concentrate on what you were saying.

**FITZGERALD:** Well, I do have an incredibly boring voice. I was just saying . . . what's the catch?

*Pause.*

**TED:** Sorry! I didn't get it there either.

**REILLY** (*very dynamic voice*)**:** Ted, I was just thinking, the Tea-master thing . . . there must be some sort of catch.

**TED:** A catch? No, there's no catch. Watch this.

*Ted slides a cartridge in. Immediately there is a massive grinding noise that goes on for ages, blocking all other noise out. It finishes and Ted takes out the cup.*

**TED:** Y'see? Perfect. Now, perhaps you could all tell me what you thought of my speech.

*Jack bursts in. The priests return to their chairs. The older priest is sitting on Jack's chair. Jack walks calmly to his chair and sits down on the old priest, crushing him against the chair. Jack doesn't seem to notice.*

**TED:** Ah, Father Jack? Could you, ah . . . there's actually someone . . .

**JACK:** Wha—?

**TED:** There's someone . . . ah . . . you all right, Father?

**PRIEST:** Yes, I . . . it's actually quite hard to breathe . . .

*Jack looks around in confusion, wondering where the voice is coming from.*

**TED:** Father, could you just . . .

**PRIEST** (*red-faced and husky-voiced*)**:** I really am finding it quite hard to breathe . . .

**TED:** Just stand up!

*The priest wheezes unsettlingly.*

**JACK:** What?

**TED:** Dougal, quick! Put on that music!

**DOUGAL:** What?

**TED:** Put on the music that makes Father Jack stand up!

*Dougal bends over the record player. After a moment, 'La Marseillaise' starts up. Jack cocks his head, then slowly, uncertainly, stands up. Ted pulls the still-gasping priest away.*

**TED:** Sorry about that. For some reason, that bit of music always makes Father Jack stand to attention.

**JACK:** Up! Up! Up!

**TED:** Yes. Father Jack likes us all to stand when that comes on.

**JACK:** Sing!

*Cut to a wide shot of them all. Jack stands proudly to attention while the others sing along half-heartedly to the words. Fade down.*

SCENE 34 INT./EVENING 5
SET: PAROCHIAL HOUSE
*Fade up. The men are still standing up. They mumble the end of the song in a very unconvincing manner, trailing off and overlapping each other. Father Cleary walks over to Jack, holding a cracker.*

**JACK:** Again, again, again.

**CLEARY:** Father, will you have a go of this with me?

*Jack, slightly confused, reaches out for the cracker. Cleary grips it and pulls back. Jack looks confused and angry. He starts pulling hard.*

**JACK:** Arrrch! GERRAWAY!!!

*Jack stands up and leans backwards with the cracker. Cleary starts to look uncertain.*

CLEARY: No, Father, it's just a bit of fun.

JACK: Aaarrrggghhh!!!

*Jack punches Cleary and takes the cracker. He holds it up in the air with a victorious yell, then runs towards the window and tries to jump out. However, he simply whacks against it and falls back on to the floor.*

TED: Ah, yes, we sort of thought Father Jack was jumping through that window a little too much, so we put in Plexiglass. Anyway! My speech! Tell me what you thought of it.

DOUGAL: Will we have a look at the Christmas film?

PRIESTS: Yaaaayyy!!!

*Dougal switches on the television. All the priests flutter excitedly.*

TV ANNOUNCER: That was *Indiana Jones and the Last Crusade*. And now, a special extended Latin Mass from Saint Martin's Cathedral in Dublin.

*The mood descends a notch or two. Ted and Dougal look at each other.*

TED: Oh . . . great . . . Mass.

*We see that the other priests aren't terribly enthusiastic either. They ad lib fake keenness. Ted and Dougal sit, pretending to pay attention to the Mass. They occasionally shift their eyes to look at the other priests. Everyone is quite obviously bored out of their minds, sneaking guilty looks at each other.*

TERRY: God, I've just remembered. I've got to do something terribly important . . . (*They all look at him.*) Actually what I have to do, I've, I've just remembered. I have to go and phone this fella on Death Row I befriended recently. He's being executed tomorrow for mass murder so I'd say he's very low at the moment.

TED: God almighty. And did he do it?

*Terry wasn't expecting this question. He thinks about it.*

TERRY: I don't know . . . yes.

BILLY: Do you need any help, talking to him?

TERRY: Ah . . .

BILLY: 'Cause, he might get hysterical and start crying, and then I could say, 'Pull yourself together, man!'

TERRY: All right.

*Pause.*

FITZGERALD: There's been a big accident. So I should go, too.

*They all look at him.*

FITZGERALD: I got a phonecall there when . . . you were all . . . somewhere else. So I should go.

BILLY: We're all off, so!

*Todd enters.*

BILLY: Father Unctious, are you coming? I could give you a lift.

TODD: Eh . . . no. I'll stay a while. Oh fantastic . . . Mass. Father Ultan Crosby is doing the Mass. (*He nods at the television.*) I'm a huge fan of his. He gives good Mass.

BILLY: He what?

TODD: He really knows how to work the altar. (*He watches the set in admiration.*) Look at that chalice work . . . effortless.

REILLY: Anyway, we'll be off. See you all again.

ALL PRIESTS: Bye, thanks, etc. . . . .

TED: Bye! Thanks for coming to my awards ceremony where I won an award!

*The priests leave. Ted and Dougal turn round and watch the television. Ted looks over at Todd, who smiles in an 'I'm really enjoying this' kind of way. Ted smiles, gives him a wink and sinks further in his seat. Fade down.*

SCENE 35A INT./LATER THAT EVENING 5
SET: PAROCHIAL HOUSE
*Fade up. Ted, Dougal and Todd are sound asleep. From behind the sofa, a groggy Jack stands up. He looks at the television, which is still showing the Mass. He looks at the three, goes over to the set and switches the channel.*

ANNOUNCER: Now on BBC1, the director's cut of *Jurassic Park* with extra dinosaurs.

SCENE 36 INT./NIGHT 5
SET: TED AND DOUGAL'S BEDROOM
*Ted and Dougal are in bed. Ted looks very grumpy.*

**TED:** Well, that was a fantastic day.

**DOUGAL:** It was, Ted, wasn't it? What a brilliant day. Fantastic fun! That was one of the best Christmas Days ever!

**TED:** I was being sarcastic, Dougal.

**DOUGAL:** Oh, right. Ah, so was I.

**TED:** I don't think everyone was nice enough about my speech. Actually, I was glad when they left. You could *feel* the begrudgery and the jealousy leaving the room with them. (*He whispers slightly.*) And what's that fella doing, still here? I didn't invite him to stay. Did you?

**DOUGAL:** Huh?

**TED:** No, actually I barred you from inviting anyone after that tramp stayed for a week. Remember that? When I was away?

**DOUGAL:** He wasn't a tramp, Ted. He was the Prime Minister of France.

**TED:** No, he wasn't, Dougal. He just lied to you.

**DOUGAL:** Oh, actually, he did, yeah. And he stole the video.

**TED:** Todd Unctious, Todd Unctious . . . I don't remember him at all. Who the hell is he?

**DOUGAL:** Maybe he had a nickname. You know, like Terry Wogan.

**TED:** Terry Wogan? What's his nickname?

**DOUGAL:** What? (*Pause.*) Oh, you mean that's his *real* name!? Ah, well, don't let it worry you, Ted. He'll be gone tomorrow.

*There is a knock on the door. Father Todd sticks his head round the door.*

**TODD:** There y'are!

**TED:** Aha! Hello, there!

*Todd comes in. He is wearing white Y-fronts and nothing else. Ted pulls the covers up slightly in an embarrassed, slightly guarded way. Dougal does the same.*

**TODD** (*to Dougal*): Look at you, lyin' in there like a big eejit. Ha, ha!

*Ted and Dougal make quiet, polite 'ha, ha', noises. Todd stands between the beds, hands on hips, legs apart.*

**TODD:** Here we are now, anyway. All the lads.

**TED:** Yes . . . yes . . .

*Todd sits at the end of the bed.*

**TODD:** Just like the old days, eh? Do you remember all the fun we used to have in the showers?

*He picks up a towel and flicks it at Ted playfully. Ted cowers.*

**TODD:** Do you still have the big old hairy arse?

**TED:** Ah, fluff, Todd. It wasn't hair. It was a bit of downy fluff.

**TODD:** Ah, God . . . memories. Do you remember you all mitched off to that Dana concert? I couldn't go because I was recovering from a massive car accident. Did I ever show you the scar?

*He walks over to Ted and points to a scar stretching down his leg from his boxer shorts. His leg is possibly a little too close to Ted's face for his liking. Ted pretends to take in the scar while looking at everything else in the room.*

**TODD:** Y'see, there . . .

**TED:** God, yes . . .

**TODD:** See that little crescent shape . . .

**TED:** Phew. Yes.

**TODD:** . . . And this series of . . . Can you see them? . . . Tiny indentations along my inner thigh . . .

**TED:** That's . . . that's really . . .

**TODD** (*tracing it with his finger*): And they run all the way up there to my groin . . .

**TED** (*jumps out of bed*): Whoah! What do you say we all go to the pictures? I feel like going to see a good film.

**TODD:** Ted, it's half one in the morning.

**TED:** Oh, right.

**TODD:** No, you go off to sleep. I was just wandering around. Sometimes I can't sleep at night and I need a good walk to calm meself down. You don't mind, do you?

**TED:** No, no. You do that.

**TODD:** Good night, so. And . . . Happy

Christmas, Ted.

*He holds his arms out. Ted realises that Todd wants a hug. Like a man condemned, he opens his arms and Todd embraces him. Ted's not having the greatest time of his life. Todd disengages. He does some pretend boxing and laughs. Then he leaves the room.*

**TED:** Well, I'm not moving out of here until tomorrow. I don't want to bump into that weirdo walking around the house in his nudiness. Goodnight, Dougal.

SCENE 37 INT./NIGHT 5
SET: PAROCHIAL HOUSE
*Jack comes into the living room, in his dirty, rotten pyjamas, and turns on the light. He walks over to the fireplace and picks up a massive bottle of whiskey and a funnel. As he walks back, he steps in front of the award and the floorboards creak. There's a bump from upstairs, we hear footsteps running down the stairs, and Ted bursts into the room wielding a tennis racket.*

**TED:** Get away from that award!

**JACK:** Feck off!

**TED:** Oh, Father, it's you. Right. Eh, turn off the light before you go up, won't you? And please, don't slam the door.

*Jack makes a grunting noise. Ted leaves the room and Jack follows him. He stops at the light, gives the unseen Ted the finger and goes out of the room, closing the door gently behind him. But before it closes, he thinks better of it, and slams the door.*

SCENE 38 INT./NIGHT 5
SET: TED AND DOUGAL'S BEDROOM
*Ted and Dougal hear the slam and jump with the shock.*

SCENE 39 EXT./NIGHT 5
SET: PAROCHIAL HOUSE
*The slam causes loads of birds to burst from the trees.*

SCENE 40 INT./NIGHT 5
SET: CANADIAN SKI RESORT
*We see Larry Duff, in a neck brace and lots of plaster. He hears the slam, and turns his neck slightly.*

**LARRY:** Aaaaaowww!

*We hear a low rumble. Larry looks puzzled. He tries*

*to turn and sees . . . an avalanche starting. The avalanche roars down and mingles with Larry's scream.*

SCENE 41 INT./NIGHT 5
SET: PAROCHIAL HOUSE
*Back to the living room. Pause. We hear a small shuffling noise. Cut to the grille in the ceiling over the award. It is moved to one side. Cut back to the living room. Pause. Suddenly, with a 'zzzzzz' noise, a figure descends into shot, suspended from wires, right in front of the award. He is dressed in cool 'Mission Impossible' cat-burglar gear. He is suspended directly in front of the award. He sticks a suction cup on to the glass and starts running a glass cutter around it. Suddenly there is a noise. He pulls on something and shoots back up with the same 'zzzzzz' noise. Mrs Doyle comes into the room, looking shifty. In one hand she holds a screwdriver. She goes up to the Teamaster, opens it and starts fiddling about inside it. We hear things breaking and snapping.*

**MRS DOYLE:** Heh, heh, heh . . .

*She finishes and walks out. The figure descends immediately with the 'zzzzzz' noise and gets back to work. He suddenly hears a noise and pulls the control for his wires; it brings him halfway up, but then something snaps with a 'ping' noise and he's stuck there, pointing slightly head-downwards.*

*Dougal enters the room, carrying a glass of milk, and turns on the light. The burglar waits for the worst. Dougal walks over to the television, completely oblivious of the figure hanging and turning slightly, right beside him – and switches it on. He sits down to watch. The burglar hangs there, silent and confused. We hear the dialogue from the television.*

**MAN 1** (*American accent*): . . . What's wrong, McKenzie?

**MAN 2:** I don't want you to panic . . . but there's a dangerous burglar in the house.

**MAN 1:** What?!

**MAN 2:** In fact, he may be in this very room. Hiding.

*Dougal looks a bit spooked. He turns around, checking there's no one behind him.*

**MAN 2:** A burglar. In the room, you say. My God.

**MAN 1:** Yes. In fact, I think it's safe to say that

the burglar is definitely in the room.

**MAN 2:** But where could he be?

**MAN 1:** There he is!

**MAN 2:** Where?

**MAN 1:** Right there, man! Use your eyes!

*Dougal squints at the television, trying to see him.*

**MAN 1:** THERE!

*Dramatic music. Both Dougal and the burglar jump with the shock. Dougal squints again, looking at the screen.*

SCENE 42 INT./NIGHT 5
SET: TED AND DOUGAL'S BEDROOM
*Ted tosses and turns. He wakes up. He looks at Dougal's bed. Dougal isn't there. Ted shakes his head and gets out of bed.*

**TED:** Dougal, Dougal, Dougal . . . you'll have nightmares . . .

SCENE 43 INT./NIGHT 5
SET: PAROCHIAL HOUSE
*The burglar is still hanging from the wire. He stays perfectly still. Dougal hears Ted coming down, turns off the television and stands up. The burglar finally gets his harness thingy to work and whizzes up into the air, out of shot. Ted comes into the room.*

**TED:** . . . Dougal, I thought I told you not to watch that film . . .

**DOUGAL:** No, Ted, I wasn't watching it. I just came down to . . . to . . . ah . . . (*He looks at his milk.*) . . . carry the milk . . . around.

**TED:** Go on. Up to bed with you.

*Dougal skips out. Ted is about to follow him when he looks over at his award. He goes to it and takes it out of the case, poses with it, and then starts walking around the room in an extraordinarily poncy way, like a particularly vain king or Pope with his sceptre. He looks absolutely ridiculous.*

*In the background, Todd (the burglar), trying desperately to adjust his harness, starts slipping down into shot. Finally he hangs there, unable to do anything. He looks at Ted, who is now standing very close, with his back to him.*

**TED:** Ah, Your Holiness, hello. Mr De Niro, Bob. I enjoyed you in *The Godfather II*. Ah,

President Robinson, well done on everything. (*He turns around so that his nose almost brushes Todd's.*) Ah, Todd. (*Beat*) Aaaaarrrrgggghhh!!!

SCENE 44 INT./DAY 6
SET: PAROCHIAL HOUSE
*Ted is talking to Sergeant Hodgins.*

**HODGINS:** He won't be doing any more burglaries where he's going.

**TED:** Where's that?

**HODGINS:** Well . . . prison.

**TED:** Of course, of course, sorry . . . But Sergeant, how did he know so much about me?

*Todd is being led out.*

**HODGINS:** I'm curious about that myself . . . Unctious, if that is your real name.

**TODD:** I already told you it wasn't.

**HODGINS:** Did you? Oh, right, sorry. Forgot. Tell us how you knew so much about Father Crilly.

**TODD:** Is this off the record?

**HODGINS:** Of course.

**TODD:** I was in Cellbridge a few days ago, got to talking to this old priest in a bar . . .

SCENE 45 INT./NIGHT X
SET: AMERICAN BAR
*We see Todd, listening to someone in a bar. We see a grizzled old priest like Tom Waits in another ten years - leaning on a bar in front of a bar sign for 'Miller' or another American brand. We hear country/honky tonk music in the background. Over this, Todd's narration continues, but we hear occasional snatches of the old priest's dialogue too - rising up through the gaps in Todd's spiel.*

**TODD:** . . . he was cagey at first, but a few shots of J.D. and he was singing like a bird . . .

**OLD PRIEST** (*in hokey American accent*): The Golden Cleric, they call it givin' it to an old pal of mine . . . Ted Crilly . . . met him on Dollymount Strand . . .

**TODD:** . . . as I listened, a plan formed in my head. We drank long into the night, me paying,

of course, him spilling his guts on the subject of a certain Father Ted Crilly . . .

**OLD PRIEST** (*drunker*): . . . got a mane of white hair kinda like you'd get on a mule . . . used to wet his bed in Saint Colm's . . . (*gestures with fingers*). . . big hairy ass . . .

**TODD:** The longer he talked, the better it got . . .

**OLD PRIEST:** . . . 'resting in his account', heh, heh . . . lives with a pig-ignorant old timer called Jack Hackett, and a poor, strange idyut-boy name of McGuire. . .

SCENE 46 INT./NIGHT X
SET: SLEAZY HOTEL BEDROOM
*The old priest flops onto the bed. A pair of hands come into shot and starts to pull off his trousers.*

**TODD:** After that, all I needed was the right costume . . .

**OLD PRIEST** (*almost unconscious*): . . . five-bedroomed house . . . Ted sleeps directly above living room . . . no alarm system . . .

*We see Todd putting the trousers to one side. Fade down. Fade up, and Todd is putting on the last of the other priest's clothes in front of the mirror. He looks exactly the same as when he was in his own clothes. He sizes himself up.*

**TODD:** Perfect.

SCENE 47 INT./DAY 6
SET: PAROCHIAL HOUSE
*Back to Ted, Todd and Hodgins in the living room.*

**TED:** But, you're a priest. I mean, why?

**TODD:** It's a long story. I used to be like you, a completely average, bog-standard, run-of-the-mill priest. But then I won first prize in the

County Westmeath Priest of the Year Competition. I guess it went to my head. Before I knew it, I was hitting the altar wine too much, going easy on people in Confession, getting backhanders for doing quicker Masses. All I wanted was trophies and prizes, and the one that really got me hard was the Golden Cleric . . .

**TED:** No, no, no, Todd. Sorry, what I was going to ask was . . . you're a priest. Why did you wear the other priest's clothes?

**TODD:** Oh. I'm not sure. It was just goin' that way.

**HODGINS:** Well, I've got bad news for you, so-called Todd Unctious. That wasn't off the record! I'm using that as evidence against you!

**TODD:** Oh! That's completely unfair!!

**HODGINS:** Take him away.

*A policeman leads him out through the doorway. Dougal enters.*

**TED:** Thank you, Sergeant!

**HODGINS:** There'll be a reward in this, Father! You both should be very proud of yourselves.

**TED:** A reward. Well. Not such a bad Christmas after all.

**MRS DOYLE** (*offscreen*): Well done, Father!

*We see Mrs Doyle on the dangerous window ledge. She finishes adjusting something and then jumps off. Instead of falling, however, she just hangs there. We realise that she is using the burglar's wire contraption when she pulls something and lowers gently to the floor.*

**TED:** That's a handy old thing, isn't it, Mrs Doyle? Modern technology is great, isn't it?

**MRS DOYLE:** Oh, yes, Father, thanks again. It's the best Christmas present ever!

**TED:** Well, what about the tea-making machine?

**MRS DOYLE:** Oh . . . yes . . .

**TED:** I'll go and crank it up now.

*He walks over and slips in a cartridge. It makes its usual horrible noise. Mrs Doyle looks worried. Then it starts making another strange noise, exactly like someone hacking up a particularly horrible ball of phlegm and spitting it into a cup.*

**TED:** Euuch. What was *that*? I didn't like that sound at all. Sorry, Mrs Doyle, we'll have to get it fixed.

**MRS DOYLE:** No, Father, don't! Please!

**TED:** What?

**MRS DOYLE:** Father, I *like* the whole tea-making thing. You know, the playful splash of the tea as it hits the bottom of the cup . . . the sheer unbridled excitement of adding the milk and seeing it settle for a brief moment on the surface, before it gently filters down through the rest of the cup, changing the colour from dark brown to . . . a kind of lighter brown. Perching an optional Jaffa Cake on the saucer . . . like a proud soldier standing to attention beside a giant . . . cup of tea . . . Just think, Father. Remember all the great times we've had, when I used to make the tea . . .

*We see Ted's expression turn to one of nostalgia.*

SCENE 48 INT./DAY X
SET: PAROCHIAL HOUSE
*We see loads of flashbacks of Mrs Doyle offering teas to Ted. They're all exactly the same – Ted makes the same 'Ah, tea!' gesture in each one – but her aprons are a different colour. We hear accompanying nostalgic music.*

SCENE 49 INT./DAY 6
SET: PAROCHIAL HOUSE
**TED:** Mrs Doyle, you're right. Tea out of a machine is like . . . milk from a baby's bottle. A baby doesn't want milk from a bottle, he wants it from his mother's . . . (*He realises he has made an analogy he doesn't want to continue.*) Anyway, Mrs Doyle, why don't you make us both a *normal* cup of tea?

**MRS DOYLE:** Right-O, Father. And don't worry, it'll be 'tea-riffic'.

*Everyone laughs as in a Lassie film, heartily and for too long. Mrs Doyle leaves the room. They all stop laughing.*

**TED:** 'Tea-riffic'. Bloody hell. You know, Dougal, being in the priesthood – it's not about awards and glamour. It's about hard graft. It's about applying yourself to the spiritual needs of your parishioners. You know, that Todd Unctious fella there . . . that could have been me.

**DOUGAL:** Really? Ahhh . . . that would explain a lot. *Pause.*

**TED** (*beat*): I don't think you quite picked up on what I meant there.

*Dougal looks even more confused. The telephone rings. Dougal picks it up.*

**TED:** I could have turned into a bad priest, like him. Selfish, arrogant, not giving a damn about my parishioners.

*Dougal puts his hand over the mouthpiece.*

**DOUGAL:** Ted, it's Mrs Gilcuddy. She wants you to do one of those remembrance Masses.

**TED:** I'm not in.

**DOUGAL** (*into the receiver*): Ah, he's not in at the moment. All right, so, bye.

*He throws the receiver on to the table.*

**TED:** Dougal, I'm sorry about my recent silliness. I think you deserve this award as much as me.

**DOUGAL:** Oh, well, Ted, thank you. That's brilliant. Thanks very much.

**TED:** So . . . will I put it back in the case?

**DOUGAL:** Better, I suppose.

**TED:** And my name on the plaque, we needn't bother changing that.

**DOUGAL:** No. I know the award's mine, and that's good enough for me.

**TED:** I think I'll run the bath. That'll calm me down after the day.

**DOUGAL:** OK, so.

*Ted leaves the room. Dougal makes sure he's gone, then walks over to the trophy. He picks it up (there is a creaking noise) and starts walking around with it in a very poncy way. Dramatic close-up of Dougal. He starts laughing in a vaguely mad-scientist-type way.*

**DOUGAL:** Heh, heh, heh . . . HEH, HEH, HEH . . . HAAA, HA, HAA, HAAA, HAAAAA!!!! . . .

*He is cut short when he sees Ted standing at the doorway, looking puzzled.*

**TED:** What are you doing, Dougal?

**DOUGAL** (*back to normal*): Oh, nothing. Just having a bit of a laugh.

**THE END**

# aRe you RIGht theRe, father teD?

**GRAHAM:** The great thing about an imaginary location such as Craggy Island is that it can expand and contract according to our needs. So in one episode we can say it's as small as four football fields, and in another it can be so big as to support a Chinatown that Ted has somehow never stumbled upon. The only constant is that it doesn't have a west side – that fell into the sea in Episode One.

The opening scene, which finds Ted in a delightful new parish, is actually an echo of the very first scene in Episode One, when Ted was asking Jack whether he could possibly say Mass at any time in the future. It's impossible to imagine Jack saying Mass, I know. We decided early on, in fact, that you would never see any of them saying Mass or doing any proper priestly business. It didn't feel right, somehow. I'd like to say we had some high-minded purpose in writing this one, but really we were just trying to be funny. If it does comment on racism at all, then fine. I'm really not sure what kind of comment we could possibly be making . . . racism is bad, perhaps? Pretty controversial stuff!

**ARTHUR:** This started with an idea, at that time unrelated to a theme, that Ted would pull a Chinese face without knowing that there were Chinese people watching. Then we realised this could tie in with one of our really old ideas – and possibly one of our first – that Craggy Island had been harbouring a Nazi for fifty years without anyone knowing. There *is* a connection between Nazism and Rome: after the war, there was some sort of Nazi escape route that led to the Vatican.

Another take on the racist theme, and a further embarrassment for Ted, is the way the Craggy Islanders react. They think they ought to become zealous racists – which is exactly the opposite of what Ted wants. It's the reverse of their reaction in *The Passion of Saint Tibulus*, when Ted actively wanted them to follow his example – which they spectacularly failed to do.

Someone asked why Jack keeps hiding in cupboards and clocks in the episode. It's this condition he developed. We called it claustrophilia: an addiction to small places.

## PART ONE

SCENE 1 EXT./DAY 1
SET: ANOTHER PAROCHIAL HOUSE
*We see a lovely Parochial House in beautiful surroundings. Trees, nice lawn, etc. Birds sing in the trees and it's a beautiful sunny day. We see a caption that reads 'Castlelawn Parochial House, Dublin'.*

SCENE 2 INT./DAY 1
SET: ANOTHER PAROCHIAL HOUSE
*A modern but cosy-looking Parochial House. Ted is sitting with a glass of port in one hand, looking at some notes on his lap. An older, kind-looking priest sits nearby, smoking a pipe. A man in a nice suit is poring over some ledgers on a table in the background.*

**TED:** What about Tuesday? Can you do the eleven o'clock?

**OLD** (*posh, south Dublin accent*): Ted, I'll do the eleven and the twelve. You should have a rest after that weekend away.

**TED:** Well, Paris does tend to tire me out. Thanks, Father!

*A younger priest bounds in. He has a white sweater tied around his shoulders.*

**YOUNG** (*posh accent*): I'm off for a game. Ted, care to join me?

**TED:** No, thanks, Darren! What time are we off to the Curragh for the races?

**DARREN:** I suppose after lunch. Oh, and Mrs Dunne hopes you like pheasant!

**TED:** I love pheasant! (*Father Darren bounds off.*) Ah, yes, this is what it's all about. A fine port, beautiful surroundings and intelligent company.

**OLD:** Did you not have all that at your last parish?

**TED** (*darkly*): No.

**OLD:** Dublin seems to suit you, though. You've got a newfound gleam in your eye.

**TED:** Oh, yes, I'll be staying here for a good while . . . as long as I don't somehow mess it up for myself by doing something stupid!

*The man at the table turns round. He peers over the top of half-spectacles.*

**MAN:** Most of these accounts are in order, Father Smith, but I wonder if I could ask Father Crilly a thing or two about some of these things he's put down under 'expenses' . . .

SCENE 3 INT./NIGHT 1
SET: FRONT DOOR
*The front door opens, revealing Dougal.*

**DOUGAL:** TED!!!!!

*We see Ted standing there in the rain, carrying two suitcases, dripping wet, miserable.*

SCENE 4 INT./DAY 2
SET: PAROCHIAL HOUSE
*Ted is sitting at the table, looking grumpy. The house seems to have become very grim since he's been away. We hear a constant squeaky, repetitive noise coming from somewhere in the room.*

**TED:** What's that incredibly annoying noise?

**DOUGAL:** That's Renaldo. It was a bit lonely without you, Ted, so I got a hamster instead.

**TED:** Yes. Can I ask, though . . . does he ever stop running in that *fecking* wheel?

*We see a hamster in a wheel. This is where the spinning, squeaky noise was coming from. Dougal is sitting at the table, mending a tiny bicycle.*

**DOUGAL:** No. (*He holds up the bicycle.*) Ever since he rode this into his feedtray, he's had to use the wheel. But don't worry, I think there's just something wrong with the brakes.

*Ted tries to take this in.*

**TED:** Does he ever stop, though? You'd think Tommy Lee Jones was after him.

*Dougal continues to work on the bicycle.*

**TED:** How long has Jack been living in there?

**DOUGAL:** Ah, he started just a few days after you left.

*Pause. Ted sits there, still in the same depressed slump. The wheel squeaks away relentlessly and in the background we can see the wheel spinning.*

*Suddenly Jack calmly gets out of a chest that was sitting in one corner of the room, walks over to the table and takes a sandwich from it. Then he goes back to the chest and climbs inside. Ted watches all this dispassionately.*

TED: Maybe he's agoraphobic . . .

DOUGAL: Jack? Scared of fights? I don't think so, Ted.

*Ted walks to the window and looks outside. Suddenly Mrs Doyle falls off the roof outside, passing by the window on her way. Ted stares out dispassionately. Pause.*

TED (*almost to himself*): Mrs Doyle just fell off the roof. (*Pause.*) I think I might go out, Dougal – visit Father Fitzpatrick. I think he has a book belonging to me . . .

*Ted puts on his coat. He is stopped halfway by the hamster's wheel suddenly speeding up, like a washing machine on spin-cycle. The hutch starts shaking. Ted watches, mesmerised.*

SCENE 5 EXT./DAY 2
SET: SEAMUS FITZPATRICK'S PAROCHIAL HOUSE
*An old, grumpy-looking priest, Father Seamus Fitzpatrick, is looking through a shelf of books. In the background Wagner music plays on a stereo. There are two doors in the room, one leading out into the hall, the other closed and padlocked.*

FITZPATRICK: . . . Let's see, let's see . . . (*We see Ted standing nearby. Fitzpatrick takes an old, dusty book from the shelf.*) . . . Ah, yes . . . *Humanae Vitae* . . . I sometimes leaf through it just to remind myself how far we've come . . . (*He puts it back on the shelf, then starts running his finger along the line.*) . . . The Celebration of the Christian Mystery . . . Daeus Canida . . . Ventra Mepolo . . . where is it, where is it . . . ah . . . Stephen King's *The Shining*. (*He takes it down and hands it to Ted.*) Here you are . . .

TED: Did you like it?

FITZPATRICK: . . . Well . . .

TED: Well, the one with the vampires is much better. But *Firestarter* is very good. It's about this psychic girl who can start fires on people just by looking at them. I'll get that one for you if you want.

FITZPATRICK: Ah . . . no. Thank you.

TED: OK, so . . . thanks for the tea! I'll see you next time we, ah . . we . . . Sorry about this, Father, but . . . if you don't mind me asking . . . what have you got a padlock on that door for? Is there something 'top secret' in there?!!

FITZPATRICK: Oh, my collection!

TED: Yes! I heard you have an interest in, ah, what was it? War memorabilia and all that.

FITZPATRICK: That's right, yes. Do you want to have a look?

TED: I'd love to!

*Fitzpatrick starts unlocking the latch. He opens the door. We don't see the whole room all at once – just one 'exhibit' at a time. First of all, they stop in front of a shell-casing with a Nazi insignia on the side.*

FITZPATRICK: This'd be from a German gun during the advance on Russia. See that? You see there's where the hammer strikes the shell-casing . . .

TED: Gosh, that's very interesting . . .

*They move on to another 'display'. In it we see lots of helmets.*

FITZPATRICK: These are helmets – infantry, mostly . . .

TED: These would be German as well, wouldn't they?

FITZPATRICK: That's right.

*The next exhibit is a full S.S. uniform on a tailor's dummy.*

TED: You don't have anything from the Allied side at all, do you?

FITZPATRICK: No, no, no. I wouldn't be interested in that type of thing, to be honest.

*Cut wide to reveal the room in its entirety. Nazi banners and flags lie everywhere. There is a massive swastika hanging over the whole display. Ted looks ever so slightly worried.*

TED: Right! Well, that's my curiosity satisfied . . .

*Fitzpatrick puts an arm round Ted's shoulder, and shows him a photograph.*

FITZPATRICK (*ignores him*): This man here, see him there beside the Führer? Sigmund Hoff. Did you know Sigmund would be the German equivalent of Seamus? That'd be *my* name if I'd been born in Germany . . . Stalingrad. God, we put up a great fight there.

TED: *We?* . . .

FITZPATRICK: We? Sorry, oh, no, I mean the Germans. Look. This is one of the last photographs taken of Herr Hitler. He's signing a few death warrants here.

TED: Yes, ha, ha . . . Funny how you get more right wing as you get older . . . anyway . . . It's great, all this stuff —

FITZPATRICK: A lot of people aren't too sure about it when they see it. But you seem genuinely interested.

TED: Oh, yes. I am genuinely interested.

*Ted is backing away and he steps on something. We hear an old man screaming. Ted realises he has stepped on someone's foot. What Ted thought to be another display covered by a blanket is in reality an old man.*

OLD MAN: Aaarrgh!!! Was ist das?

FITZPATRICK: What are you doing in here! I told you, no sleeping here!

*The man says something in German. Fitzpatrick*

responds in German. The man starts crying. He attempts a Nazi salute but Fitzpatrick grabs his arm and places it back by his side.

FITZPATRICK: This is just an old friend of mine, Ted. I'll see you again . . . (*The old man starts singing 'Deutschland über Alles'.*) Good luck Ted!

TED: Ah . . . yes . . . goodbye!

*Ted leaves, the two men shouting behind him.*

SCENE 6 INT./DAY 2
SET: HALL
*Ted is passing by a grandfather clock. He notices that it is showing the wrong time. He looks at his own watch, then adjusts the hands on the clock. As he moves it to four, we hear a muffled clank of the bell inside, followed by 'feck!'. The muffled bell sounds again, and we hear 'arse!' It rings again, we hear 'drink!'. Ted opens the front of the clock. We see Jack, who looks at Ted for a moment or two, then slowly closes the door.*

SCENE 7 INT./DAY 2
SET: PAROCHIAL HOUSE
*Dougal is reading a book. Ted walks in. He goes to the mantelpiece, puts his finger on it, and notices a lot of dust. He then runs his finger more slowly along the shelf and we cut to reveal that a large pyramid of dust has formed where his finger has stopped.*

TED: Right! That's it! I'm not living in filth any more! Dougal, we have to get this place cleaned. And look at you! Look at that hole in your tanktop. What if the parishioners saw that?

DOUGAL: Where, Ted— Ah, God, would you look at that—

*He stands up to examine a tiny hole in his sweater. He turns around while still looking at it and there is a massive hole in the back, one that exposes everything from shoulders to waistline. Ted sees something else.*

TED: And this here, look! A perfectly square bit of black dirt on the window. (*We see that it is a perfectly square bit of black dirt.*) How on earth can you get a perfectly square bit of black dirt on a window? Surely that's practically impossible!

DOUGAL: It's just, Mrs Doyle's back is very bad since she fell off the roof. She can't do any cleaning.*

TED: Well, then . . . damn it, I'm just going to come out and say it . . . We're going to have to clean the place ourselves!

DOUGAL (*gobsmacked*): What!!!!

TED: You heard me! Are you with me, Dougal?

DOUGAL: Well . . . yeah!

TED: Then let's go! Let's clean this mother!

DOUGAL: Yeah!

*They look around, unsure of what to do. The energy level drops back to zero before our eyes. Ted picks up a can of beer, carries it over to the bin, and drops it in, but cautiously, as if he's not sure he's doing it right.*

DOUGAL: What about that bit of the lamp that came off? I could pick that up.

TED: Good idea.

*Dougal picks it up slowly. He seems delighted to have accomplished this difficult task.*

DOUGAL: Wow.

TED: Well done, Dougal. (*Pause.*) I'm bored now.

DOUGAL: Yeah.

*Ted takes the lamp off him.*

TED: Dougal, look. (*He puts the lampshade on his head. He smiles and does a pathetic 'Chinaman' impression. Dougal doesn't laugh.*) I am Chinese, if you please . . . Come on, Dougal! Lighten up!

*He turns around, still doing his impression, and freezes. Outside, looking through the window with hurt and disappointed looks on their faces, are three Chinese people: a man, a woman, and their son, who looks about seventeen.*

TED: Uh . . . (*The Chinese people turn sadly and move away from the window. Ted's mouth drops open.*) Wha . . . wha . . . who . . . Dougal!! There were Chinese people there!

---

*In the final version, we inserted a scene here showing Mrs Doyle falling off the roof.

DOUGAL: Oh, right, yeah.

TED: They — I mean . . . what? What is . . . I mean . . .

DOUGAL: That's the Yin family. They live over there on the other side of the island.

TED: But . . . since when have Chinese people been living on the island?

DOUGAL: There's a load of them there in that Chinatown area.

TED: Chinatown area – there's a Chinatown on Craggy Island? But they . . . I wouldn't have . . . I wouldn't have done a Chinaman impression if I thought a Chinaman would actually see me doing a Chinaman impression!

DOUGAL: Why not, Ted?

TED: Because . . . because it's racist! They'll think I'm a racist! (*Putting on his coat.*) I've got to catch them and explain that I'm not a racist.

DOUGAL: You'd better be quick, Ted. They're getting into their car!

SCENE 8 EXT./DAY 2
SET: OUTSIDE PAROCHIAL HOUSE
*Ted is in front of the car. The engine has started and the driver is revving aggressively. Ted is in front of it, his hands outstretched.*

TED: . . . and basically, if I don't stretch my eyes like that from time to time, I get this thing the doctor calls 'fat eyes' . . . (*The driver starts beeping the horn furiously and revving towards Ted.*) . . . so I hope you wouldn't think that this'd be anything of a racial nature . . . (*He has to hop out of the way as the car goes past. He starts running alongside the car.*) . . . So I'm glad we cleared that up. Come again! See you, bye!!

*The car has driven off.*

SCENE 9 INT./DAY 2
SET: PAROCHIAL HOUSE
*Later the same day. Ted comes into the living room.*

DOUGAL: There you are, Ted. Where were you?

TED: I just went to order some stuff for the

house, get rid of this tat. Dougal, you don't think I upset those Chinese people earlier?

**DOUGAL:** I don't know, Ted. It's like the time when we had that variety show and you decided to do that impression of Stephen Hawking.

**TED:** Well, he's the last person you'd expect to turn up. That was a million-to-one chance. God, he can fairly move in that wheelchair when he's angry.

**DOUGAL:** Don't worry about it, Ted. (*He*

*points at Ted's bag.*) Ah, did you go to Habitat?

**TED:** No. Habit Hat. Like Habitat it sells soft furnishings, but also clothes for priests. It used to be called Habits and Hats, but when priests stopped wearing hats in 1965, they changed the name and started to sell soft furnishings instead. Instead of hats.

**DOUGAL:** Does it not get confused with Habitat, though?

**TED:** No, that's never happened. Except just there, when you did it.

**DOUGAL:** So, anyway, what stuff did you get?

**TED:** I got some priests' socks. Really black ones.

**DOUGAL:** I read somewhere – I think it was in an article about priests' socks – that priests' socks are blacker than any other type of socks.

**TED:** That's right. Sometimes you see lay people wearing what *look* like black socks, but if you look closely, you'll see that they're very, very, very, very, *very, very, very* . . . dark blue.

**DOUGAL:** Actually, that's true. I thought my Uncle Tommy was wearing black socks, but when I looked at them closely they were just very, very, very, very . . . *very, very, very, very* . . . dark blue.

**TED:** That's right. Don't ever get black socks from a normal shop, Dougal. They'll shaft you every time.

*Ted leaves. Dougal looks worried at this final thought.*

SCENE 10 EXT./DAY 2
SET: ROAD
*Ted comes out of the house. He sees Colm Matthews, an old farmer, walking along the road. He is some distance away, so he has to shout.*

**COLM:** Hello, there, Father!

**TED:** Ah, Colm, hello! Off on a stroll?

**COLM:** I am! Same as yourself!

**TED:** Good, good!

**COLM:** I hear you're a racist now, Father!

**TED:** What?!!

**COLM:** How'd you get interested in that type of thing?

**TED:** Who said I was a racist?

**COLM:** Everyone's saying it, Father. Should we all be racists now? What's the official line the Church is taking on this?

**TED:** No, no . . .

**COLM:** Only, the farm takes up most of the day, and at night I just like a cup of tea. I mightn't have the time to devote myself full time to the old racism. Who are we against, anyway?

*An old woman, Mrs Carberry, comes on the scene. She also stops several yards away.*

**MRS CARBERRY:** Good for you, Father!

**TED:** What? Oh, Mrs Carberry . . . what?

**MRS CARBERRY:** Good for you! Well, someone had the guts to stand up to them at last. Coming over here, taking our jobs and our women, and acting like they own the place. Well done, Father! Good for you! Good for you! I'd like to feckin' . . . (*She is apoplectic with rage. In an attack of physical inarticulacy, she punches the air suddenly as if attacking several people.*) FECKIN' GREEKS!!!!

**COLM:** It's not the Greeks, it's the Chinese he's after.

**TED:** I'm not after the Chinese!

**MRS CARBERRY:** I don't care who we get, as long as I can have a go at the Greeks. They invented gayness!

**TED:** Look, we're not having a go at

anybody! I'm not racist! All right? God!

*Ted storms off. Colm and Mrs Carberry look at each other. Then Colm walks off. Mrs Carberry has another brief attack.*

**MRS CARBERRY:** FECKIN' GREEKS!!!!

*Pause. Mrs Carberry turns to Colm.*

**MRS CARBERRY:** How's Mary?

**COLM:** Oh, she's fine. She got that job.

**MRS CARBERRY:** Great!


SCENE 11 EXT./NIGHT 2
SET: PUB
*Ted looks very unhappy. He sees the pub and decides to go in.*


SCENE 12 EXT./NIGHT 2
SET: PUB
*Ted walks in. The pub is buzzing with activity. The noise suddenly stops. Ted freezes. The pub is filled with about thirty Chinese people, and they've all stopped to look at him: men holding pints of Guinness to their mouths, some old lads playing Mah-jong. Ted stands there and laughs uncertainly.*

**END OF PART ONE**

\* \* \*

**PART TWO**

SCENE 13 INT./DAY 3
SET: A HOUSE
*The Yin family home. Father and son are having an argument.*

**FATHER:** That is my final word.

**SON:** Father, be reasonable.

**FATHER:** I will not.

**SON:** Father, you must realise. The old ways are dying. This is a new world. The young have ideas of their own, roads they must travel—

**FATHER:** No. I am sorry, but there is nothing in gangster rap that appeals to me. It's just noise. Now maybe some of the West-Coast rappers, some of the lighter stuff like DJ Jazzy Jeff— (*The telephone rings.*) Hold on. (*He answers it.*) Hello? (*It is Ted on the line.*)

**TED:** Is that the Yin dynasty? Family! I mean family!

**FATHER:** Yes, this is Sean Yin.

**TED:** This is Father Ted Crilly.

**FATHER:** Oh . . .

**TED:** I just wanted to say how sorry I am about . . . I think there's been a *huge* misunderstanding.

**FATHER:** Father Crilly, I'm sure you meant nothing by it.

**TED:** Why not drop round to the Parochial House and we can have some tea or a few drinks and clear the whole thing up?

**FATHER:** Yes, yes. OK, Father. That would be nice.

**TED:** Right . . . I'll see you in a while, then. (*He puts the telephone down.*) Ah, ha, Dougal! That's everything cleared up. They're coming round this afternoon. I'll just be really nice to them, and people will stop saying I'm a racist. Great! Nothing can go wrong!

**DOUGAL:** Fantastic! So the story is, you're not a racist.

**TED:** Yes! What? No, it's not a 'story'. I'm not a racist!

**DOUGAL:** So if anyone asks me if you're a racist, I'm supposed to say . . . ?

**TED:** You're not supposed to say anything!

*Mrs Doyle enters. She is still walking delicately, arms out from her sides, and she pushes a tea tray along the floor by giving it little kicks.*

**MRS DOYLE:** Hello, everyone! Father Crilly, I hear you're a racist.

**DOUGAL:** No, Mrs Doyle. He's *not* a racist.

*Dougal winks ostentatiously at her.*

**TED:** I'm not! I'm not a racist! Mrs Doyle, we've got to do something for your back. You can't go on like this. (*He walks behind her.*) All right, I'm going to try something . . .

**MRS DOYLE:** No!

**TED:** Don't *worry*, Mrs Doyle.

*Pause. Ted starts gingerly trying things.*

**MRS DOYLE:** Ahhhhhhaaaaaahhhh!!!!!!! AHHHH!!!! OH, JESUS, MOTHER MARY AND JOSEPH! OH MY GOD! DEAR GOD, MAKE THE PAIN GO AWAY!

**TED:** All right! All right! OK, now, just relax . . . (*He takes her neck in a sort of choke hold. She starts whimpering.*) Don't worry . . .

**MRS DOYLE** (*tiny whimper*): Ohh, nooo, nooo, nooo . . .

**TED:** Mrs Doyle, just relax!

*Ted wrenches her neck the other way with a single move and a cracking sound. Pause. Ted looks worried.*

**MRS DOYLE** (*frozen in this final position*): Oh . . . oh, yes, that's much better.

**TED:** Are you sure? You look a bit . . .

*She starts to move off, sideways, frozen in an absolutely horrendously painful-looking stance.*

**MRS DOYLE** (*starts to move off, sideways*): No, no . . . this is great! I'll be fine now, Father . . .

**TED:** All right, maybe I should try . . .

**MRS DOYLE:** No! Seriously, Father, that's made all the difference. I feel twenty years younger . . .

*She crabwalks from the room. Dougal is at the window.*

**DOUGAL:** Ted, the Chinese people are coming.

**TED:** Oh, right . . . where are they? (*He throws a few cigarette packets, beer bottles and other bits of rubbish into the bin. He notices the black mark on the window.*) Oh, feck it, this big mark is still here. Never mind . . . (*He waves through the window to the Chinese people.*) Hello! Hello!

SCENE 14 EXT./DAY 3
SET: OUTSIDE HOUSE
*The father and son are approaching.*

**SON:** I don't know why we have to talk to this fascist.

**FATHER:** Now, come on, it may just have been . . .

*They see Ted and start to wave, but stop short when*

they notice something.

SCENE 15 EXT./DAY 3
SET: WINDOW
*Cut to their point of view of Ted. From this position, the black mark on the window is directly below Ted's nose, and looks like a little Hitler moustache. Ted's waving resembles a Nazi salute.*

SCENE 16 EXT./DAY 3
SET: OUTSIDE HOUSE
*Father and son both frown. The son turns angrily and storms away. The father follows.*

SCENE 17 INT./DAY 3
SET: PAROCHIAL HOUSE
*Ted stops waving.*

**TED:** Where are they going? (*Ranting.*) My God! I invite them up here, and then they won't even let me tell them my side of the story! . . .

*Cut to a shot from the other side of the window. Ted's angry hand gestures make him look like a wildly gesticulating Führer.*

SCENE 18 INT./NIGHT 3
SET: TED AND DOUGAL'S BEDROOM
*We shouldn't be quite sure where we are at first. Jack is lying on the ground, in near-darkness, asleep with a smile on his face. The camera pulls back and rises to reveal that he is under Ted's bed. Ted and Dougal are in bed, Ted is sitting up and looking anxious.*

**TED:** This is terrible. Everyone thinks I'm some kind of Nazi racist. But I'm not. You know, one of my favourite songs is 'Ebony and Ivory'. I almost bought that when it came out. Ohh, what can I do? . . .

**DOUGAL:** Ted, here's an idea right off the top of my head. I haven't thought it through, so it's probably not brilliant, but what the hell, I'll just talk and see what comes out. You ready?

**TED:** Hold on a second and I'll strap myself in.

**DOUGAL:** How about some kind of festival celebrating all the different cultures of Craggy Island? You could organise it, say a few

words, and then people will think you're a fantastic man, rather than a big racist.

*Pause.*

**TED:** My God.

**DOUGAL:** What?

**TED:** That's a good idea!

**DOUGAL:** No, it's not!

**TED:** It is, Dougal! It is!

**DOUGAL:** No, I'm sorry, Ted, I just can't accept that I had a good idea. You're just being nice.

**TED:** Dougal, you know me, I'd be honest with you. I mean, haven't I told you in the past when your ideas were crap? . . .

**DOUGAL:** Yes . . .

**TED:** . . . Because, frankly, you're not a hugely intelligent person.

**DOUGAL:** If anything, Ted, that's an understatement.

**TED:** Exactly. But this one, this is actually good.

**DOUGAL:** Ted, there's probably something wrong with it. You just haven't thought it through.

**TED:** Yes, but . . . usually your ideas . . . you immediately know that they're crap. I mean . . . (*He snaps his fingers.*) . . . like *that*.

**DOUGAL** (*rubbing his chin*): Yes . . .

**TED:** OK, you've had a brilliant idea. But just break it down for me a bit more. So what would an event celebrating all the different cultures of Craggy Island actually be like?

*Pause. Dougal stares straight at Ted.*

**DOUGAL:** What?

**TED:** What would the day involve? I mean, yes, a celebration. But what kind of celebration? What form could it take? (*Dougal looks a bit stressed.*) What would it—

**DOUGAL:** Ted, I want out.

**TED:** What do you mean?

**DOUGAL:** I went too far, too soon. I didn't know what I was getting into.

**TED:** Dougal, just relax.

**DOUGAL** (*stands up and picks up his duvet*): No, Ted. I didn't know you had to follow up a good idea with lots more little good ideas. I'm sorry. I'll sleep in the spare room.

**TED:** Dougal —

**DOUGAL** (*at the door*): I'm sorry.

*He leaves. Ted sighs and turns out the light.*

**TED:** GOODNIGHT, THEN, DOUGAL!

**DOUGAL** (*from outside*): GOODNIGHT!

*Pause.*

**JACK:** Goodnight.

**TED:** Goodnight, Father — Aaarghhh!*

*Ted jumps out of bed, turns on the light and looks at his bed, terrified.*

SCENE 19 INT./DAY 4
SET: SEAMUS FITZPATRICK'S PAROCHIAL HOUSE
*This is the Parochial House we were in earlier. We are in the small room filled with Nazi memorabilia. Father Fitzpatrick is berating the old priest.*

*This may be unclear – Jack's under the bed.

**FITZPATRICK:** You old fool. I've sheltered you for fifty years, and you've never once made me a cup of tea!

**OLD MAN** (*German accent*): You make the tea. I do the washing up!

**FITZPATRICK** (*gasps*): When have you ever done the washing up?

**OLD MAN:** I did it for all of 1947 and 1973.

**FITZPATRICK** (*gasps*): Oh! You liar! You kept dropping the plates and going (*Dreadful German impression.*) 'Ach, I am so tired. I never washed plates when I was with the Wehrmacht! Blah-di-blah-di-blah. . .' Oh! You're driving me insane! I'm going to take a valium.

**OLD MAN:** I want one, too!

**FITZPATRICK:** Why must you ape my every move? Oh, all right!

*He takes out a bottle, empties two pills into his hand and gives one to the old man. They both down the pills with a glass of water.*

**FITZPATRICK** (*splutters*): Wait! This isn't valium! These are the cyanide pills we kept for emergencies! You stupid fool! You put the cyanide pills beside the valium! That's just asking for trouble!

**OLD MAN:** Oh, shut up!

**FITZPATRICK:** You shut up! We're going to die in fifteen seconds!

**OLD MAN:** Well, that's just fine by me.

**FITZPATRICK:** Good. It's fine by me, too.

**OLD MAN:** I'm glad it is.

**FITZPATRICK:** Good. I'm glad, too.

**OLD MAN:** Good.

**FITZPATRICK:** Good.

*They walk away from each other in a huff, then drop down dead.*

SCENE 20 INT./DAY 4
SET: STAIRS
*We see Mrs Doyle at the top of the stairs, her back still arched uncomfortably so that she's feeling her way down. We see her foot about to step on the tiny hamster bicycle. She steps on it and falls down the*

*stairs.*

**MRS DOYLE:** Oh, Mother of God! Oh, Jesus, Mary and Joseph! Oh, God help me!

*She lands at the bottom of the stairs, going out of shot, and then jumps back up into shot.*

**MRS DOYLE:** I'M CURED!!!!!

*Ted and Dougal come into the hallway, putting on their coats.*

**TED:** What happened, Mrs Doyle?

**MRS DOYLE:** I stepped on the hamster's bike and fell down the stairs, Father.

**TED:** Dougal, I told you to put that bike away safely!

**DOUGAL:** I did! I put it back in the cage!

**MRS DOYLE:** Don't worry, Father! I feel fantastic! This is great! I forgot my head could go right round like this!

**TED:** All right, well, listen, that delivery from Habit Hat is coming today, so when it arrives, give Father Jack . . . where is Father Jack?

**MRS DOYLE:** I think he's up the chimney.

**TED:** Right.

**MRS DOYLE:** Will I burn him out, Father?

**TED:** Good God, no. The smoke's back up and it'll be all over the house. No, leave him be – he's just going through a phase. Just leave his new clothes out when they come, or he'll be spreading dust all over the place like a big atomic cloud.

**DOUGAL:** God, yeah, it'd be like Hiroshima all over again.

**TED:** God, yes. But, Dougal, to be honest, we should never have brought him there in the first place. Anyway, Mrs Doyle, put all the stuff up . . . all the new . . . rugs and the . . . things for the . . . chairs . . . I don't know, that's your 'thing' really. I wouldn't know anything about all that sort of stuff, because I'm a man. Anyway, we're off to the celebration of Craggy Island's ethnic diversity.

SCENE 21 EXT./DAY 4*
SET: PAROCHIAL HALL
*We see an exterior shot of the parochial hall. A banner outside reads 'Tonight – Special Event – a Celebration of Craggy Island's Ethnic Diversity'.*

SCENE 22 INT./DAY 4
SET: PAROCHIAL HALL
*We see a wide view of the hall. All the Chinese population are present, including the Yin family. The teenage Yin is wearing headphones. Rap music seeps out from them. Ted addresses the congregation. There is a white screen behind him.*

**TED:** Welcome. Wilkommen. Bien venue. (*He says welcome in about six different languages.*) It's an honour and a privilege for me to present this celebration of the wide diversity of cultures that exists on Craggy Island today – namely, Chinese people, and people from Craggy Island . . . I have prepared a short slide presentation to reflect this multicultural mix, so without further ado, I shall start the show.

*The lights go off. Ted presses a button. The first slide is projected on the wall behind him. It shows Ted with his arm around a black man. The man is normally dressed, wearing an Aran jumper and smiling.*

**TED:** This man visited the island a few years ago. I forget his name, but I got on very well

*We deleted this scene from the final version.

with him. Just thought I'd throw that in at the start . . .

*Cut to a shot of the unresponsive audience. Ted presses another button. Another slide, this time of a Maori.*

**TED:** The Maori . . . (*Long pause.*) I'm sorry. Don't know how that got in there. Sorry about that, folks. Of course, there are no Maoris on Craggy Island.

**MAORI** (*insulted*): Hey!

*Cut to a Chinese man in the audience.*

**CHINESE MAN:** Will there be any free drink at this?

**TED:** Yes, there will be a limited supply of free drink afterwards.

**CHINESE MAN:** It's probably feckin' Harp.

*Ted carries on, oblivious. Another slide, this time of Chairman Mao.*

**TED:** Chairman Mao, Secretary of The Communist Party of China, one of the biggest Communist parties in the world, and in my view the best.

*Another slide comes up. It is Mr Miyagi from 'The Karate Kid'.*

**TED:** Mr Miyagi from *The Karate Kid*. One of my favourite films. Not because of the Karate Kid himself, but because of Mr Miyagi. Not a day goes by when I don't remember one of his words of wisdom. For instance, (*solemnly*) 'You look revenge, better start by digging two graves' and 'You make good fight, earn respect. Then nobody bother you.'

*Next slide. It is Kato from the Pink Panther films, fighting with Peter Sellers.*

**TED:** Kato! Where would he spring from next?

*Next slide. David Carradine.*

**TED:** Kung Fu. Named after his art. And played by the actor David Carradine.

*Next slide. Ming the Merciless.*

**TED:** Ming the Merciless.

*The Maori and the Chinese man look at each other, confused. The next slide is of a big crowd of Chinese people.*

**TED:** But best of all, the Chinese people themselves. Look at them there. They're great. Well done to you all! I applaud you for your great strength in times of adversity, such as the One Hundred Year's War, and the Cultural Revolution. A great bunch of lads. And lasses of course – mustn't forget the Chinese ladies. Right, I think I've addressed all aspects of Chinese culture . . .

*A slide of Ted comes up, followed by a slide that reads 'Not a Racist'. This sequence of two slides repeats while Ted speaks.*

**TED:** . . . And I'd like to thank you all for coming. It's been a great night . . . If anyone wants a word with me afterwards, feel free to come over and have a bit of an old chat . . .

*He rambles on, the two slides repeating behind him.*

SCENE 23 INT./DAY 4
SET: PAROCHIAL HALL
*Everyone is standing around drinking. The father and son are still there.*

**FATHER:** Well, the slide show was a big pile of crap . . .

**DOUGAL:** Ha! Told you, Ted!

**FATHER:** But the free drink is appreciated. Thank you, Father Crilly.

**TED:** I just wanted to clear things up. I'm not a fascist, I'm a priest. Fascists go round dressing in black and telling people what to do. Whereas priests . . . (*Long pause. Ted has no idea what to say next.*) More drink!

**EVERYONE:** Hurray!

SCENE 24 INT./DAY 4
SET: PAROCHIAL HOUSE
*Mrs Doyle is leading a young man into the living room. He has a huge box that he is dragging behind him.*

**MRS DOYLE:** Anywhere around there. Would you like a cup of tea?

**MAN:** Oh, no, thanks. I have a kind of allergic reaction to it. It's very rare but pretty serious. If I drink tea there's a seventy per cent chance that I'll die.

**MRS DOYLE:** Well, I'll make you a cup anyway, in case you change your mind.

**MAN:** Eh, thanks anyway.

*He leaves. Mrs Doyle turns her attention to the large box that the delivery man left. She opens it up and takes a letter out of it. She looks at the letter, frowns, then looks into the box and frowns.*

SCENE 25 INT./DAY 4
SET: PAROCHIAL HALL
*A few of the Chinese men are playing traditional Irish music on bodhrans, tin whistles and fiddles. They're pretty good. Cut to Ted with the rest of the Chinese. Dougal looks on in confusion.*

**TED:** To China!

**EVERYONE:** Hurray!

**FATHER:** To Craggy Island!

**EVERYONE:** Hurray!

**TED:** More drink!

**BARMAN:** I'm sorry, the bar is closed.

**TED:** Tsk. I tell you what, how about everyone comes back to my place?!

**EVERYONE:** Hurray!

**DOUGAL:** Wait! I need to go to the toilet first.

**EVERYONE:** Hurray!

SCENE 26 INT./DAY 4
SET: PAROCHIAL HOUSE
*Mrs Doyle opens the door.*

**EVERYONE:** Hurray!

**TED:** Mrs Doyle, we have guests! (*Aside.*) Did that stuff come?

**MRS DOYLE:** Oh, yes, Father. I felt so fantastic, I put it all up in less than an hour. And there was this letter . . .

*Ted takes the letter, going towards the door of the living room. The excited Chinese people huddle behind him.*

**TED:** Letter? (*He reads it.*) Dear Father Crilly, on the instructions of our recently deceased client, Father Seamus Fitzpatrick, here are some items which he specified you should have . . .

*Ted absent-mindedly opens the door.*

SCENE 27 INT./DAY 4
SET: PAROCHIAL HOUSE
*Ted enters the room, followed by all the Chinese people. They all stop talking. Ted continues reading, oblivious to the fact that the entire room is covered in swastikas, Nazi memorabilia, etc.*

**TED:** . . . In the event of his death . . .

*He looks around at last. He doesn't do anything. There is a stunned silence. We then hear a 'ching-ching' noise. Ted moves one of the Chinese people to one side and the hamster, riding his little bicycle, cycles across the floor and past the group of men, into the hallway. It rings the bell again once it's in the hallway. Pause.*

**TED:** I can explain everything. (*He looks into the hallway, into which the hamster has disappeared, then back into the room loaded with Nazi stuff.*) Actually . . . no, I can't.

POST-CREDIT SEQUENCE
SCENE 28 INT./DAY 4
SET: A HOUSE
*Back in the Yin home, father and son are watching the television. The telephone rings. The father goes to answer it. The son eats a sandwich.*

**FATHER:** Hello?

*It is Ted on the line, looking hugely frantic.*

**TED:** Ah, hello, have you opened that present yet?

**FATHER:** No. Looking forward to it, though. A year's supply of Whyte & Mackay whisky! How very generous of you!

*We see a big box behind him, with 'Whyte & Mackay Whisky' written on the side. Cut back to Ted. We see there is a huge pile of empty whiskey bottles in one corner of the room.*

**TED:** Yes, the problem there is, y'see . . . well, basically . . . Father Hackett's been having this rather unusual problem . . .

*As Ted speaks, we see Jack, dressed in full S.S. gear, getting out of the box. The son's mouth hangs open, watching this. Jack drunkenly walks over to the table, grabs a bit of sandwich, then walks back and gets inside the box.*

**FATHER:** All right, Father. Bye! (*He turns to the son.*) Apparently, we're not to open the box.

*The son looks at him, a piece of meat hanging from his mouth.*

**THE END**

# Chirpy Burpy Cheap Sheep

**GRAHAM:** This episode began life as something entirely different. The plot originally started with Ted and Dougal on an open-topped bus that was on a sightseeing tour of Craggy Island. The tour was terrible. They were exposed to the elements and it started raining, so they headed downstairs. But they were prevented from getting downstairs by a little dog barking like mad at them at the foot of the stairs. That's it. We thought we could make a plot out of that. We liked the idea for about a morning, but couldn't see where it would go (actually, I defy anyone to see where that could go). Finally we decided that the only thing we could keep was the title – which was at that stage *The Beast of Craggy Island* (a reference to the little dog) – and instead invent a *Hound of the Baskervilles*-type story, with Ted as Sherlock Holmes and Dougal as Dr Watson. So the original title had to go.

There's a nod to Stanley Kubrick in this episode. When Chris the sheep is looking at the two farmers and the camera pans from mouth to mouth, it's a straight copy from the scene where Hal lip-reads in *2001*. Also, the names of the farmers, 'Giant', 'Hud' and 'Fargo' come from three of our favourite wide-open-spaces movies.

**ARTHUR:** This doesn't exactly have an airtight plot, so don't look too closely. While we were happy with Ted and Dougal's story, we really didn't know what to do with Jack and Mrs Doyle. In the end, Jack being oddly affected by leap years gave us a chance to show him in a different guise – and one highly appropriate to Frank Kelly. Frank is actually very nimble, very light on his feet, so it was a pleasure to show him dancing. Mrs Doyle ended up doing the opposite – dragging her feet and making the most appalling din when walking. The theory is that she always makes that noise but they've only just noticed it.

Towards the end of this script, the Beck video reference (during Ted's denouement scene) is from Beck's video for their song *Devil's Haircut*. We wanted to copy the way the image freezes and zooms electronically into details you didn't notice before, but in our version, we put in ridiculous shots with fur coats, 'baa' sounds, party hats and crowns.

## PART ONE
SCENE 1 EXT./DAY 1
SET: FIELD
*We see a sign that reads . . . ' "King of the Sheep"*
*Weigh-in '98 – Officials and Competitors Entrance'.*

SCENE 2 INT./DAY 1
SET: TENT
*We see various shots of sheep being 'weighed in.' Cut*
*to a lone sheep standing in a sheep pen. Cut to a*
*farmer, Fargo Boyle, leaning over the gate of the pen*
*looking very fondly at the sheep. Another two*
*farmers, Giant Reid, and Hud Hastings, join him.*

**GIANT:** Hello, Fargo.

**FARGO:** Ah, Giant, Hud, hello.

**HUD** (*looking at his sheep*)**:** You have Chris
looking great for the contest.

*We see Ted turning up. He waves to Fargo.*

**FARGO:** Thanks, lads. Father Crilly! Hello,
there!

*He goes off towards Ted.*

**TED:** Fargo, how's The Champ?

**FARGO:** Ah, he's great. Few quid on him this
year, Father?

**TED:** Oh, yes. Put the entire annual heating
allowance on him to win.

**FARGO:** But if he doesn't win, what does that
mean, Father?

**TED:** Oh, well, we won't have any heating for
the year. But if the rest of the year stays as
warm as the summer, we're laughing! But
come on, it's Chris! He's The Champ! Talk
about a safe bet! See you, Fargo!

*Cut back to Hud and Giant.*

**HUD:** Giant, have you heard about this
creature going around terrorising sheep on the
island?

*As Hud continues to talk, the camera zooms slowly*
*between them, in on the sheep.*

**GIANT:** No. Tell me more.

**HUD:** They say it's as big as a jaguar.

**GIANT:** The *car?!!*

**HUD:** No, the big cat thing. And its face is all

teeth – big sharp teeth as sharp as a knife. And
it makes a howling sound that seems to come
from the very gates of hell . . . And its favourite
food is mutton. Mutton from sheep.

**GIANT:** Has it killed yet?

**HUD:** No, but it's only a matter of time . . .

*Fade out on close-up of a sheep's face.*

SCENE 3 EXT./NIGHT 1
SET: SHEEP PEN
*The sheep is asleep. It 'baas' uncomfortably in its*
*sleep. We hear the voices of Hud and Giant.*

**HUD'S AND GIANT'S VOICES:** Mutton
from sheep . . . Has it killed yet? . . . Only a
matter of time . . . Its face is all teeth, all teeth,
all teeth . . .

*The sheep wakes up with a start. We hear a distant,*
*unearthly howl . . .*

SCENE 4 EXT./DAY 2
SET: PAROCHIAL HOUSE
*Establishing shot of the Parochial House. We hear*
*various atmospheric sounds of birds and so on.*

SCENE 5 INT./DAY 2
SET: PAROCHIAL HOUSE
*Inside, the sound of birds, etc., is much, much louder.*
*Cut to Dougal sitting on the ground beside the record*
*player. He is looking at an album cover, 'BBC Sound*
*Effects Volume 4'. Ted is sitting down, reading a*
*newspaper. He turns the page, and instead of the*
*noise of the pages turning, we hear loads of pots and*
*pans rattling. He coughs, and we hear the sound of a*

*machine gun.*

**TED:** Dougal, give the album a rest now.

**DOUGAL:** Ah, Ted, come on. It's brilliant! I think people will soon give up listening to pop music, and listen to this type of thing instead.

**TED** (*chuckles*)**:** You know, when I hear some of the things in the charts today, I wonder if that's not happening already!

**DOUGAL:** What? This is so good, though, isn't it, Ted? They've got all kinds of things. As if by magic, I can create a big crowd of invisible ducks . . . (*He moves the stylus arm. We hear a steam engine.*) Or take you to darkest Africa . . . (*We hear an explosion.*) Or bring you into a spooky castle on a stormy night . . . (*We hear sounds of a car revving up.*) God, it's fantastic.

**TED:** Dougal, come on now, please!

*We hear the telephone ringing.*

**TED:** Is that the phone ringing or is it another sound effect?

**DOUGAL:** It's the phone. Unless someone else is playing a sound-effects record.

*Ted picks up the telephone.*

**TED:** Hello, Craggy Island Parochial House. Father Ted Crilly speaking.

SCENE 6 INT./DAY 2
SET: FARGO'S LIVING ROOM
*We see Fargo the farmer.*

**FARGO:** Father Crilly, Fargo Boyle here.

**TED:** Ah, Fargo. How's the prizewinner doing? We're all counting on you to come through for us again!

**FARGO:** Father, that's what I . . . Could you drop by later. I . . . need to speak to you urgently . . .

**TED:** Certainly, Fargo. What seems to—

*We hear the dial tone. Fargo has hung up.*

**TED:** Dougal, I have to go. Something's up with Fargo Boyle. I think there might be something wrong with The Champ.

*Mrs Doyle enters the room. She looks a little jittery and a little tired.*

**TED:** Mrs Doyle, are you all right? You look terrible. Doesn't she, Dougal?

**DOUGAL:** Awful, Ted.

**MRS DOYLE:** Ah, I didn't get much sleep, Father. I thought I kept hearing a terrible howling noise.

**DOUGAL:** Oh, that'd be the Beast.

**TED:** What's this now?

**DOUGAL:** God, Ted, have you not heard? Everyone's been talking about it . . . except you and me, obviously.

**MRS DOYLE:** There's something terrible on the moors, Father.

*Dougal plays a brief burst of spooky, old-style, flying-saucer sounds. Ted gives him a look and Dougal stops.*

**TED:** Moors? We don't have any moors.

**MRS DOYLE:** Well, then, there's something terrible roaming about the place where normally there would be moors. They say . . . it might . . . be a kind of giant fox!

*Dramatic thunder sound.*

**TED:** Dougal!!!

**DOUGAL:** Sorry!

**TED:** Well, I'm sorry, but I'm not going to be taken in by this type of nonsense. Do you remember that panic last year, when everyone was worried about The Small Man of Rochree?

**MRS DOYLE:** Well, he was a very small man, Father.

**TED:** That's not unusual in itself, Mrs Doyle. I myself have known many small men and they're just the same as the rest of us. Nothing to fear there at all.

**DOUGAL:** It couldn't be Jack, could it? You could see how someone would mistake him for a big mad cat.

**TED:** No, don't forget that during leap years Father Jack is very much affected by the changing of the seasons. For a short while, a marvellous serenity enters his life, and he is at one with nature.

SCENE 7 EXT./DAY 2
SET: FIELD
*Cut to Jack, looking clean and rosy-cheeked, running through a field. He sniffs some flowers, pats a little girl on the head, and rolls around with some puppies.*

SCENE 8 INT./DAY 2
SET: PAROCHIAL HOUSE
*Cut back to Ted.*

**TED:** Ah, yeah, he's great when he's in this mood. If only it lasted a bit longer.

SCENE 9 EXT./DAY 2
SET: FIELD
*We see a load of cans of Special Brew on the ground. Jack is throwing up in a bush. He stands up and we see he is completely back to normal. He picks up a puppy and wipes his mouth with it.*

SCENE 10 INT./DAY 2
SET: PAROCHIAL HOUSE
*Mrs Doyle sees something on the table.*

**MRS DOYLE:** Oh, look, there's my scissors . . .

*She walks out of the room. As she walks, we hear a hideous slurping, popping and gurgling noise.*

**TED:** Dougal, I said turn the record off!

**DOUGAL:** But . . . it is off . . .

*Dougal is putting the disc back in its sleeve. They look at the door through which Mrs Doyle went. They look a tad horrified.*

SCENE 11 INT./DAY 2
SET: FARGO'S HOUSE
*Ted is talking to Fargo Boyle. Dougal stands nearby.*

**TED:** What do you mean Chris won't be in the competition? He's The Champ. You *have* to enter him.

**FARGO:** All this talk of the Beast has got to him. His nerves are shot. I took a photo of him this morning . . .

*He starts taking it out.*

**TED:** His nerves? Fargo, it's a sheep.

**FARGO:** He always had a very artistic

temperament, Father.

**TED:** But, I mean, he's not a concert pianist. He's a sheep. I don't see how— (*Fargo shows him the photograph.*) Oh, my God . . . this is Chris?

*Fargo hands Ted the photograph. We don't see it. Fargo nods gravely.*

**FARGO:** I mean, when you compare it with what he looked like last year . . .

*He hands Ted another photograph.*

**TED:** It's like . . . it's like two completely different sheep!

*We see the photographs. There is no discernible difference between the Chris of old and the new Chris.*

**FARGO:** All this talk of the Beast has got to him. He's off his food, he's not sleeping, and he's started . . . burping.

**TED:** Burping? Can a sheep burp?

**FARGO:** They're not supposed to burp, I know that! And look at him . . . look at the rings around the eyes; the bored, unhappy turn of the mouth; the sad, dirty texture of his wool.

**TED:** What the hell happened to him?!

**FARGO:** Sheep can sense things, Father.

**TED:** That's very true. (*To Dougal.*) I read once they can feel evil vibrations in the air. In that respect they're very like plants or cars. My God, look at the old Chris . . . (*He smiles as he looks at the first photo.*) Those playful laughlines round the eyes . . . his fluffy coat of fur . . .

**DOUGAL:** Wool.

**TED:** Whatever . . . his confident black lips . . or whatever you call those things round their mouth. His cheeky grin. Yes, the whole feeling of 'sheep okayness' is there.

*Fargo's composure cracks a bit.*

**FARGO:** Oh, Father, what am I going to do? (*He holds up the second photograph.*) That *thing* out there, that's not Chris! I want Chris back!

**TED:** Don't say that, Fargo! He needs you now more than he's ever needed you! Come on! I want to see him!

**FARGO:** He doesn't want to see anybody.

**TED:** Fargo, that's an order! Take me to see Chris The Unhappy Sheep!

SCENE 12 EXT./DAY 2*
SET: SHEEP PEN
*We see a very average-looking sheep standing in a pen. Ted, Dougal and Fargo are standing looking at him. The sheep burps loudly.*

**FARGO:** Oh, God! . . .

*Another shot of the sheep. Fargo spins round to Ted.*

**FARGO:** Where is your kind, benevolent God now, Father?!! Where is he?! Tell me this, would a just God allow this to happen to Chris?!

*The sheep burps.*

**TED:** Ah, now, come on—

**FARGO:** It's all God's fault!

**TED:** Well, it's easy to blame God for everything, Fargo. Certainly he's let me down loads of times. (*Bitterly.*) I mean, *loads* . . . but you just have to presume that he knows what he's up to.

**FARGO:** I want to believe you, Father. But it's the eternal Catholic dilemma. I think it was Saint Thomas Aquinas who was tortured by doubts . . .

---

*We deleted this scene from the final version.

**TED:** Yeah? Great. Anyway, best not to think about any of that stuff at all, I find.

**FARGO:** But if God allows these terrible things to happen, how can we say he is benevolent?

*The sheep burps. Ted looks very uncomfortable.*

**TED:** Look, let's just concentrate on the job at hand—

**FARGO:** But how can there be a God if—

*Dougal suddenly yells out and falls to the ground.*

**TED:** Dougal! What's wrong!

**DOUGAL:** It's my stomach, Ted! I think I've been poisoned!

**TED:** Fargo, quick! Call Doctor Sinnot! Call Doctor Sinnot!

*The sheep does one long, long burp.*

SCENE 13 INT./NIGHT 2
SET: TED AND DOUGAL'S BEDROOM
*Dougal is in bed, reading happily. Ted comes into the room and takes off his dressing gown.*

**TED:** Well . . . good job, Dougal! That was a number three, though. I asked for number one.[†]

**DOUGAL:** Sorry about that, Ted.[†]

**TED:** Let's do a quick run-through now . . . Someone's asking me the difficult questions about religion . . . blah di blah di blah . . . and I give you the signal . . .[†]

*Ted sticks out one finger.[†]*

**DOUGAL:** Ted, I've just remembered! You have to go and do a big Mass!![†]

**TED:** Very good. And . . .[†]

**DOUGAL:** Ah . . . the top half of the island's on fire and they need your help with the dead.[†]

**TED:** Great, and number three's the poison thing.[†]

**DOUGAL:** God, Ted, what do you think about this Beast affair? Are you scared?[†]

**TED:** No, I think it's just . . .[†]

**DOUGAL:** They say it's as big as four cats. And it's got one leg that it can retract into its body so it can leap up at you better. And it lights up at night. And it's got four ears and it uses two of them for listening and the other two are kind of backup ears. It's got claws the size of cups and you can't leave it by itself or it goes mad, and then if it goes near water it goes a kind of purple colour, and it's got a fear of stamps. And it can reproduce the smell of fifteen different types of cats . . . Oh, and it's got magnets on its tail so if you're made out of metal it can attach itself to you. And instead of a mouth it's got two faces . . .*

**TED:** It's only a legend, Dougal. It doesn't exist.

**DOUGAL** (*sarcastically*)**:** Right, Ted. The way the Phantom of the Opera doesn't exist.

**TED:** The Phantom of the Opera *doesn't* exist, Dougal. Look, I'm not going into this 'what does exist, what doesn't exist?' debate with you again. But I'm going to have to insist you add those last two examples to the chart.

---

[†] We deleted this from the final version and the scene began instead with Ted telling Dougal what a bad state Chris the sheep is in. To which Dougal replies that if he were a sheep, he'd be watching his back too.
*Ardal got bored saying this last line as written and changed it on the night without telling us he was going to do so, to, 'Instead of a mouth it's got four arses...', which was just fine by us.

**DOUGAL:** But, Ted! . . .

**TED:** Dougal!

*Ted hands Dougal a marker. Dougal sulks a little and walks over to a big chart on the wall that reads:*

THEY DON'T EXIST
Loch Ness Monster
Frankenstein
'Evil' Badgers
Magnum PI
Crocodile Dundee
Darth Vader

*Dougal starts adding Phantom of the Opera to this list.*

**TED:** I'm more worried about that bet I put on Chris being crowned King of the Sheep.

**DOUGAL:** You don't think he'll win, then?

**TED:** Come on, Dougal, you saw him. Damn. Ah, well, it's just the heating budget. I see this warm weather lasting a long, long time. (*He hears thunder outside.*) Oh, no, I forgot! Weather *changes*! I'll have to see if John and Mary will let me take my money back tomorrow.

**DOUGAL:** I might drop down with you and see if they've got Volume 5 of the *BBC Sound Effects* album.

**TED:** Fair enough. Good night, then, Dougal.

*Ted turns off the light. We hear a low, distant howl. Ted turns on the light. Dougal is in bed beside him. They look at each other, scared.*

SCENE 14 EXT./DAY 3
SET: JOHN AND MARY'S SHOP
*Ted and Dougal approach the door.*

**DOUGAL:** . . . and when it yawns it sounds like Liam Neeson chasing a load of hens round inside a barrel . .

**TED** (*nudges him*)**:** Hold on, Dougal. Hello, Fargo.

*Fargo, who is coming out of the shop, looks at them sadly. He gives a slight wave and walks on, depressed. Ted sighs.*

**DOUGAL:** . . . And it has no knuckles.

SCENE 15 INT./DAY 3
SET: JOHN AND MARY'S SHOP
*We see John slamming the door of a broom cupboard.*

**JOHN:** And you can stay in there until you learn some feckin' manners!

**MARY:** Let me out! You bastard!

*Just as the door closes, we see Mary banging her head on the low ceiling of the cupboard.*

**MARY:** Ow!!!!

*He locks the door, opens the window and throws the key out.*

**JOHN:** I've thrown the key away! How do you like that?! Eh?!

*Ted and Dougal enter the shop.*

**TED:** Hello, John! (*There is a banging from the cupboard.*) Ah . . .

**JOHN:** HELLO, FATHER CRILLY, HELLO, FATHER McGUIRE.

*The banging stops. Ted and Dougal are a little shocked by the loudness of his greeting.*

**TED:** Eh . . . Where's Mary?

**JOHN:** Oh, she's away at her mother's.

*There's a bumping noise from the cupboard.*

**MARY:** Ow!!!!

*Pause.*

**TED:** Is . . . is there someone in the cupboard?

*Pause.*

**MARY** (*from the cupboard*): Hello, Fathers!

**TED:** Mary?

**JOHN:** Ah, Mary, I forgot you were there! I thought you were at your mother's.

**MARY** (*from the cupboard*): Ah . . . no, I didn't go to my mother's after all. I'm in the cupboard.

**TED:** Mary . . . what are you doing in there?

**JOHN:** Eh . . . Oh, I know! It's because of this Beast of Craggy Island thing. I thought Mary would be safer in the cupboard.

**MARY** (*from the cupboard*): That's right. I'm better off in here.

*Pause.*

**MARY:** What can we do for you, Father?

**TED:** Ah, a pack of twenty Carrolls, please.

**MARY** (*from the cupboard*): Certainly, Father.

**JOHN:** I'll get them, love. You stay in the cupboard.

*John goes to look for them.*

**TED** (*to an offscreen John*): John . . . can I have a word? . . .

**MARY** (*from the cupboard*): Is Father McGuire there?

**DOUGAL** (*oblivious to anything unusual*): I am! Hello, Mary!

**MARY** (*from the cupboard*): It's a lovely day, isn't it, Father?

**DOUGAL:** Oh, yes . . .

**MARY:** You're looking great, anyway.

*Over to Ted and John.*

**TED:** I really need to get this money to the girl for this operation . . .

**JOHN:** Father, I'm sorry but . . . once a bet is put on, I can't cancel it.

**TED:** I wouldn't ask normally but . . . think about it, John. If you had no kidneys . . .

**JOHN:** So this woman has no kidneys at all?

**TED:** No. It's very sad.

**JOHN:** But if she has no kidneys, wouldn't

she be dead?

**TED:** Well, she has one kind of kidney the doctors threw together for her. It's made out of GoreTex, I think . . .

**JOHN:** I'm sorry, Father. A bet's a bet. It's a pity you didn't wait, Father. The odds have lengthened to twenty to one, due to his nervous troubles. Anyway, your cigarettes.

**TED:** Oh, right, thank you.

**DOUGAL:** Ted, they don't have the sound-effects album. Tschoh! We might as well just go.

**MARY:** Bye, Fathers!

*They leave.*

**MARY:** Well, I hope you're satisfied!

**JOHN:** Ah, shut up!

*A fist smashes through the cupboard and smashes John in the head.*

SCENE 16 EXT./DAY 3
SET: JOHN AND MARY'S SHOP
*Ted and Dougal see Giant Reid cycling by on his tatty bike. He wears a big fur coat, like something Bud Flanagan might have worn.*

**TED:** Look, there's Giant Reid. Hello, Giant!

*Giant sees them and starts to cycle off hurriedly. The coat hampers this and the sight is oddly ridiculous as he shambles off. He also tries to hide his face with one of his hands.*

SCENE 17 INT./DAY 3
SET: PAROCHIAL HOUSE
*Ted and Dougal enter. They sit down. Ted is deep in thought.*

**DOUGAL:** What are you thinking about there, Ted? You should see the big serious look on your face!

**TED:** Dougal, this changing weather business has got me worried. What if it does get cold in winter? All our heating budget is tied up in that load of quivering mutton.

**DOUGAL:** Well, Ted, I can't see anything we could do. It's pointless even thinking about it. You're only wasting your time. There's nothing we can do about the situation, and that's it. We

just have to accept it. There's nothing we can do. Accept the fact. That's it.

**TED:** How about we bring Chris here for a few days? The change might do him good.

**DOUGAL:** Oh, wow!!!! What a brilliant idea! Ted, you're a genius! Fantastic! I knew there'd be something we could do! Didn't I say it!? Didn't I say it to you there a second ago?

**TED:** No, you didn't. In fact, you said the exact opposite. That there was absolutely nothing we could do.

**DOUGAL:** Actually, Ted, you've done this to me before, so I took the liberty of taping the conversation. Let's have a listen . . .

*He presses the 'play' button.*

**DOUGAL'S VOICE:** . . . Anything we could do. It's pointless even thinking about it. You're only wasting your time. There's nothing we can do about the situation . . .

*Pause.*

**DOUGAL:** I stand corrected.

SCENE 18 INT./DAY 3
SET: PAROCHIAL HOUSE HALLWAY
*We see Fargo leading Chris into the hall.*

**TED:** There he is now, anyway!

*Chris burps.*

**FARGO:** I'm still not sure about this, Father.

**TED:** Don't worry, Fargo. By the next time you see him, he'll be a new sheep. If not, we'll make him into a jumper and a few chops! *(Fargo just looks at him.)* I'm terribly sorry. That was tasteless. I'm terribly, terribly sorry.

**FARGO:** I'll be off then, Father.

**TED:** OK, so, Fargo. And seriously, if there's one place he can be sure of a bit of peace and quiet —

*There's a rumble and a roar as Jack falls down the stairs, causing as much noise as can be imagined. He demolishes all the railings as he descends. He finishes off by destroying a vase on a table with his foot. He stands up, looks dazedly at Ted and Fargo, and wanders off into another room in an exaggeratedly grand, vaguely pompous way.*

**TED:** I think it would be an insult to you if I finished that sentence.

*Fargo leaves.*

**DOUGAL:** God, Ted. Poor old Chris. Do you think he'll ever be himself again?

**TED:** 'Course he will, Dougal. It could be a long process, though. We're just going to have to try very, very hard to cheer him up. And remember, not a word about B-E-A-S-T-S.

**DOUGAL:** Not a word about breasts?

**TED:** No. Not a word about . . . (*He does an impression of the Beast. He makes growling noises and shapes his hands like claws.*) . . . rowwr. The rowwwwr.

*We see this from the sheep's point of view. Ted is going 'rowwwr' and pulling a face. The sheep looks up into the camera.*

### END OF PART ONE

\* \* \*

### PART TWO

SCENE 19 INT./DAY 4
SET: PAROCHIAL HOUSE
*Ted is wearing a tracksuit. Mrs Doyle is serving tea.*

**MRS DOYLE:** You're up early, Father.

**TED:** Well, we're off to try and get Chris into shape for the competition.

**MRS DOYLE:** Do you think that our new guest would like some tea, Father? The little sheep fella?

**TED:** I don't think they drink tea, Mrs Doyle. Unless you have some special Sheep Tea!!

**MRS DOYLE:** Yes.

**TED:** What?

**MRS DOYLE:** I do have some Sheep Tea in the kitchen.

**TED:** Really?

**MRS DOYLE:** Yes.

**TED:** Oh . . . oh, right. Well . . . give . . . give him some of that, then.

**MRS DOYLE:** OK, so!

*She potters off. Dougal comes in, yawning and rubbing his eyes.*

**DOUGAL:** God, Ted, do we have to get up this early?

**TED:** Has to be done, Dougal. Right. It's almost midday. That gives us half an hour before lunch.

**DOUGAL:** What are we going to do to cheer him up, Ted?

**TED:** Well, we'll try a few different things. And I'll keep a diary of how he progresses. Are you wearing a whistle? Oh, that won't do you any good, Dougal.

**DOUGAL:** Why not?

**TED:** Sheep can't hear high sounds such as whistles or women in hysterics. They can only hear very low sounds, like . . . (*he half-whispers*) farts. (*We hear a burp. Chris the sheep is in the room.*) Right, there he is. Now remember, Dougal, we've got to get him from looking like this . . . (*he throws down on to the table the photograph of the 'unhappy' Chris he was given by Fargo*) . . . to looking like this. (*He throws down a photograph of the 'happy' Chris. Fade this into . . .*)

SCENE 20 EXT./DAY 4
SET: LAKE
*We see Chris the sheep, standing motionless in a boat in the middle of the water. Ted and Dougal look at him.*

SCENE 21 INT./DAY 4
SET: TABLE
*A Polaroid of Chris the sheep is thrown down on the table. Written underneath it is 'Day one'. Sad music accompanies this.*

SCENE 22 INT./DAY 4
SET: PAROCHIAL HOUSE
*We see loads of album covers on the living room floor – Brian Eno ambient records, Cocteau twins, The Orb, and so on – pan along these until we see the sheep wearing a pair of headphones. Ted and Dougal look on, expectant and hopeful.*

SCENE 23 INT./DAY 4
SET: TABLE
*A Polaroid is placed on top of what has now become a small pile of photographs. It has 'Day four' written on it. The sheep looks exactly the same, but the music is more hopeful.*

SCENE 24 EXT./DAY 4
SET: ISOLATION TANK CENTRE
*We see a sign reading 'Lonesome Float Ltd. Craggy Island's Premier Isolation Tank Centre'.*

SCENE 25 INT./DAY 4
SET: ISOLATION TANK CENTRE
*We see the sheep wearing an oxygen facemask and floating happily in one of the tanks. Ted and Dougal stand beside it. A lab technician in a white coat takes notes.*

SCENE 26 INT./DAY 4
SET: TABLE
*Another photograph, on which is written 'Day Seven'. The photograph of the sheep looks exactly the same, but the music does a kind of 'ta-daaaaa' thing, as if the difference is remarkable.*

SCENE 27 INT./DAY 4
SET: PAROCHIAL HOUSE HALLWAY
*Ted opens the door to a hopeful-looking Fargo.*

**FARGO:** Hello, Father. Did you? . . . Is he? . . .

**TED:** I'm sorry. We tried everything.

**FARGO:** Ah, well . . . I suppose I'd better take him home.

*Ted leads him into the living room, where Dougal is*

*waiting. The sheep is standing there. Fargo looks at him for a second, then gives an excited, joyous yelp.*

**FARGO:** Ahhh!

**TED:** Ahhh-haaaa!!! Gotcha!

**DOUGAL:** Ahhh-haaaa!!!!!

**FARGO** (*delighted*): What did you do?!!!! What did you do?!!!

**TED:** Oh, you know, just did my best . . .

**FARGO:** Oh, I don't know what to say! Father, can I buy you a drink to celebrate?

**TED:** Ah . . .

**FARGO:** Come on. I know you won't let me pay you anything . . .

**TED:** Well, actually, I've been meaning to talk to you . . .

**FARGO:** So at least let me buy you a drink in the pub.

**TED:** Yes. Interesting you brought up the issue of payment —

**FARGO:** One drink, Father! It's the least I can do!

**TED:** Yes, it may well be. The thing is, I am a bit low at the moment —

**FARGO:** That's settled then! You're coming for a drink!

**TED:** Oh, all right, then. Dougal, you mind Chris until we get back. And keep your eye on him. Don't let him wander off.

**DOUGAL:** Ah, come on, Ted. He's a fully grown sheep. How am I going to lose him? He's not going to fall through a crack in the floorboards!

**TED:** Sampras fell through a crack in the floorboards.

**DOUGAL:** Ah, Ted, Sampras was a rabbit . . . and it was a big crack.

**TED:** It was an ordinary crack until you widened it because you thought that Sampras had fallen down through the normal-sized crack.

**DOUGAL:** I didn't know where he was. I thought he . . .

**TED:** Shut up, Dougal. Just keep an eye on Chris. Keep that front door closed.

**DOUGAL:** OK, Ted.

*Ted and Fargo leave. Dougal looks at Chris.*

SCENE 28 INT./NIGHT 4
SET: PUB
*Ted and Fargo are sitting at the bar. Fargo's a bit drunk.*

**FARGO:** He's the best feckin' sheep ever. His little sheep face . . . and you have to say, great sense of humour . . . not a bad dancer, actually . . . Strangely enough . . .

**TED** (*not drunk, a little uncomfortable*): Really . . . Great . . .

**FARGO:** He only cost twenty-three pounds! Twenty-three! There's some clause where I'll have to pay more if his image is ever used on stamps, but still . . . that's a great bargain for such a happy sheep.

*Ted notices Hud Hastings, the second of the two farmers we saw earlier, sitting at a table a short distance away. There are two beautiful girls with him, and he wears a crown on his head.*

**TED:** Is that Hud Hastings?

**FARGO:** Yeah . . .

**TED:** Isn't he . . . is he wearing a crown? (*He gets up and approaches Hud.*) Hello, there, Hud.

*Hud immediately stops laughing and looks vaguely guilty.*

**HUD:** Ah. Yes. Hello there, Father.

*He indicates with a quick jerk of his head that the two women should leave. They click away on their high heels, looking sulkily at Ted.*

**TED:** Hud . . . are you . . . are you wearing a crown?

**HUD:** Ah, yeah. I am. So what? That's not a sin is it? If I want to wear a crown?

**TED:** No, it's—

**HUD:** Then just mind your own business!

*He storms off towards the girls. Ted looks at him, confused.*

SCENE 29 EXT./NIGHT 4
SET: PAROCHIAL HOUSE
*Fargo stops and waves. Very, very drunk by now.*

**FARGO:** Yadaa . . . yaaa . . . blaaaa . . .

**TED:** Yes, yes! Bye, now!

*Ted turns. He sees that the front door is wide open.*

SCENE 30 INT./NIGHT 4
SET: PAROCHIAL HOUSE
*Dougal is sitting in a chair, smiling happily, doing nothing. Ted enters the living room.*

**TED:** I notice, Dougal, that the front door is wide open.

**DOUGAL:** Oh, it is, yes. Ted.

**TED:** Yes. And I see that we are currently without sheep.

**DOUGAL:** Oh . . . ah . . .

**TED:** I told you to keep that door closed! God, Dougal!!!

**DOUGAL:** Ah, now, Ted, just hold it there.

*Dougal takes out his tape recorder, but is interrupted by a terrible howling noise.*

**TED:** What was that?!

**DOUGAL:** The Beast!

**TED:** Come on!

*They run out of the room.*

SCENE 31 EXT./NIGHT 4
SET: PAROCHIAL HOUSE
*They come out of the house.*

**DOUGAL:** Ted, how will we know which way he went?

**TED:** Sheep, like all wool-bearing animals, instinctively travel north where it's colder and they won't be so stuffy. So we have to go north.

**DOUGAL:** Which way's north?

*Long pause.*

**TED:** I don't know. (*We hear another howl.*) Quick!

*Ted and Dougal run in the direction of the howl.*

SCENE 32 EXT./NIGHT 4
SET: WOODS
*We hear howling. Ted and Dougal are behind a bunch of rocks.*

**TED:** It seems to be coming from all around us. (*He looks up.*) The Sioux Indians in the Arizona desert used to be able to pinpoint the exact location of buffalo by looking at the position of the moon . . . and then putting their ears to the ground.

*He puts his ear to the ground while closing one eye and pointing his thumb upwards to the moon. Pause.*

**DOUGAL:** Actually, Ted, maybe the sound is coming from that stereo.

*We see, in the tree right next to them, two speakers dangling from the branches of a small tree. Between the branches is a stereo system. Ted stands up. The side of his head is covered in muck. Ted and Dougal approach the record player. Ted lifts the needle off. The sound of the Beast stops. It's replaced by the sound of burping.*

**DOUGAL:** Ted, it's Chris!

**TED:** Is he all right?

**DOUGAL:** He's fine. He must have realised it was just a big stereo hanging from a tree.

**TED:** Let's bring him home, Dougal. I think I'm beginning to figure out what's been going on . . .

SCENE 33 INT./DAY 5
SET: PRESENTATION AREA
*A rather posh event, rather like the BAFTA Awards.*

*Everyone wears tuxedos, etc. We see Hud, Giant and Fargo, each standing with their respective sheep – Hud's and Giant's sheep are black. A sort of jury are talking among themselves. Then the head of the jury stands up.*

**JUDGE:** Well, it's been an easy decision. There's one out-and-out winner and rather than waste time with a speech, I'll get on with the job of announcing the winner who today has come first in this competition to see who the winner is of the King of the Sheep competition . . . that we have all come to today with nerves jangling wondering who indeed will it be who wins the prize of King of the Sheep. The winner of this year's King of the Sheep is—

**TED:** STOP!

*Everyone turns. Ted is standing at the back of the tent.*

**JUDGE:** Good God! What is the meaning of this?

**TED:** This contest is a sham and a fraud and a sham!

**JUDGE:** What! How dare you!

**TED:** There has been a deliberate and scurrilous attempt to sabotage this high-profile sheep competition. And those responsible are in this very room . . . *Giant Reid and Hud Hastings!!!!*

*General hubbub. One distant 'fucking hell'.*

**HUD:** You'd better have something to back that up with, Father!

**TED:** Oh . . . I do. I do. You were the ones who constantly chatted nonchalantly of the so-called Beast of Craggy Island, always within hearing distance of Chris the sheep.

*Flashback shows this:*

*(Note: The term 'Beck shot' in the following descriptions refers to the effect in the Beck video for the song 'Devil's Haircut' and the Nike advertisement of freezing on a wide shot and then zooming in on one particular frozen image.)*

*Beck shot: wide shot of earlier conversation between Hud and Giant; zoom in on Hud and Giant, then on to sheep.*

**TED:** . . . And it was you who used a copy of *BBC Sound Effects Volume 5* to add weight to your fanciful claims. A naïve sheep could not help but be convinced by the late-night roarings of 'Terrible Monster Type A'.

*Beck shot: a hand placing an album on a turntable. Zoom in on the words on the record label – 'Track 1: Terrible Monster Type A'.*

**JUDGE:** Well. Well, well, well. What a pretty picture Father Crilly has painted. How dare you bring shame on this celebration of sheep!

**TED:** Don't be too hard on them . . . I'm sorry, I don't know your name—

**JUDGE:** Alan.

**TED:** Don't be too hard on them, Alan! They were simply pawns. The real villain of this piece I have yet to reveal. But I now will reveal him. It was . . . (*He spins and points.*) Fargo Boyle!

*General hubbub. One 'fucking hell'.*

**FARGO:** What? That's nonsense. I'll just go now and take my trophy . . .

**TED** (*the following over a montage of the events described*): It was you who was disappointed at the poor odds Chris was receiving.

*Beck shot: Fargo looks at a newspaper headline that reads 'Champion sheep odds-on favourite'. He looks worried.*

**TED:** You who planned to manipulate those odds by sabotaging your own sheep, and then staging a miraculous recovery on the day of the competition.

*Beck shot: Fargo slipping some money to a delighted Hud and Giant.*

**TED:** You who paid Hud and Giant to talk about the Beast in front of Chris.

*Beck shot: Fargo leaving John's and Mary's shop. Zoom in on guilty face and then on the sound-effects record under Fargo's arm.*

**TED:** You who bought the BBC sound-effects record just before Dougal had a chance to.

*Beck shot: wide shot of a field. Freeze and zoom in on Ted and Dougal and the sheep, all wearing party hats and laughing in a jolly manner.*

**TED:** You who gave the sheep to me, knowing that as a priest with an intuitive understanding of sheep I could nurse him back to normal. You, Fargo! You! You! You! You!

*Fargo begins to say something, but then turns and sees Chris standing around, no different from at any other time he's been standing around.*

**FARGO:** Chris! It's not true! It's not true, I tell you! (*Chris just stands around.*) No, don't – DON'T LOOK AT ME!! DON'T LOOK AT ME!!!

*Fargo slumps down on to the ground.*

**TED:** You stood to make a fair profit, didn't you? But you didn't count on the vanity of your accomplices . . . using their newfound wealth to buy a fur coat, and a crown.

*Fargo sobs.*

**JUDGE:** Should I call the police, Father?

**TED:** No. He's lost the trust of his sheep. That's enough punishment for a farmer who deals primarily with sheep. Now, if you'll excuse me . . there's a bit of a stench in here and I need some air.

*He walks out, leaving the three farmers crestfallen and ashamed.*

SCENE 34 EXT./DAY 5
SET: TENT
*Ted comes out to where Dougal is waiting. He lights*

a cigarette. Dougal sees Chris off to one side.

**DOUGAL:** What'll happen to Chris?

**TED:** I don't know, Dougal. It's a cold world out there and he's just been metaphorically shaved of his wool.

*A young girl with her family sees Chris. She runs up to Chris and hugs him.*

**GIRL:** Mammy, Daddy! It's a lovely sheep. Can I keep it?

**FATHER** (*with pipe*): 'Course!

*They bundle it into a car and drive off. Chris looks out of the back of the window as it departs. Ted looks at this and gives a little wave.*

**TED:** You know, Dougal . . . maybe it isn't such a cold world after all.

*They walk off into the sunset.*

**DOUGAL:** One thing, Ted . . . if Chris has been disqualified, doesn't that mean you've lost the heating allowance money on the bet?

*Dougal walks off, leaving Ted alone.*

SCENE 35 INT./DAY 5
SET: PAROCHIAL HOUSE
*We see Ted in a woolly hat and mittens and warm-weather gear.*

**TED:** It's a radical step, Dougal, but it is very, very cold.

**DOUGAL:** See you in three months, Ted.

*Credits start over . . .*

*Ted gets into a cardboard box filled with straw. He packs the straw in around him and closes the box. Dougal gets into a similar box.*

*Credits end.*

*The box opens.*

**TED:** Actually, better go to the toilet first.

**THE END**

# speed 3

**GRAHAM:** We thought, 'How can we make a worse sequel than *Speed 2*?' and Dougal on an exploding milk float sounded promising. We worked backwards from that joke. What's Dougal doing on a milk float? He got a job working as a milkman. What happened to the last milkman? He was fired for fooling around with the local women while on the job. How was he found out? The babies have started growing facial hair. How does Ted know about the facial hair? He was judging a bonny baby competition. So we worked backwards until Ted walks into the room covered in baby sick.

The brick was inspired by my recent move into a new flat whose previous owner had left a brick on the floor, which he had been using to prop the front door open. I started thinking about what a strange thing it was, this brick on the floor. Take a brick out of its natural context and it becomes an ode to uselessness. Ah . . . I am aware how this story manages to be both insane and boring, by the way . . . so, that gave us the idea of this brick that keeps popping up and getting in the way. Until they find a use for it at a crucial moment. I'm telling you all this to illustrate how inspiration can come from the most boring places, and also to give you a small insight into the nightmare that is my life.

**ARTHUR:** The milkman who sleeps with housewives has all those 1970s connotations of Dick Emery, the *Confessions . . .* films and Benny Hill, which is possibly why we introduced some of the more risqué lines here – like the milkman wondering if he can put his giant tool in Mrs Doyle's box. That's really quite un-*Ted*. But what *is* very Ted (the character) is what he considers to be a practical solution to Dougal's plight. When all else fails, he turns to religion, and a Mass is conducted alongside the float (here's an instance of 'spot the writer' – I'm one of the priests saying Mass). That's so typical of Ted: when religion is the last thing that's needed, he suddenly finds his faith. And when that fails, they watch *The Poseidon Adventure* because Gene Hackman played a priest in it. This is supposed to be a *practical* solution, so they watch the entire film.

I'm very fond of this episode and, while it contains a lot of silliness, it provides one of the best illustrations of the dynamic within the Parochial House. They are, effectively, a family, with Ted as the father, Dougal as the son, Mrs Doyle as the mother and Jack as the grandfather. We thought we'd illustrate this by having Ted becoming emotional about Dougal striking out on his own to do his milk round.

## PART ONE

SCENE 1 INT./DAY 1
SET: PAROCHIAL HOUSE

*The living room is empty, except for Jack sleeping in one corner. We hear the front door opening and closing, then immediately Ted's and Dougal's voices.*

**TED** (*from outside*): . . . even to talk to me! I don't want to hear it!

**DOUGAL** (*from outside*): Ted, I'm so sorry.

**TED** (*from outside*): You're judging a baby competition, you're not supposed to get them agitated! This happens every year and I'm sick of it!

*Ted and Dougal come in. Ted is covered in a white, gooey, milky substance. It is in his hair, on his shoulders and down his front.*

**DOUGAL:** I was just playing with them, Ted!

**TED:** Playing with them? You were doing this! (*He makes a vigorous shaking motion.*) You were agitating the babies! It was like Schumacher celebrating a win! Next time, when you're given a baby, just check that it doesn't have two heads, and hand it to me, and I will return it to its mother.

*Ted dries himself off with a cloth. They both look exhausted. They flop down in chairs – Ted unbuttoning his collar so that it hangs off.*

**DOUGAL:** I thought the standard this year was rubbish.

**TED:** It was awful all right. A lot of very sloppy babies who looked as though they really couldn't be bothered.

**DOUGAL:** I can't even remember who won. Who did win?

**TED:** Ah, just some baby. I can't even remember it's name now. They all looked the same. If they couldn't be bothered being a decent standard of babies, then why should I break my bottom judging it. And the hairiness of some of those babies. That was a very hairy baby parade.

**DOUGAL:** Exactly, Ted. If people aren't even going to shave their babies before they come out . . . I mean . . .

**TED:** Well, normally, you wouldn't have to shave a baby. It's like their hormones have

gone mad.

*Ted crosses over to the table but as he goes, trips over something.*

**TED:** AAH!!! What the hell was— Mrs Doyle, did you put a brick in the middle of the floor?

*Mrs Doyle enters. She is wearing a lot of make-up and a dress that is frillier than usual.*

**MRS DOYLE:** I did, Father.

**TED** (*taking in the new look*): Eh . . . Well . . . Why?

**MRS DOYLE:** I thought it might be a good place for your paperclips. You can put them in that hollow there.

**TED:** But why in the middle of the floor? Why not on the desk?

**MRS DOYLE:** I got the idea in a magazine. Look.

*She opens a glossy magazine called 'Design Today'. We see a photograph of a studio flat with a brick in the middle of the floor. A yuppie couple sit on a designer sofa in the background. The headline reads 'A new look for autumn – brick enlivens dull floor'.*

**TED:** Yes, well, that may be all very well for Will Self or one of those fellas, but I like the traditional aspect of not putting bricks in the middle of the floor.

*He puts it on the desk. Mrs Doyle is staring out of the window.*

**MRS DOYLE:** EEP!

*She has seen something out of the window. She jumps up with excitement and runs from the room.*

**TED:** Mrs Doyle is looking very . . . different today.

**DOUGAL:** Was it definitely Mrs Doyle?

**TED:** Yeah . . . what's going on?

SCENE 2 EXT./DAY 1
SET: PAROCHIAL HOUSE

*A milkfloat pulls up. We see two stickers on the back, which read 'World's Greatest Lover' and 'My Other Car is a Porsche'. We see a chain hanging around a hairy chest. The milkfloat stops. A cigarette falls on the ground beside it and is stubbed out by a leather boot/fashionable Italian shoe.*

SCENE 3 INT./DAY 1
SET: KITCHEN

*Mrs Doyle is in the kitchen. There's a knock on the door and she jumps. She checks herself in the mirror one more time and then opens the door.*

*Pat Mustard, the milkman, leans in. He is big, beefy, has his shirt open to reveal a hairy chest and a medallion, and sports big sideboards connecting to a handlebar moustache.*

**PAT:** Oh, sorry, I was looking for Mrs Doyle.

**MRS DOYLE:** It is Mrs Doyle!

**PAT:** Wha'? I thought you were Marilyn Monroe!

*Mrs Doyle giggles girlishly. Pat walks by her and puts two pints of milk on the table.*

**PAT:** A few more pints for you.

**MRS DOYLE:** Oh, great! We're a bit low, actually.

**PAT:** There's more where that came from.

*Mrs Doyle giggles girlishly.*

**PAT:** I tell you, I shouldn't really be here. The police are after me.

**MRS DOYLE:** They're not!

**PAT:** Yeah. I'm so gorgeous, they want to put me under arrest. They think the women'll be after me, and there'll be no one to make the tea.

*Mrs Doyle giggles girlishly. Pat pulls up his trousers*

to reveal a massive bulge in his groinal area. Mrs Doyle steals one quick look.

**PAT:** Actually, Mrs Doyle, I'm a bit sad at the moment. I have to go to a funeral.

**MRS DOYLE:** Oh, no. Really?

**PAT:** Yeah, me last girlfriend. She died from exhaustion!

**MRS DOYLE:** Really? What was she doing?

**PAT:** Well . . . ah . . .

*Ted sticks his head around the door.*

**TED:** Hello.

**MRS DOYLE:** Oh, Father, this is Pat Mustard, the new milkman.

**TED:** Oh?

**PAT:** Yeah, just took over the south side of the island. Thought I'd spread meself around a bit . . .

**TED:** Mrs Doyle, you need to do a bit of dusting in Father Jack's room. And there's a huge cobweb in the shed that needs removing.

**MRS DOYLE:** Oh, right, Father.

**PAT:** I'll be on my way then, Padre . . .

*Ted flinches a bit.*

**PAT:** . . . Off on me rounds.

*He leaves, whistling as he goes.*

SCENE 4 INT./DAY 1
SET: PAROCHIAL HOUSE

*Ted enters, holding a cup of tea. Dougal has a blackboard set up. As the following conversation takes place, he writes on it with a stick of chalk.*

**TED:** We have a new milkman, Dougal.*

**DOUGAL:** Oh, yes. I saw him goin' on his milkfloat the other day. God, I wish priests could go round on things like that. You know, if milkmen can have those things, I don't know why priests can't.*

**TED:** Well, they use them to deliver milk, Dougal. Priests don't deliver milk in a professional capacity.*

**DOUGAL:** Well, we could use them to deliver things that priests deliver . . . What do you call those things? . . . Sacraments. We could deliver those. I don't know, Ted . . . as you get older, you start asking yourself if . . . you know, if you should start thinking about getting a job.*

**TED:** Dougal, you have a job. Being a priest is a job.*

**DOUGAL:** Ah, Ted . . . *

**TED:** It is! It's as much a job as being a milkman is – actually, it's more important than being a milkman. Much more important. Milkmen just deliver the milk. We deliver the milk . . . that comes from God.*

*He sees that Dougal has written 'My name is Father Dougal McGuire' on the blackboard.*

**DOUGAL:** Right, Ted. Watch this. Looks like an ordinary blackboard, doesn't it?

**TED:** Yes . . .

**DOUGAL:** That's what I thought. But watch this . . . (*He takes a duster and wipes off the letters.*) You see! You can rub off the letters!

**TED:** Well . . . you can do that with every blackboard, Dougal.

**DOUGAL** (*puzzled*)**:** What?

*Ted takes a sip of tea. We see that it is very milky. Mrs Doyle enters, carrying a can with 'Cobweb-Remover' written on it.*

**TED:** That's very milky tea, Mrs Doyle.

**MRS DOYLE:** Well, yes, I thought you might like more milk . . . in your tea . . .

**TED:** This is almost an all-milk cup of tea, though. I mean . . . (*He tastes it.*) Is there actually any tea in here at all?

**MRS DOYLE:** Well . . . no.

**TED:** Anyone would think you were trying to use up more milk so that Pat Mustard can come here more often.

**MRS DOYLE:** Ha, ha, ha, ha! Actually, Father, Pat is very interesting. On the weekends he's a swimming instructor at the pool. And he fought in Vietnam, and he's a former Mr Universe and he taught Elvis Presley to play karate.

*We deleted these lines from the final version.

**TED:** Well, it sounds to me like he's telling you a few 'tall tales'.

**DOUGAL:** Well, Ted, I'm very cynical, as you know, but I do find all that a bit hard to believe. Especially that 'swimming instructor' business.

**MRS DOYLE:** Well, Father, it's not my place, I know, but it sounds to me like you're a little bit jealous.

**TED:** Jealous? Of Mr Milky Man? I very much think not.

*He is.*

SCENE 5 INT./NIGHT 1
SET: TED AND DOUGAL'S BEDROOM
*Dougal has a little table in front of him as he sits in bed. Ted is sitting up in bed, reading something.*

**TED:** What are you doing, Dougal?

**DOUGAL:** I was looking at some of the hairy babies from today. There's something about them . . .

**TED:** Let's see.

*He crosses over for a look. We see the photos lined up. One baby has sideboards, another has long hair coming from the back of a bald head. The third has a very faint moustache.*

**TED:** Well . . . oh, my God . . .

**DOUGAL:** What?

**TED:** Well . . . this is a terrible thing to say but . . . if you took this baby's moustache, this baby's head and this baby's sideboards and put them together . . . I think you'd get Pat Mustard!

**DOUGAL:** You're right, Ted! Do you think the babies are copying his style?

**TED:** No, Dougal. It's more likely that . . .

*He looks at Dougal. Dougal has a very innocent face on.*

**TED:** It's more likely that Pat Mustard has been . . . (*Dougal still looks innocent.*) . . . well . . . delivering more than dairy products . . .

**DOUGAL:** No! You mean he's been . . . (*Ted looks expectant.*) . . . he's been . . . I can't . . . oh! Ho-hoh! Of course . . . but . . . so he . . . no,

*God . . . (Pause.) He's been what?*

**TED:** I think we should do a little detective work, Dougal. Find out exactly what this Pat Mustard fella is up to.

SCENE 6 EXT./DAY 2*
SET: ROAD
*Pat Mustard is coming down the road in his little milkfloat. Cut to a house in the road. Pat Mustard is knocking on the door. It opens and a tarty-looking woman appears in a negligée and pink slippers. 'Confessions of a Window Cleaner' type 1970s music plays.*

SCENE 7 EXT./DAY 2*
SET: ROAD
*We see Ted pulling up in a car. He wears shades.*

SCENE 8 EXT./DAY 2*
SET: HOUSE
*Pat Mustard is talking.*

**PAT:** . . . Thought it was Marilyn Monroe . . .

SCENE 9 EXT./DAY 2*
SET: ROAD
*Cut to reveal that Ted is actually right beside the pair. They turn to look at him. Ted looks away innocently, which is hard considering he's right beside them.*

*Pat walks up to Ted and raps on the window. Ted doesn't answer. He keeps looking the other way.*

*Pat raps again. Ted, still pretending not to notice Pat, turns the ignition in his car and drives slowly away, not looking at Pat once.*

SCENE 10 EXT./DAY 2*
SET: HOUSE
*From the point of view of the woman opening the door, we see a door opening to reveal Pat waiting.*

**PAT:** . . . Marilyn Monroe!

*In the background, Ted cycles by, from left to right, in and out of shot. Pat hands the woman some milk.*

**PAT:** There's more where that came from.

*Ted cycles back in the other direction.*

**PAT:** Actually, I shouldn't be here because I'm

*\*We deleted this scene from the final version.*

wanted by the police . . .

*Ted cycles back in the other direction. A car is coming straight for him and beeps its horn. Ted swerves out of the way and heads straight for Pat. Pat is brushed to one side and Ted cycles up into the house and behind the camera.*

**PAT:** Are you all right, Father?

*Ted doesn't say anything. He just backs out in a pathetically slow way.*

**PAT:** Do you want something? Father? Can I help you? Father?

*Ted doesn't say anything. He just rights his bicycle and cycles off.*

SCENE 11 INT./DAY 2†
SET: PAROCHIAL HOUSE
*Dougal and Ted are in the living room. Ted is pacing up and down.*

**TED:** That milkman is definitely up to no good with the women of the parish. Soon half the population will have been spawned by Pat Mustard. And they'll all be marrying each other in twenty years' time.

**DOUGAL:** Like Michael Jackson and Lisa Marie.

**TED:** They're not brother and sister . . .

**DOUGAL:** No. No, they're not, are they? Why did I think they were?

*Jack enters. Ted walks behind him, trips over something, and goes headfirst into the wall.*

**TED:** What's this bloody brick doing on the ground again?

*Jack yanks a piece of string attached to the brick and it jumps out of Ted's hand, landing on his foot.*

**TED:** Aaaah!!!

*Jack continues pulling the brick after him on a piece of string. He sits down, picks up the brick, and puts it on his lap.*

**TED:** What's going on there?

† We also deleted this scene from the final version but kept the theme of Jack being very fond of the brick, then suddenly tiring of it and throwing it at Ted and inserted it in scene 18.

He throws the brick at Ted. It hits him with a loud 'conking' sound. Ted falls out of shot.

SCENE 12 EXT./DAY 2
SET: PAROCHIAL HOUSE
*Ted comes out of the house and decisively throws the brick in the bin. He goes back into the house. Mrs Doyle comes out to put out some empty milk bottles. Coming back, she notices the brick in the bin. She takes it out.*

**MRS DOYLE:** Tsk!

*She wipes the brick and brings it back in.*

**END OF PART ONE**

\* \* \*

**PART TWO**

SCENE 13 INT./DAY 2
SET: KITCHEN
*Mrs Doyle is sitting at the kitchen table with Pat. Ted comes in.*

**MRS DOYLE:** Hello, Father. Pat was wondering if he could put his massive tool in my box.

**TED:** What!! How dare y—

**PAT** (*lifts up a giant wrench*)**:** It's too big for the milkfloat. I'll pick it up tomorrow.

*Mrs Doyle puts it away in a metal box.*

**TED:** Mrs Doyle, could you leave us for a moment.

**MRS DOYLE:** Oh . . . yes, OK.

*She does do. Ted spins on Pat.*

**TED:** I know what you're up to, Pat Mustard. There's some hairy babies on Craggy Island, and I think you're the hairy babymaker.

**PAT:** Oh, yeah? I think you need proof for that kind of accusation, Father. And I'm a very careful man, Father. A very careful man.

**TED:** Except when it comes to taking precautions in the bedroom, Pat.

**PAT:** You wouldn't be advising the use of artificial contraception, would you Father?

**TED:** Yes, I . . no, I . . . If you're going to be . . . I . . . of course . . . you . . .

**DOUGAL:** Jack's got very fond of that brick, Ted. They're great pals. He's a brilliant pet actually. Jack doesn't have to feed him or look after him or show him any affection like you'd have to with normal pets. It might catch on, actually, having bricks as pets.

**JACK:** I LOVE MY BRICK!

*He hugs it affectionately.*

**TED:** But it's fun showing pets affection. That's the whole point of them. I mean, what do you think pets are for?

**DOUGAL:** Eh . . . ah, just . . . someone to talk to when you're down. Someone to get advice from.

**TED:** You don't usually get advice from animals, Dougal. Anyway, I'm off. I won't rest until I've caught Pat Mustard 'on the job', so to speak. And I don't mean the job of being a milkman. I mean . . . the job of getting on top of women . . . which isn't really a job . . . but you know what I mean . . . (*He sees Jack hugging the brick with a blissful smile on his face.*) Oh, well . . . if Jack's found a new friend in a brick, then I suppose we should be happy for him.

**JACK:** AH, FECK IT! FED UP OF BRICK!

(*He goes quiet. There is an unnaturally long pause.*)
Just . . . feck off.

PAT: You can keep following me, Father. But
you have to be up very early in the morning to
catch me. Very early in the morning.

SCENE 14 EXT./DAY 3
SET: STREET
*A caption comes up that reads 'Very early in the
morning'. We see two houses next to each other. Pat
comes out of one house and zips himself up. This
turns into a frozen image and we hear a click. Cut to
Ted taking the shot from his car with a camera with
an amazingly long lens.*

PAT: God, I really enjoyed riding Mrs O'Dowd.

*Pat opens a milk carton and throws it back.*

TED (*gasps*): Did you get that, Dougal?

*We see Dougal with a pair of earphones on and a
radar-type device pointing out of the window. Dougal
gives the thumbs up.*

PAT (*finishes milk*): Now to ride Mrs Reilly.

TED: God almighty. He really is quite reckless
this early in the morning. (*Pat goes next door.*)
Right. Now we wait.

DOUGAL: I'll put the volume up as loud as I
can in case I can hear inside the house.

*He does so, the radar still pointing out of the
window. A truck passes by and sounds its incredibly
loud horn. Dougal's eyes cross as the sound hits him.
He faints. Ted, in the front seat, doesn't notice.
Suddenly the door of the house opens.*

TED: Oh my God!

*Pat comes out, not wearing any trousers. He has very
hairy legs. He gets in his milkfloat then, stops and*

*bounds back to the house. The door opens.*

**PAT** (*to woman*): . . . Forgot me feckin' trousers! . . .

SCENE 15 INT./DAY 3
SET: PAROCHIAL HOUSE
*A well-dressed civil-servant type, Mr Fox, is looking as Ted puts a succession of photographs down in front of him. Mrs Doyle is nearby, listening in.*

**FOX:** Right . . . yes . . . that's disgusting. I . . . shameful . . . I've never seen anything like this . . .

**TED:** These were all taken in the course of one morning . . .

**FOX:** Dear God . . . disgraceful . . .

**TED:** Look at him there, Mr Fox. Have you ever seen anything like that?

**FOX:** No, I have not. (*He stands up straight.*) All right, how will we do this? . . . How about . . . two pounds each for this, this and this, and a tenner for the rest.

**TED:** Eh . . . I wasn't trying to sell them to you. I just wanted to show you what one of your employees got up to on his round.

**FOX:** Oh! Oh, my God, yes!

**TED:** . . . Why? What did you think . . .?

**FOX:** I completely misread the situation! Please just . . . yes, this is *disgraceful* behaviour. This employee shall be removed from his job straight away. Thank you for bringing this to our attention, Father Crilly.

**DOUGAL:** Who's going to deliver the milk now?

*As Mr Fox replies, Mrs Doyle calmly walks over to the table, slides one photograph off and quietly, calmly, leaves the room with it.*

**FOX:** Actually, next week is a big week for us. We recently agreed to ease the milk-surplus problems of the newly liberated Eastern European republic of Krovtonova by buying seventeen thousand tons of milk from them. Pat's sacking couldn't have come at a worse time.

**DOUGAL:** It's terrible to think of all that lovely milk floating around and going sour,

with no one dropping it off anywhere. I wish I could do it.

**FOX:** Well, Father, we could certainly trust you. You are, after all, a man of God.

**DOUGAL:** A what?

**FOX:** A priest.

**DOUGAL:** Well, yeah. (*Sulkily.*) Thanks for reminding me. (*He perks up.*) But I'd love to be a milkman for a while. That'd be fantastic. God knows, I do flip all around here.

**FOX:** Not a bad idea! You could certainly fill in for a while.

**TED:** I'm not sure. Father McGuire has other duties in the parish.

**DOUGAL:** Like what?

*Very long pause.*

**TED:** I'm not sure what the rules are on priests becoming milkmen. Let me look it up. (*He goes to the bookshelf, grabs an absolutely huge book from high up and flips through it very quickly.*) Hmm . . . apparently it's OK. Well . . . I really don't know, Dougal. God knows what sort of damage you could do on a milkfloat. How fast can those things go?

**FOX:** Pretty fast. Our new model can reach speeds of nearly ten miles an hour.

**TED:** Yeah, you see, that's pretty fast . . .

**DOUGAL:** But, Ted, I wouldn't be going that fast anyway! Unless there was an emergency! And what type of emergency could happen on a milkfloat! Oh, please let me, Ted. Please, please, please, please, please, please!

**TED:** Well . . . all right.

**DOUGAL:** Yes! I'm going to deliver bread!

**TED:** Milk.

**DOUGAL:** Milk! I'm going to deliver milk!

SCENE 16 INT./DAY 3
SET: PAROCHIAL HOUSE HALLWAY
*Mr Fox stands at the door. Ted is adjusting Dougal's scarf.*

**TED:** . . . And make sure you keep warm.

**DOUGAL** (*impatient whisper*): *Te-ed*, not in

front of Mr *Fox*.

**TED:** . . . And stay on the left side of the road.

**DOUGAL:** *Duu-uuh! I kno-ow!*

*Ted licks a hankie and tries to wipe something off Dougal's face. Dougal wriggles uncomfortably. Cut to Mr Fox watching all this in complete wonderment.*

**DOUGAL:** Stop it!

SCENE 17 EXT./DAY 3
SET: PAROCHIAL HOUSE
*Dougal is sitting in the milkfloat. Mr Fox stands to one side.*

**FOX:** All right, Father . . .

**DOUGAL:** Ah, no, today I'm not Father. I'm . . . ah, Milkman.

**FOX:** Right, ah, Milkman. I'd better take you through the workings of the old float here.

**DOUGAL:** Right.

**FOX:** That turns it on, that makes it go and that steers it.

**DOUGAL:** Rrrrrright.

**FOX:** OK! You're ready to be a milkman! You'd better get going, actually – milk gets sour, you know. Unless its UHT milk, but there's no demand for that because it's shite.

**TED:** Actually, I might as well be the first customer! Two pints please, Milkman!

**DOUGAL:** Oh. Right. OK. Right. Two pints. Right. Here we go. Right. Two pints.

*He picks them up and hands them to Ted.*

**TED:** Well! Thank you very much. (*Pause. Everyone just stands there.*) Actually, I just realised, we don't need any. Can I give this back?

*Cut to Dougal driving out of the gate. He waves back at Fox and Ted. Ted looks worried.*

**FOX:** He'll be fine, Father.

*Ted wipes away a little tear, nods and goes into the house.*

SCENE 18 INT./DAY 3
SET: PAROCHIAL HOUSE
*Ted enters. He picks up the book he had earlier and*

*puts it back, high on the shelf. Another book takes his interest. He starts to pull the book out and we see the brick on top of it. It falls and conks him on the head.**

**TED** (*intense pain*): OH, MY GOD!!!!!

*The telephone rings. He picks it up.*

**TED** (*still in pain*): Hello. Craggy Island Parochial House. Father Crilly speaking.

SCENE 19 INT./DAY 3
SET: TELEPHONE BOX
*Pat is in the telephone box, telephone to his ear. He's not wearing his uniform any more, but a tracksuit. Cut back to Ted.*

**PAT:** It's me, Father. Y'ignorant bastard . . .

**TED:** Who's that? Is that you, Pat?

**PAT:** It's me all right. I've got a score to settle with you, ye baldy fecker.

**TED:** Don't use that type of language. And I'm not bald. I've got a lovely head of hair.

**PAT:** You got me sacked, and now I'm having to yank meself off round the clock 'cause I'm not getting any proper sex with girls.

**TED:** Well! If you're going to use that kind of language! . . .

**PAT:** Wait! Don't hang up! I've got something to tell you. I've put a little present on that milkfloat your little friend took off me. Something to remember me by. A bomb.

**TED:** What?

**PAT:** That's right, Father. A very special bomb. When your little friends gets over four miles an hour, the bomb will be armed. But when he goes back under four miles an hour . . .

*Pat makes a low, exploding sound. Ted moves the earpiece away in confusion.*

**TED:** Pat, I lost you there. What'll happen if it goes under four miles an hour?

**PAT:** It'll blow up.

**TED:** Oh, no! Dougal!

*He throws down the telephone. Pat doesn't notice.*

*We deleted this and replaced it with Jack and the brick from scene 11.

**PAT:** Oh, yes. Your little friend is going to go boom . . .

SCENE 20 EXT./DAY 3
SET: ROAD
*We see the speedometer of Dougal's float. It reads just under four miles an hour. Dougal stops the float and takes two pints from the back. He approaches the door of a customer.*

**DOUGAL:** Mrs Millet . . . Two pints for her . . . two pints of milk . . .

*It bursts open. We see a naked woman revealed.*

**WOMAN:** Pat! FATHER! Oh, my God!

*She covers her breasts up. Dougal, still concentrating on the order, hands over the two bottles. She covers her breasts with them.*

**DOUGAL:** Two pints. Two pints. Two pints . . . there you go! Bye, then! (*The mortified woman closes the door.*) Hah! Right, who's next . . . ? Mrs Gleason.

SCENE 21 EXT./DAY 3
SET: ROAD
*Ted's car is speeding along. Ted is inside.*

**TED:** Come onnnnn . . . onnnnnnnnnn . . .

*The car roars over a hill.*

SCENE 22 EXT./DAY 3
SET: DOORWAY
*The door opens. We see another naked woman. Dougal hands over the milk.*

**DOUGAL:** Morning, Mrs Gleason!

*The woman, totally shocked, slams the door.*

**DOUGAL:** I'll leave it out here then!

*He tootles away.*

SCENE 23 EXT./DAY 3
SET: ROAD
*Ted is driving along. We see, from his point of view, Dougal's milkfloat up ahead.*

SCENE 24 EXT./DAY 3
SET: STREET
*We see Dougal driving along. The speedometer is just about to reach four miles an hour. Ted drives the car up alongside Dougal.*

**TED:** Dougal! Are you going over four miles an hour?

**DOUGAL:** Ah, Ted, I'm doing fine, leave me alone.

**TED:** Are you doing over four?

**DOUGAL:** Ah . . . not yet . . . now I am.

*We see the speedometer hitting four.*

SCENE 25 EXT./DAY 3
SET: UNDER MILKFLOAT
*We see a device. A green light turns red. We see that the device is connected to explosives that run the entire length of the bottom of the milkfloat.*

SCENE 26 EXT./DAY 3
SET: ROAD
*Ted is driving along.*

**TED:** Oh, no! Dougal, listen to me! There's a bomb on the milkfloat!

**DOUGAL:** A bomb? Right. Who's that for?

**TED:** No, you're not supposed to deliver it to anyone! It's going to go off and kill you!

**DOUGAL:** Ah, I'm sure there's nothing to worry about. It's probably there for a reason.

**TED:** Pat Mustard put it there because I got him sacked! When you go under four miles an hour it'll go off – the bomb will go off! Have you got that?!

**DOUGAL** (*hyperventilating*)**:** Oh, God! Help! I don't want to be a milkman any more!

**TED:** You'll be safe as long as you don't slow down!

**DOUGAL:** Oh, no, Ted! (*He points out something ahead of him: pile of cardboard boxes in the middle of the road.*) It's a big bunch of boxes in the middle of the road!

**TED:** Just stay over four!

*Ted drives up ahead and stops near the rubbish. In the background we see the milkfloat getting nearer. Ted jumps out of the car and starts moving the boxes away. Dougal's getting nearer.*

*Ted clears away more boxes, huffing and puffing. He moves them directly across the road in front of his car. Dougal is getting nearer.*

*Ted takes a break for a second to catch his breath. The milkfloat gets nearer.*

*Ted resumes picking up the boxes. He piles them up on the other side of the road. One drops off. He carefully replaces it. Dougal closes his eyes, ready for impact. Ted clears away the last box just in time and the milkfloat drives slowly past.*

**TED:** Go! Go! Go!

*Ted jumps into his car. Cut to the boxes. Ted rams his car through them.*

*Dougal is driving along. Ted drives up beside him.*

**TED:** Just get to the roundabout and start circling it! I've got to have a think!

*Ted pulls over to the side of the road.*

**DOUGAL:** TED!!!!

SCENE 27 INT./DAY 3*
SET: PAROCHIAL HOUSE
*Ted bursts into the living room and slides up to the telephone. He punches out some numbers. Mrs Doyle enters.*

**MRS DOYLE:** What in the name of goodness gracious me is going on?

**TED:** I'm calling Father Darsoley. Dougal's in trouble and he might be the only person who can help.

**MRS DOYLE:** Oh yes, he helped the police with that hostage thing last year. I forget how it ended.

**TED:** He tried reverse psychology on the terrorists. He said something like, 'Oh, go ahead, kill them all! Who cares about them?!'

**MRS DOYLE:** Oh, dear God! Did it work?

*Ted pauses. He hangs up the telephone.*

**TED:** Actually, no, it didn't. I'll try Father Beeching. He did an evening course in counterterrorism when he was in Wicklow.

*He starts dialling again.*

*\*We deleted this scene from the final version.*

SCENE 28 INT./DAY 3
SET: A PAROCHIAL HOUSE
*A priest comes to the telephone. This is Father Beeching.*

**BEECHING:** Hello, Barren Island Parochial House, Father Beeching here!

**TED:** Derek, I need your help. Dougal's got a job as a milkman and the previous milkman has put a bomb on the milkfloat that'll go off if the milkfloat goes under four miles an hour!

**BEECHING:** Yes. That is a problem. Well, don't panic, Ted. We'll find a way through this. But in the meantime, is there anything we can do to lift his spirits? Anything to keep his morale up?

**TED:** We have to do something practical. Something that will really help Dougal.

**BEECHING:** Wait! I've got it!

SCENE 29 EXT./DAY 3
SET: ROAD
*Dougal is driving along. We see him from the side. Suddenly (albeit slowly) another milkfloat drives up alongside him, driven by a priest. The back of it has been taken off, so that it's sort of like a flatbed truck on the back of a truck. We see Ted, Father Beeching and another priest, Father Clarke, all dressed in vestments. A couple of altar boys are there as well. Father Beeching stands at the podium, Ted and Father Clarke sit down at the side of the altar.*

**BEECHING:** The Lord be with you.

**TED AND CLARKE:** And also with you.

**DOUGAL** (*to himself*): Oh, no! Mass!

**BEECHING:** The Mass today is being offered for Father Dougal McGuire, who finds himself in a most trying and unfortunate situation. We pray that God will protect him from . . . (*The milkfloat jolts and Beeching falls over. He stands up again.*) . . . from harm at this time and deliver him to safety.

**ALL:** Amen.

*He sits down. The other priest, Father Clarke, steps forward.*

**CLARKE:** A reading from the letter of Saint Paul to the Corinthians: 'Verily do I say to you . . .'

*Dougal, despite himself, pays attention.*

SCENE 30 INT./DAY 3
SET: TELEPHONE BOX
*Pat is still on the telephone.*

**PAT:** . . . Oh, yeah . . . they'll be peeling him off the walls for weeks to come . . .

SCENE 31 EXT./DAY 3
SET: ROAD
*Ted is now speaking.*

**TED:** The Mass has ended. Go in peace to love and serve the Lord.

**EVERYONE:** Amen.

**TED:** DOUGAL! THERE'S THE ROUNDABOUT!

*Dougal drives on. They stop.*

**TED:** Dougal, keep driving round and round! Everything's going to be OK!

**DOUGAL** (*offscreen*): I'm getting dizzy, Ted!

**TED:** Don't get dizzy! (*To the other priests.*) All right, we've got to come up with a plan. Back to my house, and step on it!

*The van drives off, incredibly slowly, Ted holding on to the side.*

MONTAGE SEQUENCE
*Ted drawing a complicated diagram on the board.*

*Dougal driving in circles.*

*Ted arguing with the other priests.*

*A battery level about to go into the red.*

SCENE 32 INT./DAY 3
SET: PAROCHIAL HOUSE
*Ted is looking at the other priests.*

**TED:** That's the idea?

**BEECHING:** It's the best we've had, Ted!

**TED:** Another Mass? That's our best idea?

**BEECHING:** Well, I thought the other one went very well.

**TED:** He needs help, not Mass! He needs physical lifting off the milkfloat, not spiritual lifting of his . . . spirits. There's a time for Mass and a time for action. And this is a time for action!

**BEECHING:** Ted's right! Another Mass at this point would just waste time! We could sit here all night discussing the merits of saying Mass or not saying Mass, but we'd just be wasting precious time, and time is precious at the moment! It's the one thing we can't afford to waste! We can't afford to waste any more time sitting around here talking!

**CLARKE:** I agree with Father Beeching. We can't talk about this any longer. Father Dougal's out there, in trouble and we're the only ones who can help him. Sitting round here talking about whether another Mass would be wasting time is just wasting time! We've got to do something!

*Pause.*

**BEECHING:** Is there *anything* to be said for saying another Mass . . .? Just a small one. God, I love saying Mass.

**CLARKE:** Listen to him! Any excuse!

**TED:** For God's sake! Will you all just shut up and help me come up with a *practical* solution!

*Mrs Doyle comes in.*

**MRS DOYLE:** Tea for everyone! Father Beeching, biscuit or cake?

**BEECHING:** Biscuit or cake . . . biscuit or cake . . . let's see . . .

*Pause.*

**TED:** For God's sake, hurry up, man!

**BEECHING** (*flustered and panicky*)**:** Don't rush me! Eh . . . eh . . . biscuit, no cake!

*Cut to Jack in his chair listening to the telephone.*

SCENE 33 INT./DAY 3
SET: TELEPHONE BOX
*Pat is still on the other end.*

**PAT:** I've seen the damage a bomb can do. It can blow your face on to the other side of a tree . . .

*Jack looks intrigued. Cut back to the others.*

**BEECHING:** . . . Well, it worked for them! And they saved *hundreds* of people. We just have to save one!

**TED:** It's not the same thing. That was a big building that caught fire. You can't apply the same criteria to rescuing a priest from an explosive milkfloat. And besides, they had Paul Newman and Steve McQueen.

**CLARKE:** God almighty. It's so long since I saw it, I forgot Steve McQueen was in it.

**BEECHING:** Yes, he plays the fire chief.

**TED:** WAIT A SECOND! I'VE GOT IT! *THE POSEIDON ADVENTURE*!

**CLARKE:** What?

**TED:** GENE HACKMAN PLAYS A PRIEST IN IT!

*Ted goes to a cupboard and fishes out a video box. He takes the cassette out of the box and slams it into the*

*machine. He turns out the lights. They sit down to watch the film. We hear the music beginning.*

SCENE 34 EXT./NIGHT 3
SET: ROUNDABOUT
*Dougal is jerking himself back awake every now and again.*

SCENE 35 INT./NIGHT 3
SET: PAROCHIAL HOUSE
*The film ends. Ted stands up and turns on the light.*

**TED:** That was no help at all.

*Everyone mumbles agreement.*

**BEECHING:** He didn't even say Mass.

**TED:** All right, let's go down to the roundabout. Maybe we'll think of something there.

*They all stand up and head to the door. Ted trips over something and the rest go flying this way and that.*

**TED** (*holding up brick*)**:** This feckin brick! (*He runs out but then walks slowly back in.*) Wait a second . . . I've got an idea.

*He looks back at the brick, then back at the blackboard, then at the brick again. During the following speech he starts drawing something on the blackboard in a passionate, assured manner, so the speech is punctuated by the clicking and scratching of the chalk.*

**TED:** Yes! Gentlemen, Father McGuire is propelling the milkfloat by exerting a small amount of pressure on the accelerator. If we could replace his foot with an object that would exert the same pressure, we are in the position to safely remove Father McGuire from the vehicle. The pressure exerted can be effectively produced by a heavy object.

**BEECHING:** You mean . . .

**TED:** Yes! We put the brick on the accelerator.

*Ted steps back from the blackboard. He has written, 'We put the brick on the accelerator.'*

SCENE 36 EXT./NIGHT 3
SET: ROUNDABOUT
*Dougal is nearly asleep at the wheel. Ted comes running up alongside him.*

TED: Dougal!

DOUGAL (*snapping awake*): Aaaaaahhhhh!!!!

TED: Sorry! Probably a bad idea to shout at you when you've . . . got all those explosives under you. Anyway! We've got an idea, but you've got to trust me! Take the milkfloat up to nine miles an hour!

DOUGAL: Ted, I want to be a priest again.

TED: And you will be, Dougal! It's not really for you, this type of thing, is it?

DOUGAL: No, I don't like it at *all*.

TED: All right, when I say step off the milkfloat, step off the milkfloat, all right?

DOUGAL: But what if it goes under four?

TED: I've got a plan. It's too complicated to explain to you at the moment so you'll have to trust me. Just brace yourself and keep saying, 'I want to be a priest again.'

DOUGAL: I want to be a priest again. I want to be a priest again. I want to be a priest again . . .

TED: Step off the milkfloat!

*Ted waits until Dougal is well into the mantra, then guides him off the milkfloat. He quickly slams the brick on to the accelerator.*

TED: Now, run, Dougal, run!

*The milkfloat trundles away in a straight line off the roundabout and towards a telephone box.*

SCENE 37 INT./NIGHT 3
SET: TELEPHONE BOX
*Pat is still in the telephone box, talking, he thinks to Ted. We see the milkfloat trundling towards him.*

PAT: Oh, yes, when that milkfloat goes off, you'll hear it all the way to . . .

SCENE 38 EXT./DAY 4
SET: NORTH POLE
*An Eskimo standing beside a sign that reads 'The North Pole' hears a far-off explosion. He looks around, puzzled.*

SCENE 39 INT./NIGHT 3
SET: PAROCHIAL HOUSE
*We see the telephone receiver on the ground. The tone is making a static type of noise. Mrs Doyle sees it, then puts it back in its cradle.*

SCENE 40 INT./NIGHT 3
SET: TED AND DOUGAL'S BEDROOM
*Ted hands Dougal a cup of cocoa. Dougal is wrapped up cosily, sitting in bed and reading a pile of comics.*

DOUGAL: Thanks, Ted.

TED: That's OK. Are you sure you don't want any milk in it?

DOUGAL: Oh, no, no. I'll stay off the milk for a while. God, thank— (*He takes a sip.*) Aaargh! . . . Thank God that's over. Why did I ever want to be a milkman? You should stick to what you're good at, and I'm good at being a priest.

TED: Eh, yes . . .

DOUGAL: It's scary out there, Ted. In the real non-priest world.

TED: Not every job is as dangerous as being a milkman, Dougal.

DOUGAL: No, Ted, I feel safer here.

TED: All right. Good night, Dougal!

*Ted leaves the room. Dougal puts his cocoa and comics to one side, then lies down. He opens his eyes, and beside the lamp we see a tiny toy milkfloat. He looks at it for a second, sighs, and then turns out the light.*

*Almost immediately, the light comes on again. Dougal sits straight up in bed.*

DOUGAL: THOSE WOMEN WERE IN THE NIP!

POST-CREDIT SEQUENCE
*Ted takes big plastic bag of rubbish outside. He looks up at the moonlit sky. Everything is back to normal. He smiles. He sees what he thinks is a comet in the sky. It makes a descending whining sound. It gets louder. Ted suddenly looks alarmed.*

TED: OH NO!!!

*He is hit in the face by the brick and falls to the ground. The brick, slightly charred from the explosion, but still intact, lies beside him.*

**THE END**

# the mainland

**GRAHAM:** Richard Wilson unconsciously inspired this plot. Arthur and I were invited to see Le Cirque du Soleil at the Albert Hall and he was sitting right in front of us, watching acrobats performing extraordinary gymnastics and tricks. During the break, Arthur said that it would just be terrible – so tasteless and wrong – to lean forward every time one of the acrobats did something interesting and say, 'Eyyy don't *believe* it!' in the style of Victor Meldrew. Just imagining it made us curl up in embarrassment, and then we realised that Ted should do it. He would think it so amusing and original – it was perfect for him.

Directing Richard Wilson was terrifying, but he was terribly nice. At the end, when he appears at the door, we stood around for about five minutes talking about how he should say the famous line. We wanted the ultimate 'I Don't Believe It!' and we stood around the Parochial House location listening to him try out various versions. It was a very strange moment in my life . . .

**ARTHUR:** It made sense to base this episode on the mainland. Apart from the fact that it provides an adventure for the Craggy Islanders, it simply wouldn't have worked on the island itself. Everyone's so insane that we couldn't have had a proper AA meeting, and Mrs Doyle's tea-shop fight works because it's witnessed by normal people, as is Ted's fight with Richard Wilson. The mainland provides far greater scope for embarrassment: on the island Ted is the voice of sanity, but here he's as strange as the other Craggy Islanders.

He's not quite as strange as Jack however. I know we're not supposed to laugh at our own jokes, but we loved Jack on the mainland – when he reads the 'Feckarse Industries' chart at the optician's and also when (Graham's favourite scene, this) someone from the AA meeting tries to stop him having a drink in the pub and the camera cuts straight to the shot of an ambulance.

I'm slightly ashamed to say that the idea for the briefcase came from someone who approached us in a pub and asked us if we'd look after his briefcase for a minute. Graham turned to me and said, 'If someone came up and stole it I wouldn't do anything, would you?' I said, 'No'...We were trying to make each other laugh, I think, but we knew that Ted *definitely* wouldn't do anything.

## PART ONE

SCENE 1 INT./DAY 1
SET: PAROCHIAL HOUSE
*We hear the closing music to 'One Foot in The Grave'. Dougal is smiling away. Ted walks in with his coat on. He throws Dougal's coat over.*

**TED:** Come on, Dougal, turn off the video.

**DOUGAL:** OK, so, Ted. That's a great show, though, isn't it? He's mad, isn't he, Ted? 'I don't believe it!' he says.

**TED:** Ha, ha. Which one were you watching?

**DOUGAL:** What?

**TED:** Which episode of *One Foot in The Grave* were you watching? Was it the one with the ventriloquist dummy? I love that one.

**DOUGAL:** Eh . . .

**TED:** Dougal, you've just finished watching it. Do you not remember anything from it?

*Pause.*

**DOUGAL:** I don't believe it! Ha, ha, ha! That's what he says.

**TED:** Right. Anyway, Dougal, hurry up, we're off to the mainland.

**DOUGAL:** Hurray! Why?

**TED:** We have to go the betting shop and collect my winnings. Four hundred quid on Father Liam Rice winning that limbo competition . . . Ha ha! What they didn't know is there's something wrong with his back! He always walks like that!

**DOUGAL:** I don't believe it!

**TED:** Ha, ha! I don't believe it! Ha, ha, ha!!!!

SCENE 2 INT./DAY 1
SET: PAROCHIAL HOUSE HALLWAY
*Ted and Dougal emerge, and start putting on their coats.*

**TED:** You'll have to get that mended, Dougal. There's a little hole in your tanktop, there.

**DOUGAL:** Really, Ted? (*Pause.*) I don't believe it!

*They both laugh.*

**TED:** Brilliant, Dougal.

**DOUGAL:** Can we go to the caves, then, Ted? After we go to the betting shop? I love the caves. They must be one of the great wonders of the world. Who do you think built them, Ted? The Egyptians? Or the Romans, or who?

**TED:** Well, it'd be the Irish if anyone, Dougal. Although I don't think anyone actually built them. They just kind of . . . became caves.

**DOUGAL:** Ah, Ted . . . you know I love the caves. Can we go, can we? Please, please, please, please, please, please!!!

**TED:** All right, Dougal, we'll go to the caves.

**DOUGAL:** Fantastic. Going to the caves. I don't believe it!

*They both laugh.*

**TED:** Stop, Dougal. Honestly . . .

*They try to be serious.*

**TED:** I don't believe it!

*They both crack up again. Mrs Doyle emerges, pushing Jack in his wheelchair.*

**MRS DOYLE:** Here we are now!

**DOUGAL:** I don't believe it!

*Ted and Dougal laugh. Jack is confused.*

**JACK:** Drink!

**TED:** Not now, Father. We're going to the opticians in Roundskin, remember? To get you a nice pair of glasses.

**DOUGAL:** I don't believe it!

*They laugh again.*

SCENE 3 EXT./DAY 1
SET: PAROCHIAL HOUSE
*Ted, Dougal, Mrs Doyle and Jack come out of the house. Dougal is pushing Jack in his chair.*

**MRS DOYLE:** We should all be very careful on the mainland. There's so much crime around. Arsonists and muggers everywhere. My friend Mrs O'Dwyer was robbed last week.

**TED:** Oh, no! How much did they get?

**MRS DOYLE** (*beat*)**:** No, I don't think you understand, Father. She was robbed. They stole her.

**TED:** Oh . . . I see.

**MRS DOYLE:** It's a terrible thing when old people can't walk down the street for fear of being stolen.

**TED:** It is.

SCENE 4 INT./DAY 1
SET: CAR
*Ted and Dougal are in the front. Dougal is sticking his head out of the window and letting his tongue hang out like a dog's. (Note: Could Dougal have a slightly longer tongue than is normal?)* \* *Mrs Doyle and Jack are in the back.*

**TED:** Come on, Dougal, I don't want any accidents.

**MRS DOYLE:** Oh, there's Mrs Dineen. You can drop me off here, Father.

**TED:** Right so . . .

*Ted pulls up in his car beside a woman who looks very like Mrs Doyle standing outside a shop. The woman potters up to Ted's window. Ted rolls it down.*

**MRS DINEEN:** Hello, Father Crilly!

**TED:** Hello, Mrs Dineen.

**MRS DINEEN:** What?

---

\*We tried this. Didn't work.

**TED:** Hello!

**MRS DINEEN** (*nods after a moment, smiling*)**:** Yes.

**MRS DOYLE** (*through the window*)**:** Will we go to the tea shop, Mrs Dineen? We can have a bit of a chat there.

*Mrs Doyle opens the door and starts to get out.*

**TED:** All right, goodbye, then!

*Ted looks around for Mrs Dineen. No sign of her. Ted looks puzzled, then drives off.*

SCENE 5 INT./DAY 1
SET: CAR
*We see that Mrs Dineen is in the back of the car, where Mrs Doyle was sitting.*

**TED:** God almighty, can you imagine spending any more time with those tw—

*He sees Mrs Dineen in the rear-view mirror and slams on the brakes.*

SCENE 6 EXT./DAY 1
SET: CAR
*A few minutes later, the car screeches away again, leaving Mrs Dineen and Mrs Doyle by the side of the road.*

SCENE 7 INT./DAY 1
SET: OPTICIAN'S
*There are eye charts, spectacle frames, etc. The*

*optician, Thelma Fox, addresses Ted.*

**THELMA:** So what happened to his last pair of glasses?

**TED:** No idea. He was just out of the house a few minutes, and when he came back, they were gone. He can't seem to hold on to a pair.

SCENE 8 EXT./DAY X
SET: PAROCHIAL HOUSE
*Cut to a flashback. Jack, wearing glasses, is in his wheelchair outside the Parochial House. A bird sweeps down and takes the glasses off his nose, makes a loud squawking sound and flies off with them. Jack flails wildly with his arms.*

*Cut to the bird arriving back at its nest (complete with eggs, etc.) with the glasses in its beak. It drops the glasses into the nest. We see about ten other pairs there as well. The nest is completely constructed from pairs of glasses.*

SCENE 9 INT./DAY 1
SET: OPTICIAN'S
*Back in the optician's.*

**TED:** Oh, it's a real pain. He's always bumping into furniture and knocking things over.

**THELMA:** Yes. And how's his eyesight?

**TED:** That's not great, either.

**THELMA:** All right. I'll give him another test and we'll see what we can do. Give me about an hour.

**TED:** OK, so . . . Come on Dougal, time to collect my winnings . . .

SCENE 10 INT./DAY 1
SET: TEA SHOP
*Mrs Doyle and Mrs Dineen are sitting at a small table.*

**MRS DOYLE:** . . . You remember Mrs Kiernan . . . ? She was walking to the shops the other day and a man came over to her and killed her and stole her pen.

**MRS DINEEN:** Killed her?

**MRS DOYLE:** Well, they think so – they're keeping her in for tests.

**MRS DINEEN:** Oh, dear.

**MRS DOYLE:** I was looking at the News there and they had this thing about how robbers outnumber normal people in Kildare. And murderers outnumber the robbers, so there's more murdered people there than people who aren't murdered.

**MRS DINEEN:** Well, you know what happened to old Mr Sweeney . . . These young fellas broke into his house and started messing with him . . . ruffling his hair and all types of nonsense. Calling him an ould fella . . . and they put a bra on him.

**MRS DOYLE:** Oh, poor Mr Sweeney, he wouldn't like that. I heard there were two hundred cases of forced transvestism involving Mr Sweeney last year.

**MRS DINEEN:** Oh, it's terrible. What's the world coming to?

*The waiter comes to the table. Mrs Dineen and Mrs Doyle snatch up their bags protectively. They look very wary.*

SCENE 11 INT./DAY 1*
SET: PUB
*Dougal and Ted are sitting at a table in an alcove. Ted is counting his winnings from the betting shop.*

**TED:** Ha! Ha! Ha!

*The barman notices Ted laughing, frowns suspiciously, then goes back to his newspaper. Sitting near Ted is a city type, with a briefcase. We see a wide shot of the rest of the pub. There is only one other person present, sitting in a corner of the pub. Ted has a pint of Guinness in front of him. Dougal has a fizzy orange.*

**DOUGAL:** God, Ted, I'm starving. I'm so hungry . . . (*He looks scared.*) There's no chance . . . I couldn't die? From the hunger?

**TED** (*sighs*)**:** Not immediately, no. Not for a couple of hours, anyway. Have a look at the menu.

*Dougal looks at the menu. The city gent leans over to them.*

**MAN:** Excuse me, could you keep your eye on my briefcase for a minute?

**TED:** Yes, yes, of course. Secret documents?

*We deleted this scene from the final version.

**MAN:** Ha, ha, no.

**DOUGAL:** What's in the case, then?

**TED:** Dougal!

**DOUGAL:** What?

**MAN:** Well, I work in the bank over there, and—

**TED:** No, no, really. We don't need to know. We'll just keep an eye on it. (*The man gets up and goes into the Gents.*) God, Dougal . . .

*A man sitting in the corner immediately stands up, walks over to the briefcase and picks it up. Cut to Ted and Dougal, glasses raised to their mouths. They're too stunned to react. The big man picks up the briefcase and walks out of the pub. Ted can't seem to take this in at all.*

**DOUGAL:** Ted . . . the man just took the briefcase.

**TED:** Uh . . .

**DOUGAL:** The briefcase we were supposed to be looking after for that fella.

*Ted seems to be still trying to assimilate all this information in his head. He starts to say something several times, but can't quite manage it. We hear the sound of the hand dryer from inside the toilet. Ted and Dougal look around at the door of the Gents.*

**TED:** Dougal, let's run away.

**DOUGAL:** But what about our food?

**TED:** No, Dougal, we're running away. I've been weighing the various pros and cons and I think that running away is . . . the way to go here.

*They both get up. Ted pulls Dougal out of shot after him.*

SCENE 12 INT./DAY 1
SET: OPTICIAN'S
*The optician comes over to Jack and takes away a metal contraption covering his eyes.*

**THELMA:** Well, I'm very confused, Father. Your eyesight seems to be . . . better than ever before. You read right down to the very last line and even I can't see that one.

*From another angle, we see the eyechart. It looks like this:*

# DRINK
## DRINKDRINK
### DRINKDRINKDRINK
#### DRINKDRINKDRINKDRINK
##### DRINKDRINKDRINKDRINKDRINK
###### DRINKDRINKDRINKDRINKDRINKDRINK

*Ted enters the room.*

**TED:** Are you finished with him yet?

**THELMA:** Well, I'm amazed. He seems to have perfect eyesight.

**TED:** Really? (*He sees the eye chart.*) Ah . . . well, I think I know what might have happened. You see, Father Jack has a great fondness for saying that particular word.

**THELMA:** Oh, I didn't know. It's the first time I've used this eyechart, actually. I got it free with a promotional crate of Carlsberg.

DOUGAL: Hey, do you have anything to eat? Like a plate of chips or a burger or a few chops? I'm out of me head with hunger.

THELMA: Ah . . . no. I'll just get another chart . . . Sorry about this, Fathers, this might take some time.

*She leaves the room. Dougal stands up.*

DOUGAL: Come on, Ted, let's go to the caves while we're waiting. Oh, no! I'm still starving! Maybe we should get something to eat first. God, I *really, really* want to go to the caves. But at the same time, I'm *really, really* hungry. God, I don't know what to do first! Oh, God, Ted!

TED: Well, they have a snack-bar place at the caves.

DOUGAL: Oh, really? Great. No need to worry. Sorry if I seemed a bit over-anxious there.

*They leave. Thelma comes back in.*

THELMA: This one was given to me by Slovakia's premier lens manufacturers – Feckarse Industries . . .

*She turns it round. It's like the 'Drink' chart, except it has 'Feck' and 'Arse' written all over it. Ted and Dougal leave.*

SCENE 13 INT./DAY 1
SET: TEA SHOP
*Mrs Doyle is still chatting away to Mrs Dineen. There are a whole stack of cups on the table in front of them.*

MRS DOYLE: Oh, God, no, don't ever try to be one of those have-a-go heroes . . .

MRS DINEEN: Well, I was surprised at my own strength. I heard this arm snap, and then it was just a case of lying on top of him until the filth arrived. (*She takes out her purse.*) We'd better go, Mrs Doyle. I'll get this.

*Mrs Doyle takes out her purse as well.*

MRS DOYLE: No, Mrs Dineen. Put that away. I'll get this one.

MRS DINEEN: No, you won't, don't be silly. I'll pay.

MRS DOYLE: No, no, no, no, no, you won't. Put that away.

MRS DINEEN: No, don't be stupid, Mrs Doyle.

MRS DOYLE: No, no, no, no, no, no, no, no, no . . .

MRS DINEEN: Now, just . . . put your money away . . .

MRS DOYLE: *You're mad!* No, no, no, no, no, no, no, no . . .

SCENE 14 EXT./DAY 1
SET: CAVES
*We see a sign that reads:*

'VERY DARK CAVES'

'IT'S ALMOST LIKE BEING BLIND!'

*Tourists are milling about, taking photographs, and so on. Dougal is photographing Ted beside the sign for the toilets.*

TED (*sees something*): God almighty . . .

DOUGAL: What?

TED: Look who it is! It's yer man!

*Cut to reveal Richard Wilson, enjoying the scenery.*

DOUGAL: Who?

TED: Yer man from *One Foot In The Grave*! The 'I don't believe it' man!

DOUGAL: Oh, wow!

TED: God, that's amazing. Look at him there. (*Pause.*) Ha, ha . . . Do you know what he'd love?

DOUGAL: What?

TED: He'd love it if someone came up to him and said his catchphrase.

DOUGAL: Oh, yeah, Ted, he'd love that! You should definitely do that!

TED: Should I?

DOUGAL: Oh, yeah, he'd *love* that! I'd say no one ever does that to him! He'll think you're hilarious!

TED: It would be good, wouldn't it?

DOUGAL: Seriously, Ted, that is a *fan-tastic* idea. This is one of those times when I'm absolutely one hundred million per cent sure that you'd be doing the right thing. I can safely say you definitely, *definitely* won't regret doing that.

**TED:** You know what? I'm going to do it!

**DOUGAL:** Brilliant, Ted!

**TED:** Will I?

**DOUGAL:** Yeaaaahhh!!! Go on!

*Ted creeps away from Dougal and walks up to Richard Wilson, who is looking the other way. Ted looks back at Dougal one more time. Dougal gives him the thumbs-up. We see all this from Dougal's point of view, from a distance.*

**TED:** Eyyyyyyyyyy don't belieeeeeeve it!!!!!!!

*Dougal sees Richard Wilson turn around and start to shout something at Ted, and then attack him. Ted protects himself. A few caves staff arrive on the scene and start holding Richard Wilson back. Ted cowers as Richard escapes, grabs Ted by the jacket and starts pulling it over his head. The staff are finally able to hold Richard back. Ted slinks back towards Dougal.*

**RICHARD** (*in the distance*): . . . KICK YOUR ARSE! . . .

*Ted arrives back with Dougal. He looks completely shellshocked.*

**DOUGAL:** What'd he say? Did he laugh?

**TED** (*quietly*): No. Not really, no. No. No, he didn't. No. No. No, no, no. Ohhhhhhhh, no. No. No. I'm going to sit down now.

SCENE 15 INT./DAY 1
SET: OPTICIAN'S
*Jack is wearing a new pair of glasses. He seems happy. The optician shakes hands with him.*

SCENE 16 EXT./DAY 1
SET: OPTICIAN'S
*Jack leaves the optician's. A bird swoops down and attacks him, knocking him over. It takes his glasses and flies away. Jack gets up. We see from his point of view that everything is a blur. He walks a short way, coming to a sign beside an open door,*

**JACK** (*reading*): Dri . . . Drink? Drink!!! Drink!!!!

*He goes into the building. We see now that the sign reads 'Had enough of drink? Join Alcoholics Anonymous. Meeting 4 p.m.'*

SCENE 17 INT./DAY 1
SET: TEA SHOP
*Mrs Doyle is on top of Mrs Dineen. She is holding out a tenner to a waiter.*

**MRS DOYLE:** Take the money! TAKE THE MONEY!

**MRS DINEEN:** PUT YOUR MONEY AWAY!!!

*She grabs it from Mrs Doyle. We see nearby a member of staff on the telephone.*

**MANAGER:** Hello, police?

SCENE 18 INT./DAY 1
SET: ALCOHOLICS ANONYMOUS
*About six people and Jack are sitting in a very bare room. One man, Peter, is standing.*

**PETER:** . . . That was when I was drinking over a pint of vodka a day.

**JACK:** Yes!

**PETER:** Yes. All I could think about was where the next drink was coming from . . .

**JACK:** DRINK!

**PETER:** I didn't give a damn about my wife or kids.

**JACK** (*disgusted*): Nyaaahhhh!!!!

**PETER:** But now, with your help, I'm coming through it. I'm just taking it one day at a time.

*He sits down. Everyone applauds. The chairman, Ronald, stands up.*

**RONALD:** Thank you, Peter. Now, I notice we have a new member of the group today. Father? Do you want to tell us your story?

*Jack stands up unsteadily.*

**JACK:** DRINK! (*Everyone nods understandingly.*) DRINK! (*Jack is a little put out. No one seems to be giving him any drink.*) DRIIIIIIIINK!!!!

**RONALD:** We hear you, Father. Let it all out.

**JACK:** DRIIINK!!!! DRIIIIIIIIIIINK!!!! (*He gets down on his hands and knees.*) DRIIIIIIIIIIIIIIIIIIIIIIIIIIIIIIIIIIIIIIIIIINK!!!!!

*People are softly wiping away tears and nodding.*

**PETER:** It's so true. So true . . .

SCENE 19 INT./DAY 1
SET: CAVES
*The tour guide stops in front of some rocks.*

**TOUR GUIDE:** And this rock here is actually granite.

**TED:** How long would that be there?

**TOUR GUIDE:** Many millions of years.

**TED:** Really? As long as that? That is fascinating.

**DOUGAL:** How come the rocks are all different sizes?

**TOUR GUIDE:** Well, you know . . . rocks are generally different sizes.

**DOUGAL:** Wow. I'm finding out all kinds of things I never knew about rocks.

*The tour guide moves on. More people join in.*

**TOUR GUIDE:** . . . Of course, at this time, most of the world would have been submerged under water.

DOUGAL: How did everyone breathe?

TED: They'd have some sort of apparatus . . .

DOUGAL: Oh, right. Wow! Look at that rock there!

*He wanders off.*

TOUR GUIDE: Anyway, the fossils were creatures that used to live at a depth of twenty thousand fathoms . . .

TED: Wow. I don't believe it.

*A man in front of Ted turns around. We see that it is Richard Wilson.*

WILSON: YOU AGAIN!

*Cut to Dougal looking at a rock. He hears the fracas and turns to watch it. We see, from a distance, people holding Richard Wilson back. Ted and Dougal escape and run away. Richard Wilson looks flustered and angry. The tour guide comes over to him.*

TOUR GUIDE: I'd better send someone after them. That part's not open to the public . . . Mr Wilson, can I just say how sorry I am about all the, all the, eh . . .

RICHARD: Oh, please. Just so long as I don't hear that bloody catchphrase again. Ha, ha.

*Pause. Close-up of the tour guide. He is smiling inanely, as if suppressing something.*

TOUR GUIDE (*his silent thoughts*): Oh, God. I really, really, want to say it. Eyyyyyyy don't believe it!

TOUR GUIDE (*guiding Richard Wilson away*): Anyway, there's lot of places around where you can get a bit of peace and quiet for the rest of your holiday . . .

SCENE 20 INT./DAY 1
SET: CAVES
*Ted and Dougal come around a corner.*

TED: I was sure we came in this way.

DOUGAL: God, Ted, I'm so hungry. I'm beginning to hallucinate.

TED: Dougal, don't exaggerate . . . (*We see Ted from Dougal's point of view. He is dressed as Abraham Lincoln.*) . . . and stop worrying. We'll be out of here in no time. Right, let's try over here . . .

SCENE 21 INT./DAY 1
SET: ANOTHER PART OF THE CAVES
*They walk along a little further. Dougal hears something behind them. He keeps looking around.*

DOUGAL: Ted . . . Ted, what's that?

TED: What's wh— (*They hear a low moaning noise.*) I don't . . . I don't know . . .

*The noise grows louder. Ted's eyes widen as he sees something. Cut to his point of view. We see coming around the corner a classic 'sheet' ghost.*

TED AND DOUGAL:
Aaaaaarrrrghhhhhhhhhh!!!!

*The ghost stops, then whips off his pillowcase head. It is Noel Furlong. He has a beard. He looks delighted.*

NOEL: TED!!!!!!!!

TED AND DOUGAL:
Aaaaaarrrrghhhhhhhhhh!!!!

**END OF PART ONE**

\* \* \*

**PART TWO**

SCENE 22 INT./EVENING 1
SET: CAVES
*We see Noel standing in the centre of a group of people. Ted, Dougal and the Saint Luke's Youth Group – Tony Lynch, Jerry Fields (both bearded) Janine Reilly and Nuala Ryan. Noel is singing. (Note: In the following, he acts out the words in a very theatrical way.)*

NOEL: 'Bom, bom, bom, bom, bom, bom, bom, bom . . .
I see a little sillhouetto of a man
Scaramouche, Scaramouche will you do the fandango?
Thunderbolt and lightning, very very frightning!
ME! GALLILEO, GALLILEO, GALLILEO, GALLILEO, FIGARO, MAGNIFICO,
I'm just a poor boy, nobody loves me.
He's just a poor boy from a poor family,
Spare him his life from this monstrosity,
Easy come, easy go, will you let me go?
Basmillah! No! We will not let you go. Let me go!
Basmillah, will not let you go. Let me go!
Basmillah, will not let you go. Let me go!

No, no, no, no, no, no, no, no!
Oh, mama mia, mama mia, mama mia, let me
go.
Beelzebub has a devil put aside for me,
For me,
For meeeeeeeeeeeeeeeeeeeeeeeeeeeee!!!!!!!!'

*He finishes. No response. Everyone looks very fed up.
Pause.*

**TED:** . . . As I was saying. I think the thing to
do is try and find an exit before the caves close
for the evening.

**TONY:** Good idea, Father.

**TED:** How long have you been in here?

**TONY:** Two days now, Father. At least, I think
it's two days.

**NOEL:** We've been having a great laugh!

**TED:** It's just I wouldn't like to be here too long
. . .

**NOEL:** He wouldn't like to be here too long!
Would you listen to him! I suppose if he doesn't
get back to Craggy Island they'll all turn into
devil worshippers or something!

**TED:** No, it's just, I think everyone would
actually like to get out of here and get
something to eat and go home.

**NOEL:** Who can screech the loudest? Let's
have a screeching competition! I'll go first . . .
(*He emits a 'Jurassic Park' type screeching sound.*)

Ha, ha, ha! Gerry Fields, your go!

**GERRY:** I'd rather not, Father.

**NOEL:** Oh, go on. (*He screeches again.*) It's easy
peasy!

**TED:** Father, I really think we should think
about getting out.

**NOEL:** Oh, God, maybe you're right, Ted. If we
don't get out, we might have to eat each other!

*Dougal sits up when he hears this and looks very
interested indeed.*

**NOEL:** Like in that film *Alive*, where they get
into the plane crash and then they have to eat
all their friends. Look! Here's me eating Tony!

*He starts miming, as if he's eating something, with a
jokey look on his face.*

**NOEL:** Yum, yum, yum, yum, yum. And this'd
be Tony! 'Oh, no, get off me! I'm not dead yet!'
and I'd be like, 'But I'm hungry, Tony!' and
Tony'd be goin', 'No, no, go away!' Ha, ha, ha!
Wouldn't you, Tony? And this'd be Tony's
parents, hearing that I've eaten Tony. (*He mimes
a boo-hoo crying action.*) 'Oh, no, why'd you eat,
Tony? He was our only son!'

*Tony looks very, very distressed at this.*

**NOEL:** 'But Mr and Mrs Lynch, I was hungry!'
Ha, ha, ha! And then they'd be at the funeral,
and I'd be going, 'Best not show me head for
the m—'

**TONY** (*suddenly*)**:** WILL YOU SHUT UP! WILL
YOU! WILL YOU PLEASE SHUT UP! WILL YOU
SHUT UP! SHUT UP! *SHUT UP!*

*Pause.*

**NOEL:** OOOOOOOOOOOoooooooooo!!!!!!
Someone got out of the wrong side of the bed
this morning! I wonder who that could be . . .
(*He points behind Tony's back.*) Come on, let's
have someone else for the screeching
competition . . . Janine Reilly, oh, she'd love a
go. Go on there, it's easy . . .

*He screeches again. There is a slight rumbling in the
background.*

**TED:** Eh, Noel . . . I wouldn't do that.

*Noel ignores him. We see bits of rock falling from the
ceiling of the cave.*

NOEL (*screeches again*): Ha, ha, ha!!!

TED: Seriously, Noel! . . .

*He screeches again. Some rocks fall. Ted and Dougal jump out of the way. We hear a crash and everything goes black. Fade out.*

*Fade back. We see a pile of rocks and rubble. Noel's hand is sticking out of the rubble and gesticulating happily. We hear his voice from under the rubble.*

NOEL: . . . So it was me, Father Collis and Father Duggan, and you'd think, wouldn't you, that someone like Chris Evans wouldn't want to hang around with the likes of us – especially when he's in that sort of condition. And you'd be right! He didn't want to hang around with us. He didn't want to hang around with us *at all*. What was that colourful phrase he used? Oh, that's right, 'If you don't get out of my house right now, I'll call the police.'

TED: Noel, sorry to interrupt, but are you not worried about being trapped under that big pile of rocks?

NOEL: Not at all, Ted. Sure aren't you here to keep me company? And the Youth Group will be back with help any moment. They said that they were just going to find the tour guide, tell them that I was buried under a pile of rocks, and come right back!

SCENE 23 INT./EVENING 1
SET: AIRPORT CHECK-IN DESK
*An air hostess.*

AIR HOSTESS: Right, that's four tickets to

Paraguay. It leaves through Gate Three in an hour.

*We see the Youth Group, looking anxious.*

TONY: An hour? No! We have to leave now! NOW!

*The rest of the Youth Group try to calm him.*

SCENE 24 INT./EVENING 1
SET: CAVES
*We hear Noel's voice from the rockpile.*

NOEL: . . . but I *liked The English Patient*. Very confusing and far-fetched and very, very boring, but it was my kind of film. And now I suppose you could say I'm in that type of situation that Kristin Scott Thomas found herself in . . . (*We gradually pull back to see that Ted and Dougal have gone.*) . . . I liked *The Piano* as well. Did you see Harvey Keitel running around in the nip!? God! Did you see that, Ted? (*Pause.*) Ted?

SCENE 25 INT./EVENING 1
SET: ANOTHER PART OF THE CAVES
*Ted is looking ahead. Dougal comes up behind him.*

TED: I hate leaving Noel, but we're doing him no good sitting around listening to him screech.

DOUGAL: At least he'll be safe under that big pile of rocks.

TED: Let's just get out ourselves – then we can worry about Noel. God . . . where's this exit?

*Dougal takes his coat off. His tanktop has unravelled, leaving only a sort of tanktop bra.*

DOUGAL: Aahhh!! Ted, my tanktop has turned into some sort of woman's bra!

TED: What? It's after unravelling. Oh, my God, Dougal! We can find our way back with this! You obviously snagged this on something – if we follow it back, we can find our way out! Ha, ha!!!!

*Ted stands still and starts winding the thread around his hands.*

TED: Oh, thank God, Dougal! We'll be out in no time! Ha, ha!!!

DOUGAL: Ted, should you be winding it up like that? Or should we be following it?

TED (*still winding*): What?

**DOUGAL:** Well, what use will it be once you've finished winding it up?

*Ted continues winding, looking at Dougal, looking at the thread, looking at Dougal, his smile slowly disappearing. After a few moments, he comes to the end of the thread. He looks at it.*

**TED** (*beat*): I DON'T BELIEVE IT!!!!!!!!!!!!!!!!!!!!!!

SCENE 26 INT./EVENING 1
SET: CAVES
*Ted's words rebound off the walls of the caves in different locations. Ted and Dougal travel down various tunnels.*

*Finally we see Richard Wilson with the tour group.*

**TED'S WORDS:** I DON'T BELIEVE IT! I DON'T BELIEVE IT! I DON'T BELIEVE IT!

*Richard puts his hands over his ears and starts to scream.*

SCENE 27 EXT./EVENING 1
SET: PUB
*Jack is walking past the pub.*

**JACK:** PUB! DRINK!!!!

*He wanders in. A moment later, Ronald, from the AA meeting, walks past. He notices something. We see that he sees Jack through the window sitting at a table. Jack is pouring himself a large glass of whiskey. Ronald gasps and runs in to the pub.*

**RONALD:** Don't do it, Father!

*Jack is about to put the glass to his lips when Ronald reaches into shot and grabs Jack's arm.*

**JACK:** ROWARRRREEEE?????

**RONALD:** I won't let you do it, Father. You can beat me, you can kick me, but I'm not going to—

SCENE 28 EXT./EVENING 1
SET: ROAD
*Shot of an ambulance speeding past.*

SCENE 29 EXT./EVENING 1
SET: CAVE EXIT
*Ted and Dougal come into the open, looking very bedraggled. They see someone in a one-piece outfit very*

*like the ones all the tour guides wear. Ted grabs him.*

**TED:** Listen, there's someone been buried in the caves. He's all right, but I really think you should get someone in there quickly. Thank you. Please hurry. Come on, Dougal. I want to get away before they rescue him.

*They walk away. The man in the outfit shrugs and turns to pick up a large bin. He throws it into the back of a nearby bin-truck and jumps up on the back. He is driven away. Ted and Dougal don't notice this.*

SCENE 30 INT./EVENING 1
SET: CAVES CAFE
*Dougal and Ted are queuing up for food, sliding a tray along the rail. Dougal is piling things on to his plate, hopping with the excitement. Ted's mobile phone rings.*

**TED:** Hello?

SCENE 31 INT./EVENING 1
SET: POLICE STATION
*A policeman is on the telephone.*

**POLICEMAN:** Hello. Is this Father Crilly?

**TED:** Yes. This is him. Or rather, this is me. This is . . . yes, this is Father Crilly. I *am* Father Crilly, is what I'm trying to say.

**POLICEMAN:** We've been trying to contact you all night. Do you know a Mrs Doyle? Full name. Mrs (*Telephone interference.*) . . . Doyle.

**TED:** Do I know a Mrs (*Telephone interference.*) . . . Doyle? Eh . . . (*Sensing trouble.*) I'm not . . . let me think . . .

**DOUGAL:** Ah, we do, Ted.

**TED:** OK, yes, yes. She's our housekeeper.

**POLICEMAN:** Well, I need you to come to the police station. She's been in a spot of trouble.

*We see Mrs Doyle and Mrs Dineen in a cell in the background. They both look dishevelled and have scratch marks on their faces.*

**MRS DOYLE:** Now, Mrs Dineen, if there's a fine or anything, I'll pay it.

**MRS DINEEN:** No, no, no, no, no . . .

*Cut back to the policeman on the telephone.*

**POLICEMAN:** OK, thank you, Father.

*He puts down the telephone. Another policeman emerges, bundling Jack through the door.*

**MRS DOYLE:** Father Hackett!

*The policeman takes this in.*

SCENE 32 INT./EVENING 1
SET: CAVES CAFE
*Ted puts the mobile phone back in his jacket.*

**TED:** Dougal, you're not going to be able to eat that. (*Dougal whimpers.*) We have to go and get Mrs Doyle and Mrs Dineen . . . (*Ted's phone rings again. He picks it up and nods.*) OK. (*He puts the mobile phone away.*) . . . and Father Jack out of prison. Come on.

*He ushers Dougal away. Dougal picks up a fork and makes one final stab at a chip. We go into slow motion. The chip, in extreme close-up, seesaws on the fork, accompanied by a loud creaking sound. Dougal lifts the fork to his mouth and the chip, still in close-up, starts to fall off the fork. Dougal makes a lunge for it and misses it. He roars in slow motion.*

**DOUGAL:** Noooooooooo!!!!!!!!!!!!!!

*Back in normal speed, Ted grabs Dougal and pulls him out of shot.*

SCENE 33 INT./EVENING 1
SET: POLICE STATION
*Ted is at the front desk dealing with the policeman. Another policeman is looking at Dougal, slightly bemused.*

**TED** (*To Policeman 1*): I'm very, very sorry . . .

**DOUGAL** (*To Policeman 2*): You wouldn't have a lasagne or some chicken curry or something?

**POLICEMAN 2:** No.

**DOUGAL:** OK. Well, maybe I'll just have a bag of chips. And could I have a Fanta orange as well?

**POLICEMAN 2:** I don't think you know where you are. This is a police station.

**DOUGAL:** Right . . . Hmnn . . . In that case I'll have the chicken satay and boiled rice.

*Policeman 2 looks no less confused. Meanwhile, Policeman 1 has brought Mrs Doyle, Mrs Dineen and*

*Jack round to the other side of the desk and is handing them back into Ted's care. Ted is profoundly apologetic.*

**TED:** . . . I hope you don't think this type of thing goes on all the time! We're not all criminals and troublemakers in the Church! I hope this won't stop you going to Mass!

**POLICEMAN 1:** I'm a Protestant actually, Father.

**TED:** Really? Oh . . . ah, sure . . . they're great . . .

**POLICEMAN 1:** We can overlook this bit of trouble, Father. Charges won't be pressed. But I'm afraid I'll need a sum of money as a guarantee against their future behaviour. Either that or they'll have to spend the night in the cell.

**TED:** A sum of money? Right . . . How . . . how much?

**POLICEMAN 1:** Two hundred pounds.

**TED:** Oh, well, I wouldn't have that money on me. Maybe a night in the cell would be the best option under the circumstances . . .

**DOUGAL:** Ted . . .

**TED:** Shut up, Dougal.

**DOUGAL:** Ted, you're not going to believe this, but I've got a brilliant idea! Why don't you use that two hundred pounds you won this morning? I mean, it's exactly the amount we need to get Mrs Doyle and Father Jack out! Ha, ha!!!! That bet you won! You have it there with you! Two hundred pounds. *Exactly!*

**POLICEMAN 1:** You do have it? Right, well then, we're all happy.

*Ted reluctantly reaches into his coat and extracts the money from his wallet. The policeman nods a thank you and moves off.*

**DOUGAL:** Never mind, Ted, you've still got two hundred pounds left.

**TED** (*to Dougal*): Well, I must say . . . There was a time when the police in this country were *friends* of the Church. Drunk driving charges quashed; parking tickets torn up; even turning a blind eye to the odd murder. But now . . .

*As he continues on his tirade the man who owns the briefcase comes up to the desk and begins talking to Policeman 2.**

**BRIEFCASE MAN:** Hello, I'd like to report a stolen briefcase . . .*

*Cut back to Ted talking to Dougal.**

**TED:** . . . 'Oh, no, Father, I'm afraid you *were* doing ninety miles an hour.' I don't know . . . it's the criminals they should be after, not the clergy.*

*Back to the briefcase man.**

**BRIEFCASE MAN:** . . . And I said to two *priests*, of all people, 'Could you keep an eye on this for me?' And they were the ones who ran off with it.*

**POLICEMAN 2:** Yes. This is just a hunch, but it wouldn't be those two men over there?*

*He turns and looks amazed.**

**TED:** Believe me, this won't go unreported. I'll be writing a letter to . . . some bishop or something, telling him exactly how far we have fallen from those days of innocence when priests could get away with anything.*

*He notices that the briefcase man and Policeman 2 are looking at him.**

**TED:** Ah . . . hello.*

SCENE 34 INT./NIGHT 1†
SET: POLICE CELL
*Ted and Dougal sit in their cell, miserable. Mrs Doyle is outside.*

**MRS DOYLE:** Don't worry, Father. We'll have you out in no time! All we have to do is raise another two hundred pounds. (*Ted, sadly, resignedly, hands over the other two hundred pounds to Mrs Doyle.*) Oh! Well . . . what did I tell you? Officer!

*Food is slid in through the gap.*

**DOUGAL:** PRISON FOOD!!!

*Dougal is about to eat when the cell door opens.*

**POLICEMAN:** All right, come on, you're free to go.

*Dougal is about to chow down when Ted grabs him and pulls him out of the cell.*

SCENE 35 EXT./DAY 2
SET: COUNTRY ROAD
*Richard Wilson is walking along a country road. He inhales deeply, at peace at last. Despite this, he seems a bit lost. He consults a map, and when we cut we reveal the Parochial House nearby. The map doesn't help him, so he sets off towards the house.*

SCENE 36 INT./DAY 2
SET: PAROCHIAL HOUSE
*Jack, Dougal and Ted are present. Dougal is eating a plate of chips, Ted is reading a newspaper.*

**TED:** What did I say, Dougal? God, there's always trouble when we go to the mainland. I must make a note of never, ever going there again. Unless it's completely unavoidable. Which it isn't. Unfortunately.

SCENE 37 EXT./DAY 2
SET: PAROCHIAL HOUSE
*The front doorbell rings. Ted comes into shot and opens the door. We see Richard Wilson standing there. He turns around.*

**RICHARD:** Hello, I'm terribly sorry, but— (*He takes in the fact that it's Ted.*)

I DON'T BELIEVE IT!!!!!!!!!!!!

POST-CREDIT SEQUENCE
SCENE 38 INT./NIGHT 2
SET: CAVES
*The mound of rocks. Noel is still under it. We hear him singing.*

**NOEL:** 'Fat-bottomed girls, they make the rocking world go round . . .'

**THE END**

---

*We deleted these lines from the final version.
† We deleted this scene from the final version.

# escape from victory

**GRAHAM:** More film references. The title's an obvious one, and the opening, where Ted is stripped down to his vest, destroying his house and looking for bugs, is a straight lift of the end of *The Conversation*, a Coppola movie that Arthur and I love.

During the filming of the match, I spent most of the time shouting '*SLOWER!*' at the elderly footballers. We used four types of football; a normal one, one that was weighted so that it would move slowly, one that had water in it to make it wobble like a very, very old person and another that had a camera attached to it. Even with the wobbleball, the men sped about after it like excited puppies – I guess the instinct to run after a ball is hard to suppress. Mrs Doyle's friends were mostly extras, delightful well-mannered girls from Clare who were all willing to scream abuse at the players. There's a great half-time match discussion with Mrs Doyle and her two friends in this draft. We had to lose it due to length, sadly, but it's a neat little scene. Arthur and I have a very loose style of writing, which sometimes leads to shows being overlong. It suits us until we have to lose something like this from the final edit.

**ARTHUR:** This is probably one of the most insane plots in the series, and it's another example of a crazy situation being deliberately badly set up, as in the case of Ted saying that only a 'completely ludicrous' situation could demand a remote-control wheelchair and a pair of false arms – we love making our intentions clear in this way.

When we were plotting the episode we came up with the idea of forfeits rather than Dick and Ted's usual cash bet. We got a pleasant jolt when we realised that we could end the show with our first 'To Be Continued . . .' This was fortunate, not only because it cut a long story in half, but also because the words 'To Be Continued' seemed to lend the line, 'You have to kick Bishop Brennan up the arse!' a gravity it didn't deserve and gave us, I think, a solid, satisfying ending.

## PART ONE

SCENE 1 INT./DAY 1
SET: PAROCHIAL HOUSE

*The living room looks pretty wrecked, with furniture overturned and some wallpaper stripped off the wall. Ted takes a picture off the wall and looks behind it. He throws the picture on the floor. We see that he is wearing a vest, looking very nervous and suspicious. He grinds out a cigarette in a big pile of cigarettes.*

SCENE 2 INT./DAY 1
SET: PAROCHIAL HOUSE HALLWAY

*Dougal comes in through the front door. He has a suitcase.*

SCENE 3 INT./DAY 1
SET: PAROCHIAL HOUSE

*Dougal comes into the living room. Ted is pulling up a floorboard and looking underneath it.*

**DOUGAL:** Ted! How are ya?!

**TED** (*jumps up*): Dougal! Hello there! Did you have a good time?

*Ted nods his head, indicating silently for Dougal to say 'yes'.*

**DOUGAL:** What?

**TED:** Great! Great! (*He is furiously writing something on a piece of card.*) I'm so glad to hear that. Everything here has been fine. Nothing's wrong at all. There's no problem here at all.

*He holds up the card, on which he has written, in capital letters, 'WE'RE BEING BUGGED'. Dougal takes it, frowns, looks up at Ted, then turns the card around and writes something on the back. After a moment, he holds it up. He has written, 'WHAT?'.*

*Ted takes the card back and writes something. His side of the card now reads, 'I SAID WE'RE BEING BUGGED'.*

**TED:** So, how was the school reunion? (*He whispers.*) Keep talking.

*He sees a plug plugged into a socket, with a wire leading off somewhere.*

**DOUGAL:** Ah . . . (*He clears his throat.*) . . . I was at the old school reunion . . .

**TED** (*to himself*): Where does this go . . . ?

*He picks up the wire and follows it. It leads to the door. He opens the door and follows it out.*

SCENE 4 INT./DAY 1
SET: PAROCHIAL HOUSE HALLWAY

*Ted follows the wire into the hallway and up the stairs. He looks up the stairs.*

SCENE 5 INT./DAY 1
SET: PAROCHIAL HOUSE HALLWAY

*Dougal shouts up after Ted, still very confused.*

**DOUGAL:** Eh . . . well, it was all right. It was weird, though. Everyone's changed so much, I hardly recognised them . . .

*Dougal trails off. He looks confused. Mrs Doyle enters, sticking her head around the door cautiously.*

**MRS DOYLE:** Father, do you think a cup of tea might calm you down? . . .

*She sees that he's gone and then sees Dougal. She runs up to him. She is worrying a succession of paper handkerchiefs to pieces.*

**MRS DOYLE:** Father, Father, oh, you're back at last, oh, thank God . . . Oh, dear, oh, dear, oh, dear, oh, golly, oh golly . . .

**DOUGAL** (*oblivious*): Hello, Mrs Doyle!

**MRS DOYLE:** Oh, Father, you've got to do something. He's gone mad. It's this football thing.

**DOUGAL:** God almighty, is it that time of the year again?

**MRS DOYLE:** Yes, and for some reason, he's got it into his head . . . Well, he just thinks Father Byrne is up to something . . . trying to find out Father Crilly's tactics for the match. It's only a stupid game of football, for goodness sake!

**DOUGAL:** Mrs Doyle, I'm sorry, but no. I have to say no. I'm sorry, I don't want to be rude, but no. There's nothing stupid about football. And there's nothing at all stupid about the annual All Priests Five-a-Side Over Seventy-Fives Indoor Football Challenge match. (*Beat.*) Against Rugged Island.

SCENE 6 INT./DAY 1
SET: UPSTAIRS LANDING
*Ted follows the lead to Jack's bedroom.*

SCENE 7 INT./DAY 1
SET: JACK'S BEDROOM
*Ted comes into the room. He lifts the lead and sees that it goes up to a tiny, white electric fan that Jack is fanning himself with in a rather fey way. He looks at Ted in confusion. Ted looks annoyed and closes the door.*

SCENE 8 INT./DAY 1
SET: PAROCHIAL HOUSE
*Mrs Doyle and Dougal are in the living room.*

**MRS DOYLE:** Please, Father, please do something. I can't stand seeing him like this.

**DOUGAL:** Well . . .

*Ted comes into the room.*

**TED:** Anyway, Dougal, you were saying? About your school reunion?

**DOUGAL:** Oh, ah . . . Well, I didn't recognise many of them. And, do you know what? They all became firemen! I was the only one who wasn't a fireman! Can you believe that?

*Ted stops.*

**TED:** Em . . . you're sure you hadn't gone to a fire station or something by mistake?

*Pause.*

**DOUGAL:** Ahhhhhhhhhh . . .

*Ted returns to his mad, paranoid business. He starts pulling up a floorboard.*

**DOUGAL:** Ted, come on, you're going a bit mad, there.

*Ted makes an urgent 'shut up' gesture.*

**TED:** What? I'm sure I don't know what you're talking about. I'm absolutely fine!

There's nothing wrong with me at all.

*He unscrews a lightbulb and looks in the socket.*

**DOUGAL:** Ted, I'm going to have to do something, and you won't like it. But it's for your own good. Are you ready?

**TED:** Hmm . . . ?

**DOUGAL:** You won't like it, Ted, I just know it. Call it female intuition, or whatever the male equivalent of female intuition is, but this isn't going to go down well in the Ted camp at all.

**TED** (*not really paying attention*): I think—

*Dougal slaps Ted in the face.*

**DOUGAL:** Sorry, Ted. You were going a bit mad.

**TED:** What the— What are you— (*Pause. He looks around.*) Oh, my God. Oh, my God, look at this place! What have I done? What have I done? I've got to get a hold of myself. God almighty . . . I suppose I've never been able to get over last year. Do you remember? When Dick tried to find out about our tactics using the Internet? Remember? He printed all those details about us? And then someone in Holland accidentally sent us loads of hard-core pornography?

*They drift off for a nostalgic moment.*

**DOUGAL:** But Ted . . . being bugged by Dick Byrne! I don't think that's very likely now, do you? Come on, Ted, look at you! You look terrible.

**TED:** I've been having a lot of trouble getting any sleep. I'm going to try this stuff, 'Dreamy Sleepy Nightie Snoozy Snooze' . . .

**DOUGAL:** 'Dreamy Sleepy Nightie Snoozy Snooze'?

*Ted produces it – a bottle of green fluid with its name on the label.*

**TED:** Yes. It's a bran-based, alcoholic, chocolate sleeping-aid. It's banned in most European countries, so that means it's very good.

**DOUGAL:** In the meantime, Ted, I'll go and buy us an ice-cream. That'll calm us both down.

**TED:** Yes, that'd be nice. Where are you going to get an ice-cream, though?

**DOUGAL:** There's an ice-cream van outside . . .

**TED:** Is there?

*He looks out of the window.*

SCENE 9 EXT./DAY 1
SET: NEARBY FIELD
*We see an ice-cream van.*

**TED:** It'll never sell much out there . . .

SCENE 10 INT./DAY 1
SET: ICE-CREAM VAN
*Cut to inside the van. Father Dick Byrne is crouched beside a large radar dish type thing in the back of the van. He is wearing headphones and is dressed in a white coat. Father Cyril McDuff is in the front seat. Dick takes off his earphones and slams them down.*

**DICK:** They're on to us, Cyril! Let's go!!!

*Cyril slams his foot down and the ice-cream van roars off, playing a slow nursery rhyme as it does so.*

SCENE 11 EXT./DAY 1
SET: FOOTBALL FIELD
*We see Ted and Dougal at the side of the pitch.*

**TED:** Come on, Father Bigley! Get your arse in gear! Father Whelan, come on! You can move faster than that! Get into it! For missing the target from there you need shooting!

*Cut to reveal three very old and frail-looking priests kicking balls very slowly at an equally frail-looking goalkeeper.*

**BIGLEY:** Are we nearly finished? I'm very tired! I'm ninety-seven!

**TED:** Good God, that's an awful defeatist attitude, Father Bigley! I'm holding you back for extra training! You'll stay here till seven. Do fifteen laps of the pitch.

**BIGLEY:** But . . .

**TED:** Off you go . . .

*Father Bigley reluctantly heads off at an incredibly slow pace around the pitch.*

**TED** (*to Dougal*): God, I don't know. The

attitude of those lads. There was a time when the Over Seventy-Fives team put their hearts into it.

**DOUGAL:** I suppose these days they're too busy with their computer games and their Nike trainers.

**TED** (*not listening*): Yes, God, there's a distinct lack of pace in the team this year. And Dick Byrne's lot have a new fella that's supposed to be flip hot. An Italian fella.

**DOUGAL:** Ah, yes, the Italians know football all right. And, of course, the world of fashion! God, do you remember that fella who was so good at fashion they had to shoot him?

**TED:** Where's Nick Doorley? God almighty, our first training session and our star player can't be bothered to turn up. We're relying on his almost telepathic understanding with Father Jack to knock in a few goals. If anything happened to him, well, we'd be up to our necks in flip. And with this new fella on Dick's team, we need Nick at the very peak of his powers.

SCENE 12 INT./DAY 1
SET: A MORGUE
*We see the body of an ancient priest laid out in a coffin. Pull back to reveal Ted beside a middle-aged priest. This is Father Niall Haverty. This morgue is very minimal, very white, with expensive, stylish fittings and track lighting.*

**TED:** So, there's no way he'll be able to play?

**NIALL:** No. He's dead.

**TED:** Right. (*Pause.*) It's completely out of the question, then. (*Niall thinks this is rhetorical.*) Is it? It's completely out of the question?

**NIALL:** What? Oh, yes, yes, completely out of the question.

**TED:** Right. (*Pause.*) Wait . . . You . . . you don't hear breathing, do you?

**NIALL:** No, Ted, seriously, he's long gone.

**TED:** Right. Actually, Nick was a very dear friend of mine . . . Do you mind if I have a few minutes alone with him?

**NIALL:** Of course.

*He leaves the room and closes the door behind him.*

*We go with him into a small reception area. After a second, we hear a thumping noise from inside the room. Niall frowns and re-enters the room. Ted is holding Father Nick beneath the arms, pulling his fists to his chest in a resuscitating movement. He sees Niall and stops.*

**TED:** I thought I had something going there for a moment.

**NIALL:** Ah, come on, Ted, you're clutching at straws, man!

**TED:** Ah, you're right. Sorry, Father Nick.

**NIALL:** I told you, Father, he can't hear you, he's gone! C'mon, lads . . .

*Some men in suits come in and take the coffin out. Ted watches this sadly.*

**NIALL:** Ted, come on, cheer up. Look, have you seen my new watch? I got it from a catalogue. Look, if you press this button here, it tells you the time in Singapore. In Chinese! And then if you want to go back to normal time, you just press this here . . . (*He presses something a few times. This is accompanied by soft bleeping noises.*) . . . That's weird . . . it's supposed to . . . got the feckin' calculator now . . . come on . . . ah! And there you go, back to normal time. Half past ten.

**TED:** It's a quarter to two, Niall.

**NIALL:** Is it? Hold on a second and I'll set it to the right . . . to the right time . . . oh . . . God, the thing is fecked . . .

*He starts pressing buttons again.*

**TED:** That's an unusual-looking television.

**NIALL:** Ah, yeah, it's great, isn't it? It's voice activated. Tell it to come on, there.

**TED:** What?

**NIALL:** Say, 'I want to watch the television' or something.

**TED:** Ah, no, Niall, it's a bit mad.

**NIALL:** Go on!

*Pause.*

**TED:** I want to watch television!

*Nothing happens.*

**NIALL:** That's weird . . . it's supposed to . . .

come on there, now, television! COME ON! HE WANTS TO WATCH TELEVISION! COME ON!

**TED:** Niall, you've got to stop buying this catalogue stuff. It never works. The only thing you got that ever worked was that remote-controlled wheelchair.

**NIALL:** Yes, that worked perfectly, didn't it?

**TED:** But what use is it? You'd probably have more use for those joke fake arms you got!

**NIALL:** Oh, those things! They seemed funny at the time . . . Also, they reminded me of my own arms.

**TED:** Fake arms! Honestly, Niall! What the hell kind of situation could possibly require either a pair of fake arms or a radio-controlled wheelchair? Only, I would imagine, a completely ludicrous one.

**NIALL:** Yes. Anyway, Ted, do you think you can win the match without Father Nick?

**TED:** I don't know. He had a great partnership with Father Jack up front. God, if Dick Byrne won again . . .

*The telephone rings. Ted picks it up.*

**TED:** Hello?

*We hear Father Dick Byrne's voice from the other end.*

**DICK:** I *am* going to win again, Ted!

**TED:** Ha! I wouldn't be too sure of that, Dick! I think we've— Wait a second! How did you know I was here?!

*We hear a click and a dial tone. Then, from outside, we hear the ice-cream van's bells dwindling again. Ted runs to the window and shakes his fist.*

**TED:** Damn you, Father Dick Byrne!

SCENE 13 INT./DAY 1
SET: PAROCHIAL HOUSE
*Dougal is wearing a tracksuit, kneeling down and going through the contents of a trainer's kit bag. Jack is asleep in his chair. He snores loudly. Ted is looking through 'The Over Seventy-Fives Priests Five-A-Side Rulebook'.*

**TED:** Do you know what we need, Dougal? We need another Father Pinky Flood.

**DOUGAL:** Well, yeah . . . (*He looks nostalgic.*) Who is he, Ted?

**TED:** The greatest over seventy-fives player ever. He was to over seventy-fives football what George Best was to the world of players who were . . . average-age-type players. An absolute legend in the world of asthmatic, arthritic, hardly-able-to-move footballers with no teeth.

**DOUGAL:** There must be *someone*, Ted.

**TED:** I was just talking to Father Ned Fitzmaurice. He had a terrible stroke and fell from the roof of his house last week. He can hardly move. There's no way round it – I'll have to put him in goal.

**DOUGAL:** Oh God, Ted. I can't wait to get into the old physio's role again. Spraying things on to people's legs and running on to the pitch with the magic sponge. And doing all 'physio' type things.

**TED:** Yes. When they're injured, Dougal. (*Beat.*) Part of the skill of a physio is to wait until someone is injured before chasing after them with a sponge.

**DOUGAL:** Right.

**TED:** And while we're at it . . . Do you know exactly what the sponge does, Dougal?

*Pause.*

**DOUGAL:** . . . It . . . soaks up . . . germs . . .

**TED:** No, that's quite, quite wrong. Dougal, don't take this the wrong way, but . . . I don't want you to be a physio this year.

**DOUGAL:** Ted, if you don't want me to be physio this year, just come right out and say it.

**TED:** Ah . . . OK . . . Actually, Dougal, I was thinking of a new role for you, this year.

**DOUGAL** (*apprehensive*): Right . . .

**TED:** Yes. Very much a step-up in the whole off-the-field back-up-support team structure. An organisational change, you could call it.

**DOUGAL** (*apprehensively*): What is it, Ted?

**TED:** Eh . . . it's a very important job. One to which I'm sure you'll be able to bring all your qualities . . . ah . . . I want you to keep an eye on the corner flags. Make sure no one steals them.

*Dougal looks at Ted very seriously, then breathes a massive sigh of relief.*

**DOUGAL:** Oh, thank God for that! Phew! I thought you might be giving me something completely stupid to do, but wow! Watching the corner flags! Big responsibility!

*Jack snores unusually loudly. Ted and Dougal look at him. Mrs Doyle enters with her tray of tea.*

**MRS DOYLE:** Football! Football! Football! What you men see in it at all, I don't know! A load of men kicking a bit of leather around a field! Tscha! I don't know . . . you men. The things you think are great fun! Like going to the films. A load of men sitting around looking at films. And rollercoasters! A load of men in a big rollercoaster going up and down on a metal track. And fishing! A load of men fishing! And sailing. A load of men in a boat, floating about in the water! And shouting! A load of men going around shouting! And so forth.

**TED:** Hah, there's more to football than you think, Mrs Doyle. Here, I got you this book . . .

*He hands her a book, 'Understanding Football for Women'. The cover features a drawing of a buxom lass in a clench with a Ryan Giggs type in a Manchester United strip, a blazing fire in the background, all drawn in a romantic-novel style.*

**MRS DOYLE:** Ooh. All right, Father. I'll get on top of it right away.

*Mrs Doyle goes out.*

**DOUGAL:** God, Ted, he's been like that for a good long time. He wouldn't be dead again, would he?

**TED:** No, I don't think so. He's already died once, and it's very unlikely that he'd die again. God almighty . . .

**DOUGAL:** I hope he wakes up in time for the match, Ted. He looks like he's unconscious.

**TED:** Oh, I'm sure he's just dreaming of his old sporting days . . .

*Cut to Jack. We fade into his dream.*

SCENE 14 EXT./DAY 1
SET: TABLE
*We see Jack at a table. He has 'Judge' written on a piece of card in front of him.*

*We pull wide to see him sitting beneath a banner with 'Wet T-Shirt Competition' written on it. Some women are in the foreground, their backs to us, being sprayed by another woman wielding a hose.*

SCENE 15 INT./DAY 1*
SET: PAROCHIAL HOUSE
*Ted sees something in one corner of the room. It is a video camera with a red light on, pointing at them and humming quietly.*

**TED:** Dougal . . . how long has that video camera been there?

**DOUGAL:** What video cam— Oh . . . I don't know . . .

**TED:** Dick Byrne! Well, Dick, see how you like this!

*He smashes the video camera to smithereens.*

**DOUGAL:** Oh, wait, Ted, now I remember. That's actually your video camera. I thought I might do a fly-on-the-wall documentary about the match.

**TED:** What . . . It is my video camera!

*The telephone rings. Dick Byrne is on the other end.*

**DICK:** Hello, Ted!

**TED:** Oh, hello, Dick . . .

**DICK:** Ted, I was thinking . . . rather than a cash bet this year, how about some sort of forfeit?

**TED:** NO CASH BET! YOU BETCHA!!! I mean, yes, OK, if you're scared of losing . . . What kind of forfeit?

**DICK:** Oh, I've got a few ideas. But when you lose, you *have* to do it. No backing out, Crilly!

**TED:** Very well. One condition. Nothing illegal.

**DICK:** Agreed. And by the way, Ted, don't worry about the video camera. You can have a lend of *mine* if you want.

**TED:** Oh, thanks very much, Di— Wait a second! How did you know I smashed up my video camera?!

*The line goes dead.*

*We deleted this scene from the final version.

**TED:** Right . . .

**DOUGAL:** Ted! Where are you going?

**TED:** I'm going to find a way to shut Dick Byrne up once and for all!!

*He leaves the room. We see this from the point of view of a black-and-white camera hidden in one corner of the room.*

### END OF PART ONE

\* \* \*

### PART TWO

SCENE 16 INT./DAY 2
SET: PAROCHIAL HOUSE
*Dougal has a corner flag propped up in the middle of the room. He's staring at it intently. Ted comes in, rubbing his hands together.*

**TED:** Well! Today's the day! (*Dougal doesn't say anything – he's concentrating too hard on the flag.*) Got the hang of it yet, Dougal?

**DOUGAL:** It's harder than you'd think, Ted. (*He turns to talk to Ted. Mrs Doyle enters, sees the flag, frowns, picks it up and carries it out of the room.*) The trick is to— (*He turns and sees that the flag has gone.*) Aaaaghh!

*He starts to look around desperately for the flag. Mrs Doyle returns and approaches Ted.*

**MRS DOYLE:** Well, Father, I have to say that book you gave me has got me really interested in football. It's brilliant! I even put a little bet on this season.

**TED:** Oh, great! Who'd you bet on?

**MRS DOYLE:** It's an accumulator bet. Arsenal to win the league, Inter Milan to win Serie A by four points from Fiorentina with Ronaldo not scoring less than thirty goals, Kevin Keegan resigning from Fulham before the end of the season, Wimbledon getting relegated, but not finishing last – I have Southampton to finish last – Jimmy Hill to grow back his beard to balance that moustache (that's just a bit of fun, that one), and how the final Premiership table will look. First, Arsenal; second, Manchester United; third, Liverpool; fourth, Chelsea; fifth, Newcastle . . .

*Ted leaves the room as she continues speaking.*

SCENE 17 INT./DAY 2
SET: PAROCHIAL HOUSE HALLWAY
*Ted enters the hallway. Dougal is looking around desperately. He spots Ted and stands up.*

**DOUGAL:** Ah, hello, Ted. I'm just . . . eating . . . my . . . breakfast.

**TED** (*admonishingly*)**:** Dougal . . . that's a fib. What are you really doing?

**DOUGAL:** I . . . I . . . I've lost the flag, Ted! I'm sorry! I just put it down for a second and the next thing it was gone! I'm so sorry! Ted, you've got to give me another job! I can't take this one! It's too much, too soon! Oh, God, Ted, I can't do it! I just can't do it.

**TED:** Dougal, there's no such word as can't.

**DOUGAL:** Yes, there is. It's short for cannot. I cannot do it, Ted! I simply cannot!

**TED:** Dougal! Eye of the tiger. Just remember that at all times! Eye of the tiger!

*A beat, then Dougal nods bravely.*

SCENE 18 INT./DAY 2*
SET: PAROCHIAL HOUSE
*In the living room, Ted, Dougal and Mrs Doyle are looking very anxiously at a still-very-much-asleep Jack.*

**DOUGAL:** God, Ted, do you think he'll wake up in time for the match? It starts in six hours. I'm getting worried.

**TED:** This is a bit unusual, all right. Let's try old faithful. (*He holds up a CD case.*) Ah, yes. Never fails.

*Mrs Doyle, Dougal and Ted put on protective earwear. Mrs Doyle and Dougal hide behind the sofa, as if they're going to witness a nuclear explosion. Ted turns on the CD player, and then runs behind the sofa to join the other two.*

SCENE 19 EXT./DAY 2*
SET: PAROCHIAL HOUSE
*We hear from inside the house 'Smoke on the Water'. It is very, very, very loud.*

SCENE 20 EXT./DAY 2*
SET: NORTH POLE
*We see an Eskimo outside his igloo. We hear the*

*distant, faraway strains of 'Smoke on the Water'.*

SCENE 21 INT./DAY 2†
SET: PAROCHIAL HOUSE
*We see various objects in the room rattling with the noise. Ted turns off the music, and takes off his headphones. Dougal and Mrs Doyle emerge from behind the sofa.*

**TED:** God, this is very serious. I wonder . . . (*He sees something on the ground behind Jack's chair.*) Wait a second . . . Oh, my God! (*He runs over and picks something up. It is an empty, oversized bottle with 'Dreamy Sleepy Nightie Snoozy Snooze'.*) He's drunk an entire bottle of 'Dreamy Sleepy Snoozy Nightie Snooze'!

**DOUGAL:** Yes, Ted. But why is he still asleep?!

SCENE 22 EXT./DAY 2
SET: SPORTS HALL
*We see Dick Byrne's team. Everyone is very old, and can barely kick the ball, except for a player on the Rugged Island team, Father Romeo Sensini. He is very bronzed, with a thick mane of white hair; he looks super fit and wears a pair of cool shades. Dick watches as a mini-van pulls up. Ted and Dougal get out of it. Ted wears a massive Alex Ferguson-like manager's all-weather coat. Dougal wears a tracksuit. Dick and Cyril sidle up to Ted.*

**DICK:** Well, there he is, Ted. Father Romeo Sensini.

*We see Sensini being approached by two equally old women. He signs autographs for them in an offhand sort of way.*

**DICK:** He has seventeen caps for the Vatican Over-Seventy-Fives. Very fit. Only drinks very, very fine wine. Can walk up two flights of stairs unassisted. Only needs one nun to help him get out of a chair. You won't have a chance.

**TED:** Hah! That's what you think, Dick. We've put Father Hackett through a rigorous training schedule and he's never been fitter.

---

*We deleted this scene from the final version.
† Following the deletion of scenes 18–20, the contents of this scene were incorporated into the previous scene.

*Dick snorts and moves off. Cut to darkness. A door opens and we see that we're in the back of the van with the five players. The five men in the back gasp for air as soon as Ted opens the door.*

**TED:** Sorry, Fathers! Probably a bit stuffy in there.

*The men start to crawl out of the van. They reveal Jack, lying on the floor. Dick approaches Ted.*

**TED:** Whatever you do, Dougal, don't let Dick—

*Dick comes into shot.*

**DICK:** Aha! Yes, Jack looks like a major threat, all right. Hmmmn, we may have counted our chickens too soon.

*He turns round and laughs his head off. Cyril joins in and starts laughing, too, even though he has no idea what he's laughing at. His laughter dwindles as Dick looks at him with disdain.*

**CYRIL:** Ha, ha . . . ahhhh . . . chickens . . .

*He shuts up.*

SCENE 23 INT./DAY 2
SET: VAN
*Ted is looking at Jack.*

**TED:** Father! Father! Please wake up! Oh, what are we going to do?! OH!!! I can't believe we're in this completely ludicrous situation! (*Ted stops short.*) Wait a second! That's it!

SCENE 24 INT./DAY 2
SET: SPORTS HALL
*Cut to the pitch. The captains of each team are watching as the referee flips the coin.*

**REFEREE:** What's that? Can anyone see that?

**BIGLEY** (*bends to look, then straightens*)**:** It's some kind of coin.

*Cut to Mrs Doyle, who is joined by Mrs Norton.*

**MRS NORTON:** God almighty, Mrs Doyle. How could you be interested in this type of thing?

**MRS DOYLE:** That's what I thought. But look at this.

*She hands Mrs Norton 'Understanding Football for Women.' Cut to Ted on the sidelines. He is talking*

*anxiously into his mobile phone.**

**TED:** Sorry to ring again, Niall, but I'm getting worried.†

*Cut to Niall on the other end of the line.†*

**NIALL:** No need to worry at all, Ted. Just look out for a white van. I'm amazed it hasn't got there already.†

**TED:** They're just about to kick off! Oh, no, wait!†

*We see a white van pulling up outside. Ted sees it through the door. It has the following written on its side: 'NICK OF TIME DELIVERIES'.†*

**TED:** Great!†

*He hangs up. Cut back to the referee.†*

**REFEREE:** Father McGuire, you're a man short. If he's not here by kick-off time, I'll have to award the match to Father Byrne's team. And where's your manager?†

**DOUGAL:** Ah. He had to go to the toilet. He's . . . ah, got diarrhoea.†

**REFEREE** (*cringes*)**:** I'm sorry, I'll have to give Father Byrne a walkover . . . Father Byrne?†

**DOUGAL** (*hears something*)**:** Wait!†

**REFEREE:** What's that noise?†

*Cut to the doors of the stadium. There is a mechanical noise, growing louder. After a moment, to a burst of celebratory music, Jack speeds in, still asleep, in his mechanical wheelchair. Dick comes up to the referee.†*

**DICK:** This can't be allowed, surely!†

*Ted follows in through the door. He has fake arms.†*

**REFEREE:** I'll look at the book . . . (*He consults his book, 'The Over Seventy-Fives Priests Five-A-Side Rulebook'.*) I can't see anything about wheelchairs . . .†

**TED:** Oh, they're definitely allowed. There's a precedent. Turn to page 166.†

*The referee turns to page 166. We see an old picture, circa 1920s, showing an old-priests match. In an old bath chair is a fearsome old priest, wielding a stick.*

---

*We deleted the previous two sentences from the final version.
†We deleted this from the final version.

*Ted flips his fake hand on to the picture.*[†]

**TED:** There. (*Ted realises he shouldn't be showing off his fake hand and flips it away.*) Father Pinky Flood.[†]

*There is a reverent hush.*[†]

**TED:** The greatest over seventy-fives priest footballer there ever was. This was his testimonial game against a Hungarian/Polish selection. He had a massive stroke during the pre-match warm-up, but he was still determined to play. He was held in such esteem that the referee let him play in a wheelchair.[†]

**REFEREE:** Well, I suppose, if there's a precedent . . .[†]

**TED:** Great![†]

**DICK:** *Grrrr!* It's not fair![†]

*1. Kick-off*[†]

*2. One priest kicks the ball to another (Father Bigley). The ball moves terribly, terribly slowly. We see a moving-camera position from just behind the ball. As it rolls towards Bigley, we can see him looking afraid. It hits his foot and he falls over. We see that Ted is fiddling with a remote control under his jacket. His arms look very fake. We see Jack shifting around in his wheelchair, still unconscious, in a corner.*

*3. We see Father Romeo Sensini gain possession. He makes for the goal.*

**TED:** Close him down! Close him down!

*4. A priest very slowly starts to make towards Sensini. Sensini dribbles very slowly around him.*

**TED:** He's running rings around you!

*Sensini gets past the old man. He approaches the goal. Jack is blocking his way, asleep in his chair. Ted fiddles with the remote control under his coat and Jack makes towards Sensini. Without pausing, Jack goes right past Sensini and through the door by which he just came in. Meanwhile, Sensini is still moving slowly towards goal. Mrs Doyle approaches Ted.*

**MRS DOYLE:** Sensini's got an open goal, Father. If you don't do something quick, he'll score in a matter of minutes.

*We see Mrs Norton finishing 'Understanding*

*Football for Women'.*

**MRS NORTON** (*making managerial hand gestures*)**:** Out! Out! Push out!

*She hands the book distractedly to a cleaning woman, Mrs Cavanagh, who is mopping a floor nearby. She starts leafing through it. Sensini finally kicks the ball with a tremendous grunt. The ball travels incredibly slowly towards the line.*

*Very, very slowly it comes to a stop just on the line. We see the ball on the line. A very tense moment. Cut to Ted looking hugely anxious.*

*5. Father Whelan (from Ted's team) then very slowly moves from out of shot and kicks the ball away.*

*Cut back to Mrs Doyle and Mrs Norton. Mrs Cavanagh is still leafing through the book.*

**MRS DOYLE:** Where did he come from?!

**MRS NORTON:** Great defending!

*6. The ball goes to Father Bigley (Craggy Island).*

**TED:** Get rid of it! Get rid of it!

*Bigley looks around, confused.*

**BIGLEY:** What?

**TED:** Don't look at me! Keep playing!

**BIGLEY:** I'm ninety-seven!

*Bigley leaves the ball and takes a step or two towards Ted. Behind him, Sensini moves very slowly towards the ball.*

**TED:** Turn around! Concentrate on the game!

**BIGLEY:** Is that Father Crilly? Hello, Father!

*Cut to the spectators.*

**MRS DOYLE:** Someone's going to have to get tighter on the Italian.

**MRS NORTON:** The tension is almost too much to bear. Tell me when he gets possession.

*Mrs Norton turns around and hides her eyes. Mrs Doyle watches the match. We stay on this for about thirty seconds.*

**MRS DOYLE:** Now.

*Mrs Cavanagh finishes the book.*

**MRS CAVANAGH:** Go wide! Go wide!

*7. Sensini has possession of the ball and heads towards the goal. Cut to Ted. He looks alarmed. We see the wheelchair coming back through the door and heading straight for Sensini. A shot of Ted making an 'ouch' face as we hear a 'crump' sound. Cut to Sensini on the ground holding his leg. The referee blows his whistle.*

**TED:** Penalty! Damn!

*Sensini puts the ball on the penalty spot. He strikes coolly, and we see a shot from the ball's point of view. The ball very slowly goes one way while the goalkeeper goes the other.*

**MRS DOYLE:** He's sent the keeper the wrong way!

*The ball goes into the net. We see Dick Byrne, Cyril, etc., jumping up and down with excitement.*

**DICK:** GOAL!

**CYRIL:** What's that, Dick?

**DICK:** We're going to win, Cyril. I think I'll want a souvenir of this day . . . Get me one of those corner flags.

**CYRIL:** Yes, Dick.

*He walks out of shot. Ted looks downcast. He fiddles with the remote control.*

**TED:** God, this remote control is tricky.

*Dougal is standing near one of the flags. Cyril approaches. Dougal watches him warily. They do a little suspicious dance around the flag. The referee blows his whistle. It is half-time.*

SCENE 25 INT./DAY 2
SET: DRESSING ROOM
*The players sit around, exhausted.*

**TED:** Right! I know you're tired. I know you want to go home. I know you're due back in the home by eight. But remember one thing – you're carrying the whole of Craggy Island on your shoulders.

*Father Whelan puts up a finger.*

**WHELAN:** Eh—

**TED:** Metaphor, Jim.

**WHELAN:** It's just, my back—

**TED:** Jim, metaphor, don't mean it literally. Try not to jump into the flow here.

SCENE 26 INT./DAY 2*
SET: CAFE-TYPE AREA
*Mrs Doyle and Mrs Norton, with Mrs Cavanagh to their right, are sitting in what look strangely like half-time match-discussion positions.*

**MRS CAVANAGH:** Mrs Doyle, an exciting first half. Any thoughts?

**MRS DOYLE:** Sensini's not getting picked up. The problem is he's got a free role in midfield. He's pulling the centre half all over the place.

**MRS CAVANAGH:** Lack of pace certainly a problem for Craggy Island.

**MRS NORTON:** It's not just lack of pace. Some of that marking from set pieces . . . you wouldn't see that in a school playground.

**MRS DOYLE:** That corner they had just before half-time—

**MRS NORTON:** The defending on that was a joke.

**MRS DOYLE:** You can't have the full backs staying on the post like that. You've got to have them push out, or they're leaving their front two onside. That's naïve defending. Do that too often and you'll get punished.

**MRS CAVANAGH:** Anyway, let's return to what should be a very exciting second half.

SCENE 27 INT./DAY 2
SET: CHANGING ROOM
*Ted is still in spiel mode.*

**TED:** All right, I want you all to go out there

*We deleted this scene from the final version.

and play the greatest game of what's left of your lives! I want you to take Dick Byrne's team and rip them to shreds!

**WHELAN:** Eh . . .

**TED:** Again, Jim, metaphor. Now, get out there and lick some arse! Kick! Kick some arse! Just go! Now!

SCENE 28 INT./DAY 2
SET: PLAYING FIELD
*The referee blows his whistle. Father Whelan is standing around, not really knowing what's going on. The ball comes towards him and stops at his feet. Sensini comes into shot and tackles him roughly. Cut to Ted, as we hear Whelan scream and then a whistle blow. Ted stands up and runs to where some players have gathered around the fallen Whelan.*

**TED:** This looks bad. It could be broken.

**WHELAN:** No, no, I don't think it's broken. I'll play on. Don't want to let the side down.

**TED:** Good man!

**WHELAN:** I might just have a little rest first.

*He settles into a little snooze. Cut back to Dougal and Cyril. Cyril is trying to sneak up backwards on the flag. Dougal swoops in and discourages him at a vital moment.*

*Cut back to the match. One priest passes to another. Cut to Jack in his chair. We hear a kicking sound and the ball lands in Jack's lap.*

**TED:** Go, Father Jack! Go!

*We see Jack's chair accelerate through the players and steam through the Rugged Island goal.*

**TED:** Yaaaayyy!!!

*We see Mrs Doyle, Mrs Norton and Mrs Cavanagh clench their teeth and fists. They are surrounded by ten Mrs Doyle-alikes pointing and chanting.*

**MRS DOYLE AND HER COTERIE**
(*chanting*): You're all very quiet over there, you're all very quiet over there . . .

*8. Rugged Island kick off again and Jack steams through, gaining possession. He's heading straight for goal.*

*9. Sensini runs up and boots something on Jack's wheelchair. Smoke starts issuing from it and it goes round in a circle then heads towards the door again.*

*Jack goes through it for the last time.*

**TED:** Foul, Ref, surely!

**REFEREE** (*making a gesture with his hands*): Play on!

*10. The ball wanders into the path of Bigley.*

**TED:** Open goal! Go on, Father Bigley!

**BIGLEY:** What?

**TED:** Don't look at me. You've only got the goalkeeper to beat!

*11. We see this from behind the goal. Bigley kicks the ball. It slowly rolls under the keeper and into the goal. The final whistle is blown.*

**TED:** Whhhhhhhaaaayyyy!!!!!!!

**BIGLEY:** Have I done something wrong?

*Much joy. Ted and Mrs Doyle run out and celebrate. Cyril makes one more stab at stealing the flag. Dougal stops him again. Cyril walks off, defeated. Dougal beams happily, a job well done.*

SCENE 29 INT./DAY 2*
SET: DRESSING ROOM
*Ted and Dougal approach Dick and Cyril. The referee stands between them. Ted's fake hands hang uselessly by his side.*

**CYRIL:** Six nil. God, we had it easy out there.

**DICK:** We lost two one, Cyril. Ted, I have to say, we've had our arguments down through the years but you played a good game.

*During this speech, we cut to Dougal's, Niall's and the referee's admiring expressions.*

**DICK:** Seeing your team out there, pulling together for the common good, well . . . it made me realise how much time we've wasted

---

* In the final version of this scene, Ted tells Dick his forfeit and Dick and Cyril go home, leaving Dougal and Ted to open champagne with the referee. It is he who notices something amiss when Dougal forces Ted to take a glass of champagne. A new scene was then added with Ted and Dougal back at the Parochial House. His ruse discovered, Ted must do Dick's forfeit, and in the final version the scene ends with a disbelieving Ted reading his forfeit out loud.

on our stupid rivalry. I accept my defeat, because it came at the hands of a better man. Put it there, Ted.

*Ted stands there, his plastic hands hanging uselessly by his side. Long, long pause.*

**TED:** No.

**REFEREE:** *No?*

**TED:** No.

**DOUGAL:** Ted, I didn't understand any of that speech, but even I know Dick's trying to make friends!

**TED:** Yes, but—

**DICK:** No, I understand. You think it's another trick. But listen to me, Ted. No more tricks. Take my hand and I will never, never let it go.

**TED:** Right . . . Ehh . . . Dick, I, too, wish to put our rivalry to one side. But I would rather do that . . . with a nod. Dick, please accept my nod of friendship.

*He nods.*

**DICK:** Ah, Ted, come on, shake hands. It'll make me feel better.

**DOUGAL:** Ted, I don't know what's wrong with you . . . (*Ted makes urgent facial expressions to remind Dougal of the hands.*) Shake his hand, Ted. What's wrong with you at all?

**MRS DOYLE** (*incredibly savagely*): DON'T DO IT, FATHER!!!!

*Pause. Everyone is looking at Ted. He finally gives in and does a little jerk to swing his hand into Dick's. Dick catches it and shakes it, smiling warmly at Ted.*

**DICK:** Now . . . let's hear it, what's the forfeit?

**TED:** Well, Dick, in the light of that lovely speech, what's say we go without the forfeit?

**DICK:** Oh, no, I don't think so. I believe the referee has the envelopes containing the forfeits?

*Dick absent-mindedly scratches his face with Ted's now-detached fake hand. He notices it.*

**DICK:** What the—

*He looks down at Ted and sees where the hand is missing. He examines Ted's other hand. Fake. He pulls aside Ted's coat and sees Ted's hand holding the remote control. Pause. Dick's face gradually darkens.*

**DICK:** You . . . you little cheating fibber!! I always knew you were a dirty little sneaky cheatbag! How *dare* you sully this holy football ground with cheating! You . . . cheating priest!

*Ted hangs his head. Cyril approaches Dick.*

**CYRIL:** Dick . . .

**DICK:** Just one second, Cyril. I want to get one last look at Crilly, just so the next time I think there's a cheat around, I'll know what to look for. (*He looks Ted up and down, shaking his head.*) There. I'm finished.

**CYRIL:** Great. I just wanted to know . . . even though we lost, do we still have to give all that money to their goalkeeper?

*Dick just looks at Cyril while Ted's face lights up.*

**TED:** Ahhhhhhhhhhhhhhhhhhhhhhhh-hah! Well, well, well, well, well, well, well, well, well, well, well, well, well, well, well, well. Bribery, the most dishonest form of corruption there is. Even worse than swindling or fraud or prostitution rackets or skimming money off a parish account and putting it in a high-interest, special-needs savings account for a few years before moving it back . . .

**DOUGAL:** Oh, ho!

**TED:** Shut up, Dougal . . . Oh, much worse than that! I should have known. You . . . briber . . . or whatever the word is.

**DOUGAL:** Right.

**REFEREE:** Well. I think you're both a disgrace. And I think you should both do your forfeits

**TED:** Fine by me.

**DICK:** Oh, me, too.

*The referee opens one of the envelopes.*

**REFEREE:** Father Byrne and Father McDuff first. Your forfeit is . . . oh, good God . . . Father Byrne has to kiss Father McDuff on the cheek.

*Dick looks incredibly bored by this.*

**DOUGAL:** Haaaaaaa!!!!! Ahghhghaaa!!!!!! WHAT A BRILLIANT IDEA TED!!!!! HA, HA, HA, HA!!!! Ted, you're a genius!!!!! I can't wait to see that!!!!

*They both laugh in a very childish, superior way. Dick enters into shot.*

**DOUGAL:** Oh, God, Ted, how did you think of that?! That's just the best—

**DICK:** . . . Did it.

**TED** (*beat*): What?

**DICK:** I did it.

**TED:** But . . . but we didn't see it.

**DICK:** Well, they all saw it.

**TED:** Oh. (*To the crowd.*): Was it funny?

*Everyone shrugs half-heartedly. The referee opens the other envelope.*

**REFEREE:** And now Father Crilly . . .

**DOUGAL:** Don't worry, Ted. It'll never be as good as your one.

**REFEREE:** You, Father Crilly . . . (*To Dick.*) Is this right? (*Dick nods, smiling. The referee looks concerned but reads on.*) You . . . Father Crilly, by this time next week . . . you have to . . .

*Close-up on Ted. Dick steps forward and grabs the letter from the referee's hand.*

**DICK:** Crilly . . . You have to . . . KICK BISHOP BRENNAN UP THE ARSE!!!!!!

*Freeze on Ted's look of horror. Words come up on the screen: 'To Be Continued'.*

POST-CREDIT SEQUENCE
*We see a quiet road and hear a low mechanical noise. After a moment Jack passes by, still unconscious in his chair. Tilt up to reveal a sign that reads 'Pier'.*

**THE END**

SERIES THREE ⊕ EPISODE SIX

# kicking Bishop Brennan up the arse

**GRAHAM:** Our idea of kicking someone up the arse and then pretending nothing had happened was influenced by a story told about the painter Magritte. Apparently, after he met a potential suitor for his sister, he brought him into the sitting room, kicked the suitor in the behind and then pretended that absolutely nothing had occurred – just to see what would happen. It's an intriguing concept. What would you do in that situation? And how long would it take you to become absolutely convinced that you had indeed been kicked? We thought it would work especially well here because of the relationship between Ted and Brennan. The latter knows Ted is *terrified* of him, so it would take him ages to make the intellectual leap of registering an attack.

That one idea drives the whole plot of this episode, so we had to expand it as much as possible. That's why we introduced Bishop Jessup, the sarcastic bishop. We needed a reason for the first attempt to fail. That sequence – Ted's run-up and subsequent leap out of the window – was originally supposed to be filmed in slow motion. Somehow it didn't work, so on a hunch someone suggested running it at the proper speed, and it was perfect. Jessup's fate – being locked in Jack's underpants' hamper – originally had the ending you'll see in this draft, but it was funnier on paper than in rehearsal. In the end, we decided to keep it simple and ended up with a nod to *The Vanishing*, which, if you haven't seen it, is one of the scariest films ever made.

**ARTHUR:** Len (Brennan) is extremely egotistical, so we used that as the reason for his arrival – Dick, knowing this, tells him that an apparition of his face has appeared on a skirting board. And that basic idea is not quite as ridiculous as it might seem. The Church is always investigating apparitions, many of which are totally bizarre and some of which are recounted in a book called *Beyond Belief* by Liam Fay, a friend of ours. Brennan's apparition was inspired by a passage in that book when an apparition of Jesus appears on a little girl's bedroom door and ten days later, the Virgin Mary follows suit by turning up on her built-in wardrobe . . . But other apparition stories really are beyond belief, like the sensation generated by an American advertisement for spaghetti. It was claimed in some quarters that the image of a forkful of spaghetti was, in fact, the face of Jesus. It *did* actually look like Jesus, but would he really appear in spaghetti?

So, getting Brennan to the Parochial House wasn't a problem, but we had to keep him there. Hence Mrs Doyle saying that he'll have to stay the night because they're 'taking in the roads' and storing them in a warehouse until the rain stops. It's another of those surreal aspects of Craggy Island, like the west side falling into the sea, that are best heard and not seen. They simply wouldn't work if we tried to show them, or went into them in any detail whatsoever . . .

## PART ONE
SCENE 1 INT./DAY 1*
SET: SPORTS HALL
*An American 'NYPD Blue' voice comes up over black.*

**VOICEOVER:** Previously on *Father Ted*.

*We then see cut-together scenes from 'Escape from Victory', but the scenes are filmed in the style of 'NYPD Blue' – the camera 'finding' the people who are speaking a near-documentary style. First of all, the referee scolding Ted and Dick.*

**REFEREE:** Well. I think you're both a disgrace. And I think you should both do your forfeits.

**TED:** Fine by me.

**DICK:** Oh, me, too.

*Then, the revelation of Ted's forfeit.*

**REFEREE:** You, Father Crilly . . . (*To Dick.*) Is this right? (*Dick nods, smiling. The referee looks concerned but reads on.*) You . . . Father Crilly, by this time next week . . . you have to . . .

*Close-up on Ted. Dick steps forward and grabs the letter from the referee's hand.*

**DICK:** Crilly . . . you have to . . . KICK BISHOP BRENNAN UP THE ARSE!!!!!!

*The camera finds Ted, looking shocked, then looks at his hand for no reason, then looks at Dougal, who is looking straight at the camera.*

*'NYPD Blue' style drums lead us into titles . . .*

SCENE 2 EXT./DAY X
SET: EDGE OF A VOLCANO
*We see a round volcano-hole. A little smoke comes up from the hole, with a flow of red lava around the rim. We see Ted – looking like a priest in a Graham Greene novel, unshaven, unwashed, etc. – being led up to the edge by two natives. We hear distant, menacing drums.*

**TED:** Ah, now, lads, come on.

**WARRIOR:** Xatl, the Volcano God, is angry. We must appease his wrath.

---

\* In the final version, this scene was altered to incorporate the changes to the final scene of *Escape from Victory*, footnoted on page 324.

**TED:** Volcano God! What kind of nonsense is that? Look, come on, I'll ask you one more time . . . Would you not give Catholicism a try?

**WARRIOR:** It'll never catch on here. We don't agree with the Pope's line on artificial contraception. It's the 1990s, for goodness sake.

*They throw Ted in. He screams as he goes. A native woman (actually Mrs Doyle in a grass skirt and a bra made out of leaves) approaches the edge of the volcano.*

**MRS DOYLE** (*looking down the volcano*): Cup of tea, Father?

*Cut to Ted in the Parochial House. A startled look on his face. We hear Mrs Doyle's voice offscreen.*

**MRS DOYLE:** Father? Cup of tea? God, Father, what's wrong with you? You're a million miles away.

**TED:** Hmm? Oh, I'm sorry, Mrs Doyle. I was just thinking about my next parish.

**MRS DOYLE:** You're not leaving us, Father?

**TED:** Well, Bishop Brennan is always threatening to send me somewhere unpleasant, and this time he just might go through with it. You see, I'm going to kick him up the arse.

**MRS DOYLE:** Ah, sure I'm sure he won't mind that, Father. He'll probably love a big hard kick up the arse.

**TED:** I'm not sure if he will, Mrs Doyle. And he certainly won't like *me* kicking him up the

arse. I'm on the horns of a dilemma. Very big horns sticking out of a giant dilemma cow.

*Dougal rushes in with a newspaper.*

**DOUGAL:** Ted, Ted, wait'll you hear this! You are not going to believe this! (*He reads aloud.*) Clint Eastwood has been arrested for a crime he didn't . . . oh, wait, no, it's a film.

*Ted sighs.*

**TED:** There was a time, Dougal, when that type of frankly . . . mental misunderstanding would have irritated me quite a lot, but now . . . (*He sighs deeply.*) To put it very bluntly, Dougal, the flip's hit the fan.

**DOUGAL:** Do you really have to kick him up the arse, Ted?

**TED:** I lost the bet, Dougal, and I have to do the forfeit. Do you remember last year, when Dick Byrne lost the darts tournament? He had to say 'bollocks' very loudly in front of President Mary Robinson. Well, he's not going to let me off this one.

**DOUGAL:** You're right, Ted. There's a code of honour involved. (*Pause.*) You could lie to him.

**TED:** No, he insisted you have to take a photograph as proof. (*Beat.*) Oh, God, Dougal! What am I going to do? I like this parish!

**DOUGAL:** Do you?!

**TED:** Well, no, but God, you should see some of the other parishes! Some of these places, you can only get three channels! And one of them's in Irish! And what if they send me abroad?

*Jack snorts loudly.*

**TED:** Father Jack. How can I leave Father Jack? Look at him there, drunk out of his mind, sleeping in his own filth, ready to lash out and whack someone if they get too close. I'll really miss him!

**DOUGAL:** But Ted, look at it this way. Bishop Brennan has only come to visit us twice in the last three years. He hates us, Ted. He thinks we're all a bunch of big eejits. Especially you, Ted. He thinks you're the biggest eejit of them all. Head honcho eejit number one. You never know. He may never come here again.

*The telephone rings. Ted looks at it for a moment or two, then answers it.*

**TED:** Hello? Yes. OK. (*He puts the phone down.*) That was Bishop Brennan. He's coming tomorrow.

**DOUGAL:** Oh, no, why?

**TED:** Well, what I gathered from that conversation is that Father Dick Byrne has told Bishop Brennan of a miraculous vision appearing in the skirting boards in the Parochial House here. He has told Bishop Brennan that within the woodgrain of the skirting boards you can clearly see what appears to be a perfect likeness . . . of Bishop Brennan.

**DOUGAL:** You found out all that just there?

**TED:** Yes, he's very excited about it.

**DOUGAL:** Wow . . . God, I must have a look. (*He goes over to the wall, throws himself on to the carpet and looks at the skirting board.*) Oh, God, I see it! It's him, Ted, it's him! It's just like Len! A big frown on him and all!\*

**TED:** No, it isn't, Dougal. Firstly, it's in the spare bedroom not the living room, and secondly, Dick Byrne made up the whole

---

\* We deleted these lines from the final version.

thing to lure Bishop Brennan here under false pretences.*

**DOUGAL:** What? Oh, right. (*He gets to his feet.*) That's one of those weird things, though, isn't it, Ted? The way Our Lord and Our Lady and all that crowd pop up on household furniture and in other mad places where you wouldn't expect them. Like the Turin Shroud. Or that time I saw God's face in that Weetabix. Do you remember I showed it to you?*

**TED:** It reminded me more of Leonard Nimoy. But people see anything they want in those things. (*He picks up a magazine. It has an advertisement for spaghetti.*) I mean, look at this . . . This to me looks like Elle Macpherson giving Kylie Minogue a piggy back.*

*He tears out the picture and slips it in his pocket.*

**DOUGAL:** . . . Maybe they just get fed up there in Heaven. They decide to go on a little tour of household appliances and sundry items. Do you remember that fella in Sligo? There was an image of Padre Pio in his wig. And Saint Martin De Porres appearing in those triangular teabags in Clare.*

**TED:** It's weird all right. It's one of those areas of Catholicism that's frankly . . . well, a bit mad.*

**DOUGAL:** Sure the whole Catholic thing is a bit of a puzzler, isn't it, Ted?*

**TED:** Careful, Dougal . . . But Len appearing on a skirting board . . . I bet he's just dying to see his big face on a bit of wood.*

**DOUGAL:** I'm a bit afraid of Len, Ted.*

**TED:** Hah! Join the club! But I'm not going to worry about it. The worst thing would be . . .*

SCENE 3 INT./NIGHT 1
SET: TED AND DOUGAL'S BEDROOM
*Ted and Dougal sitting up in bed with the light on. We hear occasional thunder outside and heavy rain.*

**TED:** . . . just to keep thinking about it, and becoming so anxious and obsessed that you can't sleep. I mean, that'd be just . . . Dougal? (*We see that Dougal is asleep.*) Dougal!

**DOUGAL** (*waking up suddenly*): What! God, that was weird. What happened there? The last thing I remember is . . . feeling very drowsy and tired . . . and then . . . God, I don't remember anything after that at all.

**TED:** Yes. It's called sleeping, Dougal. You do it every night. I don't know why you're finding it so easy to drop off. Tomorrow – today, in fact – you are going to be taking a photograph of me kicking Bishop Brennan up the arse. He won't like that either, you know. I mean, would you like someone taking a photograph of you being kicked up the arse? Put yourself in his place.

*Dougal thinks. His face gradually darkens.*

**DOUGAL:** I wouldn't like that at all!

**TED:** I thought you wouldn't!

**DOUGAL:** Who do they think they are? Taking photographs of me being kicked up the arse!

**TED:** Exactly! Now, imagine the 'they' you're talking about is me and you, Dougal. And imagine Bishop Brennan just said what you said there, and is as angry as you are now.

*Dougal, still angry, thinks for a second. Then he looks scared.*

**DOUGAL:** Oh, no!

**TED:** Exactly!

**DOUGAL:** Oh, God, Ted!

**TED:** It's a terrible situation, Dougal. But I'll just have to do it, and hope for the best.

**DOUGAL:** That's the spirit, Ted! I feel much better now. What were we worried about at all?!

**TED:** And his PA's coming. Father Jessup. The rudest priest in Ireland. He's bound to say something. I'd say one of the first duties of a personal assistant would be to point out when his boss has been kicked up the arse.

**DOUGAL:** Ted, when Len comes round—

**TED:** Dougal, stop right there. You've got to remember, don't call Brennan 'Len'. He's a bishop. What shouldn't you call him, Dougal? Let's get this right.

**DOUGAL:** Len.

**TED:** Very good. Now, just remember that.

**DOUGAL:** Len, Len, Len, Len, Len, Len, Len, Len, Len, Len, Len . . .

**TED:** OK, now, let's just get a good night's sleep.

*He thumps his pillow. He turns the light off and puts his head on the pillow. However, it's still as bright as it was when the light was on.*

**TED:** Oh, God, it's morning! We must have talked all night! At least we'll still have a few hours before the—* (The alarm goes off.)* Oh, God! Well, I set it a bit early so we'd have plenty of time before Bishop Brennan—* (The doorbell rings.)* Oh, God!

SCENE 4 INT./DAY 2
SET: PAROCHIAL HOUSE HALLWAY
*Mrs Doyle is walking to the door. Ted runs down the stairs, whispering fiercely.*

**TED:** Mrs Doyle! Stall them for a few seconds! . . . Dougal, come on!

*They run into the living room, yanking their clothes on. They are still a long way from being presentable. Ted throws his pyjama bottoms out of shot. Mrs Doyle opens the door. We see Bishop Brennan and Father Jessup. It is raining outside. They are very wet.*

**MRS DOYLE:** Hello!

**BRENNAN** *(to Jessup)*: This is the housekeeper.

**JESSUP:** Hmmm . . .

**MRS DOYLE:** Your Grace, is that a hat you're wearing?

**BRENNAN:** It's called a mitre.

**MRS DOYLE:** Is it?

**BRENNAN:** Yes.

*Pause.*

**MRS DOYLE:** Well, that's enough 'stalling'. Come on in!

SCENE 5 INT./DAY 2
SET: PAROCHIAL HOUSE
*Mrs Doyle opens the door for Len and Jessup. They walk in and see Ted and Dougal, both wearing half-moon spectacles and both looking over a large book, 'The Catechism of the Catholic Church'. Ted is pointing at something over Dougal's shoulder.*

**TED:** That's true, Dougal, and you can see the importance of the Eucharist in the Mass from what Saint Paul says here . . .

**DOUGAL:** The way I see it . . .

**BRENNAN** *(to Jessup)*: Pretending to talk about religion. *(To Ted.)* Crilly.

**TED:** Ah!

**DOUGAL:** Len—

*Len bristles.*

**DOUGAL:** —d me a fiver, will you, Ted?

*Ted catches on and does so.*

**TED:** Certainly, Father McGuire. A fiver for you. Don't forget to pay me back! Ha, ha.

**BRENNAN** *(to Jessup)*: This type of thing, twenty-four hours a day. *(To Ted.)* I'll make this short, Crilly. Show me the likeness and I'll be off. I have to go off to Rome tomorrow for an audience with the Pope.

**DOUGAL:** I love those programmes. Did you see the one with Elton John?

**BRENNAN:** You shut up. Aah! Damn! That car journey has played havoc with my . . . lower back . . .

**TED:** Sore around that whole area, yeah?

**BRENNAN:** Yes.

**TED:** Well. Better make sure no one . . . does anything to it. Hello, Father Jessup. Helping out Bishop Brennan, then?

**JESSUP:** No, I'm up in space doing important work for N.A.S.A.

*He raises eyes to heaven.*

**BRENNAN:** Show me this thing, Crilly.

**TED:** It looks very like you, Your Grace.

**BRENNAN** *(a bit flattered)*: Does it?

**TED** *(jokily)*: You're far better looking

though. I don't mean that . . . in an intimate way, of course . . . Nasty day, isn't it? . . . Did you come by the new road?

**JESSUP:** No. We went round by Southern Yemen.

*He raises his eyes to heaven.*

**TED:** Anyway . . . Oh, before you have a look at the skirting board, Your Grace . . . would you mind if Father McGuire took a few photographs? Dougal, get the camera there.

**DOUGAL:** Oh, right . . .

*Dougal takes a camera from the table. Ted goes over to him. They start whispering to each other very conspiratorially. Cut to Jessup and Brennan looking at Ted and Dougal.*

**BRENNAN** (*notices Jessup looking at him*): Oh, this is nothing. Nothing!

*Dougal then wanders around the room trying to look casual, taking a few photographs.*

**TED** (*terrified*): Right . . . I suppose . . . I suppose we'd better go . . .

*Ted and Dougal let the other two go first. They look at each other. Dougal is terrified. They hug. Jessup and Brennan turn around and see this.*

**BRENNAN:** This is a new one.

SCENE 6 INT./DAY 2
SET: SPARE ROOM
*Brennan and Jessup enter. Ted and Dougal follow.*

**TED:** Before we look at it, perhaps we should say a prayer.

*Brennan sighs.*

**BRENNAN:** No, Crilly, let's just . . . Oh, yes, very well.

*They all bow their heads.*

**TED:** Oh, Lord, at this time of great joy for Bishop Brennan, when you have seen fit to put his face in the skirting boards of our house, let us reflect on the gift of forgiveness. You are the most forgiving of all gods.

**BRENNAN:** Of all gods? What other gods are there, Crilly?

**TED:** Eh . . . false gods.

**BRENNAN:** All right, carry on.

**TED:** And who could not forget that wonderful scene at the end of *Jesus of Nazareth* when Robert Powell, playing you, forgave them for they knew not what they did. Do . . . do you remember that, Your Grace? How forgiving Our Lord was . . . What he said there . . .

**BRENNAN:** Get on with it, Crilly.

**TED:** Yes, of course . . . Oh, Lord, heap blessings upon wise Bishop Brennan, the best bishop in the world by miles. For he endureth without spite, Amen. There it is, Your Grace. Have a look at it. It's under the window there.

*We see a piece of ordinary-looking skirting board. There are a few swirls in the grain that could, if stared at really, really hard, possibly resemble some sort of face. Brennan goes over and leans down to see it. Jessup bends over as well. Ted gets a view of his arse. His eyes widen.*

**BRENNAN:** I don't see anything, Crilly . . .

*Ted sees his chance. We see Ted, in a very dramatic slow motion, run up behind Brennan. Very dramatic music. Then we see Ted's expression turn from determination to terror; he turns in mid flight and heads towards the window. His momentum takes him through the frame and we hear a dwindling 'Aieeeee . . .' Cut back to normal speed. Brennan looks up.*

**BRENNAN:** What happened there?

**JESSUP:** Crilly . . . just . . . he . . . jumped through the window.

*Brennan goes over to the window and looks outside.*

**BRENNAN:** Crilly? Crilly . . . are you out there? What's going on? Why did you jump through the window?

*He looks at Dougal. Dougal can't think what to say.*

**DOUGAL:** *An Audience with Lily Savage.* That was good as well. But the Pope . . . that'll be great.

*Ted enters through the door, slightly out of breath.*

**BRENNAN:** Crilly, there you are! Why did you jump through the window?

*Long pause.*

**TED:** Jump through the window? I didn't jump through the window, did I?

**JESSUP:** You did. You jumped through the window.

**TED:** Oh, right. Eh, it was because of shock. I saw your face! Did you not see it in the skirting board?

**BRENNAN:** No.

**TED:** God, did you not see it? I thought it smiled at me. Did you see it, Dougal?

**DOUGAL:** No.

**TED:** Did you not?

**DOUGAL:** Definitely, definitely not. I'm absolutely *positive*.

*Ted winks furiously at Dougal. Dougal looks terribly confused.*

**TED:** You must have seen it!

**DOUGAL:** Ahhhh . . . no. But I saw Ted winking . . .

**TED** (*quickly turns from Dougal*): God, it was extraordinary. And do you not notice the sort of holy smell in the room?

**DOUGAL:** Ted, that might just be Jack's underpants hamper. (*We see a horrible pile of*

*dirty, horrible underpants overflowing from a hamper. We hear flies buzzing around it.*) I'll put it back in his room.

*Dougal gingerly picks it up and exits with it. Ted goes over to the skirting board.*

**TED:** Look at that. God, it really is uncanny. I'm surprised you're not appearing on more things, actually, since you're such a top-of-the-range bishop.

**BRENNAN:** It's just an indistinct squiggle, Crilly.

**TED:** Actually, the image usually is at it's best around twelve. It's *very* clear then. You can even pick out the laugh lines around your mouth! And a bit of stubble! The old image mustn't be using the old Gillette G2!

**BRENNAN:** I think this really is a waste of time.

*He exits very quickly. Jessup accompanies him. Dougal and Ted follow quickly.*

SCENE 7 INT./DAY 2
SET: PAROCHIAL HOUSE
*The entourage enters the living room.*

**TED:** . . . I think you should look at it again tomorrow.

**BRENNAN:** No, Crilly. Now, where's my coat . . . ?

*Mrs Doyle comes in.*

**MRS DOYLE:** Your Grace, Father Crilly! I just heard on the News that they've taken the roads in.

**BRENNAN:** They take the roads in?

**TED:** Yes. When the rain is bad, they store the roads in a warehouse on the east of the island.

**BRENNAN:** Why do they take the roads in?

**TED:** Well . . . they get wet.

**BRENNAN:** What! I have to go to Rome tomorrow to see the Holy Father!

**DOUGAL:** Oh, they repeat those things all the time . . .

**TED:** Oh, they'll have built new roads by then. But you might have to stay the night.

**BRENNAN:** Bollocks!

**MRS DOYLE:** Will I make up the beds in the spare room?

**JESSUP:** No, we'll sleep outside in a ditch.

*He rolls his eyes. Mrs Doyle looks confused.*

**MRS DOYLE:** Eh . . . OK, so. Would you like a cup of tea, then?

**JESSUP:** No, I want to die of thirst.

**MRS DOYLE:** Really? OK, so . . .

**TED:** Mrs Doyle, I think Father Jessup was being . . . maybe a bit, ha, ha . . . sarcastic?

**MRS DOYLE:** What? Were you being sarcastic, Father Jessup?

**JESSUP:** No, I really do want to die of thirst.

**MRS DOYLE:** Ah, were you being sarcastic there?

**JESSUP** (*sarcastic*): No, I wasn't.

*Ted brings Mrs Doyle aside.*

**TED:** Mrs Doyle, I know it's confusing, but just do the opposite of what Father Jessup says.

**MRS DOYLE:** OK, so. (*To Jessup.*) So you *would* like a cup of tea.

**JESSUP** (*exasperated*): Oh, of course I want a cup of tea!

**MRS DOYLE:** Ah, go on.

**JESSUP:** Yes, I will.

**MRS DOYLE:** Ah, go on, have a cup.

**JESSUP:** Yes, I will! I want one!

**MRS DOYLE:** Are you sure? Have a little cup.

**JESSUP:** I want a cup of tea!

**MRS DOYLE:** You'll only want one later if you don't have one now.

**JESSUP:** But I want one now!

**MRS DOYLE:** One cup. Have one cup.

**JESSUP:** Oh, forget it! I don't want one now!

**MRS DOYLE:** Great!

*She starts pouring him a cup. Jack wakes up and sees Brennan.*

**BRENNAN:** Ah, the Kraken awakes. Did we disturb you, Father Hackett?

**JACK:** Arse biscuits.

**JESSUP:** What? How dare you talk to His Grace like that. Apologise immediately!

*Jack does an impression of a timid little bunny.*

**JACK** (*baby voice*): Awwwww . . . I'm so, *so* sorry.

*Ted turns to Dougal.*

**TED:** Now, *that's* sarcasm.

### END OF PART ONE

\* \* \*

### PART TWO

SCENE 8 INT./NIGHT 2
SET: TED AND DOUGAL'S BEDROOM
*Ted and Dougal are lying in bed. Ted has a newspaper.*

**TED:** Dougal, there's no way I'm going to be able to kick Bishop Brennan up the arse. He's just too scary. I'd rather take my chances in another parish. (*He turns the page in his newspaper. A headline reads, '200 priests fall to death in another parish'.*) Oh, God!

**DOUGAL:** Ted, I might have a way you can kick Bishop Brennan up the arse and get away with it.

**TED:** If you did, Dougal, that would make you the most intelligent person in the world. Do you think that's likely?

**DOUGAL:** Ha, ha, I wouldn't go that far. I'm no Jeffrey Archer, I don't care what anyone says, but . . . well . . . Why don't you just kick him up the arse, and then act like nothing happened?

**TED:** What, and just hope he doesn't notice it?

**DOUGAL:** Ah, no, Ted, he will notice it. After all, you're giving him a kick up the arse.

**TED:** That's right. I'm giving him a big kick up the arse.

**DOUGAL:** But . . . I mean . . . well . . . look at it like this. How scared are you of Bishop Brennan?

**TED:** Very scared.

**DOUGAL:** Exactly. So how likely would it be for you to kick him up the arse?

**TED** (*thinks*): Well . . . not very likely at all.

**DOUGAL:** Exactly. So when you kick him up the arse, just carry on like nothing happened. He'd *never* believe that you'd be brave enough to kick him up the arse. He'd think he just imagined it.

*Ted looks at Dougal, amazed.*

**TED:** My God. It's so stupid it just might work! (*He gets out of bed.*) Dougal, I'm going to do it! I'm ready! As God is my witness, I will kick Bishop Brennan up the arse!

*There is a banging on the wall.*

**BRENNAN:** CRILLY! WILL YOU KEEP THE NOISE DOWN IN THERE!

*Ted jumps into bed and pulls the covers up over himself. The bedclothes quiver.*

SCENE 9 INT./DAY 3
SET. SPARE BEDROOM
*Ted and Brennan enter the room. Jessup lingers at the door.*

**TED:** . . . I just think it might be worth having one more look. You never know . . .

**BRENNAN:** I think I'll have to have a word with Dick Byrne for wasting my time.

**TED:** Well, things might pick up. You never know.

**BRENNAN** (*sighs*): Right. Let's see.

SCENE 10 INT./DAY 3
SET: CORRIDOR
*Jessup sees Jack going towards his room, fag hanging from his mouth. He carries a bottle of Bailey's.*

**JESSUP:** Hey! That's not yours. That belongs to His Grace! Give that back. (*Jack regards*

*Jessup coolly.*) Don't you look at me like that! You give that back or there'll be trouble.

*Jack turns and goes into his room. Jessup follows.*

**JESSUP** (*offscreen*): Come back here! What are you . . . No! No! Stop!! Aaaaargghhh!!!

*Jack's door slams shut loudly.*

SCENE 11 INT./DAY 3
SET: SPARE ROOM
*Brennan is bending over. He hears the scream and turns.*

**BRENNAN:** What was that?

**TED:** Hmm? Oh, probably mice or something. Do you see anything?

**BRENNAN:** No . . . I . . . Wait a second. There seems to be . . . I mean, it looks like some sort of crude watercolour painting of a man in a bishop's hat.

*From Brennan's point of view, we see the drawing. It is very crude indeed.*

**TED:** Really?

*Ted kicks Brennan up the arse. Dougal pops up outside the window, takes a photograph – it flashes momentarily – and ducks down again. Brennan freezes, a look of frozen amazement on his face.*

**TED:** Let me have a look. (*Ted bends down to look. Brennan looks at him in the same, frozen way.*) Ah, you're right. (*He stands up straight.*) I tell you what must have happened. Dougal probably didn't want you to be disappointed, so he must have drawn that himself. Ah, he meant well. (*He starts leading Brennan, who is walking like a zombie, to the door.*) Anyway, I suppose you'll want to be off, catch that ferry . . . We'll order you a taxi . . .

SCENE 12 INT./DAY 3
SET: PAROCHIAL HOUSE HALLWAY
*Dougal comes through the front door, slightly out of breath, hiding his camera behind his back. He hears Brennan and Ted coming down and looks up.*

**TED:** . . .so! Off to Rome to meet the Pope then. I bet you're really looking forward to that!

*They come down the stairs. Brennan is still in shock.*

**DOUGAL:** Did you see anything?

**TED:** No, nothing there at all, sadly. You were right, it was all a wild goose chase. I don't know what that Dick Byrne's up to at all. You really ought to have a word with him. Where's Father Jessup?

**DOUGAL:** Maybe he went on ahead? . . .

**TED:** Oh. OK, so, see you soon, Your Grace. Come back as soon as you can! (*They open the door and usher him out, Brennan still walking like a zombie.*) Bye!!

**DOUGAL:** Bye!!!

*Pause. They peer through the letterbox. We hear a car starting up and moving off. Pause. Ted and Dougal look at each other.*

**TED** (*hardly believes it*): I think we've done it.

SCENE 13 INT./DAY 3
SET: TAXI
*The taxi driver looks at Brennan.*

**TAXI DRIVER:** Your Grace! Your Grace, are you all right?

*Brennan stares ahead. We see the car speeding into the distance.*

SCENE 14 INT./DAY 3
SET: PAROCHIAL HOUSE
*Ted is opening a bottle of champagne. Celebratory music blares from the hi-fi.*

**TED:** You were right, Dougal. He didn't notice a thing! Ha, ha, ha!

**DOUGAL:** You gave him a really hard kick up the arse, and he didn't realise it at all!

**TED:** Maybe . . . maybe I didn't kick him up the arse . . .

**DOUGAL:** No, Ted, I took the photograph, remember.

**TED:** You're right! I did do it! Ha, ha! And I really went for it! I got a big rush of adrenalin just at the last moment and I gave him an even bigger kick up the arse than I meant to. God, I can't believe we got away with it . . . More champagne! I need more champagne!

Ha! Ha! Ha!

SCENE 15 INT./DAY 3
SET: AIRPORT
*A woman at a check-in desk.*

**WOMAN:** Did you pack these bags yourself, Your Grace? (*Beat. Cut to Brennan, still staring into the distance, open-mouthed.*) Your Grace?

**BRENNAN:** Whu . . . ?

**WOMAN:** Did you pack these bags yourself?

*Cut back to Brennan. He is still staring into the middle distance.*

SCENE 16 INT./DAY 3
SET: PAROCHIAL HOUSE HALLWAY
*Jack leaves his room and goes down the stairs, passing by Mrs Doyle.*

**MRS DOYLE:** Father . . .

**JACK:** Arse!

*Mrs Doyle carries on, then hears something from Jack's room.*

**JESSUP** (*from Jack's room*): Help!

*Mrs Doyle frowns and opens the door.*

SCENE 17 INT./DAY 3
SET: JACK'S BEDROOM
*Mrs Doyle comes in.*

**JESSUP:** Oh, thank God! Help me!

*We see the underpants hamper, fastened up, with underpants coming out of the side and Jessup's face just visible through a slot at the front.*

**MRS DOYLE:** Father Jessup, what are you doing in there?

**JESSUP:** Hackett locked me in here! The smell! Dear God!

**MRS DOYLE:** Are you not terribly uncomfortable in there?

**JESSUP:** Of course it's uncomfortable!

**MRS DOYLE:** Oh, right, you're being sarcastic.

**JESSUP:** I want to get out!!!

**MRS DOYLE:** Fair enough!

She starts to close the door.

**JESSUP:** Where are you going?! Help me!

*The door closes.*

SCENE 18 INT./DAY 3
SET: PAROCHIAL HOUSE
*Ted is really, really, really drunk. He is standing in front of a chair. Dougal looks a little bored.*

**TED:** This iss . . . dis isss what I did, Dougal . . .

*He kicks the chair, then sticks out his tongue, makes a raspberry sound and gives the chair the V-sign with both hands. Ted stares at the photograph of him kicking Brennan.*

**TED:** First thing tomorrow, Dougal . . . get this shot blown up. Arright? Ten by six. And I want two hundred copies for all me friends . . . feckin . . .

*He makes the raspberry sound again. Jack enters the room.*

**TED:** Feck off!!!!

*Jack, terrified, backs out.*

SCENE 19 INT./DAY 3
SET: PLANE
*An air hostess approaches Brennan.*

**AIR HOSTESS:** Have you finished your meal, Your Grace? (*Brennan is sitting in his chair, knife and fork held out at odd angles,*

staring into the middle distance.) Your Grace?

**BRENNAN:** Whu—?

**AIR HOSTESS:** Have you finished your meal?

**BRENNAN:** Whu . . . nuh . . .

*The air hostess frowns and walks away. Brennan sticks his knife into some jam. He looks distracted again. We cut to see that he has smeared jam all over the palm of his hand. He looks down, takes this in vaguely, then resumes his staring position.*

SCENE 20 INT./DAY 3*
SET: PAROCHIAL HOUSE
*Ted is staring glassily at Dougal.*

**TED** (*slurring his words terribly*): Put it on . . .

**DOUGAL:** Fair enough, Ted.

*Dougal puts a little paper crown on Ted's head.*

**TED:** I'm king o' thu wurld. I'm king o' thu wurld . . .

**DOUGAL:** I think it's time for bed, Ted.

**TED** (*like a ten year old*): 'Time for bed . . .'

SCENE 21 INT./DAY 3
SET: VATICAN
*A line of bishops. Brennan is on the end, still staring into the middle distance. From behind, we*

---

*We deleted this scene from the final version.

see the Pope moving along the line, his aide introducing him to the different bishops. Finally he gets to Brennan.

**AIDE** (*Italian accent*): . . . and from Ireland, this is Bishop Len Brennan.

*The Pope holds out his ring for Brennan to kiss it. Beat. Brennan suddenly gasps.*

**BRENNAN:** He *did* kick me up the arse!!!!!!!!

*He pushes the Pope on to the ground and runs out of shot. He runs a little way, then stops and takes out a mobile phone. In the background we see people trying to help the Pope up.*

**BRENNAN:** Get me on the first plane back to Ireland! Now, Goddamit!

*He turns distractedly while waiting for the person on the other end of the line to continue talking. The other bishops are watching him in an admonishing way.*

**BRENNAN:** What are you looking at?

SCENE 22 INT./MORNING 4
SET: TED AND DOUGAL'S BEDROOM
*Ted wakes up. He looks very, very much the worse for wear. He sits up and rubs his head, stands up and walks to the window. He opens the window and takes a few deep breaths. Then his eyes widen.*

SCENE 23 EXT./MORNING 4
SET: OUTSIDE PAROCHIAL HOUSE
*From Ted's point of view, we see a car pulling up. Brennan gets out of the car and runs to the house like a bat out of hell, an unfeasibly long cloak extending behind him.*

**BRENNAN:**
CRIIILLLLLLLLLYYYYYYY!!!!!!!!!

SCENE 24 INT./MORNING 4
SET: TED'S AND DOUGAL'S BEDROOM
*Ted looks mortified.*

**TED:** Oh, no!

SCENE 25 INT./DAY 4
SET: FRONT DOOR
*In a flash, Brennan charges through the door, knocking it off its hinges.*

SCENE 26 INT./DAY 4
SET: TED AND DOUGAL'S BEDROOM
*Ted bounces up and down on the balls of his feet, looking round the room, making noises like a frightened monkey and trying to spot a hiding place. Suddenly Brennan kicks in the door. We see him hold this 'kicking position' for a moment, then he marches in. Ted is nowhere to be seen.*

**BRENNAN:** Crilly!!!!

*Brennan opens the cupboard doors. There is no one there. He looks around, then sees a pair of feet sticking out from under the bed. He smiles and walks over.*

**BRENNAN:** Crilly . . . (*No response.*) Crilly, I know you're under the bed. I can see you.

*Pause.*

**TED:** Bishop Brennan?! Hello! God almighty, what brings you back?

**BRENNAN:** Crilly, come out from there. Now.

*Pause.*

**Ted:** No.

**BRENNAN:** No? I'll give you ten seconds, Crilly.

**TED:** It's just . . . I think I see another vision of you, Bishop Brennan . . . These bits of fluff seem to be arranging themselves into a sort of 'Bishop' formation . . .

*Brennan reaches down and starts to drag Ted out from under the bed. Ted tries to hang on with his fingernails.*

**TED:** Ah! Hello! God, great to see you back. What brings you here?

**BRENNAN:** What brings me here? Well . . . the fresh air . . . the company . . . the view of the big pile of sludge from my room . . . but, number one on the list, I suppose, would be the matter of you kicking me up the arse. Yes, I think that would be the one I'd prioritise.

**TED:** Kicking . . . what? But . . . when did I kick—

**BRENNAN:** DON'T TRY MY PATIENCE, CRILLY!!!!! (*Ted cowers.*) YOU KICKED ME UP THE ARSE! TRY TO DENY IT AND I'LL HAVE YOU FED TO THE DOGS – if you have dogs.

TED: But why would I do that? You'd kill me!

BRENNAN: You're damn right I would!!!

TED: I would never, ever kick you up the arse. Sure I think you're great!

*Brennan pauses.*

BRENNAN: Well . . .

TED: Are you absolutely sure you're not making a terrible, terrible mistake? Do you think that could be possible?

BRENNAN: I don't . . . well, I admit it did seem unbelievable.

TED: It's unbelievable because it didn't actually *happen*. I swear, Bishop Brennan, on my life, on everything I hold dear, on my religion, on God and all the saints and angels in heaven . . . I did *not* kick you up the arse.

BRENNAN: Hmm . . . well . . . maybe I . . . maybe I need a holiday . . . Maybe I've been imagining things.

TED: You *have* been imagining things. Have a holiday! You *deserve* one!

BRENNAN: Shut up, Crilly.

TED: Okey dokey.

SCENE 27 INT./DAY 4
SET: PAROCHIAL HOUSE HALLWAY
*Brennan is at the front door.*

**TED:** Well, come back soon.

**BRENNAN:** No.

*Brennan leaves the house. Dougal approaches Ted from behind. He has lots of photographs.*

**DOUGAL:** Ah, Ted, I got those copies you wanted—

**TED:** Shut up, Dougal! Shut up! Bye, Bishop Brennan!

**DOUGAL:** But that one you wanted blown up, the six by ten, where do you want that?

**TED:** What do you mean, where do I want it? Bye, Bishop Brennan! We love you!

SCENE 28 INT./DAY 4
SET: PAROCHIAL HOUSE HALLWAY
*Brennan is walking away from the house. He gets to his car and opens the door, then turns casually around. His face assumes his earlier, frozen look. He drops his keys. Cut to his point of view, so that we see a massive photograph, six foot by ten foot of the exact moment when Ted kicked Brennan up the arse, propped against the wall of the house beside where Ted is standing waving. Ted notices that Brennan is looking at something. He walks out from the house a little way, then turns to look at what Brennan's looking at. He sees the photograph. He whimpers slightly.*

*Brennan recovers and starts after him. Ted begins running. Brennan is gaining on Ted.*

*Ted falls over, and starts to get up. As he does so, Brennan catches up with him and kicks him. Cut to a low-angle shot, looking up. Ted flies about forty feet into the air, arcs, and crashes to the ground.*

POST-CREDIT SEQUENCE
SCENE 29 INT./DAY 4
SET: HAMPER
*We are inside the hamper. Jessup looks uncomfortable and afraid, hugging his knees. Underpants are bunched up around him. Suddenly the underpants are brushed to one side and a priest with a scraggly bear sticks his head out.*

**JESSUP:** Aaaargh!

**SCRAGGLY PRIEST 1:** Calm yourself, my son. You need your wits about you if we're to escape.

*Another priest sticks his head out.*

**SCRAGGLY PRIEST 2:** Escape? Escape? You crazy old fool! We shall never escape from this place!

*Another priest sticks his head out.*

**SCRAGGLY PRIEST 3:** What news of the war? Is it true the Allies have taken France?

*Jessup screams.*

**THE END**

# night of the nearly dead

**GRAHAM:** This arose from our desire to come up with a character for Patrick McDonnell, a plan which backfired on us somewhat. Writing it was like giving birth to a baby who needed extensive surgery to survive: constant rewrites were needed because we were never quite sure what the episode was about. In retrospect, we were perhaps too concerned with bending and shaping the plot around Patrick's character, Eoin McLove, until there was very little shape left.

I liked the sudden revelation in the final draft that part of Eoin's problem was that he didn't have a willy. That was Patrick's idea, but we really didn't do anything with it (or indeed without it). We just gave Patrick the go-ahead to say it, more or less on a whim. I think this is a good indication of the weakness of the episode. If it had been tightly plotted, or indeed, made any sense as a story at all, we probably wouldn't have had space for the line.

**ARTHUR:** This episode *is* flawed and in hindsight it might have been better to concentrate on Dougal's relationship with Eoin. Yet that would have had its own problems, as we'd already tackled the theme of Dougal and a friend by introducing Father Damo in *Old Grey Whistle Theft*.

I enjoyed Jack's out-of-character speech about beasts in the night, but it revealed one of the problems we were beginning to have with *Ted* and the reason we planned this to be the final series. Basically, the fact that all the characters (apart from Ted) were rather extreme caricatures was beginning to make it more and more difficult to come up with new things for them to say. This might explain Jack's outburst. But you can only play the out-of-character card once per series, and the fact that we were playing it at all pointed out the problem to us.

## PART ONE

SCENE 1 INT./DAY 1
SET: PAROCHIAL HOUSE

*On the television we see an Oliver Sacks-type psychologist on his hunkers beside a patient who sits in a rocking chair. A caption comes up that reads 'Doctor Oliver Sacks'. They are both outside on a porch in a sunny Caribbean-type location. The patient looks very like Jack.*

**SACKS** (*to camera*): Strange, short emissions which the patient shouts out seemingly involuntarily . . .

**PATIENT:** FIRK!

*Jack sits bolt upright in his chair, confused.*

**PATIENT:** ARPSE!

**JACK:** ARSE!

**PATIENT:** GRALS!

**JACK:** GIRLS!

*Dougal switches channels. Jack waits for a second, cocking his head to hear more, then, when nothing else comes, immediately slumps into sleep again. Ted comes in and sits down with a book.*

**TED:** Dougal, there's nothing on. Why don't you read a book or something?

**DOUGAL:** Oh, all right.

*Ted sits reading. After a moment, we pull back to reveal Dougal sitting beside and behind Ted reading the same book. Ted notices this.*

**TED:** No . . . Dougal. Read a different book.

**DOUGAL:** Actually, Ted, it's been a few minutes. I'll see if there's anything good on now.

*He goes back to the television.*

**TED:** Honestly, Dougal, you've got to broaden your mind a little bit. Just for once you should try turning the TV off and reading a book. You're missing out on a whole world of thought and ideas and experience.

**DOUGAL:** What are you reading at the moment?

**TED:** I'm re-reading it, actually. (*He holds it up*) It's William Shatner's *Tek Wars.*

*Dougal presses another button on the remote control. We see a country singer, Eoin McLove, in full flow, finishing a song. His name appears on a glittery backdrop behind him. Eoin is a fresh-faced man with the voice of a six year old.*

**EOIN:** ' . . . My broookkken-hearted heart . . .'

**DOUGAL:** Oh, NO! This *eeeejit!*

**EOIN:** . . . 'is running around like a duck, it used to go "bibbety-bop", but now it goes "cluckety-cluck."'

*Cut to a shot of the audience, which is made up of middle-aged or elderly women. Mrs Doyle bursts from the kitchen and slides a good six feet into the room.*

**MRS DOYLE:** It's Eoin! Oh, Father, isn't he lovely!

**DOUGAL:** Tschoh! Ghod! Thscha!

*As Mrs Doyle watches Eoin, she adjusts her clothes constantly in a nervous, compulsive way. Jack sees Eoin. He looks disgusted.*

**JACK:** Uuugggghhhh!!!!

*Cut back to Eoin. During the instrumental break in the song, he passes the microphone from hand to hand.*

**MRS DOYLE:** He's a brilliant dancer as well!

*The song comes to an end and the audience cheers wildly.*

**EOIN:** Now, it's time to announce the winner of the fabulous poetry competition. You had to write a poem about me, and the prize is that I call round to the winner's house to have a lovely cup of tea.

**DOUGAL:** Ech! Ghod, can you imagine that? Oh, Ghod!

**EOIN:** So over I go to my Poetry Corner.

*He moves out of shot. He arrives back in shot in what is obviously the same bit of set, but with 'Poetry Corner' written on a banner behind him. Mrs Doyle looks very expectant.*

**EOIN:** OK, here it is. This is my favourite one. And the standard was very high indeed. This is the winner, anyway:

'Eoin Mclove is his name,
Singing songs is his game,

Some day I will say hello,
And for a cup of tea we will go."

*The audience of old women goes 'Ahhhhh' and applauds gently.*

And the winner is Mrs O'Neill from Kildare. And it says here she's a hundred and ten years old! She also asks me what my favourite things in the world are, and I'd have to say . . . jumpers . . . and cakes! Oh, no, look at this! (*He bends down out of shot and comes up with a puppy. The puppy has a little cast on its leg.*) It's a little puppy with a broken paw. I'd better go home and nurse it back to health. Goodbye, everybody!

*Applause. Mrs Doyle sighs deeply.*

**TED:** Hard luck, Mrs Doyle. Maybe next time.

**MRS DOYLE** (*to Ted*)**:** Have you heard his latest album, Father? *Wispy Afternoons*? I'm going to go into the kitchen and stick it on the cassette recorder. Oh, God, I love him so much, I can't even wait to get into the kitchen.

*She leaves the room.*

**TED:** Women!

**DOUGAL** (*jumps up*)**:** Where?!

**TED:** No, I mean (*With a chuckle and a shrug.*) 'Women!'.

**DOUGAL:** Oh, right, yeah. 'Women!'

**TED:** Tscha!

**DOUGAL:** Tscha!

**TED:** You can't live with them, and you can't live without them!

**DOUGAL:** Yeah! (*Pause.*) But there definitely aren't any women in here? . . .

**TED:** No, you're fine. You know what, I could write a poem and send it in to that show. After all, let's face it, the kind of poetry Mrs Doyle writes is bound to be *hopeless.*

**DOUGAL:** Oh, Ted! It'd be very unhip for a Parochial House if that fella came over here.*

**TED:** Dougal, it's not a priority for a priest to worry about how hip their parish is. I mean, 'The Man Himself' was probably regarded as being a bit of a square when he was alive.*

**DOUGAL:** Really, Ted?*

**TED:** Yes, Dougal. But after he was nailed to a cross, people began to think 'I see what he was on about.'*

**DOUGAL:** God almighty. Johnny Cash was nailed to a cross?*

**TED:** What? No – Jesus! The Man Himself is Jesus!*

**DOUGAL:** Oh, right . . . I was thinking of 'The Man in Black.'*

**TED** (*to himself*)**:** I think I *will* write a poem for Mrs Doyle. It'd be great to hear something I wrote read out on television. Something with a little depth, not one of those birthday-card greetings you usually get on that show.*

**DOUGAL:** What are you going to write it about?*

**TED:** Ah, Dougal . . . inspiration can come from so many places . . .*

SCENE 2 INT./DAY 1
SET: MONTAGE
*We see Ted, a pair of half-moon glasses on the end of his nose, a pen in his mouth, thinking. A thought strikes him, and he writes something down.*

*A drooping, dying flower. A petal falls off it. Ted looks at it, wipes a tear from his eye and writes*

---

*We deleted these lines from the final version.

*something down.*

*A little urchin begging for money. Ted sees him, looks sad, writes something down and then goes off without giving him any money.*

*Ted in the foreground, Mrs Doyle in the background doing something on the windowsill. She falls off and Ted laughs softly, shakes his head and writes something down.*

*A dog, crouching down to do a poo outside the Parochial House. Cut to Ted watching through the window. He writes something down.*

*Cut to a close-up of the letter. We see the words,*

*'The Eoin McLove show
RTE, Dublin.'*

SCENE 3 INT./DAY 1*
SET: OFFICE
*Start off on the same shot of envelope. Pull back to see a policeman and a woman – Patsy – looking at the letter. Posters of Eoin McLove cover the wall.*

**PATSY:** But you understand why we called . . .

**POLICEMAN:** Yes, but I really wouldn't worry. Someone this simple-minded couldn't pose any real threat.

**EOIN:** I want extra security!

**POLICEMAN:** Really, I think this is just the work of a confused child, or someone who's quite seriously retarded.

SCENE 4 INT./DAY 2
SET: PAROCHIAL HOUSE
*Ted and Dougal come into the living room in their dressing gowns, yawning.*

**MRS DOYLE:** EOINMcLOVECMNGTOCR-AGGYISLAND!H'SCMNGTOCRAGGYISLAND!

**TED:** Mrs Doyle, calm down. What was that again?

**MRS DOYLE** (*deep breath*): EoinMcLOVE'S Cemming TOCRAGGYISLANDCRAGGY ISLANDCOMING! He read out my poem!

**TED:** Your poem? Well, Mrs Doyle, I wrote it as a sort of a surprise, but it was actually

---

* We deleted this scene from the final version.

my poem . . .

**MRS DOYLE:** No, it was mine.

**TED:** I'm . . . I'm sorry, Mrs Doyle but . . . I don't think so. What was the first line?

**MRS DOYLE:** 'Eoin McLove has a happy face.'

**TED:** That's not my poem!

**MRS DOYLE:** No, it's mine!

**DOUGAL:** I'm *hugely* confused, Ted. The only thing that I can think of that must have happened is that Mrs Doyle's poem was better than yours. But that couldn't be, could it, Ted? That your poem just wasn't as good as Mrs Doyle's. That just couldn't happen, could it?

*Close-up of Ted. He looks very uncomfortable. An end-of-scene jingle sounds.*

**DOUGAL:** Could it?

**TED:** Shut up, Dougal!

SCENE 5 INT./DAY 2
SET: SHOP
*We see an absolutely huge box, about the size of a box that might contain a widescreen television, with 'Tower Teabags. The teabags shaped like a tower. Contents 40,000' written on it. It's on top of a shelf and Mrs Doyle is trying to pull it out. A little further down the aisle, we see two women gossiping and looking at Mrs Doyle. One of the women starts moving towards Mrs Doyle, sliding along as if on casters. She has her handbag held up in a prissy way and her mouth is pursed, also prissily. She silently glides up to Mrs Doyle. This is Mrs Boyle.*

**MRS BOYLE:** When's he coming?!

**MRS DOYLE** (*jumps*): Aieeee!!!!

**MRS BOYLE:** When's he coming? Tell us!

**MRS DOYLE** (*recovering*): I can't say. It's a secret.

**MRS BOYLE:** Thursday? . . . (*Mrs Doyle remains stony-faced.*) Friday? (*Mrs Doyle remains stony-faced.*) Saturday? (*Mrs Doyle remains stony-faced.*) Sunday? (*Mrs Doyle's face, despite all her efforts, goes mental.*) Aha!!!

**MRS DOYLE:** Eoin wouldn't like anybody

to know. You won't tell anybody, will you?

**MRS BOYLE:** I swear I won't tell anyone. May I be struck down with every disease that it is possible for a middle-aged woman to suffer from. And you and I know, Mrs Doyle, that's a hell of a lot of diseases.

*During this speech, she glides backwards.*

SCENE 6 EXT./DAY 2
SET: ROAD
*Mrs Boyle bursts out of the shop and walks along the road excitedly. She approaches a woman, Mrs Kierans, who is dressed like herself (scarf, coat, carrying a shopping bag) but is kicking a football up against a wall.*

*Cut to a long shot of the scene. We don't hear their conversation. Mrs Kierans listens to Mrs Boyle for a moment and then looks very interested. Mrs Boyle starts walking off again.*

*Cut to a red line on a map. As the red line travels all over the island, we see superimposed shots of Mrs Boyle's feet walking along at an amazingly fast rate. Also we see . . .*

*Mrs Boyle on the telephone, then another woman on the telephone, hearing the news she is relaying.*

*The red line travels to a location on the map. With 'Telegraph Office' superimposed, we see Mrs Boyle at one of those Morse-Code type things; she taps away, the same expression on her face. The red line travels to another location with 'Pigeon Sanctuary' superimposed; we see Mrs Boyle rolling*

*up a little note and putting it in to a tube on a pigeon's leg. We see loads of pigeons taking off.*

*The red line travels to a location with 'Internet Café' superimposed. Mrs Boyle is tapping away at a computer, the same demented expression on her face. (She doesn't look at the screen, or the keyboard – just types and maintains her expression.)*

*We see the words 'You have new E-Mail. Access?' coming up on a screen and flashing, an 'OK' information box is selected and the words 'Eoin McLove' travel across the screen, ending the montage.*

SCENE 7 INT./DAY 3
SET: MIRROR
*A mirror somewhere in the Parochial House. Mrs Doyle is putting on lipstick. She purses her lips in front of the mirror, seems satisfied and smiles. When she smiles, we see lipstick all over her teeth.*

**MRS DOYLE:** Eeeek!

SCENE 8 INT./DAY 3
SET: PAROCHIAL HOUSE
*Ted is sitting in a chair, looking grumpy. He and Dougal hear Mrs Doyle's 'Eek'. Ted looks up to where he imagines her to be.*

**DOUGAL** (*goes to the window*): I think he's just pulled up, Ted. God – the good news is that he's only able to afford a crappy blue Ford Fiesta. Imagine going round in that thing.

**TED:** That's my car, Dougal.

**DOUGAL:** Oh, right. Still, you know what I mean.

SCENE 9 INT./DAY 3
SET: MIRROR
*Mrs Doyle is still at the mirror.*

**TED:** MRS DOYLE! HE'S HERE!

*Mrs Doyle hears Ted and runs her lipstick halfway up her face.*

SCENE 10 INT./DAY 3
SET: LIMOUSINE
*Eoin and Patsy, his manager, are in the limo, which has stopped outside the Parochial House.*

*Patsy is in the driver's seat.*

**EOIN:** Is this the place? What is it? A kind of a mental hospital?

**PATSY:** No, it's a Parochial House. This week's winner is the priests' housekeeper. Better go and prepare the ground.

*Eoin, now sucking his thumb, nods his head.*

**EOIN:** What's the story, then? Do I have to walk to the door?

**PATSY:** Yes.

**EOIN:** I have to walk to the door meself?

**PATSY:** Yes, Eoin, you have to walk to the door yourself.

*Eoin looks very unhappy. He looks around for a moment, then, with quite a lot of effort, breaks off the headrest from the seat in front of him. Pause.*

**PATSY** (*to herself*): Sheesus . . .

SCENE 11 INT./DAY 3
SET: PAROCHIAL HOUSE
*Patsy is talking to Ted and Dougal. Jack is sitting in his chair in the background.*

**PATSY:** Mr McLove will not allow any photographic record of the event, except one official picture for advertising purposes. Mr McLove will not sign autographs in ink. Mr McLove is not an equal-opportunities employer.

*Patsy's mobile phone rings.*

**PATSY:** Hello.

*We hear Eoin's voice on the end.*

**EOINE:** Hello. Is Patsy there?

**PATSY:** Yes, Eoin. This is Patsy.

*Cut to Eoin outside the living-room door, standing in the hallway.*

**EOIN:** This is Eoin here. I'm in the hall now. Is someone going to let me in or will I knock on the door, or what?

**TED:** Now, Dougal, he's our guest. Let's do this for Mrs Doyle . . .

**DOUGAL:** Yeah, I know, I know . . .

*Patsy opens the door. Eoin steps in. Jack sees Eoin.*

**JACK:** Feck!

**EOIN:** Hello. I'm Eoin McLove.

**TED:** Hello, Eoin. You're very welcome. (*Indicates Dougal.*) Father Dougal McGuire.

**EOIN** (*to Ted*): You're Father McGuire?

**TED:** No, I'm Father Ted Crilly.

**DOUGAL:** I'm Father Dougal McGuire.

**EOIN:** Hello. I'm Eoin McLove.

**TED:** That's Father Hackett.

**EOIN** (*to Dougal*): Father Hackett . . .

**TED:** No, Father McGuire.

**EOIN:** You're Father McGuire?

**TED:** No, I'm Father Crilly.

**EOIN** (*shakes hands with Ted*): Eoin McLove, hello.

**TED:** This is Father McGuire, here.

**EOIN:** I'm Eoin McLove. That's who I am, anyway.

*Jack glares at Eoin.*

**EOIN** (*to Jack*): Hello, I'm Eoin McLove.

*He steps closer to Jack. We hear what is clearly the sound of a dog growling in a threatening way, coming from Jack. (Note: At various points in the show Eoin should pass near Jack, and we hear this growl building and subsiding.)*

**TED:** Best, eh, step away there.

*Pause.*

**EOIN:** You're all priests, I see. Well done.

**TED:** Yes.

*No attempt is made by Eoin to make the following conversation private in any way.*

**PATSY:** I'll leave you alone, then . . .

**EOIN:** I'll talk to these two.

**PATSY:** Yes, Eoin.

**EOIN** (*indicating Ted*): What'll I do if the old one says something and I don't know what to say back to him?

**PATSY:** Just . . . I don't know . . .

**EOIN:** What about the thick-looking one.

He's looking at me weird.

**PATSY:** Eoin . . .

**EOIN** (*sniffs*): I smell wee. Where's that from? (*He's now beside Jack.*) It's this one. This one smells of wee.

*Patsy gives Ted and Dougal an apologetic look and leaves.*

**EOIN:** So where's the winner so I can go home and have me tea?

**TED:** Well, actually, you can have your tea here. Mrs Doyle!

*The kitchen door opens and a terrified, heavily made-up Mrs Doyle enters slowly through it. She has a tray with loads of cups and a teapot on it. It vibrates slightly. She walks slowly towards Eoin and the tray vibrates even more. She tries to say something but can't seem to get the words out.*

**MRS DOYLE:** Eghhh . . . eggghhh . . .

*The tea things are rattling very noisily now as Mrs Doyle shakes violently. With each step nearer to Eoin, it gets worse.*

**EOIN:** Hello.(*Mrs Doyle shakes all the tea things off the tray, wobbles around for a while and then collapses out of shot.*) I don't want tea off the carpet. I want proper tea. Where's my tea?

SCENE 12 EXT./DAY 3
SET: GATE OF PAROCHIAL HOUSE
*The camera angle is very low. We see the house through the gate. Two middle-aged female legs move into shot. Then another pair. Dramatic music accompanies this.*

**END OF PART ONE**

* * *

**PART TWO**

SCENE 13 INT./EVENING 3
SET: PAROCHIAL HOUSE
*Mrs Doyle is sitting down in Ted's chair, still looking terrified. Eoin sits across from her on the sofa. Ted and Dougal are also present. Eoin is looking carefully at his watch, mouthing something to himself. Stay on this for a while.*

**EOIN:** . . . Fifty-eight . . . fifty-nine . . . sixty! (*Stands up.*) Right, that's our twenty minutes up. I'm off. Don't try to stop me.

*Ted starts making 'hint-hint' motions towards Mrs Doyle with his head.*

**TED:** Eh . . . did you like your tea, Eoin?

**EOIN:** What? Yeah, I don't know, whatever. I want to go home now. It's getting dark outside.

**DOUGAL:** You're not afraid of the dark, are you? It's only because the sun goes . . . Eh, it . . . there's this . . . eh . . . it . . . something to do with clouds?

**TED:** Our part of the earth is turned away from the sun.

**DOUGAL:** That's it, yeah. And, what was it? The clouds can't get through? . . .

*Eoin gets up to leave.*

**EOIN** (*struggling with the door*): How do you work this door handle? Is this a new kind of door handle? I'm used to the ones that go round.

*Ted takes him gently aside.*

**TED:** Before you go, Eoin . . . was there another poem that was very good this week?

**EOIN:** What? No.

**TED:** You sure?

**EOIN:** The only other letter I can remember was from this lunatic. We had to call the police because it was so demented. Anyway, I'm going to stop talking to you now, because I don't know what else to say to you.

*Eoin opens up his mobile phone and dials.*

**EOIN:** Hello, is Patsy there?

SCENE 14 INT./NIGHT 3
SET: PAROCHIAL HOUSE
*Cut to Patsy waiting in the hallway. She answers her mobile phone.*

**PATSY:** Yes, Eoin. This is Patsy.

**EOIN** (*as he comes into the hallway*): It's Eoin McLove here. Get the car and pull up right outside the door, so I don't have to walk far. (*Patsy starts going towards the door, followed by Eoin. Both are still on their mobiles. Ted follows* *behind.)* I want to be able to walk right into the car without touching the ground.

**PATSY:** Eh . . . I don't think that's going to be possible, Eoin.

**EOIN:** What? You're breaking up there. Why is not going to b— (*They are now standing next to each other talking on their mobile phones, both looking out of the window. Ted arrives on the scene.*) What? Why not? Oh, God.

SCENE 15 INT./NIGHT 3
SET: PAROCHIAL HOUSE
*We see that there are fifty little old ladies outside the house. One, with big bottle-thick glasses, snaps her head up when she hears the door opening.*

**WOMEN:** Hello, Eoin! Hello there, Eoin, etc.

*Ted walks to one side of Eoin.*

**TED:** Eh, hello, ladies . . . we'll be away now . . . Dougal, get around that side of Eoin.

*They start walking slowly towards the car. The women start following at a distance. The men see the limo waiting ahead. Ted and Dougal stand on either side of Eoin and start walking quickly towards it. The women advance towards them.*

**TED:** Better pick up the old pace a bit . . .

**EOIN:** Oh, God, here they come. What's on their mind at all?

*They are easily able to outrun the women. They approach the limo. The door of the limo opens.*

**TED:** Here we go . . .

*Eoin gets in. We suddenly see that there are about seven old women in the car. The woman in the driver's seat turns around.*

**OLD WOMAN** (*sinister*): Hello, Eoin.

**EOIN:** Aarrgh!

*Eoin jumps out of the car.*

**TED:** OK, OK. We'd better get back inside.

*The women in the car turn the headlights on. From above, we see the old women slowly approaching Ted, Dougal, Eoin and Patsy in a big, slow, horrible movement.*

**EOIN:** I'm scared. It's like a big tide of jam

coming towards us. But jam made out of old women.

**TED:** There's a lot of them, but they're slow. Dodge between them!

*Ted, Dougal and Eoin run towards the old women and then thread through them. The old women grab at Eoin but miss him. Ted reaches the door first.*

**TED:** Come on!

*Eoin falls over. The women start to advance towards him.*

**EOIN:** Oh, God!

*Ted runs back and grabs him. They run towards the door. The women start to advance towards them. They run through the door just before the women can catch up, and they slam it shut.*

SCENE 16 INT./NIGHT 3
SET: PAROCHIAL HOUSE HALLWAY
*Eoin relaxes against the door.*

**EOIN:** Oh, thank God.

*Suddenly a hand smashes through the window in the door and grabs Eoin around the neck. More hands follow and start grabbing madly in the air, some of them grabbing hold of Eoin.*

**EOIN:** Help!

*Ted grabs Eoin and tries to wrestle him away from the hands.*

**TED:** Dougal!

*Ted stretches his hand out to Dougal. Dougal smiles and waves at Ted.*

**DOUGAL** (*cheerily*): Hello!

**TED:** No, Dougal, I mean 'help', not 'hello'.

**DOUGAL:** Oh, right.

*Dougal goes over and whacks some of the hands. Jack comes out and sees this. He goes back into the living room.*

**TED:** Ow! That's actually *my* hand, Dougal. Try hitting some of the women's hands.

**DOUGAL:** OK, yes. Sorry, Ted.

*Jack comes out of the living room with a chair and glass of whiskey. He sits on the chair and sips his whiskey, enjoying the scene.*

SCENE 17 INT./NIGHT 3
SET: PAROCHIAL HOUSE
*It is later on. The living room is gloomy. Ted sits by the window and lifts the curtain occasionally to look out. Patsy is talking on her mobile phone. A grandfather-clocky-type ticking noise is in the background.*

**PATSY:** Battery's dead. Oh, God! What about your phone?

**TED** (*shakes his head*): I think they've cut the lines.

*Pause.*

**JACK:** 'They lie in wait, like wolves. the smell of blood in their nostrils, waiting, interminably waiting . . . and then . . .'

*Ted looks at Jack, dumbfounded at this eloquence. Jack slumps back to sleep.*

**DOUGAL:** He's right, Ted.

**TED:** Miss Bartley, we've got a problem. And you know what my motto is when I've got a problem? I'm going to solve that problem. (*Pause.*) Well, it's not really a motto, it's more a sentence. But anyway . . . here's the problem. We're surrounded by a bunch of thirty elderly women. (*Pause.*) Actually, when you put it that way, it doesn't sound so bad. Maybe we should just walk out.

**PATSY:** No, I don't think so. I've never seen someone mothered to death before, and it's not going to happen now, not on my watch.

**TED:** To be honest, he's got no one to blame but himself. When you've got album covers like this, you're just asking for trouble.

*Ted holds an album cover up. It's called 'Eoin McLovenotes' and features Eoin dressed as a baby*

with his arms outstretched.

SCENE 18 INT./NIGHT 3
SET: PAROCHIAL HOUSE
*Meanwhile, Dougal and Eoin are in the kitchen.*

**EOIN:** I'm hungry. Where's the jam?

**DOUGAL** (*gasps*): You're not supposed to eat before dinner.

**EOIN:** You shut up. I'm Eoin McLove. I can do what I like.

*Eoin finds a pot of jam and gets a small spoon. Then he gets a bigger spoon and starts digging out spoonfuls and eating it. Dougal stares at him. Eoin stares back, eating the jam.*

SCENE 19 INT./NIGHT 3*
SET: PAROCHIAL HOUSE
*Ted is examining a pipe. The mood is calmer now. Patsy looks at him.*

**PATSY:** You're a pipe man, Father.

**TED:** Ah, well . . . I thought I'd try it out. To be honest, I'm a bit disappointed by the amount of spit involved. You see, there's a build-up . . . sorry, that's disgusting. I don't know how you put up with your man. He'd drive me mad.

**PATSY:** Oh, he's all right. He's just so used to being taken care of he's going through some sort of second childhood.

SCENE 20 INT./NIGHT 3
SET: PAROCHIAL HOUSE KITCHEN
*Eoin's face is now covered in jam. Dougal is still staring at him. Ted comes in. Dougal points at Eoin.*

**TED:** Eoin!

**EOIN:** Wha'?

**TED:** Don't eat the jam from the jar. Get inside the other room there.

**EOIN:** You leave me alone. I can have you killed.

*Ted pushes Eoin out. Dougal waits a moment, then goes over to the jam. He picks up a spoon and*

---

*We deleted this scene from the final version.

*starts licking it. Ted comes in and gives him a look. Dougal notices him and jumps with the fright.*

**DOUGAL:** Just, eh . . . cleaning the spoon.

*He licks it again and holds it up to the light.*

SCENE 21 INT./NIGHT 3*
SET: PAROCHIAL HOUSE
*Close-up of Ted smoking his pipe and reading a newspaper. We pull back to reveal Patsy on the sofa doing some knitting. Dougal and Eoin are also revealed, on the floor playing a game of draughts.*

**EOIN:** I'm bored. Can I go home?

**PATSY:** We can't go anywhere, Eoin. Those women are still outside.

*Dougal goes to the window and looks outside.*

**DOUGAL:** Tsk . . . I'm no good at judging the size of crowds, but I'd say there's about a million of them out there.

**TED:** Well . . . more like forty, Dougal . . .

*Eoin walks to the window and looks out.*

**EOIN:** Still there. Why don't they leave me alone? Do you know what they send me as well? Big bras. Sure I have no need for them. I'd have to be very hard up for clothes to wear big bras. God almighty . . . This came in the post this morning. Look at the size of it. (*He reaches into his travel bag and pulls out a bra about the size of a widescreen-television screen.*) That'd fit two women.

*Mrs Doyle walks in. Eoin jumps with the fright.*

**EOIN:** Aaaah! Don't do that again! What's she doing in here, anyway? She should be out there with the rest of those eejits.

**TED:** Eoin! Don't be mean to Mrs Doyle! She's one of us!

**EOIN:** She's making me nervous. Tell her to get out.

**TED:** Mrs Doyle, maybe you should go and make some tea.

*Mrs Doyle leaves, looking utterly crestfallen. Eoin goes over and prods Jack.*

**EOIN:** Hey, wake up. (*He starts poking Jack.*) Wake up. Why are you asleep? Wake up and do something interesting.

**PATSY:** For God's sake, Eoin. Give it a rest.

**TED:** I really wouldn't do that, Eoin.

*Eoin continues to push and poke Jack.*

**EOIN:** Why not? I can do what I like. You're not the boss of me. (*He pokes Jack again a few times. Jack wakes up and stares at Eoin balefully.*) Hey, you, wake up. Do something interesting.

*Cut to Ted as we hear the sound of a wild animal on the attack, mingled with Eoin's screams. Ted can't look, and he slowly turns and walks to the window. He looks out of the window for a moment or two, then turns around as the sounds subside.*

*Jack is asleep again. On the ground beside him is Eoin, tied up in his own jumper like a particularly gaudy Easter egg. All the jumper's 'orifices' have been tied together, so nothing can be seen of Eoin.*

**EOIN** (*muffled*): What's going on? I'm bored again. Let me out.

**DOUGAL:** Ha, ha! He looks like a big Easter egg!

*Ted, Dougal and Patsy laugh in an American film-type way. Ted puts his pipe in his mouth to complete the picture.*

*We deleted this scene from the final version.

SCENE 22 INT./NIGHT 3
SET: PAROCHIAL HOUSE
*Patsy is at the window. She starts shaking.*

**PATSY:** I CAN'T STAND IT! THEY'RE SO QUIET. WHY ARE THEY SO QUIET?!

**TED:** Patsy, snap out of it!

*A brick comes through the window. Everyone dives. Patsy screams. Ted recovers and picks up the brick. There is paper wrapped around it. He unfolds it and we see that it has 'Tell Eoin we think he's lovely' written on it. Mrs Doyle enters. She has a cake tin in her hand. She goes over to Ted, right up to his ear and whispers in it. We hear a very low murmur coming from her lips.*

**TED:** What is it, Mrs Doyle?

*Mrs Doyle whispers again. Ted gets up. She still whispers in his ear at an annoyingly close distance, as if she's glued to his ear. Ted frees Eoin from his jumper with difficulty.*

**TED:** What? What? Yes . . . yes. Eoin, Mrs Doyle wants to know if you'd like a cake.

**EOIN:** Who?

**TED:** Mrs Doyle. This woman here.

**EOIN:** Oh, right.

*Ted is now walking around, bent over, as Mrs Doyle continues to whisper in his ear.*

**TED:** Eh, it's banana. She says she knows that's your favourite.

**EOIN:** Oh, God, yeah, I love that. I'll eat that. No one else is getting any. This is all for me. (*He digs into it with a knife. He pulls away a slice, but there is some resistance. There seems to be something baked in the middle of the cake.*) What's goin' on?

*Mrs Doyle, with a pleased, excited yelp, whispers in Ted's ear.*

**TED:** Oh, my God.

**EOIN:** What's happening? I'm scared.

**TED:** I'm not sure how to tell you this . . . (*Eoin is pulling something out of the cake with a horrified expression.*) Mrs Doyle has, in an unusual move . . . baked a jumper in the cake.

*Eoin pulls it out with difficulty. It is indeed a jumper, with loads of cake bits sticking to it.*

**EOIN:** I'm going to get sick. This is horrible. This is the worst thing that's ever happened to me. I'm not wearing a cake jumper. And I'm not eating a jumper cake. This is terrible. Oh, my God.

*Mrs Doyle looks crestfallen.*

**TED:** Right! I've had enough of this. You don't have to eat the cake, or wear the jumper, but you will stop acting like a baby right now and thank Mrs Doyle or I will personally throw you outside and let those women deal with you how they will. And believe me, if that happens, a jumper cake is the least of your problems. *Got it?!*

*Eoin is shocked by this. He sees Ted is serious. He turns and sees that Mrs Doyle is leaving the room sadly.*

**EOIN:** Eh . . . you . . . (*Mrs Doyle stops.*) . . . Thanks for the . . . eh . . . cake-jumper thing.*

*Mrs Doyle beams.*

**MRS DOYLE:** Are you going to try it on?*

*Eoin pauses, looks at Ted, then sighs and puts it on. He smiles.*

**EOIN:** God, it's brilliant.*

*He gives Mrs Doyle a kiss on the cheek. Mrs Doyle passes out. Eoin immediately starts scratching himself.*

**EOIN:** There's bloody cake bits all over the place!*

---

* We deleted these lines from the final version.

SCENE 23 INT./NIGHT 3
SET: PAROCHIAL HOUSE

*Ted is still thinking hard. We see Eoin in the corner of the room, asleep, sucking his thumb. Patsy is asleep, too. Ted and Dougal are conspiring together in another part of the room.*

**TED:** We have to get him out of here. You know what we need? Some kind of distraction. Something to lead them away from him, and then he could escape. Some kind of misleading event. What could it be?

*Pause.*

**DOUGAL:** I know!

**TED:** What?

**DOUGAL:** A 'diversion'. That's what it's called. A 'diversion'.

*Pause.*

**TED:** I know it's called a diversion! I'm not asking you what it's called! I'm asking what the diversion should *be*! God almighty! Right, come on. Ideas, ideas.

*Pause. Jack looks as if he's about to say something, then changes his mind, then leans forward, then changes his mind. Ted notices this movement, as does Dougal. They look at him and silently wait for him to speak. Finally, he leans forward and puts one finger in the air in a 'how about this?' type gesture.*

**JACK:** Arse! Feck! Drink! Girls!

**TED:** Yes . . . thank you, Father Jack.

**TED:** We need more concrete ideas than that. What do older women like?

**JACK:** My cock in a burger bun.

*Pause as they take this in.*

**DOUGAL:** Do you know what they really, really love, Ted?

**JACK:** My cock in a burger bun!

**DOUGAL:** A great game of bingo. What about luring them into some kind of giant game of bingo?

**TED:** Right. How would we do that?

**DOUGAL:** Well. We could make up some bingo cards on our printing press, and then . . . Oh.

**TED:** Yes. It's the lack of a printing press that stops us there, Dougal. Plus we have no bingo balls. Or a big, glass, bingo-ball-dispenser thing that blows out the bingo balls. Or a microphone. Or, in fact, any bingo paraphernalia at all.

**DOUGAL:** Damn! So near and yet so far!

*There is a noise from the window. Ted goes to it and lifts the curtain. About four old women are grouped together, looking in. They motion in a friendly way for Ted to open the window.*

**TED:** No way. You just go home! Go on! Shoo!

**WOMAN 1:** Oh, Father, we just wanted to tell you what a brilliant Mass you did last week.

**TED:** Oh . . . oh, well, thanks very much. I was very happy with the sermon actually . . .

**WOMAN 2:** Oh, yes, how did it start again?

**TED:** Oh, what was it . . . 'I believe it was the actor Nick Berry who said . . .'

**WOMAN 1:** Sorry, Father? It's very hard to hear you through this window . . .

**TED:** Oh, right . . . (*He opens the window. They lean in.*) 'I believe it was the actor Nick Berry who said . . .' (*More women start filling the window.*) Actually . . . could you move back from the window there . . .

**WOMAN 1:** Where's Eoin?!

**TED** (*gasps*): You're not interested in my sermon at all!

**WOMAN 2:** We don't want any trouble, Father. Just send out the boy.

**TED:** I'm not sending out anyone. You lot should be ashamed of yourselves.

**WOMAN 1:** Ahh, look, there he is asleep.

**WOMAN 2:** Ahhhhh! He's lovely!

**WOMAN 3:** Aaaaahhhh!!!

**WOMAN 4:** Aaaaaahhhhhh!!!!

*They start pushing their way through the window. Patsy wakes up.*

**PATSY:** What are you doing? Why is the window open?!

*The women are struggling through.*

**TED:** I can't hold them back! Upstairs! Get upstairs!

*They all run to the living-room door, except Jack, who is asleep. Cut to a map of the house, like a blueprint. We see a red line travelling through the hallway, then up the stairs, then into Ted and Dougal's bedroom.*

SCENE 24 INT./NIGHT 3
SET: TED AND DOUGAL'S BEDROOM
*Ted and Dougal come into the room. There are more women coming through the upstairs window.*

**TED:** Back! Back!

*The red line goes into a room labelled 'Bathroom'.*

SCENE 25 INT./NIGHT 3
SET: PAROCHIAL HOUSE BATHROOM
*Ted, Dougal, Patsy and Eoin come into the room. They lock the door.*

**TED:** Oh, God, what do we do now?

SCENE 26 INT./NIGHT 3
SET: PAROCHIAL HOUSE
*The living room is now full of middle-aged women, walking around like zombies, bumping into walls and furniture, and chanting 'Eoin, Eoin'. Jack wakes up and looks around, confused.*

SCENE 27 INT./DAY 4
SET: PAROCHIAL HOUSE BATHROOM
*The four are sitting around, looking anxious.*

**PATSY:** Oh, God, what are we going to do? I'm not so worried for ourselves, Father. But the little ones. They have their whole lives ahead of them.

*Dougal and Eoin sit on the side of the bath, looking sheepish. The door starts thudding, straining against the lock with each blow. Finally it bursts open. The women are revealed. Some of them move in. From somewhere outside, we hear a cock crow. Ted looks outside, through the window.*

*We see that it is dawn, and the light is getting brighter.*

**TED:** Ladies, it's after seven. I think your husbands might be wondering where their breakfasts are? After all, I don't think you can expect a man to cook a few sausages and rashers for himself. (*The old ladies pause.*) Remember last year, Mrs Dunne? Your husband tried to make some toast and he burnt the house down. And Mrs Collins, when Mr Collins tried to make the bed on his own, didn't he lose a leg?

*The old ladies very slowly reverse out through the doorway. Ted, Dougal, Eoin and Patsy breathe a huge sigh of relief.*

SCENE 28 INT./DAY 4
SET: PAROCHIAL HOUSE
*Eoin and Patsy are ready to leave. Eoin has a suitcase with him.*

**EOIN:** Right, we're off.

**TED:** Eoin, did you have those suitcases with you when you came?

**EOIN:** No, they're yours. I just liked a lot of stuff here and I thought I'd pack it up and take it off with me.

**DOUGAL:** Oh, that's very cheeky.

**EOIN:** Patsy will pay for it. I'm just taking everything, and that's it. Come on, Patsy.

*He goes out through the door with the cases.*

**PATSY:** I'm sorry he was so much trouble, Father.*

**TED:** Oh, no . . . (*He looks at Dougal.*) I'm used to it . . .

**PATSY:** Bye, Father . . . (*She goes to leave. As she approaches the door, she turns.*) Father . . . you've been very kind to us. I wonder if you'd like to come to the show next week? Father McGuire tells me you're always trying to get on television.

**TED** (*coy*): Oh, no . . . that's not true.

**DOUGAL:** It is true, Ted. You're *always* trying to get on television. You told me that

---

*Eoin's line 'I have no willy.' was inserted here in the final version.

it was your number-one ambition in the world.

**TED:** Did I? Oh, yes, I might have said that . . . jokingly, probably. I'm not really that bothered . . .

**PATSY:** There's a new part of the show where we get an audience member up on stage to take part in a quiz. There's a cash prize . . .

**TED:** I'll do it! Even though I'm not that interested. (*Pause.*) Do you know what the viewing figures are exactly?

**PATSY:** About two million.

**DOUGAL:** Not bad, Ted. When you were on that religious show there were only about thirty watching.

**TED:** Well, no one watches religious programmes. They're so dull. And it was up against the O.J. Simpson verdict. Can you imagine what those thirty people were like?

**PATSY:** If you do well, you could win five hundred pounds.

*She leaves. Ted looks delighted with himself.*

**TED:** Five hundred pounds . . . five hundred pounds.

SCENE 29 INT./DAY 5
SET: TELEVISION STUDIO
*Ted is sitting in a chair, wearing a T-shirt. Eoin stands beside him with a question card in his hand.*

**EOIN:** Well, Father, you've got four out of five right on your specialist subject, William Shatner's *Tek Wars*, so if you get the general-knowledge question, the five hundred pounds will be yours. All right . . . (*He reads the card.*) Oh! People will think this is rigged. What was the present Pope's original name before he took the name John Paul?

*Ted freezes. Under his breath he mutters something like 'For fuck's sake'. We stay on Ted's tortured face. The end credits roll over this. Finally . . .*

**TED:** Jim?

**THE END**

# GOING TO AMERICA

**GRAHAM:** I found out that Dermot had died the day after we filmed this, a show we had already decided would be the last *Father Ted*. The shock was indescribable. I had to call Arthur and tell him, and a few days later we had to go in and edit this episode, still reeling. Dermot was great in this episode, probably the best I've ever seen him, and I think on some unconscious level he was keeping himself going until the end of the series (in the same way that people often get sick at the end of a long location shoot). It's still unbelievable to Arthur and me that he's not here anymore.

Our original idea for the ending (published in this script) was to have Ted joining the suicidal priest on the window-ledge. Dermot's death wasn't the whole reason we decided not to use the scene. It just didn't work, and it would have been terrible to end the series on a joke that didn't work. Our alternative, to show a clip from every episode in reverse chronological order, seemed far more apposite. Even though Ted is stuck on Craggy Island forever, and he'll never have any of his wishes come true, there's something familiar and reassuring about a place that never changes.

**ARTHUR:** The idea of having a brash priest at the centre of an episode had been with us almost from the beginning. It ties in with a theme we liked, that of religion as a commercial activity, which brings us to Buzz Cagney. Buzz was based on someone I'd met a wedding; a desperately arrogant man who went to America and bought heavily into the 'work hard, play hard and reap rewards'ethic. We were originally going to take that idea even further and make a promotional video for Buzz's parish which featured American priests playing computer games and working out in a gym. Ted wouldn't have been able to resist the luxury of that.

## PART ONE

SCENE 1 INT./DAY 1
SET: CONFERENCE ROOM

*We see a banner that reads 'It's great being a priest!*
*'98'. Below it, a group of priests are standing,*
*facing a window. There is much worry and concern*
*on their faces. Cut to outside, where we see a priest*
*standing on a ledge, occasionally glancing down.*
*From his point of view, we see cars far down below.*
*A priest, Father Alan, steps forward.*

**ALAN:** Father! Father, please come in!

**KEVIN:** Don't come near me! I'll jump!

**TED:** Let me through! (*The crowd parts and*
*reveals Ted. He walks over to Alan.*) I'll take care
of this, Alan. (*Alan moves back.*) Kevin? Kevin,
what's going on for goodness' sake?

**KEVIN:** I can't go on!

**TED:** Don't be silly now, Kevin!

**KEVIN:** What's the point of living? We're all
going to die anyway!

**TED:** Nonsense! We're not going to die!

**ALAN:** Yes, we are, Ted.

**TED:** Well, yes, but not for years.

**KEVIN:** It's pointless! What am I a priest for?
What an utterly useless waste of time. I'd be
more use sweeping up roads.

**TED:** Well, would you listen to him?!! It's
fabulous being a priest! Think of all the
comfort you bring to the sick and the dying,
for instance! They love it! They can't get
enough of it!

**KEVIN:** I've never heard one word of thanks
from the sick or the dying. They're an
ungrateful shower of bastards. I haven't got
one friend in the world and I'd be better off
dead.

**TED:** You have a room full of friends in here,
Kevin! Father Alan here, for instance!

**ALAN:** I've never met him before.

**TED:** Well . . . (*He speaks to the priests.*) Who
knows him? Anyone? No? All right. I'm your
friend, Kevin!

**KEVIN:** Really?

**TED:** You better believe it! Now, come on,

stop this nonsense!

**KEVIN:** I suppose . . . yes . . . I'm coming
in . . .

**PRIESTS:** HURRAY!

*Kevin gets a shock and starts to fall off the ledge.*
*Ted jumps forward and catches him. He starts to*
*drag him up on to the ledge. Meanwhile, Alan is*
*approached by a tanned, good-looking, well-to-do*
*priest with an American accent. His name is Buzz*
*Cagney.*

**BUZZ:** That priest . . . what's his name?

**ALAN:** Why, that's Father Ted Crilly.

**BUZZ:** Crilly, eh? Thank you . . .

**ALAN:** And who are you? (*Alan turns around,*
*but the priest has gone.*) What the . . .?

*The priest suddenly appears again.*

**BUZZ:** Sorry, I went over there. What did
you say?

**ALAN:** I said, who are you?

**BUZZ:** My name's Cagney. Buzz Cagney. And
I think I might have a proposition for this
'Father Ted Crilly'.

*Ted has finally managed to pull Kevin up into the*
*room.*

**TED:** There you go.

**ALAN:** Is he all right?

**TED:** He's fine.

**ALAN:** Good.

*All the priests immediately go back to talking, as if nothing had happened.*

**KEVIN:** Thank you, Father. I . . . I don't know what came over me. I get a bit depressed.

**TED:** Oh, don't mention it. Eh . . . I hate to bring this up now, but that twenty quid you owe me . . . do you remember? . . . if you have it . . .

**KEVIN** (*reaching into his pocket*): Oh, of course!

**TED:** Sorry!

**KEVIN:** No problem. It . . . oh, wait, I might not have it on me. Could you wait until tomorrow?

**TED:** Yes, yes . . . as long as, eh . . . ha, ha . . . as long as you'll still be around!

**KEVIN:** Ha, ha!

*Ted doesn't join in with Kevin's laughter. He was being serious.*


SCENE 2 EXT./DAY 2
SET: CHURCH
*Ted is talking to Dougal as the parishioners file past them out of church. He shakes hands with passing parishioners as he talks.*

**TED:** . . . And then Harrison Ford jumps off the plane, and fires back up at the plane as he's falling!\*

**DOUGAL:** Wow! It sounds great!

**TED:** I'd go again if you want to see it this weekend.

**DOUGAL:** Great!

*Mrs Doyle is one of the parishioners.*

**TED:** Oh, Mrs Doyle, when you go home, Father Kevin will be there. He's staying until this depression, or whatever it is, lifts.

**MRS DOYLE:** Oh, right. So I shouldn't say anything that might depress him?

**TED:** Yes, stay away from war and death and that whole *Mirror* pension-fund area.

———————————————

\*This same imaginary film is discussed in an episode of *Seinfeld*.

**MRS DOYLE:** All right. I'll stick to things like puppies and cushions.

**TED:** Puppies and cushions. I'm in a better mood already.

*Mrs Doyle goes off. A parishioner, Eugene, stops to speak to Ted.*

**EUGENE:** Father, that sermon today, frankly it bored the arse off me.

**TED:** Well, Eugene, I'm not here to entertain you. If you want that type of thing, go to see Jean-Michel Jarre or someone.

**EUGENE:** What the hell was it about, anyway?

**TED:** It was . . . (*He can't remember.*) What was the first line again?

*Eugene, disgusted, moves off.*

**TED:** God, I don't know why I bother . . . What was my sermon about today? Do you remember?

**DOUGAL:** Sorry, Ted, I was concentrating too hard on looking holy.

**TED:** Oh, well. To be honest, I don't give a toss.

*Dougal is slightly shocked.*


SCENE 3 INT./NIGHT 2
SET: PAROCHIAL HOUSE
*Ted, Dougal and Kevin are playing Snakes and Ladders in the living room.*

**TED** (*taking his go*): Ha! Well . . . this is much more fun than killing yourself, isn't it, Kevin?

**KEVIN:** S'pose . . .

**TED:** Oh, come on, Kevin, cheer up. That's me and Dougal's job now – we're in the Smile Brigade. Not the fire brigade – the Smile Brigade! We'll keep you happy and cheery until you can go to the bank.

**KEVIN:** Go to the bank?

**TED:** Go home. I meant go home. Now, come on, Kevin, things will get better. You wait and see!

*Kevin throws a dice. He moves his counter.*

**TED:** Nice move, Kev. Actually, Kevin . . .

You landed on a snake there. You . . . have to go down . . .

*Kevin moves his counter down the snake. He starts weeping. Ted looks uncomfortable. Dougal thinks this is hilariously bizarre.*

**DOUGAL:** What's wrong with you?

**TED:** Dougal, there's nothing wrong . . . Kevin, are you all right?

**KEVIN** (*cries a little*): . . . Yes, yes . . . I'm all right . . .

*He is now weeping uncontrollably. Ted takes the dice and throws it. They continue playing, ignoring the weeping. It comes to Kevin's turn again.*

**TED:** Your go again, Kevin.

*Kevin wipes his face, blinks through the tears and throws the dice.*

**TED:** That's a five . . . Oh . . . another snake.

*Kevin moves his counter down the snake, weeping constantly throughout.*

**TED:** Dougal, your go.

*Dougal throws the dice.*

**DOUGAL:** Hurrah!!!!! Ha, ha! If he keeps landing on snakes then I'll win for sure!

*Ted glares at Dougal. Dougal moves his counter up a ladder. Play continues. It's Kevin's turn again.*

**TED:** Oh, very near another snake, Kevin! As long as you don't get a one!

*Kevin throws the dice. It rolls off the edge of the table and lands on the floor.*

**TED:** Ah, you're all right there, Kevin. It's a six.

**DOUGAL:** No, it isn't, Ted. It's a one! Definitely!

**TED** (*intently*): I don't think it is, Dougal.

**DOUGAL:** It is, Ted! Look! It's a one! He's going to snaketown! (*Dougal moves Kevin's counter to the top of the snake and all the way down to a lower line.*) Weeeeeeeeeeee!!!!!

*Kevin looks at this for a moment, then gets up from the table and runs off.*

**DOUGAL:** Bye! . . . What's wrong with him, Ted?

**TED:** He's a panic depressive.

**DOUGAL:** A panic depressive?

**TED:** Yes. It's like a manic depressive, only you panic as well as getting depressed. It's a combination of Waaaaaghh!!! and . . . (*He makes childish 'depressed' noises.*)

**DOUGAL:** I think he just knew who the better player was.

*Ted picks up an apple and leaves the room.*

SCENE 4 INT./DAY 3
SET: PAROCHIAL HOUSE HALLWAY
*Ted comes out of the room, idly eating an apple. Mrs Doyle is at the door, looking out at someone outside. She notices Ted.*

**MRS DOYLE:** Ah, Father?

**TED:** Mmmmmm?

**MRS DOYLE:** A visitor, Father.

*Mrs Doyle swings the door open slowly, revealing Buzz Cagney. He steps in and closes the door behind him.*

**BUZZ:** Father Crilly, hello.

**TED** (*still eating his apple*): Oh, hello . . .

**BUZZ:** My name is Father Buzz Cagney. I was at the conference the other day. I was wondering if we could have a chat . . . *I think you might be interested in a little proposition.*

*We stay on Buzz's mysterious expression and a mysterious-sounding sting plays. Beat.*

**TED** (*chews, swallows*): Sorry about that . . . eating an apple. Yeah, all right! Come in, come in . . .

SCENE 5 INT./DAY 3
SET: PAROCHIAL HOUSE
*Ted and Buzz are sipping sherry.*

**BUZZ:** . . . and then I was in Utah for a few years. Osmond country. Not a good Catholic market. Mormons there got that polygamy thing going . . . big crowd puller. Guy in the street says to himself . . . 'I'm looking around for a religion to suit my lifestyle. With the Mormons, I can have five, ten wives if I want. That's a *lot* of action.'

**TED** (*not really getting it*): Action, yeah . . .

**BUZZ:** Hard to compete against that. Then I was in Reno . . .

**TED:** Reno. I hear that's very like Wexford. I did a mass in Wexford once. Very rough crowd. Very restless. You *have* to do a good sermon there or they'll hop all over you. Where are you at the moment?

**BUZZ:** I'm in Beverly Hills.

*Ted's tongue literally hangs out with excitement.*

**TED:** Bruberly Huls? Wa . . . Wow! You landed on your feet there. I suppose Gregory Peck drops in for an old chat about his grandchildren's first communion, and then you head off for a dip in his pool.

**BUZZ:** I do meet quite a lot of celebrities, yes.

**TED:** Yeah? Like who?

**BUZZ:** Kevin Spacey. He's a nice guy. He—

**TED:** Don't know him. What about Val Kilmer? I hear he's a complete bastard.

**BUZZ:** Did you ever think of going over yourself?

**TED:** Well, I usually go on holidays with my curate, Father McGuire . . . And he can't really take the sun too well . . .

*Ted points out a row of pictures of Dougal on holiday. In every one of them his skin is a ludicrous colour of bright red. Dougal comes in.*

**DOUGAL** (*notices Buzz*): Who are you? What are you talking about?

**TED:** Oh, this is Father Buzz Cagney. He's just on a quick visit. He's from America.

**DOUGAL:** America? We were just talking about that fella, Kurt Cobain from Nirvana, earlier on. He was from America. That was weird, wasn't it? Blowing his head off with a shotgun! God, how did he manage to survive that?!

**TED:** He . . . eh, he didn't, Dougal. He died.

**DOUGAL:** Oh . . . right.

**TED:** Anyway, you go to bed, I'll be up in a minute.

**DOUGAL:** All right, Ted. Goodnight!

*Dougal leaves.*

**BUZZ:** You'll be up in a minute?

**TED:** Yes, we sleep together. So who else do you know?

*Mrs Doyle enters.*

**MRS DOYLE:** Hello, everyone! Father, are you looking forward to dinner?

**TED:** Hmm? Oh . . . yes, I suppose so.

**MRS DOYLE:** I think you'll enjoy dinner tonight. You do like pheasant, don't you, Father?

**TED:** Pheasant? God, yes, I love pheasant!

**MRS DOYLE:** Well, that's a little clue as to what you'll be eating for dinner. The thing you'll be eating likes pheasant as well!

*As Mrs Doyle talks, she puts on a protective visor and sits down on a chair in front of Jack. Buzz sees this and looks puzzled. Ted turns to Mrs Doyle.*

**TED:** What are— Oh, Mrs Doyle, you're not doing his nails now, are you?

**MRS DOYLE:** I have to, Father. He's been worrying the armrests again.

*We notice that there are two big piles of stuffing coming out of the armrests of his armchair.*

**TED:** Oh, all right. Slip this on, Buzz.

*He hands Buzz an old-style motorbike helmet. Buzz, puzzled, puts it on. Ted puts one on too.*

**TED:** Anyway, Buzz, you were saying . . .

**BUZZ:** Eh . . . yes, I was curious . . . How much money did this parish bring in last year?

**TED:** How much money? God, I don't know. I suppose in an average month we'd take— (*Mrs Doyle clips a nail and the living-room window shatters as if a bullet has gone through it. Buzz jumps with the shock.*) Tsk. Another bloody window gone – I suppose we'd take in about a hundred and fifty pounds in collections. Maybe two hundred. (*Another nail is clipped and raps sharply against Ted's helmet.*) Mrs Doyle? Aim into the wall, *please*.

**BUZZ:** Two hundred pounds . . . what's that? Not even four hundred dollars. Do you know what I'd do with four hundred dollars? I'd wipe my ass with four hundred dollars.

**TED:** Good God. But . . . can that still be accepted as legal tender?

**BUZZ** (*not listening*): My parish made two million dollars last year. That's a lot of sherry and steak dinners.

*He raises his glass and salutes Ted briefly. Just as he's about to raise it to his mouth, another nail is clipped and the glass shatters.*

**TED:** Mrs Doyle! Seriously, now, do it later!

**MRS DOYLE:** Oh, all right, Father.

*Mrs Doyle leaves. Ted and Buzz take off their helmets.*

**BUZZ:** I want to show you something. This is a brochure for Saint John's parish, Beverly Hills. This is the parish grounds.

*Buzz picks up a brochure. He holds it in front of Ted, blocking his face. Ted starts leafing through it.*

**TED:** Whoah! Is that the Hollywood sign in the background?

**BUZZ:** Uh-huh. All the usual features . . . (*He starts turning pages.*) . . . heated swimming pool in the basement . . . computer-games room . . . revolving restaurant giving you . . . I dunno, I suppose a pretty good view of the Hollywood Hills . . . it's really very nice.

*He takes the brochure away. Cut to a two-shot of Ted and Jack. Ted is sitting with his head cocked to one side, mouth open and drooling slightly, just like Jack.*

**BUZZ:** Ted . . . the other day I saw how you dealt with that suicide guy. You were the *Iceman*. Supercool. I liked what I saw, Ted. How would you like to work with me in L.A.? In a satellite parish to Saint John's?

**TED:** What? You mean? . . . L.A.? Dear God in . . . (*Dougal walks in, dressed in his pyjamas. Ted and Buzz stop talking. Dougal, a little confused, walks over to take a football annual off the table, then walks out again.*) . . . heaven! That'd be fantastic! Do you really think you could swing it?

**BUZZ** (*nods*): It's a good parish, Ted, and if you work hard, the rewards are there.

**TED** (*disappointed*): Yeah . . . spiritual rewards.

**BUZZ:** No! Real rewards!

**TED:** Really? Great!

**BUZZ:** It's the land of opportunity, Ted. You want something, you can get it.

**TED:** Well, I want it!

*Buzz raises his hand in the air to move his hair back. Ted mistakes this as an invitation to give Buzz a 'high five' and starts to do so. But he misses and slaps Buzz in the face in a rather embarrassing way.*

**END OF PART ONE**

\* \* \*

**PART TWO**

SCENE 6 INT./MORNING 4
SET: PAROCHIAL HOUSE LIVING ROOM
*Ted is on the telephone.*

**TED:** Really? It's official? Yes! Yes, great news! OK! Thank you, Buzz, *thank* you!

*He puts the telephone down and makes a 'yesssssss' gesture. He is so excited that things keep occurring to him and the excitement is renewed. He sits down and then has to stand up again. He runs to the door, then stops.*

**TED:** No . . . no . . . one step at a time. Get them all together . . . Dougal, Father Jack, Mrs Doyle . . . *I'm going to America!!!!!*

*He jumps up and down with excitement. Kevin comes through the door.*

**KEVIN:** Ted, could I speak with you a moment?

**TED:** Sure!

*They sit down at the table.*

**KEVIN:** Father, I'd like to thank you for talking me down off that ledge. It was very good of you. I can't pretend I'm any happier, I'm afraid. The world still looks to me a very dark, unpleasant place—

**TED:** YES!!!! (*Ted has jumped out of his chair. He walks around the room, talking to himself.*) I'll need to get all my stuff brought over somehow, but that won't be a problem. I'm sure the Washington parish can . . . Kevin! Hello! What can I do for you?

**KEVIN:** Eh, yes, I just felt I should tell someone where my thoughts have been leading me these last few weeks. Down some very dark and disturbing alleys . . . I think I'm experiencing what you might know as the dark night of the soul.

**TED:** Hold on a second, Kevin, do you mind if I put on some music?

**KEVIN:** What? Oh, no . . . go ahead. (*Ted goes to the record player.*) You see, I've begun to be plagued by doubts. Doubts about . . . oh, God! I mean . . . what if none of it's true? (*The music starts up. It is 'Shaft' by Isaac Hayes.*) What if there's nothing out there?

**TED:** 'Shaft'!

**KEVIN:** Sorry, Father?

**TED:** This is such a great song.

**KEVIN:** Yes . . . anyway . . . I just keep thinking about all the terrible, awful things that happen to people . . . War, famine, that whole *Mirror* pension-fund thing . . . (*Mrs Doyle comes into the room, hears the previous line, and turns and goes straight out again, an embarrassed look on her face.*) . . . and it just makes me despair—

**TED:** 'Who's the private dick who's a sex machine with all the chicks? Shaft!'

*Ted starts grooving silently to the music, a million miles away. Kevin realises that Ted's not going to be much help, and sighs. After a moment, he starts to listen to the music. He starts slowly, gently grooving, his head bopping up and down.*

**TED:** I love this bit . . . 'Daga, daga, daga, dang, daga, daga, dang.'

*The music pours out. Ted looks at the album cover*

*and grooves slightly. Kevin stares at the record player. He smiles.*

**KEVIN:** I do like this song, actually.

**TED:** Aw, it's great. Mrs Doyle got it at a car-boot sale.

*They groove for a while.*

**BOTH:** Shaft!

*They groove for a while longer. The song ends.*

**TED:** Sorry, Kevin. You were saying?

**KEVIN** (*smiling to himself*): Hmm? Actually . . . no, it doesn't matter. Thank you, Ted. I'd better be going home, actually. Do you want that twenty?

**TED:** Yea – actually, keep it.

**KEVIN:** Really? Oh. Thanks, Ted!

**TED:** No problem!

*Kevin leaves. Ted jumps up and down with happiness.*

SCENE 7 EXT./DAY 4
SET: PAROCHIAL HOUSE
*Kevin walks away from the house, the theme of 'Shaft' still playing in his head. He smiles happily.*

SCENE 8 INT./DAY 4
SET: PAROCHIAL HOUSE
*Dougal comes in, dressed in his pyjamas.*

**DOUGAL:** Yes, Dougal, I have some very good news. I've been asked to go and work in America!

**DOUGAL:** Really? As what?

**TED:** Well . . . as a priest . . .

**DOUGAL:** A priest, great. That's more or less the same as what you do here.

**TED:** Yes . . .

**DOUGAL:** God, America! Fantastic! When are we going?

**TED:** When are we – what?

**DOUGAL:** I am going, aren't I? You wouldn't . . . you wouldn't leave me behind, would you?

*Ted looks at Dougal. From Ted's point of view, we*

*see that coming out of the collar, where Dougal's head should be, is a puppy. Cut back to Ted.*

**TED:** Well . . . ah . . . yes.

**DOUGAL:** Brilliant, Ted!

*Mrs Doyle comes in.*

**DOUGAL:** Mrs Doyle! Wait'll you hear this! Ted's been offered a job in America and we're all going with him!!!!

**MRS DOYLE** (*makes squeaky noise*)**:** We're geeng te Meerica? We're geeng te Meerica? We're geeng te Meerica? We're geeng te Meerica? (*By now she is holding on to Ted's collar.*) Are we? Are we really? Are we really, Father?

*Ted looks at Mrs Doyle. We see her from his point of view. He sees a ruby-cheeked little girl dressed in frills, with a pathetically hopeful look on her face.*

**TED:** Eh . . . yes . . . we . . . we're going to America . . .

**DOUGAL:** Tell Father Jack!

*Father Jack is asleep. Ted looks at him. Mrs Doyle and Dougal look at Ted expectantly.*

**TED:** Father Jack? Father Jack?

**JACK** (*wakes*)**:** ARSE!

**TED:** Eh . . . Father Jack?

*We see Jack from Ted's point of view. He is an old man in a Pringle jumper. He has the puppy we saw earlier in his lap, and the little girl has one hand on the back of the rocking chair he is sitting on. Music starts: 'I'll be seeing you in Apple Blossom time . . .' Cut back to Ted. He looks very confused.*

**TED:** Actually, I think I'd better go and have a lie down . . .

*He leaves the room unsteadily.*

SCENE 9 INT./DAY 4\*
SET: SACRISTY
*We hear the murmur of a cheering mob outside the door. It opens. The cheering becomes louder and we see some jubilant islanders outside. Ted walks through them and they clap him on the back. He comes in, followed by Buzz and two altar boys. Buzz slams the door after Ted has entered. Ted turns to the altar boys.*

**TED:** Yes! Woo-hoo! You guys! What a great mass! Buzz, what did you think?

**BUZZ:** Seeing you out there today, Ted, well . . . let me put it this way, I haven't been this excited about religion in thirty years. You really know how to work the room.

**TED:** Well, you inspired me, Buzz. (*He puts a towel around his neck, sits down and one of the altar boys starts giving him a neck massage.*) It was just one of those Masses when everything seemed to go right. I don't know what it was . . . I was just in the *zone*.

**BUZZ:** I liked the *Star Trek* joke.

**TED:** Yeah, I was trying to lighten the mood after the Offertory.

**BUZZ:** Well, people expect to be depressed after the Offertory, but nice idea. I like the way you're thinking. In the States you won't be in competition with Father Pat Shilleagh from Bally-Go-Assways anymore. You're up against Billy Graham and those Nation of Islam guys. Those mothers can put on a show like Judy Garland at Carnegie Hall. You have to grab the audience, Ted. And do you know where you have to grab them?

**TED:** Yeah. *By the balls!*

**BUZZ:** I was going to say by the shoulders.

**TED:** Oh, right, sorry. *God*, that was fantastic! I feel like going out and doing another Mass right away!

**BUZZ:** Pace yourself, Ted. I wouldn't do another Mass for a week.

*Ted nods, thinking to himself, still very high.*

**TED:** The way I feel now, I could convert gays.

SCENE 10 INT./DAY 5†
SET: PAROCHIAL HOUSE HALLWAY
*A caption comes up that reads 'One month later'. Six teenagers in T-shirts with cool band names on them are getting Ted's autograph. Ted is signing for them happily.*

\* We moved scene 12 to here in the final version.
† We deleted this scene from the final version.

TED: There you go. See you at Mass on Sunday! You will be there, won't you?

TEENAGER 1: You bet, Father! Your Masses are the greatest!

TEENAGER 2: What's the sermon going to be about?

TED: Follow not false gods.

TEENAGER 1: Oh, right. Except you, Father!

TED: Ha, ha!

*He closes the door and walks into the living room.*

SCENE 11 INT./DAY 5
SET: PAROCHIAL HOUSE
*Dougal is sitting, reading a big book called 'So you're a priest who is going to America'. Ted sees this and looks abashed.*

DOUGAL: God, Ted! One week to go!

TED: Eh . . . yes.

DOUGAL: There were some fans outside looking for you. Did you see them?

TED: Yes, it looks as though I'll have to make this Sunday's Mass all-ticket.

DOUGAL: Actually, I just realised, I haven't seen the gloomy fella around lately. Where is he?

TED: He's gone home. I think he's all right now.

SCENE 12 EXT./DAY 5*
SET: BUS
*Kevin is on a bus, smiling happily.*

DRIVER: Father, do you mind if I turn on some music?

KEVIN: No, not at all!

*He smiles happily. The driver turns a knob.*

D.J. (*from the radio*): . . . From yesteryear, 'Alison' by Elvis Costello . . . Now . . . the new single from Radiohead: 'Asleep'.

*The incredibly depressing song starts playing. Kevin listens to it, the smile slowly disappearing from his face. After a few moments, he looks totally miserable. The bus speeds off into the distance.*

SCENE 12A INT./DAY 5
SET: PAROCHIAL HOUSE
*Back to Ted and Dougal.*

DOUGAL: Ted, how come you've got really good at saying Mass and you used to be crap?

TED: I wasn't crap at saying Mass. And don't say 'crap'. It's just Buzz has been a big inspiration to me. (*Pause.*) Dougal, about this whole America thing . . . I really have to talk . . .

*Mrs Doyle enters.*

MRS DOYLE: I've arranged for the phone and electricity to be cut off, Father, and someone's coming on Tuesday to take away all the furniture and burn it in a big fire.

TED: Mrs Doyle, Dougal, Father Jack . . . I have to tell you something. I have to be absolutely honest with you . . .

DOUGAL: The money was just resting in the account . . .

MRS DOYLE (*overlapping*): . . . just resting in the account . . . yes, we know that, Father . . .

TED: No, it's nothing to do with that . . . it's . . . (*He looks at them. They look really helpless.*)

* In the final version we inserted this scene after scene 8.

. . . well . . . (*He sees them again.*) . . . the thing is . . . (*He sees them again.*) . . . what I'm trying to say is . . . (*He sees them again.*) . . . you're not . . . you're not going to be . . . able to come with me . . . (*Mrs Doyle drops a cup. Dougal's face crumples.*) . . . when I go into space. I'm going to be the first priest in space! (*Long pause.*) Yes . . . I've been selected by N.A.S.A. to be the first priest in space. So . . . well, that's the news. Just thought I'd tell you that.

**MRS DOYLE** (*obviously relieved*)**:** Oh, great. Well, that's fine.

**DOUGAL:** But Ted, how will you breathe in space?

**TED:** Oh, I'm sure they'll . . . I'll have some sort of apparatus.

**DOUGAL:** God, Ted, first America, then space! What's next!? Mars or somewhere, I suppose.

**TED:** Well, who knows.

**MRS DOYLE:** Still, as long as we can all go with you to America, Father, that's the important thing. I think if I couldn't go for any reason, I would have to say it'd be the single most crushing thing of my entire life. A disappointment like that, well, I couldn't see how I'd live with it. I might even take the ultimate step and take my own life.

**TED:** Mrs Doyle! That's a terrible thing to say!

**MRS DOYLE:** Well, it doesn't matter anyway, because I *am* going to America! Ha, ha!

**TED:** Yes. Ha, ha.

*She potters out. The telephone rings. Ted picks it up, still looking sheepish.*

**TED:** Buzz, hello! Well, just one more Mass and I'm off!

SCENE 13 INT./DAY 5*
SET: HOTEL ROOM
*Buzz is standing with a towel around his waist, just out of the shower. Room service comes in with a tray full of expensive goodies.*

**BUZZ** (*to room service*)**:** Put it on the bed . . . Yeah . . . I've been meaning to talk to you about that . . . the people here . . . Well,

you're very popular here at the moment, Ted. They're going to find it hard to let you go . . .

**TED:** What? Oh, no, they'll be fine.

**BUZZ:** I don't know. Bishop Brennan received a petition the other day begging for you not to be sent away, signed by everyone on the island, including – and this is something I find a little bizarre – you.

**TED:** That's what that was? I assumed it was something to do with getting satellite TV. Don't worry about that. I'm out of here.

**BUZZ:** Hmm. This is the thing, Ted. It might be hard for me to get you to America if you keep doing these great Masses . . . I think something drastic is called for.

**TED:** I . . . you mean . . . *throw the Mass?!!!* You're not serious! No way, Buzz! I can't!

**BUZZ:** You want a shot at the big time, you've got to throw the Mass.

**TED:** No, Buzz, no! Please don't make me do it!

**BUZZ:** I'm sorry, Ted, but it's got to be like that.

*Buzz gets up and leaves. Ted sits down, looking devastated.*

SCENE 14 INT./DAY 5*
SET: SACRISTY
*Buzz is waiting. The door leading out is opened. Outside, a group of people are looking at someone offscreen. They are very quiet. Ted passes through them. They part to let him through but they seem quietly angry.*

**TED:** Ah . . . excuse me . . . thank you . . . yes . . . (*He comes in, followed by the two altar boys, and closes the door. The altar boys won't look at Ted.*) Ah, could you take my, ah? . . .

*He holds out his stole for an altar boy to take. The boy does so, but without much enthusiasm. A man sticks his head through the door. He has an old-style hat with a card with 'Press' written on it stuck in the band.*

**PRESS:** Father, can I ask you a few questions?

---

*We deleted this scene from the final version.

**BUZZ:** He ain't talkin' to no one! Get outta here!

**PRESS:** Lotta people sayin' you threw that Mass, Fadda. What you got to say to that?

**TED:** I don't throw Masses! You tell 'em Father Ted Crilly does not throw Masses!

*Buzz goes to the door and forces the reporter out of it.*

**TED:** I coulda had that crowd, Buzz. The way I felt . . .

**BUZZ:** I know how hard that was for you, Ted, going through the forty days Our Lord spent in the desert moment by moment. You were boring the ass off me. And that nasal, annoying voice . . .

**TED:** What nasal, annoying voice?

**BUZZ:** Hmm? Oh, I mean, ahm . . . you're going to America!

**TED:** Yay!!!!

SCENE 15 INT./DAY 6
SET: PAROCHIAL HOUSE
*The living room has been cleared of all ornaments, pictures, etc. Ted walks in. Mrs Doyle is clearing stuff up.*

**TED:** Wha—?!!!

**MRS DOYLE:** Come on, Father! We don't want to be late for our plane!

**TED:** Look, there's no easy way to tell you this but . . .

*Dougal comes in carrying suitcases.*

**DOUGAL:** Ha! God, Ted! I've just been looking at my passport photo! I look hilarious! Have a look. God, I've changed a lot . . .

*He shows his passport photo to Ted. We see a photo of a baby.*

**TED:** You haven't changed that much, Dougal. Anyway, listen carefully . . .

**DOUGAL:** Look at Jack, he's so excited about going to America he can barely keep still!

*We see Jack in his chair, mouth open, asleep. We hear the clock ticking. Finally he rouses slightly in an involuntary way and makes a grunting noise.*

**DOUGAL:** You see?!

**TED:** Yes, Dougal. Seriously, I need to say something . . .

**DOUGAL:** Oh, I can't wait to hear this! Every time Ted's talked to us over the last few days, it's just been more and more good news! Now you're going to tell us you're Santa, or something!

**TED:** No, Dougal, I'm not Santa. In fact, I'm the opposite to Santa.

**DOUGAL** (*afraid*)**:** The anti-Santa?!

**TED:** I'm afraid . . . this is going to come as a terrible blow to you all . . . but I really can't put it off any longer. I have to tell you now.

*We see Mrs Doyle, Jack and Dougal staring back at him.*

SCENE 16 INT./DAY 6
SET: AIRPORT
*Ted, Dougal, Jack and Mrs Doyle come through the door. We see a sign that reads 'Departures'.*

**DOUGAL:** We'd better check in before we go to America.

**TED:** Yes, better. Ah, here's Buzz.

*Buzz approaches. He notices Ted's mad, bush-wired hair.*

**BUZZ:** Ted. What the hell's happened to your head?

**TED:** Wha—? . . . (*He remembers what he looks like.*) Oh. You don't like it? I'll put it back as it was.

*He starts trying to smooth down his hair.*

**BUZZ:** What are those guys doing here?

**TED:** Ah, they just came with me to the airport to say goodbye.

**BUZZ:** They don't think they're going as well, do they?

**TED:** Oh, God, no. I told them. I definitely made that very clear to them. I told them a million times.

**BUZZ:** Just say your goodbyes. Then you can check in and go to the executive lounge. Talk about your new parish.

*Ted goes over to Dougal, Jack and Mrs Doyle. Buzz*

*sees them shaking hands, but can't hear them. Cut away from Buzz's point of view.\**

**TED:** . . . So that's how to react when we meet people in America. Just shake hands, give them a firm greeting. Just as if they were normal Irish people. Mrs Doyle, I'll just show you as well . . . \*

*Cut to Buzz's point of view. Ted shakes hands with Mrs Doyle, then with Jack. Then he starts waving. Cut closer on Ted.\**

**TED:** And it's basically the same, left-right movement for waving. Can you try that?\*

*From Buzz's point of view, we see a confused Mrs Doyle and Dougal waving back at Ted. Ted goes over to Buzz. Jack, Mrs Doyle and Dougal look at them.\**

**TED:** Right. That's them dealt with.\*

\*We deleted these lines from the final version.

**BUZZ:** All right, I've checked in so I'll see you in the lounge. Get ready to rock!\*

**TED:** Yes! (*Buzz walks off. Ted crumples.*) Oh, God!\*

SCENE 17 INT./DAY 6
SET: CHECK-IN
*Ted is waiting in the line with Mrs Doyle, Dougal and Jack. There are about four people ahead of them. Ted is a picture of horror.*

**DOUGAL:** Oh, Ted, you know, all my life I've dreamed of something really special happening to me, and now it is. I think this is the greatest moment of my life.

**MRS DOYLE:** Me too.

**JACK:** Bras!

*The line moves forward a little more, past a potted plant – a tall shrub.*

**TED:** Oh, God!

*There is one woman in front of them. Then it is Ted's turn. He checks in. The operator starts feeding information into her computer. Ted looks desperate.*

**TED:** Dougal, Mrs Doyle, Father Jack, you go and wait in the restaurant. I'll check us in.

**DOUGAL:** Which restaurant, Ted?

**TED:** The one that isn't a Sock Shop, over there.

**DOUGAL:** OK, so.

*They all move off. Ted watches them go. Ted sneaks off. He sees Buzz at the gate.*

**BUZZ:** Ah, Ted! What's wrong?

**TED** (*doubled over*): Just a slight bit of guilt about leaving. Hold on a sec. (*He makes a horrible face, swallowing the guilt as if it were a lump of steak with nails in it.*) There it goes.

**BUZZ:** Right. Come on, Ted. There's a whole world out there to experience. Let's take the first step.

*They walk through the gate.*

SCENE 18 INT./DAY 6
SET: AIRPORT
*Dougal, Mrs Doyle and Jack are sitting down.*

**DOUGAL:** They're never going to serve us.

*Cut wide to reveal that they are in a Sock Shop.*

SCENE 19 INT./DAY 6
SET: A SCREEN
*We see a 'Departures' display. Among those listed we see: 'AL 152 LOS ANGELES GATE 27. 17.30'*

SCENE 20 INT./DAY 6
SET: AIRPORT
*Dougal, Mrs Doyle and Jack are wandering through the emptying airport. They watch people going by, pushing their trolleys and smiling.*

SCENE 21 INT./DAY 6
SET: A SCREEN
*The same as earlier except that it now reads: 'AL 152 LOS ANGELES GATE 27. NOW BOARDING'.*

SCENE 22 INT./DAY 6
SET: AIRPORT
*Dougal, Mrs Doyle and Jack are hanging around in another location. They look ever so slightly forlorn, but still hopeful.*

SCENE 23 INT./DAY 6
SET: PLANE
*Ted is sitting beside Buzz.*

**TED:** Sorry about that, Buzz. Anyway! Can't wait to get to America!

**BUZZ:** You'll like it, Ted. Going in at the deep end . . .

**TED:** Oh, great! The old swimming pool! Lovely. I packed my swimming trunks . . .

**BUZZ:** You won't have a swimming pool.

**TED:** No? OK . . .

**BUZZ:** You'll have a basketball court.

**TED:** Oh, good. That'll keep me fit, anyway.

**BUZZ:** One of the ways the parish has tried to cool tensions between the gangs in the past is through sports . . .

**TED:** Sorry, Buzz . . . stop you there for a moment . . . gangs? Did you use the word

'gangs' there? What does that mean exactly?

**BUZZ:** Well, L.A.'s gang problem is getting slightly better these days. Last year there were only five thousand, six hundred and twenty gang-related deaths.

**TED:** There's another use of the word 'gangs', which I asked about earlier. Also, I couldn't help noticing that it was closely followed by the word 'deaths'.

**BUZZ:** Yes. The good news is that drive-by shootings are down.

**TED:** Right, there I notice the word 'shootings'. *Pause.* Buzz?

**BUZZ:** Yes?

**TED:** I quit! I didn't know I was going out to America to umpire drive-by shooting tournaments. STOP THE PLANE!

**BUZZ:** It hasn't started yet, Ted.

**TED:** Well . . . even though . . . yes . . . Don't start the plane! . . . I'm getting off!

*He runs to the exit.*

SCENE 24 INT./DAY 6
SET: AIRPORT
*Time has passed, and Dougal, Mrs Doyle and Jack are asleep in their uncomfortable chairs. Ted comes up and sits beside Dougal.*

**DOUGAL** (*waking*)**:** Ted? Is that you?

**TED:** Yes, it's me. Listen . . . I've been thinking about things . . . I really think it would be better if I didn't go to America. I think we'd all be happiest back where we belong. On Craggy Island.

**DOUGAL:** Fair enough, Ted. I didn't really want to go anyway.

*Ted is taken aback. Mrs Doyle and Jack wake up.*

**MRS DOYLE:** Oh, Father, you're back. What's going on?

**DOUGAL:** Ted's decided that it would be better if we didn't go to America.

**TED:** Huh?

**MRS DOYLE:** Really? Ah, he's probably right.

**JACK:** Drink!

**MRS DOYLE:** Come on, Father, we'll go home and get you a drink.

**TED:** I thought you really wanted to go.

**MRS DOYLE:** Yes, I thought I'd be a bit more disappointed, but now you've told us, I realise that I didn't really want to go at all. In fact, I don't think I *can* go. I haven't told my sister about it.

*They get up.*

**DOUGAL:** Come on, Ted. Let's go.

*Dougal, Jack and Mrs Doyle get up. Ted slowly gets to his feet and follows them.*

**DOUGAL:** Ah, yeah, Ted. You're here to stay! With me and Mrs Doyle and Father Jack for ever and ever and ever and ever . . .

*Ted stops short.*

SCENE 25 INT./DAY 6*
SET: CONFERENCE ROOM
*We see a banner that reads* 'It's still great being a priest!' *Below it, a group of priests are standing, facing a window. There is much worry and concern on their faces. Cut to outside, where we see Kevin standing on a ledge, occasionally glancing down. From his point of view, we see cars far down below. The group of priests parts and Ted comes through them. He goes to the window and climbs out. He ushers Kevin along the ledge.*

**TED:** Move up a bit.

**THE END**

---

*In the final version we replaced this scene with a montage of clips from every previous episode of *Father Ted*.

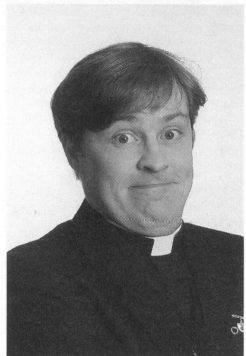